Mainland China

Westview Special Studies

The concept of Westview Special Studies is a response to the continuing crisis in academic and informational publishing. Library budgets are being diverted from the purchase of books and used for data banks, computers, micromedia, and other methods of information retrieval. Interlibrary loan structures further reduce the edition sizes required to satisfy the needs of the scholarly community. Economic pressures on university presses and the few private scholarly publishing companies have greatly limited the capacity of the industry to properly serve the academic and research communities. As a result, many manuscripts dealing with important subjects, often representing the highest level of scholarship, are no longer economically viable publishing projects--or, if accepted for publication, are typically subject to lead times ranging from one to three years.

Westview Special Studies are our practical solution to the problem. As always, the selection criteria include the importance of the subject, the work's contribution to scholarship, and its insight, originality of thought, and excellence of exposition. We accept manuscripts in camera-ready form, typed, set, or word processed according to specifications laid out in our comprehensive manual, which contains straightforward instructions and sample pages. The responsibility for editing and proofreading lies with the author or sponsoring institution, but our editorial staff is always available to answer questions and provide guidance.

The result is a book printed on acid-free paper and bound in sturdy library-quality soft covers. We manufacture these books ourselves using equipment that does not require a lengthy make-ready process and that allows us to publish first editions of 300 to 1000 copies and to reprint even smaller quantities as needed. Thus, we can produce Special Studies quickly and can keep even very specialized books in print as long as there is a demand for them.

About the Book and Editor

Over the past several years, Mainland China has undertaken reforms in various domestic areas, including culture and society, education, the economy, and the Communist Party. In addition, since September 1982 Peking has begun to pursue an independent course in foreign relations. In this volume, based on the Thirteenth Sino-American Conference in Taipei, contributors provide a penetrating analysis of the problems Peking faces in trying to implement reforms and of possible future developments in its domestic and foreign policies.
In Part 1 they examine ideological theory and practice, party reform, the Hong Kong question, political corruption, population controls, and cultural and educational problems.
Part 2 includes discussion of the Mainland Chinese economic system as a whole, the issue of special economic zones, and agricultural reforms. The final part focuses on China's foreign policy, looking specifically at Peking's relations with India and Western Europe and at the Washington-Peking-Moscow triangle.

Dr. Yu-ming Shaw is the director of the Institute of International Relations, Taipei, and professor in the Graduate School of International Law and Diplomacy at National Chengchi University. He is the editor of Power and Policy in the PRC (Westview, 1985).

Published in cooperation with the
Institute of International Relations,
Taipei, Taiwan

Mainland China
Politics, Economics, and Reform

edited by
Yu-ming Shaw

Westview Press / Boulder and London

Westview Special Studies on China and East Asia

All rights reserved. No part of this publication may be reproduced or transmitted in any form or by any means, electronic or mechanical, including photocopy, recording, or any information storage and retrieval system without permission in writing from the publisher.

Copyright © 1986 by Westview Press, Inc.

Published in 1986 in the United States of America by Westview Press, Inc.; Frederick A. Praeger, Publisher; 5500 Central Avenue, Boulder, Colorado 80301

Library of Congress Catalog Card Number: 85-51582
ISBN: 0-8133-0267-6

DS
779.16
M35
1986

Printed and bound in the United States of America

The paper used in this publication meets the minimum requirements of the American National Standard for Permanence of Paper for Printed Library Materials Z39.48-1984.

6   5   4   3   2   1

Contents

Preface ix

PART ONE
POLITICS IN THE PRC

1   The Chinese-type Socialist Road: Theory
and Practice, *Hsien-yun Chao* 3

2   The Nature of Chinese Communism and the
Prospects for Teng's Reforms, *Cal Clark* 37

3   Studies in the Republic of China on
Communist China Affairs, 1949-1979,
Tai-chun Kuo 69

4   Party Rectification in Post-Mao China,
Lowell Dittmer 103

5   The Mousetrapping of Hong Kong: A Game
in Which Nobody Wins, *Chalmers Johnson* 121

6   Kleptocracy on Mainland China: A Social-
Psychological Interpretation, *Alan P.L. Lui* . . . 157

7   Higher Educational Charters in Mainland
China, *C. Montgomery Broaded* 173

8   Chinese Intellectuals and Party Policy,
Lynn T. White III 205

9   Policy Implications of Population Dynamics
in the PRC, *Wen Lang Li* 257

10   Socialist Spiritual Civilization and
     Cultural Pollution: The Problem of Meaning,
     James T. Myers 277

PART TWO
ECONOMICS IN THE PRC

11   Mainland China's Economic System: A New Model
     or Variations on an Old Theme?
     Robert F. Dernberger 331

12   Mainland China's Special Economic Zones,
     Jan S. Prybyla 367

13   Review of Studies on the Mainland Economy,
     K. C. Yeh 393

14   How Well Did U.S. Economists Understand
     Communist China's Economy? *Ramon H. Myers* 421

15   Agricultural Reform in Mainland China:
     Problems and Prospects, *Feng-hwa Mah* 443

16   Agriculture in Mainland China: Reform and
     Problems, *Ting-chung Ch'en* 471

PART THREE
FOREIGN POLICY OF THE PRC

17   The Evolution of Communist China's Foreign
     Policy, *Ch'ing-yao Yin* 499

18   Peking, Moscow, and the Indian Subcontinent:
     Cards, Triangles, and Possible Rapprochement,
     Richard J. Kozicki 527

19   Paris and London: Between Washington and
     Beijing, *Douglas T. Stuart* 553

20   Sino-Soviet Relations and the Asian Quadrangle,
     1984, *William E. Griffith* 587

21   Co-opting China: The Realization of an
     American Dream? *Peter Van Ness* 607

22   The Washington-Moscow-Peking Triangle: An
     Analysis, *Bih-jaw Lin* 627

23   Interpretations of Mainland China's Recent
     Foreign Policy, *Harold C. Hinton* 649

About the Contributors 661

Preface

Over the past several years the People's Republic of China (PRC) has undertaken reforms in various domestic areas, including those of party, culture, society, education, and the economy. Also, since September 1982, the PRC has spoken of pursuing an independent course in foreign relations. These reforms and changes offer a challenging subject for examination. A group of well-known scholars from the United States and the Republic of China (ROC) addressed this topic in Taipei, Taiwan, in June 1984 at the Thirteenth Sino-American Conference. Sponsored by the Institute of International Relations, the conference that generated this book provided valuable insights into and analysis of the problems the PRC faces in implementing current reforms. Possible future developments in its domestic and foreign policies were also considered.

I thank the cosponsors of the conference for their support and Westview Press for publishing these papers. I am indebted to many friends and colleagues at the Institute of International Relations for their assistance in the organization of the conference and the publication of the proceedings. My predecessor, Dr. King-yuh Chang, planned and ran the conference from beginning to end; we all owe him our gratitude.

Yu-ming Shaw

Part 1

Politics in the PRC

1
The Chinese-type Socialist Road: Theory and Practice

Hsien-yun Chao

A NEW SLOGAN IN SUBSTITUTION FOR THE
"FOUR MODERNIZATIONS"

    The term "Chinese-type socialist road," or "socialism with Chinese characteristics," made its first formal appearance in Teng Hsiao-p'ing's opening address to the Twelfth Chinese Communist Party (CCP) National Congress on September 1, 1982. In the period between the Third Plenary Session of the Eleventh CCP Central Committee in December 1978 and this congress, the same concept was generally referred to as "Chinese-type modernization." By substituting "Chinese-type socialist road," Teng seems to have attached more importance to the political significance of the Four Modernizations.

    In a communiqué issued on December 22, 1978, the Third Plenary Session of the Eleventh CCP Central Committee stated that in the early years after the founding of Communist China, especially after the socialist transformation had been basically completed, Mao Tse-tung had instructed the whole Party to shift the focus of its work to the economy and the technical revolution. The communiqué also announced that the Party would shift the focus of work to socialist modernization in the following year.[1] At that time, Teng had already gained the upper hand over Hua Kuo-feng in the struggle for the leadership.

    Teng himself indicated the basic direction of the socialist transformation. In an address to the CCP's Theoretical Work Discussion Meeting on

March 1, 1979, he asserted: "In the past, in launching the democratic revolution, we had to adopt methods suitable to China's conditions and follow the trail that Comrade Mao Tse-tung had blazed of 'using the rural areas to encircle the cities.' Now, in promoting our modernization program, we must also adopt methods suitable to China's conditions and blaze a Chinese-type trail to modernization."[2] At the same time, he emphasized: "In order to realize the Four Modernizations in China, we must, in the field of ideology and politics, uphold the four basic principles. This is a fundamental prerequisite to the realization of the Four Modernizations. These four basic principles that we must firmly uphold are: the socialist road, the dictatorship of the proletariat, the leadership of the Communist Party, and Marxism-Leninism and Mao Tse-tung thought."[3]

In the same speech, Teng also warned that "Marxist ideological and theoretical workers cannot be divorced from politics." He added:

> By politics, I refer to the general situation of class struggle at home and abroad, i.e., the fundamental interests of both the Chinese people and other people in the world in the living reality of struggle. I cannot imagine that a person who is divorced from the general political situation, who does not study the general political situation, and who does not appraise the real development of the revolutionary struggle can ever become a Marxist or theorist.[4]

He further expounded:

> Scientific socialism is developing in the living reality of struggle; so are Marxism-Leninism and Mao Tse-tung thought. We, of course, shall not retrogress from scientific socialism back to utopian socialism; nor shall we allow Marxism to remain at the level of personal judgment of a few decades or more than a hundred years ago. Therefore, we should use basic theories

of Marxism-Leninism and Mao Tse-tung thought to study the new situation and solve new problems.[5]

People who became accustomed to hearing Mao Tse-tung and Lin Piao's criticism of the "biggest power-holder within the Party taking the capitalist road" during the early stage of the Cultural Revolution, those who are familiar with Teng Hsiao-p'ing's theory of "white and black cats" in particular, or those who know well how the Gang of Four accused Teng--without mentioning his name--of capitulating to the bourgeoisie at home and to imperialism abroad during the movement to criticize the <u>Water Margin</u> may think that Teng was insincere in his speech to the Theoretical Work Discussion Meeting, or they may be surprised at Teng's tendency to dogmatism. However, this speech is included in the <u>Selected Works of Teng Hsiao-p'ing</u> as an important document that the whole Party should study, which shows that Teng was really serious, and therefore, the speech deserves our attention.

Finally, in his opening address to the Twelfth CCP National Congress, Teng formally instructed all Chinese Communists to "integrate the universal truth of Marxism with the concrete realities of China, blaze a trail of their own, and build a socialism with Chinese characteristics."[6] The formula of combining the universal truth and concrete realities can be traced back to the Seventh CCP National Congress in April 1945. In his report to that congress, Liu Shao-ch'i defined Mao Tse-tung thought as "teachings which unite the theories of Marxism-Leninism with the actual practice of the Chinese revolution."[7] Now, Mao is dead, but Teng continues to employ the same formula by suggesting the integration of the universal truth of Marxism-Leninism with the concrete realities of the Chinese mainland. He has not explained what ideology he wants to create, but it is clear that he intends to establish the concept of lineage that Mao was the leader of the Chinese-type revolution and that he himself is the leader of the Chinese-type socialist construction. He is eager to succeed Mao as "the great teacher" of Communist China.

For this reason, a study of the so-called socialism with Chinese characteristics, from both theoretical and practical perspectives, will help us understand where Communist China is going under Teng's leadership.

TENG HSIAO-P'ING'S VERSION OF MAO TSE-TUNG THOUGHT AS GUIDING IDEOLOGY FOR THE THEORETICAL BASIS

In analyzing the Teng faction's current theory on building socialism with Chinese characteristics, I prefer to begin with a review of the heated debate on the elimination of bourgeois rights in the period from October 1958 to April 1959. The debate was provoked by the publication in the People's Daily on October 13, 1958, of an article by Chang Ch'un-ch'iao entitled "Eliminate the Idea of Bourgeois Rights." It ended in April 1959 when the First Session of the Second National People's Congress elected Liu Shao-ch'i to replace Mao as state chairman for the purpose of correcting the errors of the Three Red Banners.

In his article, Chang Ch'un-ch'iao recalled the life of military communism of the Worker-Peasant Red Army, which was characterized by the supply system. He stated that those people who, in line with the principle of material profit advocated by the economists, favored the implementation of a graded wage system gave top priority to money instead of to politics. He contended that instead of arousing the people's enthusiasm for production, material incentives encourage the people to compete for fame and profit, to become proud of extravagance and waste, and to become divorced from the masses. He emphasized that because of the bad influence of material incentives, some unsteady elements would degenerate into bourgeois rightists and embezzlers. Therefore, he favored the launching of a struggle to thoroughly eliminate bourgeois rights.[8]

The people who disagreed with Chang Ch'un-ch'iao thought that there was nothing wrong in introducing the wage system as it was naturally suitable to the conditions of those days. They blamed Chang for completely negating the historical significance of the wage system, and they contended that it was inappropriate to identify the wage system with the grade system.[9]

When Chang's first article in this debate on eliminating bourgeois rights was published, the editor of the <u>People's Daily</u> added a note to show that the paper was on his side, which indicated that Mao agreed with Chang. The editor's note conceded that Chang had brought up an important problem and that his views were by and large correct.[10] A later note suggested that the article written by those on the opposite side of the debate "approved Chang's appraisal of the supply system but held that there was nothing wrong in implementing the wage system after Liberation as it was a natural product suitable to the conditions of those days."[11]

The editor's note reflected Mao's views because, at that time, he was bent on promoting the movement to establish people's communes, on running public canteens, and on introducing the supply system. The life of military communism of the Worker-Peasant Red Army advocated by Chang conformed with the needs of the movement. In other words, Chang's views were in line with Mao's wishes.

The debate was further extended to include such questions as "distribution according to labor,"[12] "commodity production in a socialist society,"[13] the "weakening, restriction and elimination of bourgeois rights,"[14] the "principle of material profit,"[15] "relations between mental and manual labor,"[16] and "relations between commodity production and the law of value."[17] Now that Teng is calling for building socialism with Chinese characteristics, all of these questions have once again become themes of heated ideological and theoretical discussions on the Chinese mainland.

As the failure of the Three Red Banners became more and more obvious, the views represented by Chang's article gradually gave way to the opposite opinions. In its communiqué issued on December 18, 1958, the Sixth Plenary Session of the Eighth CCP Central Committee announced that the people's communes were to be readjusted and that Mao would not be a candidate at the next election for state chairman.[18] Chang Ch'un-ch'iao and the other people who held views similar to his were silenced. The discussion on bourgeois rights resumed a few years after the Lin Piao incident in September 1971. The third issue of <u>Red Flag</u> in 1975 published Yao Wen-yuan's article entitled "On the Social Basis of the Lin Piao Anti-Party Clique," and the next issue of the same magazine published "On Exercising All-Round Dictatorship over the Bourgeoisie" by Chang Ch'un-ch'iao. Then, a struggle to eliminate bourgeois rights, to "cut the bourgeois tail," was launched. By that time, Mao had perfected his theory of continued revolution under the dictatorship of the proletariat, and Chang Ch'un-ch'iao's theory on bourgeois rights served as a theoretical explanation of Mao's theory of continued revolution.

During the debate in 1958 and 1959, Teng Hsiao-p'ing defended the wage system, contending that the introduction of a low-wage system was aimed at creating more employment opportunities and accelerating the development of production in society.[19] After Mao stepped down from the leadership, Liu Shao-ch'i and Teng adopted such measures as "three freedom and one contract" and "using economic methods to handle economic affairs" to correct the errors of the Three Red Banners. By and large, these measures reflected the viewpoints of those people who had disagreed with Chang Ch'un-ch'iao during the bourgeois rights debate. During the Cultural Revolution, they were listed as proof that Liu and Teng were guilty of taking the capitalist road, and they became popular again only after Teng gained the upper hand over Hua Kuo-feng at the Third Plenary Session of the Eleventh CCP Central Committee at the end of 1978.

The first point that is noteworthy in this theoretical struggle is that during the debate in 1958 and 1959, both sides based their arguments on Marxism-Leninism and Mao Tse-tung thought, and now Teng Hsiao-p'ing continues to insist on inheriting and developing Mao Tse-tung thought. The <u>Selected Works of Teng Hsiao-p'ing</u> is publicized as the "guiding ideology for CCP members--a new sequel to Mao Tse-tung thought"[20] and "a national construction program for building socialism with Chinese characteristics and an inheritance and development of Mao Tse-tung thought."[21]

The second interesting point is that in 1958 and 1959, although each side held that the views of their opponents were wrong, there were no accusations of "pursuing revisionism," "practicing dogmatism," or "taking the capitalist road." Mao and Chang Ch'un-ch'iao began to accuse Liu Shao-ch'i and Teng Hsiao-p'ing of pursuing revisionism and taking the capitalist road only after the beginning of the Cultural Revolution and Teng started to label Chang's views as dogmatism only after the downfall of the Gang of Four. It is quite interesting that some scholars of Chinese Communist affairs are using Mao's judgment that Liu and Teng were capitalist roaders to evaluate Teng's line and policies since the Third Plenary Session of the Eleventh CCP Central Committee while other observers are using Teng's criticism that the Gang of Four was practicing dogmatism to evaluate Mao and Chiang Ch'ing's line and policies during the Cultural Revolution. This trend toward adopting the attitudes of the Chinese Communists themselves in their intra-Party struggles in the study of the lines and policies of various factions on the Chinese mainland deserves our special attention.

We should not use empty semantics to analyze the guiding ideology or the theoretical basis of Teng Hsiao-p'ing's concept of building socialism with Chinese characteristics. For instance, it is inappropriate to discuss whether the concept is "revisionist," whether it is "taking the capitalist road," or whether it is a "rightist" or a "leftist" line. We should examine its content and development.

In the current movement to promote socialist construction with Chinese characteristics, Teng and his followers, of course, have to propose some theories to justify their policies, and they have already gone beyond the limits of the earlier debate. In those days, only economic problems were involved; now all other aspects must also be taken into consideration. In fact, thinkers and theorists who belong to the Teng faction have made strenuous efforts to produce a series of new theories over the past few years. To sum up, these theories expound the following points:

1. The substitution of socialism for

capitalism is an inevitable result of social development. Although this is an old Marxist theory, it serves a new purpose on the Chinese mainland, because if this premise is not affirmed, both "socialism" and "communism" will become meaningless and the Teng faction will have no reason to promote Chinese-type socialism. Therefore, the Chinese Communists have brought out the old theory again in these words:

> The substitution of socialism for capitalism is a natural product of social development. This is an objective law that cannot be altered by the will of human beings. The proletariat is the representative of social productive forces. Its economic position decides that it will inevitably become the grave-digger of capitalist systems and the creator of a Communist society. The proletarian class struggle against the bourgeoisie will inevitably lead to the dictatorship of the proletariat. The Russian Revolution ushered in a new era of proletarian revolution under imperialist rule and blazed a new historical trail to socialism for the nations where capitalism is not yet developed. That the semi-colonial and semi-feudal old China went through new democracy to socialism was the result of the protracted struggle of the Chinese people under the leadership of the Chinese Communist Party which, in the light of China's special historical conditions, integrated the universal truth of Marxism with the concrete practice of the Chinese revolution. It is the victory and development of scientific socialism in China.[22]

This argument has provided the theoretical basis of Teng's call for "adhering to the Four Basic Principles."

2. It is historically inevitable that underdeveloped countries are the first to develop into socialist societies. In recent years, some people on the Chinese mainland have advocated a theory of "prematurity" and a theory of "making up the

missed lesson." They have quoted from the Manifesto of the Communist Party that "united action, of the leading civilized countries at least, is one of the first conditions for the emancipation of the proletariat." They have also referred to the five social forms that, according to Marxism-Leninism, represent the order of social change in the history of social development. They hold that in carrying out socialist revolution and socialist construction, China jumped over the capitalist stage and reversed the historical order of social development. They therefore contend that a premature revolution was launched in China and that the Chinese people must make up the missed lesson of capitalism. This tactic of quoting from Marxism-Leninism to oppose the Communist regime is an important sign of the development of liberal and democratic ideas on the Chinese mainland. To meet this challenge, the Chinese Communists have proposed the theory that underdeveloped countries are the first to launch the revolution, an argument that was presented in an essay by Wang Ching-ch'un.[23]

In his essay, Wang says that some people have misinterpreted the Marxist-Leninist idea that socialist revolution occurs first in civilized countries. He criticizes this misinterpretation as being mechanical and says that these people try to use the formula to undermine the practice of revolution. He contends that Marx and Engels talked dialectically about the order of revolution in strict accordance with changes in objective and subjective conditions. He asserts that not all countries have to follow the order of social development Marx and Engels proposed and that it is fully possible for a backward race or nation to jump over certain historical stages and enter directly into a social form that human society has already developed. He uses the example that the United States built up a typical capitalist society without going through the feudal stage. He emphasizes that as the socialist system has already been realized in the present era of proletarian revolution, it is not only possible but also historically inevitable for some underdeveloped or backward countries to jump over the historical stage of capitalism and effect a direct transition to socialism. He states that imperialism (the highest stage of capitalism) is corrupt and dying and that the reason why it still survives is that it uses the enormous amount of surplus profit that its monopolistic position has enabled it to earn to delay the outbreak of revolution within a country. He adds that because of this survival, backward countries must first rise in revolution. He concludes that if the proletariat of a backward country, under the leadership of the Communist Party, can really integrate Marxism-Leninism with the concrete practice of the country's revolution to form a solid worker-peasant alliance led by the working class, it will become the gravedigger of imperialism and its agents, such as bureaucratic capitalism and feudalism.

3. It is historically inevitable that socialist countries "coexist peacefully" with capitalist countries and utilize them, and in developing their foreign relations, the Chinese Communists advocate the Five Principles of Peaceful Coexistence. However, they regard peaceful coexistence as an expedient, and they teach the Party members and cadres that the Five Principles of Peaceful Coexistence are an important development of Lenin's concept of peaceful coexistence under new historical conditions.

In the early twentieth century, Lenin came to the conclusion that imperialism is the precursor of the proletarian revolution. He argued that in the stage of imperialism, because of increased imbalance in the economic and political development of capitalist countries, socialism cannot possibly win victories in most capitalist countries simultaneously but can only win victories in one or some capitalist countries. Therefore, he announced that the Russian Soviet Federated Socialist Republic wished to coexist peacefully with the people of various countries and use its own forces to carry out national construction. He further suggested that to rapidly reactivate and develop the national economy and promote socialist construction, the newly born socialist republic would not only need a peaceful international environment but would also need to use the advanced techniques of Western capitalist countries. However, long-term coexistence is unimaginable, and the final result will surely be the victory of one side or the other.[24] In advocating peaceful coexistence, the Chinese Communists are following Lenin's line of "the new economic policy" and Stalin's "building socialism in one country." Coincidentally, it seems that the Western capitalist countries are adopting the same tactics that they employed to deal with Lenin to handle their relations with Communist China.

4. A socialist society may conduct self-readjustment and reforms without launching a revolution during which one class is overthrown by another. In a socialist society, the proletariat is the ruling class, and it exercises dictatorship through the Communist Party. The dictatorship of the proletariat is in reality the dictatorship of the Communist Party. Under such political conditions, if a revolution is launched by one class to overthrow another, its target will surely be the government of the proletariat or of the Communist Party. Therefore, the Chinese Communists have announced that after the establishment of state power in the form of the people's democratic dictatorship on the Chinese mainland, and especially after socialist transformation had been basically completed and the exploiters had been eliminated as a class, the socialist revolution represented a fundamental break with the past in both content and method although its tasks remained to be completed. They have also emphasized that under socialist conditions, a great political revolution, in which one class overthrows anothers, can only bring grave disorder, damage and retrogression.[25]

In addition, they are making strenuous efforts to make it known that the nature of the socialist system is such that it is perfectly possible to correct all its shortcomings and defects through reform--the so-called superiority of socialism.[26] They insist that the basic contradictions of a socialist society, namely, the contradiction between the relations of production and productivity and that between the superstructure and the economic base, are completely different from those of a capitalist society. They hold that the basic contradictions of a capitalist society--which are manifested by antagonism, conflicts, and fierce class struggles--cannot be solved by the capitalist system itself and can be solved only by a socialist revolution, while basic contradictions in a socialist society are not antagonistic and can be solved through continued reform of the socialist system itself.[27]

5. The <u>Selected Works of Teng Hsiao-p'ing</u> is a national construction program for building socialism with Chinese characteristics. The <u>Selected Works</u> was published on July 1, 1983, the sixty-second anniversary of the founding of the CCP. On July 12, the CCP Central Committee issued a circular to urge the whole Party to study the work, stating that "the <u>Selected Works of Teng Hsiao-p'ing</u> systematically reflects the correct leadership of the Party represented by Teng Hsiao-p'ing." The statement that the Party is represented by Teng signifies that the book contains the viewpoints of the Teng faction, and the emphasis on the correct leadership of the Party implies that the book is a product of a struggle against an erroneous leadership and that a struggle against opposing forces will continue. The same circular urges all Chinese Communists to study Teng's works conscientiously, review their experience in recent years in connection with their actual thinking and work (veterans are urged to review their experiences gained over the past thirty years or so since the founding of Communist China), sum up lessons learned, and combat all types of erroneous ideas so as to maintain a political unity with the CCP Central Committee.[28]

On July 25, 1983, the <u>People's Daily</u> reported the appraisal of the <u>Selected Works of Teng Hsiao-p'ing</u> by the National Conference on Propaganda Work, which had closed several days before. The conference concluded that the <u>Selected Works</u> was a national construction program for building socialism with Chinese characteristics; the theoretical basis for the formulation of the Party's line, principles, and policies; and an inheritance and development of Mao Tse-tung thought. It was a starting point and a target in the struggle to build socialism with Chinese characteristics, and it not only was of great significance to the creation of a new situation in socialist modernization but also provided historical guidance for the ideological unification of the whole Party and all nationalities within the country.[29]

In addition, the Chinese Communists have created the idea of the history of the development of Mao Tse-tung thought. They have said that the period since the Third Plenary Session of the Eleventh CCP Central Committee is an important period in the history of the development of Mao Tse-tung thought because since that plenary session, Teng Hsiao-p'ing has ruled out interference from both leftist and rightist forces, has correctly appraised Mao's historical merits, has penetrated the mist that obscured Mao Tse-tung thought for a rather long period, has restored the true features of Mao Tse-tung thought, and has enhanced the further development of Mao Tse-tung thought in the practice of creating a new situation.[30]

It was to be expected that the members of the Teng faction would sum up their search for a theoretical basis for Chinese-type socialism in the <u>Selected Works of Teng Hsiao-p'ing</u>. In fact, their search in different fields and aspects for various forms of the integration of the universal truth of Marxism-Leninism and China's socialist construction was just a prologue to the presentation of the <u>Selected Works</u>. Obviously, Teng's ambition is to succeed Mao as the great teacher, helmsman, and commander of Communist China. However, political unity has not yet been achieved between the CCP Central Committee and other forces, and within the Teng faction itself, there is still controversy over whether the theory of socialist alienation can be made the theoretical basis for reforms. All of this controversy indicates that Teng's policies have not yet won general acceptance. In short, the Teng faction must continue to explore effective ways to enhance the prestige of Teng's version of Mao Tse-tung thought to act as a guide to the Chinese-type socialist road.

CONTINUED EXPLORATION AND READJUSTMENT OF THE EMBRYONIC FORM OF THE BASIC STRUCTURE

Teng and his followers have discussed in detail the theoretical aspect of the Chinese-type socialist road. However, as far as the basic structure of practical systems is concerned, the concept has been developed in only an embryonic form. Hu Ch'i-li's address on April 28, 1984, at a labor-day meeting in Peiping may serve as proof of this assertion. He stated that the line and policies adopted by the Third Plenary Session of the Eleventh CCP Central Committee and the Twelfth CCP National Congress were all correct and irreversible, and he emphasized the necessity of advancing on this road.[31] Two things are reflected in his statements. First, to build socialism with Chinese characteristics, the Teng faction must continue the search for better practical systems. Second, as some people object to the existing embryonic form of the structure and are trying to do away with it, there may possibly be changes in the future. Hu Ch'i-li also contended that to raise productivity on a large scale, a series of reforms must be introduced to change those relations of production that are incongruous with the development of productivity; those parts of the superstructure that are incongruous with the economic base; and all unsuitable management methods, activities, and ways of thinking.[32] This statement indicates that the Teng faction is not satisfied with existing reforms and will continue to institute new ones.

The Sixth Plenary Session of the Eleventh CCP Central Committee announced ten key points in relation to the correct road to socialism with Chinese characteristics. These were based on the summing up of the historical experiences of Chinese socialist modernization. Later, the Twelfth CCP National Congress summed up seven basic characteristics of socialism from the historical experiences of all Communist parties in building socialism. These ten key points and seven basic characteristics give an approximate idea of the Chinese type of socialism that the Teng faction is promoting. A resolution adopted by the Sixth Plenary Session of the Eleventh CCP Central Committee stated the ten key points of socialist modernization as follows.

1. After socialist transformation was basically completed, the principal contradiction Communist China has had to resolve is that between the growing material and cultural needs of the people and the backwardness of social production.

2. In socialist economic construction,

strenuous efforts must be made to reach the goal of modernization systematically and in stages according to the conditions and resources of Communist China.

3. The reform and improvement of the socialist relations of production must be in conformity with the level of the productive forces and conducive to the expansion of production. The task of the Chinese Communists is to create those specific forms of the relations of production that correspond to the needs of the growing productive forces and facilitate their continued advance.

4. Class struggle no longer constitutes the principal contradiction after the exploiters have been eliminated as classes. However, owing to certain domestic factors and influences from abroad, class struggle will continue to exist within certain limits for a long time to come and may even grow acute under certain conditions. It is necessary to oppose both the view that the scope of class struggle must be enlarged and the view that it has died out.

5. A fundamental task of the socialist revolution is gradually to establish a highly democratic socialist political system. It is essential to consolidate the people's democratic dictatorship. The kind of chaotic situation that prevailed during the Cultural Revolution must never be allowed to happen again in any sphere.

6. Life under socialism must attain a high ethical and cultural level. It is imperative to engage in a more diligent study of Marxist theories; strengthen and improve ideological and political work; persist in the educational policy that calls for being both red and expert, integration of the intellectuals with the workers and peasants, and the combination of mental and physical labor; and counter the influence of decadent bourgeois ideology as well as that of the remnants of feudal ideology.

7. It is of profound significance to such a multinational country as Communist China to improve and promote socialist relations among its various nationalities and strengthen national unity. To uphold the Four Basic Principles does not mean that religious believers should renounce their faith, but it does mean they must not engage in propaganda

against Marxism-Leninism and Mao Tse-tung thought, and they must not interfere with politics and education in their religious activities.

8. In the present international situation, in which the danger of war still exists, it is necessary to strengthen the modernization of national defense.

9. In external relations, it is imperative to oppose imperialism, hegemonism, colonialism, and racism; uphold proletarian internationalism; and support the cause of the liberation of oppressed nations, the national construction of newly independent countries, and the just struggles of people everywhere.

10. It is imperative to build up a sound system of democratic centralism inside the Chinese Communist Party, consolidate its organization, purify its ranks, and correctly handle its relations with other organizations.[33]

The seven basic characteristics of socialism, as summed up by the Twelfth CCP National Congress are
1. Elimination of the system of exploitation
2. Public ownership of the means of production
3. Distribution according to labor
4. A planned and proportional development of the national economy
5. A spiritual civilization with communism as the core
6. A government of the working class and the laboring people
7. Highly developed productive forces and a labor productivity higher than that in capitalist countries.[34]

Judging from all of the above points, the Teng faction's "building socialism with Chinese characteristics" involves politics, the economy, military affairs, psychology, and foreign policy. Although the central task is the development of the economy, the program also covers other spheres; although in the economic sphere, it gives top priority to the development of productive forces, it also attaches importance to other economic problems. Therefore, comprehensive observation is necessary to understand the practice of socialism with Chinese characteristics. I think it is appropriate to use the formula mentioned by Hu Yao-pang in an address commemorating the centenary of the death of Marx on March 13, 1983. Hu said: "Provided that we adhere to the four basic principles and the basic system of socialism, we will surely succeed in building socialism with Chinese characteristics by readjusting those links in the relations of production that are not in correspondence with the requirements of the economic base."[35] In accordance with this structural outline, I shall discuss Chinese-type socialism from the perspective of the transformation of the economic base, the readjustment of the superstructure, and the integration of the economic base with the superstructure.

Let us first examine the transformation of the economic base, including the forms of ownership of the means of production, the status and interrelation of various social groups in production, and the forms of product distribution. The Chinese Communists adhere to the socialist system of public ownership of the means of production and attach special importance to the leading position of a socialist economy of ownership by the whole people, which they regard as the foundation of the socialist economy and the most fundamental sign of its superiority. They do so because blindness and spontaneity exist in the economy of collective ownership and the individual economy manifests even a greater degree of blindness and spontaneity. In their opinion, only by maintaining the leading position of the system of ownership by the whole people with the state economy as the organizational form can the activities of the collective economy be guided toward socialism in such aspects as machinery and equipment, raw materials, energy, procurement and marketing, the Party's guidelines and policies, and economic levers and only by guidance and conditioning in such spheres as raw materials, commodity supply, prices, taxation, and administration can the individual economy be transformed into a necessary supplement to the economy of public ownership.[36]

In agriculture, the Chinese Communists continue to adhere to the system of collective ownership by the laboring people, but they have introduced some organizational reforms. For instance, they have separated government administration from commune management and reestablished village governments. However, in most areas, the people's communes are preserved as administrative organizations of agricultural economy, though the existence of other organizational forms is permitted.

The supplementary role of the individual economy and the collective economy of laborers in cities and towns in developing a socialist economy has already been confirmed. As the implementation of the responsibility system of contracted farm production to individual households in the people's communes and the reorganization of enterprises to improve economic results in the cities have produced a large surplus labor force, it has become necessary to introduce the individual economy and the collective economy of laborers in cities and towns to prevent the increased unemployed population from causing a social crisis.

Joint ventures using Chinese and foreign investment and special economic zones are now described as "the state capitalist economy." Their role is to absorb foreign investment and advanced technology, and the adoption of these new forms is the newest application of the dialectical law concerning the principle and tactical flexibility of socialism.

With the coexistence of such economic sectors as ownership by the whole people, collective ownership, individual ownership, and the state capitalist economy, Communist China's economy seems to have retrogressed to the period of new democracy. However, this is not so in reality, because the system of socialist public ownership still maintains a position of absolute dominance.

In the sphere of management, the Chinese Communists have introduced organizational reforms and readjusted the status and interrelation of the various sectors in socialist social production. In the sphere of production, they have confirmed the supplementary role of market regulation in the socialist economy; and they have sought to fix the limits of mandatory plans, guiding plans, and market regulation in the socialist planned economy.[37] They have acknowledged that commodity production continues to exist in a socialist society, that the products serving as the means of production in industry are commodities, that the law of value plays a regulatory role, and that competition exists under socialist conditions. They have also expanded the decision-making power of enterprises. At present, enterprises have the right to arrange the production and marketing of their products provided they can fulfill state plans and state purchase quotas. This new policy has enabled various enterprises to compete with one another and to enhance their ability to adapt to the market.[38] A change to commodity production in agriculture is regarded as a "strategic" policy, and strenuous efforts are being made to promote this change.

In the sphere of circulation, the Chinese Communists are trying to reform the highly centralized system of unified purchase and marketing of commodities within the country as well as of unified imports and exports. As far as the domestic market is concerned, attention is being paid to increasing circulation channels and reducing circulation links. Means of industrial production have begun to circulate as commodities, and some flexible methods have been introduced for the planned distribution of materials. Both collective and individual commerce have been restored, and such operational forms as ventures jointly financed by industrial and commercial organizations, by the agricultural and commercial sectors, and by industrial enterprises and trading companies have emerged. Fair trade has been restored in towns and villages, and small-commodities trade warehouses and markets that are run by individual laborers have been set up.[39] The right of conducting foreign trade has been transferred to a limited extent to lower-level trading organizations. The policy of decentralized management has been implemented, and enterprises engaging in foreign trade are allowed to keep a certain percentage of the foreign exchange they earn. In Kwangtung and Fukien Provinces, except for some particular commodities, all exports are handled by provincial-level organizations. In addition, eleven enterprises have been authorized to carry out foreign trade directly and attempt to integrate industry with foreign trade. The Import and Export Corporation under the Ministry of Foreign Trade has also adopted measures to promote imports and exports and to organize joint export ventures.[40]

In the sphere of distribution, in order to encourage enterprises and their staff members and workers to show concern for production and management and pay more attention to increasing economic results, the Chinese Communists are emphasizing the principle of material profit and linking production and management results with rewards to staff members and workers. A floating wage system without a fixed ceiling or floor for bonuses has been introduced on a trial basis in industrial enterprises. However, to prevent the indiscriminate distribution of bonuses, a method of taxation has recently been introduced under which taxes on bonuses have to be paid by the enterprises concerned. Various production responsibility systems have been implemented in rural areas to link the results of labor with income. City industrial and commercial enterprises run under the system of ownership by the whole people are also trying to implement various production responsibility systems on a trial basis. However, they are still groping for applicable methods because their conditions are quite different and the problems involved are very complicated. The financial system of a unified handling of revenue and expenditure was discontinued in 1980. Central government finance is now separated from that of local government, and each government body is responsible for its own revenue and expenditure. The central government no longer provides local governments with needed funds, and each local government has to raise funds and plan its expenditure by itself.[41] The system of substituting taxes for profits delivered to the state is another important reform. It is regarded as a form of the system of economic responsibility that reflects the relations of profit distribution between the state and enterprises.[42]

In the sphere of consumption, importance is being attached to the relations between accumulation and consumption. In March 1979, in an address to the CCP Central Committee (CCPCC) Politburo, Ch'en Yun said:

> Ours is a big country with more than 900 million people and 80 percent of them are peasants. Thirty years have passed since the victory of our revolution and the people

> are now asking for improvements in their standard of living. There have actually been some improvements, but there are still beggars in quite a number of places. This is a big problem. If it is not solved in ten or twenty years, secretaries of our Party branches in those places will be leading the people to the cities to beg for food.[43]

According to recently announced statistics, the average annual per capita peasants' income that could be used for living expenses reached 248.3 yuan in 1983, an increase of 12.7 percent over the previous year; in the same year, the average annual per capita income of staff members and workers that could be used for living expenses reached 526 yuan, an increase of 6.4 percent over the previous year, and after allowing for the rise in the cost of living index, the real income of staff members and workers rose by 4.3 percent.[44]

Without doubt, the Chinese Communists have carried out quite a number of economic reforms, and their policy of opening the country to the outside world and enlivening the domestic economy has reaped considerable results. Although the reforms, which are superficial in terms of the economic system itself, have had a rather serious impact on the socialist economy of public ownership, the Chinese Communists continue to uphold the leading position of socialist public ownership and have so far declined to make any concessions. This conflict should not be confused with the reforms. In addition, a considerable number of controversial economic issues in Communist China are old problems that were raised during the 1958 debate. But the people whose opinions are different from those of the ruling faction do not have the chance to openly publish their views, so it is very difficult to find out who they are and what channels they make their views known through. However, the struggle launched by the Teng faction against both leftist and rightist trends proves that there are indeed some people whose opinions differ from those of the Teng faction. This fact deserves our attention.

As far as the readjustment of the superstructure

is concerned, the problems involved include the dictatoship in the sphere of ideology, concrete measures to strengthen the state apparatus of dictatorship, and the true meaning of "building a socialist democracy and legal system." In the sphere of ideology, the Four Basic Principles are regarded as the four pillars of socialism, implying that the abandonment of these four principles would ruin the Party and the country. Therefore, the Chinese Communists are making tremendous efforts to combat the attitude of skepticism toward the Four Basic Principles[45] while promoting socialist spiritual civilization. The Four Basic Principles were first proposed by Teng Hsiao-p'ing in his address to the CCP's Theoretical Work Discussion Meeting on March 1, 1979,[46] and the building of socialist spiritual civilization was first mentioned in Teng's address to the Central Work Conference in December 1980. These addresses, together with his other speeches about emancipating ideology, giving play to democracy, destroying idols, and eliminating dogmatic doctrines in 1977 and 1978 (i.e., before the Third Plenary Session of the Eleventh CCP Central Committee) show that Teng has always attempted to tighten political control in the process of seizing, maintaining, and expanding power.

In September 1982, in his report to the Twelfth CCP National Congress, Hu Yao-pang asserted that communism is the core of socialist spiritual civilization. He indicated the relationship between socialist spiritual and material civilization, saying that each is the condition and objective of the other. He explained that socialist material civilization provides an indispensable foundation for socialist spiritual civilization, which, in its turn, gives a tremendous impetus to the former and ensures its correct orientation. In this respect, Teng and Hu hold identical views. Following the proposal of the Four Basic Principles, Teng abolished the people's rights to air their views freely, write big-character posters, and hold great debates by revising the Constitution of Communist China. He then suppressed "the Peiping spring" by violent means. Soon afterward, the controversy over the so-called theory of socialist alienation gradually developed into a struggle against capitalist spiritual pollution. This struggle is developing and will continue for a long period to come. Therefore, it can always be used to purge those people who hold different views, and it has already become a sign of a new "terrorism" in the ideological sphere.

As to the strengthening of the state apparatus of dictatoship, the Chinese Communists have enforced the dictatorship of the proletariat in the form of a people's democracy. They explain that

> the dictatorship of the proletariat must be enforced in a socialist society. However, owing to the different conditions of various countries, the dictatorship of the proletariat must assume different forms in different socialist countries. In our country, the dictatorship of the proletariat is exercised in the form of the people's democratic dictatorship; this corresponds to the situation in our country. It demonstrates in a concrete manner the class situation and the extensive basis of the government of our country in the current period and is a special characteristic of our government.[47]

In 1949, when the Communist regime had just been established, the people's democratic united front was the basis of the government, the Chinese People's Political Consultative Conference (CPPCC) was the highest political organization, and the Common Program of the CPPCC served as the provisional constitution of the country. In those days, it was claimed that the government was a people's democratic dictatorship. After the adoption of the first Constitution of Communist China in 1954, the CPPCC became a pure united front organization, and when the 1954 Constitution was revised in 1974, the people's democratic dictatorship became the dictatorship of the proletariat, and the CPPCC suspended all its activities. With the collapse of the united front, various "democratic parties," which were targets of united front work, were on the verge of extinction.

In 1978, the Constitution was again revised, but the dictatorship of the proletariat remained unchanged. However, the CPPCC resumed its activities, and the people's democratic united front was renamed the revolutionary united front. The CPPCC became a peripheral organization for uniting various social forces on the Chinese mainland. The 1978 Constitution was revised in 1982, and the dictatorship of the proletariat was changed back to the people's democratic dictatorship to demonstrate in a concrete manner the class situation and the basis of the government. These changes seem to suggest that Communist China has already retrogressed to 1949, or at least to 1954. However, name changes do not mean much. So long as the Four Basic Principles are upheld, there will always be dictatorship by the leaders of the CCP, no matter what form that dictatorship takes.

The Chinese Communists have always maintained the apparatus of dictatorship such as security and procuratorial and judicial organs. In recent years, a Ministry of State Security and a People's Armed Police Headquarters were set up to strengthen the existing state apparatus of dictatorship and to check the trend toward social liberalization and capitalist influences caused by opening up the country to the outside world. These two newly established organizations operate at all levels, from the center to the grass roots. Judging by this standard, Teng has adopted more repressive measures to strengthen the dictatorship than Mao did.

In the sphere of building a socialist democracy and legal system, the Chinese Communists have instituted quite a number of laws, including a Criminal Law and a Law of Criminal Procedure. Special attention has been paid to the institution of economic laws to meet the needs of promoting economic relations with foreign countries and of reforming the economic management system. However, there is still no civil law. The Chinese Communists themselves have acknowledged that their legal system is still far from perfect. The cry is often heard that "there are no laws to abide by" that "affairs are handled contrary to existing laws or according to the will of cadres" because cadres still have deep-rooted habits of bureaucratism and privilege. Since mid-1982, the Chinese Communists have adopted the policy of rounding up the criminals at a stroke and meting out serious punishments quickly, and they have resorted to political movements to solve the problem of social crimes. Thus, they have themselves undermined the legal system they have made efforts to propagate in the past few years. However, this problem is only the tip of the iceberg. The real core lies in their basic concepts of democracy and a legal system.

The Chinese Communists hold that a democratic system, on the Chinese mainland and in other countries, is an organizational and systematic way of employing violence against the people.[48] They regard laws as written provisions of the Party's policies, and they emphasize the need to proceed from the realities of the socialist economic base in building a Chinese-style socialist legal system. In other words, the socialist legal system must serve the economic base and conform with the current situation and the trend of class and class struggle.[49] To promote democracy and the legal system on the basis of such concepts cannot possibly lead to substantial progress.

MEASURES OF INTEGRATION AND CONCLUSION

In this section, I shall examine the measures the Chinese Communists have adopted to integrate the transformation of the economic base with the readjustment of the superstructure and offer my conclusion about the changing situation in Communist China.

1. A new name, i.e., the Chinese-type socialist road, has been proposed, and the development of Communist China's domestic situation since Mao's death can roughly be divided into four periods. The period from Mao's death to the downfall of the Gang of Four in October 1976 was a prologue to the power struggle within the CCP. In the period from October 1976 to the Third Plenary Session of the Eleventh CCP Central Committee in December 1978, Hua and Teng were struggling for leadership and Hua had the upper hand. During the period from December 1978 to the Twelfth CCP National Congress in September 1982, Teng gradually gained the upper hand over Hua. At the Twelfth CCP National Congress, Teng formally completed the

struggle to "substitute his own faction for the Party" and attained the leadership that he has gradually consolidated since then.

During the initial stage of this long-drawn-out struggle, Teng mainly paid attention to solving the problems left after the Cultural Revolution. Later, he emphasized settling the new problems that had arisen in the process of solving the old. His most urgent need was to get Party members to agree whether the Party's principles and policies since the Third Plenary Session of the Eleventh CCP Central Committee had been socialist or capitalist. To this end, he advanced a new theory and summed up the Party line, principles, and policies as "building socialism with Chinese characteristics." He said that it was necessary, in the current situation, to take a Chinese-type socialist road. By giving a new name to the expedient measures taken since the Third Plenary Session of the Eleventh CCP Central Committee and calling for popular support, Teng signified that the struggle to seize power was over and the struggle to consolidate power had just begun.

2. A struggle against the trend toward capitalist liberalization has been launched. This struggle has three main tasks, the first of which is to criticize the theory of socialist alienation. The people who have advocated this theory were originally theorists belonging to the Teng faction. When Teng was struggling hard for the leadership, they used this theory to explain that the Cultural Revolution and individual superstition were phenomena of alienation in a socialist society, and they said that Teng's reforms to bring order out of chaos were aimed at solving the problem of alienation. The theory of socialist alienation conformed with Teng's needs at that time, but once he had taken over the leadership, the situation changed. At present, Teng, with power in his own hands, is attempting to carve out a historical image that Mao was the leader of a Chinese-type socialist revolution while Teng himself is leading Chinese-type socialist construction. The theory of socialist alienation has become incompatible with current needs because if it is acknowledged to be correct, Teng himself will be the first example of alienation. Theorists who failed to notice this

change and continued to advocate the theory of socialist alienation, such as Chou Yang and Wang Jo-shui, have been attacked.

The second task of the struggle against the trend toward liberalization is to eliminate capitalist spiritual pollution. In their reform of the economic system, the Chinese Communists have introduced the concept of a market economy and have even applied capitalist methods in administering enterprises. An inevitable result of this Western influence is spiritual pollution, which the Chinese Communists badly want to eliminate. Therefore, they advocate the adoption of a sober and correct attitude toward capitalist economic theories. They contend that although market regulation and the law of value are economic principles that human beings have arrived at through observing the objective world, capitalist economists of modern times are in fact trying hard to "explain," defend, and cover up capitalist contradictions. They give as an example a textbook on economics written by Paul A. Samuelson, saying that in his book, Samuelson regards capitalism as an everlasting system and refrains from discussing such questions as the origin, development, and destruction of capitalist methods of production.[50] This argument shows that the Chinese Communists will not take the capitalist road.

The third task of the struggle against the liberalization trend is to attack the spontaneous trend toward capitalism. Measures such as cracking down on economic crimes and building socialist spiritual civilization have been implemented for this purpose.

3. An all-out Party consolidation movement has been launched, and efforts have been made to promote the four modernizations of cadres and the building of a three-echelon cadre contingent. The Chinese Communists have consistently emphasized that after the Party line and policies have been formulated, cadres become the decisive factor. A review of the history of the CCP intra-Party struggles shows that since the rectification movement launched by Mao in Yenan, whenever a faction gains victories in a power struggle, it routinely initiates a rectification movement within the Party to thoroughly eliminate alien elements

and to consolidate its own power base. Therefore, it was a matter of course that Teng arranged a "Party consolidation" to purge "three types of person"[51] after the conclusion of the Twelfth CCP National Congress.

The movement has gradually gained momentum since the establishment of the Central Party Consolidation Commission at the Second Plenary Session of the Twelfth CCP Central Committee in October 1983. The movement is to be divided into two stages. The aim of the first stage is the consolidation of Party organizations at and above the provincial level. So far, the study of documents on Party consolidation has been completed, and Party organizations are now required to examine themselves by the standards mentioned in the documents. In the near future, a reorganization will be conducted after experiences have been summed up and the reregistration of Party members will be carried out. However, judging by the current situation, it is possible that the movement will be reduced to the level of mere formality, and the Teng faction has not yet decided on measures to avert such a danger. After the Party organizations at and above the provincial level have been consolidated, the second stage of work will begin in Party organizations below the provincial level. At present, those Party organizations are being asked to correct themselves before consolidation work begins. The whole Party consolidation movement, which, according to Teng's plan, will be completed within three years, is part of the preparation for the convocation of the Thirteenth CCP National Congress. At that congress, there will be a further readjustment of the central leadership, so the current reforms of organizations, personnel, and systems are marks of a period of transition.

The Teng faction has adopted two measures to get the country on a Chinese-type socialist road. First, Teng wants to revolutionize leading bodies and make them younger, better educated, and more professionally competent. Second, he wants to prepare the leadership succession by building a three-echelon cadre contingent. At first, Teng divided the ranks of cadres into the first line, the second line, and the third line and asked veteran cadres to retreat to second- and third-line positions and to give up their power. Later, he proposed the idea of building a three-echelon cadre contingent with Ch'en Yun and himself as members of the first echelon and the real power-holders. In brief, there are two different methods of classification. The veteran cadres who have retreated to the second- and third-line positions are, of course, dissatisfied with Teng's measures to defend his own privileges.

4. When Lenin adopted the new economic policy after the period of "war communism," factories, mines, and enterprises were run according to a system of state capitalism. Lenin also levied a grain tax, protected rich peasants, and issued a call to "get rich." Basically, his policy, like that of the current Chinese Communist leadership, was to open up the country to the outside world and to enliven the domestic economy. However, Lenin frankly admitted that he was effecting a retreat. He explained the situation in terms of troops advancing to a position too far from base who must retreat in order to avoid going deep into enemy positions without logistic support. He said that the consolidation of the worker-peasant alliance was the base. Teng reviewed the historical experiences of the CCP and discovered that it had taken the wrong road. He has, therefore, decided to retreat to the point at which this wrong turning was taken and start again on the right road. His plan for restarting also proceeds from reestablishing and consolidating the worker-peasant alliance. In enlivening the domestic economy, he has attached great importance to readjusting rural economic policies; politically, such action may help the peasants back to the alliance.

We can also compare Teng's Chinese-type socialist road with the situation pertaining in other socialist countries. Yugoslavia is practicing market socialism, Romania has agricultural combines, and the Soviet Union is reforming its economic system on a trial basis. The Chinese Communists may learn something from the experiences of these countries, but since they are emphasizing building Chinese-type socialism, it will be impossible for them to copy directly from other socialist countries. Besides, the Chinese Communist reform of the economic system is only superficial; the core is still "Soviet style." Solving the contradiction between new measures and old systems has already become a thorny problem.

In brief, Communist governments have always upheld political dictatorship even when they have been trying to reform their economic systems. So far, no Communist country has ever metamorphosed into a free and democratic country through economic reforms. Therefore, the socialist modernization of Communist China will not automatically lead to the democratization of its politics, and without political democratization, Communist China's achievements in modernization will be a potential threat to the free world. When giving assistance to Communist China, countries of the free world should pay attention to the question of labor alienation in their own society.

5. One of the forces pushing the Chinese Communists to readjust or reform their country's economic systems is social psychology. The mainland people, feeling the easing of political pressure after Mao's death, suddenly expressed their long-cherished hope for an improvement in economic and political life, and the Chinese Communists have been forced to respond to this desire. However, the most important motive force has been the continuation of the Party line and power struggle within the CCP over the past twenty years and more. Unending controversy over the line and policies has reflected the rise and fall of different factions, which may be proved by the surprising amount of similarity between the themes of the debate during the latter part of the 1950s and those of the current theoretical controversy.

However, China today is not the China of yesterday; even the people are not the same. Once the reform of the economic system has been initiated, the mainland people know how to employ it to gain concessions from the Chinese Communists. For instance, when the agricultural responsibility system was first introduced in the rural areas, it was stipulated that contracts could be concluded only with production groups, but the people themselves implemented the system of "contracted farm production to individual households"; when the Chinese Communists approved the implementation of this system, the people went one step further and demanded the introduction of the system of "contracted farm production linking remuneration with output"; when this system was also adopted, the people went another step further and asked for the extension of the duration of contracts from one to three years, then to five years, ten years, and even longer. So far, the Chinese Communists have been forced to extend the duration of contracts to fifteen years. They describe all their concessions as resulting from the Party's respect for the creative spirit of the masses. The question now is, how far will the Chinese Communists let themselves be dragged by this creative spirit? What measures will they adopt to suppress this spirit when they feel that they may lose control of the situation because of the rapid development of social liberalization?

In recent years, the Teng faction has repeatedly guaranteed that its existing policies will not be changed. But in fact, the reforms it is promoting have not yet been completed and are always changing--now in the direction of respecting the creative spirit of the masses. However, the Teng faction will refuse to act according to this spirit and will tighten its policies again when its political control is threatened. The new crisis that may arise under such circumstances will also deserve our close attention.

NOTES

1. "Communique of the Third Plenary Session of the 11th CCP Central Committee," <u>Peking Review</u> 21:52 (December 29, 1978), pp. 6-16.
2. Teng Hsiao-p'ing, "Uphold the Four Basic Principles," in <u>San-chung ch'Üan-hui i-lai chung-yao wen-chien hsuan-pien</u> [A Selection of important documents since the Third Plenary Session] (Beijing: People's Publishing House, August 1982), p. 86.
3. Ibid., p. 87.
4. Ibid., p. 103.
5. Ibid.
6. <u>Teng Hsiao-p'ing wen-hsuan</u> [Selected works of Teng Hsiao-p'ing] (Beijing: People's Publishing

House, July 1983), pp. 371-372.

7. <u>Liu Shao-ch'i hsuan-chi</u> [Selected works of Liu Shao-ch'i], vol. 1 (Beijing: People's Publishing House, 1981), p. 332.

8. Chang Ch'un-ch'iao, "Eliminate the Idea of Bourgeois Rights," <u>People's Daily</u>, October 13, 1958.

9. Wu I, "Don't Negate the Historical Significance of the Wage System," <u>People's Daily</u>, October 17, 1958.

10. <u>People's Daily</u>, October 13, 1958.

11. <u>People's Daily</u>, October 17, 1958.

12. Ho Chih-chung, "'Distribution According to Labor' Is the Foundation of the Current Distribution System in Our Country," <u>People's Daily</u>, October 17, 1958.

13. Hu Sheng, "On Our Commodity Production at the Present Time," <u>People's Daily</u>, December 20, 1958.

14. Cheng Chi-ch'iao, "On the Weakening of Bourgeois Rights," <u>People's Daily</u>, October 31, 1958.

15. Wang P'u, "We Cannot Negate the Principle of Material Profit," <u>People's Daily</u>, January 20, 1959.

16. Yü Ch'ang-pin, "Mental Labor Must Be Integrated with Manual Labor," <u>People's Daily</u>, November 29, 1958.

17. Department of Economics and Other Departments of the Chinese People's University, "A Discussion of the Questions of Commodity Production and the Law of Value," <u>People's Daily</u>, April 3, 1979.

18. <u>People's Daily</u>, December 18, 1958.

19. Liu I, "It Is Imperative to Implement the Wage System After Liberation," <u>People's Daily</u>, October 17, 1958.

20. Hsueh Hsin, "A Sharp Weapon of Ideological and Theoretical Work--Reading Notes on the <u>Selected Works of Teng Hsiao-p'ing</u>," <u>Liberation Army Daily</u>, November 8, 1983.

21. "Studying and Propagating the <u>Selected Works of Teng Hsiao-p'ing</u> Help Cadres and the Masses to Understand the General Program of National Construction," <u>People's Daily</u>, July 25, 1983.

22. Fan Jo-yü and Chiang Liu, eds., <u>K'e-hsueh she-hui chu-i kai-lun</u> [An Introduction to scientific socialism] (Beijing: Central Party School Press, July, 1983), p. 53.

23. Wang Ching-ch'un, "On the Inevitability of Backward Countries Developing into Socialist Societies First," <u>Hsin-hua wen-chai</u> [The Hsinhua collection of essays], no. 6 (Beijing, 1983), p. 57. This article was first published in <u>She-hui k'e-hsueh chi-k'an</u> [A Collection of essays on social sciences], no. 2 (Shenyang: Liaoning Provincial Academy of Social Sciences, 1983).

24. Fan Jo-yü and Chiang Lin, <u>K'e-hsueh she-hui chu-i kai-lun</u>.

25. "Resolution on Certain Questions in the History of Our Party Since the Founding of the People's Republic of China," <u>Beijing Review</u> 24:27 (July 6, 1981), pp. 10-39.

26. Hsi Chung-hsun, "Be a New Generation with the Greatest Creative Spirit--A Speech at the Meeting Celebrating the 65th Anniversary of the May 4th Movement," <u>People's Daily</u>, May 5, 1984.

27. Shao Hua-tse, "Socialist Reforms Cannot Be Explained by the Concept of Alienation," <u>Liberation Army Daily</u>, November 19, 1983.

28. "The CCPCC Circular on Studying the <u>Selected Works of Teng Hsiao-p'ing</u>," <u>People's Daily</u>, July 13, 1983.

29. <u>People's Daily</u>, July 25, 1983.

30. Li Ming-te, "Uphold and Develop the Brilliant Model of Mao Tse-tung Thought," <u>Kwangming Daily</u>, July 2, 1983.

31. Hu Ch'i-li, "Speech at the Meeting Celebrating the May 1 International Labor Day," New China News Agency broadcast, April 28, 1984.

32. Ibid.

33. "Resolution on Certain Questions in the History of Our Party."

34. Wu Chen-k'un, "A Discussion About Building Socialism with Chinese Characteristics," <u>Kwangming Daily</u>, September 25, 1983.

35. <u>Beijing Review</u> 26:12 (March 21, 1983), p.V (as rewritten by the translator).

36. Sun Hsueh-wen, "Uphold the Leading Position of the Socialist System of the Ownership by the Whole People," <u>Kwangming Daily</u>, December 11, 1983.

37. Fan Mou-fa, "A Summary of the Investigation on Determining the Limits of Mandatory Plans, Guiding Plans, and Market Regulation," <u>Kwangming Daily</u>, April 17, 1983.

38. Ibid.
39. Hsü Ching-an, Ni Ti, and Fang Kung-wen, "New Developments of the Reform of the Economic System in Recent Years," <u>Kwangming Daily</u>, August 28, 1983.
40. Ibid.
41. Ibid.
42. Editorial of the <u>China Peasant News</u>, "Two Main Links in Perfecting the Responsibility System of Contracted Farm Production Linking Remuneration to Output," reprinted in <u>People's Daily</u>, January 20, 1984.
43. <u>San-chung ch'üan-hui i-lai chung-yao wen-chien hsuan-pien</u>, p. 74.
44. "Communique Issued by the State Statistical Bureau," <u>People's Daily</u>, April 30, 1984.
45. <u>Teng Hsiao-p'ing wen-hsuan</u>, pp. 151-152.
46. Ibid.
47. <u>Kwangming Daily</u>, September 25, 1983.
48. Second Lesson of the Broadcasting Course on Democracy, "Democracy Is a Kind of State Form," Central Broadcasting Station of Mainland China, October 13, 1979.
49. Chang Sung-yang and Wang Kuei-hsiu, "Proletarian Democracy and Proletarian Dictatorship," <u>People's Daily</u>, January 22, 1979.
50. Huang Fan-chang, "The Correct Treatment of Modern Bourgeois Economic Theories," <u>Kwangming Daily</u>, November 20, 1983.
51. The "three types of person" are those who rose to prominence by following the counter-revolutionary cliques of Lin Piao and Chiang Ch'ing in rebellion; those who are seriously factionalist in their ideas; and those who indulge in beating, smashing and looting.

2
The Nature of Chinese Communism and the Prospects for Teng's Reforms

Cal Clark

The emergence of Teng Hsiao-p'ing and his closest allies as preeminent power-holders in mainland China in the early 1980s was taken by many in the West to herald an era of major reform in Chinese politics because of the Teng faction's long-standing hostility to Maoist radicalism and because of the defeat of the leftists associated with Hua Kuo-feng and the declining power of the veteran cadres who opposed any significant political or economic change.[1] And, in fact, radical policy initiatives were clearly made in agriculture, Western economic contacts, and very briefly in freedom of political expression. Less spectacularly, Teng has clearly indicated that his principal policy goal is now economic development rather than the implementation of radical Maoist social goals and that he hopes to restructure the Party and government organizations in order to create professional bureaucracies that are capable of effectively directing the mainland toward economic development and prosperity. These reforms might be seen as a prologue to the recent program of the Third Plenum of the Twelfth Central Committee, which proclaimed far-reaching market reforms for the Chinese economy.[2]

Yet, despite these profound changes, there are still indications that Teng's reforms may remain distinctly limited. The dissident movement centered on the Democracy Wall and the constitutional commitment to the Four Great Freedoms proved quite abortive; Teng's first decentralization program in industrial planning and production was ineffective; the recent campaign against spiritual pollution--although the degree of Teng's responsibility and support for it is somewhat questionable--is certainly at variance with the liberalizing image of mainland China; and, as will be discussed in detail later, many of the political practices of the Maoist era still remain essentially unchanged.

The theme of the Thirteenth Sino-American Conference on Mainland China, which concerned the nature, extent, and permanence of Teng's reforms, then, certainly is an important and intriguing one. This chapter seeks to evaluate the question of what these reforms are likely to bring by comparing mainland China to the well-established Communist regime in the Soviet Union. Such a comparison is aimed at illuminating a series of topics: (1) the nature of communism in mainland China; (2) the strategies of Communist regimes for retaining power and creating popular allegiance, (3) the role of communism in promoting economic modernization, and (4) what these factors suggest about the probable outcomes of Teng's reforms.

This approach reflects what is called a "structuralist perspective" in social science analysis. This perspective presupposes that even though situational factors--such as Teng's true goals and motivations, the changing balance of forces in the CCP center, and the identity of the successor generation that will inevitably assume power soon--may be very important in determining short-term policy and personnel issues, they operate within constraints that stem from the basic nature or essence of the Communist regime. Thus, even if the situational factors turn out to be the most favorable for reform, the reforms may fall far short of their promise because of the structural features of the Chinese Communist system.

The first section of this chapter, then, describes the Soviet Communist system. This regime may be considered fairly successful because of its longevity, which results from a combination of factors that, ironically, have little to do with the regime's official Marxist-Leninist ideology: (1) an authoritarian form of government that in many ways is consistent with traditional Russian political culture; (2) an impressive record of economic growth that has benefited broad strata of

Soviet citizens; and (3) the regime's ability to appeal to Russian nationalism.

The second section conceptualizes the system of Chinese communism by comparing it to this Soviet model, and I argue that the Chinese Communists suffer several distinct disadvantages compared to the Soviets. The Chinese Communist regime diverges much more from the national political culture; the government has yet to create as sophisticated and workable a bureaucracy; the industrialization and modernization programs have not yet proved to be fully feasible; and the massive disruptions and persecutions of the Cultural Revolution have largely squandered the potential nationalistic support of the Chinese people. Finally, the concluding section examines the implications of the nature of Chinese communism for the long-term viability of Teng's reforms.

THE SOVIET MODEL OF COMMUNISM

Although Marxist philosophy predicted that communism would be the successor of capitalism and the culmination of world historical and economic development, Communist revolutions have occurred only in nations that have relatively underdeveloped economies. Thus, communism is best conceived as an alternate development strategy to capitalism-- one based on a similar, if not greater, exploitation of the working class and peasantry than the early capitalist pattern described by Marx (euphemistically termed "primitive socialist accumulation") and on a much greater degree of political repression than in capitalist industrializing states.

The process of Communist industrialization, however, transformed Soviet society and placed increasing pressure on many of the Communists' basic political institutions and practices. This section argues, therefore, that fundamental changes have occurred in the domestic political institutions of the Soviet Union during the post-Stalin period. The system changed from a highly personalistic totalitarian dictatorship to a complex bureaucratic oligarchy. Although the new system is quite sophisticated and has experienced marked success in leading the transformation of the USSR to a modern industrial state, it has also created a huge bureaucratic structure, and its interest in self-preservation provides a formidable obstacle to the further development of the Soviet economy and polity.³

Under Stalin, the Soviet Union was ruled by an extremely repressive system that probably merits the title "totalitarianism." Stalin gave the principal political institutions (Party, state, and secret police) overlapping responsibilities and played them off against one another, thus concentrating power in his own hands. Pervasive terror and repression were directed against both the general population and the political elites (including many who seemed absolutely loyal to Stalin) in order to preclude even the opportunity of voicing opposition and discontent. Finally, the system was highly ideological in the sense that all policies were justified in terms of Marxism-Leninism-Stalinism and that any deviation from the official state ideology was a punishable political and criminal offense.⁴

Despite the facts that the Communists claimed to have destroyed all vestiges of the czarist regime and that their official ideology of Marxism-Leninism rejected all previous philosophical and cultural norms, it is not too difficult to see that many elements in the Soviet style of rule follow the norms of the traditional Russian political culture of autocracy and absolutism. Some of the major components of this Russian absolutism were (1) a strong subordination of a "service" nobility to the czar, (2) a tight integration of the Russian Orthodox church into the czarist regime, (3) a very personalistic view of power as residing in the czar (or some other official) rather than in impersonal political institutions, (4) an acceptance of a strong government to counter both external threats and fears of internal disorder, (5) a large state role in the economy, and (6) a belief that the state should assume a broad paternalistic responsibility for both the moral and the materialistic aspects of Russian life. Thus, although the early Communist regime under Lenin and Stalin clearly extended the sphere of government control much further than in the prerevolutionary era, it was still fairly consistent with the absolutist tradition in Russia. Even the murderous excesses of Stalin had their precedent under some of the more notorious czars, such as Ivan the Terrible with whom Stalin evidently identified.[5]

Communist ideology almost mandates a strong commitment to industrialization and economic modernization since a truly classless Communist society is said to represent the final stage of economic growth. Within about three decades, between the early 1930s and the early 1960s, the Communists transformed the USSR from a backward, basically agricultural nation to an advanced, industrial economy. The twin pillars of the Soviet industrialization drive were very high rates of economic investment, probably overconcentrated in heavy industry, and a strong education program that provided the human capital for industrial expansion.

Two very distinct periods can be delineated in the Soviet industrialization drive. First, the Stalinist era saw extreme coercion, including the great purge of the 1930s; heavy-handed central direction of the economy; and the stern suppression of the standard of living to promote investment and growth. In the post-Stalin period, there was a greater reaping of the fruits of industrialization. The Soviet economic structure began to assume a more well-rounded character, economic management became much more professional, and the population as a whole benefited from a very substantial rise in the standard of living and from broad opportunities for upward social mobility.[6]

Moreover, the economic and social transformation of the Soviet Union apparently had some major political repercussions as well. Whether preordained by economic determinism or not, radical changes occurred in the USSR's political superstructure following the death of Stalin. After the interim Khrushchev period, the Soviets under Brezhnev moved toward a more stable type of bureaucratic oligarchy with some of the following characteristics:

1. A stable division of labor between Party and government positions rather than the overlapping and competitive roles of Stalin's totalitarianism

2. Policymaking based primarily on bureaucratic incrementalism rather than on the whims of individual leaders
3. The growth of a bureaucratic "interest group" system marked by continuing and at many times vigorous policy debates within specialized issue areas
4. Much more normal career patterns stressing greater job security and longevity, functional specialization, and professional performance
5. Roles for the key position of regional Party secretary that emphasized policy integration, lobbying, bargaining, and obtaining practical economic results rather than ideological purity and campaigning
6. The granting of much more autonomy, security, and influence to specialized government and Party bureaucracies
7. A style of decision making based on the competition among representatives of these functional bureaucratic interests
8. Consensus decision making both in the collective Politburo and in the resolution of interagency conflicts at lower levels
9. Substantial differences among specific issues in the degree of influence on policy outcomes exercised by lower-level initiatives
10. Attempts to check bureaucratic power by bringing together a wide range of expert opinion in the policy-formation process and by soliciting citizens' comments on government and participation in oversight activities.

Thus, the Brezhnev era was marked by the growth of a complex and differentiated political system. There was increasing emphasis upon expert and rational administration conducted according to professional norms; the dominant mode of decision making became one of incremental bureaucratic bargaining among spokesmen for various societal and sectoral interests; and the regime even tried to provide some checks on petty bureaucratism by providing avenues of political influence for both technical experts and the broader population. Such political development, furthermore, clearly made a major contribution to economic growth and the rising standard of living in the USSR during the two decades between the mid-1950s and the mid-1970s.[7]

Still, the slowdown in economic growth since the mid-1970s has clearly produced substantial increases in popular disaffection[8] and has made basic reforms of government and economic institutions increasingly vital. However, it is precisely the structure of the huge and complex bureaucratic system in the USSR that forms the largest obstacle to meaningful political and economic change because entrenched bureaucrats oppose and undermine any changes that will attenuate their personal and institutional powers. Thus, if there is any merit to the argument that economic development helped change the character of the elites in the Soviet Union, it should be noted that these beneficiaries have in turn tried to arrest the development process by preventing changes in the basic economic institutions that might make their own skills and powers obsolete--an ironic conclusion in view of the Communists' belief that all systems and elites except their own inevitably become barriers to social progress.[9]

The Communist regime in the Soviet Union, thus, has experienced a combination of successes and failures. It has promoted rapid industrialization and created a sophisticated and complex form of bureaucratic government. Yet, it is precisely its current form of government, which seems so progressive and effective by the standards of its czarist and Stalinist predecessors, that now forms a principal obstacle to the major reforms that are needed to reignite economic and social progress. This problem, in turn, has resulted in a mixed record in terms of the regime's efforts to build popular legitimacy and support. First, the Communist regime, especially in its present and much less totalitarian form, seems in line with traditional Russian norms of political authoritarianism, although today's more highly educated population seems to be beginning to resent the monopoly of power exercised by the Communist Party's top elite.

Second, and related to these traditional norms, the Communist regime has been able to stimulate substantial feelings of national patriotism. Third, economic growth has generated significant support for the regime on the basis of its performance in improving its subjects' standard of living, although increased economic problems may now be eroding popular evaluations of the government.

The picture is less rosy for other potential bases of support. Democratic governments based on popular representation and participation derive substantial legitimacy from these institutional arrangements. Although there are more avenues for participation in the USSR than many critics of communism are wont to recognize, the regime clearly elicits little such participatory legitimation. The bulk of the people see themselves as quite separate from the power-holders (<u>vlasti</u>), and there is widespread antipathy toward governmental corruption, which is one of the reasons for the often noted "nostalgia for Stalin" as a "big boss" who could keep the "little bosses" in check.[10] Officially, the Soviet regime legitimizes itself by appealing to the tenets of Marxism-Leninism. Yet, the available evidence indicates that most of the people (and many Party members as well) have become atheists in regard to the official state "religion."[11]

Adding up these pluses and minuses, it would appear that the Communist government in the Soviet Union has won the acceptance of much of the population, although its real bases of support diverge from the officially proclaimed ones and may come under increasing pressure if the domestic performance of the regime does not improve in the future. As a result, the levels of coercion and police terror have dropped greatly from the era of Stalinist totalitarian excesses. Still, political coercion and repression remain significant facts of life in the Soviet Union, even though they are now directed at active dissidents and certain suspect groups (e.g., Jews). One good indication that repression has a continued role in Soviet political life is the Communist addition of the "dual personality" to Russian authoritarian cultural traits. This is the tendency for Soviet citizens to be themselves and "human" in private settings but to adhere to political orthodoxies and rituals when in public view.[12]

THE NATURE OF CHINESE COMMUNISM

Superficially at least, China's situation would seem quite similar to the one in the USSR. Dynastic China had an authoritarian political culture; after Mao's famous lean-to-one-side speech in July 1949, the Chinese Communists explicitly announced their adherence to orthodox Marxism-Leninism and aligned themselves with the USSR; mainland China subsequently adopted basically Stalinist economic policies; and both China and the Soviet Union under communism have witnessed periods of normalcy interspersed with cataclysmic disruptions (collectivization, the great purges, and World War II in the USSR and the Korean War, the Great Leap Forward, and the Cultural Revolution in mainland China).

A closer examination, however, indicates that the nature of Chinese communism and the relationship of the regime to the Chinese people differ significantly from the Soviet case. These differences, moreover, are almost all in the direction of undercutting the developmental potential and bases of popular support in mainland China. In particular, the traditional political culture of China, while authoritarian and paternalistic in nature, is a far cry from Russian absolutism and clashes more sharply with the mores and institutions of a Communist polity than in the Soviet case; the Maoist model of communism proved far less appropriate for promoting economic development than even the brutal Stalinist system; the Great Proletarian Cultural Revolution was much more disruptive and destructive in both an economic and a psychological sense than analogous events in the USSR, such as collectivization and the great purge; and the system of government in mainland China has yet to achieve the degree of bureaucratic sophistication and rationality of the Soviet regime, which throws into some question the ability of the government in China to administer a program of rapid modernization and of economic and political transformation. The four subsections that follow discuss these topics and the problems that they create for mainland China.

The Chinese Political Culture

In terms of a developed political culture, China represents almost the other extreme from Russia. The political culture of Russian autocracy and absolutism was widely regarded as the most backward in Europe; in contrast, China's political culture has existed in a sophisticated form for well over 2,000 years and consisted of an enlightened form of bureaucratic rule by an intellectual or a scholarly elite when European culture was still in the Dark Ages. In terms of the substance of the political norms, the Russian culture stressed the power and autocracy of the czar while the Chinese culture, at least on the philosophical level, was primarily concerned with the social goals that a good government could accomplish.

The philosophical system of Confucianism gave China a common cultural heritage and form of government for over 2,000 years before the fall of the Ch'ing dynasty in 1912. Confucianism is based on a series of interdependent assumptions about the fundamental goals of society, the relationship of individuals to society, and the role of government in creating the good society. First, it is believed that the perfect society is one in which there is total peace and harmony. A second assumption is that the perfectly ordered society is one in which each individual fulfills his or her social role. Society is governed by a set of rules or rituals (the li) that defines how people in different roles should interact with one another. Third, these social roles are linked together in a primarily hierarchical structure, so a society consists of an integrated web of hierarchical social relations that begins in the family and ultimately links the individual to the highest authority in the society (i.e., the emperor). However, although the Confucian ideal of social hierarchy presupposes an authoritarian structure, it is far different from traditional Russian absolutism's concern with the right of the ruler. Rather, Confucianists believe that mutual obligations exist between inferior and superior, even in hierarchical relationships. The inferior owes deference and support to the superior, but in return, the superior must use his or her power to help and protect the inferior, thereby creating the mutual responsibilities and ties of kuan-hsi.

Unfortunately, societies do not attain this perfect state automatically, and the world's history, including that of China, has yet to produce such an ideal social order. The fourth assumption of Confucian philosophy, then, is that the "good" social hierarchy and the various social relationships and rituals that compose it can only be found by intense and extensive scholarly investigation and contemplation. More particularly, it is believed that the perfect social order did exist at the beginning of the Middle Kingdom and that human history and folly gradually corrupted and changed it, necessitating scholarly investigation and interpretation of China's classical literary, philosophical, and historical traditions. This belief further implies a fifth assumption that a person's being or value is determined by his or her inner state of knowledge about the just society and of morality in complying with the social mores and rituals involved in such a society.

Confucian philosophy was transferred to the realm of government with the sixth assumption that the primary goal of government is to promote social harmony and morality. Thus, China should be ruled by virtuous scholars who, through long study and contemplation, had come to recognize the essence of the good social order and hierarchy and who should be given broad powers over social, as well as political, life in order to promote morality and peace for the entire society.[13]

Thus, although the Chinese political culture supports an authoritarian government with powers over its citizenry that reach far beyond what is normally considered to constitute the political sphere, it is really far different from the traditions of Russian absolutism, which emphasize the autocratic powers and prerogatives of a leader. In sharp contrast, the Chinese political culture explicitly assumes that hierarchical social and political relations are based on mutual obligations and that a good government must actively promote the public welfare and the search for a just socity. These deviations from the norms of Russian absolutism, in turn, mean that a stringent political dictatorship, such as the ones implemented by all other ruling Communist regimes to date, would be far more at variance with popular political mores in China than in Russia.

In addition, this distinctive Chinese culture clashes specifically with the tenets of Marxism-Leninism in several ways that the Soviet Union's political culture does not. First, the Chinese emphasis on social stability and searching the past for knowledge of the desired social order directly contradicts the Marxist assumptions of historical progress and revolutionary change. Second, the Chinese belief that scholarship and moral rectitude are the keys to establishing the perfect social order directly clashes with Marxist materialism. Third, traditional social organizations, like the family, are highly valued by the Chinese, while being targeted for destruction by the Communists as a remnant of bourgeois and feudal society. In summary, then, the Chinese political culture would seem much less supportive of a Communist regime than the Russian one.

The Maoist Model

Mao Tse-tung has been given credit for "Sinifying Marxism," and to some extent, this attribution is true. His revolutionary strategy, which was based upon the peasantry and the countryside rather than on the proletariat and the cities, was clearly appropriate for China, and his belief that the human spirit and consciousness were supreme used the philosophical assumptions of Confucianism, albeit with a radically different content, to "stand Marxist materialism on its head." Still, the central elements of Maoism appear to be generally antithetical to the traditional Chinese culture, so Maoism is even more inconsistent than orthodox Marxism with ingrained Chinese beliefs about how politics should be conducted. A second problem facing the Chinese Communist regime is that the form of communism advocated and implemented by Mao was far less suitable for stimulating rapid economic development than the Stalinist model of communism.

Maoism was based on a series of central tenets. Some seemed to derive from orthodox

Marxism-Leninism and others from traditional Chinese thought. Rather than providing a synthesis to Sinify Marxism by making communism applicable to Chinese conditions, however, Mao's combination of these principles produced an extremism that was quite dysfunctional for economic and social development, in China or anywhere else. Parts of Maoism are, at least on the philosophical level, consistent with both Marxism-Leninism and Chinese cultural traditions. These include a basically collectivist conception of society, the belief that government should exercise broad powers to promote the moral development of the people, and a strong dose of anti-imperialism directed against the Western capitalist and colonialist powers.

Other facets of Maoism, though, ensured that the actual implementation of these principles was far different than the precepts of either Confucians or orthodox Marxists. Mao saw collectives as social classes (although not totally in the normal Marxist sense of this term) rather than as the integrated social hierarchy envisioned in traditional Chinese thought, and his emphasis on the need for continual struggle and conflict to keep society progressing--which went far beyond the normal Marxist conception of dialectical conflict as the driving force in history--was the diametric opposite of the Confucian value of social peace and harmony. Conversely, his anti-imperialism and calls for Chinese self-reliance produced a Chinese nationalism that varied a good deal from the alleged proletarian internationalism of Marxism. Moreover, his tremendous emphasis on the human spirit and consciousness, which probably derived from traditional Chinese cultural norms, clearly clashed with Marxist materialism in devising strategies for economic development and even in defining the nature of "classes" in China. Finally, Mao's beliefs that rural values were superior to urban ones differed radically from both Confucianism and Marxism.[14]

The application of these principles produced a regime that was highly ideological, hostile to normal institutional and bureaucratic organizations, and contemptuous of normal approaches (even Marxist ones) to economic development. Maoism's concern with human consciousness and continual struggle resulted in a never-ending series of campaigns aimed at producing ideological conformity through thought reform, struggle sessions, and self-criticism. Thus, instead of accepting public acquiescence--as in the Russian dual personality--Mao seemingly wanted to control all aspects of Chinese life and even thought (e.g., forcing people to engage in self-criticism of their own thoughts and dreams).

Such totalitarian controls of the people (or "masses" in Marxist parlance) carried over into the political and economic spheres as well. Mao was extremely suspicious of any regular institutional or bureaucratic organ, and he used the most radical phase of the Great Proletarian Cultural Revolution to basically destroy the normal Party and government organizations.[15] In the economic realm, despite Mao's original strategy of following a Stalinist pattern of rapid development based on heavy industry, Maoism was quite distinctive from and inferior to the Soviet model as well because Mao's opposition to professional administration, failure to provide material incentives, reliance upon crash programs, and ideas of both national and regional autarchy all inhibited economic growth and development programs.[16]

The degree to which Maoism was applied in mainland China during the life of the Chairman varied quite considerably. Once the country returned to normalcy after the Korean War, periods of relative orthodoxy and stability alternated with the upheaval and chaos of the Great Leap Forward and the Great Proletarian Cultural Revolution.[17] Still, the overall impact of Maoism both exacerbated the difference between Communist political practices and the ideals of traditional Chinese culture and undoubtedly retarded the economic growth of mainland China to a very considerable extent. Much more than even orthodox communism, Maoism produced a state of constant ideological turmoil, totalitarian controls and excesses, and attacks on traditional social institutions and ties--like family and friendship relationships--that directly contravened many of the Chinese cultural norms and thereby further estranged the people from their rulers. Furthermore, the adverse economic results of Maoism were quite substantial, unlike even Stalinist totalitarianism, which at least produced entourages of specific leaders.[21]

Debates over policies or "tendencies" are certainly easy enough to spot in the post-Stalin Soviet Union, both among top leaders and competing bureaucratic interests and among groups within a single issue sector. These policy debates have encompassed questions of sectoral resource allocation, the need to respond to consumer and citizen demands, and, more basically, "orthodox" versus "liberal" and "decentralist" strategies for promoting economic development. Important as these issues certainly are, however, there has been almost no challenge to the desirability of steady industrial growth and the development of a professional and specialist bureaucracy. Rather, the major challenge to the Soviet bureaucracy has been that it needed to decentralize and develop new skills as the USSR evolved into a complex advanced industrial society.

In mainland China, on the other hand, the question of whether a permanent specialized bureaucracy should be developed was one of the central elements in the "battle of two lines" between Maoists and pragmatists that played a prominent role in Communist Chinese politics. As a result of Mao's radical initiatives, relatively short periods of bureaucratic institution building in the mid-1950s and early 1960s were interspersed with the Great Leap Forward and the Cultural Revolution, which came close to destroying the Party and government bureaucracies. Thus, the bureaucratic structure of mainland China in the late 1970s was much less institutionalized or professionally developed and sophisticated than in the USSR.[22]

The system of bureaucratic politics seems well developed in the Soviet Union. Most cadres follow career patterns within a single functional area, bureaucratic organs have been granted substantial autonomy within these functional areas, and much of Soviet politics consists of competition among bureaucratic entities that represent the interests of their various functional areas. In contrast, most observers feel that bureaucratic politics in mainland China are much less significant, and some argue that they are almost nonexistent. The most important reason for this unimportance is Mao's blaming past horrors on individual evil leaders. The Cultural Revolution, in contrast, began with the mobilization of almost an entire generation of students to lead mainland China into a new social order. With the crushing of the Red Guards and the widespread perception that they had just been manipulated and then abandoned by Mao and the other top CCP leaders, cynicism about and alienation from the Communist system became prevalent. Ironically, these feelings evidently have been transferred to the current leaders, most of whom were disgraced and persecuted themselves during the Cultural Revolution.[20]

Form of Communist Bureaucracies

After the death of Stalin, the USSR established a fairly sophisticated and professional form of bureaucratic government. Through the centralized command economy that it administered, this bureaucratic government promoted a rapid industrial growth and a concomitant rise in the popular standard of living between the mid-1950s and the mid-1970s. However, as the USSR developed a sophisticated industrial economy that became increasingly unresponsive to crude central planning, the bureaucracy's opposition to economic and political changes that would undermine its power and status is a principal reason the Soviet Union failed to enact meaningful and increasingly necessary structural reforms.

In mainland China, however, even the first stage of bureaucratization has yet to be attained. This lack of bureaucratic institutionalization can, in turn, be explained by the nature of the Chinese Communist government and the differences between it and its Soviet counterpart. Harry Harding has argued that three major theoretical frameworks all have significant applicability for describing and explaining the nature of the Chinese Communist regime: (1) tendency analysis, which views politics as the struggle between competing policy orientations, (2) bureaucratic politics, which argues that competition among bureaucratic organs pushing their institutional interests creates the major political issues in a society, and (3) factionalism, which conceptualizes politics as the struggle for power among the personal political thereby causing the almost total loss of a generation of human capital.

In addition to the incalculable economic loss and the tremendous number of human tragedies for the millions who were politically persecuted, the Cultural Revolution had another effect--one that may be the most serious for mainland China in the long run--the pervasive distrust of and cynicism toward the regime on the part of a large segment of the population. Fox Butterfield captures these feelings perfectly:

> Chinese who came through the cataclysms of the past thirty years seemed to me like survivors. They were chastened and cynical and numb. When I asked friends how they had coped with their personal tragedies, they often answered, "Ma-mu-le" (I was numbed). "Surviving" is a word they frequently used. It reminded me of a passage [from the wallposter of Li Yizhe] . . . . "We are survivors," the three men had written. "We were once bitten by the tiger but it failed to grind us small enough to swallow. Its claws left scars on our faces, so we are not handsome."
> They spoke for the many Chinese I met who had all been clawed by the tiger.[19]

There are probably several reasons for the difference in the popular reaction to persecution by the world's two largest Communist regimes. First, the much greater acceptance of absolutism in the Russian culture might make the Russians more tolerant of repressive governments, even murderous ones. Second, the much more deleterious economic consequences of the Cultural Revolution also contributed to its greater attitudinal effects. The primary reason, though, may well be the very different nature of these events in the USSR and mainland China in terms of popular involvement. In the Soviet Union, the ravages of collectivization and the great purge were imposed on the population by a highly dictatorial police state, so that when a more moderate regime emerged after Stalin's death, Soviet citizens seemingly gave it credit for their improved economic and political situations while a base for impressive industrial growth in the Soviet Union.

The Cultural Revolution and Political Alienation

The Great Proletarian Cultural Revolution represents a watershed in the politics of mainland China. It marked, at least temporarily, a complete victory of the Maoist model of communism over the capitalist-roader policies of Liu Shao-ch'i and Teng Hsiao-p'ing; it reduced the polity and the economy to near anarchy; and, perhaps most important for the long run, it evidently shaped the basic political perceptions and assumptions of much of the mainland's population.

In some respects, the Cultural Revolution resembles the period of collectivization and the great purge under Stalin in the 1930s. There was a tremendous loss of life, which even by the most conservative estimates is counted in the millions; even the ruling Communist Party suffered massive purges, which extended throughout the government and Party organs; and there were severe economic dislocations, which wiped out previous gains in the popular standard of living.[18] Yet, the long-term results and implications of these events in the two countries seem quite different. The Cultural Revolution was much more disruptive economically and caused much greater long-term political alienation than the analogous collectivization and great purge in the USSR. The economic reasons for this difference are easy to discern. Most of the economic dislocation in the Soviet Union during the 1930s was in the agricultural sector as Stalin quite consciously extracted resources from agriculture in order to finance industrialization. Although the great purge did eliminate bourgeois experts, its general impact was to allow very rapid advancement for a group of "red experts" who were better trained and more professional than the ideologues who fell victim to Stalin's ax. In mainland China, in sharp contrast, the Cultural Revolution devastated the urban and industrial (as opposed to the rural and agricultural) sectors, led to the promotion of less educated and more ideological cadres, and totally disrupted the educational system for a decade, great hostility toward institutionalizing the regime. In addition, the very fact that the top CCP leadership was involved in constant conflict over the basic political orientation of the regime from the early 1950s until the death of Mao and the purge of the Gang of Four pushed aside normal bureaucratic politics and competition for resources. Finally, the articulation of bureaucratic interests goes against the norms of both communism and Confucianism, according to which, albeit in rather different ways, the model public official moralistically serves the common interest rather than pushing the parochial and material interests of a bureaucratic entity.[23]

Such arguments about the absence of bureaucratic politics in mainland China may well be somewhat overdrawn. Several examinations of specific policy areas or the role of specific bureaucratic agencies, for example, have shown that there are clear differences among agencies and departments in institutional mission, identity, and ideology, which normally form the core of bureaucratic politics and certainly conflict with the generalist norms of both Confucianism and communism.[24] Still, even these analyses indicate that bureaucratic politics are less developed in Communist China than in most other countries that have constructed large bureaucratic organs of rule.

Another reason for the relatively diminutive role of bureaucratic politics in mainland China is that factional politics are particularly important there, in large part because of the impact of traditional Chinese culture and psychology, which emphasize personal security and the repression of aggression through informal group ties and <u>kuan-hsi</u>. Because personal protection and security supply the prime motives for factionalism, the principal determinants of factional allegiances are not issues or bureaucratic interests but simple calculations of political power.[25] Factional politics that are oriented around the competition for power among individual leaders and their personal entourages are certainly an important part of almost any government (e.g., Brezhnev's Dnepropetrovsk mafia in the Soviet Union), but the role of political factions seems to be particularly pervasive in mainland China.

All three of these models for describing politics in a society--the tendency, bureaucratic politics, and factionalism perspectives--are clearly relevant in describing the situation in Communist China, although it is hard to separate their individual effects at times.[26] The relative applicability of these models evidently varies greatly over time periods and issue concerns.[27] Still, conceptualizing Chinese politics in terms of these three models again suggests the weakness of bureaucratic institutions on the mainland, since each model implies a different type of force that is undermining bureaucratic power and efficiency. Since a skilled and sophisticated administration is an especially vital necessity in a command economy, these characteristics of the Chinese Communist regime imply that its performance should be inferior to the record of the post-Stalin USSR.

IMPLICATIONS FOR TENG'S REFORMS

Elucidating the nature of the Communist regime in mainland China by comparing it to the model of communism in the Soviet Union should be suggestive because the reforms of the Teng Hsiao-p'ing regime are in some significant ways trying to replicate the experience of the Soviet Union in promoting economic development and building popular support. Like leaders in the USSR, Teng is attempting to win popular legitimacy through a combination of promoting economic growth to improve the popular standard of living, easing the Communist dictatorship to create a regime that is more in line with the paternalistic national culture, and appealing to feelings of nationalism and patriotism. Also like the Soviets, the Tengist strategy basically eschews the Maoist attempt to use Communist ideology to legitimate the regime, diminishes but far from eliminates police controls and coercion as a basis of rule, and makes little effort to build legitimacy, as democracies do, through granting opportunities for popular participation in politics. Teng's initial reforms can be seen as presuming a sequence: (1) political changes, especially the creation of a professional and highly skilled administrative bureaucracy, that in conjunction with (2) several structural economic reforms will produce (3) sustained economic growth, which will, in turn, create (4) popular support and legitimacy for the regime.

Teng's reforms have met with mixed success, and it is this mixture of success and failure that probably stimulated the radical proposals of the Third Plenum. However, the structural conditions that are inherent in the Chinese Communist regime suggest that a rapid transformation to a market-based economy will face even more problems than the previous, more gradual reforms. The primary thrust of the political dimension of these reforms is clearly upon improving the administrative capabilities of the regime, to be accomplished both by increasing the caliber of political functionaries and by restructuring bureaucratic organs.

To a significant extent, these reforms have been successful. Economic policy in particular seems more rational and autonomous than during the Maoist era, the professional quality of the top bureaucrats is clearly increasing, and an institutionalized process of bureaucratic administration is evidently evolving.[28] Still, even analysts who believe that considerable progress has occurred see major problems and obstacles to bringing these reforms to full fruition:

> The current package will face constraints similar to those which undermined the effectiveness of earlier attempts at reform--scarcity of appropriate material and human resources, an inadequate theory of administrative leadership, the continuing imperative of political control, the reality of firmly entrenched bureaucratic interests, and the pervasiveness of informal, personal relations-based modes of operation within the bureaucracy.[29]

The centerpiece of Teng's reforms so far has been in the economic realm, and a leading area of these reforms has been the introduction of the responsibility system in agriculture, which, when coupled with rising agricultural prices and investment, has been fairly successful in stimulating substantial increases in both agricultural production and peasant incomes. Still, there is a strong array of opponents to this program, and they might well be able to curtail it in the future.[30] The agricultural reforms have also been linked to Teng's efforts to increase popular consumption, which have proved fairly successful, especially in some of the more prosperous rural areas, and urban consumption has increased appreciably as well. Whether further gains can be sustained, though, probably depends on the success of the regime's policies for spurring industrial production.[31]

Teng has also hoped to use Western trade, investment, and technology transfer as an integral part of the Four Modernizations effort to spur economic growth. The results of these policies have been somewhat mixed. Major expansions of foreign trade and investment have certainly occurred, yet overinvestment has caused the cancellation of substantial Western contracts, the absence of a well-developed Chinese legal system creates problems for Western investors, economic negotiations with organs in mainland China tend to be quite arduous and time-consuming, and the economy has yet to prove that it can fully and efficiently integrate imported Western technology.[32]

In other areas, Teng's policies have had much less success. Substantial reforms have been proposed in the urban/industrial sector, including promoting a better balance between heavy and light/consumer industries; decentralization of decision-making authority, especially to the enterprise level; greater use of economic and market mechanisms; and some encouragement of small-scale private enterprise to help increase the level of services and consumption and to ameliorate mainland China's substantial unemployment problem. Although there has been some success in the efforts to increase private enterprise and market phenomena,[33] the reforms in the industrial sector have not proved particularly productive for a wide variety of reasons: (1) resistance and opposition from middle-level cadres who refuse to surrender their political and economic powers and from workers who fear that their "iron rice bowl" might be broken, (2) the absence of a market-determined price system, (3) irrational aggregate investment patterns after decentralization, and (4) rapidly growing state subsidies for unprofitable enterprises.[34]

This failure in the industrial reforms, coupled with the limitations on Teng's success in restructuring the bureaucracy, have probably convinced the Teng faction that only a radical market-oriented reform could break mainland China out of its present hiatus. However, the structural conditions inherent in the Chinese Communist regime suggest that a rapid transformation to a market-based economy will face even more problems than the previous, more gradual reforms.

The experience of the Soviet Union suggests that Communist regimes that come to power in less developed countries must make at least two fundamental structural transformations in their political and economic organization if they are to modernize successfully. The first is to construct a professional bureaucracy to administer the initial and extensive phase of economic growth. Once a sophisticated industrial economy and society have been created, however, a second transformation is needed--one that includes economic decentralization, a growing utilization of market mechanisms, and political liberalization. The Soviet Union has clearly made the first transformation, but, ironically, the bureaucratic institutions that it created now provide a major barrier to the reforms that are necessary for the second structural shift.

Much more progress toward economic reform has occurred in Eastern Europe, even in countries such as Bulgaria that are considered ideologically orthodox and politically subservient to the USSR. Very substantial transformations toward a market economy, have occurred in two East European states in particular--Hungary and Yugoslavia.[35] The success of economic reform in these two countries, in turn, seems to have been conditioned by two important structural factors. First, their domestic Communist Parties became much more liberal and less orthodox than the Community Party of the Soviet Union (CPSU), thereby decreasing political resistance to economic reform. Second, their market reforms were phased in in several stages over nearly two decades, so that economic dislocations remained manageable.

Teng Hsiao-p'ing's reforms contain elements of

both of these structural transformations. Initially, Teng and his colleagues are trying to create a professional bureaucracy to oversee a rapid industrialization policy. In addition to this first-stage transformation, however, Teng's reforms also try to promote economic decentralization and market mechanisms. Thus far, these reforms have met with mixed success. Strangely, the most successful parts of the reform--like the responsibility system in agriculture--have generally been of the second type of decentralist and market-oriented transformation.

In large part this limited success is because the legacy of Maoism, the Cultural Revolution, and the very strong nature of factionalism in Chinese politics is a huge bureaucratic structure that is not particularly efficient or professional. Teng hoped that his reforms would transform this bureaucracy into an institution capable of leading the economic and social modernization of mainland China, but no matter how successful the Tengist purges are, a huge bureaucracy will remain and self-interest will dictate resistance to any fundamental changes in the political, economic, and social systems. The Soviet experience from the mid-1970s to the mid-1980s indicates that an entrenched Communist bureaucracy possesses substantial powers to frustrate meaningful reform.

The decisions of the Third Plenum, then, can be seen as an attempt to circumvent bureaucratic opposition and inertia by making a radical jump toward using free-market mechanisms. There is no evidence, however, that Teng is even considering similar fundamental reforms in the political realm. The Four Great Freedoms turned out to be quite fleeting, and a recent report by Amnesty International depicts a continuing pattern of political repression and human rights violations.[36] Thus, Teng evidently intends a policy mix, like that of the Soviet new economic policy during the 1920s, which continued Communist political monopoly with economic liberalization and marketization.[37]

Rather than emulating the Soviet development model as his initial reforms did, Teng now seems to be trying to leap ahead of it by using radical economic reform and transformation to surmount the problems of bureaucratic inertia that have increasingly frustrated Soviet economic development (even if, as suggested above, he seems to be returning to a Soviet Communist past). Such an economic leap forward, however, faces several serious impediments, especially in view of Teng's simultaneous attempt to prevent similar radical change in the political arena in the hope of maintaining the basic Communist nature of the regime.

First, as present fears of rampant inflation suggest, the tremors associated with radical market reforms may be much more serious than when they are implemented in smaller stages as in Hungary and Yugoslavia. Second, Teng's failure to countenance more-far-ranging political reforms still leaves the previously discussed problems that are associated with the Communist regime unresolved, which will make it much harder to build popular support and legitimacy in China through "goulash communism" than in the Soviet Union. Third, there would seem to be a fundamental structural contradiction in the Tengist strategy of liberating the economy while still controlling the polity. A substantial movement toward an economic free market threatens the power and status of a wide range of Communist leaders--leftist ideologues in the Party and the People's Liberation Army (PLA), officials in economic ministries and planning agencies, and even such ostensible beneficiaries of the reforms as many enterprise managers who are not competent to operate in a market economy.

Thus, profound political resistance among the Chinese Communist leadership can certainly be expected--as strong and probably stronger (because more officials are affected) than the political opposition that frustrated Teng's first round of reforms. More fundamentally, it would seem doubtful that a Communist dictatorship can be maintained in the political sphere if a basically free market exists in the economic one. Thus, one may certainly wonder how far the second transformation can go if the first one is not successfully completed or even, on the basis of the situation in the Soviet Union at present, whether a professional bureaucracy might be almost as hostile to the second transformation as an ideological one.

Therefore, Teng's inability to fully effect political reforms in the bureaucratic operations of the Communist government and his failure to even attempt meaningful reform in the political monopoly exercised by the Communist Party over the general population will probably greatly impede his new economic program. Conversely, the success of a radical reform in the direction of free-market mechanisms might soon challenge the basic tenets of the political order that Teng clearly seeks to preserve. Therefore, a consideration of the structural features inherent in the present Communist regime in mainland China implies that the very nature of the current political system sets serious constraints on the degree to which the proposed economic changes can proceed. A much more fundamental political change than Teng is willing to advocate would seem necessary to permit the economic reform and growth that he wants. Consequently, President Reagan's characterization of the mainland's leadership as so-called Communists and <u>Time</u> magazine's description of that country's economy as "capitalism in the making"[38] seem rather premature.

NOTES

1. Lucian W. Pye, <u>The Dynamics of Chinese Politics</u> (Cambridge, Mass.: Oelgeschlager, Gunn and Hain, 1981), especially pp. 22-27. Shu-shin Wang, "Hu Yaobang: New Chairman of the Chinese Communist Party," <u>Asian Survey</u> 22 (September 1982), pp. 801-822, identifies a more detailed set of five factions: the reformist led by Teng, the conservative led by Yeh, the leftist led by Hua, the petroleum led by Li, and the economic adjustment led by Ch'en. For more detailed discussions of Chinese politics during this period see John Gardner, <u>Chinese Politics and the Succession to Mao</u> (New York: Holmes and Meier, 1982), and Peter Moody, Jr., <u>Chinese Politics After Mao</u> (New York: Praeger, 1983). Chang Chu-pang, "Analysis of the Personnel Elected at the 12th CCP National Congress," <u>Issues and Studies</u> 18 (November 1982), pp. 14-24; Hong Yung Lee, "China's 12th Central Committee: Rehabilitated Cadres and Technocrats," <u>Asian Survey</u> 23 (June 1983), pp. 673-691; William deB Mills, "Generational Change in China," <u>Problems of</u>

Communism (November-December 1983); Richard Nethercut, "Leadership in China: Rivalry, Reform, and Renewal," Problems of Communism (March-April 1983); and Tseng Yung-hsien, "The New Leadership in Mainland China: Shifts of Power and Policies," Issues and Studies 19 (June 1983), pp. 15-42, discuss recent changes in factional fortunes.

2. Pyco Iyer, "Capitalism Comes to the City," Time, November 29, 1984.

3. John Kautsky, Communism and the Politics of Development (New York: John Wiley, 1968), presents this developmental model for interpreting communism.

4. Seweryn Bialer, Stalin's Successors: Leadership, Stability, and Change in the Soviet Union (Cambridge: Cambridge University Press, 1980), pt. 1; Merle Fainsod, How Russia Is Ruled, rev. ed. (Cambridge: Harvard University Press, 1963); Merle Fainsod, Smolensk Under Soviet Rule (Cambridge: Harvard University Press, 1958); and Carl J. Friedrich and Zbigniew K. Brzezinski, Totalitarian Dictatorship and Autocracy (Cambridge: Harvard University Press, 1956).

5. Stephen White, Political Culture and Soviet Politics (New York: St. Martin's Press, 1979). Alexander Yanov, The Origins of Autocracy: Ivan the Terrible in Russian History (Berkeley: University of California Press, 1981), presents an interesting, if somewhat controversial, interpretation from this perspective.

6. Walter D. Connor, Socialism, Politics, and Equality: Hierarchy and Change in Eastern Europe and the Soviet Union (New York: Columbia University Press, 1979); David Lane, The Socialist Industrial State: Toward a Political Sociology of State Socialism (London: Allen and Unwin, 1976); Mervyn Matthews, Class and Society in Soviet Russia (New York: Walker, 1972); Alastair McAuley, Economic Welfare in the Soviet Union: Poverty, Living Standards, and Inequality (Madison: University of Wisconsin Press, 1979); Alec Nove, Political Economy and Soviet Socialism (London: Allen and Unwin, 1979); Alec Nove, The Soviet Economic System (London: Allen and Unwin, 1977); and Robert J. Osborn, Soviet Social Policies (Homewood, Ill.: Dorsey, 1970).

7. Jerry F. Hough and Merle Fainsod, in How the Soviet Union Is Governed (Cambridge: Harvard

University Press, 1979), present the most comprehensive overview of the Soviet political system. For treatment of the specific elements of the model of Soviet politics presented here see Jan S. Adams, <u>Citizen Inspectors in the Soviet Union: The People's Control Committee</u> (New York: Praeger, 1977); Jeremy R. Azreal, <u>Managerial Power and Soviet Politics</u> (Cambridge: Harvard University Press, 1966); Bialer, <u>Stalin's Successors</u>, pts. 2 and 3; George W. Breslauer, <u>Khrushchev and Brezhnev as Leaders: Building Authority in Soviet Politics</u> (London: Allen and Unwin, 1982); Stephen F. Cohen, Alexander Rabinowitch, and Robert Sharlet, eds. <u>The Soviet Union Since Stalin</u> (Bloomington: Indiana University Press, 1980); Theodore H. Friedgut, <u>Political Participation in the USSR</u> (Princeton: Princeton University Press, 1979); Ronald J. Hill, <u>Soviet Political Elites: The Case of Tiraspol</u> (New York: St. Martin's Press, 1977); Jerry F. Hough, <u>The Soviet Prefects: The Local Party Organs and Industrial Decision-Making</u> (Cambridge: Harvard University Press, 1969); Jerry F. Hough, <u>The Soviet Union and Social Science Theory</u> (Cambridge: Harvard University Press, 1977); Donald R. Kelley, ed., <u>Soviet Politics in the Brezhnev Era</u> (New York: Praeger, 1980); John Lowenhardt, <u>Decision Making in Soviet Politics</u> (New York: St. Martin's Press, 1981); Joel C. Moses, <u>Regional Party Leadership and Policy-Making in the USSR</u> (New York: Praeger, 1974); Robert W. Siegler, <u>The Standing Commissions of the Supreme Soviet: Effective Co-optation</u> (New York: Praeger, 1982); H. Gordon Skilling and Franklyn Griffiths, eds., <u>Interest Groups in Soviet Politics</u> (Princeton: Princeton University Press, 1971); Peter H. Solomon, Jr., <u>Soviet Criminologists and Criminal Policy: Specialists in Policy-Making</u> (New York: Columbia University Press, 1978); William Taubman, <u>Governing Soviet Cities: Bureaucratic Politics and Urban Development in the USSR</u> (New York: Praeger, 1973); and Peter Vanneman, <u>The Supreme Soviet: Politics and Legislative Process in the Soviet Political System</u> (Durham, N.C.: Duke University Press, 1977).

    8. For example, see George Feifer, "Russian Disorders," <u>Harper's</u> (February 1981), and David Shipler, <u>Russia: Broken Idols, Solemn Dreams</u>

(New York: Times Books, 1982).

9. Cal Clark and Donna Bahry, "Dependent Development: A Socialist Variant," *International Studies Quarterly* 27 (September 1983), pp. 271-293, develop this argument in much more detail.

10. Hedrick Smith, *The Russians* (New York: Quadrangle, 1976), chap. 10.

11. White, *Political Culture and Soviet Politics*, chap. 6.

12. Ibid., pp. 108-112. For illustrations of the dual personality see Smith, *The Russians*.

13. Lucian W. Pye, in *China: An Introduction* (Boston: Little, Brown, 1984), chapters 3 and 4, gives an excellent overview of traditional Chinese culture and political institutions. For more detailed treatments of the relationship between culture and politics see Wm. Theodore de Bary, *Neo-Confucian Orthodoxy and the Learning of the Mind-and-Heart* (New York: Columbia University Press, 1981); John W. Dardess, *Confucianism and Autocracy: Professional Elites in the Founding of the Ming Dynasty* (Berkeley: University of California Press, 1983); Ping-ti Ho, *The Ladder of Success in Imperial China: Aspects of Social Mobility, 1368-1911* (New York: Columbia University Press, 1962); Roy Huang, *Fifteen Eighty-Seven, a Year of No Significance: The Ming Dynasty in Decline* (New Haven: Yale University Press, 1981); Edwin O. Reischauer and John K. Fairbank, *East Asia: The Great Tradition* (Boston: Houghton Mifflin, 1960); and Richard J. Smith, *China's Cultural Heritage: The Ch'ing Dynasty, 1644-1912* (Boulder, Colo.: Westview, 1983).

14. James Chieh Hsiung, *Ideology and Practice: The Evolution of Chinese Communism* (New York: Praeger, 1970); Lucian W. Pye, *Mao Tse-Tung: The Man in the Leader* (New York: Basic Books, 1976); Stuart Schram, *The Political Thought of Mao Tse-Tung*, rev. ed. (New York: Praeger, 1969); and Raymond F. Wylie, *The Emergence of Maoism: Mao Tse-tung, Ch'en Po-ta, and the Search for Chinese Theory, 1935-1945* (Stanford: Stanford University Press, 1980).

15. A summary model of the mature Maoist system is contained in Michel Oksenberg and Richard C. Bush, "China, 1972-1982: From Revolution to Reform," in Richard C. Bush, ed., *China Briefing,*

1982 (Boulder, Colo.: Westview, 1983), pp. 11-22.
  16. Chu-yuan Cheng, China's Economic Development: Growth and Structural Change (Boulder, Colo.: Westview, 1981); Nicholas Lardy, Economic Growth and Distribution in China (Cambridge: Cambridge University Press, 1978); and Jan S. Prybyla, The Chinese Economy: Problems and Policies, rev. ed. (Columbia: University of South Carolina Press, 1981), provide excellent descriptions of the Chinese economy.
  17. See Richard C. Thornton, China: A Political History, 1917-1980 (Boulder, Colo.: Westview, 1982), for an overview history of communism in China.
  18. Hong Yung Lee, in The Politics of the Chinese Cultural Revolution (Berkeley: University of California Press, 1978), provides a detailed description of the Cultural Revolution and the shifting political factors that underlay it.
  19. Fox Butterfield, China: Alive in the Bitter Sea (New York: Times Books, 1982), pp. 19-20.
  20. Ibid.; Richard Bernstein, From the Center of the Earth: The Search for the Truth About China (Boston: Little, Brown, 1982); David Bonavia, The Chinese (New York: Harper and Row, 1980); John Fraser, The Chinese: Portrait of a People (New York: Simon and Schuster, 1980); and Helen Siu and Zelda Stern, eds., Mao's Harvest: Views From China's New Generation (New York: Oxford University Press, 1983).
  21. Harry Harding, "Competing Models of the Chinese Communist Policy Process: Toward a Sorting and Evaluation," Issues and Studies 20 (February 1984).
  22. Harry Harding, in Organizing China: The Problem of Bureaucracy, 1949-1976 (Stanford: Stanford University Press, 1981), describes and interprets the competing political orientations about the nature and structure of bureaucracy in the politics of mainland China. See also A. Doak Barnett, Cadres, Bureaucracy, and Political Power in China (New York: Columbia University Press, 1967); and Franz Schurmann, Ideology and Organization in Communist China (Berkeley: University of California Press, 1966).
  23. Pye, Dynamics of Chinese Politics, chap. 3.
  24. David M. Lampton, The Politics of Medicine

in China: The Policy Process, 1949-1977 (Boulder, Colo.: Westview, 1977), and Michel Oksenberg, "Economic Policy-Making in China: Summer 1981," China Quarterly 90 (June 1982), pp. 165-194.

25. Pye, Dynamics of Chinese Politics.

26. For example, during the battle between two lines in the early 1960s, there was clearly intense conflict between two radically different policy orientations of tendencies associated with factions supporting different leaders (e.g., Mao Tse-tung, Lin Piao, Liu Shao-ch'i, Chou En-lai, etc.) who, in turn, generally represented different organizational interests--like the Party and government bureaucracies versus the politicized military and propaganda organs.

27. Harding, "Competing Models of the Chinese Communist Policy Process," and Frederick C. Teiwes, "The 'Rules of the Game' in Chinese Politics," Problems of Communism 28 (September-October 1979), pp. 67-76.

28. Hong Yung Lee, "China's 12th Central Committee"; Mills, "Generational Change in China"; Michael Ng-Quinn, "Deng Xiaoping's Political Reform and Political Order," Asian Survey 22 (December 1982); Oksenberg, "Economic Policy-Making in China"; and John P. Burns, "Reforming China's Bureaucracy, 1979-1982," Asian Survey 23 (June 1983), pp. 692-722.

29. Burns, "Reforming China's Bureaucracy," p. 693.

30. Chu-yuan Cheng, "Economic Reform in Mainland China: Comparison to Yugoslavia and Hungary," Issues and Studies 19 (September 1983), pp. 27-54; Tang Tsou, Marc Blecher, and Mitch Meisner, "The Responsibility System in Agriculture: Its Implementation in Xiyang and Dazhai," Modern China 8 (January 1982), pp. 41-104; and David Zweig, "Opposition to Change in Rural China: The System of Responsibility and People's Communes," Asian Survey 23 (July 1983), pp. 879-900.

31. Pyco Iyer, "China: Capitalism in the Making," Time, April 30, 1984.

32. Arnold Chao, "Economic Readjustment and the Open-Door Policy," in Lin Wei and Arnold Chao, eds. China's Economic Reforms (Philadelphia: University of Pennsylvania Press, 1982).

33. Iyer, "China," and Marlene R. Whittman,

"Shanghai in Transition? Implications of a Capitalist Intrusion," *Issues and Studies* 19 (June 1983), pp. 66-79.

34. Cheng, "Economic Reform in Mainland China"; Stephen Feuchtwang and Athar Hussain, eds., *The Chinese Reforms* (New York: St. Martin's Press, 1983); Joyce Kallgren, "China in 1983: The Turmoil of Modernization," *Asian Survey* 24 (January 1984); Nicholas R. Lardy and Kenneth L. Lieberthal, eds., *Chen Yun's Strategy for China's Development* (White Plains, N.Y.: M. E. Sharpe, 1983); Dorothy J. Solinger, "Marxism and Market in Socialist China: The Reforms of 1979-1980 in Context," in Victor Nee and David Mozingo, eds., *State and Society in Contemporary China* (Ithaca, N.Y.: Cornell University Press, 1983); Wei and Chao, *China's Economic Reforms*; and Whittman, "Shanghai in Transition?"

35. Cheng, "Economic Reform," provides a good comparison of Teng's initial reforms with those that have been implemented in Hungary and Yugoslavia.

36. Fraser, *The Chinese*, pts. 3 and 4, provides an excellent eyewitness description of the rise and fall of the Democracy Wall; Lowell Dittmer, "Ideology and Organization in PostMao China," *Asian Survey* 24 (March 1984), describes the thaw and subsequent freeze in freedom of speech and ideological affairs; and Harry Anderson, "China: A Report on Peking's Political Prisoners," *Newsweek International*, October 8, 1984, summarizes the Amnesty International Report.

37. See the essay by Dr. King-Yuh Chang "Whither Mainland China: Reforms and Problems," *Issues and Studies* 20 (July 1984), pp. 13-20.

38. Iyer, "Capitalism Comes to the City."

3
Studies in the Republic of China on Communist China Affairs, 1949-1979

Tai-chun Kuo

After the provisional capital of the Republic of China (ROC) was established in Taipei, Taiwan, on December 7, 1949, it was only natural that the government there would monitor by every means possible developments occurring on the mainland under the rule of the CCP. Nationalist government experts on Communist affairs quickly noted that Peking was relying more and more on moral and material support from the Soviet Union. Realizing that the CCP lacked sufficient naval and air force power of its own, the experts were alarmed by the possibility of a Soviet-backed Communist military invasion of Taiwan. Recognizing, too, that Communist subversion had enjoyed notable success in undermining popular support in the cities and behind the Nationalist lines on the mainland during the civil war, the leaders in Taipei feared an upsurge of Communist infiltration and sabotage on Taiwan.

For these reasons, the Central Committee of the Kuomintang (the Nationalist Party) established special agencies in early 1950 to study all developments on the Chinese mainland that might tend toward subversion in or an armed attack on Taiwan and to recommend appropriate countermeasures. These agencies also began to examine the policies of the new Chinese Communist regime and to pinpoint weaknesses in the system that the Nationalist government might someday turn to its own advantage-- if its own forces were ever able to reenter the mainland.

Although the Ministry of National Defense in

Taipei assumed responsibility for intelligence-gathering activities on the mainland, the number of Communist affairs experts comprised only a small group of military officials and civilians, some of whom had even been former members of the CCP.[1] These experts relied mainly on information from Hong Kong and on Nationalist intelligence sources, but they also tapped public sources: newspapers and magazines published throughout the mainland, radio broadcasts on the mainland, Communist Party publications, interviews with refugees and defectors, and documents relating to the official relations between the Soviet Union and the People's Republic of China (PRC).

From such sources, particularly the firsthand intelligence information gathered by the ROC government, the China watchers assessed current conditions and the prospects for a change on the mainland. In the 1950s, these reports--primarily for official eyes only--were rarely circulated publicly. In any bureaucracy, a pattern often evolves of subordinates not reporting any news that might distress their superiors, and such was the case in regard to the Peking-Moscow split of 1960. Nationalist government officials continually stated publicly that Communist China merely replicated the organizations and policies that had been long established in the Soviet Union and that the foreign policy interests of the two Communist giants were one. The experts, meanwhile, had correctly interpreted the growing friction between the two powers, but they did not write about their true fears of a possible split.[2] This example merely serves to highlight the serious need to report accurate intelligence assessments when the findings conflict with foreign policy claims and threaten the personal stake a leader has in those policy positions.

By the early 1960s, a number of events had begun to take place that slowly influenced how China watching was to be conducted within the ROC. First, the split between Moscow and Peking had divided Communist parties all over the world, and the relentless expansion of a Moscow-led Communist global movement that had appeared to accelerate in the late 1940s and 1950s now seemed to be slowing down. This new development convinced many people that the danger of new Communist expansion had passed.

Second, Peking's Great Leap Forward campaign had failed, and the regime had increasingly turned inward. In doing so, Peking's leaders limited all contacts with foreign countries and especially reduced the flow of published information outside the country. These new developments were frustrating for outside observers because they meant that less information was available about one of the world's leading Communist powers just as outside interest in that power was growing more intense.

Third, in countries like the United States, a major effort was being launched to train experts on Communist China and to achieve a greater understanding of the events in that country. The sudden outpouring of new journals and books on China at that time attested to this new fascination.

Fourth, within the ROC, an interest in Communist China had rapidly spread among youths and intellectuals, and Taipei officials, in particular, had to respond to the new demands for more information about conditions on the mainland. Finally, the China watchers themselves had begun to utilize the findings of many foreign experts to improve their research procedures; some had even sent their publications to foreign scholars and received extensive critical comments. Because of these complex developments, ROC experts on Communist affairs became even more eager to prove the veracity of their reports and to debate with foreign experts about differing interpretations of events and trends in Communist China. These mixed developments, therefore, launched important changes in China watching in the ROC.

The 1960s proved to be a watershed for these changes. In 1961, the Institute of International Relations (IIR) was established and, not long after, the Institute for the Study of Chinese Communist Problems (ISCCP), both in Taipei. Both organizations made use of the small core of government in-house experts of the 1950s, and these senior China watchers quickly became the nucleus for building a new research staff. By drawing from several universities, government agencies, and the department of the military, the two organizations not only augmented their staff of researchers but expanded their libraries to include material procured from underground Nationalist intelligence operations on the mainland, Communist publications from the mainland, foreign publications on Communist affairs and on the PRC in particular, and books and journals relating to social sciences and methodology. Both institutes also began to publish their research findings in journals and monographs in Chinese, English, and other languages.

For example, the IIR publishes six journals that contain articles on China studies, international Communist affairs, and international relations in general: <u>Fei-ch'ing yüeh-pao</u> [Chinese Communist affairs monthly];[3] three monthly journals entitled <u>Issues and Studies</u> in Chinese, Japanese, and English; and Spanish and French editions of the latter on a quarterly basis. Although the contents of each journal are similar, they are not identical: The Chinese edition of <u>Issues & Studies</u> contains more articles on international affairs while the other five journals concentrate exclusively on PRC studies. Every year the IIR also publishes an index of periodicals published in the ROC relating to international affairs and Communist China studies.

Some of the notable monograph publications of this institute include a four-volume work by Warren Kuo, <u>Analytical History of the Chinese Communist Party</u>, in both Chinese and English; a list of leading Chinese Communist officials in a <u>Chinese Communist Who's Who</u>, revised and published in April 1983; a selection of important mainland official documents in <u>Classified Chinese Communist Documents: A Selection</u>, in both Chinese and English; an annotated list of key Chinese Communist terms in <u>A Comprehensive Glossary of Chinese Communist Terminology</u>; two useful reference guides to the speeches of Chinese Communist leaders in <u>Chinese Communist Internal Politics and Foreign Policies</u> and <u>Foreign Policy Speeches by Chinese Communist Leaders, 1963-1975</u>; studies on Ting Ling, Chou En-lai, and Liu Shao-ch'i; and a collection of Mao's writings entitled <u>Mao Tse-tung ssu-hsiang wan-sui</u> [Long live Mao Tse-tung's thought].

The IIR has built up a very large collection of original Chinese Communist documents such as <u>Ts'an-k'ao hsiao-hsi</u> [Reference information], CCP Central Committee reports, texts of central and local radio broadcasts, national and provincial newspapers, as well as many Russian publications relating to the international Communist movement and Soviet-PRC relations. A particularly useful feature of this library is the impressive collection of publications on Chinese Communist studies both from the ROC and from abroad, so researchers may keep abreast of Chinese Communist studies on a worldwide basis.

In the early 1960s, the IIR established exchange programs with other institutes specializing in international affairs and tried to collaborate with certain institutions on special research projects. A notable event was the initiation of the Sino-American Conference on Mainland China in December 1970, involving participants from the United States and the ROC and their presentation of papers on Communist China. The IIR cosponsored this conference with the Academia Sinica (Taipei); the Institute of Chinese Communist Affairs of the ROC (Taipei); the Hoover Institution on War, Revolution and Peace (Stanford); the Institute of International Studies of the University of South Carolina; and the Center of Asian Studies of St. John's University in the United States. This gathering represented an impressive advance from the former isolation of ROC centers watching Communist China. More significantly, perhaps, this conference paved the way for similar annual conferences to be held and rotated between the United States and the ROC.

Although members of the staffs and faculties of the major U.S. centers for China studies located in the East and Midwest have long participated in this annual international gathering, these major academic institutions have yet to cosponsor the conference. A major event occurred in 1981 when the Institute of International Studies and the Institute of East Asian Studies at the University of California, Berkeley, became cosponsors of the conference. These first conferences marked the formal cooperation between China watchers in the United States and the ROC. China watching in the ROC had come of age; it had become a respectable academic pursuit and was no longer viewed solely as an intelligence analysis activity.

In 1971, the IIR initiated the first joint conference with China watchers in Japan, which has also developed into an international gathering, rotating each year between Japan and the ROC. The IIR also has cosponsored conferences on Communist China with research institutes in South Korea, the Philippines, and West Germany.

The IIR is closely affiliated with National Chengchi University in Taipei, from which it draws many of its young staff members for further training. The pattern of cooperation has been for Chengchi University to train selected students in master's degree programs relating to international studies or Communist studies. After being selected to conduct research in the IIR, promising students may be chosen for advanced studies abroad and encouraged to obtain higher degrees, specializing in political science or international studies. These students are also expected to develop a command of foreign languages so they can communicate better with other scholars. The IIR has about seventy-six researchers, of whom thirty-three focus on Communist China affairs (twenty full time and thirteen part time). The IIR's eminent senior experts include Warren Kuo, Li T'ien-min, Chang Chen-pang, Yin Ch'ing-yao, Chu Wen-lin, and Yao Meng-hsuan.

The other major organization, the Institute for the Study of Chinese Communist Problems, has about eighty researchers, of whom seventeen are senior China watchers, including Tsai Hsiao-ch'ien, Hsüan Mo, Chen Yü-ch'ang, Hsiao Yeh-hui, and Lin Chen. The ISCCP has five research groups focusing on analyses of the Communist Party, the PRC's political system, and its military, economic, and cultural affairs. The ISCCP differs from the IIR in one notable respect--it concentrates considerable effort on collecting relevant PRC documents such as tabloids published during the Cultural Revolution by the Red Guards, texts of central and local broadcasts of Chinese mainland radio since 1949, and microfilmed texts of local broadcasts from May 1956 until December 1974.

The ISCCP issues two monthly journals: <u>Chung-kung yen-chiu</u> [Studies on Chinese communism] and <u>Ta-lu kuan-ch'a</u> [Monitoring the mainland]. It also publishes a yearbook entitled <u>Chung-kung nien-pao</u> [Yearbook on Chinese communism], a detailed reference book covering events, statistics, and profiles of the Communist leaders as well as charts on government and Party administration. This yearbook is now in its seventeenth edition.

Finally, the ISCCP also publishes monographs such as <u>Mao Tse-tung's Military Thought and the People's War</u>, <u>The Cultural Revolution and the Intellectuals</u>, and other studies. Notable works in Chinese containing original documentation include, just to name a few, <u>Lin Piao shih-chien yuan-shih tsu-liao hui-pien</u> [Collection of original documents on the Lin Piao affair] and the sixteen-volume <u>Ta-lu ti-hsia k'an-wu hui-pien</u> [Compilation of underground literature on the Chinese mainland].

A third notable center is the Hui Lu Research Center. Affiliated with the ROC's Bureau of Investigation, this center probably has the largest collection of documents relating to the early history of the CCP outside of Communist China. These materials include a large number of classified Party documents and memoranda that pertain to the Kiangsi-Soviet period as well as to the days when the CCP had moved to Yenan and other North China bases. The Hui Lu Research Center houses a research staff of about eighteen of whom six are senior experts. It publishes a monthly journal called <u>Kung-tang wen-t'i yen-chiu</u> [Communist problems studies] and a weekly digest, <u>Fei-ch'ing chai-yao</u> [Communist affairs]. A large number of original Communist Party documents have been published under such titles as <u>Tang-ti chien-she</u> [The Construction of the Chinese Communist Party] and <u>Nung-min yün-tung</u> [Peasant movements]. The orientation of this center is historical and primarily related to the pre-1949 period of CCP affairs.

Containing more than 400,000 books, pamphlets, journals, and newspapers, the center holds such rare items as the important CCP journal <u>Tou-cheng</u> [Struggle] as well as other periodicals such as <u>Tang-ti sheng-huo</u> [Party life], <u>Lieh-nin ch'ing-nien</u> [Leninist youth], <u>Chung-kuo kung-jen</u> [The Chinese worker], and <u>Chieh-fang</u> [Liberation]. A large quantity of intra-Party documents that circulated among the membership during the Kiangsi-Soviet period and when the Party had moved to Yenan is also available. There are other archives in the ROC that contain similar types of material such as the <u>Shih-sou-shih</u>, or the archives of the late Vice-President Ch'en Ch'eng, and the Historical Archive

Commission of the Kuomintang Central Committee. All of these centers contribute to the richness of Chinese Communist historical documents in the ROC for the pre-1949 period.

At the Institute of Mainland China Affairs (IMCA), the research staff concentrates mainly on current affairs in Communist China. Most of the publications produced by this staff, consisting of about thirteen researchers, are circulated among government officials as well as other China watchers in the ROC. The IMCA is under the Chinese Mainland Affairs Commission, an organization supervised by the Central Committee of the Kuomintang.

Just as Chinese Communist studies rapidly developed in the United States during the 1960s and 1970s, an impressive expansion in staff and facilities took place in the ROC. In the 1950s, only about fifty experts worked full time on this subject; by the 1970s, the number was close to a hundred and fifty. These researchers were selected for China watching on the basis of their demonstrated understanding of Chinese history and culture; they are also expected to be well versed in Marxist-Leninist theory and the history of the Chinese Communist Party and to have received training in social science as it has developed in the West, particularly the United States. By these standards, it would seem that the more educated pool of experts are located at the IIR; more than a half of its staff have an M.A. degree or higher.

As previously mentioned, the majority of the research staff members of the IIR are selected from students of the Graduate Schools of East Asian Studies or Political Science or Diplomacy at the National Chengchi University. The remainder are selected from graduate students who have studied abroad, many of whom have earned doctoral degrees. As a result of this upgrading of academic qualifications in the past two decades, a new generation of China watchers is gradually replacing the cadres of elders who predominated in the 1950s but continued to work into the 1960s and 1970s. Many of that early group are now retired, or about to retire, and the younger generation of China watchers will approach their work from different perspectives and with diverse skills. Some members of this new group who have already distinguished themselves are Yung Wei, who works mainly on the methodology of China studies, and Chao Hung-tse and Wu An-chia, who work on the history of the Chinese Communist Party. Others are Chou Yu-shan, Liu Sheng-chi, and Chiang Chen-ch'ang, who have written principally on culture and society under Communist rule. Theorists like Chiang Hsin-li have primarily worked on Communist ideology and theory; Yeh Po-t'ang concentrates on PRC foreign policy.

A unique aspect in the ROC is the remarkable success the researchers have had in procuring rare documents from Communist China, some of which are noted below. Although U.S. China watchers have not utilized these materials as might be expected, these published documents have constantly been used by ROC China watchers in interpreting mainland China affairs.

In 1966, Henry G. Schwarz referred to a small newsletter called <u>Reference Information</u> (<u>Ts'an-k'ao hsiao-hsi</u>), which was circulating among the members of the hierarchy of the CCP to keep them well informed about events occurring in other parts of the world. Schwarz mentioned a leading authority on Communist China who had "never heard of anyone outside of the mainland having copies" of <u>Reference Information</u>,[4] and the U.S. China watching profession now learned about this newsletter for the first time. Schwarz had even written to libraries in the United States with major Chinese collections to ask whether other copies than the few in his possession were available. They informed him that none had been acquired. In the ROC, however, China watching experts had been reading <u>Reference Information</u> throughout the 1950s, and copies abounded. These experts also recognized this newsletter's function among the CCP elite. They never publicly discussed the newsletter, taking it for granted that the CCP leadership kept its members informed about the outside world in a very selective way. What was long known in the ROC was never fully realized in the United States until the mid-1960s.

As early as the 1950s, ROC China watchers were reading intra-Party documents that had circulated within the CCP Central Committee, at other important CCP meetings, and among lower organs of the Party and government--all obtained through government intelligence operations. One such document pertained to Peking's preparations to intervene in the Korean War.[5] Another collection pertained to Lienchiang County in Fukien, and these documents were acquired during the night of March 4, 1964, in a Nationalist commando raid.[6] These materials referred to the official policies of fourteen rural communes in that county and shed considerable light on how seriously the Chinese Communist authorities viewed the new rural problems that had been created by the disastrous Great Leap Forward. These documents made it possible to identify new rural organizations and to understand how they had operated in the countryside since their establishment in 1958. Still another collection of fascinating records, called the Landing Craft Documents, reveals how, after the Great Leap Forward, PLA units helped the Party deal with severe food shortages, and these documents also contain information on the declining morale among Party members.[7]

ROC China watchers also had the opportunity to read the texts of both the CCP's Party constitution and the Constitution of the People's Republic of China even before Communist officials made them public.[8] The ISCCP published documents released by the CCP Central Committee concerning the Lin Piao incident in the April 1972 issue of <u>Chung-kung yen-chiu</u>, reprinting by photo offset <u>Chung-fa</u> [Central Committee] Document no. 4 (1972), which contained information on Lin Piao's aborted coup and his death.[9] Three months later, the same journal printed additional documents pertaining to the report, which also included "The Struggle for Crushing the Counter-Revolutionary Coup of the Lin-Ch'en Anti-Party Clique" and the "Outline of 'Project 571.'" The latter document describes how Lin and his associates tried to oust Mao Tse-tung.[10]

The number 571, or <u>wu-ch'i-i</u> in Chinese, signifies "armed uprising." The document, drafted by Lin Li-kuo (Lin Piao's son) and his associates, mentions how political power would be seized throughout the country, argues the justification and inevitability of an armed uprising, describes the favorable conditions as well as the various difficulties that the activists would confront, points out the importance of timing if the project is to succeed, and discusses various strategies that could be used. Although some experts outside the ROC doubted the veracity of Chung-fa Document no. 4 and the other appended material when they were published, even Chou En-lai referred to the same material in his political report at the Tenth CCP National Congress, in August 1973.[11]

According to Chang Chen-pang, then at ISCCP and in charge of authenticating the validity of these documents, the reason Chung-kung yen-chiu did not publish the appended material along with the Central Committee's Chung-fa Document no. 4 in April 1972 was because a few pages were missing from the document "Outline of 'Project 571,'" which also was an original and a true Central Committee report. Some time later, another intelligence agency of the ROC obtained a handwritten copy, which made it possible to authenticate the original set of documents. Although several words were still missing, it was now possible to understand the document in its entirety. It is noteworthy that only the IIR, through its two English language journals, Facts and Features (a biweekly) and Issues & Studies, had translated and published a total of 249 classified Chinese Communist Party documents by the end of December 1979.[12]

One final example will illustrate still further the remarkable access to Communist Chinese documents ROC researchers have. On July 23, 1974, the newspaper Kwang-ming jih-pao devoted its entire second page to an article, "Interpretation and Commentaries to Ku-fen (Solitary Exasperation)" of Han Fei-tzu, a distinguished philosopher during the period of the Warring States of the third century B.C. The article was authored by Nan Chung, one of a group of anti-Maoists during the anti-Confucius campaign of 1974. The article praised the Ku-fen text as a "political treatise full of a combative spirit" and analyzed the contradictions and struggles between the new and the old political forces in China at that time. The article went on to say that the Ku-fen treatise was "of very prominent and immediate significance when published in its time, as well as today" and that anyone "reading the treatise would be inspired and enlightened." Its authors, in referring to the ancient text, stressed, in effect, the notorious political despotism of that period. They were thus trying indirectly to expose Mao Tse-tung's dictatorship and the corrupt activities of his Party cadres. They cited the following passage in the Ku-fen text to make their point: "If, in a state, the ruler himself has made great mistakes and his vassals have committed great crimes, it is impossible to believe that such a state will not soon perish." Such allusions were clear attacks on Mao and his supporters in the Chinese Communist Party.

On the same day, however, someone on the Kwang-ming jih-pao staff spotted the article, alerted the newspaper directors, and the daily immediately recalled all unsold papers. Although a new edition was issued, Nationalist agents had already acquired a copy of the first one. Both editions were later examined by ROC experts, and they gave the experts the vital clues they needed to support their contention that the intra-Party factional struggle still raged on the provincial level throughout the country.

Important Red Guard tabloids and the big-character wall posters that appeared in leading cities gave further clues to the violence and internal disputes that raged in mainland China on and off during the late 1960s and the 1970s, and this information also surfaced in ROC journals devoted to China watching. This evidence and the other examples cited show that ROC experts have long possessed a vast storehouse of original documentation acquired directly from Communist China.

The first group of China experts in the 1950s included people who had participated in the Communist Party movement and understood its internal operations and the character of the Party membership. These same experts--reading huge quantities of mainland documentation every day--could understand the code language that was so often used in these documents, so it is not surprising that they would develop some very definite interpretations about the character and behavior of the mainland regime. It is to that descriptive "ideal" that I now turn.

THE CHINESE COMMUNIST TOTALITARIAN SYSTEM

There has been no previous attempt to examine the great amount of literature written about Communist China by ROC China watchers, and my approach is merely a preliminary attempt to present a synthesis of their findings. First I present six fundamental and interrelated propositions.

1. The CCP has completely dominated the state and through its organs--especially the military and the Public Security Bureau--it has tried to control all action and behavior of the people. Such control, however, has led to the bureaucratization of society and the creation of a stratum of privileged people who are dependent upon Party power.

2. The CCP, however, has been enormously influenced by the leadership of a single man, Mao Tse-tung, who eventually came to exert a dictatorial role over the Party and the state alike. Certain structural features of the Party permitted power to be concentrated in the hands of Mao and his followers.

3. Because the Party leadership and the rank and file were always composed of a mixture of Marxist-oriented intellectuals, rural poor, and social deviants, the behavior of these Party members was influenced by their powerful and charismatic leader, Mao, but many also craved power, privilege, and security and frequently supported other Party leaders who opposed Mao.

4. Therefore, there were constant powerful tensions between the dominant leader, Mao, and the other Party leaders. Such an intra-Party elite power struggle has always characterized the CCP and will continue to do so as long as the Chinese Communist Party tries to maintain total dominance over the state and society.

5. Because the Party has been, and still is, faction ridden and obsessed with maintaining its dominance over the state and society, a peaceful, gradual transition to a different kind of political system cannot occur without great violence.

6. Finally, because the Party and the state have greatly reduced private property rights, the economy has experienced serious dysfunctions, such as low productivity and enormous economic waste,

and Chinese cultural values have greatly deteriorated.

ROC China watchers have constantly warned their readers, and perhaps unconsciously reminded each other as well, that to understand CCP aims and behavior requires a thorough reading and a practical understanding of how the CCP acquired power, has controlled its members, and has ultimately dominated the people under its rule. One has to grasp the essence of Party tactics and the theories that its leaders constantly cite, such as the "endless class struggle" and "the omnipotence of war," as well as know how the CCP applies dialectical thinking to Party policies. Warren Kuo has informed his readers of this necessity in these words:

> In order to analyze Chinese mainland issues, we often must resort to the same dialectical logic which the Communists have used. . . . That logic had proved to be effective for studying the CCP's intra-Party struggle and Party personnel changes by using such concepts as the "law of contradiction," and the principle of "dividing one into two"; we also can examine the continuous violence on the mainland by using their theory of "endless class struggle"; we can appraise Party behavior by referring to "struggle-criticism-transformation (tou-p'i-kai)" and "one strike and the three-anti movement"; we can interpret how power has shifted within the Party and the state by the theory of "continued revolution"; we can also analyze the CCP's foreign policy and the Party's concept of coexistence with other states by their "united front tactics" and other double-dealing techniques.[13]

At a seminar on the methodology for studying Communist China held in Taipei in June 1982, Yin Ch'ing-yao, Ts'ao Po-i, and Chao Hsien-yün concurred that even though training might differ in regard to textual analysis, the study of Communist behavior, and matters of Communist ideology, it is necessary for China watchers to develop a profound knowledge of Marxist-Leninist theory, the use of dialectical logic, and the history of Communist parties in general.[14] Chao Hsien-yün, in particular, emphasized that "dialectical logic is especially useful for analyzing material issued by the Communists."[15] Cheng Hsüeh-chia and Li T'ien-min asserted that two prerequisites for undertaking Communist China studies are a thorough comprehension of how the Communist systems in different countries actually work and an ability to differentiate among the special characteristics of Chinese Communist Party control over the state and society.[16]

With these injunctions in mind, it should be noted that ROC experts have placed primary emphasis on the capability of the CCP to dominate the state and society in a totalitarian fashion. After seizing power, the Party quickly eliminated the national political legislative body, ended freedom of the press, forbade freedom of movement in society, regulated choice of housing, controlled entry into work occupations, and dominated the judicial process through various state instruments and mass popular control. As far as choice within the Party is concerned, Chen Yü-ch'ang declared that "in the Chinese Communist power apparatus, the Party decides virtually everything."[17]

Because the Party has been obsessed with achieving total control over the state and society, CCP leaders have always stressed the importance of political action, and they have frequently urged that "politics takes command," implying that the driving force for all activity must be the form that political behavior takes. Throughout much of the period of CCP control, Party leaders have simply regarded the population they rule as putty to be remolded through political education and particularly the creation of a new mass ideology-- one that is uniform for all. Political campaigns have also aimed at releasing the productive power and creating an appropriate incentive structure for people to work harder and longer and to consume less. Therefore, the great political campaigns like the land reform (1950-1952), the Three-Anti and Five-Anti Campaigns (1952), the Three Reform movement (1953), the Three Red Banner Campaign (1958-1960), and the Three Revolutionary movements

(1963) were, according to Wu An-chia, initiated partly to develop the economy by releasing greater productive forces.[18] He concluded: "The Party red line had become a panacea, and political movements had been endless. As a result, these movements produced serious economic backwardness, and the inefficient economic policies associated with each [movement] constituted a primary obstacle to achieving stability."[19]

The regime has also had to depend upon military power and a countrywide secret police system to extend its total dominance over society. Warren Kuo has noted that "under the CCP's centralized leadership, the military and the police have turned out to be inseparable instruments for governing the people and identifying any possible enemies opposed to the Party."[20]

Such pervasive Party control, however, led to a massive bureaucratization of society, which replaced private exchange through free associations and markets. Without any strong checks on bureaucratic control and privilege, small fiefdoms of bureaucratic power quickly emerged, and this power was exercised by only a few members of a privileged class that took its rights for granted. Warren Kuo has observed the following: "The principal malpractices by the Party leaders are those of bureaucratism, the excessive concentration of power into the hands of a few, patriarchal leadership, lifelong tenure for cadres holding positions of leadership, and all kinds of special privileges."[21] Wu An-chia, too, has noted that the establishment of a Party dictatorship created widespread bureaucratism and a society without any formal law.[22]

Just as this Communist Party rules the Chinese people very differently from any previous regime, its dominant leadership style of governance and ideology represents an aberration in Chinese political history. According to ROC experts, Peking's rulers rely excessively upon foreign political theories, particularly the Marxist-Leninist interpretations that evolved in the Soviet Union and have been borrowed from that Communist state as "exported products of the Soviet Communist revolution."[23] Even this Sovietized Marxist theory has been further modified by Communist leaders like

Mao Tse-tung and then imposed upon his followers. Consequently, those Chinese Communists who prided themselves as followers of Mao practiced an "excessive, leftist-oriented and fiercely adventuristic type of Marxism-Leninism."[24]

Because of this two-stage transmutation of Western Marxist theory--first by Soviet Communists and later by Mao and his supporters--ROC experts on Communist affairs have contended that the Maoist leadership and its policies bore no relationship to traditional Chinese statecraft principles and political philosophy. Many ROC experts have therefore been stunned and dismayed to read accounts by China watchers in the West that stress the continuities between Maoist political-cultural goals and Chinese political-cultural traditions. Teng Kung-hsuan has pungently stated, "We are most astonished about the theory that Maoism should be regarded as an extension of China's cultural tradition rather than as an imported ideology."[25] Teng went so far as to argue that the Peking regime bears a close similarity to the Stalinist regime, its key organizations and policies being greatly influenced by the Soviet experience of the 1920s and 1930s. He said that the "inception organization, and growth of the CCP were planned and hatched all along by Soviet Russia; in particular, Stalinism exerted a profound influence upon Mao."[26]

To differentiate the post-1949 Communist regime from previous Chinese political systems, ROC experts stress that the new regime under the Communist Party has never represented a change in dynasty or simply another ordinary government. Instead, the Communist Party has tried to impose a completely different social system upon the people. Second, the Communist theories developed in China pertaining to continuous class struggle, the need for violent revolution, and the justification for a proletarian dictatorship are entirely incompatible with former Chinese political rules for governance. The rules were that the ruling elite should practice benevolence, seek to establish social harmony, and stress a proper morality and personal ethics. Finally, such political campaigns as the catastrophic Cultural Revolution (1966-1976) simply showed the contempt Mao and others had for Chinese political traditions.[27]

Even so, Mao and his followers were Chinese. Having borrowed from the experience of the Russian revolution and the writings of Lenin and Stalin in transforming Communist ideas to conform to China's reality, Mao and other leaders reflected a highly negative strain of Chinese political culture: Machiavellian skills, despotism, and unbridled cruelty. Warren Kuo has tried to explain the process in these terms:

> Mao Tse-tung was deeply imbued with the dark side of traditional Chinese society and he engaged in the same dictatorial practices of the ancient tyrants of Chinese history. In building up his control over mainland China, Mao really created a personality cult as well as introduced a personal style of dictatorship that is based upon using absolute power exceeding that of any other tyrant in Chinese history.[28]

ROC experts have placed considerable importance on Mao Tse-tung's one-man autocratic rule. Chu Hsin-min found Mao to be a person obsessed by contradictions and egomania;[29] for Warren Kuo, Mao was "obsessed by super-egotism";[30] and Hsing Kuo-ch'iang considered Mao a man of a "radical and unstable mentality."[31]

But if Mao was obsessed with power and, unlike previous Chinese tyrants, employed it in unlimited ways, he also eulogized the great upheavals, especially those fomented by the peasantry, that toppled monarchs and replaced them with new leaders of greater power. Yung Wei declared that "it was the peasant revolts in Chinese history in which Mao found his deepest empathy and identification."[32]

That peculiar combination of ideas that Mao developed from his reading of foreign Communist sources and his penchant for selecting the practical tactics used by Chinese political leaders to outsmart their rivals accounted, in the eyes of the ROC China watchers, for much of Mao's intense desire to transform the world. But the Communist Party organization also allowed Mao a special latitude to achieve a supremacy over his colleagues and rivals that previous Chinese rulers had never attained. Warren Kuo has described how the special structural features of the Communist Party allows individuals to accumulate enormous power without being accountable to anyone.

First, the Party has always been ruled by an inner core of leaders whose power has never been curtailed by any institutions within the Party:

> Because the plenum of the Central Committee of the CCP is not annually held and meetings of the Politburo are rarely convened, the decision-making power naturally falls into the hands of those within the Standing Committee of the Politburo. . . . The Party Chairman, in turn, can exercise absolute power in the Standing Committee.[33]

Second, the Party chairman also dominates the Party's Central Committee. Once that committee decides upon a particular policy, all Party members are compelled to comply:

> The very fact that the CCP persists in subordinating the individual to the organization, the minority to the majority, and lower organs to higher organs, creates the favorable conditions for the Central Committee to behave in an absolutist manner. To make matters worse, it is the Chairman of the Central Committee who has the last say in everything. . . . The actual processes of policymaking within the top elite, in reality, negate collective leadership.[34]

Finally, these structural elements of the Party make it possible for a dictator to emerge and impose his personal style of leadership. Given a man of Mao's capabilities and strong personality, it was easy for him to gradually build a personality cult of leadership:

> The dictatorial traits inherent in the Chinese Communist hierarchy will never change. Viewing the current Chinese Communist apparatus in this perspective explains how Mao could establish a tightly controlled organization, instill iron discipline, and subordinate individuals

> to the Party. . . . [Such conditions
> demanded] the sacrifice of individuals
> to the Party dictatorship. Because Mao
> personally took over the reigns of the
> Party, Party dictatorship became tanta-
> mount to being his personal dictatorship.[35]

For these reasons, ROC China watchers believe that Mao and his leadership clearly counted and that no historical analysis of the post-1949 period can ignore his monumental influence upon Party affairs and upon society itself. But Mao could not have acquired such enormous power if the organizational structure and behavioral norms within the Party had not combined to allow the concentration of power in the hands of the supreme leadership.

The Party also has other features that ROC experts believe have to be related to the special combination of Party development, the strong personality of Mao, and the Leninist features of Party organization. These features consist of a blend of different social groups committed to employing violence in which the ends justify the means.

The Party has never appealed to the industrial working class. In the formative years of the Party, membership came primarily from disgruntled students and alienated intellectuals--many with a distinct Marxist ideological orientation--who hated authority and sought power to transform society according to their utopian ideals. After the Party left the cities and switched to guerrilla warfare in remote areas, various social deviants and community outcasts joined its ranks and became committed to using violence to achieve Party goals. Cheng Hsüeh-chia has observed that ever since the Party's August 7, 1927, conference, when the CCP leaders adopted a policy of rural violence, the "Party consisted mainly of peasants and rascals" and was not a party of urban industrial workers or proletarians.[36] In July 1971, Kung Teh-liang wrote:

> For the past 20-odd years, peasants have
> occupied roughly 70 percent of the total
> CCP membership; if intellectuals are
> included, the figure is more than 80 per-
> cent. With these non-proletarian, petty

bourgeoisie elements in its ranks, the CCP has always been plagued by "intra-Party contradictions."[37]

This new social mixture greatly contributed to a pattern of deviant behavior that represented the worst features of Chinese social behavior:

> By inheriting the traits of the peasants, rascals, and the petty bourgeoisie, the CCP was inclined to such characteristics as seeking revenge, engaging in sabotage, and resorting to force. Party members tended to indulge in Leftist, adventuristic policies. The Three Red Banner campaign and the Cultural Revolution were events which in part represented this particular social background and behavioral traits of the CCP.[38]

Without the social-moral constraints that are usually so widespread in Chinese society to check individual greed, deceit, and violence, these new Party members brought with them their moral relativism and a willingness to submit to the new code of morality demanded of them by the Party leadership.

Therefore, the existence of a powerful leader bent on becoming an autocrat, a Party that contained no institutional checks on the accumulation of power by a few leaders, and a membership that represented the most undesirable behavioral traits in society combined to produce cleavages and tensions within the CCP among different leaders and their supporters. Factions or groups often formed, dissolved, and re-formed again. They competed with each other for power--with the winner taking all and the loser being purged--so that the CCP was constantly subjected to group rivalry and factional struggle for power and influence within the Party. Li T'ien-min put it this way: "The purge is one of those measures used by the Communist Party for consolidating its organizations, or, to be more specific, a procedure which the ruling stratum of the Communist Party uses to substitute for elections."[39]

ROC experts place great significance upon this

particular Party pathology, which they contend will exist as long as a Party structured like that of the CCP tries to rule China. One expert wrote:

> The history of the Chinese Communists is one of intra-Party struggle. . . . Intra-Party struggle is not only a built-in feature of the CCP, it is also a mechanism by which the power-holders compete with each other to consolidate their control. Looked at in this way, all intra-Party struggles are basically power struggles, but they have been carried out under the guise of ideological-line struggles.[40]

Certainly some Party leaders, like Mao, have insisted upon a political style of action that is conducive to continual competition for Party power.

This competition should be viewed in two ways. First, the Party leadership has always stressed daily struggle by encouraging members to criticize each other as well as their own thinking and conduct. Such criticism can be friendly or rancorous, but this persistent habit is bound to put Party members on their guard to strike at their opponents first rather than wait to be criticized, and thus lose credibility and respect in the eyes of others.

Second, tactics and ideas matter. The different debating positions or viewpoints in regard to Party goals and policies are typically labeled as the Left or the Right course of political opinion or action. From this kind of classification of political action, it is a simple step to refer to a particular political tactic or course of action as being "the leftist line" or "the rightist line."

Therefore, arguments over how key problems confronting the Party should be resolved through political action are continually phrased in the metaphorical language of a "line struggle" between a "rightist" or a "leftist" leader, his faction, and the political solution they advocate. Consequently, Party debates always take the form of struggles among intra-Party leaders and their factions over which particular political course of action or "line" the Party should take, and such debates can become strident and brutal as opponents keep changing sides, hurl accusations at each other, and often use devious methods of humiliating their rivals. Warren Kuo has contended that such debates merely reflect an underlying struggle for the reins of Party power: A leader and his faction can impose his ideas, his will, and his tactics upon opponents:

> All evidence indicates that while everyone of the [Party] struggles began as differences over "line," they always ended as a struggle for leadership in which either one group of new power-holders or another emerged victorious to defeat the other challengers. It seems only reasonable to say that any difference of "line" between rival factions are merely of secondary importance and that the struggle for power is of primary importance.[41]

To win any debate over which political line the Party should adopt, a majority of the Party leaders have to convince enough opponents to vote for the majority view, impose that view upon the Central Committee, and then influence the membership. The struggles over political line among the top leaders of the Politburo's Standing Committee can take many forms, ranging from friendly discussion and a show of hands to a vicious use of force to crush and purge opponents, even sending them to languish and die in prison. In 1966, for example, Mao organized the Red Guards and called in the PLA to impose his course of political action upon his rivals in the Politburo. Of course, this struggle made it possible for many military officers to assume positions of power in both the Party and the state, and thus hold more power than Mao wanted. As Mao perceived that the Party was being taken over by the military, he had to undertake other moves to reverse the trend.[42]

By denying that leadership disagreements over which political line to follow never really matter, some ROC experts have gone so far as to assert that the so-called line struggles can be interpreted simply as naked power struggles between particular leaders. For example, when Lin Piao died in 1971, Mao Tse-tung announced that the conflicts between Lin and himself had been "the severest line struggle since the founding of the CCP." But, according to Yao Meng-hsuan, "there has never been a Lin Piao 'line' in the CCP's history," and he interprets this event as merely the end of a bitter struggle for power.[43] In similar vein, Kung Teh-liang has observed: "Every power struggle has been concealed by reference to a two-line struggle. . . . The so-called leftist, rightist, counter-revolutionist lines have merely been used by Mao to label his enemies or to eliminate dissent within the Party."[44] If debates simply conceal the struggle for Party power to impose a course of action upon rivals, have any specific tactics been developed by competing leaders and their factions to win such struggles?

ROC China watchers have often referred to the "united front" tactics of Mao and the CCP as a means by which a weaker contender can wear down and isolate a stronger rival and eventually gain supremacy in the struggle. Warren Kuo and others have referred to countless times in the pre-1949 period when Mao used this strategy to assert his power whenever he was outvoted in the Central Committee. A tactic that worked well for Mao to checkmate his rivals within the Party certainly could be utilized against enemies outside the Party. The application of the united front tactics during the Sino-Japanese War and in the struggle with the Nationalist Party are too well known to reiterate here, but ROC China watchers have been adamant in their claims that the CCP has continually used these tactics as a strategy in conducting Peking's foreign policy.

After a meticulous study of PRC publications pertaining to united front tactics, ROC experts like Warren Kuo suggested the following key elements. First, the enemy must be clearly identified by differentiating between the primary enemy and secondary or weaker enemies. To deal with the primary enemy, one has to make compromises on a temporary basis and cooperate with the secondary enemy, even if on a weak alliance basis, to marshal all power to deal with the primary enemy. In effect, this tactic really means teaming up with tomorrow's enemy to eliminate today's more powerful opponent--with an eye to crushing the secondary enemy some time in the future. Second, this tactic also means adopting a sequential set of activities to crush one's enemies on a one-by-one basis. Essentially, one deals with a series of enemies by aligning with several weaker ones, uses this alliance to crush the primary enemies, and finally turns against one's allies and crushes them. Third, this strategy involves relying upon both alliance and struggle at the same time. When the CCP offers friendship to either a party or a state to form an alliance against a common, superior foe, it is really utilizing this alliance on a short-term basis and will scrap it when expedient.[45]

Kuo has warned that in foreign policy affairs or when dealing with the CCP on any political, military, or economic matter, one should never take its public statements at face value:

> In line with their principle of dialectics, the Communists can devise and modify their tactics depending upon how time, space, and conditions change. If certain objective conditions are required, they will unequivocally negate what they asserted yesterday. Therefore, any public statements by the Communists are hardly credible.[46]

Warning that PRC statements of foreign policy should be reviewed critically as united front tactics, Yin Ch'ing-yao has stressed that such tactics were used by the CCP to deal with its enemies when it rose to power in China and are being applied in foreign policy to compensate for the PRC's position of weakness in the world. Yin has maintained that "the united front tactics are a disguised form of Mao's class struggle."[47] When the PRC established diplomatic relations with the United States as of January 1, 1979, ROC experts warned that Peking's overtures to cooperate with the United States against the Soviet Union had to be understood as a part of their united front strategy. Hsiang Nai-kwang said, "We avoid their traps in negotiations that merely conceal a ploy of united front-type struggle."[48] Having linked the regime's foreign policy design to tactics long used by Party leaders to unseat their rivals, whether within the Party or outside it, ROC experts found a compelling relationship between intra-Party power struggles and the continual political crisis in the Communist body politic.

This crisis stems from several pathologies. First, the Communist Party is constantly being subjected to factional struggle in the ranks of the top leaders and is continually changing its political policies. Within the Communist Party, members can feel only an endless insecurity as they try to ally with this or that faction so they can retain their power and guaranteed privileges. Party members are constantly being scrutinized and tested by their peers, and if found wanting, they are disciplined, punished, or purged. Members have to be especially careful to conceal any "fatal" flaws about their family or social background, their personal relationships, and their individual views that might be used by Party rivals to humiliate and disgrace them, thereby ruining their Party careers.

Second, the Party has thus far not been successful in legitimizing its rule over the country. ROC experts have maintained that the Party has ruled mainly by virtue of its power and control over society. Because of continual policy changes, creation and dismantling of institutions, and switching leaders from one position to another, the Communist Party has failed to develop any routine procedures that would inspire popular confidence in either the Party or its leaders. These two pathologies of Party factional struggle and continual changing of Party line have created uncertainty, fear, and cynicism throughout mainland China.

ROC experts also contend that it is virtually impossible for this kind of a totalitarian regime to evolve into a different kind of political system without great disorder and violence. Because Party leaders constantly compete for the mantle of leadership, strong leaders come and go without any single leader ever arranging for a successor according to prescribed procedures. Further, because the Party holds total power, it is unlikely that it will ever relinquish power peacefully to other groups. Therefore, political change can take place only by the violent seizure of power by some group inside or outside the Communist Party.

After the turbulence of 1966-1967 and the Ninth National Congress in April 1969, many foreign observers concluded that the Chinese Communist regime would enter a new, stable era of governance, and CCP leaders at that National Congress had indeed demonstrated a show of Party unity. ROC China watchers, however, saw no prospects for a peaceful, stable era; they warned that the Cultural Revolution had not really ended but, rather, was entering a new stage of struggle. They foresaw no end to the Peking leaders' fomenting revolution in other Asian countries and continuing to quarrel among themselves on the sharing of Party power.[49]

Again, after the Tenth CCP National Congress in August 1973, many Western experts expected that political stability would result and that more attention would be devoted to matters of economic development. ROC experts, however, suggested that this congress did not end the internal struggle within the Party and that it merely was the starting point for a new power struggle among Party factions.[50]

ROC experts see no mechanism within the Communist Party for the membership to have checks and balances against leaders who accumulate excessive Party power. Because the Party supposedly represents the proletarian dictatorship over society, the ROC experts ask, how can Party leaders be expected to establish institutions that curtail or limit their power? Furthermore, the China watchers believe that any organizations that try to form outside of Party control or supervision will only be crushed by the Party or various instruments of the state. They strongly assert, therefore, that the only way this political system can be replaced is by the forcible removal of the Communist Party from power. There does not seem to exist any means within the Peking regime by which a peaceful fundamental transition to a different political order can ever take place.

CONCLUSION

Many ROC experts on Chinese Communist affairs might not agree with all the elements of this "ideal" type, and they might even take issue with several of them. Interviews with leading ROC experts and a careful reading of the major journals on PRC affairs, however, have corroborated the ideal type presented in this chapter.

The older generation of China watchers worked in the 1950s with government intelligence documents and published their findings for government use. Apart from their close relationship with the intelligence community in the ROC, many of these experts had personally been acquainted with leading Chinese Communist officials and had even worked with them in political activities. They also had other strengths. They understood Chinese political behavior, culture, and language, so they could read between the lines and extract additional meaning from Communist Party documents. Therefore, when these experts analyzed intelligence information from the mainland, they were able to interpret it in ways that are very different from the way people with a social science training and perspective would interpret it. Whether they would have interpreted these same documents very differently if they, too, had had a background in the social sciences is a question I cannot answer, but I doubt it.

Beginning in the early 1960s, a second generation of Communist affairs experts emerged, some of whom had been trained by their seniors and had received social science training abroad. They began to challenge the traditional approach of their older colleagues, contending that the application of Western social science methods not only was desirable but would prove to be more insightful and useful for policymakers. Then in the seventies a third generation of researchers came on the scene, even better trained in social science methodology and quantitative techniques but naturally having less understanding of the former realities of the mainland and lacking the rich personal experience and empathy of the first generation of experts.

Let me set forth some key characteristics about these Chinese Communist affairs experts in the ROC. First, these researchers have the ability to understand Chinese political culture and language, which enables them to read enormous quantities of Chinese Communist documents and public media matter and to understand the complexity of the material. Second, these China watchers have been very fortunate to be the recipients of a vast storehouse of intelligence information, which gives them access to CCP Central Committee documents and other records that reveal intra-Party debates and the maneuvering of even the top leaders themselves.

Third, several senior experts have even had personal ties with the Chinese Communists, especially those in the top leadership, or they have had the experience of dealing firsthand with the CCP. Therefore, they are extremely sensitive to and able to understand key Communist terms and cliches, and they are able to understand the real meaning of the original documents, the true intentions of their authors, the complex political activities within the CCP, and the behavior of the Party cadres themselves.

Perhaps of even greater significance, these ROC China watchers implicitly believe in and use the ideal type (described as the Chinese Communist Totalitarian System) in order to understand the major developments and general behavior in mainland China. This ideal type stresses the importance of holding power in the regime and the fact that the dominant political activity is that of consolidating and wielding political power. Therefore, the concern for power also means the struggle for power, so the power struggle has become a way of life. By viewing mainland developments in this way, ROC researchers tend to stress the dysfunctions of the Communist system and describe at great length Communist China's numerous socioeconomic pathologies, such as economic waste and inefficiency, low living standards, and the disintegration of the traditional culture. They also tend to ignore recurring complex patterns in the relationship between the state and the society, patterns that a social science methodologist might prefer to give high priority.

But this latter defect has not seriously flawed their research findings. Revelations by PRC leaders and the new findings reported by Westerners since 1979 have also described these same dysfunctions and pathologies. Moreover, that new information now strongly confirms the veracity of the ideal type presented above as accurately interpreting general characteristics and trends in the system since its founding.[51] If the ROC experts produce credible scholarship that is so accurate, why have their central findings never been taken seriously by the majority of the China watchers in the West? Why are their findings continually ignored by their Western counterparts? Why, too, do Western experts ignore so many of the Communist Party documents that are published and stored in the ROC when few reliable Communist documents have ever been obtained by Westerners? These questions deserve serious consideration, because the answers will certainly shed some light on why so much of Communist China watching that has been done by Westerners appears to have been flawed.

To be sure, studies in the ROC on Chinese Communist affairs can be improved, and at this time, this work is at a very important crossroads in its gradual evolution. But wouldn't the research of Western scholars also be improved if they began to make greater use of the CCP material that is available in the ROC, and wouldn't greater cooperation between Western and ROC researchers be the correct way to try and achieve a greater understanding of the dynamics of change in Communist China?

NOTES

1. To protect the individuals concerned, those who had had affiliations with the Chinese Communist Party are not identified.
2. Evidence for this assertion is based on private interviews with leading ROC experts on Chinese Communist affairs.
3. <u>Chinese Communist Affairs Monthly</u> is the English title used in the ROC, but a strict translation should read <u>Communist Bandit Intelligence Monthly</u>.
4. Henry G. Schwarz, "The <u>Ts'an-k'ao hsiao-hsi</u>: How Well Informed Are Chinese Officials About the Outside World?" <u>China Quarterly</u>, no. 27 (July-September 1966), p. 56.
5. Warren Kuo, <u>Tui-fei tou-chen shih-shih</u> [Facts on the political struggle against the Chinese Communists] (Taipei: Bureau of Investigation,

1963), p. 153.

6. The documents were later published by the Bureau of Intelligence, Republic of China, in 1970. An English version has been made available by the Hoover Institution.

7. Landing Craft Documents are collected at the Institute for the Study of Chinese Communist Problems, Taipei.

8. On November 5, 1970, major newspapers in Taipei published the entire text of the revised draft of the Constitution of the People's Republic of China, which was to be approved by the Fourth National People's Congress in January 1975.

9. Chung-kung yen-chiu [Studies on Chinese communism] 6:4 (April 1972), pp. 4-5.

10. Chung-kung yen-chiu 6:7 (July 1972), pp. 1-12, 98-102.

11. "The Political Report Given by Chou En-lai at the 10th CCP National Congress," Chung-kung yen-chiu 7:9 (September 1973), pp. 38-40.

12. The Chinese language Fei-ch'ing yüeh-pao [Chinese Communist affairs monthly] has also published a number of such documents.

13. Warren Kuo, "Mainland China Studies in the R.O.C.," Proceedings of the First Sino-American Conference on Mainland China (Taipei: Institute of International Relations, 1971), pp. 13-16.

14. "Seminar on Methodology of Communist China Studies," China Times Magazine, July 4-10, 1982, pp. 57-62.

15. Ibid., p. 62.

16. Cheng Hsüeh-chia, A Review of the Chinese Communist Party in the Past Thirty Years (Taipei: China Times Press, 1980), pp. 1-56; Li T'ien-min, "A Study of the Chinese Community Personality" (Paper presented at the Second Sino-American Conference on Mainland China, 1972).

17. Chen Yü-ch'ang, "The Political Theories of the Chinese Communists," Monograph on the CCP Politics (Taipei: Institute of International Relations, 1973), p. 11.

18. Wu An-chia, "The Nature of the Chinese Communists," Chin-tai Chung-kuo [Modern China] (February 1983), pp. 171-173.

19. Ibid., p. 163.

20. Warren Kuo, "Personal Dictatorship or Collective Leadership?" Issues & Studies 10:12

(September 1974), p. 48.

21. Warren Kuo, "Reforming the Chinese Communist Leadership System," *Proceedings of the Tenth Sino-American Conference on Mainland China* (Berkeley: University of California, 1981), p. 41.

22. Wu An-chia, "Nature of the Chinese Community," p. 168.

23. Tsui Chui-yien, "Does Mao Tse-tung's Thought Originate in Chinese Tradition?" *Issues & Studies* 4:7 (April 1968), pp. 1-8, and Teng Kung-hsuan, "Maoism vs. Chinese Cultural Tradition," *Issues & Studies* 4:9 (June 1968), pp. 1-8.

24. Hsing Kuo-ch'iang, "A Brief Analysis of Mao Tse-tung Thought After Mao's Death," *Issues & Studies* 12:11 (November 1976), p. 55.

25. Teng Kung-hsuan, "Maoism vs. Chinese Cultural Tradition," p. 1.

26. Ibid., p. 7.

27. Warren Kuo, "Mainland China Studies in the R.O.C.," pp. 13-16; Tsui Chui-yien, "Does Mao Tse-tung's Thought Originate in Chinese Tradition?"; and Teng Kung-hsuan, "Maoism vs. Chinese Culture Tradition."

28. Warren Kuo, "Factional Dissension in Communist China," *Issues & Studies* 16:9 (September 1980), p. 12.

29. Chu Hsin-min, "Mao Tse-tung's Personality Model and Behavior Rule," *Tung-ya chi-k'an* [East Asian quarterly] 10:3 (January 1979), pp. 134-144.

30. Warren Kuo, "Personal Dictatorship or Collective Leadership?" p. 51.

31. Hsing Kuo-ch'iang, "Brief Analysis of Mao Tse-tung Thought," p. 61.

32. Yung Wei, "Culture, Ideology, and Elite Conflict: Toward a 'Middle Range' Interpretation of Chinese Communist Behavior," *Proceedings of the Third Sino-American Conference on Mainland China* (Taipei: Institute of International Relations, 1972), pp. 1-15.

33. Warren Kuo, "Personal Dictatorship or Collective Leadership?" p. 53.

34. Ibid.

35. Ibid., pp. 52-53.

36. Cheng Hsüeh-chia, *From the Cultural Revolution to the Eleventh CCP National Congress* (Taipei: Li-ming Publishing Company, 1978), p. 14.

37. Kung Teh-liang, "A Brief Review of CCP Activities During the Past Fifty Years," *Issues & Studies* 7:10 (July 1971), p. 39.

38. Warren Kuo, "Communist China in the Post-Mao Period: Possible Development of the Power Struggle," *Issues & Studies* 12:11 (November 1976), p. 4.

39. Li T'ien-min, "The Big Struggle on the Chinese Mainland," *Issues & Studies* 2:11 (August 1966), p. 7.

40. Yeh Hsiang-chih, "A Review of the CCP's Intra-party Struggles," *Chung-kung yen-chiu* 6:11 (November 1972), p. 4.

41. Warren Kuo, "Possible Outcome of the Recent CCP Intra-party Struggle," *Fei-ch'ing yüeh-pao* 19:12 (June 1977), p. 8.

42. Chang Chen-pang, "The Evolution of Mao-Lin Clique's Strategy to Seize Power," *Fei-ch'ing yüeh-pao* 10:3 (April 1967), pp. 13-19; also Chang Chen-pang, "The CCP's Intra-party Struggle After the CCP Tenth National Congress," in *Monograph on the CCP's Intra-party Struggle* (Taipei: Institute of International Relations, 1973), pp. 658-676.

43. Yao Meng-hsuan, "Issues of the CCP Intra-party Struggle," *Fei-ch'ing yüeh-pao* 16:2 (April 1973), p. 13.

44. Kung Teh-liang, "Brief Review of CCP Activities in the Past Fifty Years," p. 39.

45. Warren Kuo, "Peace Offensives and the United Front Tactics," *Issues & Studies* 15:3 (March 1979), pp. 14-15.

46. Warren Kuo, "Personal Dictatorship or Collective Leadership?" p. 43.

47. Yin Ch'ing-yao, *PRC's Foreign Policy and Foreign Relations* (Taipei: Institute of International Relations, 1973), p. 21.

48. Hsiang Nai-kwang, "Historical Lessons of the Chinese Communist Negotiation Policy," *Chung-kung yen-chiu* 6:8 (August 1972), p. 55.

49. Chang Ching-wen, "An Analysis of the Members of the Ninth CCPCC," *Fei-ch'ing yüeh-pao* 12:3 (May 1969), pp. 14-17; Kung Teh-liang, "A General Analysis of the Ninth CCP National Congress," *Fei-ch'ing yüeh-pao* 12:3 (May 1969), pp. 7-13; Yao Meng-hsuan, "Some Questions Concerning the Ninth National Congress of the CCP," *Issues & Studies* 5:10 (July 1969), pp. 16-30.

50. Hsiao Yeh-hui, "Power Infrastructure of the CCP Top Level Hierarchy and Its Future Direction of Struggle," <u>Chung-kung yen-chiu</u> 6:9 (September 1972), pp. 5-9; Kung Teh-liang, "A Comprehensive Analysis of the Tenth CCP National Congress," <u>Fei-ch'ing yüeh-pao</u> 16:8 (October 1973), pp. 7-13; Yin Ch'ing-yao, "The Tenth CCP National Congress and Peiping's Foreign Policy," <u>Fei-ch'ing yüeh-pao</u> 16:9 (November 1973), pp. 13-19.

51. See Harry Harding, Jr., "From China, with Disdain: Trend in the Study of China," <u>Issues & Studies</u> 18:7 (July 1982), pp. 12-39, and Chalmers Johnson, "What's Wrong with Chinese Political Studies?" <u>Issues & Studies</u> 18:6 (June 1982), pp. 12-18.

4
Party Rectification in Post-Mao China

Lowell Dittmer

The Party rectification campaign launched by the Chinese Communist Party in 1982 represents an interesting attempt to come to terms with several of the dilemmas that have faced the new leaders since they initiated their ambitious reform program at the Third Plenum of the Eleventh Central Committee (CC). First and foremost is the issue of whether a Party rectification campaign per se can be made politically viable in light of the Party's general repudiation of the campaign approach to policy implementation. On the negative side of this question are the well-known adverse features of the mass movement, which risk alienating either the masses (if the movement is too tightly regimented) or the elites (if the masses are given license to attack the elites spontaneously). On the affirmative side is the functional need for some technique to arouse apparently enthusiastic and widespread support for new policies.[1] Can an organization that is accustomed to a crusade mentality be placed on a more orderly and routine footing without impairing its morale? Also urgently needed is some effective way to monitor and correct cadre abuses without giving free rein to anarchic reactions against authority.

The fact that Party rectification continues to qualify as a type of campaign, however restricted in compass and tactically modified, also raises the question of the proper role of the masses--that is, the non-Party citizenry--in its implementation since in previous campaigns, the masses played an important role--sometimes lauded, sometimes deplored. The fact that the Party rectification campaign never really got into high gear until the mass movement to clear up spiritual pollution and promote a socialist spiritual civilization gathered momentum implies that the question whether the Party can really rectify itself <u>by</u> itself is still moot.

The Party rectification in question has been launched only recently and is still in its incipient stages, so any attempt to answer questions about it is necessarily preliminary and tentative. But in view of the facts that this is the first Party rectification campaign to have been undertaken in the post-Mao era and that it aspires to be among the most significant of such undertakings since the Yanan Zhengfeng movement (with which it is frequently compared), it is appropriate--in fact, inevitable--that questions be asked. The following brief survey will consist of three parts: a look at the preparations for the campaign, a preliminary assessment of the progress of implementation to date, and a concluding section dealing with the campaign's broader implications.

PREPARATIONS

The Party rectification campaign has been in the offing for some time, and preparatory measures have been unusually elaborate. The problem was discussed as early as December 1978 at the Third Plenum, and in fact, the Central Disciplinary Inspection Commission was established at that time (under the chairmanship of Chen Yun) in order to take effective countermeasures against the congeries of abuses that are generally categorized under the term "unhealthy work style." Deng Xiaoping's reform faction won a significant victory at the Third Plenum, but its position was yet by no means secure, and its members no doubt wished to consolidate their power against the prospect of a leftist counterattack. Even on the right, among their presumed supporters, they saw problems--in an infatuation with democracy and a liberalizing tendency that threatened discipline and implicitly challenged the legitimacy of the proletarian dictatorship.

Thus in February 1980, at the Fifth Plenum of the Eleventh CC, the Party adopted a set of "Guiding Principles for Intra-Party Political Life" in an effort to establish a normative basis for rectification, and on November 12, 1981, Deng Xiaoping made an important speech at a Politburo meeting on the rectification of work style in which he identified its principal targets for the first time. These were the "three types of person" (san zhong ren): the remnant elements of the Lin Biao-Jiang Qing counterrevolutionary clique, those who had gained power during the Cultural Revolution through "rebellion," and the "smash and grabbers." It will be noted that all of these types happened to be "leftists" (bearing in mind that the Democracy Wall activists had by this time been reclassified under this epithet because of their rambunctious tactics). Deng also drew attention to the problem of serious overstaffing in the Party, citing statistics to show that there were more than 600,000 cadres in the organs directly under the central authorities of the Party and the state and more than 1,000 people at or above the vice-ministerial level.[2]

Party rectification was then formally announced at the Twelfth Party Congress in September 1982. In his report to this congress, Party Secretary Hu Yaobang said that the rectification and consolidation of the Party (consolidation began to receive stronger emphasis than rectification, no doubt because the prospect of the latter had alarmed some people) would begin in the latter half of 1983 and last for three years. The objective would be to achieve a fundamental turn for the better in the work style of the Party. This was only one of three "fundamental turns for the better," the others being "turns" in the nation's finance and economy and social customs. But the Party's work style was given top priority: Only through Party rectification and an improvement in Party work style could a fundamental improvement in social customs or in national finance and economic matters be achieved.[3] At the same meeting, Deng Xiaoping also emphasized the significance of Party consolidation and the rectification of work style, calling it one of the four guarantees of China's success in achieving the Four Modernizations, but he somewhat pessimistically predicted that such efforts would have to continue until the end of the century.

It may be surmised that the most enthusiastic supporters of the rectification at this point were still the so-called practice faction (<u>shijian pai</u>) led by Deng Xiaoping, which may tentatively be divided into two subgroups. Having just delivered a severe, but not fatal, setback to the "whateverists" (<u>fanshi pai</u>), both subgroups were justifiably concerned about a possible counterattack from the Left and united in their determination to preempt this threat. In the absence or extenuation of such a common threat, the senior veterans--such as Chen Yun, Wang Zhen, Bo Yibo, and Deng Liqun--were primarily concerned with the restoration of order; though they were in favor of economic reform, they were concerned about the corruption and ideological confusion they perceived to be flowing in through China's new open door and intent upon staunching it. The younger reformers--led by Hu Yaobang and Zhao Ziyang and including Wan Li and Wang Zhaoguo among the civilian cadres and such recently upward mobile military cadres as Zhang Tingfa, Qin Jiwei, and Hong Xuezhi (Zhang rose after the Third Plenum; Qin and Hong were both promoted after Hu Yaobang became general-secretary)—had more ambitious career objectives that transcended the tenures of office of their superiors, in pursuit of which more thorough rectification of the veteran Left would be expedient. As group patron, Deng Xiaoping alternatively displayed sympathy for both subgroups, which resulted in an ambiguity that is typical of his position since the Third Plenum.

Throughout the winter of 1982-1983, the Party conducted experiments in preparation for the campaign; the experience gained therein would be summarized and used as guiding principles in the subsequent implementation. In the central government apparatus, ministries and commissions under the State Council conducted rotating training classes for Party members to study various documents in preparation for the campaign, primarily the new

Party Constitution; by the end of March 1983, twenty-seven ministries and commissions were in the process of conducting rotational training "by stages and in groups," and other units were preparing to do so.[4] The CC sent out work teams to seventeen provinces, municipalities under the jurisdiction of the central government, and autonomous regions to help solve the problems encountered in the course of experimentation. For example, Beijing Municipality selected a number of units in the municipal Party committee organs, the industries, the capital-construction system, the financial and trade system, the countryside, and urban areas as experimental places for Party rectification work and sent leading cadres down to the relevant departments of the district and bureau Party committees to participate in the process.

According to a survey and an analysis of the 3,658 Party branches in Beijing Municipality that was conducted in conjunction with this experiment, fewer than one-third of the branches were fully satisfactory; about 60 percent were deemed average, and 10 percent were considered backward, of which some were paralyzed or semiparalyzed. The main problems encountered were factionalism, lack of a forthright ideological line, an attitude of doubt and resistance toward Party policies (particularly policies introduced since the Third Plenum), an inclination to take advantage of one's office to pursue personal privilege, and an inclination to take advantage of decentralization with respect to superiors so that each might do whatever he or she thinks is right and to take the posture of "whatever I say goes" with regard to subordinates. Of the 650,000 Party members in Beijing, 310,000, or 48 percent of the total, had joined the Party before the Cultural Revolution, 250,000 (38 percent of the total) had joined during the Cultural Revolution, and 90,000 (14 percent of the total) had joined after the collapse of the Gang of Four. The impact of the Cultural Revolution was still considered a major threat; some cadres even said, "Why should Party members have to lead in pursuing our work; why can't the masses take the lead?"[5]

Yet far from experiencing any such upheavals,

this preparatory period appears--from the slim evidence available--to have been dedicated exclusively to the supervised study of documents, and there was considerable reluctance to air local problems. Hunan Province, for example, reported that from November 1982 until July 1983, only eight units were assigned as experimental places for Party rectification work, a process that was carried out in sequence. In three advanced units, the work of Party member registration and election of leading groups had been completed and the experience was being summarized; of the other five units, some were comparing and inspecting, some testing and evaluating personnel in the leading groups. Development of the experimental work was "not balanced," the major complaint being "slackness," not "bold enough to face confrontation."[6]

In any event, a total of more than 580 different types of grass roots Party organizations in the twenty-nine provinces, municipalities under direct central governance, and autonomous regions had carried out some form of Party consolidation work since the Twelfth Congress. From January to August 1983, about 92.4 percent of the Party members were reportedly sent to receive training; in the PLA, 92.6 percent of all Party members received such training from early 1983 to September 1983.[7] In May 1983, the CC convoked a Symposium on the Work of Party Consolidation to coordinate these preliminary efforts. On July 1, People's Daily published an editorial, "Resolutely Overcome the Unhealthy Tendencies Within the Party," asking Party committees at all levels to strengthen their leadership of the experiments and to lay a sturdy foundation for the forthcoming rectification.

IMPLEMENTATION

The next major watershed in the development of the Party rectification campaign was the Second Plenum of the Twelfth CC, which was conducted on October 11 and 12, 1983, after a two-day preparatory meeting. This session marked the passage from the experimental stage to the application of rectification to the Party at large. Both Deng Xiaoping and Chen Yun gave important speeches stressing the campaign's significance. On October 11, the plenary members passed "The Decision of the CC of the Communist Party of China on Party Consolidation," which outlined a relatively detailed prospectus for the campaign under nine separate headings. Rectification would last for three years and be conducted in two stages. During the first stage, beginning in the winter of 1983, work would focus on the consolidation of Party organs of the leading bodies at the central, provincial, municipalities under central governance, and autonomous region levels. At the same time, provincial Party committees were to be enjoined to run experimental areas of Party rectification at the county (<u>xian</u>) and sub-provincial prefectural (<u>zhou</u>) levels. During the second stage, beginning in the winter of 1984, the work would stress the consolidation of all Party organs at the district and grass-roots levels.[8]

The organization of the campaign represents a contrast to (and an implicit rejection of) the campaign practices of the Cultural Revolution and, more generally, the period of Mao's ascendancy.[9] Thus the Decision warned against excessive zeal: "attention should be paid to guard against the erroneous practice of the past of ruthless struggle and merciless attack. It is absolutely impermissible for anyone to take advantage of the Party consolidation to whip up factionalism to persecute others, to make false charges or to retaliate against others against whom he bears a grudge."[10]

The movement is to proceed <u>fen qi fen pi</u> ("stage by stage and group by group"), as in the Socialist Education Campaign of the early 1960s, thereby avoiding nationally coordinated, simultaneous "wavelike advances." It is to move "from top to bottom," both in terms of the Party hierarchy as a whole and within each individual unit. A special central steering committee (<u>zhongyang zhengdang zhidao weiyuanhui</u>) was set up under the chairmanship of Hu Yaobang to lead the campaign.[11] It did not appear to develop a network of subordinate committees that paralleled the Party-state hierarchy, as in many previous campaigns, nor was it to send out the work teams that had become so notorious during the Cultural Revolution; it could however send out liaison teams to the various units to observe (without actively interfering) and make reports. The central steering committee was to hold meetings in the winter of 1983 or the spring of 1984 to discuss questions concerning the strengthening of work on the ideological front. In each Party organization, rectification would be carried out by the leadership of the Party unit itself, which would then report to its superior organization for official approval.

In terms of overall objectives, rectification would involve a struggle on two fronts, tacitly shifting from Hu Yaobang's 1982 emphasis on the inherited sins of the Cultural Revolution to at least equal billing for cadre corruption (usually considered a rightist deviation). The Decision set forth four main tasks for the campaign: the achievement of ideological unity, the rectification of Party work style, the strengthening of discipline, and the purification of the Party organization.

Ideological unity would be achieved through the intensive study of designated documents, attended by criticism and self-criticism. Aside from the Decision itself, study documents would include a primer for Party members, a collection of important post-1978 documents (such as those of the Third Plenum or the constitution of the Twelfth Party Congress), a selection of Mao's writings on the Party's work style and organization, and <u>The Selected Works of Deng Xiaoping</u>, of which no fewer than 40 million copies have been published since July 1983 (which happens to coincide precisely with the number of Party members).[12] Much was made at the Second Plenum of an article by Chen Yun, originally published in Yanan in December 1939, "To Study Is the Responsibility of the Communist Party Members", as well as his "Comments on the Draft of the 'Resolution on Party History'" and his speech "Concerning the Problem of Two Deviations by Party Art Workers,"[13] so his <u>Selected Works</u> will presumably be studied as well. Once the period of study and education is considered complete, each Party organization will submit to an acceptance test (a written examination, to which most cadres are hardly accustomed) administered by a superior organization.

The rectification of Party work style is to be based on the Four Basic Principles, which were first enunciated by Deng Xiaoping in March 1979. Taking a cue from Deng Xiaoping, the Decision again defined the main targets as the "three types": those "who rose to prominence by following the counterrevolutionary cliques of Lin Biao and Jiang Qing in 'rebellion,' those who are seriously factionalist in their ideas, and those who indulged in beating, smashing and looting."[14] To the original san zhong ren, however, the Decision added an additional six candidates for disciplinary sanction: those who have stubbornly resisted the policies of the CC adopted since the Third Plenum; those who have committed grave economic crimes; those who have committed serious mistakes but refuse consistently to correct them; those who do not have a correct ideological consciousness, create splits, do not have a sense of responsibility, and are not career minded; those unprincipled "good old boys"; and those who do not have any political integrity and are in a state of inertia.[15]

The original three types were all leftists, whereas the additional six might be assumed to be more broadly distributed, perhaps including many of the veteran cadres who composed Deng's core constituency of Cultural Revolution victims. The last-named category might be expected to be particularly ubiquitous; of the 21 million Party and government cadres, it is estimated that only about 20 percent have a college education and 30 percent some professional competence.[16] For those cadres whose cultural level is low, organization departments at all levels are urged to work out training programs that are in line with the practical conditions and requirements of their local areas.

The third task, strengthening Party discipline, involves an attack on economic criminals. For those cadres whose unhealthy work style is manifested in such traits as bureaucratism, seeking private gain at public expense by exploiting one's office, or committing economic crimes, severe sanctions are in order. According to the

"Report on the Attack on Serious Criminal Activities in the Economic Field" issued by the Central Disciplinary Inspection Commission, a total of 192,000 cases of economic crime were exposed and investigated between January 1982 and April 1983. These cases involved 71,000 Party members, about 8,500 of whom have been stripped of Party membership.[17] In addition to Party disciplinary actions, sanctions include criticism and self-criticism, administrative measures, and legal sanctions.

The final task, purification of the Party organization, involves reregistration of all 40 million Party members. Some Party members will be permitted to reregister, some may have their registrations postponed pending further educational efforts, and some will not be allowed to register and will have their names removed from the Party entirely. It has been widely anticipated that reregistration will involve a sweeping purge of people who moved upward during the Cultural Revolution as they compose the "three types of person" categories that are designated as prime targets.

There are at present about 40 million Party members, attached to 2.5 million Party organs from the grass roots level to the CC, of whom about 9 million are cadres. About 18 million were recruited before the Cultural Revolution, and 4 million have been recruited during the post-Mao period, which leaves 18 million who were recruited during the Cultural Revolution decade. Although all in this group must be considered vulnerable, their liability has been somewhat extenuated by certain passages in the Decision. When rectification was first broached in 1982, its political aspect was quite prominent, but in 1983 it was stipulated (in the Decision) that the criterion for determining whether someone was one of the "three types" is the actual damage done to the Party and the people in the case at hand, not the historical background of the person (i.e., membership in a particular faction during the Cultural Revolution). In contradistinction to previous movements, there would be no quotas for the number of either punishments within or expulsions from the Party. All disciplinary measures must be approved by the Party's organization at the next highest level.

In the course of implementation, the rectification campaign has thus far proceeded through two phases. The first phase, initiated at the Second Plenum of the Twelfth CC, lasted through the end of 1983. In addition to the Decision, the work of this phase was defined by Central Document no. 1, issued October 24, 1983, which contains various study materials, and by Central Document no. 4, issued on December 12 to the various liaison groups (<u>lianhuayuan xiaozu</u>), the leaders of which were called to a high-level conference with the steering committee.

Inasmuch as this phase of the campaign coincided with a campaign to clear mental pollution, which was also formally launched at the Second Plenum, many of its themes were drawn from this simultaneous mass movement. In fact, although the Decision indicated that rectification would be pursued without mass involvement[18] (whereas in some previous campaigns, such as the Hundred Flowers or the Cultural Revolution, the distinction between "inner" and "outer" had been lost), there was some tendency to merge the two movements. This inclination, for example, was evident in the speeches given at a forum for democratic parties that was convened by the CC from October 21 to October 26, which solicited the views of these non-Party notables on both Party rectification and spiritual pollution. Luo Qiong put the two campaigns in tandem in a written statement to veteran cadres on November 24, and even Bo Yibo, vice-chairman of the Standing Committee of the Central Steering Committee, indicated that the clearing of mental pollution was part of the work of inner-Party rectification.[19]

The second phase of the campaign began in early 1984. Hu Yaobang, who had been in Japan at the time of the initiation of the Spiritual Pollution Campaign, and had been conspicuously silent about it after his return, signaled the shift as early as October 25 when he defined the rectification in terms of promoting good things and overcoming the current negative side. What was the current negative side? Ignoring the "three types of person," he defined the negative side in terms of economic criminals, lawbreakers, those who abused power for selfish reasons, and followers of Lin Biao and Jiang Qing.[20] At the session of the Standing Committee of the National People's Congress held in early December, the Spiritual Pollution Campaign aroused strong controversy and was not brought to a vote. In an interview with French journalists on January 25, 1984, Hu again discussed his view of the purpose of the rectification movement, and the newspapers correspondingly shifted their emphasis from spiritual pollution to "bad Party work style" (<u>bu liao zuofeng, bu zheng zhifeng</u>). Also in January, when <u>People's Daily</u> reported on the progress of the campaign at various levels, the emphasis was almost entirely on study documents, with no indication of any personnel changes. The main objective of the rectification campaign was now defined as ensuring that cadres work conscientiously and competently--with increasing emphasis on the latter, more apolitical, criterion.

How can this apparent moderation of the campaign be accounted for? One possibility is that the lower-level cadres, who may be assumed to comprise most of the "three types of person" eligible for purge in the first instance, were simply too skillful in redefining campaign objectives, mobilizing local support, etc., to be dislodged. There is some question as to what proportion of the 18 million Cultural Revolution recruits were really devotees of the Gang of Four and what proportion were simply politically ambitious and upwardly mobile; there is also some question how many radical loyalists managed to survive the three-year campaign against them in 1977-1980. Another possibility is that Hu Yaobang simply wished to avoid a struggle that might quickly become a generation conflict between veterans and youth, thereby adversely affecting the recruitment base of this erstwhile chairman of the Communist Youth League.

IMPLICATIONS

Both outside commentators and the responsible authorities themselves have often compared the current rectification to Mao's original <u>Zhengfeng</u> movement at Yanan in 1942-1944. In many ways, the analogy is apt. Both campaigns were launched to consolidate a major shift of Party line and to build political support for a new regime--Mao Zedong's at Yanan and that of Deng Xiaoping and (more pertinently) Hu Yaobang and Zhao Ziyang in the present instance. Whereas the Yanan movement anticipated the seizure of power on the mainland, the current campaign looks forward to the realization of the Four Modernizations. Publication of Deng's <u>Selected Works</u> on July 1 recalls the heavy reliance on Mao's writings (for the first time) in the 1940s.

Although too little is really known about the Yanan movement, let alone the ongoing one, to permit a tenable comparison, it seems to me that the present campaign is essentially different. Zhengfeng seems to have been the first concerted rectification campaign, and the technique was still sharp at that point, so it could be pushed ruthlessly ahead without all the trepidations that seem to burden the current program. The regime is now attempting to embark on reform in a context in which reform, because of its inherently incalculable consequences, evokes fears of a resurgence of radicalism. Thus, the regime proceeds only with extreme caution, moving ahead only to backtrack at the first sign of adverse consequences.

The regime confronts a series of dilemmas and problems to which traditional expedients provide no fully satisfactory solution and for which the suitability of untried new proposals is quite uncertain. These problems range from quite practical political problems to more abstract developmental dilemmas. Among the former is, How should the young people who participated in the Cultural Revolution be dealt with? The current consensus is that the Cultural Revolution was an unmitigated disaster, which has commonly been translated to mean that all the people who rose against the "Party persons in authority taking the capitalist road" are now considered villainous. The "three types of person" category abets this construal. And yet the young people whom Mao inspired to overthrow evil and make way for a brave new world were unquestionably political idealists whose ideals were then seasoned by their experiences in the factional wars or during their tenure in the countryside. For all they lack in formal education, they do tend to make up contemporary China's most politically sophisticated generation since the revolution. They were at Tiananmen to honor the memory of Zhou Enlai, and they provided vocal mass support for Deng Xiaoping during his rise against the "whateverists" in 1978-1979. Now that Deng's position is secure, it might be possible to suppress this troublesome constituency without adverse consequences, yet there is certainly a need for youthful enthusiasm in a system that still operates on the seniority system, if only to exert pressure on entrenched bureaucrats.

Which brings us to the second practical problem: How can the venality that is inherent in any large-scale bureaucracy be rectified? To rely on internal controls such as criticism and self-criticism seems to be inadequate, and even the attempt to construct an external control hierarchy (viz., the Central Disciplinary Inspection Commission [CDIC] and its subordinate agencies) has not yet had impressive consequences. The notion of a "campaign" to correct bureaucratic abuses is very unpopular because of the havoc campaigns wreak without permanently solving problems, and yet, if there is no means whereby the people can monitor the bureaucracy, it seems unrealistic to expect the bureaucrats to keep their own house in order. There have been some encouraging efforts to utilize letters to the editor in newspapers and letters to the CDIC to bring attention to conspicuous abuses, and perhaps more will be done along these lines.

The more general problem is, of course, how to make the transition from a revolutionary, charismatic regime to an institutionalized, "routinized" modernizing system without a crisis of confidence. Although perhaps economically ineffectual, Mao Zedong thought has been linked with public morality in China so long and so well that to repudiate it is fraught with more risk to the system's legitimacy than Khrushchev's repudiation of Stalinism. The leaders are accustomed to implementing those policies they deem important through crusadelike movements, in which a constantly evolving consensus is generated by an evolving repertoire of slogans; for them to shift abruptly to a bureaucratic proceduralism, based on rule-governed implementation with a relatively fixed, codified consensus means risking apathy, loss of political momentum, elitism, and corruption. Such a dilemma had not yet emerged at the time of Yanan. The flaws in the campaign approach were then not yet apparent; even more important, there was no bureaucratic alternative.

It is the presence--indeed, the inescapability-- of this alternative that is so decisive at this stage in China's development. Implicit in the Deng Xiaoping "reform" regime's criticism of the late Maoist era and in the whole thrust of its plans for the future is the assumption that institutional vested interests must not be incautiously assailed. They may be expediently rearranged, but the interests and functions they serve must still be taken into account. This assumption has given rise to a sort of crypto-pluralism that promises to change the face of Chinese politics. The actors will still be a small group of elites in Beijing, but their political power will be defined, not by their ties to an ideologically defined informal network (faction), but by their links to a functional system in the division of labor. The way politics will be conducted is by "floating" or attempting to "capture" already available issues by pre-emptive definition. The way one can determine whether an issue has been effectively captured or not is whether the particular definition imposed generates a politically influential constituency. Rather than actively mobilizing mass support an elite will now "angle" for such support in much the same way that someone angles for fish, trying one rhetorical lure after another.

Perhaps the most effective practitioner of this technique in recent Chinese politics has been the PLA. Six weeks before the Sixth Plenum of the Eleventh CC, at which Hua Guofeng was to officially lose his chairmanship of the Party, <u>Liberation Army Daily</u> published an article criticizing Bai Hua by name for the filmscript

"Bitter Love." This article was scrupulously ignored (as far as outsiders can determine) during the plenum, but shortly afterward a campaign was launched against Bai Hua, and it was followed by other campaigns against bourgeois liberalization and in favor of building a socialist spiritual civilization. Again in 1982, on the eve of the Twelfth Party Congress, a military propagandist named Zhao Yiya published an article simultaneously in Liberation Army Daily and Shanghai's Liberation Daily entitled "Communist Ideology Is the Core of Socialist Spiritual Civilization," in which he argued that ideology was of more importance than culture or education. This attempt to preempt the Party "line," coming even after the latter had been ratified by the Politburo at the Seventh Plenum of the Eleventh CC, was too bold and was met with sharp criticism, but it fits the emerging pattern.

The "struggle between two fronts" format provides a rich field of ambiguity for these politics of rhetorical preemption, for it places the correct "line" between two forbidden alternatives, leaving unclear which poses the greater danger. Representatives of either side will attempt to preempt the particular rhetorical formulation that best approximates their interests and turn it against its logical antithesis. Thus, during the opening phase of the Party rectification movement in the fall of 1983, the two fronts consisted of spiritual pollution on one side, which implies an attack against the Right (against the intellectuals), and Party rectification on the other, which originally implied an attack against the Left (against the cadres). Struggle on both fronts was launched concurrently, and the relationship between these two struggles is complex and obscure. The two struggles are at once compensatory and competitive, as higher cadres try to use Party rectification to purge younger radicals and the latter emphasize the struggle against spiritual pollution. One possible interpretation is that Deng Xiaoping launched the campaign against spiritual pollution as a sop to the Left in order to generate sufficient support to pursue Party rectification. But such an interpretation is only preliminary, and any final reckoning must await the conclusion of the two campaigns. What seems interesting at this point are the emergent patterns.

NOTES

1. See the vindication of the campaign approach in Shen Baoxiang, "Do Not Exaggerate the Concept of 'Political Campaign,'" Jiefang ribao [Liberation daily] (Shanghai), November 21, 1981, p. 4.
2. Chang Chen-pang, "Peip'ing's Rectification of the Party Work Style," Issues and Studies (hereafter IS) 18:5 (May 1982), pp. 1-5.
3. Ming pao, November 30, 1982, p. 5.
4. Guo Xuan, "Strengthen the Education of Party Members and Do a Good Job of Preparing for Party Rectification," Renmin ribao [People's daily] (hereafter RR), April 22, 1983, p. 3.
5. See note 3.
6. Ming pao, July 7, 1983, p. 5.
7. New China News Agency report, October 13, 1983, and October 18, 1983.
8. "The Decision of the CC of the Communist Party of China on Party Consolidation," Beijing Review 26:42 (October 17, 1983), p. 2.
9. See David S.G. Goodman, "The Second Plenary Session of the 12th CCP Central Committee: Rectification and Reform," China Quarterly, no. 97 (March 1984), pp. 84-91.
10. Beijing Review 26:42 (October 17, 1983), p. 9.
11. Important members included Bo Yibo (vice-chairman), Deng Liqun, and Wang Zhaoguo.
12. Beijing Review 26:28 (July 11, 1983), pp. 5-6, and New York Times, September 30 and November 20, 1983.
13. Guangming ribao [Enlightenment daily], July 25, 1983.
14. See note 8.
15. "To Accelerate the 'Four Modernizations': Construction of the Leading Body with the Spirit of Reform," RR, July 22, 1983, p. 1.
16. RR, December 11, 1983, and January 6, 14, 21, and February 7, 1984; Far Eastern Economic Review 122:50 (December 15, 1983), p. 23.
17. Chang Chen-pang, "Party Consolidation and

Work Style Rectification," <u>IS</u> (August 1983), pp. 1-5.

18. The Second Plenum stated that "on no account should the past erroneous practices of 'letting the masses consolidate the Party' or letting non-Party members decide issues in the Party be repeated" <u>Beijing Review</u> 26:42 (October 17, 1983), p. 7.

19. <u>RR</u>, January 6, 1983, p. 1. To be sure, Bo may have been trying to damp down the campaign against spiritual pollution rather than heat up the Party rectification campaign.

20. <u>RR</u>, October 25, 1983, p. 1.

5
The Mousetrapping of Hong Kong: A Game in Which Nobody Wins

Chalmers Johnson

The term NIC, pronounced "nick" and meaning "newly industrialized country," entered the vocabulary of international politics and economics during the 1960s and 1970s. It referred to the astonishing performance of the East Asian capitalist developmental states--namely, Hong Kong, Singapore, Taiwan, and South Korea. All four were characterized by relative political stability, complex combinations of quasi-authoritarian politics and capitalist economics, very high-speed economic growth, an equitable distribution of income, and a high level of education. In the space of two decades, these four NICs achieved the highest per capita incomes in East Asia, exceeded only by Japan. During 1982, per capita gross national products (GNPs) were (in U.S. dollars) Japan $9,684, Hong Kong $5,390, Singapore $5,220, Taiwan $2,587, Korea $1,720, and the PRC circa $300.[1]

However, by mid-1984, Hong Kong was in serious trouble. The term NIC still applied, but it had become clear that a new term referring specifically to Hong Kong would soon be needed. Within the category of NICs, Hong Kong was in the process of becoming what I propose to call a CRIC--a "collapsing recently industrialized country." Hong Kong's transition from NIC to CRIC was due entirely to its having been mousetrapped by modern Chinese history. From 1982 to 1984, Hong Kong allowed its future to become entwined with the passions of Chinese nationalism, above all with the emotional goal of "unification of the motherland," and it soon discovered that the entry of these symbols into the discussion meant that Hong Kong itself had no future at all. Even the PRC, as we shall see, may have wanted to avoid negotiating over Hong Kong in terms of the unification of the motherland, but once that idea had intruded itself into the discussion, there was no way the trap could be avoided. The heritage of China's victimization by Western imperialism is still so potent that whenever it becomes an issue in current politics, the outcome is virtually foreordained regardless of whether that outcome damages every party's interests. It was an error to let the past dictate the future in the case of Hong Kong, but this error contains an even more serious warning for Taiwan, the largest by far of the three great NICs built by the overseas Chinese: There is no way to win a direct fight with Chinese nationalism. If one cannot command the nationalist issue, then it must be finessed or avoided.

Hong Kong, it must be understood at the outset, is not really a British colony. It is a Chinese city-state that has found it profitable and expedient to sail under a flag of convenience, rather like an American or a Japanese or a Hong Kong ship's being registered in Liberia or Panama. The British themselves have long acknowledged Hong Kong's anomalous status. On June 22, 1983, the queen, in her speech opening Parliament (written for her by Prime Minister Thatcher's government), clearly distinguished among the cases of the Falklands, toward which Britain has "obligations"; Gibraltar, toward which Britain has "commitments"; and Hong Kong, toward which Britain has "aims." The Labour party has long wanted to be rid of Hong Kong, which it regards as an economic competitor of British industry, and Mrs. Thatcher's government faces no domestic political or popular pressure from any quarter to achieve a particular outcome in the negotiations over Hong Kong.

One reason why Hong Kong should not be regarded as a British colony is that there are virtually no British colonialists there. The territory's population is 98 percent Chinese. In fact, Britain's true interest in Hong Kong is best revealed by the several U.K. nationality acts and regulations going back to 1951, the most recent of which came into effect on January 1, 1983. They deny British citizenship, and therefore rights of settlement in the United Kingdom, to natives of Hong Kong as well as to the many Chinese immigrants to the territory who have only residence permits. What Britain most wants to avoid is a reverse colonization of the British Isles by Hong Kong Chinese. Even the PRC agrees that Hong Kong is not a colony. In March 1972, as one of its first acts after being seated in the United Nations, Beijing requested that the UN's Special Committee on Colonialism delete Hong Kong and Macao from its list of territories for which independence should be sought.

Hong Kong is a member of that class of cities and territories whose de jure status is irrelevant in comparison to their de facto functions. Such places often occupy niches adjacent to larger nations or groups of nations, and they come into being to accomplish important tasks or to relieve significant pressures that their larger neighbors find useful but that their legal rigidities or ideological pretensions prevent them from acknowledging. Historical examples of such places include Trieste, Danzig, and Beirut before 1975; present-day ones include Miami, Monaco, Las Vegas, Bermuda, and the Cayman Islands, and of course the oldest continuous regime in East Asia, Macao, which dates back to the sixteenth century.[2]

Hong Kong was not built by the British any more than Taiwan or South Korea was built by the Japanese. Both Hong Kong and Taiwan were built by Chinese exiles and emigrants from the PRC (joined, in the case of Taiwan, by a large local population that does not want "unification with the motherland"). Hong Kong has a 140-year history as a British trading post, but its significant history dates from 1949, when the Communists conquered the mainland, and from 1951, when the United Nations imposed an embargo against trade with the PRC because of its actions in the Korean War. Hong Kong then began to serve its three great functions: first as a place of refuge for Chinese fleeing the Communists, second as a major source of hard currency earnings for mainland Chinese exports that could not be sold in such quantities anywhere else (such as Chinese foodstuffs, medicines, and water), and third as a financial and manufacturing center serving the entire Pacific Basin and the rest of the world. In 1982, all three roles were as important as they had ever been over the previous thirty years. It is sometimes forgotten that between 1977 and 1980, well into the period of China's post-Mao reforms, more than 400,000 people from the mainland entered Hong Kong to live and work. The ending of Hong Kong's ability to perform its true functions will have enormous consequences, not just for the people of Hong Kong, but for all the nations of the Pacific Basin.

What do I mean when I say that Hong Kong has been mousetrapped by Chinese history? On June 25, 1983, in a meeting in Beijing with deputies from Hong Kong and Macao to the National People's Congress (and well after Prime Minister Thatcher's historic visit), Deng Xiaoping responded to a question about why he could not just maintain the status quo in Hong Kong by saying, "If I agree to prolong the lease, I will become the second Li Hongzhang."[3] In an entirely different context, on August 15, 1983, Communist Party General-Secretary Hu Yaobang commented to a group of Japanese newspaper executives: "We consider the so-called three Hong Kong treaties to be unequal. But it is a fact that the treaties exist. Moreover, it is clearly written that the expiry date is June 30, 1997. Therefore, we do not intend to bring forward or postpone this date. We will recover Hong Kong on July 1, 1997. As far as China is concerned, our attitude is one of respect for history."[4]

It must be noted that this "respect for history" is highly selective. The history that Hu and other Chinese leaders regard as relevant is the history of the three treaties--Nanking (1842), the Convention of Peking (1860), and the ninety-nine-year lease dating from July 1, 1898--each of which was a watershed in the Qing dynasty's nineteenth-century encounters with Western imperialism. The history that does not interest the current leaders in Beijing is how Hong Kong has developed since 1950 and the PRC's own sorry record of harebrained experiments with economic development and social control, each of which resulted in more emigration into Hong Kong. Similarly, it may be noted that PRC leaders also lean very selectively on history in their claims to Taiwan--stressing the island's cultural unity with the mainland but ignoring its remarkable achievements since the end of the Japanese occupation.

It is hard to imagine that any Chinese or foreigner would characterize Deng Xiaoping as a second Li Hongzhang, so why did Deng raise the comparison? We do not know, but there are at least three plausible explanations, any one or a combination of which would be decisive. First, Prime Minister Thatcher broached the question of the treaties with Deng, and no Chinese political leader could afford merely to let the matter pass. Second, even though Deng and other economic reformers have strong incentives not to disturb the status quo in Hong Kong, they are vulnerable to charges of being "soft on nationalism" in internal political conflicts. And third, Chinese nationalism is consciously being used by the PRC in order to defuse the "public opinion card" (the Communist press's term for a possible mobilization of Hong Kong mass sentiment against a British transfer of sovereignty to the PRC) and in order to soften up Taiwan, which is the ultimate target of the Hong Kong campaign. Each of these elements requires further discussion.

It is possible that Deng would have preferred to avoid any mention of the treaties in talking about the future of Hong Kong. He knows full well that from 1949 to 1982, during much of which time he himself was a high policymaking official in the mainland government, the PRC consistently maintained the anomalous status of both Hong Kong and Macao for its own good and sufficient reasons. In 1974, at the time of the Portuguese revolution, Beijing turned down Portugal's offer to return Macao, and the following year, the PRC signed a treaty with Portugal establishing China's sovereignty but providing for Portugal's administration of the territory.

The PRC's reasons for tolerating separate enclaves on its southern borders have been primarily economic. During the thirty-one years between 1950 and 1980, mainland China's overall foreign trade balance was in deficit only twelve years. But if trade with Hong Kong is excluded from the calculation, the PRC would have recorded substantial deficits for twenty-four of the thirty-one years. As Y. C. Jao puts it, "Broadly speaking, China is using its trade surplus with Hong Kong to finance its deficits with other countries."[5] Table 5.1 summarizes China's economic stake in the Hong Kong market.

Table 5.1. PRC net foreign exchange earnings from Hong Kong (millions US $)

	1977	1978	1979	1980
Trade surplus	1,741.4	2,259.5	3,034.1	4,407.2
Remittances	394.9	477.3	562.9	673.7
Tourism	223.5	367.5	819.4	951.8
Investment profits	367.8	461.0	609.9	824.9
Total	2,727.6	3,565.3	5,026.3	6,857.6
Percent of total PRC foreign exchange earnings	29.3	31.7	31.8	36.5

Source: Y. C. Jao, "Hong Kong's Role in Financing China's Modernization," in A. J. Youngson, ed., China and Hong Kong: The Economic Nexus (Hong Kong: Oxford University Press, 1983), p. 58.

Hong Kong's value to China's economic modernization is greater today than at any time during the past three decades. Professor Jao concedes that the loss of revenues from Hong Kong would not be fatal to the PRC's modernization, given the absolute size of the Chinese economy, but it would certainly "represent a disastrous setback."[6] Why then should Deng Xiaoping, the leader of the current economic modernization effort, worry about being called a Li Hongzhang when no one ever raised the charge against Mao Zedong or Zhou Enlai in earlier years? During 1982 and early 1983, most people in Hong Kong regarded the answer to this question as so obvious, particularly considering the current era of mainland "reform," that they believed Hong Kong's future was secure. Their view came to be known locally as the "doctrine of the sweet peaches." Huang Chin-ming explains, "Whether Hong Kong can maintain the status quo depends on whether the people of Hong Kong can continuously produce 'peaches' which are to the liking of their masters, and feed them with these peaches one by one."[7] Ironically enough, during 1982 Hong Kong even gave Britain a sweet peach in the form of a HK $20-million contribution to the welfare fund for families of soldiers killed in the Falklands war.

Why hasn't this theory of clear economic interest held up? There are several reasons, all interrelated but separable for purposes of discussion. First, the efforts regarding economic development in the PRC may not have as high a priority as is commonly supposed outside of China. The relaxation of economic controls is surely aimed as much at refurbishing the political legitimacy of the Communist Party as at seriously promoting sound economic growth. Even Donald Zagoria, in a highly optimistic survey of Deng's reforms, concedes, "There is still no coherent strategy [in the PRC] for combining plan and market and the problems of running a mixed system are bound to be enormous."[8]

Closely related to this point, there is ample evidence that the leaders in Beijing seem to be seriously misinformed about the Hong Kong economy and its sociopolitical foundations. For one thing, most senior leaders in Beijing (as distinct from lower-level analysts in the research institutes) appear to get most of their information about Hong Kong from the Hong Kong Communist press, and needless to say, the Ta kung pao and Wen wei po serve up their own versions of sweet peaches. For example Fei Yiming, the well-known publisher of the Hong Kong Ta kung pao and a member of the Standing Committee of the NPC, writes: "Did some people not say that the Chinese could not rule Shanghai well? Facts have shown that the Chinese are completely capable of ruling Shanghai well. Since they can rule Shanghai well, they can also rule Hong Kong well."[9] Fei, a long-time resident of Hong Kong, knows this statement is nonsense. Until the death of Mao, Shanghai was either the scene of Red Guard pogroms or a ghost town and as poorly run a place as there was on earth. In fact, Hong Kong is living testimony to what Shanghai might have been if it had not been ruled by the Communists. Fei is, of course, correct in that the local Chinese are able to rule Hong Kong quite effectively, but his reference points should have been Singapore and Taipei, not Shanghai. The question is, Do his readers in Beijing know that?

Other evidence of the PRC's misunderstanding can be found in its repeated references to mainland "aid" to Hong Kong's prosperity. The following extract from Xinhua (Beijing) is typical:

> In mid-May last year [1982], transportation on some sections of the Beijing-Guangzhou railway were disrupted by floods. Even so, supplies to Hong Kong continued thanks to the efforts made by inland provinces. For instance, Hunan and Jiangxi Provinces rushed pig supplies to Hong Kong by road; Shandong and Liaoning Provinces shipped cattle on the hoof by sea; while Guangdong and Fujian Provinces and Guangxi Autonomous Region also shipped supplies of fresh but perishable goods. As a result, although the Beijing-Guangzhou railway service was suspended for about two weeks, supplies of daily necessities for Hong Kong were not affected. It is obvious that without the uninterrupted supply of daily necessities from the Chinese mainland at stable prices for years, Hong Kong's inflation would have been worse and its cheap labor market would have lost its material basis.[10]

In the same vein, Cao Weilan, the deputy director for economic affairs of the Hong Kong office of Xinhua News Service (the PRC's de facto consulate in Hong Kong), has gone on at length about "China's sacrifices to help maintain Hong Kong's prosperity and stability," his main examples being mainland investments in Hong Kong (from which the PRC earns interest) and "the supply of Hong Kong's toilet paper"![11]

Perhaps the best example of the air of

unreality in PRC comments about Hong Kong is the
ongoing war of words over whether horse racing
and mahjong will be permitted after reversion.
At first, horse racing was said to be "an unhealthy colonial activity and will be banned";
then Liao Chengzhi said it was all right so long
as the word "Royal" was removed from the title of
the Royal Hong Kong Jockey Club at Happy Valley.[12]
Even when Beijing's pronouncements are apparently
intended to reassure the people of Hong Kong,
virtually all of them have a quality of blandness
and generality that seems to worry the residents
more than silence. Margaret Ng, perhaps the most
astute commentator on the scene, has often wished
aloud that the mainland government would quit
saying, "Don't worry," since it worries her more
than anything else they say.[13]

It is possible that Deng and his colleagues
do not understand the Hong Kong economy, over-
estimate their ability to run it, and are misinformed about it by their own minions. Still,
none of these possibilities seems a sufficient
reason to have overturned the PRC's thirty-year-
old policy of keeping hands off Hong Kong while
profiting from its prosperity. Let us turn,
therefore, from a consideration of the economic
connection to how, precisely, the fear of being
labeled a Li Hongzhang arose. One line of
speculation, for which there is some evidence, is
that during 1982, Deng had no fixed policy on
Hong Kong but was reacting to a badly misconceived
opening shot by Margaret Thatcher.

In May 1982, in preparation for the Thatcher
visit in September, Humphrey Atkins, deputy to
then-British Foreign Secretary Lord Carrington,
observed that the initiative in the Anglo-
Chinese talks about 1997 came from the British
side. "The Chinese," according to Atkins, "are
addressing their minds to the problem. They gave
me to understand they will be studying the line
they should take. . . . They don't have a decided
position on Hong Kong. They did not give any
assurances beyond the fact that the particular
attributes of Hong Kong, its free port and its
centre of business and commerce and trade, were
going to be taken very much into account."[14]
According to this view, the British government,

with the strong backing of the Hong Kong Chinese establishment, undertook to negotiate Hong Kong's future in 1982 because the timing seemed especially propitious. There was a Tory government in London, Mrs. Thatcher had just fought and won the Falklands war, Deng Xiaoping seemed to be at the peak of his power, and China had launched a major campaign of economic reform and was becoming more open to the democracies. The conditions seemed perfect to negotiate a <u>perpetuation</u> of British administration in Hong Kong after the lease expired.

What went wrong was a combination of bad luck, poor summit preparations, and sheer incompetence. During her visit to Beijing in September 1982, Mrs. Thatcher adamantly supported the legality of the nineteenth-century treaties, and she even went so far as to characterize the history of Anglo-Chinese relations as one in which "cultural and scientific contact went from strength to strength through the 19th and early 20th centuries." One imagines that she had never heard of the mainland activities of Lord Elgin, "Chinese" Gordon, or Sir Robert Hart. Roy Jenkins, leader of the Social Democratic Party, seemed to utter no more than the simple truth when he said that Thatcher had provoked a "pointless, premature, and potentially damaging argument."[15]

According to this line of reasoning, the Iron Lady tried to mousetrap Deng but succeeded only in tripping herself. Deng had no choice but to contradict her views. Xinhua hardly let her get out of Beijing before it started the counterattack:

> It must be pointed out that these treaties which involve the Hong Kong area were products of British imperialism's "gunboat policy" and invasion of China in the 19th century. These treaties, which were forced on the Chinese people, provide an ironclad proof of British imperialism's plunder of Chinese territory. The Chinese people have always held that these treaties are illegal and therefore null and void. . . . Whoever today tries to cling to these unequal treaties will only awaken the

memories of the British imperialist
invasion of China in the minds of the
people of China, Britain, and the whole
world.[16]

Xinhua's blast is, of course, the standard Chinese version of their country's nineteenth-century history. There is nothing Communist about it. Every Chinese schoolchild born in the twentieth century has read it, and the authorities on Taiwan could hardly take exception to it, since it is also their version. Indeed, shortly after the Thatcher trip, the Far Eastern Economic Review quoted David Chou, deputy director of the Institute of International Relations in Taiwan, as saying, "Every Chinese would like to see the end of colonialist rule in Hong Kong."[17] Thus, Mrs. Thatcher had unintentionally placed the negotiations concerning Hong Kong on the worst possible basis. She had made Hong Kong a touchstone of Chinese nationalism. Whether Deng was irritated or pleased by this turn of events is a subject to which I shall return, but it is clear that he could not let the insult pass.

There is a variation on this argument, and it belongs to the second category of explanations of how Hong Kong got caught up in the "unification of the motherland" mousetrap. This view emphasizes that Deng and his associates in Beijing were preoccupied with other matters during 1982. Their major concerns were with reforming the Party, replacing the old guard with younger leaders, and removing the last vestiges of Maoist institutions. The big event of the year for Deng was the Twelfth Congress of the Chinese Communist Party, September 1-11, 1982, at which he did not do nearly as well in the inner-Party infighting as he had hoped. Equally important, Deng's opponents had been sniping at him for months over his handling of the arms-sales-to-Taiwan issue with the United States and the textbook controversy with Japan. The timing of Thatcher's visit, September 22-25, thus was not nearly as propitious as foreign journalistic opinion suggested. What Deng did not need at this time was another "national prestige" issue (as well as a possible opening for his internal enemies), particularly one like

Hong Kong, which, if mishandled, could do serious damage to the regime's economic development plans.

Nonetheless, Mrs. Thatcher arrived and started talking about the validity of the unequal treaties. Even if Deng had agreed with her that they were all valid, Hong Kong would still have lost 89 percent of its territory in 1997 according to the terms of the third treaty. It was a subject that should never have been mentioned. But once Thatcher raised the issue, Deng had to move at once to seize the high ground before his opponents could use it against him. According to this view, the real issue is not unification of the motherland but factional politics in Beijing, in which conflicting claims of patriotic purity are important weapons for both Deng and his opponents. As soon as Deng and Thatcher started talking about the legality of the treaties, all rationality about the future of Hong Kong and its usefulness to China flew out the window.

There is, however, a third possibility. From the moment Mrs. Thatcher visited Beijing, the PRC launched a full-blown, well-coordinated campaign of united front tactics aimed at accomplishing several things. These were to acquire Hong Kong on the PRC's terms, to make the British cooperate, to prevent internationalization of the issue, and above all, to keep the local population docile and divided. These tactics suggest that Beijing's strategy toward Hong Kong is part of a larger, high-priority foreign policy to associate the Communist regime with Chinese nationalism and to bring Taiwan under PRC control. Some foreign observers believe that economic modernization is the top priority of the mainland regime and that this priority will cause it to modify its campaign to "unify the motherland."[18] The evidence from Hong Kong indicates precisely the opposite: The regime is prepared to pay the price in terms of economic setbacks so long as it can prevail in moving toward its main goals. Hong Kong is thus not a secondary issue; it is part of the primary PRC foreign policy strategy. What happened in Hong Kong and how it happened offer clues as to what is in store for Taiwan over the coming years.

Despite thirty years of analysis, foreign

observers of Communist China still do not seem to understand a united front campaign or to recognize one when it occurs. This myopia is, of course, one of the goals of such a campaign: the camouflaging of the regime's real foreign policy aims behind a facade of spontaneity and popular support. Some of the key elements of a united front campaign are

1. The creation and use of front organizations and personalities in the target area
2. The creation of a panoply of vague but plausible-sounding slogans and the use of them to avoid spelling out the PRC's true policies
3. Mobilization of the PRC's propaganda apparatus to attack and undermine the positions of the regime's current negotiating partner and to isolate that partner
4. Exploitation of rules agreed on in advance (e.g., secret negotiations, no publicity) in order to put the negotiating partner on the defensive
5. "Gong banging"--that is, going public with "nonnegotiable demands," making unilateral statements, manipulating the foreign press, controlling the agenda, involving the highest and most newsworthy personalities of the regime even though they are not participants in the negotiations, and setting deadlines
6. Use of side deals and carrot-and-stick ploys--e.g., offers of expanded trade with the PRC in return for cooperation, sensitivity to the career interests diplomats have in successful negotiations, promises to third parties in order that they not support an ally, and assistance to foreign political leaders in reelection campaigns via visits to the PRC.

Each of these elements occurred in the united front campaign aimed at Hong Kong, and the PRC's use of "people-to-people" diplomacy and news leaks outside the agreed negotiating forum are detailed in the Appendix to this chapter. Despite the formal secrecy of the Anglo-Chinese negotiations, the PRC's rock-bottom position became known as early as October 1982.[19] The elements are (1) recovery of both sovereignty and administration over Hong Kong--i.e., nonacceptance of the Macao formula; (2) special administrative region status for Hong Kong after 1997 under Article 31 of the PRC Constitution of 1982; (3) "Hong Kong people rule Hong Kong" (gangren zhigang), but with no details released about how this system is actually to work; and (4) promises of no basic changes in local socioeconomic patterns for "a long time," perhaps as long as fifty years. Even though Hong Kong analysts knew of this position from the beginning, the PRC regime took great care to introduce it slowly, piece by piece, and to make it appear that it represented only a reasonable response to extreme British positions.

For their part, the British began with the belief that they could negotiate an extension of the lease, thereby perpetuating the status quo into the next century. They held to this position from September 1982 until about June 1983, while the Chinese blasted them as imperialists and colonialists and denounced Mrs. Thatcher as a "stinking woman."[20] With the start of the so-called second phase of negotiations in July 1983, the British gave up trying to maintain the status quo and sought instead to achieve the Macao solution--i.e., Chinese sovereignty (zhuquan) but British administration (zhiquan). The adoption of this line by the British led to the high tide of the Chinese united front campaign.

For three months, Beijing and the local Hong Kong leftist press hammered away at the national humiliation involved in the British proposal, local leftist personalities declared it insane, and a steady stream of visitors to Beijing (including former British Prime Minister Edward Heath, whom Mrs. Thatcher had defeated) were told how unreasonable it was. The culmination of this phase was "Black Friday and Saturday," September 22 and 23, 1983, when the Hong Kong dollar hit its all-time low of HK $9.55=US $1.

Beijing accused the British of playing the economic card (jingji-pai) and adamantly rejected the idea that the flight of Hong Kong currency might reflect a loss of confidence on the part of the people of Hong Kong. Nonetheless, it was subsequently revealed that one of the biggest buyers of U.S. dollars during the panic was the PRC's own local agent, the Bank of China, which was trying to protect its hard currency earnings.[21] About this time, the PRC announced that if there was no agreement by September 1984, it would proceed unilaterally to announce its own plans for Hong Kong.

In November the British threw in the towel. The Chinese propaganda campaign immediately ceased, and cordiality returned to the negotiating sessions in Beijing. The negotiations continued, but now the British were simply trying to nail down a few details of gangren zhigang or otherwise find a fig leaf to cover their withdrawal. On April 20, 1984, British Foreign Secretary Geoffrey Howe announced in Hong Kong what everyone had known for six months: "The terms of an agreement have yet to be worked out, but it is right for me to tell you that it would not be realistic to think of an agreement that provides for continued British administration in Hong Kong after 1997."[22] To some observers, the whole situation seemed very reminiscent of the 1973 negotiations between Washington and Hanoi over the fate of South Vietnam.

There are many interesting facets of the Hong Kong negotiations that can be mentioned only briefly here. One is the fact that the British apparently never threatened to break the negotiations off even though their position was hopeless from the start; this eagerness to be agreeable of course gave the upper hand to the other side. Another aspect is the eerie silence maintained throughout the whole period of negotiations by Hong Kong's two biggest foreign investors, the United States and Japan. There is some evidence that the PRC privately assured them they would profit from a British withdrawal.[23] A third curious item was the highly publicized visit during August 1983 of Xu Jiatun, ex-governor of Jiangsu and the new director of the NCNA bureau in Hong Kong, to the notoriously seedy enclave in Hong Kong's New Territories known as "the walled city of Kowloon." This is an area of disputed sovereignty under the 1898 lease, but if Xu meant to hold it up as an example of Chinese administration, his case was even more embarrassing to the PRC's cause than Fei Yiming's reference to Shanghai.[24]

There is, however, one element of the negotiating process that must be dealt with in detail since it concerns the interests of the people of Hong Kong--and, by extension, the interests of the people in other overseas Chinese communities such as Taiwan. In Hong Kong, this issue came to be known as the problem of the "three-legged stool." During September 1982, Mrs. Thatcher played into the hands of the Chinese by allowing the initial talks to dwell on the treaties, but she also did one other thing that worried them a great deal. She said publicly that any Anglo-Chinese agreement on Hong Kong had to be acceptable to three different parties: the PRC government, the British Parliament, and the people of Hong Kong. She and later British spokesmen used the metaphor of a three-legged stool--if any one of its legs was not sturdy, the stool would collapse. As it turned out, the issue of the consent of the Hong Kong people, or, more precisely, the likelihood that if genuinely consulted (e.g., via a plebiscite), they would turn down any agreement that the PRC found acceptable, was virtually the only real negotiating chip the British ever had. They never used it, largely because the PRC devoted so much attention to attacking it and to dividing Hong Kong public opinion.

One problem emerged at once and still exists. Although Mrs. Thatcher promised to consult the people of Hong Kong, virtually no official institutions exist that make it easy for her to do so. As Evan Luard wrote in 1962 about the history of Hong Kong:

> Although in time Chinese unofficial members were nominated for the Legislative Council and the Executive Council, the Chinese population in practice were no more able,

>nor more eager, than their European counterparts to exercise any effective control over the way they were governed. The constitution of the island remains today in all essentials exactly what it was when it was introduced on the colony's establishment in 1843. The two councils are still, as then, controlled by official or nominated members.[25]

Twenty years after these words were written, the situation was only slightly changed with the addition of district boards and more unofficial members on the two councils. On February 24, 1984, however, a bombshell exploded in the tiny apolitical world of Hong Kong when Roger Lobo, a senior unofficial member of the Legislative Council, demanded an open council debate on the Anglo-Chinese negotiations before a final agreement is signed. The PRC was quick to react as it does not want any form of democratic input into the negotiations. Liang Weilin, chairman of the Guangdong Provincial CPPCC, declared, "They can debate anything, past or present, local or foreign, from the southern sky to the northern land . . . but the Hong Kong issue is between the British and Chinese governments."[26]

The greatest flap over the three-legged stool arose during the summer of 1983, when the second round of monthly negotiating sessions began. The British added to their negotiating team Sir Edward Youde, the governor of Hong Kong and a former ambassador to Beijing. At a press conference on July 7, Youde responded to a question about whom he would be representing in the talks: "I am the governor of Hong Kong. . . . Indeed I represent the people of Hong Kong. Who else would I represent?" The Chinese Foreign Ministry gave its answer to this question the next day: "Mr. Youde will take part in the talks as a member of the British Government delegation. Therefore he can only represent the British Government in the talks."[27] The PRC also took action. It denied a visa to Beijing for Peter Tsao (Ts'ao Kuang-yung), the director of the Hong Kong Government Information Service, who was to have accompanied Youde. Tsao had already irritated the PRC by saying to a British newspaper in May that if Hong Kong's future involved coming under PRC sovereignty, he himself would emigrate. The British made no protest over these developments: Youde joined the team as a British government official, Tsao stayed in Hong Kong, and no representative of the people of Hong Kong participated in the negotiations.

The PRC holds to the view that <u>it</u> is the representative of the people of Hong Kong, who are understood to be "Chinese compatriots." This claim, however, brings us to the most important issue in the whole Hong Kong dispute, what the people of Hong Kong actually think, and we have the evidence of five scientifically conducted public opinion polls taken between May 1982 and April 1983. One of the earliest polls found that "maintenance of the status quo" was the preferred solution for 70 percent of the population. A later poll, taken in April 1983, found 95 percent in favor of no change. Only 42 percent thought that Hong Kong's becoming a "special administrative region" of China was acceptable to them, but when the question was phrased as "returning Hong Kong to China," support fell to 26 percent. Perhaps most revealing, "No fewer than 22 percent of those polled [in June 1982]--most of them in the 15-34 age group--would 'try every means to leave' if Hong Kong reverted to China, a figure that would translate, the poll organizers say, into 710,000 people seeking to leave."[28]

Given this sentiment, it is not surprising that the PRC wants nothing to do with public opinion polls, Legislative Council debates, official or unofficial referendums, or any other forms of what it calls the "public opinion card." More important, however, the Communists have been very successful in countering and confusing public opinion. The essence of their tactics on this front is to identify themselves with "China," avoiding all mention of the Chinese Communist Party and characterizing their Chinese opponents as traitors to the lofty and idealistic goal of "reuniting the motherland." Margaret Ng offers the most incisive analysis of how this tactic has worked in Hong Kong:

Criticize "China" publicly as in any respect inferior to the West, however reasonable the criticism, and be prepared for a storm of bitter, loud, and rude protest. Associating something with "China" or "Chinese" has the power of turning any issue quickly into a highly emotive one. Turning on the cultural identity is like turning on a heavy smokescreen, making everyone argue in the darkness of non-reason. "Is self-administration for Hong Kong feasible?" is a question perfectly capable of a reasonable discussion. Turn it into "Is there any reason why Chinese people cannot govern Hong Kong as well as--or better than--the British?" and your discussion is doomed. Ask "Would you like to have the PRC govern Hong Kong in 1997?" and you may have a reasonable discussion. Ask "Should China have sovereignty over Hong Kong?" and even those who see this as meant to be a thinly shrouded version of a previous question will keep mum. The power of evoking the Chinese identification has been seen time and again, even within the past year, even apart from the 1997 question. . . . Anyone who does not recognize this identification as a great political weapon should have his head examined.[29]

The PRC's adroit exploitation of this "great political weapon" has effectively prevented the formation of any kind of solidarity among the people of Hong Kong to try to influence their own fates. Decisions to stay in Hong Kong, to leave, to transfer assets abroad, or to prepare an escape route are being made privately, household by household, and not as part of any political protest. Even the Communists have noted the phenomenon of Hong Kong millionaires' visiting the PRC and publicly applauding reversion but then privately moving their funds out of Hong Kong as soon as they return home.[30] So long as the PRC can keep the population unmobilized and divided, it faces no real obstacles to its takeover plans. And the foreign powers, particularly the Anglo-American democracies, interpret such a lack of public outcry as an acknowledgement of the legitimacy of the PRC's claims, especially since it serves their interests vis-à-vis the PRC to do so.

What, then, are the people of Hong Kong actually doing about the future? For the most part, they are exploring what the "1997 industry" has to offer. This exploration includes real estate forums sponsored by North American interests (usually with seminars on immigration requirements thrown in); working to get at least one member of the family established abroad in some capacity; agreeing to international marriages, a "thriving business" according to the London *Economist*; and transferring funds out of Hong Kong. According to one reliable estimate, net foreign-currency liabilities rose by HK $7.6 billion during the first half of 1983 alone.[31] Every new shock simply provides more business for the 1997 industry, the latest being the decision on March 28, 1984, by Jardine, Matheson, to shift its headquarters to Bermuda. Ironically enough, Jardine's great competitor, Sir Pao Yue-kang, the shipping magnate, had already moved his business to Bermuda, including his joint ventures with the PRC.

Meanwhile, hundreds of PRC cadres are arriving in Hong Kong, easily recognizable by their new Western-style suits, and many residents are preparing for the takeover. One interesting sidelight of the collapse of the Hong Kong real estate market has been a shift in the demand within high-rise apartment buildings from penthouses or apartments with a grand view of the harbor to flats no higher than the fifth floor above street level. The reason is, as an old friend explained to me: "Have you ever seen a Chinese Communist elevator that worked properly? Come 1997 we'll have to be able to walk up."

Let me conclude with two general points. First, nationalism--not economic reform, the PRC's opening to the democracies, or liberalization--is the primary political principle of the PRC today. Deng Xiaoping is, in fact, trying to rebuild the legitimacy of the Party on this foundation. Even though the major foreign powers, particularly the democracies, are aiding Deng in this effort, Chinese nationalism, as it extends beyond the boundaries of the PRC, will prove to be as dangerous a force for the democracies as it is for the PRC's neighbors. The recent history of the PRC parallels similar developments in the USSR, where the Communist Party has also become more nationalist and interested in preserving its own position than ideological.

Second, in his speech in Ottawa, Canada, in January 1984, PRC Premier Zhao Ziyang said: "All the policies we are going to adopt towards Hong Kong can also be applied to Taiwan, and even more. Reunification is the most pressing task for us and we hope to strive for peaceful reunification at an early date." Taiwan has thus been adequately warned. The danger is a united front campaign that is even more extensive than the one directed against Hong Kong. Taiwan must be prepared to counter such a campaign, including its insidious manipulation of Chinese cultural nationalism, which is actually a trap set for overseas Chinese by the Communists. The Taiwanese targets of the coming united front campaign must be prepared to nullify the "legal" and cultural weapons the PRC plans to use against them. Above all, popular mobilization and self-determination are indispensable. The failure of the people of Hong Kong to become politically involved in their own fate has sealed that fate. These are the lessons from Hong Kong, which--barring unforeseen developments--is already lost. Nonetheless, the Hong Kong case does afford a twelve-year insurance policy, during which time the other overseas Chinese communities can get their own houses in order.

APPENDIX

Partial Listing of Beijing-Hong Kong "People-to-People" Meetings and Declarations in Conjunction with Confidential Anglo-Chinese Negotations, September 1982-December 1983

O = Official meeting   U = Unofficial meeting

	Type	Date	Details
1.	O	9/22-25,1982	Thatcher visits Beijing, initiates talks on Hong Kong.
2.	O	9/26-28	Thatcher visits Hong Kong, first British prime minister ever to do so.
3.	U	10/29	Property tycoons meet with NCNA Hong Kong, are assured of status quo for fifteen years.
4.	U	11/1	HK Trade Development Council told in Beijing that a plan should be worked out "in the next one or two years."
5.	U	11/20	Liao Chengzhi explains to visiting factory owners the idea of gangren zhigang ("Hong Kong people rule Hong Kong").
6.	U	12/1	Liao Chengzhi tells visiting group of industrialists that PRC has long considered gangren zhigang.

7.	U	12/10	Zhao Zhiyang and Gu Mu discuss economic cooperation with Gordon Wu and Cheng Yu-tung, leading Hong Kong developers. Liao Chengzhi meets Hong Kong delegates to CPPCC and NPC. Xi Zhongxun, Politburo member and ex-governor of Guangdong, reassures Trade Development Council.
8.	U	12/16	Cheng Yu-tung and Gordon Wu return, say Zhao Ziyang is aware of Hong Kong people's anxiety.
9.	U	1/7, 1983	Ji Chaozhu, counselor of PRC embassy in the United States, says future governor of Hong Kong must be Chinese.
10.	U	1/10	Heung Yee Kuk party leaves for talks in Beijing.
11.	U	1/18	Li Tse-chung, director of Hong Kong Wen wei po (pro-PRC), attacks "three-legged stool."
12.	U	2/11	U.S. Secretary of State George Shultz, in Hong Kong after PRC trip, is "hopeful."
13.	U	3/13	PRC tells Britain that Hong Kong will play vital part in South China Sea oil exploration.

14.	U	4/5	Nearly 140 Hong Kong and Macao residents elected to provincial or national NPC and CPPCC committees, leave 5/31 for Canton and Beijing.
15.	U	4/9	Labour MP Roland Moyle says after trip to PRC that Hong Kong is to be ruled by Hong Kong people following reversion of sovereignty to the PRC.
16.	U	4/11	John Young, Hong Kong university lecturer back from trip to PRC, says Hong Kong to have "mini-constitution" after 1997.
17.	U	5/1	Hong Kong center-right magazine Pai hsing discloses that Liao Chengzhi told visiting academics that 1997 is date for reversion, not before or after.
18.	U	5/12	Liao Chengzhi receives thirty New Territories businessmen, rejects the three-legged stool idea. Shanghai economic delegation visits Hong Kong.
19.	U	5/16	Xu Jiatun, Party CC member, ex-governor of Jiangsu, and director designate of NCNA/HK, receives industrialists in Canton. Allen Lee, Selina Chow, and Stephen Cheong,

			legislative councillors, leave for Beijing; Xi Zhongxun tells them on 5/22 that PRC will handle Hong Kong issue with great care.
20.	U	5/29	PRC tells visiting Hong Kong journalists that Hong Kong will be a special administrative region "for a long time" after PRC gains sovereignty.
21.	U	6/6	Zhao Ziyang tells NPC that PRC will recover Hong Kong sovereignty "at an opportune moment and take appropriate measures to maintain its prosperity." Wang Daohan, mayor of Shanghai, says Shanghai and Hong Kong should work together.
22.	U	6/17	Xu Jiatun in Beijing declares that Chinese sovereignty over Hong Kong is non-negotiable.
23.	U	6/20	Newsweek says Deng Xiaoping told Thatcher in September 1982 that an agreement should be reached in two years. Newsweek says this statement was disclosed by Hu Yaobang to U.S. professor Parris Chang.
24.	U	6/22	Wang Daohan says Shanghai can help Hong Kong.

25.	U	6/25	Deng Xiaoping meets Hong Kong delegates to NPC and CPPCC; all delegates follow PRC line.
26.	U	6/30	New director of NCNA, Xu Jiatun, arrives in Hong Kong.
27.	O	7/1	Joint Anglo-Chinese statement: second phase of talks to begin 7/12. British negotiators: Sir Percy Cradock, ambassador to PRC; Sir Edward Youde, governor of Hong Kong; Robin McLaren, political adviser. Chinese negotiators: Yao Guang, vice foreign minister; Li Jusheng, deputy director, NCNA/HK; Lu Ping, Western European Department adviser.
28.	U	7/9	Peter Tsao, director Hong Kong Government Information Services, denied visa to Beijing.
29.	U	7/11	Winston Yang, U.S. academic, tells of talk with Deng Xiaoping. Deng said Hong Kong's future lies in PRC's hands: "to deny this is to deny reality and to create a dangerous illusion."
30.	O	7/12-13	First round of second phase of official negotiations.

31.	U	7/19	Xu Jiatun tells a reception for leftists at NCNA/HK that a "fair and reasonable" solution is in the works.
32.	O	7/25-26	Second round of official negotiations. Talks described as "useful."
33.	U	7/29	Group of Hong Kong postsecondary students returns from Beijing with draft of terms for Hong Kong special administrative region. Confirmed 10/14 in Denny Huang-Ji Pengfei talks.
34.	O	8/2-3	Third round of official negotiations. Phrase "useful and constructive dropped. Qi Huaiyuan, Foreign Ministry spokesman, refuses comment. Hong Kong leftist press propaganda barrage begin
35.	U	8/7	Xu Jiatun, with full NCNA publicity, takes walk in walled city of Kowloon.
36.	U	8/13	Leftist Motor Transport Workers' Union supports PRC's claim of sovereignty.
37.	U	8/15	Hu Yaobang tells Japanese newspaper *Mainichi* that PRC will take over Hong Kong on July 1, 1997--first mention of a definite da

38.	U	8/17	Beijing names Ji Pengfei, ex-foreign minister, head of Hong Kong and Macao Office, Overseas Chinese Affairs Commission, NPC Standing Committee; more Hong Kong unions back Beijing.
39.	U	8/26	Xu Jiatun tells dinner gathering not to worry, PRC has policies to maintain Hong Kong's stability.
40.	U	9/10	Deng Xiaoping tells former Conservative Party PM Edward Heath that future looks good, sovereignty is non-negotiable. In Hong Kong on 9/13, Heath walks out of meeting with unofficial members of Legco, who dub him "Deng's mouthpiece."
41.	U	9/21	Wu Xueqian, PRC foreign minister, says Britain must drop "rigid" attitude. Shi Liang, PRC legal specialist and chairman of China Democratic League, accuses Britain of trying to continue ruling Hong Kong after 1997. Huan Xiang, another PRC legal specialist visiting Hong Kong, says PRC wants to stabilize deteriorating economy.

42.	O	9/22-23	Fourth round of official negotiations. Phrase "useful and constructive" not used. "Black Friday and Saturday": HK dollar hits lowest point (US $1=HK $9.55).
43.	U	9/30	Ji Pengfei affirms September 1984 "deadline" for agreement or PRC will declare its terms unilaterally. Brands as liars people in Hong Kong who say that the public does not welcome rejoining motherland.
44.	U	10/10	He Ying, vice-chairman of Overseas Chinese Affairs Commission, says sovereignty of Hong Kong "admits of no discussion." Renmin ribao urges Britain to be more "realistic."
45.	U	10/12	Malaysian PM Mahathir comes out in favor of PRC position, first foreign head of state to do so.
46.	U	10/14	Denny Huang, urban councillor, reveals contents of 9/27 talk with Ji Pengfei, who gave fullest picture yet of Chinese plans.
47.	O	10/19-20	Fifth round of official negotiations; said to be "useful and constructive." Leftist propaganda barrage abates.

48.	U	10/28	Henry Kissinger in Hong Kong says United States must keep out of Hong Kong question.
49.	U	11/1	Head of Hong Kong Polytechnic University returns from Beijing, says Ji Pengfei is optimistic.
50.	U	11/12	Qi Huaiyuan reaffirms September 1984 deadline. New Territories District Board delegation leaves for Beijing where Ji Pengfei tells them on 11/15 that Hong Kong will be unchanged for fifty years after 1997, based on "mini-constitution."
51.	O	11/14-15	Sixth round of official negotiations; "useful and constructive."
52.	U	11/21	Ji Pengfei reiterates PRC's position to delegation from Hong Kong and Macao.
53.	U	11/24	In Japan, Hu Yaobang reassures PM Nakasone on foreign investments in Hong Kong.
54.	U	12/1	Ji Pengfei meets Chinese Reform Association of Hong Kong.
55.	U	12/2	Xu Jiatun says PRC will reveal details of mini-constitution before September.

56.	U	12/3	Peng Zhen, chairman of NPC, says PRC Constitution does not require that Hong Kong become socialist.
57.	O	12/7-8	Seventh round of official negotiations; "useful and constructive."
58.	U	12/10	Delegation of Hong Kong Observers meets Ji Pengfei, says they want post-1997 British link. Leftist press strongly attacks Observers.

NOTES

1. Japan Institute for Social and Economic Affairs, *Japan 1983: An International Comparison* (Tokyo: Keizai Koho Center, 1983), pp. 1, 9.

2. For a brilliant treatment of the history of Macao's and Hong Kong's ambiguous sovereignty, see Austin Coates, *A Macao Narrative* (Hong Kong: Heinemann, 1978), pp. 84-107.

3. "Deng Answers Queries on Hong Kong's Future," *Pai hsing* (Hong Kong), no. 52 (July 16, 1983), trans. Foreign Broadcast Information Service (hereafter FBIS), July 21, 1983, pp. W1-W4. The fear of becoming "a second Li Hongzhang" appears in many mainland comments on Hong Kong; see, e.g., *Pai hsing*, no. 32 (September 16, 1982), FBIS, September 24, 1982, pp. W3-W9. Li Hongzhang (1823-1901) was a prominent reformer, diplomat, and statesman during the last decades of the Qing dynasty. His actions in leasing the New Territories to Great Britain during the so-called concessions scramble were more a reflection than a cause of China's humiliations in the nineteenth century--see, inter alia, Immanuel C. Y. Hsü, *The Rise of Modern China*, 3rd ed. (New York: Oxford University Press, 1983), pp. 348-355.

4. Hong Kong *Wen wei po*, as discussed in *Far Eastern Economic Review*, August 25, 1983, p. 14.

5. *Far Eastern Economic Review*, January 20, 1983, p. 39.

6. Y. C. Jao, "Hong Kong's Role in Financing China's Modernization," in A. J. Youngson, ed., *China and Hong Kong: The Economic Nexus* (Hong Kong: Oxford University Press, 1983), p. 60.

7. Huang Chin-ming, "Hong Kong at its Historical Turning Point," *Pai hsing*, no. 32, (September 16, 1982), FBIS, September 24, 1982, p. W8.

8. Donald S. Zagoria, "China's Quiet Revolution," *Foreign Affairs* 62:4 (Spring 1984), p. 895.

9. *Far Eastern Economic Review*, December 3, 1982, p. 13; also see ibid., March 8, 1984, p. 24.

10. "All-out Support of Chinese Mainland Crucial to Hong Kong's Prosperity," Xinhua (Beijing), September 24, 1983, FBIS, September 26, 1983, p. E2.

11. *Far Eastern Economic Review*, August 18,

1983, p. 12; also see ibid., March 8, 1984, p. 24.

12. Pai hsing, no. 32 (September 16, 1982), FBIS, September 24, 1982, p. W5; South China Morning Post, November 29, 1982, pp. 1, 30; "Liao Chengzhi on Hong Kong People Ruling Hong Kong," Wen wei po, November 22, 1982, p. 2.

13. Margaret Ng (Wu Ai-i), "The Second Stage of Anglo-Chinese Talks," Ming pao, July 14, 1983, p. 17.

14. Far Eastern Economic Review, May 21, 1982, p. 24.

15. For the Thatcher and Jenkins statements, see ibid., October 8, 1982, p. 9.

16. "China's Stand on Hong Kong Issue Is Solemn and Just," Xinhua (Beijing), September 30, 1982, FBIS, October 1, 1982, p. E1.

17. November 12, 1982, p. 72.

18. For example, Donald Zagoria: "A China committed to reform will also continue to be a China with a strong interest in peace and stability abroad--because a reforming China needs a peaceful and stable international climate. Such a China is also more likely to be less xenophobic and therefore more pragmatic on some of the currently most sensitive national issues such as the future of Taiwan and Hong Kong" ("China's Quiet Revolution," p. 903).

19. See Lu Keng, "Hong Kong Self-Rule by the Hong Kong People," Pai hsing, no. 34 (October 16, 1982), pp. 12-15, FBIS, October 28, 1982, pp. W1-W4. This article contains the PRC's bottom-line position, the one the British agreed to in late 1983.

20. Cheng ming (Hong Kong), no. 61 (November 1, 1982), pp. 16-17, FBIS, November 5, 1982, p. W1.

21. Renmin ribao, September 24, 1983, p. 4 FBIS, September 27, 1983, pp. E1-E3; Far Eastern Economic Review, October 6, 1983, p. 20; Xinhua, (Beijing), September 22, 1983, FBIS, September 23, 1983, pp. E2-E5.

22. Los Angeles Times, April 21, 1984; Economist (London), April 21, 1984. Also see the Economist, April 7, 1984, pp. 17-18.

23. Economist, November 12, 1983, p. 92.

24. On the background of the walled city, see

Evan Luard, Britain and China (Baltimore: Johns Hopkins Press, 1962), pp. 180, 183. On Xu's visit, see Far Eastern Economic Review, August 18, 1983, p. 14, and South China Morning Post, December 27, 1983.

25. Luard, Britain and China, p. 179.
26. Far Eastern Economic Review, March 8, 1984, p. 26.
27. Ibid., July 21, 1983, p. 12; Xinhua, July 8, 1983, FBIS, July 11, 1983, p. E1.
28. Far Eastern Economic Review, August 20, 1982, pp. 14-15; Chi-xi nien-dai yueh-kan [The Seventies monthly] (Hong Kong), June 1983, pp. 11-12; ibid., July 1983, pp. 39-42; and D. K. Lewis, "The Prospects for Hong Kong," Conflict Studies (London), no. 142 (1982), pp. 17-19.
29. Margaret Ng, "Cultural Pride of the Hong Kong Chinese," South China Morning Post, August 25, 1983.
30. Pai hsing, no. 33 (October 1, 1982), p. 5, FBIS, October 6, 1982, p. W2; ibid., no. 52 (July 16, 1983), pp. 3-4, FBIS, July 21, 1982, p. W3 (comment on "big capitalists" by Deng Xiaoping).
31. Economist, November 12, 1983, pp. 91-93. For a report on a large real estate fair, see "The Money Keeps On Coming from Hong Kong," San Francisco Chronicle, March 16, 1984.

6
Kleptocracy on Mainland China: A Social-Psychological Interpretation

Alan P. L. Liu

Since the early 1970s, Peking's political meteorologists have reported two gusty, adverse, and persistent winds enveloping mainland China. At higher altitude is the "Party wind" (tangfen), the main elements of which are privilege seeking, factionalism, and venality. "Venality," I submit, is a better term than corruption to refer to the numerous cases of malfeasance, misfeasance, and nonfeasance committed by Party cadres; corruption suggests a fall from a previously attained high standard, which is not a part of the history of the Chinese Community Party.[1] At lower altitude, on the ground of mainland China, blows another wind, the "social wind" (she hui fengch'i), the chief characteristics of which are incivility, crime, mass bribery, extortion, superstition, and gambling.

A rather unique survey was conducted in the city of Changsha in 1981 on people's "expenses for cultivating human relationship" (jen-ch'ing-ch'ien), i.e., bribery. Of the 100 families surveyed, 99 had paid such money in 1981 (from January to November), the average payment being eight yuan per month, one-fifth the monthly wage of an ordinary Chinese.[2] These were cash payments only; the cost of sending gifts for the same purpose was not included. This result reminds one of the crucial distinction between "corruption in societies" and "corrupt societies" made by the Indian scholar Rajaratnam: "There is a world of difference between corruption in societies and corrupt societies. In the former case what we

157

have are lapses from what is essentially an honest society. In the latter case corruption becomes not only an essential part of the dynamics of society but also an unavoidable means for accumulation of wealth, power, influence, and even prestige in that society."[3]

All of these phenomena, from factionalism to bribery and gambling, stem from acute "anomie" in Chinese Communist society and politics. In this chapter, I shall account for the rise of anomie in Communist China in terms of the history of the Communist Party, the leadership of Mao Tse-tung, social background of Communist leaders and cadres, and the social impact of Chinese Communist rule on mainland China. My conclusion will deal with the Communist Party's measures to cope with venality in government.

ANOMIE AND DEVIANT BEHAVIOR

Anomie as used in this chapter has two meanings. It means, first of all, "a social condition characterized by a general breakdown, or absence, of norms governing group and individual behavior."[4] Second, anomie refers to "a social condition characterized by the existence of norms which conflict to such a degree that individuals and groups are confused by being faced with the dilemma that conformity to some norms insures violation of others."[5] The first meaning of anomie is used by Parsons who writes that anomie is the "polar antithesis of full institutionalization." Specifically, anomie rises because of a breakdown of value sharing and people's motivation to commit to the role expectations of society.[6] Parsons, however, cautions that anomie, just like institutionalization, is a variable, being a matter of degree in conrete societies. The second meaning of anomie is used by Merton, who sees numerous deviant forms of behavior such as crime, superstition, and gambling as a response to conflict of norms-- "differential access to economic success goals, combined with a generally uniform expectation for economic success, will result in anomie among those persons with the least opportunity to achieve such success."[7]

Anomie in the Chinese Communist context throws into relief its political and elite origins that neither Parsons nor Merton stress. Another dimension of anomie that is accentuated by the Chinese Communist system is that it is a relative concept. That is, anomie from the vantage point of the formal community might not be anomie from the vantage point of the informal community. Since on mainland China there have not been consistent values and role expectation in the formal system, the Chinese people revert to their private system of conduct. So, in the latter context, there is no anomie--bribery and establishing a patron-client relationship are the norms of the private and informal system that substitutes for the formal system of Chinese communism.

THE CHINESE COMMUNIST REVOLUTION

Perhaps one of the most important causes of anomie in any political system is an overwhelming emphasis on personality instead of on procedural authority. As some U.S. students of public opinion point out, any political system whose members judge policies and programs according to their presumed authors or supporters will be affected by elements of caprice, lability, and unprincipledness.[8] Herein lies the most important root of the anomie in the present Chinese Communist political system.

In retrospect, even before the victory of the Chinese Communist Party in the Chinese civil war, the Chinese Communist revolution had already been turned into a private enterprise. Instead of the victory of the Party in 1949, it was actually the victory of Mao. The Party was merely Mao's instrument. In this connection, the Chinese Communist revolution conforms in both form and substance to traditional Chinese revolutions. Liang Ch'i-ch'ao has observed that the classical Chinese revolutions have seven unique characteristics. First, Chinese revolutions in history have been "private" in contrast to the "public" character of Western revolutions. Traditional Chinese revolutions have been led by individual leaders who regarded the revolution as a personal undertaking. Western revolutions, however, have been staged in the name of an organized group such as the Parliament in the English civil war of 1642-1651, the Estates General in the French Revolution, and the thirteen colonies in the American War of Independence. Second, traditional Chinese revolutions have been motivated by pursuit of personal ambition instead of, as in the West, defense of group interest. The latter is for self-defense whereas the former is for personal aggrandizement.

Third, in traditional China, revolutions were organized by the upper or the lower classes; Western revolutions have been organized by the middle class. Fourth, in terms of the number of participants, Chinese revolutions have typically consisted of numerous rebel groups whereas Western revolutions, from the beginning, have been unified in a single group. Fifth, Chinese revolutions have lasted much longer than Western revolutions and, hence, have caused more casualties than the latter. Sixth, traditional Chinese revolutionaries fought not only with the old imperial authority but also with each other, whereas in the West, revolutions have mostly focused on a monarch. Seventh, Chinese revolutions facilitated foreign conquest of China whereas Western revolutionaries were capable of resisting foreign aggression.[9]

Although Liang makes the personalistic nature of Chinese revolutions explicit only in the first two points, the theme of personalism is implicit in the remaining five characteristics, and it is the egoistic nature of traditional revolutions that accounts for the type and number of participants and the induction of foreigners into Chinese revolutions. In some instances, Chinese revolutionaries enlisted the assistance of barbarians in order to overcome other Chinese revolutionary groups. That the Chinese Communist revolution conforms very closely to the traditional pattern is self-evident, and the personalistic or egoistic motif of that revolution was formally expressed during the Seventh Congress of the Chinese Communist Party in 1945. Ironically, it was the late Liu Shao-ch'i who brought forth and legitimized the Maoist imprint on the Party.

Like other ambitious leaders, Mao was

disciplined enough to control himself while in pursuit of power, but once he attained power, Mao felt no need to discipline himself. From then on he would use the Party and the state as his personal instruments to carry out his maximum program. The history of the PRC since 1949 is littered with Mao's riding roughshod over the interests and opinions of other leaders. The career of any Party leader was determined by one overriding factor: his or her conformity to Mao's wishes.

Moreover, beginning with the Great Leap Forward, Mao, in a desperate mood (because he had blundered in the Hundred Flowers Campaign) to establish his brand of socialism in China, resorted to what I call "strategic corruption." That is, Mao would support and promote any national and sub-national Party leader, regardless of the latter's method of operation, so long as he or she implemented Mao's program--be it the commune, the Ta Chai Brigade, or "support-to-the-left" during the Cultural Revolution. Rectitude was the least of Mao's considerations. He was willing to use hoodlums, albeit he referred to them as "the daring elements" (yung-kang fen-tzu).[10] The most prominent examples of Mao's "strategic corruption" technique (similar to Waterbury's "planned corruption")[11] are Liu Chien-hsun of Henan Province during the Great Leap Forward, Chen Yung-kuei of the Ta Chai Brigade, and Wang Hung-wen during the Cultural Revolution. Mao's handling of the "four cleanups" campaign in 1962-1964 leaves one little doubt as to his scheme of priority, i.e., his program concerning the rectitude of cadres.

Thus, anomie or deviant behavior on mainland China originated during Mao's leadership. Indeed, it was Mao whose behavior was anomic in that because of his overwhelming commitment to his own program, he did not care about the means of its implementation. Mao's conduct was anomic in another sense, which is expressed in the Chinese saying luan yung wei hsin ("abuse of a leader's prestige and authority"). The U.S. scholar Hollander has conceptualized leadership behavior in terms of "credit" and "debit." The past merits of a leader are treated as credits against which a leader might charge debits in the form of idiosyncratic behavior.[12] In Mao's case, he greatly "overdrafted" his credit in the Party and let his idiosyncratic behavior supersede Party convention (that is, if the CCP has a clear and well-defined "Party convention").

Since Mao set the example, other subnational leaders followed. The result is that the behavior of many lower Party cadres is scarcely different from "the daring elements" (those who "beat, smash and loot"). Their venality is only now being flushed out by the Party, and the efforts of the higher leaders are constantly being thwarted by the pervasive factional alliances among the lower leaders.

Thus, the history of the Communist Party of China and Mao's leadership bear out the observations by Rogow and Lasswell: (1) If the leadership of the institution does not serve as a model of rectitude, the people belonging to or serving in the institution may "yield willingly or without much resistance" and (2) if the membership of an institution does not collectively enforce standards of rectitude, the tendency toward individual corruption is increased.[13]

SOCIAL BACKGROUND OF CHINESE COMMUNISTS

The second source of venality or anomic behavior in Communist China has to do with the social composition of the Communist Party. Several U.S. scholars have suggested that social or class structure has consequences for the frequency of venality or corruption in a society. Rogow and Lasswell, for example, have observed that "a background of severe deprivation may encourage the use of power in corrupt forms as a means of acquiring and maintaining environmental control,"[14] and Andreski has pointed out that in Latin America, the long-established property-owning classes, being long-established, confine corruption to within certain limits.[15] Huntington is explicit about the impact of class on corruption: "A highly articulated class or caste structure means a highly developed system of norms regulating behavior between individuals of different status. These norms are enforced both by the individual's socialization into his own group and by the expectations and potential sanctions of other groups. . . . Corruption, consequently, should be less extensive in the modernization of feudal societies than it is in the modernization of centralized bureaucratic societies."[16] In a similar vein, Scott contrasts corruption in stable elite systems, such as England and Thailand, with corruption in unstable elite systems, such as Indonesia. In the latter case, corruption takes the "hand-over-fist pattern" because of the lack of security and fragmentation of the Indonesian elite.[17]

Seen in the foregoing perspective, Chinese Communist corruption belongs to the same category as Indonesia's or Huntington's "centralized bureaucratic societies." The members of the upper echelon of the Communist elite were petty intellectuals who revolted against the old Confucian ethic without, however, establishing a code of ethic among themselves, and these elites are influenced by the Soviet leaders' "cult of power" and "cult of personality." On the lower level of the Communist Party, most cadres were deliberately recruited from among poor peasants whose background was certainly marked by long deprivation. Moreover, as the leaders of the Communist Party nowadays admit, these cadres with a less acculturated background were not given adequate education or culture once they were assigned leadership duties. Mao explicitly objected to cadres' receiving formal education, preferring "learning while practicing," so the style of Chinese Communist cadres is that of the nouveaux riche. The best description came from the ideologue of the Gang of Four, Yao Wen-Yuan, who attributed to the veteran cadres the attitude that "they [the capitalists] have grabbed, let me have a go too."[18]

The absence of a code of honor or system of norms among Chinese Communist leaders, high or low, is best exemplified by the crass and criminal behavior of their children who have become a distinct class on mainland China. Zhou Enlai was quoted by the Communist Youth League paper as warning Communist cadres not to let their children degenerate the way that the children of the Manchu elite did.[19] Mao also expressed concern about the children of cadres as early as 1961.[20] The many cases of criminal deeds, especially sex crimes, that were exposed after 1977 involved a significant number of the children of Party cadres, the Hsiung brothers in Hangchow being the most notorious case. The crass conduct of the children of Party cadres is but a reflection of the moral shallowness of their parents. Historically, a true aristocracy puts a premium on the cultivation of their children--European and English royalties subject their children to rigorous tests and education so that the honor of their class is maintained--but there is no tradition of honor in the new aristocracy of the Chinese Communist Party. Theirs is the crass style of the nouveaux riche.

The grasping nature of the Chinese Communist cadres has not of course been confined to the lower echelons or the youngsters of cadre families. Topmost Party leaders such as Chiang Ch'ing and her colleague K'ang Sheng, were notorious for looting art and treasures from public institutions in the style of Hermann Goering of Nazi Germany. Chiang and K'ang were reported to have taken from a Peking municipal office artworks that had been confiscated from private homes by the Red Guards during the Cultural Revolution.[21] If one questions the credibility of these post-Mao reports, then I should mention an instance involving Marshal Chu Teh. While visiting a handicraft factory for export goods in 1975, Chu expressed a keen appreciation of a shell engraving. Subsequently the factory sent the engraving to Chu as a gift. Chu was reported to have rejected it, but his rejection was portrayed in the press as an extraordinary happening.[22] These examples are nothing more than the natural expression of the PRC's being a "proprietary state."

Taking their cue from the Communist elites, the Chinese people have responded in kind. Thus, we read reports in the Chinese press of instances of mass looting of factories that were ordered to close because of the present leaders' policy of retrenchment. In this connection, we are reminded again of Liang Ch'i-ch'ao's comment on the sad state of Chinese public morality. He wrote:

> For several thousand years, our race lived

under autocratic regimes. If a person
wants to advance himself, he must resort
to deceit and falsehood. If he desires
to protect himself, he must resort to
servitude. Those who have these qualities
occupy a superior position in our society.
Those who lack these qualities do not
survive and hence do not pass on their
virtues to their children. Hence it is
the ethos of the survivors who have
given our society its collective
character.[23]

SOCIAL IMPACT OF COMMUNIST RULE

Liang Ch'i-ch'ao was not alone in seeing the
causal relationship between the character of a
regime and public morality. Rogow and Lasswell,
for example, have written that corruption arises
as young people find themselves penalized if they
try to live up to proclaimed norms when they
compete with less scrupulous adults in society.[24]
The thirty-some years of Communist rule on mainland China have impressed upon Chinese people,
the youth in particular, two things: insecurity
due to violence or inconsistent role-expectations
and the all-or-nothing nature of political power.

The integration and stability of any society
depend, among other factors, on a few key symbols
or values and stable role expectations. The
history of the Communist rule of mainland China
is marked by continuous and inconsistent elite
manipulation of key symbols such as "socialism,"
"class," or "mass line." The Cultural Revolution,
for example, repudiated wholesale the values and
institutions that had been established by the
Communist Party. Chinese youths have been utterly
confused about their proper role in society. They
were called upon by the Party to commit themselves
to patriotism and education in the early 1950s,
"red and expert" in the late 1950s, patriotism
and learning once more in 1963-1965, "revolution
and rebellion" during the Cultural Revolution and
"intellectual education equal to bourgeois
education" in the 1970s. In a similar vein, the
role of the Chinese intellectuals has been subject

to "in" and "out" treatment repeatedly throughout the thirty-some years of Communist rule. Other examples can be cited to illustrate the normlessness of Chinese Communist social policy, such as "a socialist factory being not for production only" that was trumpeted by the Left during the Cultural Revolution. About the only group whose role has not been subject to such inconsistency is the peasantry and its members are the beasts of burden all the time.

The lack of a stable pattern of norms under Communist rule is accompanied by a high frequency of violence. This connection can best be shown in the campaigns that the Communist Party has launched. As the editor of the China News Analysis pointed out in 1974:

> A growth of violence has been noticeable through the sequence of political campaigns. The suppression of counter-revolutionaries was extremely violent, but as soon as the enemies of the Party had been exterminated, a note of civility was sounded--a State Constitution, regularion of courts and prosecution and even a kind of a jury. But this moderation, introduced in 1954, was short-lived. The su-fan purge in 1955 ignored legal niceties. In 1957, Mao in a famous speech legalized his own old doctrine of the division of the Chinese people into enemies and friends. The cultural revolution exalted the notion of violence. Huge red guard organizations were fighting one another. Very rough language was used.[25]

Thus, every Chinese citizen feels himself or herself to be isolated in a lawless and hostile world in which violence and bloodshed are endemic. Not only is he or she surrounded by hostility and violence, each is also subject to an impersonal, indifferent, and often predatory bureaucracy whose power over the citizens is vast. To adapt to this environment, the knowledgeable ones find "patrons" for protection and obtain goods and services through "the back door." The uneducated ones find solace (if possible) in superstition and gambling. But all of them, educated or uneducated, fall back on the kinship tie and personal connections. These are the natural reactions of people wherever the conditions of violence, hostility, and anarchy are found.[26]

However, as in the role expectation in China in which, amid inconsistencies, the role of peasant has not been subject to change, so it is with basic values. In the three decades of Communist rule of mainland China, one value remains overwhelmingly important--power. After the purge of the Gang of Four, the present leaders of the Communist Party openly criticized the widespread attitude among Party cadres, young ones in particular, that with power everything can be obtained (yu ch'üan chiu yu yi ch'ieh).[27] A forum was convened in the Ministry of Petroleum in 1978, and it denounced the saying of one of the early staff members of the Gang of Four, Wang Li, that "a man can be a minister at twenty. How impressive and awe-inspiring power is!"[28]

It is clear from the foregoing that power in Chinese Communist political culture is predominantly used venally.[29] Second, the implicit essence of power in Chinese Communist references is "naked power," which, as defined by Lasswell and Kaplan, is "nonauthoritative power openly exercised."[30] "It is power not accepted as authoritative by those over whom it is exercised, but nevertheless submitted to."[31] In other words, naked power is acquired by violence. Moreover, say Lasswell and Kaplan, naked power "tends to be exercised in situations where current political myths tend to be widely rejected."[32] That is, anomie and naked power are two sides of a coin. The best example of this power motif in the Chinese Communist political system is the Party elites that have risen to power in a dramatic fashion, such as the Gang of Four.

MEASURES TO CONTROL VENALITY

Although the present Chinese Communist leaders have made some major attempts to counter the widespread venality in government, there are three important limitations to their efforts. The first is a lack of consistent legal standards to deal with those individuals who are corrupt. For example, on January 8, 1984, the People's Daily publicized two cases of corruption. One, on the first page, was about a deputy Party secretary of a Hunan tobacco factory who not only was corrupt but had also tortured and committed other forms of violence against others. But no sanction was applied to this man until the exposé by the People's Daily. On page 3 of the paper was another report about a manager of a Canton tobacco factory who had received bribes. In this latter case, the manager was executed. In almost every case of corruption, the courts take a back seat to the Party Commission of Discipline Inspection. In other words, the Communist Party prefers retaining vast discretionary power to genuine legality, so the formal system of handling venality in government continues to facilitate normlessness.

The second limitation to the campaign of eliminating political venality concerns the structure of the Chinese Communist political system. The centralist and unitary nature of the system ensures that any flaw quickly permeates the system. The consequence is that, presently, there is no institution in the Chinese Communist government that can be upheld as an example of rectitude. In a pluralistic and decentralized system, one can always find some institutions with a reputation of incorruptibility that is long established, and hence, they can serve as the moral centers of society. For example, as Rogow and Lasswell have pointed out, in the United States, "the president, as the spokesman for our best traditions and aspiration, and the justices, as the collective symbol of the supreme law of the Constitution, have been forced by role and position to uphold the highest ethical standards."[33] One can not point to any Chinese Communist counterparts to the justices or the office of the president in the United States. In fact, as I have already mentioned, venality on mainland China started from the very top office—when Mao was chairman of the Communist Party. Despite all the professions by the post-Mao leaders as to their

opposition to the "cult of personality," there is
no effective check on the idiosyncratic behavior
of Party leaders.

A third fundamental limitation to the present
drive to stem the tide of venality in China is the
absence of a new "spiritual pillar" in mainland
Chinese society.[34] The formal values trumpeted by
the Communist Party have been largely repudiated
by the population, which is reflected by the
significant phenomenon of ridiculing and even
persecuting "model" or "advanced" persons on mainland China. It is true that in every society
outstanding personalities tend to draw detractors.
However, judging by the way the Chinese Communist
news media describe the ill treatment that many
"model" people have encountered (some have suffered
nervous breakdowns), we can only conclude that
their treatment represents a general rejection of
and a hostility to the values advocated by the
elites. In this moral vacuum between the rejected
formal values and the absence of any new ones,
many people in China turn to the immediate,
private, and concrete things in life. So the
Chinese Communist press publishes public sentiments such as "money is the medal of society"
or "money is the wheel that makes society move."[35]
To use the language of political meteorologists,
the social and political climate on mainland China
remains highly favorable to venality and anomie.

Nevertheless, as some people have argued,
there are some mitigating factors that might
reduce the amount of venality on mainland China.
For example, to the extent that venality was
caused by Mao's conduct, his death removed this
particular cause. Second, if the present venality
is one result of an overcentralized system, then
the reforms of Teng Hsiao-ping after 1980 in the
direction of restraining central power ought to
have a salutary effect on corruption. Moreover, it
has been pointed out that not every authoritarian
and centralized political system is equally prone
to widespread venality. The most outstanding
example of a relatively nonvenal bureaucracy is
that of Singapore, whose political system can not
be regarded as pluralistic. Finally, it is
argued that insofar as the venality on mainland
China has been caused by an extreme scarcity of

consumer goods, then the post-Mao reform in national priority--toward production of more consumer goods--ought to gradually reduce the incentive to be corrupt. In the final analysis, whatever the post-Mao regime on mainland China does, as long as it reduces insecurity and scarcity of goods, it will have the effect of substantially reducing venality.

There is, however, one stumbling block to the Chinese Communist regime's attempt to control venality. That is, the Chinese Communist political system, being the fruit of a long armed struggle, is essentially a system that is based on spoils. A visiting Chinese economist from the mainland observed to a U.S. sociologist: "The viability of the American economic system is based on buying off the poor so yours is basically a welfare economy. The viability of our economic system is based on corruption; we buy off the elites." Unless this fundamental element of the Chinese Communist political-economic system is changed (and the prospect of such change is not certain if the Soviet system is used as an example), venality will remain an integral part of the society and politics of mainland China.

NOTES

1. See, for example, the writings of Wang Shih-wei and Ting Ling on the conditions of privileges in Yenan in 1942 as reported in Wang Chien-min, Chung-kuo-kung ch'an-tang shih-kao [History of the Chinese Communist Party], vol. 3 (Taipei: Cheng-chung Shu-chu, 1965), pp. 299-312. See also Liu Tse-chiu, "Letter to Huai District Party Committee on Question of Study," in Cheng-feng wen-hsien [Anthology of Party reform documents] (Hong Kong: Hsin-min-tsu Ch'u-pan-she, 1949), pp. 299-318. The various expressions of bureaucratism are already evident in Liu's letter of 1944.

2. Ming Pao Daily News, February 2, 1982, p. 1, based on Remin ribao [People's daily] of January 31, 1982.

3. Sinnathamby Rajaratnam, "Bureaucracy versus Kleptocracy," in A. J. Heidenheimer, ed.,

Political Corruption: Readings in Comparative Analysis (New York: Holt, Rinehart and Winston, 1970), p. 547.
   4. Thomas Ford Hoult, Dictionary of Modern Sociology (Totowa, N.J.: Littlefield, Adams and Company, 1969), p. 21.
   5. Ibid.
   6. Talcott Parsons, The Social System (New York: Free Press, 1964), p. 39.
   7. Marshall B. Clinard, Sociology of Deviant Behavior, 3d ed. (New York: Holt, Rinehart and Winston, 1968), p. 35. Clinard's explanation is based on Robert K. Merton, "Social Structure and Anomie," in Merton, Social Theory and Social Structure, rev. ed. (New York: Free Press, 1964).
   8. V. O. Key, Jr., Public Opinion and American Democracy (New York: Alfred A. Knopf, 1963), pp. 247-253.
   9. Liang Ch'i-ch'ao, Yin-ping-shih wen-chi [Ice parlor anthology], vol. 1 (Taipei: Hsin-hsin She Chu, 1955), sec. 1, pp. 193-194.
   10. Mao Tse-tung ssu-hsiang wan-sui [Long live the thought of Mao Tse-tung], no. 2 (reprinted materials) (Washington, D.C.: Center for Chinese Research Materials, n.d.), pp. 591, 592, 595.
   11. John Waterbury, "Endemic and Planned Corruption in a Monarchical Regime," World Politics 25:4 (July 1973), pp. 533-555.
   12. E. P. Hollander, "Conformity, Status, and Idiosyncracy Credit," Psychological Review 65:2 (March 1958), pp. 117-125.
   13. Arnold A. Rogow and Harold D. Lasswell, Power, Corruption, and Rectitude (Englewood Cliffs, N.J.: Prentice-Hall, 1963), p. 59.
   14. Ibid., pp. 34-35.
   15. Stanislav Andreski, "Kleptocracy as a System of Government in Africa," in Heidenheimer, Political Corruption, p. 356.
   16. Samuel P. Huntington, "Modernization and Corruption" in Heidenheimer, Political Corruption, p. 496.
   17. James C. Scott, Comparative Political Corruption (Englewood Cliffs, N.J.: Prentice-Hall, 1972), pp. 79-83.
   18. Yao Wen-yuan, "On the Social Basis of the Lin Piao Anti-Party Clique," Peking Review 18:10

(March 7, 1975), p. 8.
19. As reprinted in Renmin ribao, April 22, 1979, p. 3.
20. Mao Tse-tung, Ssu-hsiang Wan-sui, pp. 351, 390.
21. Renmin ribao, May 28, 1977, p. 2, and December 22, 1980, p. 4.
22. Renmin ribao, April 25, 1979, p. 3.
23. Liang Ch'i-ch'ao, Yin-ping shih-wen-chi, p. 97.
24. Rogow and Lasswell, Power, Corruption, and Rectitude, p. 70.
25. China News Analysis, no. 951 (March 1, 1974), p. 2.
26. Compare, for example, the reaction of Chinese people under Communist rule to that of the Italian people in southern Italy as discussed in Jeremy Boissevain, "Patronage in Sicily," in Heidenheimer, Political Corruption, pp. 141-149.
27. Renmin ribao, September 21, 1979, p. 3.
28. Renmin ribao, November 18, 1978, p. 3.
29. Foreign Broadcast Information Service--People's Republic of China, June 6, 1978, p. L1.
30. Harold D. Lasswell and Abraham Kaplan, Power and Society: A Framework for Political Inquiry (New Haven: Yale University Press, 1963), p. 139.
31. Ibid.
32. Ibid., p. 140.
33. Rogow and Lasswell, Power, Corruption, and Rectitude, pp. 63-64.
34. Chi Hsin, "Establish New Spiritual Pillar," Ch'ih-shih Nien-tai [The Seventies], no. 7 (1980), pp. 29-32. See also, Flora Lewis, "Can China Stabilize?" New York Times, November 11, 1980, p. A15.
35. Wang Chih-yu, "Is Money the Medal of Society?" Renmin ribao, December 16, 1983, p. 8.

7
Higher Educational Charters in Mainland China

C. Montgomery Broaded

As an institution, education functions most generally in modern and modernizing societies as a system of legitimation (Meyer 1977). It functions both as a societal theory of knowledge (legitimizing certain kinds of knowledge as authoritative) and as a theory of personnel (legitimizing particular persons as carriers of authoritative knowledge and, hence, as qualified for incumbency of particular occupational positions). Schools are, in this view, seen as possessing certain socially recognized charters, and they can bestow the status of "graduate" to persons who pass through them successfully. Graduates of different types of schools are then socially recognized as possessing certain rights and privileges (and perhaps obligations, as well) in society.

One of the most important of these rights and privileges, of course, involves the kinds of occupations for which graduates are perceived to be qualified. Different kinds of schools provide their students with different kinds and levels of knowledge and skills, to be sure. But perhaps more important, different kinds of schools are perceived by both students and the overall society to allocate their graduates to significantly different kinds of futures, and students tend to adopt attitudes and self-concepts that are appropriate to the futures to which they expect to be allocated upon graduation.

As educational systems expand in modernizing societies, they become increasingly differentiated and tend to adopt some form of tracking (Karabel 1972). Also with educational expansion, social groups that previously could not gain entry to the education system become able to do so. However, they often find that the elite jobs for which they thought they would be qualified remain out of reach because of educational inflation (Collins 1977; Dore 1976). There is a general tendency for young people to be distributed within stratified educational systems (or excluded from them) according to their families' positions in society's overall stratification order (Bowles 1977; Karabel 1972). As Kelley and Klein (1977, p. 86) point out:

> Throughout the world, well-educated, high-status families are much more successful in getting their children educated. . . ; they provide encouragement and role models, teach linguistic skills and academic skills, force their children to work harder, and the like. Schooling is usually expensive, both in direct costs (fees, supplies, clothing, etc.) and indirect costs (income the student could otherwise have earned); prosperous families can better afford these costs.

The belief that the expansion of a "modern" educational system will contribute greatly to economic development has been one of the main ideological supports for allocating considerable state resources to such expansion, but the connection between education and modernization remains a matter of debate (see, for example, Simmons 1979). It is an issue that was fiercely debated in mainland China during and after the Cultural Revolution. Education was one of the primary institutional targets of the Cultural Revolution, and strong efforts were made to remake the educational system in the early and mid-1970s in order to have it conform to the Maoist strategy of economic development. This "revolution in education" included a fundamental challenge to the importance of high-level educational credentials in modernization efforts and sought to shift the emphasis toward a more politicized and "vocationally" oriented curriculum.

This chapter reports some of the results of a content analysis of articles on higher education published in People's Daily during the 1970s, which was a very important decade in terms of educational policy and economic development strategy. It began with the implementation of wide ranging reforms in education that were intended to alter the mixture of types of higher education institutions and to increase the access of formerly disprivileged groups--such as peasants and workers--to educational opportunities. However, a critical juncture was reached in 1976 with the death of Mao Zedong and the purge of the Gang of Four, and the 1970s ended with a sweeping program of counterreforms that sought to restore much of the pre-Cultural Revolution education system and, indeed, to strengthen some of its more hierarchical aspects.

This chapter takes a systematic look at the issue of differentiation in mainland China's higher education system during the 1970s, considering the kinds of schools emphasized in the press, the emphasis given to various economic and political-ideological goals of higher education, and the extent to which particular kinds of goals are regularly associated with particular kinds of schools. This approach provides a way to investigate the charters of different kinds of schools at different times. Finally, to the extent possible with very limited data, I explore the question of whether students from different social backgrounds are systematically associated with one or another type of higher education institution. Before presenting the relevant results of my study, however, some words about how the study was conducted are in order.

RESEARCH DESIGN AND METHODOLOGY

Content analysis techniques were used to investigate seven major dimensions of higher education policy, and of those seven, three are most relevant to the concerns of this chapter. First, the structure of the higher education system is explored by assessing the relative emphasis placed on different kinds of higher education institutions at different times during the 1970s. A fundamental distinction is made between what are called here the "traditional" and the "nontraditional" schools. (These school types have also been called "regular" and "irregular" [bu zhenggui] schools, or standard and nonstandard schools.)

Second, the goals or end-states, to which higher education is intended to contribute are explored. For convenience of presentation, these are divided into two main types--economic goals and political-ideological goals. Some goals are not so easily classified, however; for example, the goal of creating people who are both "red and expert" certainly contains both political-ideological and economic components.

Third, the background characteristics of students are explored as far as possible, since articles in People's Daily frequently use only the most general terms to describe the social backgrounds of students. I will focus on students identified in the press as coming from worker backgrounds, peasant backgrounds, and "worker-peasant-soldier" backgrounds (gong-nong-bing xueyuan) or as educated youth (zhishi qingnian).

Three one-year periods during the 1970s were selected for study: 1971, 1975, and 1978. One-year periods were chosen to ensure that a full educational cycle was included in each measurement period. The year 1971 was selected because it was the first year following the Cultural Revolution in which large numbers of colleges and universities reopened after having been closed since mid-1966. Thus, the Cultural Revolution reforms in education could be expected to receive considerable attention in the official press.

The year 1975 was selected because it was the year prior to the purge of the Gang of Four, and the policies expressed in this year could be considered to represent the preferences of the Maoists (the Cultural Revolutionary Left as they have been called) among the Chinese leadership. The year 1978 was selected because it was long enough after the purge of the Gang of Four for the new regime to have clearly established its own policies in the sphere of education.

Because the present study is concerned with higher education policy at the national level, the central Party newspaper, People's Daily (Renmin ribao), was chosen as the medium from which articles about higher education would be selected for content analysis. People's Daily represents the voice of the central Party leadership in mainland China, and it communicates the preferences of the central Party leadership to other parts of the society.

The particular articles to be subjected to content analysis were selected by referring to the yearly index to People's Daily, the Renmin ribao suo-in. For 1971 and 1978, all articles appearing on the front page were included in the sample, and a table of random numbers was used to select an additional twenty and twenty-three articles, respectively, from the articles on the inner pages. For 1975, front-page articles were so numerous that approximately half were selected at random for inclusion in the sample, and an additional fifteen articles from the inner pages were also selected at random.

The sample for 1971, then, consists of twenty-nine articles containing 378 paragraphs and 1,698 individual sentences, headlines, and internal headings. The sample for 1975 consists of thirty-nine articles, containing 307 paragraphs and 1,480 individual sentences, headlines, and internal headings. The sample for 1978 consists of thirty-six articles containing 331 paragraphs and 1,360 individual sentences, headlines, and internal headings.

The specific items to be coded from these articles were derived inductively by reading many articles from each year and compiling extensive lists of items related to each of the major dimensions of higher education policy. These lists were then consolidated, and a trial analysis of several articles from each year was conducted. On the basis of the difficulties and ambiguities encountered during the trial analysis, several of the coding categories were modified. This refined set of coding categories was then used to code the entire sample of articles for each year. Each article was read in Chinese, sentence by sentence, and the presence or absence of each category of analysis was noted for each individual sentence.

In the presentation of the results of the analysis, two kinds of frequencies are utilized to provide information about the relative importance attached by the central leaders to discrete aspects of higher education policy. The sheer volume of references to each item is summarized in a "rate of reference per 1,000 sentences of text coded" for each year. (The raw frequencies of occurrence are not directly comparable because a different number of sentences was coded for each year.) It is assumed that items which are mentioned quite often in the press are more important to the central leaders than are items that are mentioned only seldom. It is possible to assess the generality of the central leaders' concern about particular aspects of higher education policy by considering the proportion of articles about higher education in each year that include at least one reference to those aspects. An item that appears in a high proportion of all articles is assumed to be more generally important to the leadership than an item that appears in a low proportion of the articles.

It is also useful to move beyond a consideration of discrete categories of analysis to compare the patterns of association between two or more items across time. In looking at patterns of co-occurrence of two or more items of interest, the sentence is too small a unit of analysis, and the article is too large. The paragraph, however, provides a meaningful unit that generally has a fairly high level of conceptual integrity. In looking at the co-occurrences of items within paragraphs, it is important to keep in mind that the items could be expected to occur together a certain number of times on the basis of chance alone. Thus, what is really of interest here is the magnitude of the deviation of the observed frequencies of co-occurrence from the frequencies that would be expected on the basis of chance alone. Chi square is utilized as the test of independence in the tables examining the patterns of co-occurrence.

RESULTS AND DISCUSSION

Table 7.1 displays the frequency with which various kinds of higher education institutions were mentioned in People's Daily in 1971, 1975, and 1978. Both the rates of reference per 1,000 sentences of text coded and the percentage of articles containing at least one reference to each type of school are presented. The table is divided into two parts--the traditional (or regular) higher education institutions and the nontraditional (or irregular) schools.

The traditional schools are roughly equivalent to colleges and universities in Western countries, after which many of them were modeled. They are generally financed by the central or provincial governments; they offer a fairly extensive and advanced curriculum; they have generally been in existence for many years; they draw their students from large geographical areas; and their graduates, except in times of political upheaval, can generally expect to attain well-rewarded positions.

The nontraditional institutions are generally run on a localized basis; for example, factories or communes operate schools for their own workers, who return to their original work posts or units after completing their training. As the policy of "from the commune or factory to the commune or factory" indicates, these schools are explicitly opposed to serving as channels of mobility into the occupational elite. They often do, however, provide opportunities for short-range mobility within a particular enterprise. An unskilled laborer, for example, might move to a semi-skilled or skilled position after a period of training.

There is some question, of course, both within mainland China and elsewhere, about whether these nontraditional educational efforts can properly be considered institutions of higher education. But the press refers to them as workers' universities and agricultural colleges, and in the early and mid-1970s, the Cultural Revolutionary Left sought to make the traditional schools more like the nontraditional ones.

Among the traditional institutions, scientific-technical universities were referred to much more

Table 7.1. Types of higher education institutions mentioned in People's Daily, by year

	Rate of Reference Per 1,000 Sentences of Text Coded			% of Articles Referring Once or More to Each Type		
	1971	1975	1978	1971	1975	1978
Traditional Institutions						
Scientific-technical universities	19	24	49	55	28	53
Medical schools	12	3	16	21	5	22
Comprehensive universities	6	19	9	21	18	25
Teacher training colleges	2	9	11	7	15	19
Agricultural universities	1	46	4	3	33	8
Total	40	101	89	93*	72*	58*
Nontraditional Institutions						
July 21 workers' universities	32	112	20	17	33	19
Communist Labor University	31	11	2	3	8	8
Short-term training courses	18	52	12	21	44	14
Spare-time industrial colleges	4	9	4	10	18	11
May 7 agricultural colleges	0	17	7	0	13	14
Spare-time agricultural schools	0	15	4	0	17	7
Total	85	216	49	38*	72*	28*
N of sentences coded	1,698	1,480	1,360			
N of articles coded				29	39	36

*Asterisked figures indicate the percentage of articles that refer to any one or more of the traditional or nontraditional schools, rather than a total of the figures above them.

often in 1978 than in 1971 or 1975. In 1975, references to scientific-technical universities appeared in only 28 percent of the articles coded, compared with 55 percent for 1971 and 53 percent in 1978. Medical schools, too, were mentioned in the press much less often in 1975 than in either 1971 or 1978. Both scientific-technical universities and medical schools can be considered bastions of a technocratic ideology that people with high-level educational credentials do indeed possess "authoritative knowledge" and, hence, have a legitimate claim to have a large say in socially consequential decision-making processes, an ideology that was under heavy attack by the Cultural Revolutionary Left during 1975. By 1978, of course, a technocratic ideology was being vigorously promoted by the post-Gang of Four regime.

Also notable among the traditional institutions is the great emphasis on agricultural universities during 1975. Although the development of the agricultural sector of the Chinese economy was an important goal throughout the 1970s, the contribution of higher education to this goal was given considerably more emphasis in 1975 than in either 1971 or 1978.

Among the nontraditional schools, July 21 workers' universities received a great deal of press attention in 1975. These schools are run by large factories to increase the technical knowledge of their workers as well as to inculcate the proper ideological stance and world view among the workers. References to the Communist Labor University were fairly numerous in 1971, but all of the references were concentrated in a single long article. Thus, the Communist Labor University was not among the institutions about which the central leadership exhibited a general concern. In keeping with the emphasis on agriculture during 1975, references to May 7 agricultural colleges and to spare-time agricultural schools were more numerous in 1975 than in the other years.

The total rates of reference for traditional and nontraditional schools can give an indication of the relative importance the central leaders attached to these kinds of schools in the three years under consideration. In both 1971 and 1975, the total rate of reference to nontraditional schools is approximabely double that for the traditional schools. In 1978, on the other hand, the combined rate for the nontraditional schools is considerably lower than that for the traditional schools. Thus, in 1971 and 1975, there was much greater emphasis on the kinds of educational experiences that sought to improve applied productive skills (and to impart socialist values) and were explicit in their rejection of education's serving as a channel of mobility into elite occupations. In 1978, the post-Gang of Four regime had clearly reestablished the traditional schools as the most important part of the higher education system as a whole. Furthermore, the key point system had been restored and expanded, thus increasing the hierarchical nature of the higher education system.

ECONOMIC GOALS OF HIGHER EDUCATION

What is higher education expected to contribute to society? This is a fundamental question whose answer is open to debate. Education in most societies is expected to contribute to the economic health and development of the country by transmitting important skills to the young. But it also has an important role to play in political socialization and, in the case of mainland China, societal transformation. These are the expectations of the central leadership, of course. For individuals, education is often seen as a way of improving one's chances in life. This individual motivation has, until recently, been considered completely illegitimate by the central Party leaders in China, and individuals were obligated to express their interest in higher education in terms of their desire "to build socialism."

Table 7.2 displays the frequencies with which various economic goals of higher education were mentioned in People's Daily in 1971, 1975, and 1978. Looking first at the rate of reference per 1,000 sentences of text coded, it is clear that the goal of increasing production and solving

Table 7.2. Types of economic goals of higher education mentioned in People's Daily, by year

Economic Goals	Rate of Reference Per 1,000 Sentences of Text Coded			% of Articles Referring Once or More to Each Goal		
	1971	1975	1978	1971	1975	1978
Increase production; solve immediate production problems	91	93	21	62	67	39
Develop qualified human resources	39	53	84	55	62	58
Serve the advancement of science and technology	37	15	60	45	28	56
Economic development; creation of a strong country	16	35	72	48	54	50
Increase agricultural production	12	72	3	21	54	11
Create people who are both "red and expert"	7	6	14	24	15	31
N of sentences coded	1,698	1,480	1,360			
N of articles coded				29	39	36

immediate production problems was the most salient concern during both 1971 and 1975 and that considerably less importance was attached to it during 1978. The goal of developing qualified human resources shows a pattern of increasing importance as the 1970s progressed, as does the goal of economic development and the creation of a strong country. The latter goal, of course, is closely connected with the Four Modernizations campaigns of the late 1970s.

The goal of serving the advancement of science and technology is interesting in that the lowest rate of reference occurs in 1975 and the highest appears in 1978. The advancement of science and technology, of course, has something to do with the advancement of scientists and technicians. During 1975, even more so than during 1971, the Cultural Revolutionary Left was involved in an effort to depress the status of "bourgeois experts" with high-level educational credentials; hence, it attached little importance to the advancement of science and technology, unless such advances were made by experienced workers inspired by the thought of Mao Zedong. The great importance attached to increasing agricultural production during 1975 is reflected again in Table 7.2 as this goal was mentioned in slightly more than half of the articles coded for 1975.

The same patterns noted for the rates of reference are reflected for the most part in the data on the percentage of articles mentioning various goals. However, it is interesting that for both the goal of economic development and the goal of developing qualified human resources, the rates of reference increase considerably in the course of the 1970s but the percentage of articles containing references to these goals remains fairly constant. Thus, these goals are a more salient part of the articles in which they appear in 1978 than they are in 1971, and 1975 is intermediate between the two.

The patterns described thus far have to do with the goals of higher education in general, and some shifts across time are clearly evident. But what of the differences between traditional and nontraditional schools? Are some of these goals systematically associated with one or the other of these types of schools? Do the patterns of association change across time? These questions are addressed by looking at the co-occurrences of references to traditional and nontraditional schools with references to the economic goals of higher education. In this portion of the analysis, the paragraph is used as the basic unit, and Tables 7.3 and 7.4 show both the observed frequency of co-occurrence and the expected frequency of co-occurrence for each of the school types and the various economic goals of higher education.

Looking first at the traditional schools in 1971 (Table 7.3), it is clear that none of the associations differ a great deal from what would be expected on the basis of chance alone. For the nontraditional schools in 1971 (Table 7.4), both the goal of developing qualified human resources and the goal of increasing agricultural production appear in the same paragraphs with references to nontraditional schools significantly more often than would be expected on the basis of chance alone.

In 1975, the observed frequency of co-occurrence of the goal of increasing production and solving immediate production problems is slightly lower than expected for the traditional schools and somewhat higher than expected for the nontraditional schools. Although neither of these differences achieves statistical significance, they are consistent with the image of nontraditional schools emphasizing knowledge that can be applied directly to the productive process. As was true for 1971, the goal of developing qualified human resources occurs together with references to nontraditional schools significantly more often in 1975 than would be expected on the basis of chance.

A striking difference in the charters of traditional and nontraditional schools is evident in the schools' 1975 associations with the goal of economic development and the creation of a strong country. This goal occurs significantly more often than would be expected with references to traditional schools and significantly less often than would be expected with references to nontraditional schools. This goal is a much more general and abstract one than, for example, the

Table 7.3. Traditional schools by the economic goals of higher education (observed and expected frequencies of co-occurrence), by year

Economic Goals	1971 Obs'd.	1971 Exp'd.	1975 Obs'd.	1975 Exp'd.	1978 Obs'd.	1978 Exp'd.
Increase production; solve immediate production problems (90, 72, 23)	7	8.3	17	19.0	4	5.0
Develop qualified human resources (48, 55, 76)	7	4.4	12	14.5	24	16.5*
Serve the advancement of science and technology (44, 17, 56)	5	4.1	4	4.5	15	12.2
Economic development; creation of a strong country (22, 40, 64)	2	2.0	18	10.5*	14	13.9
Increase agricultural production (15, 42, 4)	1	1.4	19	16.1	1	0.9
Create people who are both "red and expert" (8, 5, 17)	1	0.7	1	1.3	0	3.7

*p < .05

Note: Figures in parentheses refer to the number of paragraphs in 1971, 1975, and 1978, respectively, that contain at least one reference to a particular goal. Traditional schools were referred to in 35, 81, and 72 paragraphs, respectively.

Table 7.4. Nontraditional schools by the economic goals of higher education (observed and expected frequencies of co-occurrence), by year

Economic Goals	1971		1975		1978	
	Obs'd.	Exp'd.	Obs'd.	Exp'd.	Obs'd.	Exp'd.
Increase production; solve immediate production problems (90, 72, 23)	23	19.8	36	29.3	7	2.0
Develop qualified human resources (48, 55, 76)	22	10.5**	42	22.4**	4	6.7
Serve the advancement of science and technology (44, 17, 56)	7	9.7	5	6.9	3	4.9
Economic development; creation of a strong country (22, 40, 64)	7	4.8	9	16.3*	0	5.6*
Increase agricultural production (15, 42, 4)	9	3.3*	24	24.8	1	0.9
Create people who are both "red and expert" (8, 5, 17)	3	1.8	3	2.0	3	1.5

*$p < .05$ **$p < .01$

Note: Figures in parentheses refer to the number of paragraphs in 1971, 1975, and 1978, respectively, that contain at least one reference to a particular goal. Nontraditional schools were referred to in 83, 125, and 29 paragraphs, respectively.

goal of increasing production and solving immediate production problems. Thus, this result is consistent with the image of traditional schools contributing to goals that are somehow outside or beyond a concern with skills that are immediately applicable to production.

Turning to 1978, a fundamental shift is evident in the fact that the goal of developing qualified human resources occurs together with <u>traditional</u> schools much more than would be expected on the basis of chance. (In 1971 and 1975, this goal had been strongly associated with the nontraditional schools.) The change should be seen in the context of other changes in higher education policy in the post-Gang of Four period, including the renewed emphasis on traditional schools, the downplaying--if not downgrading--of the nontraditional schools, and the central role attached to technical expertise in achieveing the Four Modernizations. The press argued that for scientists and technicians, the "road was long, the responsibility heavy" (<u>dao yuan, ren zhong</u>). It seems clear that a rather higher level of technical expertise was implied in the term "qualified human resources" in 1978 than earlier.

Nontraditional schools continued to be seen as places where the goal of increasing production and solving immediate production problems could be served. However, not a single reference to the more general and abstract goal of economic development occurred together with a reference to nontraditional schools in the 1978 data.

POLITICAL-IDEOLOGICAL GOALS OF HIGHER EDUCATION

Education has been expected to contribute to a wide range of political-ideological goals as well as economic goals in mainland China, but the salience of the political-ideological goals has varied a great deal from one period to another. This variation in concern with political-ideological goals is reflected in the data in Table 7.5. What is immediately apparent is that most of the political-ideological concerns of 1971 and 1975 were mentioned very seldom, if at all, in 1978. Only the goals of transforming students'

Table 7.5. Types of political-ideological goals of higher education mentioned in People's Daily, by year

Political-Ideological Goals	Rate of Reference Per 1,000 Sentences of Text Coded			% of Articles Referring Once or More to Each Goal		
	1971	1975	1978	1971	1975	1978
Transform students' consciousness	59	105	25	65	92	25
Restrict the influence of capitalists and their thought	25	33	0	34	44	0
Increase the power of workers	23	27	0	34	23	0
Serve the socialist revolution	21	23	20	31	44	36
Promote class struggle	16	30	0	52	44	0
Consolidate the dictatorship of the proletariat	14	62	3	31	67	8
(Criticism of) seeking personal career advancement	9	24	0	38	31	0
Increase the power of the laboring people (laodong renmin)	12	11	4	31	13	8
Increase the power of peasants	2	8	0	7	13	0
Graduates spread political ideology	2	14	0	10	31	0
N of sentences coded	1,698	1,480	1,360			
N of articles coded				29	39	36

consciousness and serving the socialist revolution were mentioned with any appreciable frequency in 1978, and both of these goals are sufficiently vague to permit widely varying interpretations.

Another clear pattern in the yearly rates of reference to political-ideological goals is that many of them appear much more often in 1975 than in 1971. Items related to the general issues of class conflict and class struggle appear with great frequency in 1975, with somewhat lesser frequency in 1971, and virtually not at all in 1978. Transforming students' consciousness was the goal most often mentioned in People's Daily in all three years, but the intensity of concern with this goal was clearly greatest in 1975 and least in 1978.

Several of the remaining political-ideological goals seem to be interrelated, and the cluster around the general issue of conflict between the "bourgeoisie" and the "proletariat." Schwartz (1970) has suggested that the Maoists among the central leaders tended to use the phrase "dictatorship of the proletariat" to designate the dominance of the forces of good over the forces of evil. Proletarian virtues of selflessness and total commitment to the collectivity, austerity, and so on are not necessarily connected with particular class bases; rather, they can be developed in anyone. Likewise, "bourgeois" values can develop anywhere, including in the Party and the proletariat.

In 1975, there was an intense campaign to consolidate the dictatorship of the proletariat, meaning that people who personified the proletarian virtues should monopolize positions of power in the society. The corollaries of this emphasis on the dictatorship of the proletariat were an increased concern with the imagery of class struggle and with the need to restrict the influence of capitalists and of capitalist thought. A related item has to do with criticisms in the press of young people who seek higher education primarily to benefit themselves rather than to "serve the people." This concern was much more common in 1975 than in 1971. Part of the increase in concern with this issue is probably due to the fact that there were few graduates of the newly reopened colleges and universities in 1971 while in 1975 there were many. Thus, many students were finding out in concrete terms what kinds of futures their schools could allocate them to.

It should be pointed out that college and university students were selected through the recommendation process rather than competitive examinations during the early and mid-1970s. Thus, their levels of ideological awareness and commitment, their political behavior, and their class backgrounds should have played a large part in their selection. It is perhaps a testament to the corrosive nature of higher education that these students had to be reminded in 1975 that seeking self-advancement through higher education was illegitimate. In both 1971 and 1975, People's Daily articles about higher education referred to the goal of increasing the power of factory workers vis-à-vis technicians and technical experts. This is another facet of the Cultural Revolutionary Left's attacks on professional credentials and cultural capital acquired through higher education.

In general, then, articles about higher education in People's Daily contained a much wider range of political-ideological goals in 1971 and 1975 than in 1978. Further, the concern with these political-ideological issues was considerably more intense in 1975 than in 1971, which probably reflects the fact that the Cultural Revolution reforms in education were being vigorously criticized in many quarters. For example, Zhou Rongxin had been appointed education minister early in the year, and he made numerous speeches condemning the Cultural Revolution reforms and calling for their abolition (Gardner 1977). The Cultural Revolutionary Left then used its control over the central media to launch a counterattack against "right deviationist efforts to reverse correct verdicts." Many of the themes of this counterattack are reflected in the data for 1975 in Table 7.5.

To what extent are these different political-ideological goals associated with one or another of the school types? Put differently, how similar are the charters of traditional and nontraditional schools in terms of the political-ideological goals of higher education? Tables 7.6 and 7.7 present

Table 7.6. Traditional schools by the political-ideological goals of higher education (observed and expected frequencies of co-occurrence), by year

Political-Ideological Goals	1971		1975		1978	
	Obs'd.	Exp'd.	Obs'd.	Exp'd.	Obs'd.	Exp'd.
Transform students' consciousness (66, 99, 27)	4	6.1	22	26.1	1	5.9*
Serve the socialist revolution (30, 29, 22)	1	2.8	6	7.6	2	4.8
Restrict the influence of capitalists and their thought (29, 38, 0)	2	2.7	12	10.0		
Increase the power of workers (27, 22, 0)	0	2.5	3	5.8		
Promote class struggle (24, 36, 0)	2	2.2	6	9.5		
Consolidate the dictatorship of the proletariat (22, 71, 4)	3	2.0	25	18.7	1	0.8
(Criticism of) seeking personal career advancement (13, 26, 0)	1	1.2	10	6.9		

*$p < .05$

Note: Figures in parentheses refer to the number of paragraphs in 1971, 1975, and 1978, respectively, that contain at least one reference to a particular goal. Traditional schools were referred to in 35, 81, and 72 paragraphs, respectively.

Table 7.7. Nontraditional schools by the political-ideological goals of higher education (observed and expected frequencies of co-occurrence), by year

Political-Ideological Goals	1971 Obs'd.	1971 Exp'd.	1975 Obs'd.	1975 Exp'd.	1978 Obs'd.	1978 Exp'd.
Transform students' consciousness (66, 99, 27)	17	14.5	32	40.3*	1	2.4
Serve the socialist revolution (30, 29, 22)	10	6.6	9	11.8	0	1.9
Restrict the influence of capitalists and their thought (29, 38, 0)	6	6.4	7	15.5*		
Increase the power of workers (27, 22, 0)	10	5.9	13	8.9		
Promote class struggle (24, 36, 0)	5	5.3	12	14.7		
Consolidate the dictatorship of the proletariat (22, 71, 4)	3	4.8	22	28.9*	0	0.4
(Criticism of) seeking personal career advancement (13, 26, 0)	1	2.8	5	10.6*		

*$p < .05$

Note: Figures in parentheses refer to the number of paragraphs in 1971, 1975, and 1978, respectively, that contain at least one reference to a particular goal. Nontraditional schools were referred to in 83, 125, and 29 paragraphs, respectively.

the observed and expected frequencies of co-occurrence of references to the school types and the political-ideological goals of education.

For 1971, there are no pronounced patterns of association of these goals with either the traditional or the nontraditional schools. The most that can be said is that the goals of transforming students' consciousness, of serving the socialist revolution, and of increasing the power of workers occur together with references to nontraditional schools somewhat more than expected, but the differences do not achieve statistical significance.

For 1975, the interrelated items of transforming students' consciousness, consolidating the dictatorship of the proletariat, restricting the influence of capitalists and their thought, and criticism of seeking higher education for personal career advancement all occur together with nontraditional schools significantly less than would be expected on the basis of chance. At the same time, there are mild tendencies for most of these items to occur more than expected with the traditional schools.

This pattern of results for 1975 suggests that the Cultural Revolutionary Left saw the traditional schools, but not the nontraditional schools, as the places where the conflict between "proletarian" and "capitalist" world views was most acute. The patterns of results for both the economic and the political-ideological goals of higher education support the view that the traditional schools were chartered to allocate students to the kinds of futures that could be considered "social advancement" while the nontraditional schools were not. The Cultural Revolutionary Left apparently believed that the traditional schools represented the greatest threat to its vision of China's future. The "authoritativeness of knowledge" (to use Meyer's term [1977]) had to be held in check and subordinated to proletarian virtue.

By 1978, of course, the Gang of Four had been swept from power, and most of the Cultural Revolution reforms in education had been reversed. The press continued to refer occasionally to the need to transform students' consciousness and to the importance of serving the socialist revolution, but references to other political-ideological goals were very infrequent. The 1978 articles sampled did not contain a single negative comment about seeking higher education for personal career advancement, and references to the imagery of class struggle were notably absent. The relatively few references to political-ideological goals tended not to occur in the same paragraphs with references to either traditional or nontraditional schools.

STUDENT BACKGROUNDS AND THE SCHOOLS

Meyer (1977) argued that students have at least a general idea of the kinds of futures to which their schools are chartered to allocate them and through anticipatory socialization, they tend to adopt attitudes and self-concepts that are appropriate to their probable futures. Bowles (1977) and others have suggested that young people tend to be channeled into different levels of stratified educational systems depending on their social origins and that the schools reinforce class subcultures learned in the home. Upon graduation, students move into the occupational structure at levels that generally correspond to their origins.

It is clear that traditional and nontraditional schools in mainland China have rather different--if overlapping--charters in terms of the goals to which they are intended to contribute and the levels of the occupational structure to which they can allocate their students. The question that remains is, To what extent are students distributed among traditional and nontraditional schools according to their social origins? People's Daily articles about education provide very limited data about the background characteristics of students, but Table 7.8 shows the frequencies with which students were referred to as being from a worker background, a peasant background, or a "worker-peasant-soldier" (gong-nong-bing) background or as being "educated youth."

Again, 1971 and 1975 seem very different from 1978. During the early and mid-1970s, the

Table 7.8. Types of student backgrounds mentioned in People's Daily, by year

Student Type	Rate of Reference per 1,000 Sentences of Text Coded			% of Articles Referring Once or More to Each Type		
	1971	1975	1978	1971	1975	1978
Worker	52	59	4	38	46	11
"Worker-peasant-soldier"	41	20	2	48	23	6
Peasant	11	31	2	24	51	8
Educated youth	1	21	6	3	21	14
N of sentences coded	1,698	1,480	1,360			
N of articles coded				29	39	36

Cultural Revolutionary Left was committed to increasing the numbers of students in colleges and universities who were from the urban lower classes and the peasantry, and standardized entrance examinations were abandoned in favor of the recommendation model of student recruitment. Students had to have worked in a factory or a commune for two or more years and to have the recommendations of their local work and Party units. Measures of academic ability or achievement such as school grades or examination scores carried little weight in the selection process.

The data in Table 7.8 would seem to support the contention that young people of proletarian backgrounds enjoyed greater access to higher educational opportunities in the early and mid-1970s than at the end of the decade. However, the classifications of students are potentially misleading because of the practice of reclassifying as workers or as peasants young people from urban areas who had spent two or more years in factories or on communes as part of the rustication program.

It is also difficult to say to whom the appellation of worker-peasant-soldier student is applied. This is clearly a normative designation that reflects the Cultural Revolutionary Left's commitment to increased opportunities for proletarian young people. But such a catchall category can hide a multitude of divergences from official prescriptions. The most probable of these divergences is the large-scale use of influence by cadres to have their own or their friends' children recalled from the countryside and assigned to colleges and universities. Kent (1981) estimates that "almost all" of the students in one teachers' college in 1975 were the children of cadres, and the Chinese press was full of accounts in the mid-1970s of cadres "going by the back door." Several writers have suggested that while the recommendation process was intended to benefit the children of worker and peasant backgrounds, it operated primarily to the benefit of cadres and their families (see, for example, Bratton 1979; Shirk 1979).

This phenomenon was the topic of a satirical play, <u>If I Really Were</u> (<u>Jiaru wo shi zhende</u>), which was performed in Shanghai in the late 1970s and subsequently banned. In it, a rusticated youth nearly succeeds in having himself recalled from his miserable village life by pretending to be the son of a Central Committee member. His deception is discovered, and he winds up in a lot of trouble, but he questions what the outcome would have been "if he really were" what he had pretended to be.

Li Xiaozhang, the protagonist of the play, would be considered an educated youth, that is, an urban youth who had been rusticated upon graduation from lower or higher middle school. By the middle of the 1970s, well over 10 million urban youths had been transferred to rural villages or state farms (see, for example, Bernstein 1977), and only a small proportion of them had any chance of returning legally to the cities for employment or further education. Large numbers of educated youth returned to the cities illegally, however, and serious problems of delinquency and unemployment resulted. There were numerous problems with the program in the rural villages as well, and these mounting problems probably account for the increased official attention to educated youth in 1975 that is reflected in Table 7.8.

Table 7.9 shows the extent to which these different student types tend to co-occur with traditional and nontraditional higher education institutions. For 1971, both workers and peasants are mentioned together with nontraditional schools significantly more often than would be expected on the basis of chance alone. Worker-peasant-soldier students, on the other hand, were mentioned significantly more often in the context of traditional schools.

For 1975, workers are again strongly associated with the nontraditional schools, but peasants are referred to significantly more often than expected in the context of traditional schools. This result is due primarily to the great number of references to agricultural universities in 1975; of the eighteen paragraphs referring both to traditional schools and to peasants, twelve of the cases involve agricultural schools.

Worker-peasant-soldier students were mentioned in conjunction with traditional schools only

Table 7.9. Student backgrounds by school types, by year

Student Type	1971				1975			
	Trad'l.		Nontrad'l.		Trad'l.		Nontrad'l.	
	Obs'd.	Exp'd.	Obs'd.	Exp'd.	Obs'd.	Exp'd.	Obs'd.	Exp'd.
Worker (55, 49)	6	5.1	24	12.1*	9	12.9	41	19.9**
"Worker-peasant-soldier" (44, 25)	12	4.1*	5	9.7	8	6.6	2	10.2**
Peasant (13, 32)	2	1.2	8	2.8*	18	8.4**	14	13.0
Educated youth (--, 18)					5	4.7	16	6.7**

*$p < .05$ **$p < .01$

Note: Figures in parentheses refer to the number of paragraphs in 1971 and 1975, respectively, that contain at least one reference to a particular student type. Traditional schools were referred to in 35 and 81 paragraphs, and nontraditional schools were referred to in 83 and 125 paragraphs, respectively.

slightly more than expected in 1975, but they were mentioned in conjunction with nontraditional schools a great deal less than expected on the basis of chance. Whatever the actual composition of the worker-peasant-soldier student body, collectively they were clearly the winners in the competition--as a result of the recommendation process--for the scarce places in China's traditional higher education institutions in the early and mid-1970s. This group probably did include substantial numbers of genuine workers, peasants, and soldiers, but it seems likely that the major beneficiaries of the recommendation process were the children of China's political elite. They may have participated in the rustication program along with other urban youths, but they had the good class background and the connections to get themselves recalled after a few years in the countryside.

On the other side of the coin, the educated youth were clearly the losers in the competition for college and university spaces. Although others were recalled to the cities, they were expected to put down roots in the countryside. The central authorities sought to quench their thirst for further education with correspondence courses in Mao thought, rural electrification, and the like.

In 1978 there were very few references to any of these student types in People's Daily articles about higher education. The post-Gang of Four regime moved rapidly to restore standardized examinations as the most important criterion (but by no means the only one) in the student selection process. The press freely admitted that the numbers of students from worker and peasant backgrounds had declined and suggested that this was true because education at home had taken on added importance because of the Gang of Four's disruption of the schools. Under these circumstances, young people from well-educated, usually urban, families had a decided advantage on the admissions examinations. Because intellectuals were redefined to be "part of the working class," however, the regime could still claim that a very high proportion of college and university students were from proletarian backgrounds. In 1978, then, the central leaders clearly saw distinct economic roles for the traditional and the nontraditional schools, and they offered a meritocratic ideology to legitimize the distribution of students between these two kinds of schools.

CONCLUSION

This chapter has examined the social charters of traditional and nontraditional higher education institutions in mainland China at three different times during the 1970s. During the early and mid-1970s, the Cultural Revolutionary Left proclaimed its desire to create a unified higher education system based on the part-work, part-study model, and it implemented (or tried to implement) a number of changes in the higher education system to make the traditional schools less elitist and more similar to the nontraditional ones and to raise the standing of the nontraditional schools.

Despite these attempts, however, it seems clear that the writers for People's Daily continued to perceive that these kinds of schools were fundamentally different in terms of the societal goals they were intended to serve and in terms of the levels of the occupational structure to which they could allocate their graduates.

The fundamental Maoist mistrust of "authoritativeness" based on high-level educational credentials is reflected in the fact that many of the political-ideological concerns I have discussed were focused on the traditional schools in 1971 and especially 1975 while the economic mission of the traditional schools was less clearly defined than that of the nontraditional schools.

This chapter began with a discussion of John Meyer's view that education functions most generally as a system of legitimation. A "modern" educational system had been developing in China for about a century when the Cultural Revolution began, but during the Cultural Revolution decade, the legitimacy of the traditional schools was attacked on several fronts. Since the overthrow of the Gang of Four in 1976, however, China's central leaders have done everything they can to restore the prestige and the legitimating functions of the traditional higher education institutions. Experts are accorded a central place in the achievement of the Four Modernizations, and "authoritative knowledge" is not viewed by the current leadership as a threat to the revolution.

Both the traditional and the nontraditional schools are perceived by the current leadership to have important, although different, economic functions to perform. Their charters are well defined and probably widely socially accepted. The issue that seems likely to recur in mainland China is the one of access to educational opportunities in the traditional schools. The emphasis on selflessness that was a central part of proletarian virtue was greatly eroded in the 1970s, and as striving to improve one's own social standing becomes more acceptable, students who fail in the competitive entrance examinations may, rather than blaming their own individual weaknesses, raise a new round of challenges to the fairness of the examinations.

REFERENCES

Bernstein, Thomas P. "Urban Youth in the Countryside: Problems of Adaptation and Remedies." China Quarterly 69 (March 1977), pp. 75-108.

Bowles, Samuel. "Unequal Education and the Reproduction of the Social Division of Labor." In Jerome Karabel and A. H. Halsey, eds., Power and Ideology in Education, pp. 137-153. New York: Oxford University Press, 1977.

Bratton, Dale. "University Admissions Policies in China, 1970-1978." Asian Survey 19:10 (October 1979), pp. 1008-1022.

Collins, Randall. "Some Comparative Principles of Educational Stratification." Harvard Educational Review 47 (February 1977), pp. 1-27.

Dore, Ronald P. The Diploma Disease. London: Allen and Unwin, 1976; Berkeley: University of California Press, 1976.

Gardner, John. "Chou Jung-hsin and Chinese Education." Current Scene 15:11-12 (1977), pp. 1-14.

Karabel, Jerome. "Community Colleges and Social Stratification: Submerged Class Conflict in American Higher Education." *Harvard Educational Review* 42 (November 1972), pp. 521-562.

Kelley, Jonathan, and Herbert S. Klein. "Revolution and the Rebirth of Inequality: A Theory of Stratification in Postrevolutionary Society." *American Journal of Sociology* 83:1 (1977), pp. 78-99.

Kent, Ann. "Red and Expert: The Revolution in Education at Shanghai Teacher's University, 1975-76." *China Quarterly* 86 (June 1981), pp. 304-321.

Meyer, John. "The Effects of Education as an Institution." *American Journal of Sociology* 83:1 (July 1977), pp. 55-77.

Schwartz, Benjamin. *Communism and China: Ideology in Flux*. New York: Atheneum, 1970.

Shirk, Susan. "Educational Reform and Political Backlash: Recent Changes in Chinese Education Policy." *Comparative Education Review* 23:2 (June 1979), pp. 183-217.

Simmons, John. "Education for Development Reconsidered." *World Development* 7 (1979), pp. 1005-1016.

Unger, Jonathan. *Education Under Mao: Class and Competition in Canton Schools, 1960-1980*. New York: Columbia University Press, 1982.

8
Chinese Intellectuals and Party Policy

Lynn T. White III

Intellectuals can happily exist without any government policy. They easily make their own "policies" toward officials. Their occupation is to try, in their heads, rearrangements of traits to see things that are potential in nature and personalities, not just society.[1] Governments lay a claim on them, but their interests are broader.

A Chinese philosophical tradition nonetheless holds that "the truly great is he who is capable of rectifying what is wrong with the ruler's heart." A Western one holds that rational thinking in politics is a peculiarly human thing to do.[2] Neither of these traditions makes ideas subject to politics. If anything, they do the reverse. As the <u>Analects</u> say, "The scholar is not a tool."[3]

China's past has bequeathed its intellectuals, for better or worse, a special relationship to government. One of several diverse Chinese trends of thought (the Confucian one) was so successful in preaching behavior that its tenets informed a relatively stable and predictable bureaucracy for centuries, even as rulers and dynasties came and went.

China developed public tests for identifying people who were especially adept at comparing mental forms, who were good at ideas. The tests checked their expertise mainly in a specific body of ethical thought but were general enough to provide some index of their agility in juggling other symbols too. Tensions in the official ideology lent it flexibility,[4] and its increasing prestige over time created for Chinese intellectuals a political price, and task, that were unique in the world, for mere scholars. Intellectuals have not been so credited with the survival of any other large polity, and no other has lasted so long. China's heritage is a burden for both rulers and thinkers.

DEFINITIONS AND PROJECT

This chapter aims to give an overview of recent Chinese Communist Party (CCP) policies toward intellectuals. The definition of intellectuals (zhishi fenzi) is problematic. A Communist Shanghai dictionary defines them vaguely as "People who have a relatively high level of culture."[5] In the current vernacular of the PRC, the term refers to any school-leaver. But in times of radical campaigns, when intellectuals have been in political disrepute, school-leavers of a proletarian origin have declined the title. Occasional usage restricts the term "intellectuals" to high-level scientists, journalists, professors, and artists.[6]

There have been elaborate official efforts to define "high-level intellectuals" (gaoji zhishih fenzi),[7] but the most realistic statement admits there is "no fine line" between particularly expert thinkers and other educated people.[8] The 1982 census shows that only six-tenths of 1 percent of the PRC's population has ever attended college, and the census counts nearly a quarter of the population--23.5 percent--as "illiterate."[9] The Chinese intelligentsia might include more than the university graduates, and it would hardly include the illiterates. As for the large group in between, their inclusion would depend on whether they use mainly their brains or their brawn. An article in Red Flag, the Party's theoretical journal, estimates that China now has 25 million intellectuals--although it does not specify how that number was determined.[10] The most practical approach is to emphasize the distinctive activity of thinkers: their symbol juggling.

This chapter covers four main topics. First,

it looks at the recent history of China's thinkers. The intellectuals' personal backgrounds during the Cultural Revolution, the Anti-Rightist movement, and the wars of the 1930s and 1940s all deeply condition their attitudes now. Second, it discusses the living and working conditions of intellectuals in recent years: their housing, income, and most important, the extent to which they have or lack the freedom to find and communicate knowledge in their fields. Third, it examines the general legitimacy or illegitimacy of intellectuals in PRC society. This topic is the broadest one, and it pervades all sections of the chapter, but particular analysis of it is possible by looking at the 1981 resolution on Party history. Fourth, the recent Spiritual Pollution Campaign is explored because of the light it throws on tensions in CCP definitions of proper and improper thinking.

MODERN BACKGROUND

To ask what is the government's policy toward intellectuals? is really to ask what one group of intellectuals thinks of another--because some of them are officials. Although I will focus here on recent policies, these cannot be understood without considering the hopes and fears of the same people (both governmentalists and independents) since their youth. There is no realistic way to treat this subject without a quick historical summary.

The Chinese Communists began as visionaries during the May 4 movement after 1919. They were a group of urban intellectuals whose theoretical interests in social problems and organizational forms developed especially in large cities during the 1920s. This experience was essential to their later successes elsewhere.[11]

During Chiang Kai-shek's campaigns against the CCP, which forced the Long March, the Party almost vanished. From 1934 to 1936, its membership fell ten times,[12] and the number of Party intellectuals also decreased. Student uprisings against concessions to Japan soon reversed this trend, and the "December 9 generation" contained many people who sympathized with the CCP. (Much later, during the 1957 Anti-Rightist movement and the 1966-1968 Cultural Revolution, many December 9 intellectuals became the object of severe attack.)[13]

Communist leaders fancied the idea that philosophy should swirl from the dusty caves of Shensi, and ex-schoolteacher Mao Zedong liked to phrase political and military policies in grand theoretical terms. By 1939, as some Chinese intellectuals fled to Yenan from cities Japan had seized, the Central Committee resolved to absorb them into CCP work and to instill them with the "viewpoint of the people" so they could "get along with the veterans."[14] A rectification movement, culminating in 1942, was partly aimed at intellectuals, and it provided a context for Mao's Yenan Forum on Literature and Art. The teacher-Chairman insisted that the main job of people who work with their brains is to support socialism, the wave of the future--and thus to support the CCP.[15]

Intellectuals educated from the mid-1930s to 1949, during the years of foreign attack and then civil war, naturally wanted to strengthen and unify China. Some opposed the Kuomintang at that time, but knowing that the Communists were illiberal, they hoped they could act as a "loyal opposition" in a socialist regime.[16] The pre-1949 background of the current senior Chinese intellectuals involved sharp early patriotism and sharp political frustration. There is no space in this chapter to provide details, but this background made the later CCP attack on intellectuals even more painful. This history made the intellectuals doubt their own past political wisdom, not just their stances on issues for which they were criticized.

After 1949, the war in Korea gave the Communists an unexpected opportunity to mobilize the services of many urban intellectuals whose capitalist or landlord class backgrounds often inclined them against the Party. Communist plans to amalgamate universities, schools, newspapers, and hospitals--and to insist on conformity in all expression--received a tremendous boost from patriotic propaganda about Chinese deaths in

Korea. Much was made of the alleged danger to China's integrity that was posed by the approach of the U.S. Army. This situation (and the accompanying campaigns to define corruption more strictly among businessmen and bureaucrats, to control inflation, and to clean up the cities) allowed the Party to recruit a much broader spectrum of urban intellectuals to its cause than it had reached before.[17]

Dissidents also suffered more severe repression during and after the Korean War. Campaigns against urban counterrevolutionaries increasingly focused not on secret society leaders, who were mostly true-blue proletarians, but on dissenting thinkers. For example, the 1955 attack on the writer Hu Feng was indistinguishable from the general campaign to eliminate counter-revolutionaries at that time.[18] Coercion alone could not, however, serve all CCP goals.

By 1956, the Party had moved to more systematic planning for intellectuals. That year saw many policies which reappeared in the late 1970s: Local "two-year plans" established time limits for the completion of intellectual tasks. Libraries were slightly improved, political study sessions for intellectuals were supposed to be fewer, and some Party memberships were offered to distinguished scientists and academics.[19] "Liberal" 1956 saw more efforts to keep track of intellectuals and encourage their contributions to the socialist society.[20] The 1956 resemblances to present policies are numerous enough to raise questions about how much basic change there has been since that time.

The 1957 denouement--the Hundred Flowers Campaign and then the Anti-Rightist movement--created keen distrust of the Party, which was so severe that it lasts until now. This chapter is hardly the place to attempt to detail the Hundred Flowers Campaign,[21] but liberal intellectuals' later political expression was sharply constrained by their feeling that the Party betrayed them in 1957. It had promised safe conduct through a period of criticizing bureaucrats, but it reneged on that promise. A few wary protesters had said: "We fear someone will be writing things down." "Some people may pervert the truth." "We could air our views, but of course it would have no effect."[22] Shi Hui, a movie director, was coaxed into nothing more than the logically elegant assertion, "Only lies are safe."[23] The CCP has attempted mobilization movements for intellectuals in later years, but the slogan, Let a hundred flowers bloom; let a hundred schools of thought contend--though resurrected several times since 1957--has never again made that garden grow.

After the Anti-Rightist movement, CCP policy continued to fluctuate, but it was no longer safe for anybody to advertise "loyal opposition." Intellectuals who refused to support the Party in 1957 were labeled "rightists" (and the vast majority of all rightists in China were intellectuals).

In the mass propaganda of the early Great Leap Forward, intellectuals were less particular objects of attack than they had been during the Anti-Rightist movement. Much of the Communist and non-Communist elite of urban China was ordered to decamp to market cities, smaller offices, or more rural places after the traumas of the Hundred Flowers and antirightist criticisms. This situation created an administrative infrastructure for decentralization to the middle levels, which was the essence of the Great Leap.[24] College graduates, like activists and Party members, were among the first groups to be "sent down" during this campaign,[25] and most non-CCP rightists stayed in the villages much longer, on average, than Party members did. Some intellectuals with the rightist stigma became permanent peasants.

Intellectuals in the urban areas were also required to aid the leap for communism: A writers' group vowed to produce "1,000 original literary works and 1,500 lyrics for songs" in the following two years. A theater promised to create sixty-eight new plays and to act them all over the countryside. A film director thought a high Party official's "recommendation" that he do thirty-five films was "exciting"--even though he lacked enough good scripts. As officials reminded him, "This was chiefly due to his not having brought the matter up for discussion with the masses."[26]

By 1961, when this age of heroism had ended

in economic depression, the Party decided it was time to implement a policy of letting one hundred flowers blossom together and one hundred schools of thought contend. The tension among Party intellectuals (centering on criticisms of Mao through praise of the Ming figure Hai Rui) was real enough, and it has been well documented.[27] But non-CCP intellectuals, who might well have faulted the skips of the Great Leap, were sent into required seminars with set-piece topics according to discipline: Biologists discussed genetics; economists debated how one might best explain the imminent collapse of the U.S. economy; historians contended about the Three Kingdoms figure Cao Cao (rather than anybody Ming); and newspapers "took responsibility for promoting contention" about Cao Cao.[28] The early 1960s, even after the depression ended, were years of general reticence among non-CCP intellectuals. Many still were rightists.

During the Cultural Revolution, intellectuals became the "stinking old ninth" (chou lao jiu) category among class enemies. Teachers and journalists suffered badly during the first months of the mass movement, in the spring and summer of 1966. Party officials then knew some group had to be criticized--but they did not yet know it was to be themselves. Not only were thinkers condemned, thinking was too. Research and creativity with symbols became objects of scorn in official propaganda, and intellectual activities were said to offer "a refuge for those who refuse to dirty their hands."[29] Propagandists tried, in effect, to redefine the meaning of intelligence itself. A Chinese student was expelled from the People's University for having ideas like these:

> Chinese education and re-education are. . . not to uplift a man in spirit, but to suppress him, to make him dumb and humble. . . . [Its products] cannot be described as intellectuals, for they don't know how to think. They cannot do the country much good, but are quite capable of putting down those who think. . . . At meetings, they have but to rehearse the same phrases, trembling for

> some slip of the tongue. What a dulling exercise! . . . We have to go over a small article five or even ten times, until we feel stupid, repeating every sentence over and over again.[30]

In this chapter, I cannot hope to do justice to the Cultural Revolution's treatment of intellectuals;[31] a single example will have to suffice. One of the most egregious attacks on an intellectual during the Cultural Revolution was against the famous writer Lao She. During a raid on his house, as youths were burning his books and trying to force him to help throw tomes on the fire, his wife got into a fight with them. Lao She attempted to protect her and was involved in scuffling. He reportedly took his own life during the Red Guards' presence in his house.[32]

Despite the sharpness of the Cultural Revolution, its principles were not entirely novel. The Anti-Rightist movement of 1957 had set the tone, which was heightened and brought to a conclusion in the Cultural Revolution. Even more people were then named rightists, schools and universities were disrupted even more severely and for longer periods, and by the time the Gang of Four finally fell, many Chinese intellectuals' will to serve their country had been sapped by years of personal vilification. Practically everyone now agrees that too much talent and too many years were wasted.

Among urban Chinese college graduates, according to a careful estimate, 11 percent had been legally sentenced and punished by law for political errors by the mid-1970s, and fully 33 percent had been criticized in public. Among all high professionals, 11 percent had been sentenced and punished, and twice as many had been criticized.[33] These proportions are much greater than in China's population as a whole, and since they refer only to formal, officially sanctioned acts against the persons involved, it is certain that many more Chinese intellectuals were hurt and constrained by fear in the CCP campaigns before Mao's death. All these movements, especially the Cultural Revolution, affected most Chinese thinkers, not just a few.

In this context, an intellectual tended to seek close friends whom he could trust and from whom he could acquire the political information necessary for self-protection.[34] The situation forced intellectuals to restrict their frankness to very small networks of trusted friends, and their will to aid all of China and to participate in public life, which had been evident before the severe campaigns and before mid-century, was largely overwhelmed by the official attacks.

THE PARTY'S NEED TO REMOBILIZE INTELLECTUALS

Although CCP policies toward intellectuals have fluctuated since Mao's death, the Party's general aim has been to rekindle their enthusiasm so that socialist China might have their services. Hesitancies in implementing this goal have been numerous, but the old mid-1950s' hope that useful thinkers could be good Communists has seen a renaissance in the post-Mao years.

I shall treat different kinds of policies separately. First, the removal of rightist labels has been essential to any further Party dealings with thinkers. Many intellectuals, long publicly insulted, came to feel their social legitimacy (and that of their activities and institutions) was as important as their social effect. The campaigns had contracted their interests, and it would be unrealistic to talk about larger ideals before discussing the removal of rightist labels. Second, the intellectuals' current living conditions, housing, and income are important to examine. Third, it is necessary to see how jobs are allocated to intellectuals and the extent to which they have or lack academic freedom to do their work.

I shall pay more attention to professors and scientists than to writers and artists, mostly because Hsüan Mo has recently provided a fine summary on CCP policies toward literature and art.[35] My focus will be the extent to which the Party allows intellectuals to get on with their inherent tasks.

THE INTELLECTUALS' STIGMA

Removing rightist labels has, since 1957, been necessary to any serious CCP policy toward intellectuals--but there is evidence that many mid-level Party bureaucrats still feel threatened by ex-rightist intellectuals in the same units. The bureaucrats must be ordered by high leaders to come to terms with the thinkers they know best. Deng Xiaoping tried to send them signals by speaking at the first session of the All-China Science Conference on March 18, 1978. Deng said, "The modernization of science and technology is the key to the Four Modernizations," and he averred that the only difference between brain workers and handworkers was the different labor roles assigned to them. Therefore, the intellectuals "were becoming" part of the proletariat, and some were already ordinary workers.[36]

The removal of labels from most, if not all, rightists had to accompany this effort to mobilize intellectuals. The number of high intellectuals who needed such labels doffed was great, but the Party was very slow to publish any procedures.[37] All sixty-three rightist high cadres in the Ministry of Public Security were rehabilitated early,[38] apparently before the means were published.

In thirty-five ministries, commissions, and special agencies of the State Council, which employed half of all "high-level intellectuals in state organs in Peking," over 90 percent of the rightists were able by 1982 to remove their noxious hats.[39] In this same group, 241 husband-wife couples were reunited, and 2,300 intellectuals received better housing.[40] Surprisingly few (244 of a nonreported total) of this group had joined the Party by 1982, but 28 percent of the "high-level scientific and technical personnel" had been admitted to leadership groups (lingdao banzi).

Over half of the 2,000 intellectuals in the Chinese Academy of Social Sciences had run into political trouble during the Anti-Rightist movement and the Cultural Revolution, and by the middle of 1979, 800 of them had been rehabilitated. Relatively few (45) rightists were still employed in the academy, but of those that were, almost all

(44) had been absolved.[41]

Interview information indicates the label-removal process had several aspects, some of them problematic. The most obvious difficulty was that many rightists died before the late-1970s' absolutions, sometimes for causes related to the political attacks against them. Their families were helped by the new procedures, but the victims themselves were not in a position to benefit.

For the living, the official papers on an ex-victim's rightism were returned to him or her, usually from the files (dang-an) of the work unit's public security branch. The ex-rightist would receive a resolution (jielun) indicating several points. It would say the victim had been incorrectly classified as a rightist, and it would assure that the preconviction salary level would be restored. Many 1979 resolutions also provided that the previous job could be assumed (provided the person was not beyond retirement age)--but later resolutions omitted this clause, because the police were reluctant to restore urban household registrations (hukou) to rightists who had spent decades in rural villages. Finally, in many cases where the local unit's Party bureaucrats had not changed since 1957, the resolution contained a sentence to the effect that the ex-victim had said or done some wrong things (even though he or she should not be called a rightist for these mistakes). The local bureaucratics badly needed such a clause lest their own earlier actions in classifying the rightists now be declared groundless.

Because of the inclusion of this last item, some presumed ex-rightists refused to sign the documents removing their labels. Taking old papers from personnel files did not completely solve the problem anyway, since copies of the resolutions were always put in the dossiers.[42] Intellectuals and their offspring could never be sure that these certifications of their previous stigma would not be held against them, if the political winds changed.

Party members who had been declared rightist (these were practically all intellectuals) were treated more leniently. Their memberships were restored. Often their wages had been reduced in

1957, but unlike non-CCP rightists, they received reimbursements (bufa gongci) for all the years of incorrect classification. This windfall, which in most cases was considerable, followed the precedent of reimbursement for bureaucrats who had suffered salary cuts during the Cultural Revolution. It allowed CCP ex-rightists and their families to live in high style, and it caused resentment among many rehabilitated non-Party rightists.[43]

Some high cadres think that "repressing academic talent is a crime" and that a "system for handling the repression of talent" is needed.[44] Others, however, think differently. Vice-Premier Bo Yibo, who is old enough to be frank, declared in a prominent speech that "some leading cadres" still do not trust (bu xinren) scientists and technicians.[45] By 1982, the State Council and CCP Central Committee had resolved that central Party and state cadres should all study under famous specialists.[46] In 1980, for example, "central leading comrades" from the CCP Secretariat and State Council were required to attend lectures on ten set topics, including "Modernization and Environmental Protection," "Space Technology and the Modernization of the National Defense," "The Role of Mathematics in Modern Construction," "The Scientific Control of Population," and "Resources and their Rational Use."[47] One stated goal was to make the cadres intellectuals (zhishi hua), but the enthusiasm of most mid-level and some high cadres for this change remained open to serious question.[48]

The legitimacy of intellectuals might also be increased if more of them were given leadership jobs. The Party's theoretical journal Red Flag has urged the bureaucracy to "select excellent talents from among intellectuals boldly,"[49] and it has been said that the leadership needs a "rational structure of intelligence" (heli de zhili jiegou) in terms of specialists, ages, educational levels, and general ability and character.[50] A few intellectuals, such as Liu Daoyu, who became president of Wuhan University at the age of forty-eight (still in his cradle by PRC standards for such posts) became models.[51]

The loud public ado greeting "young" President
Liu's inauguration should lay to rest any notion
that the tradition of geriatric leadership,
nurtured now by both the Communist and Confucian
traditions in China, is in any danger of dying.
At least Liu is a scholar, however, not just a
Party figure.

Lower-level intellectuals lost their stigma
less readily, because local cadres can still
discriminate against teachers. Reporters in
Peking continue to hear stories such as the
following from the summer of 1983:

> Liu Zhonghou was in the middle of giving
> a zoology lesson, when the door to her
> classroom swung open. The young Sichuan
> teacher found herself under attack from
> seven people wielding whips, knives, and
> sticks. After bludgeoning her unconscious,
> her assailants fled. Despite the serious-
> ness of the attack, Mrs. Liu's story was
> ignored by the police because the local
> judicial official had made it clear that
> he was not interested in the "problems"
> of intellectuals.[52]

This case came to the attention of the national
newspaper for intellectuals, Guangming ribao,
but even so, only one of the assailants was tried.

When three woman teachers were beaten up,
in Huairou County near Peking, the education
minister held an interview to make clear this was
a despicable but not isolated event. He said that
"the destruction of school property and the
insulting and beating of school employees are
phenomena that still come up all the time. . . .
Some leading departments still don't completely
pay attention to the problem; there are even some
who wink at (zongrong) or support such bad
people."[53]

When Hebei earthquake expert Liu Bingliang
was declared "antileadership" by the leaders of
his local unit, he appealed to higher levels
several times, but only after much red tape was
he relieved of this label.[54] From June 21 to
July 23, 1982, Guangming ribao received 100
letters to the editor detailing similar cases of

maltreatment,[55] and a directive in the People's Daily ordered the "conscientious solution of problems in investigating work with intellectuals."[56] Each local jurisdiction was given the outline of a report it should submit concerning these matters, and the need for such rules only highlights the continuing stigma that many local CCP cadres still attached to intellectuals.

DEGREES, TITLES, RANKS, AND
PARTY MEMBERSHIPS

One means to recruit thinkers is to educate more of them. The slow restoration of PRC universities in the 1970s was not thoroughgoing until 1978 when the entrance examination system was restored. "Key-point" universities and schools were designated (as they had been in the 1950s), and they were even slightly financed. Teaching research groups were established to write new textbooks, and curricula included more science and less politics.[57]

Communists expect relatively reliable intellectuals to come from the proletariat. The CCP thus launched a special effort to find "model workers" who might do well in university studies, even of the new, more academic sort. For the few who were found, all actions were still affirmative: The usual age restrictions on university entrance were relaxed so that the worker-matriculates could be older. Their previous grades were not quite so high as those of nonmodel-worker admittees, in these years of rigorous competition. Above all, they continued to receive their factory salaries, at full rate, as they pursued degrees.[58]

Graduate programs were restored to train higher intellectuals. Only in 1980 did the PRC government authorize the granting of graduate degrees. Before 1949, Chinese universities had done so, and many of the older intellectuals had received degrees from foreign universities. The PRC awarded no Ph.D.s or M.A.s in the 1950s, despite extensive discussion of the possibility that it might.[59] The policy statement creating a degree system had to be resolved by the Standing Committee of the National People's Congress, and it was not announced until February 14, 1980.⁶⁰ Details of the procedure for granting degrees were not made public until mid-1981 when the PRC granted its first doctorate.⁶¹ This event was not celebrated until a year later, because only then did the number of new Ph.D.s become noticeable (eighteen in the whole country!). At the same time, 15,000 students received M.A. degrees, and 320,000 became baccalaureates.⁶²

Titles, if not academic degrees, were also established in these years for engineers and scientists. Ever since Stalin, Communist states have tried to make intellectual circles into officially financed institutions, with ranks and medals and much imagining that politicians can be tasteful arbiters of thought. In late 1979, China's State Council passed temporary regulations on the proper titles of engineering and technical cadres,⁶³ and elaborate accompanying documents gave the criteria for evaluations and promotions.⁶⁴ For scientists and technicians, the first steps toward creating similar classifications were taken in mid-1980.⁶⁵ Such measures were put on the books for professors and teachers, medical doctors, journalists, agricultural technicians, and even social researchers. By 1982, the elaboration of such schemes was worthy of East Germany, at least on paper.

Lest hierarchy be unclear between people in different fields accustomed to different rank names, the People's Daily printed tables to relate titles from diverse professions. One can tell from these tables, for example, that a "high-level correspondent" (gaoji jizhe) outranks a mere "master in economics" (jingji shi), whereas an "editor" (bianji) has to give way before the correspondent, but not before the economist.⁶⁶ What these ranks did to improve thinking is unclear, but Confucius and Walter Ulbricht, from different viewpoints, would nonetheless both have been charmed.

Party membership is undoubtedly a sign of status in the PRC. Soon after 1949, and after most rectification movements, it was possible for some intellectuals to enter the Party if their class background were favorable or their skills impressive. But at other times, especially during major political campaigns, CCP membership has been very difficult for intellectuals to obtain. By 1978-1979, the Party was relatively open. High leaders, including Hu Yaobang, were concerned that the Cultural Revolution had egregiously invaded intellectuals' lives, and making Party membership available to them was one way to offer amends. The People's Daily reported that some intellectuals who had suffered during the late 1960s and early 1970s received their Party memberships too late: "only after they had made their contribution and had died."[67]

Because Party admission is a prolonged process involving consultations among at least three layers of the bureaucracy, mid-level functionaries who disliked particular intellectuals (or had had past conflicts with them) could often blackball their application for admission. As the People's Daily commented in 1983:

> The Party's policy on admitting intellectuals is far from being realized. The reality is that many intellectuals are applying for admission into the Party, and they are being refused. Under the sway of "leftism" some Party members even fear that more intellectuals in the Party will change its nature. They stubbornly hold to the view that intellectuals are working hard only for their fame and profit, and they are applying for admission into the Party out of ulterior motives.[68]

Intellectuals at lower levels lose their stigma less readily than those at high levels, because many Party leaders have local conflicts with the former. Although it has been claimed that 36 percent of intellectuals are Party members,[69] the evidence suggests that most of these are schoolteachers and that the portion of high intellectuals who are Party members is considerably less than 10 percent.[70] Even if Hu Yaobang or other Peking leaders wish to change this situation, they seem unable to do so.

INTELLECTUALS' LIVELIHOODS AND CONDITIONS OF WORK

As early as 1977, investigation groups were launched to look into the living conditions of employed intellectuals, apparently as part of the official effort to reforge links with them after the Cultural Revolution. Many published reports on these investigations have come from Peking, probably because the local organs there are subject to high bureaucrats. One group, investigating Peking secondary-school teachers, found their wages averaged only about fifty yuan per month (plus slight supplementary benefits), and at one school, teachers who had completed their own education in the early 1960s still averaged only forty-two yuan. These were all state schools; at private "people-run" (minban) institutions, the salaries are lower. The investigation group also found that teachers' housing conditions in 20 percent of the cases were "totally difficult" (shifen kunnan), and as many more were classed "ordinarily difficult" (yiban kunnan). Ten percent of the teachers were married but could find no housing.[71]

Problems of this kind were especially severe for middle-aged intellectuals (zhongnian zhishi fenzi). If they were educated during the Great Leap or Cultural Revolution, their qualifications for work were often not as high as those of older or younger cohorts, and funds to upgrade their training were generally not available.[72] According to one large survey of middle-aged intellectuals in East China, "First, their salaries are low," and they usually have to support either parents or children in the same household. In Shanghai, for example, many such families have to spend thirty or forty yuan each month on food alone. "Second, their housing is inadequate." Husband, wife, and children all must use one table, and teachers cannot begin to prepare lessons until everyone else has gone to sleep.[73] "Third, their health situation is generally not good." Fourth, they have no opportunity for further training. A spokesman said that even in Shanghai, China's most cosmopolitan city, 70 percent of the 350,000 "employed intellectuals" suffered conditions such as these.[74]

Even among high intellectuals, the situation is not much better. Some recreational facilities, formerly restricted to senior cadres, were opened to them shortly after Mao's death, and bonuses and prizes were established for academic research.[75] A 1982 survey of a number of prestigious institutions, including Qinghua University, still found many difficulties for these middle-aged intellectuals, however. At Qinghua University, 64 percent of the 2,300 instructors were between the ages of forty and fifty-five. The survey described their income and housing in terms scarcely more glowing than for the secondary teachers, and it mentioned additional problems too: Intellectuals have to spend more hours "washing clothes, shopping for food, and cooking" than the optimal use of their time for society would indicate. The report even said: "Because the burdens of middle-age intellectuals are heavy and their means of livelihood are deficient, they become exhausted and diseased so that their level of health deteriorates. In many units, the death rate (siwang lü) of middle-age intellectuals even equals or exceeds the alarming level among old people."[76]

Short of a major change in official budgeting to benefit intellectuals' institutions (a change that has not occurred) the means to solve these problems are not obvious. A recent reform to increase incomes does allow scientists to consult outside their main work organizations, sometimes on a private basis, and they are paid quite legally for such services. When the minister of labor and personnel was asked why experts did not do much consulting, despite the legalization of scientific and technical work outside employment (yeyu keji laodong), the minister indicated that bureaucrats in regular work units wrongly stopped wages or discriminated against their employees who received extra money in this way. Once again, there is obvious conflict between intellectuals and Party bosses in local units, and the central government admits it is unable to prevent such conflict.

Contract or responsibility systems, now used by peasants, became available to some intellectuals in 1983 and 1984. Arts troupes especially

are encouraged to make contracts (hetong) with
schools, factories, or other institutions to
provide performances. Among the expected benefits,
the minister of culture has not hesitated to
mention that "since state subsidies are down,
individual incomes can be up."[77] He also said
the responsibility system would "develop the
activism of performers" and would give them more
incentives to act.

Contracts are also available in academic
institutions. Professors and researchers at
Shanghai's Jiaotong University are encouraged to
hire themselves out to factories, whenever
possible,[78] but by no means does all of the revenue from such activity accrue to the individuals
who do the work. Jiaotong charges a hefty overhead (60 percent) on many contracts. Factory
technicians can also engage in consulting on the
side, and many articles have commended spare-time
jobs.[79]

Work-time cross appointments nonetheless have
come in for criticism. A survey of the institutes
in the Shanghai branch of the Chinese Academy of
Sciences during 1979 gathered information on the
cross appointments of 205 scientists. One-third
of them (67) had posts in five or more of the
institutes. These double-job (jianzhi) cadres
were concentrated in the higher echelons,
especially as institute heads or deputy heads
(more than half of whom had appointments at ten
or more institutes).[80] One problem with this
arrangement is that too much time is spent at
meetings, too little doing research.

Official efforts to improve the working
conditions of intellectuals, and especially to
improve information exchange among their groups,[81]
took the form of a campaign. Practically all the
changes, however--the increased incomes, the
encouragement of spare-time work, the slight
budgetary improvements for educational institutions, the awards and titles, the airing of
complaints about intellectuals' bad housing--
were déjà vu. These changes can also be found
in the policies of 1956 and early 1957[82]--the
characteristic of campaigns is that they end.
Many recent movements in China have restrained
intellectuals less than most other people (this

situation is particularly true of the birth control campaign,)[83] but China's thinkers have been around long enough to know their political environment can deteriorate quickly. They could once again lose their role or use (zuoyong).

SHIFTING JOBS AND "SEND-DOWN"

Livelihood benefits to intellectuals come at a price. The state, especially through university and school placement offices, still allocates all graduates to jobs, and there is no guarantee that a work assignment will be located where the graduate cares to live. By 1984, at least one university assigned employees elsewhere, without their consent.

This policy was a feature of the 1956 liberalization too. A prominent example then was the effort to move Shanghai's Jiaotong University to Xian.[84] "Democratic parties" were especially charged to organize the send-down (xiafang) of intellectuals who were part of their memberships; and in 1982, there were special efforts to encourage their rustication to distant provinces.[85] By 1983, the State Council approved a resolution to send intellectuals to poor and border areas.[86] But most sent-down intellectuals, in the early 1980s[87] as in the 1950s,[88] went to rural areas or smaller cities less far away.

Some intellectuals were also sent to help in factories, but they were not always accorded a warm reception by the managers: "Some leading comrades acknowledge the slogan that intellectuals are part of the working class, but their deep thoughts take intellectuals to be 'aliens,' and always unreliable ones at that. . . . They even take the real virtues of some intellectuals to be faults."[89]

By 1984, schools such as Shanghai's Jiaotong University had become models for sending not just graduates but also staff to other institutions. In a five-year campaign of "management reform," Jiaotong sent more than 500 professors and instructors to other places—firing them in a very nontraditional way, if they were selected but did not agree to go.[90] There was no pretense in this campaign that the intellectuals had volunteered to move. They were given a maximum of three months' salary at Jiaotong (and an offer of a job at a single other place); then their employment was ended.

In 1984, the send-down rules tightened for graduates also. The People's Daily reported openly that by March, 162 university graduates in Shanghai had refused to go to jobs outside the city. Their distribution plans (fenpei fang'an) moldered in the files of the Higher Education Bureau, and they did not leave. Since the pretense of voluntarism had long since disappeared, the bureaucrats took steps. They assured the refusers that they would never receive help in finding any other jobs. They forwarded the household registrations to neighborhood committees, and they published a list of refusers among state enterprises and asked that none be hired for a period of five years.[91] Finally, they said that "the comrades of the Higher Education Bureau hope that the units where the graduates' heads of household are employed will help do ideological work among the heads of households thoroughly, and thus support obedience to the state allocation."[92]

The renewed emphasis on official job allocation for intellectuals only apparently contradicts another trend of the past few years: a revival of procedures by which educated people can apply for jobs on their own. In 1981, the national CCP newspaper allowed that various "personnel departments can explore the establishment of organs such as 'talent companies' (rencai gongsi) and 'employment reception stations.'"[93] Job allocations, made by officials who know nothing about the fields in which they are assigning intellectuals, have caused obvious inefficiencies; so newspaper articles have suggested that either each heading cadre should get an education or (more feasibly) experts should be given power in such decisions.[94] The alternative option, involving a free market in which people can search for their own jobs has increased in legitimacy because of uncertainty that the bureaucrats could handle their task.

There were, of course, restrictions on this

policy. Intellectuals were not free to move from small cities to larger ones; they were encouraged to do the opposite.[95] The restriction on joint employment (jianzhi) might apply to some job searches launched by individuals, but the presumption against working in multiple units was relaxed--when technicians could transfer information from one to another.[96]

Pervasive conflicts between intellectuals and Party members provide one reason for the stress on transfers and the official encouragement allowance of new job applications. Since Party cadres are usually not removable from their fiefs, but intellectuals with whom they have long histories of tension cannot serve productively there, moving the technical experts elsewhere is sensible administration. Lin Mu, chief of the Scientific and Technical Cadres Bureau of the Labor Ministry, wrote a Guangming ribao article enthusiastically praising any means to bring about "rational movement" of his charges from job to job.[97] If this movement can be accomplished under the state plan, he approves it. But if free applications, decentralized hiring agencies, and even personal initiatives are necessary, that black cat might catch the mouse, too. High-level official enthusiasm for job circulation is often expressed in terms of its value for technical information exchange, but long-term personal rivals who are intellectuals and bureaucrats in the same unit often spend too much time thinking about each other rather than about their work.[98]

INTELLECTUALS' ACADEMIC FREEDOM

Although housing and income are important to Chinese intellectuals after so many years of neglect, the degree to which they can express what they think is even more important. Freedom of expression is almost prerequisite to freedom of thought, because if they can communicate intellectuals give each other ideas over time. During and after the "democracy period," November 1978 to March 1979, even official newspapers admitted this much. The Peking Daily carried an article claiming that "a socialist state cannot have 'thought crimes.'" This article quoted the PRC Constitution and supposed it to be serious--not just the clause about freedom of speech but also an article that prohibits certain activities as counterrevolutionary.[99] The newspaper said:

> The key, here, is that we must distinguish between the expression of thought (sixiang yanlun) and activity (xingwei). There is a difference between thought and activity. To explore problems, express opinions, and hold views are among the basic rights of citizens, protected by the Constitution; there is not a bit of similarity between exercising these rights and committing a crime. "Speech is the sound of the heart" (yan wei xin sheng), and speech and writing represent forms of thought.[100]

This view, though published officially, was contradicted even in 1979 by top leaders.

In 1979, an unnamed Red Flag commentator laid down four principles considered necessary to China's modernization: supporting the socialist road, the dictatorship of the proletariat, the leadership of the Communist Party, and Marxism-Leninism/Mao Zedong thought.[101] Should these principles of obedience or the principles of frank speech be the last word? Intellectuals could only guess. The more restrictive set of principles was linked to the main campaign of the time (the modernization drive), whereas the more liberal set was in the Constitution. Would the law or the campaign prevail, when they conflicted?

Intellectuals are especially interested in the freedom to pursue and publish their professional ideas. Lin Mouhan (who was purged as a counterrevolutionary in 1967 and did not reappear until a decade later as the vice-minister of culture)[102] raised three haunting questions. "First, are some themes not permitted to be written? Second, are some personalities, for example 'middle characters' [zhongjian renwu in literature], not to be described? Third, are some artistic styles, for example tragedy, not to be used."[103] Lin answered that all these things should be permitted.

His article was soon followed by another, published in the People's Daily by Zhou Yang (the most prominent CCP "literary bureaucrat" to criticize rightists before 1966),[104] saying much the same thing. As if the authorship of this article did not imply irony enough, Zhou entitled it "Three Great Movements for the Liberation of Thought." He compared the May 4 movement and the Yenan rectification campaign (which were hardly identical!) with 1979. The message to intellectuals was mixed to say the least. Even if a consistent principle could be found, Zhou was explicit to make it underlie a campaign only--it was temporary.

Even into 1980, after the 1978-1979 relaxation ended, defenses of scientific freedom appeared in print. Rights of hypothesis (jiashuo quan) were essential to the development of natural science; so social scientists asked why the same epistemology should not apply to human knowledge.[105] If one group of thinkers can make seeming mistakes that later prove fruitful, then why not another? Anemic professional discussions in China, especially among middle-aged researchers, were contrasted even in the Party's theoretical journal with livelier debates that Chinese noticed in other countries.[106]

These questions came out of the theoretical clouds when the Chinese Academy of Sciences established a Science Foundation (Kexue Jijin) that awarded grants for research. Competitive proposals arrived, and the foundation needed criteria to evaluate them. Undoubtedly because most applications were for natural science projects, the published standards could be unspecific with respect to social principles, but they were linked to modernization; so Deng's four strictures must have applied.

The foundation undertakes to support projects that (1) are relevant to modernization, (2) promise basic research, 3) may benefit various fields, (4) develop and apply new techniques, and (5) use current equipment efficiently and promote cooperation among units.[107] It is assumed that the main investigator's salary is paid by his or her work units, and previously acquired equipment cannot be charged against a grant. All in all, the formal rules are similar to those in other countries, and for scientific projects if not for social-scientific ones, the implementation is apparently also similar.

Human studies run into more problems as two policies are in conflict. One of them urges "seeking truth from facts" (<u>shishi qiushi</u>), which requires academic freedom. But Deng has added another, obedience to the Party, i.e., bureaucrats, and to socialism which officially includes some version of Mao Zedong thought. Here indeed is a contradiction: Free research must follow a preset (Marxist) truth. The situation becomes more like a mystery in the ecclesiastical sense as editorialists try to explain it. One of them, after identifying the antinomy clearly, affirms: "We can totally seek to unify it. . . . We certainly must unify these two things. We certainly can unify them."[108] Protesting too much suggests consciousness of the difficulty.

By 1984, organized intellectual life, especially in scientific work, became more planned. For research projects, decisions about allowable methods depend greatly on the personalities of the cadres in charge. More intellectuals have now been appointed to head research units,[109] but overall, work is still coordinated in ways similar to those of the 1950s. A science and technology responsibility system (<u>keji ceren zhi</u>) establishes the following principles: First, each unit--indeed, each research group and individual-- has a definite research plan to be finished within a specific time period. Second, the quantity and quality of results are to be measured and reported to the bureaucracy. Third, further work is approved mainly if its results can be used in factories or other institutions. And fourth, research groups may engage in contracts and share some of the income. This system is surely no cultural revolution--it is more bureaucratic than Communist. Like similar systems imposed in many nonmarket countries, it is designed to control rather than liberate thinking. Especially to the extent it is applied to humanistic and social studies, it most resembles the Soviet system.

THE PARTY RESOLUTION AND THE INTELLECTUALS

When the CCP put on its thinking cap to figure out, finally, what its policy toward intellectuals should be, it concluded with ambiguities. The "Resolution on Certain Questions in the History of Our Party Since the Founding of the PRC," adopted by the Sixth Plenary Session of the Eleventh Central Committee of the Party in mid-1981, did not condemn the repression of intellectuals quite unequivocally. The CCP policy pendulum has swung from relative tolerance to relative intolerance at various times during the years since 1978, but the resolution exemplifies an even more important phenomenon, the generator of these swings: the continuing ambiguity of attitudes toward intellectuals throughout this time. On a constant basis, the Party has tried both to mobilize and to control thinkers, even though these two goals are in deep conflict.

The resolution calls the rectification movement of 1942 "a tremendous success," without detailing why.[110] It says the Hundred Flowers line of 1957 was a "correct policy regarding intellectuals," but also,

> In the rectification campaign [of 1957], a handful of bourgeois rightists seized the opportunity . . . to mount a wild attack against the Party. . . . But the scope of this struggle was made far too broad, and a number of intellectuals, patriotic people, and Party cadres were unjustifiably labelled "rightists," with unfortunate consequences.[111]

The Party still views the Anti-Rightist movement as having been proper, even though it went too far--yet the new resolution's statement about that watershed experience offers no criterion to explain how far would have been far enough.

The resolution claims that many rightists had had their labels removed by the early 1960s[112] but that in September 1962, "Mao Zedong widened and absolutized the class struggle, which exists <u>only within certain limits</u> [emphasis added] in socialist society." The proper extent of those limits is never described.

By "the latter half of 1964, and early in 1965 . . . a number of literary and art works and schools of thought, and a number of representative personages in artistic, literary and academic circles were subjected to unwarranted and inordinate political criticism."[113] Here again, the resolution makes no attempt to define what degree of political criticism, if any, could have been warranted.

Regarding the Cultural Revolution, the 1981 Central Committee at first seems to be more forthright: "The criticism of the so-called reactionary academic authorities in the 'cultural revolution,' during which so many capable and accomplished intellectuals were attacked and persecuted, also badly muddled up the distinction between the people and the enemy."[114] But the resolution is far less clear whether any "enemy" with power really existed in the PRC by 1967. It says the Cultural Revolution was divorced from both the Party organizations and the masses--but this assertion is dubious in light of evidence that conservative Red Guards defending Party cadres in many units recruited members of those units' youth leagues and those cadres' families. There is also evidence that the most radical anticadre Red Guard groups contained some members with intellectual backgrounds, whose access to schools and jobs had been hindered by the Party's affirmative action programs in the early 1960s. These data suggest the Cultural Revolution was not divorced either from Party organizations or from the anticadre masses.

The resolution says, "Most of the intellectuals . . . who had been wronged and persecuted did not waiver in their love for the motherland and in their support for the Party and socialism."[115] Yet the Anti-Rightist movement of 1957 had made clear that sanctions on critics of the Party would be severe. Many intellectuals (especially the older ones) undoubtedly censored their expressions of dissent while others (especially young students) adopted the mixed view that bad Party cadres should be attacked even if the abstract symbols of the Party and its chairman were sacred.[116]

To its credit, the resolution does not wholly blame the Cultural Revolution on "Comrade Mao Zedong's mistake in leadership." It at least claims to seek broader "social and historical causes" and offers two: (1) "Class struggle" had been the Party's watchword during its previous periods of political success, and (2) international tension with the USSR encouraged Chinese protests against domestic "revisionism."[117] The first of these suggestions is debatable in view of evidence for the importance of peasant nationalism in the Party's rise.[118] The second ignores what was happening in Vietnam at that time, and it may overemphasize the potential of any foreign influence in the politics of this gigantic, inward-looking country.

The resolution is more persuasive when it generalizes from Mao's main fault ("he began to get arrogant") to the main problem in many Party units:

> Our Party . . . fostered a fine tradition of democracy in the anti-feudal struggle. It remains difficult to eliminate the evil ideological and political influence of centuries of feudal autocracy. And for various historical reasons, we failed to institutionalize and legalize inner-Party democracy and democracy in the political and social life of the country, or we drew up the relevant laws but they lacked due authority. This meant that conditions were present for the over-concentration of Party power in individuals and for the development of arbitrary individual rule and the personality cult in the Party.[119]

How can intellectuals be sure these faults, so broadly described in the resolution, are being cured so that intellectual expression can be free from the dictates of petty autocrats? The reduction of struggle against Party leaders after the Cultural Revolution hardly guarantees that result. Legal routinization might help, but that is inherently an ambiguous process: It could guarantee freedom for individuals and groups, but it could also become a movement to centralize and regularize repression of ideas unwelcome to Party cadres. (Stalin's codification campaign of the mid-1930s shows how laws can be antiliberal.)[120]

The 1981 resolution reaffirmed a 1978 "principle that neither democracy nor centralism can be practiced at each other's expense," and it pointed out "the basic fact that, although the exploiters had been eliminated as classes, class struggle continues to exist within certain limits."[121] No one, probably, is sure what these statements mean. Conceived functionally, they are designed to recruit intellectuals' talent and to retain the loyalties of Party members who dislike them, rather than to be clear. The proper limits of "class struggle" are undefined, and the unification of democracy and centralism is a mystical but useful tenet of CCP faith.

The resolution concludes with the "four fundamental principles, namely, upholding the socialist road, the people's democratic dictatorship (i.e., the dictatorship of the proletariat), the leadership of the Communist Party, and Marxism-Leninism and Mao Zedong Thought." Also, "Any word or deed which denies or undermines these four principles cannot be tolerated."[122] That moralistic position is likely to prevail over legal ones for some years, although CCP members seem less sure lately that they have inside information on the future and the truth.

THE SPIRITUAL POLLUTION CAMPAIGN

The clearest recent example of the Party's wariness of intellectuals is the campaign to eliminate spiritual pollution (<u>jingshen wuran</u>). This movement began in October 1983 at the Second Plenary Session of the Twelfth Party Congress,[123] and it has four tasks: to unify thought, purify work style, strengthen discipline, and cleanse organization (<u>tongyi sixiang</u>, <u>zhengdun zuofeng</u>, <u>jiagiang jilu</u>, <u>chunjie zuzhi</u>). These are all abstract; the campaign has few concrete, programmatic goals. It involves the criticism of some artists,[124] but it is mostly a propaganda movement. Formally, two spiritual faults had been the main targets: the notion that capitalist practices can help China and the notion that any proper Marxist analysis can show "alienation" between the Party and Chinese society.[125]

The gorgeous ambiguity of this movement is that these two premises underlie many concurrent Party policies in the Four Modernizations Campaign and in efforts to restore links with people, notably intellectuals, the Party has obviously alienated. The gist of the Spiritual Pollution Campaign is that although quasi-capitalist and anti-alienation policies are needed, no one must think of them for what they are. Lest socialist majesty be injured, a spade must not be called a spade.

Deng Xiaoping has been identified with this campaign from its beginning,[126] possibly to calm army and Party-legitimist doubts about the course of the Four Modernizations generally. Study groups met to read "Chairman Mao's great essay, 'Oppose Liberalism,'"[127] and the minister of culture, Zhu Muzhi, long associated with the CCP's Discipline Inspection Commission, urged the country's artists to produce more proper works.[128] For several months, the People's Daily was devoted partly to reports of economic progress and partly to exhortations against spiritual pollution.[129]

The timing of this campaign--its quick rise in October 1983 and then the reduction of its intensity during early 1984--is more problematic than its occurrence. Quasi-capitalist policies and policies to redress some grievances of alienated groups have been followed hesitantly since 1978. Why in the autumn of 1983, of all times, was there an attempt to balance these efforts with a move against spiritual pollution?

Circumstantial evidence suggests that the origins of the campaign could lie in efforts by high pragmatic-reformist and Party-legitimist leaders (such as Hu Yaobang and Zhao Ziyang, maybe backed by Deng Xiaoping, and of Peng Zhen, maybe backed by Ye Jianying) to accommodate each other when they first had to think seriously together about the PRC's future relations with China's third-most-populous and largest capitalist city, Hong Kong. The Cantonese enclaves of Hong Kong and Macao have been major conduits for

spiritual pollution. They have legendary
capitalist economies, and they lack moralistic
governments (Macao lacks much government at all.)[130]
On November 3, 1983, the People's Daily carried a
feature from the Wanzi (Wanchai) Middle School of
Zhuhai City, Guangdong:

> When you stand in front of the school,
> you can see the tall buildings of Macau
> and hear the raucous noises from the
> other shore, all a tempting world
> (huahua shijie) dazzling the eyes. In
> this peculiar environment, rotten
> capitalist ideas flow in through all
> the gullies and pipes, and the struggle
> against decay and corruption is
> especially keen.

There was no need for the People's Daily to tell
the readers about personal incomes in these
capitalist Chinese places; the grass-roots
telegraph, which they trust, had already let them
know.[131]
    The problem is that the economic prowess
of Hong Kong challenges the patriotic quality of
Chinese socialist organization. (Singapore or
Taiwan would do so too, but few PRC citizens ever
see these places--and no PRC leaders have to
decide seriously among themselves how they intend
to run administrations there.) The Spiritual
Pollution Campaign is an effort to regain, by
sheer propaganda and will, respect that the CCP
lost when it had to adopt basically capitalist and
lobbying methods to solve problems that its
previous policies had created. The campaign arose
when it did, partly because of Party uncertainties
about the huge city of Hong Kong--enviable,
capitalist, and immoral by CCP standards--that
will be within the PRC fairly soon.
    Not only the timing of this campaign, but
also the Chinese intellectuals' published contributions to it, reinforce this interpretation.
On December 11, 1983, the People's Daily carried
a full page of testimonials to the campaign. The
ex-director of the Lu Xun Arts Institute in Yenan,
a vice-president of the Chinese Academy of Social
Sciences, and the director of the State

Seismological Bureau joined others in arguing that the Party deserves support because of the progress that has been made since 1949. There was no need to mention the years or aspects of regress, because the whole point of their argument was to suggest these deserved no attention. Obedience to socialism and to the Party, they said, was a patriotic duty--and they did not say it was "still" so, because that would have raised the basic issue.

The uproar over army poet Bai Hua's filmscript Unrequited Love (Ku lian), which preceded the Spiritual Pollution Campaign, centered on the same issues.[132] A single line of that play became famous precisely because it raised the issue of patriotism alongside the hurt of Chinese intellectuals: "You love the Motherland, but does the Motherland love you?"

The Spiritual Pollution Campaign had real victims, although I have not seen any evidence these victims were physically harassed in the Cultural Revolution manner. A vice-editor-in-chief of the People's Daily named Wang Ruoshui, who had argued that alienation can exist under socialism, was fired because of his views. So was Ru Xin, the head of the Philosophy Department at the Academy of Social Sciences, who ended up contributing a series of long articles to the People's Daily entitled "Criticize Bourgeois Morality; Propagate Socialist Morality."[133] In March 1984, a poet named Xu Jingye criticized a 1981 article he himself had written praising new developments in poetry. He now castigated existentialism, self-expressionism, anti-rationalism, and imitating the West.[134] Theater directors did not know what could be safety produced. A new novel by a woman professor at Fudan University, entitled Man, Oh Man! (Ren ah! Ren!), was berated for its humanism. Even a play about Karl Marx caused problems, because it stressed his humanistic side.[135] Party thinkers seem to have been increasingly unsure about the permanent value of Marxism as a consistent basis for knowledge.

Army participation in this campaign was important. Lt.-Gen. Yu Qiuli made a prominent speech that became one of the campaign's main documents,[136] and was later designated as official study material for meetings all over the country. Many such study materials warned against carrying the Spiritual Pollution Campaign too far. They claimed this new spiritual movement for socialist civilization was different from the antipluralist hunts of the 1950s and 1960s, especially the Cultural Revolution. The gist of the late-1983 caveats might be summarized as follows:

> Don't take just any question and make it a matter of spiritual pollution. Don't take things which you haven't seen or dislike and make them into spiritual pollution without analysis. Don't resemble some comrades, who think "Spiritual pollution is a basket (kuang), and anything can be packed into it."[137]

The word kuang has a considerable recent history. With a bamboo radical, as above, it means "basket." But Yao Wenyuan, famous as a Gang of Four member in the early 1960s, prominently used a similar kuang (the same phonetic with a wood radical, meaning "frame" and implying "rules," or "the end of a coffin"). In 1962, the writer Ba Jin publicly criticized Yao, not by name but clearly, in a courageous speech at a large conference in Shanghai:

> I am a little afraid of those who, holding a coffin-end (kuang) in one hand and a club in the other, go everywhere looking for men with mistakes. . . . If anybody lets them hear some new songs or read some new writings to which they are not accustomed, they will become furious with him and bring the club right down on his head. . . . At one time, they hold literature in great contempt; at another, they place literature in high esteem and hold writers responsible for all the actions of their readers—as if a novel can thoroughly transform the spiritual aspect of a man.[138]

By 1977, Ba Jin was back in favor because of the

popularity of his novels, but the old tension between ideologues and other intellectuals had not changed just because a threatening word was treated differently or because the incumbent leaders of the CCP had somewhat rotated.

The Party's problem in the Spiritual Pollution Campaign was to instill more Communist discipline among intellectuals--just what the Gang of Four had tried to do--while dissociating itself from the recent history of repression. This was the Party's only hope of laying a claim on the intellectuals' talents, but it is a hard trick to turn. The Party had to insist on proper "analysis" before anything or anybody was condemned as "spiritually polluted," but it was also important not to specify the principles of this analysis in much detail, lest any intellectual decide to interpret the situation for himself. The upshot of the new campaign was not that socialist morals should be understood but that discussion of them should be within public bounds set by the Party. Independence in searching for the truth from the facts would subvert the official monopoly on moralizing.

CONCLUSION

The Four Modernizations Campaign has produced some tentative improvements in living and working conditions for Chinese intellectuals as well as ostentatious hoopla and speeches about intellectuals from Party leaders. The importance of thinkers for China's future development is now a policy slogan, and Deng Xiaoping himself has addressed many audiences on this topic. Lists of these speeches have been published in an obvious effort to reassure intellectuals that the regime favors them at last. In particular, since July 1977, Deng has excoriated the "two whatevers" (liangge fanshi) view of Hua Guofeng, who preferred a continuation of all Mao's policies. He has also castigated the "two assessments" (liangge guji) of a 1971 document, which claimed that before 1966 all of China's schools and universities had been dominated by the bourgeoisie and that the great majority of China's intellectuals were bourgeois.[139]

Deng has not been alone in these efforts. For example, Premier Zhao Ziyang chose to personally head the State Council's Science and Technology Leadership Group.[140] Hu Yaobang, general-secretary of the Party, is the highest leader with a relatively constant care for thinkers, according to Communists and dissidents alike. On the centennial of Marx's death, he praised the founder of communism as an intellectual, and he said such people were needed to change the world.[141] Generals Nie Rongzhen and Wang Zhen, who have some history of an interest in technology, have delivered similar speeches.[142] Even the likes of Deng Liqun, director of the Party Propaganda Department and a leader of the Spiritual Pollution Campaign, regularly deliver positive, abstract affirmations of the importance of intellectuals,[143] and economic cadres and Central Committee members do the same.[144] Li Xiannian, Peng Zhen, Song Renqiong, Chen Yun, Hu Qiaomu, and many others have contributed nice sentences about intellectuals. Even Marshal Ye Jianying (to some people, the leader most threatening to quasi-liberal policies)[145] has been heard to say positive things about thinkers.[146] Dozens of other articles cite praises from dead leaders about intellectuals--somewhat credibly from Zhou Enlai, more inconsistently from Mao Zedong. The argument for the importance of thinkers to China's progress is now published in every possible way.[147]

If words were not enough, there are models too. Ding Shengshu, a linguist at the Chinese Academy of Social Sciences who died in 1983, is to be studied for his "high loyalty to the Party, the Motherland, the people, socialism, and the Communist cause."[148] Less was said in the eulogy about his work on language reform, but he completed every task he was assigned by the Party. Another model intellectual is Zhou Qiumin, associate professor at the South-Central School of Mines and an expert in electric machines, who also died before canonization. As the People's Daily says in a long article, he participated from the age of fifteen in underground Shanghai Party organizations and was sent to study at M.I.T. for four years after 1979.[149] Jiang Zhuying, a middle-aged optics expert, died from working too hard. He was a perpetual motion machine (<u>yongdong ji</u>) because of his constant, nervous, enthusiastic efforts in research and in social work (helping mothers and children to board jammed buses, cleaning up broken glass on public streets so as to prevent bicycle-tire punctures, and many other stories).[150] Lo Jianfu, an electrical expert who was also a Party member, declined all salary increases and job promotions that were due him, took poorer housing than his comrades at the same level, refused to use the "back door" to help his son and daughter enter universities, and even went abroad and to Hong Kong without ill effects.[151] (One of the most-mooted forms of spiritual pollution is <u>Gang feng</u>, "the Hong Kong breeze.")

Sometimes a particularly trustworthy intellectual might become a less formal model, even before dying. Engineer An Zhendong, who expiated his pre-1949 membership in a Nationalist Party youth group by six years in prison, was released shortly before the Cultural Revolution only to be attacked again and put to work scrubbing toilets. After continuing to invent useful machines on a farm, An rose in a factory bureaucracy and then to the provincial level. He is now a deputy governor of Heilongjiang. His early legal conviction (for which he served a great deal of time) has been retroactively declared an unfortunate mistake. An Zhendong is not yet in the CCP, though he is much in the news.[152]

The establishment of intellectual models and speeches about the importance of thinkers for progress are refreshing after the Cultural Revolution, but they cannot substitute for a broader concept of intelligence than governments like to consider. As the classic saying goes, the scholar is still not a tool.

Some thinkers in China appreciate the value of the skills of freedom[153]--and they say so. In a 1981 issue of <u>Jiaoyu yanjiu</u> [Educational research], four coauthors grieved that

> Our higher education has been profoundly influenced by the Soviet Union of the 1960s, with its divorce of the humanities and the sciences and its establishment of

> separate schools for sciences and for
> engineering, all narrowly specialized. . . .
> The result is that students are intellec-
> tually narrow, unenlightened in their
> thinking, slow to react, short-sighted.[154]

Even the PRC will have its defenders of the skeptical, open intellect that is willing to try various values and use all styles of thought for the sake of really new understandings. Govern-ments are not very good at sustaining such intellectuals. Such people can easily become political dissidents, and imagination is worth more than organization in the thinking business.

Intellect of this sort depends on personal and social forces outside the competence of the polity. Lenin, looking back at the revolution he had made, noticed just before his death that "defects . . . rooted in the past" could undo it. (Under Stalin, they were beginning to do so, as Lenin vaguely perceived.)

> In order to renovate our state apparatus,
> we must at all costs set out, first, to
> learn, second, to learn, and third, to
> learn, and then see to it that learning
> shall not remain a dead letter, or a
> fashionable catch-phrase . . . that
> learning shall really become part of our
> very being, that it shall actually and
> fully become a constituent element of
> our social life. . . . It is high time
> things were changed. We must follow the
> rule: Better fewer, but better. We must
> follow the rule: Better get good human
> material in two or even three years, than
> work in haste without hope of getting
> any at all.[155]

Lenin was not the sort of person to admit failure, but at least, in this his very last article, he saw its shadow.

A similar uncertainty now bedevils even the official propagandists in the PRC. This is an important development of the past few years. Su Shaozhi, director of the Institute of Marx-Leninism/Mao Zedong Thought of the Chinese Academy of Social Sciences, coauthored in 1979 an article entitled "The Problem of Stages of Social Development After the Proletariat Obtains Power." Su and his coauthor, Feng Lanrui, practically argue that China is not yet a socialist society. The country still needs small-scale production, more education, and generally a modern substructure to sustain real socialism: "We are still an undeveloped socialist society (<u>bu fada de shehuizhuyi shehui</u>), still in the <u>transition</u> to socialism. It cannot be said that our economic system is already evolved or complete socialism."[156] This article, despite its jargon, is an attempt to begin the job of explaining the Cultural Revolution in social terms--and any such explanation is liable to raise questions about present problems.

The viewpoint is hardly liberal, but at least it sees the dangers of "feudal" bossism in small units, the inefficiencies of economic and even political institutions that are centralized more than the evolution of social and economic infrastructure warrants, and the extent of popular gullibility that the PRC's educational system has produced. Such a viewpoint produces policy recommendations, especially for economic and administrative problems, that strongly resemble those which would come from a Chinese liberal.

Management decentralization, the encouragement of more diverse publishing and education to enliven intellectual life in a society whose infrastructure will not support exact unity, more market-oriented pricing mechanisms, more policies taking a realistic view of the inherent cellularity of organization in an underdeveloped country--all these "tendencies of articulation"[157] could be based <u>either</u> on a neo-Marxist analysis of the sort Su and Feng presented <u>or</u> on a classic liberal one. There could be agreement on action with a decision to leave premises open (until some future problem might require they be specified). Deng Xiaoping had once said, "Whether it's a white cat or a black cat, it's a good cat if it catches mice."[158] Su and Feng expanded on that thought: By showing that Marxist grounds could be used to justify liberal policies, they implied there was, in practice, no reason to care about the color of the cat at all.

This idea has an effect on Party legitimacy, because it says there is no need for the comrades to pretend exactness (or cocksureness) about actions, including repressive ones, that might bring progress. It suggests that stubborn certainty about basic principles may hinder, not help, the real-world effectiveness of actions. Such an insight runs counter to some (not all) Chinese traditions, and it destroys the moral certainty in historical action that the Communists thought they had.

Hu Qiaomu, who has long been associated with the Chinese Academy of Social Sciences, reportedly wanted a campaign to criticize Su Shaozhi, and the fact that no witch-hunt occurred says a great deal about the state of mind of Party intellectuals now: They are no longer sure they can see the future perfectly. To a large extent, the Party legitimists' frustrations were vented later in the criticisms of Bai Hua,[159] but his filmscript could be more easily accused of antisocialism, because it was not so burdened by Marxist jargon. The diversion of the criticism may eventually prove to have as many liberating effects as its existence has constraining ones: The colorless cat is out of the bag, and if it continues to run around, the Bai Huas of the future could fare better. Over time, the new diversity of opinions in China may help to free minds.

This change will take many years. Campaigns are still the rage in China, and no one, of any political stripe, expects future ones to be entirely nonrepressive. As Vera Schwarcz has written, "An accurate reading of the mood of intellectuals . . . remains elusive as long as we fail to grasp the difference between the loud, official rehabilitation of intellectuals under way in China today and the quieter, more cautious self-healing that is being attempted by the intellectuals themselves."[160] Thinkers have long stressed memory, and self-healing comes to their Chinese community partly in the revival of symbols that predate the revolution. Students now sometimes call their teachers "earlier born" (xiansheng), a name that is more respectful than "comrade." At the lunar New Year, they again may visit their mentors' homes (bainian), and old ideas like integrity (<u>qijie</u>) and "aloofness from secular concerns" (<u>qinggao</u>) are somewhat back in style.[161] The Party might, of course, try to repress such symbols yet again, but lately it seems less certain what it wants to do; it is now running on many conflicting, ambiguous principles.

The overall conclusion is one of very muted optimism. Deng Xiaoping, and even Hu Yaobang, may be "in principle" no different from Mao or his wife Jiang. To say this alone, though, without also evaluating the intellectuals' resources, would be to miss half the picture. The intellectuals' policies toward the government are as important as the governments' are toward them. If the regime should ever wish intellectuals to think freely, that would not be the reason they would do so.

Intellectuals do not crucially oppose or support any government--that is not how their work influences most politics. If they do support a regime, it lasts or fails mainly because of other constituencies. If they try to oppose it alone, they are regularly repressed. Their power is longer term, more elusive, a matter of symbols. The social task of the Chinese intellectuals is to see China clearly and to report what they see.

NOTES

I have received extremely generous help from a research assistant and from Wu An-chia of the Institute of International Relations. All mistakes are my own.

1. Thinking is not just in the "social system"; it is also in the "personality system" (see e.g., T. Parsons, <u>Societies</u> [Englewood Cliffs, N.J.: Prentice-Hall, 1966]). Suzanne Langer argues in <u>Philosophy in a New Key: A Study in the Symbolism of Reason, Rite, and Art</u> (New York: Penguin, 1942) that art parallels the logical forms of life--and not all life is political. Artists, for example, are also intellectuals.

2. Mencius 4.A.20 in Wm. Theodore de Bary, ed., <u>Sources of Chinese Tradition</u>, vol. 1 (New York: Columbia University Press, 1960), p. 96.

A Western source is Aristotle--in the Nicomachean Ethics that man is "rational" and in the Politics that man uses his mind naturally in a community.

3. Lun Yu, Anglects, 2.xii.
4. Joseph R. Levenson, Confucian China and Its Modern Fate, vol. 2 (Berkeley: University of California Press, 1964), esp. pp. 25f. Also, Thomas A. Metzger, Escape from Predicament (New York: Columbia University Press, 1977).
5. Renmin xuexi cidian [People's study dictionary] (Shanghai: Guangyi Press, 1953), p. 201.
6. Merle Goldman, in her indispensable book, China's Intellectuals: Advise and Dissent (Cambridge: Harvard University Press, 1981), implicitly opts for restricting the definition to publish writers, scientists, university teachers, and high cultural bureaucrats.
7. Renmin ribao [People's daily] (Peking), February 2, 1956.
8. Ibid., January 30, 1956.
9. New York Times, March 4, 1984.
10. Hongqi [Red flag], no. 2 (1979), p. 32.
11. Kau Ying-mao, "Urban and Rural Strategies in the Chinese Communist Revolution," in John Wilson Lewis, ed., Peasant Rebellion and Communist Revolution in Asia (Stanford: Stanford University Press, 1974), p. 257, for example.
12. Gilbert Rozman et al., The Modernization of China (New York: Free Press, 1981), p. 275.
13. John Israel and Donald W. Klein, Rebels and Bureaucrats: China's December 9ers (Berkeley: University of California Press, 1976).
14. Mu Fu-sheng [pseud.], The Writing of the Hundred Flowers: Free Thought in China Today (London: Heinemann, 1962), pp. 213f.
15. Mao's specification of ideals in an organization (which he headed) bears a strong resemblance to Stalin's same emphasis at the same time (see James P. Harrison, The Long March to Power [New York: Praeger, 1972], pp. 334-342. For more detail on the links between disputes of the Yenan period and the post-1949 era, see Merle Goldman, Literary Dissent in Communist China (New York: Atheneum, 1971), and her "Writer's Criticism of the Party in 1942," China Quarterly 17 (January-March 1964), pp. 205-228.

16. The phrase "loyal opposition" comes from the anthropologist Fei Xiaotong (see Suzanne Pepper, *Civil War in China: The Political Struggle, 1945-49* [Berkeley: University of California Press, 1978], esp. chap. 6, "The Intelligentsia's Critique of the Chinese Communists").

17. Lynn White, "Changing Concepts of Corruption in Communist China" (unpublished paper) gives many examples of this effort.

18. Robert Loh, *Escape from Red China* (New York: Coward-McCann, 1962), pp. 165-170, gives some information on this topic. See also Ezra F. Vogel, *Canton Under Communism* (Cambridge: Harvard University Press, 1969).

19. Xinhua (New China News Agency) (Peking), March 17, 1956.

20. A census of intellectuals showed that Shanghai contained "over 10,000 higher intellectuals" (*Renmin ribao*, May 23, 1956).

21. Lynn White, "Leadership in Shanghai, 1956-69," in Robert A. Scalapino, ed., *Elites in the People's Republic of China* (Seattle: University of Washington Press, 1972), esp. pp. 313-327, contains many criticisms. See also Dennis J. Doolin, *Communist China: The Politics of Student Opposition* (Stanford, Calif.: Hoover Institution, 1964). For more background, see Goldman, *Literary Dissent*. On the question of the Party elite's intentions (which is somewhat separable from that of the intellectuals' long-term reaction), see Roderick MacFarquhar, *The Origins of the Cultural Revolution*, vol. 1 (New York: Columbia University Press, 1974), esp. pt. 3.

22. *Xinwen ribao* [News daily] (Shanghai), May 17, 1957.

23. Ibid., November 28, 1957.

24. For the results, see Franz Schurmann, *Ideology and Organization in Communist China* (Berkeley: University of California Press, 1966).

25. *Zhanwang* [Outlook] (Shanghai), January 18, 1958, p. 24, for example.

26. *Wenhui bao* [Literary news], February 2, 1958.

27. See Parris H. Chang, *Power and Policy in China*, 2d ed. (University Park: Pennsylvania State University Press, 1978); Byung-joon Ahn, *Chinese Politics and the Cultural Revolution*

(Seattle: University of Washington Press, 1976); and MacFarquhar, Origins of the Cultural Revolution, vol. 2 (New York: Columbia University Press, 1983) --among other treatments of Hai Rui and Peng Dehuai.

28. Lynn White, "Leadership in Shanghai."
29. Alain Peyrefitte, The Chinese, tr. Graham Webb (Indianapolis, Ind.: Bobbs-Merrill, 1977), p. 141.
30. A. Zhelokhovtsev, The Cultural Revolution: A Close-up (Moscow: Progress Publishers, 1975), pp. 29-30. Despite such propaganda, some passages in this book suggest that Zhelokhovtsev is able to criticize certain Soviet habits by referring to Chinese analogues. On this phenomenon among many Soviet Sinologists, see forthcoming publications by Gilbert Rozman.
31. For more, see James C.F. Wang, The Cultural Revolution in China: An Annotated Bibliography (New York: Garland Publishers, 1976). A subsidiary theme, inappropriate to this chapter, is the participation of the intellectuals' offspring in the most radical Red Guard groups because they were so frustrated at earlier discrimination in access to schools and jobs. Good interpretive literature on the Cultural Revolution is just beginning to emerge (see Stanley Rosen, Red Guard Factionalism and Cultural Revolution in Guangzhou (Canton) [Boulder, Colo.: Westview, 1982]).
32. Zhelokhovtsev, Cultural Revolution, pp. 201-202.
33. See Martin K. Whyte and William L. Parish, Urban Life in Contemporary China (Chicago: University of Chicago Press, 1984), chart on p. 282.
34. Such developments are treated in Susan L. Shirk, Competitive Comrades: Career Incentives and Student Strategies in China (Berkeley: University of California Press, 1982).
35. Hsüan Mo, "Peiping's Current Policy Toward Literature and Art." (Paper presented at the Eleventh Sino-American Conference on Mainland China, Taipei, June 1982).
36. Deng's speech is in Hongqi, no. 4 (1978), pp. 9-18.
37. Renmin ribao, January 2, 1969.

38. Ibid., January 13, 1979.
39. Ibid., April 5, 1982.
40. It would be safe to assume that not all intellectuals in the sample received better housing, i.e., that the total was greater than 2,300--probably much greater. Even if the sample were only that size, the article would imply that only about 10 percent of these Peking intellectuals were Party members. This fact compares interestingly with a statement in <u>Hongqi</u>, no. 2 (1979), p. 32, that 36 percent of all intellectuals in the country are Party members. The conclusion: A large majority of intellectuals in the Party are probably teachers outside the big cities. The portion of all high intellectuals in the Party may be well below 10 percent.
41. <u>Renmin ribao</u>, July 14, 1979.
42. This information comes from an interview, in the United States, during March 1984. Local CCP officials did <u>not</u> have to sign the absolving resolution--an act that would have been embarrassing for those people who had classed intellectuals as rightists for having criticized themselves. They could merely seal a resolution with the local unit's red-ink chop.
43. A prominent dissident of 1957, Lin Xiling, moved to Paris in 1983 and was quoted as saying, "Les cadres réhabilités se sont servis pour vivre dans le luxe, et surtout pour y faire vivre leurs enfants" ("Les vents mauvais qui soufflent sur la Chine," <u>L'Esprit</u>, December 1983, p. 73). I also spoke with Lin Xiling in Princeton, New Jersey, February 28, 1984.
44. <u>Guangming ribao</u> [Bright daily], January 21, 1980, esp. the twelfth and last recommendation.
45. <u>Renmin ribao</u>, February 19, 1981.
46. Ibid., October 14, 1982.
47. Ibid., July 25, 1980.
48. Dissident Lin Xiling guesses that Hu Yaobang may be more prointellectual than other leaders such as Ye Jianying (see note 43).
49. This is the title of an article in <u>Hongqi</u>, no. 22 (1980), pp. 15-18.
50. This is the outline of an article in <u>Guangming ribao</u>, October 3, 1980.
51. <u>Renmin ribao</u>, September 22, 1981.

52. Mary Louise O'Callaghan, "China's Educated Class Struggles for End to Harassment," Christian Science Monitor, July 21, 1983, p. 13.
53. Guangming ribao, July 22, 1982.
54. Hongqi, no. 12 (1982).
55. Guangming ribao, July 24, 1982.
56. Renmin ribao, July 26, 1982.
57. See Robert Taylor, China's Intellectual Dilemma: Politics and University Enrollment, 1949-1978 (Vancouver: University of British Columbia Press, 1981). A forthcoming book by Suzanne Pepper will provide still more information.
58. Renmin ribao, June 14, 1983.
59. The information comes from an interview at Princeton in 1984, with a knowledgeable individual.
60. Renmin ribao, February 14, 1980. A commentary by the education minister on the new regulations is also included.
61. Ibid., June 13, 1981.
62. Ibid., May 28, 1982. The names, specialties, universities, and professorial advisers of the eighteen new Ph.D.s were provided on the next day.
63. Ibid., December 30, 1979.
64. Ibid., December 28, 1979.
65. Ibid., August 4, 1980.
66. Ibid., January 13, 1982.
67. Reported in the New York Times, March 4, 1984.
68. Quoted in Christian Science Monitor, July 21, 1983, p. 13.
69. Hongqi, no. 2 (1979), p. 32.
70. See note 40.
71. Guangming ribao, September 19, 1977.
72. See Vice-Premier Bo Yibo's interview with the Beijing keji bao [Peking science and technology news] reproduced in Renmin ribao, February 19, 1981. See also Hongqi, no. 2 (1979), pp. 34-35.
73. A recent film Neighbors, by Zheng Dongtian and Xu Juming, is a scathing attack on China's housing shortage.
74. Renmin ribao, July 14, 1982.
75. Richard Curt Kraus, Class Conflict in Chinese Socialism (New York: Columbia University Press, 1981), p. 167. See also Richard P. Suttmeier, Science, Technology, and China's Drive

for Modernization (Stanford, Calif.: Hoover Institution Press, 1981), p. 39.
76. Liaowang [Lookout] 7 (July 1982).
77. Wenhui bao, January 15, 1983.
78. Renmin ribao, March 4, 1984.
79. Ibid., January 19 and August 16, 1982.
80. Hongqi, no. 21 (1980). The extreme degree of cross appointments among institute heads and deputy heads shows the scarcity of intellectuals the Party thought it could trust.
81. Renmin ribao, July 29, 1980.
82. For just a few examples, see Jiefang ribao [Liberation daily] (Shanghai), August 6, 1956; on housing, Qingnian bao [Youth news], December 21, 1956; on the "sit-and-talk" sessions of 1957, Xinwen ribao (Shanghai), especially May 4, May 15, and July 21, 1956.
83. Martin Whyte and William Parish suggest this fact in Urban Life, p. 166.
84. On Shanghai-to-Northwest rustication in general, see Lynn White, "The Road to Urumchi," China Quarterly 79 (September 1979), pp. 481-510. Although not all of the Jiaotong staff were finally shifted to Xian, a sufficient number went to form a second Jiaotong in that city.
85. Renmin ribao, May 22, 1982, based on an Xinhua report of May 21.
86. Xinhua, April 30, 1983.
87. On a move of scientists to Anhwei to make recommendations for the development of industry and agriculture, see Renmin ribao, November 27, 1980.
88. On an early move from Fudan University to northern Anhwei, for example, see Jiefang ribao (Shanghai), September 24, 1951.
89. Ibid., but a different article.
90. Renmin ribao, February 29, 1984.
91. See Martin Whyte and William Parish, Urban Life, for a great deal of material on the significance for the refusers' future income and livelihood. The information here also comes from an interview in Princeton.
92. Renmin ribao, March 3, 1984, p. 3, for this fascinating "letter from a correspondent" (jizhe laixin).
93. Ibid., January 9, 1981.
94. Ibid.

95. See Guangming ribao, April 27, 1983.
96. Renmin ribao, March 24, 1982.
97. Guangming ribao, May 23, 1982.
98. A larger problem, of course, is that the bureaucrats in a shifted expert's new unit might have developed an aversion to experts in general.
99. This statement refers to the previous PRC Constitution. The new Constitution, promulgated on December 4, 1982, provides in Article 1 that "sabotage of the socialist system by any organization or individual is prohibited" (Fifth Session of the Fifth National People's Congress [Beijing: Foreign Languages Press, 1983], p. 9). The reference to freedom of speech is in Article 35, p. 22. Article 47 (p. 27) cites "freedom to engage in scientific research, literary and artistic creation, and other cultural pursuits"--subject, presumably, to the stricture about socialism in Article 1.
100. Beijing ribao [Peking daily], August 4, 1979. Yan wei xin sheng is a classical expression; xin sheng is a bit like the French cri de coeur.
101. Hongqi, no. 5 (1975); the commentary is on pp. 11-15, but the main point is in the first paragraph.
102. Here, and for occasional reference elsewhere, see Wolfgang Bartke, Who's Who in the People's Republic of China (Armonk, N.Y.: Sharpe, 1981).
103. Lin Mouhan, "Suowei jinqu wenti" ["So-called forbidden questions"], Zuopin [Works] (Canton), no. 4 (April 1979).
104. Renmin ribao, May 7, 1979. On Zhou Yang, and literary bureaucrats in general, see Goldman, Literary Dissent.
105. See the article by Ying Guoqing and Xiao Wanquan, "Zuozhe de 'jiashuo' quan" [An Author's rights of hypothesis], Shanghai kexue [Shanghai science], no. 6 (June 1980).
106. Hongqi, no. 3 (1980), e.g., p. 37. Some prescriptions for reform in China at this time were written entirely as descriptions of common practices abroad. For example, see an article about the legal meaning of intellectual patents in Shehui kexue [Social science], no. 6 (1980).
107. Guangming ribao, March 28, 1982.
108. Renmin ribao, February 26, 1982.

109. Ibid., March 7, 1984.
110. <u>Resolution on CPC History (1949-81)</u> (Beijing: Foreign Languages Press, 1981), p. 8.
111. Ibid., pp. 22 and 27.
112. Ibid., p. 29. This statement is hard to verify independently.
113. Ibid., p. 30.
114. Ibid., pp. 34-35.
115. Ibid., p. 43.
116. An example of the first view is in Liang Heng and Judith Shapiro, <u>Son of the Revolution</u> (New York: Knopf, 1983). The more ambiguous second position is well-illustrated by Dai Xiaoai, and it became the main thesis of an article drawn from his experiences by Ronald N. Montaperto, "From Revolutionary Successors to Revolutionaries: Chinese Youth in the Early Stages of the Cultural Revolution," in Scalapino, ed., <u>Elites</u>, pp. 540f.
117. <u>Resolution on CPC History (1949-81)</u>, pp. 44-45.
118. See Chalmers A. Johnson, <u>Peasant Nationalism and Communist Power: The Emergence of Revolutionary China, 1937-1945</u> (Stanford: Stanford University Press, 1962).
119. <u>Resolution on CPC History (1949-81)</u>, pp. 46 and 47.
120. See Robert Sharlet, "Stalinism and Soviet Legal Culture," in Robert C. Tucker, ed., <u>Stalinism: Essays in Historical Interpretation</u> (New York: Norton, 1977), pp. 155-179.
121. <u>Resolution on CPC History (1949-81)</u>, p.51.
122. Ibid., p. 74.
123. <u>China Update</u> (New York), no. 12 (March 1984), p. 1.
124. For background, see Hsüan Mu's fine paper, "Peiping's Current Policy Toward Literature and Art." For recent material in English, see the series of cover articles in the <u>Far Eastern Economic Review</u> of February 9, 1984, by Ian Findlay, David Bonavia, Michel Masson, and Robert Delfts.
125. Criticism of humanism has also been a part of this campaign--partly because its prime movers found less resistance in attacking people in cultural circles, notably writers, than in attacking those in fields related to the economy.

126. <u>Renmin ribao</u>, October 31, 1983. The first sentence of the first paragraph at the top of the front page mentions both Deng Xiaophing and Chen Yun, who wanted to be well identified with the movement.
127. <u>Renmin ribao</u>, December 24, 1983.
128. <u>Ibid.</u>, November 2, 1983.
129. For example, ibid., November 12, 1983.
130. This section is influenced by my experience at the Overseas Chinese Hotel in Shekkei (Shiqi), Zhongshan County, Guangdong, in the summer of 1983, when I saw the hotel attendants greatly enjoying James Bond movies beamed by television from Hong Kong.
131. See Lynn White, "Local Newspapers and Community Change," in Godwin C. Chu and Francis L.K. Hsu, eds., <u>Moving a Mountain: Cultural Change in China</u> (Honolulu: University Press of Hawaii, 1979), pp. 76-112.
132. On this and other important works, including the play <u>If I Really Were</u> (<u>Jiaru wo shi zhende</u>) by Shanghai playwrights Sha Yexin, Li Shoucheng, and Yao Mingde, see Hsüan Mo, "Peiping's Current Policy Toward Literature and Art," esp. pp. 9f. A very different article, "Intellectuals in Literature," can be read in <u>Hongqi</u>, no. 16 (1983), pp. 24-27. I make no pretense in this chapter of "covering" recent writers; they are only mentioned alongside other intellectuals here, and complementary researches treat them more fully. A brief, recent, journalistic but good account is Ian Findlay, "Few Can Escape," <u>Far Eastern Economic Review</u>, February 9, 1984, pp. 41-42.
133. <u>Renmin ribao</u>, January 9 and 11, 1984.
134. <u>Ibid.</u>, March 5, 1984.
135. <u>China Update</u>, no. 12 (March 1984), p. 2.
136. <u>Renmin ribao</u>, December 24, 1983. The bottom of the front page is a mass photograph of hundreds of people who heard the speeches by Yu Qiuli and Deng Liqun.
137. Ibid.
138. <u>Shanghai wenxue</u> [Shanghai literature] 5 (May 6, 1962). See also Lynn White, "Leadership in Shanghai, 1955-69," in Scalapino, ed., <u>Elites</u>, pp. 334-335.
139. For example, Gong Yuzhi's article in

Hongqi, no. 19 (1983), pp. 10-17, which is translated without credit in Beijing Review 27:12 (March 19, 1984), pp. 16-20.

140. Renmin ribao, January 28, 1983.
141. Ibid., March 26, 1983; see also October 21, 1982.
142. Guangming ribao, July 18 and September 1, 1982.
143. Renmin ribao, August 22, 1982.
144. For praises to thinkers from Chen Peixian and Liu Da, see Hongqi, no. 6 (1978), pp. 41-46, and no. 1 (1980), pp. 36-38.
145. See Lin Xiling, "Les vents mauvais," for an especially juicy anecdote about Ye Jianying's use of his position to protect his malfeasant son.
146. Liaowang, 3 (March 1983).
147. To cite just a few examples, among literally hundreds of similar articles, Guangming ribao, January 8 and March 12, 1983; Hongqi, no. 2 (1979), pp. 31f, no. 1 (1980), pp. 39f., and no. 5 (1982), pp. 34f.; Renmin ribao, November 28, 1979, and January 13 and June 4, 1982.
148. Wenhui bao, April 18, 1983.
149. Renmin ribao, January 22, 1984.
150. Guangming ribao, October 10, 1982.
151. Gongren ribao [Workers' daily], November 5, 1982.
152. New York Times, March 4, 1984, pp. 1 and 18.
153. "Skills of freedom" is another, less conventional but clearer, translation of the Greek that gives us the term "liberal arts."
154. Quoted from Jiaoyu yanjiu, no. 16 (May 1981), p. 38, in John Israel, "The Ideal of Liberal Education in China," in Ronald A. Morse, ed., The Limits of Reform in China (Boulder, Colo.: Westview, 1983), p. 107.
155. This is from Pravda, March 4, 1923, tr. in Robert C. Tucker, ed., The Lenin Anthology (New York: Norton, 1975), pp. 735-736.
156. Feng Lanrui is an economist, and her husband, Li Chang, is a member of the Central Committee, a Yenan cadre, and a leading science administrator. Su's identification is confirmed by the name roster, Zhongguo Shehui Kexue Yuan [Chinese Academy of Social Sciences] (Beijing: CASS, 1983), p. 15. The experimental article is

in *Jingji yanjiu* [Economic research], no. 5 (May 1979).

157. The term is from Franklyn Griffiths, "A Tendency Analysis in Soviet Policy-Making," in H. Gordon Skilling and Franklyn Griffiths, *Interest Groups in Soviet Politics* (Princeton: Princeton University Press, 1971), pp. 335f.

158. "*Bai mao, hei mao--jua haozi de jiu shi hao mao.*" Deng was lucky to have chosen this analogy, since cats (though sometimes orange) do not come in red.

159. See the articles by Minister of Culture Zhou Weishi, *Wenyi bao* [Arts news], no. 19 (1981), and Tang En and Tang Dacheng (the two Tangs are pseudonyms for people in the Ministry of Culture) in the same issue.

160. "Reflections on the Intellectual Climate of China," in Morse, ed., *Limits of Reform*, p. 121.

161. Ibid., p. 128.

9
Policy Implications of Population Dynamics in the PRC

Wen Lang Li

INTRODUCTION

China is a land of mystery to many Western demographers. After the establishment of the People's Republic of China in 1949, the size and composition of the Chinese population remained hidden to the outside world, and for decades, the demographic community had to rely on journalistic reports about China's population concerns. The only information that was reliable to any degree was the age-sex population tabulation of the 1953 census (Aird 1982). Undeniably, there were voluminous studies on China's population programs and policies, all written in journalistic style and with great appeal to the public interest, but until recently, students of China's population could not even answer the most fundamental question, What is the birthrate in China?

The 1982 population census was a breakthrough for the demographic study of China. For the first time in Chinese history, detailed and comprehensive tabulations of demographic facts were presented to the world's demographers. At the time, the PRC government determined that census taking was important to the program of modernization and that population growth was a hindrance to socioeconomic development. Consequently, the effort and concern given to the PRC's 1982 census far exceeded those given to censuses in Western countries (Chengrui Li 1981).

This chapter will present a preliminary analysis of the 1982 census results, and there are two major reasons for the value of this endeavor. First, China's population constitutes almost one-quarter of the human race. The 1982 census reported China's population as 1,003,790,000 people; the current birthrate is 21.1 per 1,000, and the death rate is 6.6 per 1,000 (PRC, State Statistical Bureau 1983). These figures mean that China's population will increase by approximately 14,555,000 people every year, an increase that is more than the population size of three-quarters of all the nations in the world (UN 1984). Thus, analysis of the vast and growing Chinese population is a worthwhile pursuit.

A second reason why China's population is particularly intriguing to demographic students is the interplay between population phenomena and public policies. Since 1949, China has undertaken some traumatic social and political experiments that are unprecedented in recent centuries in China. At least four experiments are directly related to demographic revolutions: birth planning, health care delivery, female employment, and population dispersion programs. How effective are these programs? What are the effects of the experiments on Chinese society? We are currently unable to assess their full impact, but these questions will clearly be of great interest to historians of future generations. Nevertheless, an attempt to present some preliminary findings seems called for.

Three general topics will be discussed in this chapter. First, an assessment of the one-child family planning policy will be presented as a preliminary evaluation of the extent to which a one-child policy can be successfully implemented. Second, the mortality transition in the PRC since 1949 is examined, and I will discuss a very sensitive issue: How many humans lives have been sacrificed in the construction of the socialist state? Finally, based on the analyses of fertility and mortality, I will project the future population of China, with particular focus on evaluating how the future manpower development could affect the modernization of China. In exploring the prospects of social change in the PRC, my special concerns are human resource problems such as available workers and employment.

FERTILITY DECLINE AND ONE-CHILD POLICY

Since 1949, the PRC's population policy has undergone a 180-degree shift from pronatal to an antinatal commitment. In the first two decades of the regime, the PRC firmly adhered to the socialist anti-Malthusian doctrine. In fact, Mao Ze-dong used to designate his theory of population as the Ren-Shou-Lun ("human-hands theory"), in contrast to the Malthusian Ren-Kou-Lun ("human-mouth theory"). Mao's rationale was that the population should be viewed as a production force rather than as a consumption burden. This was not necessarily a unique perspective: Looking back to recent centuries, the traditional socialist doctrine and its predecessors have emphasized the positive function of population growth (Petersen 1971).

The decline of Mao's control in the early 1970s signified the end of the pronatal policy, and the antinatal sentiment became a formidable social force. The so-called Wan-Xi-Shao was held as the goal of birth planning in China: "Wan" meaning postponement of marriage and births, "Xi" meaning the spacing of births or children, and "Shao" meaning small family size. Apparently, the policy of Wan-Xi-Shao was not effective enough because in 1980, with the eighth draft of the Planned Birth Law, the one-child birth planning policy was officially revealed. Each couple was encouraged to have one child and to pledge they would have no more than one. The pledgers were rewarded, and the violators were penalized. Such an audacious population policy is rather unique in the world. It has won acclaim from politicians, journalists, and demographers, and many demographers have undertaken studies of it (Goodstadt 1982; Qian 1983; Saith 1981). Journalists have a tendency to equate official proclamations with social realities, and some demographers even project one-child families as the future family norm in China (Chen and Tyler 1983; Coale 1981).

The one-child family policy, if successfully implemented, would certainly be a revolution against traditional Chinese norms. The family structure would no longer be the same; interpersonal concepts such as siblings, cousins, uncles, or lineage would be discarded. In summation, the social-psychological conditions of one-child families would have a profound impact on Chinese social structure (Ching 1982). It is these concerns that lead one to ask, Can a one-child family policy be successful?

The 1982 census results do not present an optimistic picture for the success of the one-child family policy. Table 9.1 shows the total number of births in mainland China classified by the age of the mother and the birth parity. In total, there were 20,444,000 births in 1981, and 52.8 percent, or 10,774,000, were second or higher births, surely a phenomenal number. More than half of the Chinese mothers chose to have more than one child: 26 percent had their second child, and 27 percent had their third child or higher. These statistics reflect not only the attitude but actual behavior.

Table 9.1. Births by parity and age of mothers, 1981

Age of Mother	Birth Parity						
	1st	2nd	3rd	4th	5th	Total	(N in 1,000s)
15-19	.938	.060	.002	.000	.000	1.000	(377)
20-24	.751	.208	.036	.004	.001	1.000	(5,276)
25-29	.469	.323	.144	.049	.016	1.001	(10,566)
30-34	.120	.219	.268	.207	.186	1.000	(2,994)
35-39	.037	.060	.120	.192	.592	1.001	(842)
40-44	.022	.027	.047	.086	.818	1.000	(320)
45+	.039	.019	.036	.060	.846	1.000	(69)
Total	.473	.257	.129	.066	.076	1.001	(20,444)

Source: PRC, Population Census Office 1983, Table 52.

Looking at each age group, one cannot help but realize the difficulties in implementing a one-child policy. For those women who were between the ages of twenty and twenty-four, about 25 percent had a second child or higher. Officially, births for women under the age of twenty-five are discouraged or not even permitted so there is obviously a wide gap between official proclamations and social realities.

Of the more than 20 million children born in China in 1981, about 2 percent were born to mothers whose age was under twenty, and about 28 percent were born to mothers who were under twenty-five. Clearly, the problems of teenage pregnancy in China are not as severe as those in the United States, where one out of every four children are born to teenagers. Nevertheless, in China, births to women under the age of twenty-five are unacceptable for the sake of birth control and the demand for the female labor force. Thus, if "undesirable" pregnancies amount to about 25 percent in the United States, at least the same is true in China.

The analysis shows that the one-child family policy of the PRC is not likely to succeed in the foreseeable future. The prevailing fertility norm is still two children or more for at least 53 percent of the women. In addition, birth postponement (the so-called Wan-Xi-Shau policy) has not been widely accepted considering the number of women who have children while under twenty-five years of age. Taking these demographic realities into consideration, one cannot help questioning the practicality of the one-child family policy.

It is commonly understood that any public policy should not be enforced with much political severity if the objective of the policy is unrealistic as one predictable consequence of such irrational enforcement is the creation of societal inequality. Clearly, the one-child family policy is unrealistic, and if the government rigorously pursues enforcement of it, certain sectors of the Chinese society will suffer more than others. In the urban sector, the one-child policy may be successful, but in the wide rural areas, it may not. As a consequence, the highly educated families would have only one child, but the impoverished rural families would have many children. In the 1990s we may find that the urban sector is in short supply of labor while the rural sector has an abundant labor pool. The resulting rural-urban migration would further deteriorate the urban environment and widen the socioeconomic disparity between rural and urban communities.

If the one-child family policy is not realistic, what, then, should be the birth planning policy for China? Let us explore this question in light of the demographic information now available. Table 9.2 represents the age-specific fertility rates in China, and the sum of the age-specific fertility rates constitutes the total fertility rate, which, for Chinese women, is 2.615. When the total fertility rate is adjusted by the survival ratio, the result is the gross reproduction rate (see the note to Table 9.2), which represents the number of surviving children per woman. As calculated and presented in Table 9.2, the gross reproduction rate in China is 2.315, which means that every Chinese woman reproduces about 2.3 surviving children during her lifetime. Obviously, the Chinese fertility rate is not high at all compared to that of other developing countries. In fact, it is close to the level that is known as ZPG (zero population growth) in the United States.

Table 9.2. Gross reproduction rate in mainland China, 1981

Age of Mother	Population (in 1,000s) Women	Births	Birth (fertility) Rate	Survival Ratio	Gross Reproduction Rate
15-19	61,467	377	.0061	4.499	.027
20-24	36,378	5,276	.1450	4.470	.648
25-29	44,745	10,566	.2361	4.436	1.047
30-34	34,996	2,994	.0856	4.397	.376
35-39	25,605	842	.0329	4.344	.143
40-44	22,540	320	.0142	4.269	.061
45+	22,272	69	.0031	4.160	.013
Total	248,003	20,444			2.315

Sources: PRC, Population Census Office 1983, Table 52; Rong 1981, Table 2.

Note: The gross reproduction rate in this table does not follow the conventional calculations. We are interested in the number of surviving children per couple rather than the number of female births.

However, there is the possibility that Chinese fertility can be reduced further without invoking the one-child family policy. Let us make use of the demographic information presented in Table 9.1 as it can shed some light on formulating family planning policies. Guided by the Wan-Xi-Shao policy, we will agree that births for women under twenty are not desirable; births should be postponed until age twenty. In addition, we will agree that first births are reasonable for those women between twenty and twenty-four years of age but that second and higher births should be viewed as excessive. Child spacing should be enforced for the sake of the mother's health, and finally, conforming to the Shao policy, births beyond the second child for women above the age of twenty-five should be discouraged.

Thus, elaborating the Wan-Xi-Shao policy in light of the actual reproductive pattern among Chinese women we conclude that about 6,597,000 births may be regarded as "excessive" and could be discouraged without significant violation of women's rights. If intensive family planning campaigns are addressed to this target group of women with excessive births, the chances of successfully reducing fertility would be greater, and the public's acceptance of the population policy would be much higher than under the PRC's current Planned Birth Law. The Wan-Xi-Shao policy is based on much fairer and rational grounds.

If "excessive" births were avoided, the birthrate would be reduced by 32 percent, or about one-third. In other words, the birthrate in China would become about only 14 per 1,000. Following this assumption, it can be concluded that the gross reproduction rate could be reduced significantly to only 1.5 children per woman. An average of 1.5 children per couple signifies that the population growth is below the replacement level.

Table 9.3 illustrates the difference in simulated reproduction rates between the one-child family policy and the Wan-Xi-Shao policy. Under the one-child family policy, the total number of births is reduced to 9,671,000 per year, which compared to the current level of 20,444,000 births per year, means a 52.7 percent reduction. Further, the crude birthrate will fall to only 9.6 per 1,000. These statistics again suggest that the one-child family policy is an impossible task. Demographic literature has not yet reported a major country in which the birthrate has fallen to such a low level, except, of course, as the

Table 9.3. Simulated gross reproduction rate under assumptions of one-child and Wan-Xi-Shao

Age of Women	Number of Births (in 1,000s)		Birthrate		Reproduction Rate	
	One-Child	W-X-S	One-Child	W-X-S	One-Child	W-X-S
15-19	354	0	.0058	.0	.0261	.0
20-24	3,962	3,962	.1089	.1089	.4868	.4868
25-29	4,955	8,368	.1107	.1870	.4911	.8295
30-34	359	1,415	.0103	.0404	.0453	.1776
35-39	31	82	.0012	.0032	.0052	.0089
40-44	7	16	.0003	.0007	.0013	.0030
45+	3	4	.0001	.0002	.0004	.0008
Total	9,671	13,847	.2373	.3404	1.0562	1.5066

Sources: PRC, Population Census Office 1983, Table 52; Rong 1981, Table 2.

result of a catastrophe.

SOCIAL POLICIES AND MORTALITY TRANSITION

One conclusion that may be drawn from the above analysis is that a public policy must be carefully scrutinized and researched if it is to be successful. If a policy is unrealistic in light of actual social conditions, then any rigorous enforcement through political sanctions will create social dysfunctions. The price that people must pay for unrealistic social policies is high. Social dysfunctions result in human misery and even in a sacrifice of human lives.

As a revolutionary regime, the PRC has been accustomed to pursuing audacious social policies without paying much attention to actual social conditions. The one-child family policy is perhaps the best illustration. The Communists view the traditional Chinese family norms as feudalistic, whereas a small family size is considered to be good for modernization, and the rationale that a couple should be allowed only one child follows. Further, if the people decide that it is a good policy, then it should be enforced rigorously, and individuals who defy the policy objective are treated as "enemies of the people." The zealous decision makers choose to ignore such simple questions as, What are the dysfunctional aspects of the policy's implementation?

Undeniably, the traditional Chinese patrilineal preference is feudalistic and should be eradicated, but eradication of such a traditional norm through rigorous enforcement of the one-child family policy is bound to generate strong reactions and human misery. It seems all too plausible that if allowed only one child, and the infant happens to be a girl, then a couple may choose female infanticide in order to have a second chance to have a boy. Whether this scenario is likely must be carefully examined.

Table 9.4 presents the sex ratio at birth for various countries including the PRC. It is commonly understood among demographers that the

Table 9.4. Sex ratio at birth in comparative perspective

Country	Number of Births			Sex Ratio
	Total	Male	Female	
U.S.	3,612,258	1,852,616	1,759,642	105.28
U.K.	634,492	325,711	308,781	105.48
France	800,376	410,547	389,829	105.32
Japan	1,529,455	786,596	742,859	105.89
USSR	4,386,180	2,247,433	2,138,747	105.08
PRC				
Total	20,810,080	10,782,120	10,027,960	107.52
Cities	2,651,580	1,371,360	1,280,220	107.12
Towns	1,109,880	573,640	536,240	106.97
Villages	17,048,620	8,837,120	8,211,500	107.62

Sources: UN 1984 and PRC, Population Census Office 1983, Tables 19-22.

sex ratio at birth should not vary much from country to country, and exceptions to this rule are believed to result from a problem of statistical misreporting. As shown in Table 9.4, the sex ratio at birth is rather consistent among statistically advanced countries, and it appears reasonable to assume that the sex ratio at birth should be about 105.3. In other words, the proportion of females among infants should be about 48.7 percent.

Let us use this criterion to examine the sex-ratio-at-birth statistics in the PRC. Indeed, the

Chinese sex ratio at birth is much higher than expected. For the country as a whole, the sex ratio at birth is 107.52, 1.2 percentage points above the expected average. The female proportion among Chinese infants is only 48.19 percent, 0.52 percentage points below what is expected. Compared with the total number of Chinese infants of 20,810,080, the "error" proportion constitutes about 108,212 "missing" female infants. One-tenth of a million persons may or may not be statistically significant among the vast Chinese population, but these are human lives we are considering.

Examining the differentials in sex ratios at birth among cities, towns, and villages (hsiens), the common supposition about female infanticides seems to be supported. The figure is 107.12 in cities, 106.97 in towns, and 107.62 in villages. Thus, the proportion of female infants is only 48.17 percent in the villages, lower than the 48.28 percent in the cities, which is consistent with the scenario that if female infanticides are indeed encouraged by the one-child family policy, the proportion of reported female infants will be lower in the countryside than in the cities.

Nevertheless, I must hasten to add that these findings should not be taken as conclusive proof that the one-child family policy does cause widespread female infanticides. There are two points that should be taken into consideration. First, the extent of the discrepancy between reported female births and expected female births need not be equated with the number of infanticides per se. Statistical error may actually be the cause, and currently, there is no way to separate the proportion of infanticides from statistical misreporting. Second, societies of the Han culture are known to have higher sex ratios at birth, and as shown in Table 9.4, Japan's sex ratio at birth is higher than that of other countries. It would be absurd to state that female infanticides are totally caused by the Communists' one-child family policy; at most, we can surmise that the rigorous enforcement of the one-child family policy might have increased the prevalence of female infanticides.

Nevertheless, it is an undeniable fact that

the PRC's totalitarian enforcement of radical social policies has caused human misery and a horrendous number of human lives. Exactly how many human lives have been sacrificed because of erroneous social policies is a question that may not be answerable at present. A direct enumeration would be the best way to resolve the issue, but no one anticipates that the PRC regime will reveal the statistics. Thus, we have to rely on indirect measurement.

Figure 9.1 shows the birthrate and death rate in mainland China since 1950. The death rate has been steadily declining, from 18 per 1,000 in 1950 to 7 per 1,000 in 1973. Since 1973, it has not significantly changed. It is possible that the grass-roots health care delivery system in PRC, which has won international acclaim, did indeed dramatically reduce the death rate during the first twenty years of the Communist regime, but this kind of sociological innovation can be of benefit in reducing the death rate only at an initial stage. The momentum of mortality reduction is difficult to sustain unless there are dramatic medical and technological innovations. Apparently, China is still waiting for that day to come.

It is interesting to note that China's demographic transition pattern is not as clear-cut as the pattern observed in some Western societies. During the first five years of the Communists' administration, the birthrate was quite stable, around 37 per 1,000. From 1954 to 1961, the birthrate declined drastically, to as low as 18 per 1,000 in 1961, but after that year it suddenly increased, reaching 43 per 1,000 in 1963. After that high, it basically declined steadily until recent years. Interestingly enough, despite different political systems and perhaps for different reasons, the fertility rate on Taiwan has also been in decline since early 1960 (Wen Lang Li 1973).

The most spectacular irregularity in the Chinese demographic pattern is found between 1958 and 1961. During that three-year period, the birthrate declined sharply from 29 per 1,000 to 18 per 1,000, and the death rate drastically increased from 12 per 1,000 to 25 per 1,000. In

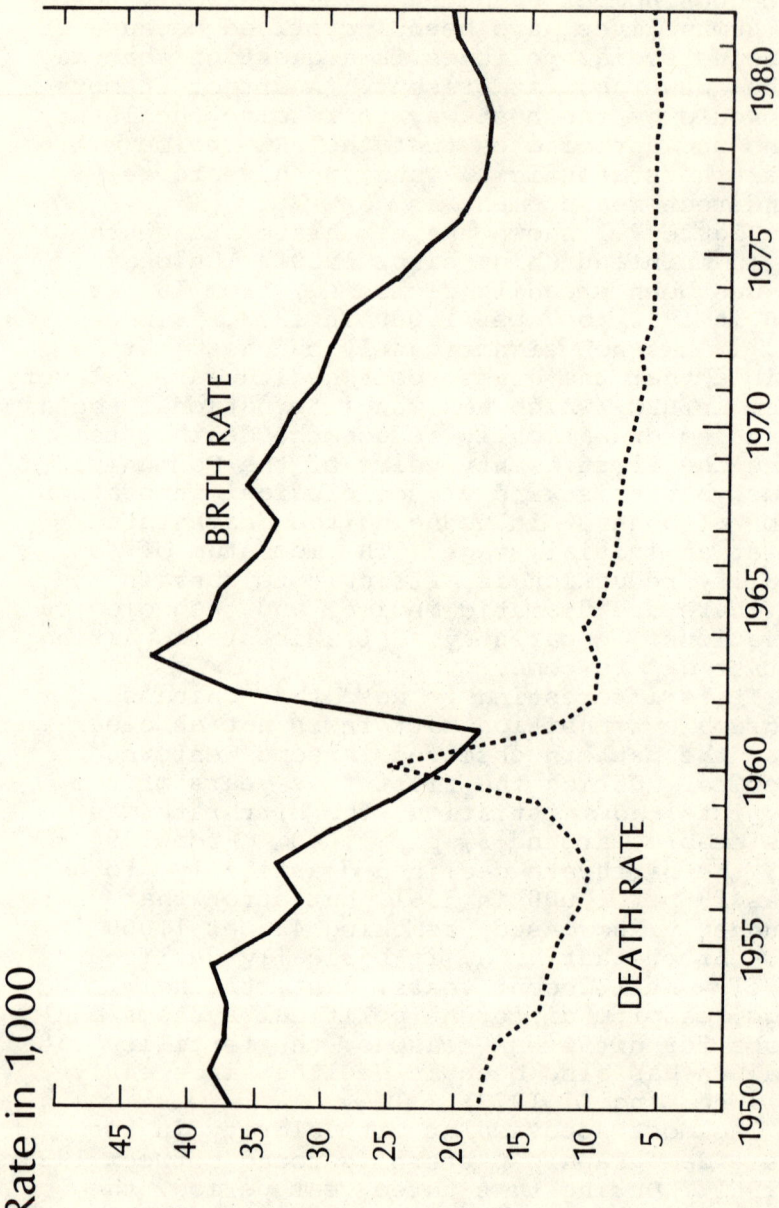

Figure 9.1: The Birth Rate and the Death Rate in China, 1950-1982

1960, there were more deaths than births. In that one year, there were 16,836,440 deaths, more than the whole population of Taiwan at that time.

The Great Leap Forward implemented what may be the most disastrous social policy in recent world history. How many human lives were sacrificed for the speedy construction of the Communist state? Let us attempt to assess this demographic tragedy in a simple mathematical way.

The rate of population increase between 1950 and 1957 was comparatively stable. For example, it was 20 per 1,000 in 1951, 23 in 1953, 20 in 1955, and 23 in 1954. The average during this "golden" period was 21.36 per 1,000. The population of China in 1957 was 646,530,000 (denoted as P_o), so without the Great-Leap-Forward we would expect that the population in 1962 (P_t) would have followed a mathematical model such as the following (population figures below are in 1,000s):

$$P_t = P_o e^{rt} = 646,530 e^{.02136 \times 5}$$

$$= 719,401$$

However, the actual population of the PRC in 1962 was only 672,950,000, a deficit of 46,451,000 people (approximately the total population of England).

Regrettably, students of Chinese society have given relatively little attention to the study of the Great Leap Forward even though voluminous studies have been made of the Cultural Revolution. In a demographic sense, the Cultural Revolution was not as detrimental as the Great Leap Forward; the sacrifice of 46 million lives during the latter period should not continue to be ignored by Sino-scholars.

PROSPECTS FOR SOCIAL CHANGE

What is to be the future development of China's population is a question of great interest to demographers. As China's population constitutes more than one-fifth of the human race, what happens to it will have a profound impact on the world. If China's birthrate is indeed declining to the level of one child per couple, then the world's population growth rate can be expected to reduce drastically. That is certainly welcome news for those people who are concerned with family planning and human environment.

Previously, two distinguished demographers attempted to project China's population on the basis of rather limited information. Ansley Coale (1981) took the position that China will adhere to the one-child family norm and prepared a set of population projections based on that assumption. His projection results call our attention to the fact that China could very well experience the problem of an aging population similar to that which is currently observed in the United States. Nathan Keyfitz (1984), on the other hand, argued that one child per couple will be much too low an estimation of the future Chinese population. Lacking the age-specific birthrate, he projected the future Chinese population based on the assumption of a constant number of births.

Both sets of projections can be further enhanced in light of the age-specific fertility rate that is now available as a result of the PRC 1982 census (see Table 9.2). We are also indebted to Rong (1981) for making available detailed life-table information calculated from the 1973-1975 nationwide PRC epidemiological survey. The survey results showed that the life expectancy was 63.6 years for Chinese males and 66.3 years for Chinese females. The low level of China's mortality, as reflected in the relatively high life expectancy, is better than that of many developing countries. Judging from the facts that the living standard of the PRC is still very low and the Chinese mortality level has been stable since 1973, it seems fair to assume that the set of survival ratios computed by Rong will be accurate at least into the near future.

Let us use $F(x)$ to denote the fertility rate at age x; $S(x)$, the survival ratio from age x to $x + 1$; $P(x)$, the initial population at age x; and $P^t(x)$, the projected population in the tth year. Then the Leslie Martrix method of population will be as follows (Wen Lang Li 1970):

$$\begin{pmatrix} F(0)S(0) & F(1)S(0) & F(2)S(0) & \cdots \\ S(1) & 0 & 0 & \cdots \\ 0 & S(2) & 0 & \cdots \\ 0 & 0 & S(0) & \cdots \\ \cdots & \cdots & \cdots & \cdots \end{pmatrix} \begin{pmatrix} P(1) \\ P(2) \\ P(3) \\ P(4) \\ \cdots \end{pmatrix} = \begin{pmatrix} P^t(1) \\ P^t(2) \\ P^t(3) \\ P^t(4) \\ \cdots \end{pmatrix}$$

Table 9.5 presents the projected results of China's population by age from 1982 to 2002 and shows that China's population will still be steadily increasing. The total population will increase from 1,004 million in 1982 to 1,073 million in 1987, 1,157 million in 1992, 1,250 million in 1997, and 1,333 million in 2002. In five-year periods, the population increase will be 69 million, 84 million, 93 million, and 83 million. On an average, the Chinese population is likely to increase by 16 million each year.

It appears that the official PRC proclamation that by the year 2000 the Chinese population will have stabilized at 1.2 billion is not likely to be realized. In the next twenty years, China's population will continue to grow. The growth rate may vary, but it will at least be comparable to the current growth of 1.5 percent per year. My estimated annual growth rates for China's population are 1.34 percent during 1982-1986, 1.51 percent during 1987-1991, 1.55 percent during 1992-1996, and 1.28 percent during 1997-2001. By the end of this century, then, the growth momentum of China's population will be slowing down, but the population size will still be increasing, not stabilizing at a fixed level.

Whether the future growth of the population will be good or bad for society depends on many considerations, one of them being the structure of that population. If a population has a high birthrate, it is likely to be burdened by a huge number of dependent children. On the other hand, if a population has a birthrate that is drastically declining, it could rapidly become burdened by a disproportionately large number of dependent old people. Neither of these two possibilities, however, appears to be applicable to China's population before the end of this century.

Table 9.5. Projected PRC population, 1982-2002
(population in 1,000s)

Age	1982	1987	1992	1997	2002
0- 4	94,717	103,399	123,358	138,986	134,209
5- 9	110,732	91,693	100,101	119,424	134,554
10-14	131,802	109,863	90,973	99,318	118,490
15-19	125,312	131,161	109,327	90,530	98,837
20-24	74,312	124,533	130,344	108,646	89,966
25-29	92,591	73,737	123,569	129,335	107,806
30-34	72,958	91,744	73,062	122,438	128,152
35-39	54,203	72,076	90,636	72,179	120,959
40-44	48,381	53,294	70,868	89,117	70,971
45-49	47,364	47,231	52,029	69,187	87,005
50-54	40,851	45,678	45,548	50,178	66,729
55-59	33,909	38,638	43,204	43,079	47,462
60-64	27,382	31,115	35,353	39,532	39,415
65-69	21,267	23,880	27,124	30,811	34,454
70-74	14,349	17,229	19,331	21,945	24,919
75-79	8,608	10,337	12,395	13,891	15,755
80-84	3,706	5,220	6,250	7,479	8,368
85+	1,344	2,426	3,406	4,055	4,831
Total	1,003,788	1,073,254	1,156,878	1,250,130	1,332,882

Sources: Calculated from PRC, Population Census Office 1983, Tables 19 and 52, and Rong 1981, Table 2.

Table 9.6 shows that the dependency ratio in China is currently expected to decline. In 1982, every 100 Chinese in the productive ages of fifteen to sixty-four were required to support an average of about 63 dependent young and old persons. By 1987, the dependency ratio will have decreased to 51 percent, and it will further decline to 49.5 percent in 1992. However, after that, it will increase to 53.5 percent in 1997 and 55.5 percent in 2002.

If the dependency ratio can be taken as an indicator of economic liability, it appears that the handicap for economic development in the PRC will be considerably lessened during the next few years, but the burden will then increase again, though it may not be as severe as that which is currently observed. In other words, if the PRC regime does not take advantage of the human capital benefit during the 1980s, the hard gained chance for economic development may disappear

Table 9.6. Dependency ratio, 1982-2002

Year	Population (1,000s)			Dependency Ratio		
	Under 15	65 and Over	15-64	Young	Old	Total
1982	337,251	49,274	617,263	54.6	8.0	62.6
1987	304,955	59,092	709,207	43.0	8.3	51.3
1992	314,432	68,506	773,940	40.6	8.9	49.5
1997	357,728	78,181	814,221	43.9	9.6	53.5
2002	387,253	88,327	857,302	45.2	10.3	55.5

Source: Calculated from Table 9.5.

during the 1990s.

During the 1980s, China's population in the productive age group is expected to increase at a rate of 2.3 percent per year before slowly beginning to decline toward the end of the decade. During the 1990s, the growth rate of China's productive force will be somewhat impeded as it is expected to be only about 1.0 percent per year.

The supposition that China's population is rapidly aging appears to be somewhat exaggerated. There is no question that the number of aged persons in China will be increasing; in fact, my estimation is that in the next twenty years, China's aged population will increase nearly 80 percent. This means a yearly aged-population growth of about 4 percent, which is certainly higher than the growth rate of total population. Nevertheless, the proportion of the aged is still relatively small in China. It was only 5 percent in 1982; by the beginning of the 1990s, it is likely to increase to 6 percent; by the year 2000, it still will not exceed 6.8 percent of the total population.

Demographically speaking, China is still a young country, and visitors to China are often impressed by the number of teenagers crowding the streets. In fact, China will continue to have a youthful population at least through this century. The youth population (ages fifteen to thirty-four) constituted 36 percent of the total population in 1982, and it is likely to increase to 39 percent in 1987. Following that, it will decrease slightly to 38 percent in 1992 and to 36 percent in 1997. Such a huge proportion of young people in the population will certainly have a phenomenal impact on many aspects of Chinese society. Whether the youth population could become a predominant social force to lead the country into becoming a more cosmopolitan and democratic state remains to be further explored.

REFERENCES

Aird, John S. 1982. "Population Studies and Population Policy in China." *Population and Development Review* 8:267-297.

Chen, Charles, and Carl W. Tyler. 1983. "Demographic Implications of Family Size Alternatives in the People's Republic of China." *China Quarterly* 89:64-75.

Cheng, Hang-Sheng. 1983. "Historical Factors of China's Economic Under-Development." Paper presented at the Twenty-fifth Annual Meeting of the American Association for Chinese Studies, Santa Barbara, California.

Ching, C. C. 1982. "The One-Child Family in China: The Need for Psychosocial Research." *Studies in Family Planning* 13:208-212.

Coale, Ansley J. 1981. "Population Trends, Population Policy, and Population Studies in China." *Population and Development Review* 7:84-109.

Goodstadt, Leo F. 1982. "China's One-Child Family: Policy and Public Response." *Population and Development Review* 8:37-56.

John Hopkins University, Population Information Program. 1982. "Population and Birth Planning in the People's Republic of China." *Population Reports*, no. 25, J577-J618.

Keyfitz, Nathan. 1984. "The Population of China." *Scientific American* 250:38-47.

Li, Chengrui. 1981. *Population Censuses in China*. Beijing: State Statistical Bureau.

Li, Wen Lang. 1970. "A Matrix Model of Population Redistribution." *Proceedings of the American Statistical Association* (Social Statistics Section), pp. 189-193.

_____. 1973. "Temporal and Spatial Analysis of Fertility Decline in Taiwan." *Population Studies* 27:97-104.

_____. 1982. "Computer Simulation of Migration and Small-Area Population." *Modeling and*

Simulation 13:1199-1203.
People's Republic of China (PRC), Population Census Office. 1983. *10 Percent Sample Tabulation on the 1982 Population Census of the People's Republic of China*. Beijing: China Statistical Publishers.
People's Republic of China (PRC), State Statistical Bureau. 1983. *China Statistical Yearbook*. Beijing: China Statistical Publishers.
Petersen, William. 1971. "The Malthus-Godwin Debate." *Demography* 8:13-26.
Qian, Xinzhong. 1983. "China's Population Policy: Theory and Methods." *Studies in Family Planning* 14:295-301.
Rong, Shou Te. 1981. "Wou Guo 1973-1975 ju Min Ping jun Qi Wang Shou Ming de Tung ji Fen Xi" [Statistical analysis of average life expectancy among our country's residents in 1973-1975]. In Beijing Economic College, ed., *Symposium of Chinese Population Science*, pp. 49-58. Beijing: China Academic Publishers.
Saith, Ashwani. 1981. "Economic Incentives for the One-Child in Rural China." *China Quarterly* 89:493-500.
Tien, H. Yuan. 1983. "Age at Marriage in the People's Republic of China." *China Quarterly* 93:90-107.
United Nations (UN). 1984. *Demographic Yearbook 1982*. New York: United Nations.

10
Socialist Spiritual Civilization and Cultural Pollution: The Problem of Meaning

James T. Myers

> *The order of history emerges from the history of order. Every society is burdened with the task, under its concrete conditions, of creating an order that will endow the fact of human existence with meaning in terms of ends divine and human.*
>
> Eric Voegelin,
> <u>Order and History</u>

> *Short of natural catastrophe, the only time life grinds to a halt or explodes in anarchy and chaos is when culture falls down on its job of constructing a meaningful hero-system for its members.*
>
> Ernest Becker,
> <u>The Birth and Death of Meaning</u>

> *Man has a profound need to believe that the truth he perceives is rooted in the unchanging depths of the universe; for were it not so, could truth be really important?*
>
> Huston Smith,
> <u>Forgotten Truth: The Primordial Tradition</u>

SIGNS, MEANING, AND POWER

> Smuggling, selling smuggled articles, embezzlement, bribery, speculation, swindling, and other illegal and criminal activities . . . have become rampant in the economic field in the last few years.[1]

> Last year, long queues of nuptial automobiles were criticized strongly by the public. So this New Year's Day saw one case of 10 beautifully decorated pedicabs, loaded with a modernized dowry including a refrigerator, TV set, sewing and washing machines, tape recorder and radio, electric fan, trunks, embroidered quilts and a variety of furniture, parading along Zhongshan Avenue in Wuhan City. Pedaled by elegantly-dressed young guests, the cab formation was surrounded by a "retinue" of young girls.[2]

> The building of socialist spiritual civilization . . . also includes resolutely eliminating all the vile social evils which had been stamped out long ago by New China but have now cropped up again.[3]

> The meaning of any utterance or sign is the response to that utterance or sign.[4]

What possible connection can these four statements have with one another? Or, more to the point, what connection can the first three have with the fourth, a statement about signs and meaning found in the introduction to Professor Morse Peckham's Explanation and Power? At first glance, there might seem to be no connection at all. Perhaps if we substituted for the last statement another of Peckham's assertions, such as "The main or central thrust of human energy is the limitation of each man's range of behavior"[5] or "Language is behavioral control and the primary mode of such control,"[6] we might begin to perceive a dim connection, for clearly the first three statements deal with human behavior and, by implication, with an attempt to direct and control that behavior. But the improvement in our understanding would probably be only marginal, and

anyway, we would be jumping the gun. Indeed, if
I am going to make a case for placing these statements together at the beginning of this chapter,
I will have to start at the beginning and proceed
systematically.

The effort to build a "socialist spiritual
civilization" and the recent complaints about
"spiritual pollution" or "cultural contamination"
in the People's Republic of China, both deal with
the control of human behavior. The first is
an effort to have individuals respond in a
certain way to certain directions; the complaints
reveal the problem of individuals' failing to
respond properly or adequately (or, in any case,
not in the desired way) to sets of directions.
The thesis of this chapter is that these problems
stem ultimately from the fundamental instability
of language itself and from the failure (ranging
from partial to complete) of human culture to
maintain "meanings" that are adequate to serve
the needs of the individual and to stabilize the
political system sufficiently to minimize the
necessity of resorting to the use of force or
political violence. In this effort, I am going
to utilize the ideas of Professor Peckham, which
seem to me especially helpful and insightful.[7]

Meaning Is Response[8]

Peckham's inquiry into the control of human
behavior was developed over a period of years in
several books and a number of essays, the most
comprehensive and systematic presentation of his
ideas coming with the publication of <u>Explanation
and Power</u> in 1979.[9] The basic building block of
his theory is the assertion that the meaning of
any sign (verbal or nonverbal) is to be found,
not in the thing itself, but in the response
the use of the sign elicits.[10] If meaning is not
immanent in the sign itself, though, theoretically
any sign could elicit all possible responses.[11]
Obviously, such a situation would make communication (not to mention human organization or even
the survival of the individual human organism)
impossible unless some way can be found to limit
the range of responses to manageable proportions.
Since meaning (response) is not immanent in the

sign, it must be learned or agreed upon.

An example of such a learned or conventional meaning may be seen in the case of language. While still in the cradle, we begin to learn the "correct" responses to verbal signs, yet we have all had the experience, even when speaking with other native users of the same set of language conventions, of being misunderstood. That is, from the point of view of the speaker, the response elicited by the utterance is inappropriate or wrong. This problem (polysemy),[12] when limited to ordinary conversation, can usually be overcome by making additional utterances and/or resorting to the use of nonverbal signs: "Not that one, _that_ one" (pointing). The resolution of this problem is a good bit less simple, however, if the meanings we attempt to stabilize are for concepts such as truth, justice, freedom of speech, socialist spiritual civilization, cultural pollution, or Lei Feng spirit.[13]

To say that the meaning of language is determined by learned agreement among speakers, however, is only a partial, incomplete, and possibly even misleading explanation of the way in which the meaning of signs is stabilized. The stabilization, or definition, of meaning is essentially an exercise in the control of human behavior, one's own as well as that of others. For words are not just the stuff of communication or of poetic or literary expression, they are directions for performance. They instruct us to _do_ something, to respond to utterances in a certain way, thus the above-quoted assertion that "language is behavioral control and the primary mode of such control."[14] If this notion is correct, then the effort to limit the theoretically unlimited range of responses to any sign and to stabilize such responses (meanings) assumes primary importance in the entire human endeavor. Here, again, we may repeat Peckham's assertion that "the main or central thrust of human energy is the limitation of each man's range of behavior."[15] Sederberg observes that: "To create a community requires controlling the range of response to situations encountered in common. The existence of shared meaning is a social puzzle to be solved not by philosophical determinations of the meaning of an event but by comprehending how human beings establish mutuality in an inherently polysemantic world."[16] Let us then turn to the question of how we attempt to channel response and thus stabilize the meaning of signs.

Redundancy, Culture, Institutions

It is Peckham's contention that the human brain is not especially good at learning and remembering, particularly in situations in which the demand to produce the learned response (behavior) is not continually repeated. That is, without regular and steady assistance, the human brain is more likely to produce a random response than a response that is appropriate to the directions received.[17] Sederberg sums up Peckham's position in this way: "The brain is not a binary, programmable, cause/effect system but a stochastic one with the capacity to randomize response."[18] Indeed, Peckham sees this capacity of the brain to produce random response as "possibly its most interesting attribute."[19] It is most certainly a key element in his explanation of the control of human behavior.

Memory is thus unreliable in establishing response, particularly in the case of language as only constant use can generate and maintain the appropriate (correct) responses necessary to read or speak that language.[20] Remembering needs help, and that help comes through repetition and reiteration: redundancy. Anyone who has ever attempted to teach a class of students or raise a child should appreciate the importance of redundancy as a pedagogical device. Peckham is thus led to the principle of cultural redundancy: "Since remembering is unreliable, since it is the consequence of the brain's capacity to produce random responses if left to itself, learned behavior can be sustained and made reliable only by constant reiteration of instructions for behavior."[21] It is redundant reiteration, without which "behavior disintegrates," that maintains meanings at the lowest level of behavior.[22] Redundancies, in turn, are maintained by culture.

Peckham defines culture as "instructions for performance"[23] or, in a more complete definition, as "those semiotic redundancy systems which maintain not merely behavior patterns but human behavior itself."[24] Elsewhere, he defines culture as "a group of individuals with the same belief system . . . [which] makes behavior predictable."[25] This definition is close to Becker's view as he sees culture as the "linguistic psychological world the human animal learns from others,"[26] the primary task of which is to provide the individual "with an ordered predictable world in which he has been trained to perform."[27] Both Peckham and Becker stress the performance dimension of culture in contrast to the more traditional "shared belief" definitions.[28] Indeed, Peckham asserts that it is precisely the job of culture to "turn behavior into performance."[29]

Culture, instructions for performance, exists in the form of explanations, that is, verbal behavior,[30] and explanation, Peckham suggests, is hierarchical.[31] These hierarchies of explanation exist in the form of "explanatory regresses," pyramids of meaning from polysemy to the final terminating concept (such as "God" or "science"), from which there can be no further appeal.[32] Each level of a regress controls the meaning of the signs or utterances on the level or levels below it, and each higher level necessarily controls a greater number of signs or utterances until, at the terminating level of the regress, such categories as God or science control everything in the pyramid.[33]

Language is inherently unstable. In fact, as Peckham observes, "Such regresses are normally anything but clear, anything but unmistakable, anything but stable."[34] How then are meanings controlled in these explanatory systems? Here Peckham introduces the notion of "policing" carried out through social institutions. Policing involves the issuance of directions about giving directions, or "metadirections."[35] Ultimately, however, the only way such meanings (response behavior) can be stabilized is by force.[36] Students of politics have, however, long recognized that the use or threat of force is itself an unstable and costly method of maintaining response behavior.[37] Indeed, there is no record of a system that was based largely or

entirely on the use of force surviving for very
long.

Peckham recognizes this problem and suggests
that culture may have developed precisely to
delay or circumvent the use of force to control
human behavior. "The suggestion is," he writes,
"that what we call culture emerged because if
force is unsuccessful in stabilizing behavior,
there is no alternative."[38] He further suggests
that "a culture is stable, it appears to follow,
to the degree that the ultimate sanctions of
physical force are obviated, postponed, or circumvented."[39] A variety of methods or strategies
for controlling behavior are thus available,
ranging along a continuum from seduction to force.
This control, in turn, is exercised through social
institutions that are hierarchically organized and
maintained by force.[40]

Not all institutions, of course, have
recourse to the ultimate sanctions at all times.
For example, we rarely kill students who fail to
generate the appropriate responses to directions
in the university. But the use of this sanction
(murder) has been sufficiently widespread in our
institutions throughout history (including the
family and religious institutions) that it should
serve to support Peckham's point. In fact, he
contends that "it is a shibboleth of liberal
thinking that no man should be executed for an
opinion, but in fact no man is ever executed or
murdered for any other reason."[41]

It may be useful to note here that there is
a distinction to be made between the notion of an
explanatory regress that is terminated by an all-powerful concept (God, fate, Chairman Mao's
thought, or whatever) and an institution (principally government institutions in this analysis)
that is terminated by force. This distinction
allows us to see the competition of explanatory
systems (regresses) across institutions or within
a single institution, such as the Chinese Communist
Party (CCP).

Those groups of sentences that we call
ideologies are systems of explanation and validation that exist for the purpose of validating
institutions. The term "ideology," Peckham tells
us, "directs our attention to those redundant

utterances which together form the ultimate explanatory rhetoric of a society."[42] The relationship between institution and ideology is thus a symbiotic one. Ideology sanctions and validates institutions, and institutions seek to sustain the coherence of the validating ideological redundancies.

Having described, albeit superficially, the methods by which we attempt to stabilize human response behavior, it must now be said that none of these efforts are more than partially successful. The problem, once again, stems from the instability of language. Instructions for performance, culturally validated explanations (validated by ideology), and ideology itself are only words and sentences—verbal behavior. Incoherence between explanation and the empirical world must develop because language cannot describe the world but can only give us directions for behavior.[43]

At the lowest level, where behavior encounters the empirical world, directions can never encompass or comprehend the total situation in which they will be carried out and are intended to control behavior. The feedback from the empirical world must cause either a shift (however slight) in the response behavior or a change in the directions. On the metadirectional level, incoherences require similar but more radical adjustment. The incoherence is necessarily more serious because of the large number of subordinate directions that are controlled by the metadirectional explanatory system. Take, for example, the situation in China during the early years of the PRC when unrestricted population growth and national development were seen to be coherent objectives. When incoherences develop, as they did in this case, it is the task of "high intellectual culture to innovate new systems of explanatory coherence,"[44] a task with which Chinese high intellectual circles are still struggling.

The resolution of explanatory incoherence is critical, because should the directions-performance system fail, human behavior would become impossible. Peckham and others see the fear of this breakdown, the fear of being unable to perform correctly to directions or to generate directions to which others can respond appropriately, as "the fundamental and pervasive human anxiety."[45] Clifford Geertz reaches essentially the same conclusion: "Man depends upon symbols and symbol systems with a dependence so great as to be decisive for his creatural viability and, as a result, his sensitivity to even the remotest indication that they may prove unable to cope with one or another aspect of experience raises within him the greatest sort of anxiety."[46] And Becker adds, "when culture falls down on its job . . . life grinds to a halt."[47]

It should be obvious that most of us are not normally threatened with behavioral disintegration. Our directions-performance system works well enough, if not perfectly. For while culture is constantly disintegrating, it is also continually being renewed by the "introduction of innovative redundancies."[48] It is possible, however, to witness the breakdown of the directions-performance system when massive negative feedback invades the system and threatens the coherence of an entire explanatory system. Such a situation results in a culture crisis and is frequently the consequence of the meeting (collision might be a better term) of two cultures, one of which is stronger or technologically superior to the other. Such is the case when "superior" colonists encounter primitive peoples, and such was the case when Western culture invaded China in the nineteenth century. Peckham, in fact, insists that there is no possibility of coexistence: "Once two modes of performance and two modes of directions come into contact, either one is destroyed--as primitives are always destroyed by more powerful explanatory systems--or both are damaged and riven with incoherence."[49]

If such a crisis in culture arises, the response will be a revolution of some other form of a cultural "revitalization" movement that seeks to construct a new system of explanatory coherences. As Anthony Wallace states, "From the standpoint of its cultural function, a revitalization movement is the process by which cultural materials which have hitherto appeared to members of society as dissonant are analyzed and combined into a new structure."[50]

To sum up, then, it is suggested that the business of culture is to validate responses, and therefore behavior, by providing culturally validated instructions for performance. Because of the brain's tendency to random response, new, innovative, or unexpected responses are constantly generated, though in most cases, but, to be sure, not all, the innovation or drift may be so slight as to go unnoticed. It is through this process (by which culturally validated innovation becomes "creativity" and that which is invalidated becomes "error")[51] that explanatory systems are renewed and adapted to the empirical world in which they attempt to direct performance. Let us turn briefly to this process of renewal and adaptation and examine the question of innovation and stability.

Feedback, Innovation, and Stability

"Cultural stability and innovation," Peckham tells us, "are irreconcilable,"[52] yet innovation must emerge from an explanatory system as a result of the "disparity between any cognitive model and the actual situation" to which it is applied.[53] How, then, do we manage this irreconcilable tension, or at least manage it well enough to muddle through? Here we must look again at the concept of feedback.

As we have seen, when explanation encounters the empirical world, incoherences develop. The individual experiences anomalies, things that do not make sense according to one's directions and expectations. These incoherences, or anomalies, we may call negative feedback. If the negative feedback is slight, the response may be to observe and forget it. Another sort of response would be to alter behavior slightly in response to the incoherence. At some point, however, if the incoherence persists, it will be necessary to alter or adjust the explanatory system that provided the directions for behavior. And, as suggested above, if the negative feedback is sufficiently widespread, it may threaten the coherence of the explanatory system at the ultimate regressive level. A cultural crisis occurs when a critical mass of individuals has "come to believe that the explanation of human experience, which is always wrong but is ordinarily believed to be right, is in fact wrong."[54] The stability of a culture over time thus depends upon the success the higher intellectuals have in adjusting the metadirectional explanatory system in response to negative feedback.

In any culture, it is the government institutions that play the primary role in resolving ideological incoherences. Such resolution (determination of meaning) occurs, not only with respect to internal inconsistencies within a particular ideology, but also in cases of conflict between two or more competing explanatory regresses. Thus, in China during the Cultural Revolution, for example, the government attempted to settle the question whether "one divides into two" or "two combine into one." More recently, the government has been faced with resolving the question whether the verbal category "socialist relations of production" properly includes the statement, "It is acceptable for one individual to hire the labor of another."

Like other institutions, government institutions seek to maintain redundancies. But because of their special task of resolving ideological incoherences in the culture, government institutions seek to sustain those ideological redundancies "which form the armory of verbal behavior used to resolve incoherences at the lower explanatory level."[55] And therein lies a problem. Government institutions have the job of resolving ideological incoherence and the "rejection or absorption of ideological rivals."[56] But where, Peckham asks, "does judgement of incoherence and innovation of rivalries come from?"[57] They do not come from the government institutions themselves, which are interested in stability and the prevention of ideological conflict. The source of such innovation is in those institutions (Peckham calls them ideological institutions) whose semiotic products are "the physical and behavioral sciences, philosophy, theology, and the arts, including decorative arts."[58]

Government institutions are therefore faced with the difficult dilemma of resolving ideological incoherence occasioned by innovation generated outside the government while, at the same time, seeking to maintain the ideological redundancies that permit them to remain in power and to carry out their functions. The techniques of science, not commitment to an ideology, Peckham suggests, are what most successfully exploit incoherence for the purpose of adjusting the metadirectional explanatory system,[59] because science links experiment with explanation.[60] The key to this technique is that the scientist, by "randomizing his behavior [experimentation], creates the conditions necessary for learning a new response which he judges to be an appropriate one."[61] But herein lies the problem. The greater the extent to which a government is committed to an ideology (and I suggest that the commitment of the government of the PRC is substantial), the greater will be its effort to prevent the "randomization of behavior within ideological disciplines" in order to prevent the "emergence of ideological innovations and critiques."[62] Committed to an ideology, such governments attempt to prevent any challenge to the ideology's coherence. As a result, all other redundancy systems are, to the fullest extent possible, brought under ideological control.

In China, therefore, we can see that any attempt to describe the central explanatory system as "scientific" is somewhat misleading. It is true that Mao exhorted his countrymen to seek truth from facts and that he wrote a major essay ("On Practice") about how explanatory systems should be modified by negative feedback, but this idea was incompatible (whether Mao realized it or not) with the dominant effort of the Party to discourage randomization of behavior and to bring under ideological control all those institutions whose job it is to innovate new explanatory ideas. Indeed, the use of the term "scientific" by the leaders of the PRC to characterize their metadirectional explanatory system (e.g., "scientific socialism") has amounted to nothing more than an attempt to draw validation for the ideology from the exceptionally high status of science as a terminating concept.[63] By its reliance on ideology, therefore, such a government cuts itself off from the most important source of adaptive innovation and, by weakening or destroying those institutions that make possible the delay or circumvention of the use of force, must, inevitably, have more frequent recourse to the use of political violence as the ultimate terminating sanction.

CULTURE AND REVOLUTION

> It was not the reality of their lives that was so unbearable. It was the hopelessness that lay behind the reality.[64]

Culture and the Individual

I have suggested that a primary human motivation is the reduction of anxiety arising from the fear of being unable to respond adequately to directions or to generate directions to which others can respond. The basis of this anxiety is the ever-present threat of the failure of culture to provide adequate directions for performance in the empirical world. Ernest Becker calls our attention to a particular dimension of the problem of anxiety. Man, he suggests, alone among the animals, lives "a whole lifetime with the fate of death haunting [his] dreams and even the most sun-filled days."[65] Becker also suggests that man endures an "existential dualism," at once "up in the stars" stalking out of nature with "a towering majesty, and yet [going] back into the ground a few feet in order blindly and dumbly to rot and disappear forever."[66] This dualism, Becker asserts, creates an "excruciating dilemma." As a consequence, man "literally drives himself into a blind obliviousness with social games, psychological tricks, personal preoccupations so far removed from the reality of his situation that they are forms of madness--agreed madness, shared madness, disguised or dignified madness, but madness all the same."[67]

All this madness is what we have been calling culture. Becker suggests that humans respond to their exruciating dilemma by creating "mythical hero-system[s] in which people serve in order to earn a feeling of primary value, of cosmic specialness, of ultimate usefulness to creation, of unshakable meaning.[68] Other writers have also noted this uniqueness of man as a symbol-using animal and the central role of symbols in man's self-ascription of value.[69] Rollo May writes that an individual's self-image is built up of symbols and that the individual "experiences himself as self in terms of symbols."[70] Becker adds that "the 'I' . . . has to take shape linguistically" and that "without speech <u>there can be no true ego</u>."[71]

All of these ideas bring us back to the point that human beings create a world of symbols through which they attempt to understand the world and their place in it, and through which they attempt to ascribe value to themselves and their actions. Becker tells us that a part of this symbolizing involves the creation of transcendent explanatory systems (hero-systems) through which humans attempt to deny the ultimate reality of their own death. But Peckham, as usual, draws us back to earth with the reminder that "psychic truths when embedded in language are no longer psychic truths but sets of directions"[72]--and, we might add, sets of directions whose inadequacy ranges from partial to complete. What happens when such directions fail the individual I have already briefly suggested in the first section of this chapter.

From the beginning of the species, Becker suggests, humans have lived in two worlds, "a visible one in which everyday action took place; and a greater, much more powerful world--the invisible one, upon which the visible one depended, and from which it drew its powers."[73] For the Chinese, over many centuries, this invisible world was largely dominated by the Confucian world view. Like all explanatory systems, the Confucian system was adapted and changed over time, but Confucius proved remarkably durable as a terminating concept stabilizing redundancies of Chinese culture over a very long period of time.

It is impossible to tell what the ultimate fate of this great explanatory system might have been, but we know what happened when it encountered the more powerful culture of the West in the nineteenth century. Lucien Bianco writes that in the three-quarters of a century from 1839 to 1916,

the Chinese "witnessed something like the crumbling
of a world, a civilization, a weltanschauung;
the death of the Confucian world view which had
been accepted by virtually every Chinese whose
income, upbringing, and leisure allowed him to look
beyond the narrow confines of his village."[74]
Indeed, the crisis of Chinese culture eventually
affected all Chinese, not just those who could
understand the failure of the higher levels of the
explanatory system.

Anthony Wallace suggests that the response
to such an explanatory failure or culture crisis
is "a deliberate, organized, conscious effort by
members of society to construct a more satisfying
culture." Moreover, the effort must be to
"innovate not merely discrete items, but a new
cultural system."[75] This response is precisely
what took place in China. The ideological
incoherences were so great, and the failure of
the cultural redundancies to maintain directions
for performance was so complete, that it was
necessary for the high intellectuals to innovate
entirely new metadirections.

It can be no accident that Chinese intellectuals selected the designation "new culture" for
their movement in 1917.[76] Nor is it merely
coincidental that the May 4 movement (1919)
heralded a renaissance, a new birth of Chinese
culture. Bianco writes, "The May Fourth Movement
called into question the very basis of Chinese
society. . . . Intellectually, the Chinese
revolution originated in the challenging of China's
cultural heritage by Western civilization. May
Fourth was the culmination of that challenge: the
brutal, wholesale repudiation of Confucianism,
the symbol of Chinese culture and Chinese history."[77]

Although the May 4 movement and the intellectual
ferment of the early decades of the century transformed Chinese culture, these cultural innovations
failed in the ultimate goal of a revitalization
movement to achieve a "new steady state."[78] The
Chinese renaissance of the 1920s was thus only a
prelude to the Chinese revolution of the 1940s.

Revolution and Charisma

It was Mao Zedong who finally succeeded in

focusing and synthesizing the disparate ideological elements into a coherent explanatory system that explained the revolution he led and validated the government it established in 1949. Central to this successful effort was Mao, the man himself, the Chairman, "the indispensable man." Edgar Snow wrote, long before the victory of the revolution, "You feel that whatever there is extraordinary in this man grows out of the uncanny degree to which he synthesizes and expresses the urgent demand of millions of Chinese."[79] In the early years of the PRC, a considerable cult began to grow up around Mao.[80] The Chairman was compared to the life-giving forces of nature, especially the sun, and he was cited as the recognized authority on everything from art to night-soil collecting.[81] Mao's image was soon found in every home, every school, every public office and factory. In many homes, it was said, his image occupied the central place on the family altar and replaced the ancestor tablets as the principal object of worship.[82] One of the most popular songs of the day proclaimed:

> The east is red
> The sun rises
> On the horizon of China
> Appears the great hero Mao Tse-tung . . .
> He is the great savior of the people.[83]

It was as "hero" and "savior" that Mao appeared in this early manifestation of the cult, which was probably to be expected in view of the fact that Mao filled the role of prophet or the charismatic leader of a cultural revitalization movement.

The concept of charisma has been subject to a variety of definitions, but central to the function of a charismatic leader is the ability to reduce the stress, anxiety, or cognitive tension associated with cultural disintegration; to resolve discontinuities; to explain the world and its meaning in a new and more satisfactory way.[84] The leader thus appears as a prophet, leading the people to a new age and a more satisfying culture. The conditions under which such prophet-leaders appear are always those of "rapid change, invalidated tradition and mass insecurity," in which the prophet points "the way out of the present state of chaos."[85]

Mao, the prophet,[86] through the manipulation of the new revolutionary redundancies, attempted to create an explanatory system in which individuals could enjoy a sense of primary self-value. The new explanatory system attempted to redefine the meaning of life and to link human action to a new "invisible world" of power. The terminating concept was no longer "Confucius" or even "China" (though the latter concept has continued to be important as a symbol of sentiment and identification), it was "history." The Chinese revolution was linked to the engine of history, and Chairman Mao was the prophet/engineer correctly forecasting and explaining the inevitable progress of the movement toward the millenium. At the height of the Great Leap Forward in 1958, the People's Daily declared: "Today in the era of Mao Tse-tung, heaven is here on earth. . . . Chairman Mao is a great prophet. . . . Each prophecy of Chairman Mao has become a reality. It was so in the past; it is so today."[87] Two years later, the same theme was stressed: "Comrade Mao Tse-tung is always able to see the essence of things and the future development, and able to point to the sun that is about to emerge from behind the clouds, to point to the coming dawn in the night and to point to the correct direction in a maze of complex surroundings."[88]

As a prophet, Mao's thought (ideological redundancies) was said to be consistently correct and victorious over erroneous thought (ideological rivals) of all kinds. Moreover, Mao was said to exemplify in his person and behavior the values that the new ideology sought to validate. He was said to be the "incarnation of Communism and truth and the symbol of invincibility."[89]

It is not uncommon, of course, for revolutionary regimes to rely on the unifying symbol of the revolutionary leader in order to endow their actions with legitimacy, that is, to have individuals follow directions for performance because they believe that those directions are endowed with the qualities of "rightness, propriety, or moral goodness."[90] The sort of authority crisis that accompanies a cultural collapse, Lucian Pye tells us, "by its very nature . . . means that power is limited by the suspicion that it lacks a proper moral base and hence lacks legitimacy."[91] Such a crisis, he notes, "calls for the creation of the myth of legitimacy for new governmental institutions."[92]

The authorizing myth (ideological redundancies) of the new revolutionary government was thus reinforced by the redundancies of the Mao cult, and Chairman Mao was projected as the exemplification of the value system that was maintained by the government-supported ideology.[93] The image of Mao as the embodiment of the revolutionary values of simplicity, dedication, and self-sacrifice was created when the Communists were still in Yan'an. Edgar Snow wrote of Mao that "he owned only his blankets, and a few personal belongings, including two cotton uniforms. Although he was a Red Army commander as well as Chairman, he wore on his collar only the two red bars that are the insignia of the ordinary Red soldier."[94] Also, "One soldier told me of seeing Mao give his coat away to a wounded man at the front. They say that he refused to wear shoes when the Red warriors had none."[95] These values (ideological redundancies) were central to the cultural revitalization movement that Mao led, and there were other people who exemplified them as well, though certainly not so perfectly as Mao did. One of these was Norman Bethune, the Canadian surgeon who died in China, who was paid a signal honor by Mao when he wrote an essay in his memory.[96] Later there developed a pantheon of revolutionary heroes, epitomized by the "ever rust-proof screw," Lei Feng.[97]

More than twenty years later, though, when the objective conditions of Mao's life and his revolution had changed considerably, perhaps fundamentally, the same image was projected:

> The door screen [of Mao's room] for protection against the sun was made of reeds, and the appointments within were very simple. Except for a bookcase full of books, a cot, a desk, and several chairs, there was nothing. Chairman Mao's clothes

> are simplicity itself. His silver-grey
> gown has been worn for several years,
> his shoes have lost their color; even
> his swim suit has been patched.[98]

There is substantial evidence that this effort enjoyed a fair measure of success in the years before 1949 and even to some extent in the early years of the PRC. Mao did seem to touch individual lives in a special way, to rekindle hope, reduce anxiety, and offer new explanations that provided many individuals with a sense of self-worth. Mao linked human action to a new invisible world of power ("communism," "history") and called upon individuals to perform miracles by drawing power from this invisible dimension.[99] This effort is what Frederick Wakeman has described as Mao's "identification of mass man with the force of nature itself" and the Chinese people as "cosmic tornados and tempests sweeping across the land."[100]

I have suggested in an earlier article[101] that it is far from coincidence that these images tend to be religious or pseudoreligious. Indeed, the literature of Mao's revolution that has been generated by both participants and observers abounds with religious imagery. Andre Malraux, for example, wrote of the "monastic bareness" of the Party assembly rooms in Yan'an, a bareness, "reminiscent of our great monasteries, which suggests an invisible power."[102] And on viewing the Museum of the Revolution in Yan'an, he made this observation: "This China, so unreligious but so strongly bound to its earth, its rivers, its mountains, and its dead, is linked to its resurrection by another form of ancestor worship, in which the history of the liberation is the gospel and Mao the son, in the sense in which the Emperor was the Son of heaven."[103] To emphasize the point, Malraux quotes the following remark made to him by Mao Zedong in 1966: "Revolution is a drama of passion; we did not win the people over by appealing to reason, but by developing hope, trust, and fraternity. In the face of famine, the will to equality takes on a religious force."[104]

But something happened. The revolution

changed direction, aborted. As the Cultural Revolution was soon to demonstrate, Mao's efforts at cultural revitalization also failed to achieve a new steady state, and many of the cultural problems that had given rise to the revolution in the first place remained to be solved.

The Fall of Chairman Mao[105]

On November 27, 1967, the Central Committee of the CCP issued the "Notification Regarding Strict Prohibition of the Reprinting of Chairman Mao's Photo,"[106] which stipulated that neither individuals nor any organization was permitted privately to reprint any photograph of Mao that had not been officially published, screened, and approved by the Central Committee. If there were not enough other signs around (the Cultural Revolution raged), this prohibition should have served notice that somehow the Chinese revolution had fundamentally changed course. The facts that even the image of the Chairman had come to be perceived by some people as incoherent and that the coherence of the explanatory system, of which the verbal and nonverbal redundancies of the Mao cult were an exemplification, was now increasingly stabilized through the use or threat of force were indicators that Mao's revitalization effort had failed.

Nor is other evidence lacking that the revolution had become conservative long before it achieved the cultural transformation at which it aimed. The much-analyzed Hundred Flowers period revealed the uneasy relationship between Chinese intellectuals and the government institutions and the effort, through force, to bring the writers (and, by extension, all of the ideological institutions, to use Peckham's terminology)[107] under the control of the government-sponsored ideology.[108] I will suggest in the next section that the situation could not have been otherwise, that the clash between government and ideological institutions, far from resulting from some sort of "mistake" or "miscalculation," was to be expected--was, in fact, inevitable--and that this tension constitutes the central dilemma facing China's modernizers.

But the best possible evidence that something had gone seriously wrong with the effort to create a new and more satisfying culture for China was provided by the onset of the Cultural Revolution. So much has been written about the chaos of this period (1966-1976) that there is no need to belabor the history of events or the cast of actors involved. Several observations, however, may be relevant to the argument that follows.

There can be little doubt that the prophet of the movement had also come to the conclusion that his revitalization movement had gone off course, or, at the very least, was far from complete and not getting any closer.[109] On the eve of the Cultural Revolution, Mao told Andre Malraux, "The thought, culture, and customs which brought China to where we found her must disappear, and the thought, customs and culture of proletarian China, which does not yet exist, must appear."[110] Mao bemoaned the "stupidities" of "corruption, law breaking, the arrogance of intellectuals, the wish to do honor to one's family by becoming a white-collar worker and not dirtying one's hands anymore."[111] "Neither the agricultural nor the industrial problem is solved," said the Chairman, "still less the youth problem. Revolution and youth must be trained if they are to be properly brought up. . . . Youth must be put to the test."[112]

At the end of this extraordinary interview, when the two were alone, Mao expressed to Malraux his sense of isolation. "I am alone with the masses," he said. "Waiting." Malraux observed, "The tone is a surprising one, in which there is bitterness, perhaps irony, and above all pride. One might think that he has spoken these last words for the benefit of others, but he has only spoken with passion since they moved out of earshot. He is walking more slowly than his illness compels him to." Mao continued, "What is expressed in that commonplace term 'revisionism' is the <u>death of the revolution</u>. . . . I have told you that revolution is also a feeling. . . . <u>Our revolution cannot be simply the stabilization of a victory</u>."[113]

The new revolution that Mao launched was once

again a type of revitalization movement, but this time it was both revivalistic[114] and nativistic.[115] The Cultural Revolution and the activities of the Red Guards, observed Pye writing at the time, meant that "those in authority have failed to live up to expected standards, and the demand of the revolutionaries is for a more complete disciplining of life."[116]

In the end, though, this movement also failed to achieve the desired cultural transformation, and the masses upon whom Mao counted seem, from the evidence of later years, to have been waiting, not for another call to arms, but for the more seductive message of Deng Xiaoping and the "modernizers." Indeed, China today (though perhaps only for the short term) appears to be firmly in the control of the very people upon whom Mao sought to vent his wrath. But while the modernizers have opened China to the world again and brought it peace and a measure of prosperity, there remains the problem of culture--instructions for performance--this time in the guise of socialist spiritual civilization.

No less an authority than Party General-Secretary Hu Yaobang has declared that "many serious problems concerning standards of social conduct now exist in our country."[117] The problem, said Hu, lies partly in "the decade of domestic turmoil [which] confounded the criteria of right and wrong, good and evil, beauty and ugliness. It will be more difficult to undo its grave spiritual consequences than its material ones."[118] It is interesting to consider the possibility that the problems which socialist spiritual civilization seeks to address, and the complaints of the campaign against spiritual pollution and cultural contamination, both reveal problems that are characteristic of what Wallace calls the "period of cultural distortion" (between the period of increased individual stress and the period of revitalization), namely, "Alcoholism, venality in public officials, the 'black market,' breaches of sexual and kinship mores, hoarding, gambling for gain, 'scapegoatism,' and similar behaviors that, in the preceding period, were still defined as individual deviancies, in effect become institutionalized efforts to circumvent the evil effects of 'the system.'"[119]

Hu Yaobang pointed to cultural problems of this sort when he declared that the building of spiritual civilization means "a fundamental turn for the better in the standards of social conduct . . . [which] includes in the main, the achievement of markedly better public order, generally improved attitudes towards all types of work and a marked decline in the crime rate. It also means putting an effective check on, and arousing universal contempt for, such unhealthy tendencies and practices as benefitting oneself at others' expense, pursuing private interests at the expense of public interests, loving ease and despising work, putting money first in everything, unscrupulous pursuit of personal enjoyment and attempting to isolate and attack advanced elements," which, one assumes, must include the Party. Hu also declared that there would be a resolute effort to eliminate the aforementioned "vile social evils which . . . have now cropped up again."[120] "All our cultural construction," Hu added, "must, of course, be guided by Communist ideology,"[121] and therein, I suggest in the next section, lies the dilemma facing China's Communist leaders.

INNOVATION AND STABILITY

>"When a society and a culture are in a condition of crisis . . . then the task of high culture is to expose the incoherences and to generate novel systems of explanation and validation."[122]

Ideology and Control

It may seem curious to some readers that this chapter returns time and again to the subject of culture crisis. The popular view would seem to have it that things are fine in China and getting better--U.S. corporations certainly seem to think so. The emphasis seems to be on stability (that is, predictability), progress, rationality (no more crazy radicalism), "modernization" (that is, getting more and more like Westerners), and the profit motive. Why, then, should I want to be a prophet of gloom and constantly draw attention to "spiritual" and "cultural" problems?

In a sense, I am only doing what I have been told to do (responding to verbal directions, though perhaps in an innovative or unanticipated way: an example of randomization of behavior) by the current leaders of the PRC who insist, time and time again, upon drawing attention to these problems. My files are fat with ideological statements about spiritual or cultural or "moral" (which is the same thing) problems. A few examples may serve to set the tone of the public expression of the cultural problem.

The Guangdong Provincial Committee of the Communist Youth League has called upon youths of the province to "further develop their Learn-From-Lei Feng and Establish-New-Habits activities so as to turn themselves into youths and children with a new spiritual civilization."[123] An item from Shanghai declared, "Selfless acts said necessary to social progress: can we be 'subjectively for ourselves' and at the same time 'objectively for others'?"[124] and from Sichuan has come, "Young people urged to build spiritual civilization," in which the secretary of the Chengdu Municipal Committee of the CCP called upon young people to "further recognize the momentous significance of 'learning from Lei Feng and creating a new trend' in the new era, develop the glorious traditions and intensively launch the 'five stresses' and 'four beauties' activities."[125] The China Daily has announced, "Institute tackling urgent problem of moral education" and revealed that "in over 200 higher learning institutions, offices or societies of moral education have been established" to deal with what is described as an "urgent need."[126]

More recently, attention has been focused on the negative or "pollution" side of the problem, and a flood of articles and broadcasts on the subject has been produced.[127] There can be no doubt that the Party takes this problem seriously, as is evidenced by Hu Yaobang's attention to spiritual civilization in his address to the Twelfth Party Congress. Indeed, said Hu, the problem is central to the future of socialism: "Socialism must possess . . . spiritual civilization with communist ideology at its core. Without this, the <u>building of socialism would be out of the question</u>."[128]

If Communist ideology is to be the core and if all is to be guided by this ideology (that is, to be brought under the control of the sanctioning ideology), an important question to be asked is, What is the nature of "those redundant utterances which together form the ultimate explanatory rhetoric"[129] of the PRC? That is, what is the content of this controlling ideology? The question is easier put than answered, for it goes to the very heart of the larger question about the nature of the culture (or hero-system, to use Becker's term) that the present government leaders are attempting to construct.

There has been no shortage of pronouncements on this subject, but the vast number of ideological sentences generated by the effort to build spiritual civilization and oppose cultural pollution, far from simplifying the task of understanding the controlling ideology, have actually confused the issue even further. A major problem involving the coherence of the highest levels of the explanatory system may serve to illustrate the point: What metadirections should control utterances regarding the category "Chairman Mao"? This is clearly no trivial matter. As founder-prophet of the movement, as its "greatest leader," and as "the reddest sun" in the hearts of his countrymen, Chairman Mao was intimately connected with the entire fabric of the explanatory system that constituted the sanctioning ideology. Great care had to be taken in innovating new meta-directions for controlling this concept lest the changes threaten the coherence of the sanctioning ideology itself. The importance of this effort can be gauged by the fact that the Sixth Plenary Session of the CCP Eleventh Central Committee devoted the bulk of its meeting to the problem and produced a lengthy document (thirty-eight single-spaced pages in translation) explaining its conclusion that while Chairman Mao was a great Marxist-Leninist, he had made serious mistakes. The former metadirectional sentences, "Chairman Mao is like the sun giving light everywhere it shines"[130] and "Today in the era of Mao Tse-tung heaven is here on earth,"[131] were replaced with the sentence, "Chief responsibility for the grave 'left' error of the 'cultural revolution,' an error comprehensive in magnitude and protracted in duration, does indeed lie with Comrade Mao Zedong."[132]

One can understand this innovation as an attempt to exemplify the new metadirections that the post-Mao leaders wish to stabilize, but that understanding does not necessarily make the new metadirections any more coherent or easy to respond to. In fact, none of their efforts seem entirely clear to me; I am not quite sure exactly what sort of response behavior the metadirections are attempting to stabilize. Efforts like the five stresses and the four beautifications and even the notion of spiritual civilization seem particularly unclear, especially if they are intended to stabilize specific response behavior at the lowest level and particularly if ultimate sanctions are to be applied for incorrect responses. My guess is that the precise response behavior called for by the new directions may be unclear to many Chinese as well.

Exemplification of Ideology

It may be useful, therefore, to turn our attention briefly to the content of ideology, and more particularly to the exemplification of this ideology, before we attempt to see what conclusions may be suggested about China's attempt to build a new and more satisfying culture. In terms of exemplifying the positive values of behavior, no model is more widely advertised than Lei Feng. For the benefit of people whose hagiography is a bit fuzzy, it might be useful to review the pertinent details of Lei Feng's life and death.

Lei Feng was born in humble circumstances and died on August 15, 1962, a soldier of the People's Liberation Army.[133] He was struck on the head by a wooden pole, which was knocked over by a truck as he was directing the truck to back away. He died of his wound. According to his biography: "Lei Feng died on duty. He lived only twenty-two years, a short but glorious life. He was born in poverty and brought up in happiness, and his life shed a brilliant light in the era of Mao Tse-tung."[134] The tremendous adulation that was soon heaped on him was occasioned by the fact that shortly after his death, it was discovered that Lei Feng had left behind a diary. That diary showed that his life had been characterized "by the communist spirit of loyalty to the motherland, the people and the Party as well as by complete selfless devotion to others."[135] In order to promote these qualities of character, the Party launched a nationwide campaign in 1963 to "learn from Comrade Lei Feng."[136]

With the passing of years and changes in the political fortunes of the people who had sponsored the campaign, Lei Feng slipped somewhat into obscurity. A children's book published in 1975 contained one passing reference to Lei Feng in a story about the importance of screws, and it was necessary to include a footnote identifying Lei Feng for the reader.[137] Thus, if name recognition cannot account for Lei Feng's recent new lease on immortality, the explanation must lie in the desire of (at least some of) the current leaders to once again stress the qualities that Lei Feng's life exemplified. These qualities included not only the selfless devotion cited above but also "excellent work" (he became the best tractor driver at one point), diligent study, taking care of public property, modesty, and thrift. It was said that he "never squandered a single cent and deposited all his savings in the bank," at one point contributing the lot toward the purchase of a tractor.[138]

But Lei is best remembered for his desire to be like a "screw that never rusts"[139] in his work. His final conversion was nearly as sudden as Saul's on the road to Damascus. A wise old worker told Lei, "Large-scale industrial production may be likened to a machine. Every shop, every kind of work, is like a machine part, a screw, and you can't do without any of them. Look, do you think a machine can work without one of its screws?" Lei Feng suddenly understood the relationship of his own small job to overall socialist construction, and as a result of this revelation, "it was with still greater eagerness that he began to drive the bulldozer." Always mindful of the Party's instructions and of Chairman Mao's admonition to maintain the Party's "tradition of simple living and hard work," Lei Feng wrote in his diary: "A screw must be frequently oiled and polished if it is to be kept from going rusty. It's the same with your thinking. It too must be frequently examined if it is to be kept from going astray."[140]

The recent campaign to emulate Lei Feng has stressed these same qualities. The Beijing Ribao declared that the "Lei Feng spirit" was needed for the four modernizations, and it cited him for his dedication to the country and to the interests of the Party: "He would do whatever the Party asked him to do. . . . Assigned a certain job, he would cherish his work and study it intensively. He was like a screw that will never rust."[141] Another article in Beijing Ribao called on young people to "be the Lei Feng of the Eighties,"[142] and a Wen hui pao article described the Lei Feng spirit as "a monument of the civilization with a socialist spirit."[143] Radio Beijing hailed the "Lei Feng spirit" and urged that "like Lei Feng, all our comrades should transform their utter devotion to the motherland and the people into actual deeds and strive to be vanguards in building socialist spiritual civilization. . . . Lei Feng's spirit will shine brilliantly forever."[144]

Despite this effort, however, the message of Lei Feng's life does not seem to be irresistible, and there appear to be few living "Lei Fengs" around. On the contrary, cynicism about "backdoor" connections and abuse of position by Party members is so widespread that these problems have also recently become themes for exemplification. The play A Warm Heart, which is said to be continually sold out, is based on the life of Zhu Boru, himself said to be a "living Lei Feng of the eighties."[145] "The message of the play," says the China Daily, "is clear: If all 40 million Party members, who make up 4 percent of the country's population, act like Liang Ziru [the character based on Zhu Boru], the Party will have the people's support forever."[146]

Another new play, Chief of the Labour and

Wage Department, is said to be a satire dealing with back-door relations. According to the China Daily, the play "directs a sharp spear at the current notion that only with connections--a back door--can one accomplish anything." The denouement occurs when the hero makes his final decision to break "the connections net" in "defense of the Party's interests and to live up to its principles."[147]

A recent film, Blood Will Always Be Warm, also features a hero who is frustrated by an "invisible 'net,'" which even includes Communist Party members who "either take overt measures or resort to subversive tactics to insure that nothing new is tried."[148] The thrust of an article about this film, which appeared in Hongqi, is that "enterprising cadres," those who "act boldly," must have their "flanks" protected by the leadership. Although this statement can scarcely be considered a call for creativity and innovation, even this limited encouragement for the randomization of behavior as the cadres "penetrate into actuality" may be a mixed blessing.[149]

The example of Lei Feng, or the more recent "Lei Feng" types, as a model for Chinese (especially the young), offers a clear picture of the sort of response behavior the leadership (or at least some important segments of the leadership) wishes to stabilize. But the negative exemplification of the drive against pollution and contamination provides an indication that aberrant behavior (that is, emphatically not of the Lei Feng type) is sufficiently widespread that one must question if the Lei Feng campaign has enjoyed any success at all. Indeed, for anyone who has lived and traveled in China, the Lei Feng campaign has an almost dreamlike quality, so out of touch does it seem with the realities one encounters. But while the negative examples of the drive against pollution and contamination seem a truer reflection of life in China, they also do not give us a very clear picture of what sort of behavior is to be encouraged.

Pollution and contamination appear to have one main aspect, "germs," which have made their way into China as a result of the recent open-door policy. There is at least a secondary problem resulting from internal bad habits left over from the pre-Communist past, as is evidenced by the discussion of the "net of ill practices." These problems are not usually treated under the headings "pollution" or "contamination," however, as those categories are reserved for externally generated germs. These germs are, in turn, divided into two categories: "The first are publications, video tapes and films with pornographic or violent contents. . . . The [second] appears in the form of academic and artistic works, sometimes mixed with information of scientific value."[150] The second type is said to have "caused more serious decay," to have resulted in "the spread of liberalism," and to have "confused many people," particularly young people.[151] This spread of liberalism is said to have caused some people to suggest that "the root of alienation lies in the socialist system itself," and it is blamed for "sowing distrust in the cause of socialism and communism and <u>the Communist Party as well</u>."[152] This is clearly no trifling matter, and we might well wonder how the Party proposes to counter the spread of the dangerous germ of liberalism. One theory proposes that instead of taking things from the West "gullibly," praising them "blindly," or absorbing them "indiscriminately," the Chinese should analyze them carefully "using the tools of Marxism."[153] What, precisely (or even approximately), these tools are, the theorist does not inform the reader. The same article goes on to cite Mao Zedong to the effect that people "should take a sniff at everything and distinguish the good from the bad before they decide whether to welcome it or boycott it." It is difficult to see how such directions can effectively stabilize behavior, even when accompanied by the widespread application of the ultimate sanction of execution, which by all accounts has increased considerably in recent months.

The confusion seems to extend from the sublime to the ridiculous--from sowing distrust of the Communist Party to the question of what sort of clothes could get the wearer in trouble. A letter to the editor of the <u>China Daily</u> assured the reader that "pretty clothes won't bring the wearer trouble"[154] and that "ideological contamination refers chiefly to certain opinions and works by a handful of people in theoretical or art and literary circles that are detrimental to the four modernizations and to the nation's stability and unity."[155]

Premier Zhao Ziyang attempted to clarify the same issue at a New York luncheon hosted by the National Committee for U.S.-China Relations and the Foreign Policy Association. In response to a question from the moderator about his suit and tie, Zhao assured the audience "with a smile that one shouldn't worry that China's opposition to 'cultural pollution will also be directed against Western suits!' After the laughter subsided, the Premier added, 'I am also in favor of ladies beautifying themselves. They can wear lipstick, earrings, and rearrange hair styles--this is not cultural pollution.'"[156] There is no record that the premier expressed himself on the question of cosmetics for men, though his further observations on the colorfulness of women's dresses in Beijing were reported to have "brought more laughter and applause." One is tempted to ask what such a presumably sophisticated audience found humorous about the premier's remarks. Such seemingly trivial (to us) matters as lipstick and fashion have been of deadly serious concern to Premier Zhao's government in the past and may well become so again. Zhao clearly did not suggest that the Party's members who sanction ideology have no interest (or rights) in regulating such matters, but the entire episode in a farcical way does illustrate--as does the above-cited letter to the editor--the point that there is presently no clear line of personal behavior beyond which individuals may transgress only at their peril.

All of these changes seem to me to indicate a stall, at least, if not a breakdown, in China's long quest to construct a meaningful hero-system or more satisfying culture. The government authorities continue to report (usually with dismay) the persistence of older, more durable systems of explanation and validation, which control by those people who sanction ideology has failed to eliminate. One article on the need for political education for peasants noted that while peasants "believe in the power of science and are trying to apply it to farming," in other matters, "concerning birth, death, age, illness and marriage, many cling to feudal superstition and outmoded custom."[157] There may be more important human concerns than birth, death, age, illness, and marriage, but I cannot imagine what they might be.

The Chinese leaders continue to treat the failure of those who sanction ideology to address these fundamental human concerns as a failure of technique that can be rectified by another "three-point education program" or a similar effort, whereas, in fact, the problem may be more fundamental. Becker suggests that "from a pragmatic point of view there must be something false about a belief system that stops short of all of man's empirical reality, and that fails when a segment of that reality fails."[158] Both Becker and Robert Bellah have suggested that only religions (or religious hero-systems) are adequate to answer humans' most general needs. Bellah suggests that it is essential for an individual or a group to have a "relatively condensed, and therefore highly general, definition of its environment and itself," particularly in situations of stress because such a conception "can provide the most general instructions as to how the system is to maintain itself and repair any damage sustained." It is precisely the role of religion, Bellah asserts, "to provide such a cognitively and motivationally meaningful identity conception or set of identifying symbols."[159] Becker offers a similar view: "The religious hero-system . . . includes the level of the invisible, the possible multi-dimensionality of reality, the problem of creation and the meaning of it. These . . . are the real dimensions of man's existence. The religious hero-system is thus the most inclusive level of generality; theoretically, anyway, this would permit organismic life to move forward almost no matter what the world did to it."[160]

If these observations are correct, they may explain both the persistence of superstition in the PRC and the failure of the sanctioning Communist ideology to provide an adequate hero-system for the Chinese people.

Stability and Change

No matter what we may think of the sanctioning ideology, though, it is the ideology that will direct China's modernization in and adaptation to a rapidly changing world. It is the system of explanation and validation that constitutes those ideological redundancies "which form the armory of verbal behavior used to resolve incoherences at the lower explanatory level,"[161] to which the government institutions are committed and which those institutions, therefore, seek to maintain against all rivals. It is also the system of explanation upon which the government's legitimacy is based, the coherence of which it must finally maintain at all costs.

"Killing," writes Peckham, "is the most effective method of social control, at least as far as the victim is concerned."[162] The effectiveness of murder or execution lies in the fact that it terminates the discussion about "meaning" (and therefore of directions for performance) once and for all. Dead men do not challenge the coherence of the sanctioning ideology. Killing is thus an important strategy for maintaining "theory" (redundancies of the sanctioning ideology) no matter what "facts" (feedback from the empirical world) emerge from a situation. But the objective is to avoid the use of force if possible.

Remember that "meanings, or culturally validated responses (the lowest level of behavior), are maintained by redundancies; redundancies are maintained by culture; culture is maintained by institutions; and institutions are maintained by force."[163] The role of culture is to provide instructions for performance and, thus, to reduce, delay, or circumvent recourse to force, the ultimate terminating sanction.[164] Directions for performance in the form of sentences (verbal behavior) can never completely describe the empirical world, however, and feedback thus constantly generates innovation. Ideology validates or invalidates this innovation, thus providing the mechanism by which the meta-directional explanatory system can be adjusted to take account of feedback from the empirical world.

It is the job of government institutions to resolve ideological incoherence, but when those institutions are themselves dependent upon maintaining the coherence of a single ideology, as is the government of the PRC, a serious problem develops. The judgment of incoherence and the generation of innovation can only come from what Peckham calls the ideological institutions, including the physical and behavioral sciences, philosophy, theology, and the arts.[165] But if the power and, indeed, the very survival of the government depend upon sustaining the coherence of a single sanctioning ideology, the government must attempt to bring the ideological institutions under the control of the sanctioning ideology, the coherence of which is threatened by outside judgments of incoherence and by innovation.

However, because cultural innovation and adaptation are necessary if culture is to provide adequate directions for performance (and thus reduce, delay, or circumvent the use of force) and if innovation is reduced or eliminated by the enforcement of the sanctioning ideology, ever-greater anomalies may develop between cultural directions and the empirical world, thus reducing the mediating role of culture and forcing the government institutions to a greater reliance on force to stabilize or maintain directions for performance. By its insistence on maintaining the coherence of the sanctioning ideology (decisive from its point of view), the government therefore cuts itself off from the most important sources of innovation in the system.

As the Chinese continually remind us, the drive for modernization in China has brought many changes since the triumph of Deng Xiaoping at the Third Plenary Session of the Eleventh Central Committee. The changes have reflected an awareness that modernization of the sort that Deng and his supporters seek to achieve requires some lessening of control by the sanctioning ideology over the various social institutions. This lessening of ideological control has been most apparent in the economic institutions, where central control has been reduced and individual and enterprise initiatives (innovation) have been encouraged. The film <u>Blood Will Always Be Warm</u>, which praises "enterprising cadres" and those who "act boldly," is an exemplification of this attitude.

There has been a marked shift in the Party's public attitude toward intellectuals as well. Deng and his colleagues seem well aware that the program of Four Modernizations requires the willing cooperation of China's intellectuals for its success. In the past, the Party has attempted to bring all intellectuals under ideological control, even those involved in technical or scientific work whose activities would seem to be only marginally threatening to the coherence of the sanctioning ideology. Writing at the time of the Cultural Revolution, Pye noted, "The Chinese are quite convinced that if scientists, economic technicians, or scholars are allowed to act according to their professional dictates, they will compromise the political system."[166] Merle Goldman also noted the "Party's inability to incorporate the intellectual community into its regime" and cites the "scientists and engineers, whose talents have been crucial to the modernization of China," who have "suffered from the harassment of the ideological remolding drives, the loss of intellectual freedom, and particularly of the management of their fields of work by untutored cadres."[167]

Intellectuals, who were classified as one of the "nine stinking things" during the Cultural Revolution, have more recently been upgraded to the status of "workers." A recent major article in the Beijing Review cites the many articles about intellectuals in Deng Xiaoping's Selected Works and asserts, "Despite the many ups and downs, Deng has indefatigably restored and developed the Party's Marxist policy of alliance with intellectuals as part of the working people."[168] There has likewise been a revival of the earlier united front concept, even to the point of resurrection of the long-defunct Chinese People's Political Consultative Conference and its membership of non-Communist leading figures.[169] In addition, since 1979, mosques, temples, and churches have been permitted to reopen, and religious properties that were confiscated or vandalized during the Cultural Revolution are being returned and repaired with government assistance. "Religious freedom" is once again proclaimed as a principle to be observed in the present stage of socialist development.

But there is a dark or troubling side to this development as well, as is evidenced by the rise in the number of executions carried out recently, many of them mass, public executions.[170] And despite Deng's efforts to include intellectuals among the working people, they are still viewed with suspicion by many Party members[171] and kept effectively under the control of the sanctioning ideology.[172] One group of well-known poets, writers, and literary critics meeting in Beijing certainly appeared to be under no illusion about the freedom of writers to randomize their behavior. The writers understood clearly that their only permissible task was exemplification of the sanctioning ideology; while they could "expose mistakes and shortcomings, the writer should encourage people to overcome them," and "works encouraging selfish attitudes are incompatible with socialist ethics."[173] After agreeing that it was not right to write "bad works," the poet Ai Qing added, "Nobody tells me what to write about." It was clear, however, that he understood where the judgment that the works were "bad" was to be made.

In the area of religious liberalization, Party ideological control is likewise pervasive. All of the priests and clergymen I met in China were wary and guarded,[174] even before the recent crackdown on the unanticipated spread of Christianity and the rapid growth in the number of converts.[175] And while the campaign against pollution has recently abated, the new target seems to be "humanism," which may amount to much the same disorder.

This backlash by the Party against the results of the liberalization or relaxation of ideology, while regrettable, is easily understood (if not actually predictable in fact) in the context of the analysis suggested here. The Party leaders recognize that their modernization plans need the innovation that can come only from the intellectuals who man the ideological institutions—the scientists, social scientists, economists, engineers, writers, philosophers, and others—and that to achieve this innovation, there must be a

lessening of ideological control. Every time
there is a relaxation of control, however, and
individuals begin to randomize their behavior in
order to create the necessary conditions for
learning a new response, the ideological innovations and critiques that result are inevitably
threatening to the coherence of the sanctioning
ideology. The new policies of the Four Modernizations require less ideological control to
permit more innovation, but that innovation is
precisely the explanation for the increase in
cultural and spiritual pollution, the rise of
humanism, and the inevitable suggestion that the
Party and its sanctioning ideology are in fact the
cause of the problems they seek to solve. It is
no mere coincidence that each time the Party has
attempted to loosen its control over intellectuals,
someone innovates the response that the Party
ought to go away and leave the Chinese people
alone.

The Party is thus caught in what appears to
be an impossible dilemma. The very sources of
innovation that hold out the promise of the sort
of future the Chinese leaders profess to want are,
in the end, unavailable to them. By giving the
ideological institutions the sort of free rein
they require to randomize and innovate, the
coherence of the sanctioning ideology is threatened. Conversely, by bringing the intellectuals
under the control of that ideology, the main
sources of innovation are shut off.

Is there no way out, then? Are the Chinese
doomed to repeat the cycles of relaxation and
represssion, muddling through much as the Soviets
have done, and creating, not a strong, powerful,
modern, vibrant China with an adequate hero-system,
but what Eric Hoffer (referring to the USSR) has
called a "global slum"? Peckham offers this
observation:

> There is one bright spot in this vision,
> and that is the possibility that govern-
> mental institutions may learn that the
> best model for all levels of behavioral
> control is science--not the commitment
> to an ideology but the exploitation of
> ideological instability. Cultural history

> is a very perilous field but it does not seem to be accidental that Western culture, which exploited the incoherence of its ultimate explanatory systems by creating modern science, is also the geographical area in which there is to be found the greatest incidence of at least a modest exploitation of ideological incoherence and instability, nor that in the culture area of the West is to be found the greatest proportion of the population which experiences the life enhancement of the negative inversions of the ultimate sanctions; economic ease, the privileges of freedom, pleasures, and the enhancement of the individual's own value (i.e., human dignity).[176]

Whether the government leaders of the PRC will "learn that the best model . . . is science" only time will tell. But for them to act on this knowledge will require the abandonment of their reliance on a single sanctioning ideology (Marxism-Leninism, Mao Zedong thought), an idealogy that legitimizes and explains their position of leadership. Control or science? I will leave the reader to judge how much control the Chinese Party leaders may be willing to relinquish in order to enjoy the fruits of science described by Professor Peckham.

NOTES

1. "Be A Sober-Minded Marxist," Beijing Review, March 22, 1982, p. 15.
2. "Costly Weddings Criticized," China Daily, February 7, 1984, p. 3.
3. Hu Yaobang, "Create a New Situation in All Fields of Socialist Modernization," Report to the Twelfth National Congress of the Communist Party of China, September 1, 1982, Beijing Review, September 13, 1982, p. 26.
4. Morse Peckham, Explanation and Power--The Control of Human Behavior (New York: Seabury Press, 1979), p. xv (hereafter Peckham 1979).
5. Morse Peckham, "The Arts and the Centers

of Power," reprinted in Morse Peckham, <u>Romanticism and Behavior--Collected Essays II</u> (Columbia: University of South Carolina Press, 1976), pp. 342-343 (hereafter Peckham 1971).
    6. Peckham 1979, p. xvii.
    7. I would be seriously remiss if I acknowledged my gratitude to my friend and colleague with only this brief reference. I owe Morse an enormous debt, and the fact that I have not learned more from him, or learned it better, is no fault of his. He has struggled manfully, heroically even--on some occasions late into the night--but more than once without notable success to elicit the proper response to his utterances from a listener whose talents and verbal skills are no match for his own.
    8. Peter C. Sederberg, <u>The Politics of Meaning</u> (Tuscon: University of Arizona Press, 1984), p. 2. Sederberg is one of the tiny band of scholars who have attempted to follow Peckham over this difficult intellectual terrain. I am indebted to him for allowing me to read the manuscript of his forthcoming book.
    9. The two books that seem to me most relevant here, in addition to <u>Explanation and Power</u>, are Morse Peckham, <u>Man's Rage For Chaos: Biology, Behavior, and the Arts</u> (New York: Schocken, 1967) and <u>Art and Pornography</u> (New York: Harper and Row, 1969 [hereinafter Peckham 1969]). The principal essays are collected in Morse Peckham, <u>The Triumph of Romanticism</u> (Columbia: University of South Carolina Press, 1970) and Peckham 1971.
    10. Peckham 1979, p. 16.
    11. Ibid., p. 36. Also see Peckham 1971, p. 343.
    12. Polysemy simply means that words can have different meanings (see Peckham 1979, pp. 12-13).
    13. I have attempted to explore this point in a more comprehensive--if extremely elementary--fashion in a textbook on the U.S. government (see James T. Myers, <u>The American Way: An Introduction to U.S. Government and Politics</u> [Lexington, Mass.: D. C. Heath, 1977], especially chap. 1).
    14. See note 6.
    15. See note 5. Ernest Becker has reached essentially the same conclusion, writing, "No

doubt man's ultimate desire is to maximize predictability of others while controlling novelty himself" (Ernest Becker, The Birth and Death of Meaning, 2d ed. [New York: Free Press, 1971], p. 91 [hereafter Becker 1971]).
    16. Sederberg, Politics of Meaning, p. 2.
    17. Peckham 1979, pp. 166-167.
    18. Sederberg, Politics of Meaning, p. 3.
    19. Peckham 1979, p. 107.
    20. This unreliability is especially easy to see in the case of a foreign language that one has learned (cf. Peckham 1979, p. 167).
    21. Ibid., p. 169. Peckham uses stop signs as a common example of such cultural redundancies. He observes: "Stop signs have multiplied enormously as automobiles have multiplied. When automobiles first came into sufficient use to start bumping into each other, it became obvious to most drivers--not all--that if they entered a main street from a street of lesser importance, it would be wise to stop or at least to slow down. Now, if the memory were reliable, it would be quite sufficient to learn that it is legally required to stop at such intersections. But, clearly, stop signs have multiplied at least as rapidly as automobiles and probably, one suspects, much faster. The driving public must continually be reminded to stop" (ibid., p. 167).
    22. Ibid., p. xviii.
    23. Ibid.
    24. Ibid., p. 183.
    25. Peckham 1969, p. 68.
    26. Becker 1971, p. 47.
    27. Ibid., p. 84.
    28. E.g., "[Culture] is the form of things that people have in their minds, their models for perceiving, relating, and otherwise interpreting them" (Ward H. Goodenough, "Cultural Anthropology and Linguistics," in Dell H. Hynes, ed., Language in Culture and Society: A Reader in Linguistics and Anthropology [New York: Harper, 1964], p. 36). The view of Peckham and Becker is much closer to the "mazeway" formulation of cognitive anthropology, e.g., "Mazeway refers to the entire set of cognitive maps of positive and negative goals that an individual maintains at a given time" (Anthony F.C. Wallace, Culture and

Personality, 2d ed. [New York: Random House, 1970], p. 15 [hereafter Wallace 1970]).
29. Peckham 1979, p. xviii.
30. There are, of course, nonverbal aspects of culture, a nation's flag, for example, some of which I shall discuss in due course.
31. Peckham 1979, p. 242.
32. Ibid., pp. 82-87. See also Peckham 1971, pp. 336-337.
33. Peckham uses the example "What do you mean by 'polysemy'? I mean 'semantic drift.' What do you mean by that? I mean 'behavioral innovation.' And so on. It will be noticed, I think, that each higher level in the hierarchy of explanatory regress is vaguer, but capable of including a wider set of terms" (Peckham 1971, p. 336).
34. Peckham 1979, p. 86.
35. Peckham 1971, p. 336.
36. Peckham 1979, p. 169, writes, "Economic deprivation, imprisonment, the infliction of pain, and killing are the ultimate sanctions for the validation of any semiotic link between sign and meaning."
37. Students of politics have long recognized that regimes based on force alone cannot long survive. Rousseau, for example, noted that "the strongest is never strong enough to be always the master, unless he transforms strength into right, and obedience into duty" (Jean Jacques Rousseau, The Social Contract and Discourses, trnas. and intro. G.D.H. Cole [New York: Dutton, 1950], Social Contract I, III, p. 6). More recently Talcott Parsons has observed that "no social system could persist through time and meet most of the functional problems which arise in it if the terms of exchange in its instrumental complex--both economic and political--were exclusively or even predominantly settled by coercion" (Talcott Parsons and Edward Shills, eds., Toward a General Theory of Action [New York: Harper, 1963], p. 220).
38. Peckham 1979, p. xviii.
39. Ibid., p. 172.
40. Ibid., pp. 184f. Peckham describes five types of institutions that he believes encompass the sum total of human activity: (1) teaching-

learning institutions, (2) value institutions, (3) economic institutions, (4) governmental institutions, (5) ideological institutions. I have no particular quarrel with this typology of institutions, but I do not propose to follow it exactly in my analysis.

41. Ibid., p. 169. I must confess that I have a problem with this formulation, especially as Peckham has also written that "an institution is a persistent mode of interactional behavior--that is, directions and performance--a persistence that may last for a few minutes when strangers meet on the street or that can last for centuries, like the Catholic Church" (1971, p. 337). It is difficult to see how the "ultimate sanctions," economic deprivation, imprisonment, and the inflicting of pain, much less the final sanction, killing, which Peckham insists is the "behavioral strategy" for "validating" the other three sanctions, could be present in a chance meeting of two strangers, though, to be sure, people are sometimes murdered by someone they encounter purely at random. However, it is clear that the institutions that interest us here are precisely those that regularly apply the ultimate sanctions, so perhaps we can defer the discussion of this problem.

42. Peckham 1979, p. 222.
43. Peckham 1971, pp. 340-341.
44. Ibid., p. 340.
45. Ibid., p. 336.
46. Clifford Geertz, "Religion as a Cultural System," in Michael Banton, ed., <u>Anthropological Approaches to the Study of Religion</u> (London: Tavistock, 1966), pp. 13-14. Ernest Becker has this to say about anxiety: "The question 'what fact is most basic to our understanding of human motivation?' can be answered with just one word: anxiety. Anxiety is a prime mover of human behavior, and man will do anything to avoid it" (1971, p. 39).
47. Becker 1971, p. 82.
48. Peckham 1979, p. 183.
49. Peckham 1971, p. 341. On the same point Becker writes, "One culture is always a potential menace to another, because it is a living example that life can go on within a value framework

totally alien to one's own" (1971, p. 82).
　　50.　Anthony F.C. Wallace, <u>Religion: An Anthropological View</u> (New York: Random House, 1966), p. 211 (hereafter Wallace 1966).
　　51.　Morse Peckham, <u>Victorian Revolutionaries</u> (New York: George Braziller, 1970), p. 207.
　　52.　Peckham 1969, p. 69.
　　53.　Ibid., p. 68.
　　54.　Peckham 1971, p. 345. Becker makes an important point: "From a pragmatic point of view there must be something false about a belief system that stops short of all man's empirical reality, and that fails when a segment of that reality fails. The religious hero-system, on the other hand . . . is the most inclusive level of generality; theoretically, anyway, this would permit organismic life to move forward almost no matter what the world did to it" (1971, p. 191). Nevertheless, the assertion that such explanations are linguistically "wrong" and can never be "right" is consistent with the explanation I am attempting here. The question whether some types of explanatory systems are more durable (and therefore more satisfactory) than others is an important one, but somewhat outside the scope of this chapter.
　　55.　Peckham 1979, p. 223.
　　56.　Ibid., p. 229.
　　57.　Ibid., pp. 229-230.
　　58.　Ibid., p. 230.
　　59.　Ibid., p. 243.
　　60.　Ibid., p. 159.
　　61.　Ibid., p. 163.
　　62.　Ibid., p. 235.
　　63.　Ibid., p. 158.
　　64.　This statement was made about the followers of Father Divine who gathered in Sayville, N.Y., during the late 1920s and early 1930s (Sara Harris, <u>Father Divine: Holy Husband</u> [Garden City, N.Y.: Doubleday, 1953], p. 26).
　　65.　Ernest Becker, <u>The Denial of Death</u> (New York: Free Press, 1973), p. 27 (hereafter Becker 1973).
　　66.　Ibid., p. 26. This is probably as good a place as any to raise the question whether there is anything "out there" or whether whatever individuals are they create themselves, with their

own intelligence. My reading of the literature is that Peckham (almost certainly) and Sederberg (for sure) would opt for the choice that individuals make themselves. If I am wrong, I am sure they will tell me. The question is undoubtedly important; indeed, some of the best minds to inhabit the planet have considered it to be the *most* important question. Nevertheless, I do not think it necessary at this point to argue, much less attempt to prove or disprove, the existence of God in order to utilize Peckham's lucid insights to assist us in a better understanding of contemporary Chinese politics. Both Peckham and Becker subscribe to a heuristic concept of truth, and both recognize the historical success of religious institutions in stabilizing cultural directions. Becker (1971 and 1972), in fact, stresses the historical need for transcendent explanatory systems.

67. Becker 1973, p. 27. Peckham calls personal preoccupations "interests" (see Peckham 1979, pp. 253-256).
68. Becker 1973.
69. Peckham 1979, pp. 198-199.
70. Rollo May, "The Significance of Symbols," in Rollo May, ed., *Symbolism in Religion and Literature* (New York: Braziller, 1960), p. 22.
71. Becker 1971, p. 28 (emphasis in the original).
72. Peckham 1969, p. 7.
73. Becker 1971, pp. 119-120.
74. Lucien Bianco, *Origins of the Chinese Revolution 1915-1949* (Stanford: Stanford University Press, 1971), p. 265.
75. Anthony F.C. Wallace, "Revitalization Movements," *American Anthropologist* 58:2 (April 1956), p. 265.
76. See Chester C. Tan, *Chinese Political Thought in the Twentieth Century* (Garden City, N.Y.: Doubleday, 1971). For the New Culture movement, see pp. 48f. The whole problem of the failure of Confucianism and of China's search for identity is brilliantly analyzed in Joseph R. Levenson's *Confucian China and Its Modern Fate: A Trilogy* (Berkeley: University of California Press, 1968). Also see Joseph R. Levenson, *Revolution and Cosmopolitanism* (Berkeley:

University of California Press, 1971), especially pp. 29-30, for the "Chinese Renaissance."

77. Bianco, *Origins of the Chinese Revolution*, pp. 27-28.

78. Wallace, "Revitalization Movements," p. 265. On the intellectual ferment focused by the May 4 movement, see Johnathan Spence, *The Gate of Heavenly Peace* (New York: Viking Press, 1981), pp. 117-123.

79. Edgar Snow, *Red Star Over China* (New York: Grove Press, 1961), p. 71.

80. I have attempted to suggest a periodization of the development of the cult in James T. Myers, "The Political Dynamics of the Cult of Mao Tse-tung," in Yung Wei, ed., *Communist China: A System--Functional Reader* (Columbus, Ohio: Charles E. Merrill, 1972), pp. 78-101.

81. Ibid., p. 83. See also James T. Myers, "Religious Aspects of the Cult of Mao Tse-tung," *Current Scene* (Hong Kong) 10:3 (March 10, 1972), pp. 1-11 (hereafter Myers 1972a).

82. Holmes Welch, "The Deification of Mao," *Saturday Review*, September 19, 1970, p. 25. Cf. Myers 1972a, p. 2.

83. Myers 1972a, p. 2.

84. The term "charisma" was originally used to signify a divinely inspired gift or gift of grace. Carl Friedrich observes that this "genuine" meaning of charisma "is rooted in a belief in a divine being and order, whereas the leadership of a Hitler or a Lenin is based on the inspirational appeal of a dynamic or even fanatical personality" (*Man and His Government* [New York: McGraw-Hill, 1963], p. 114). The modern use of the term in the social sciences derives from Max Weber's definition of the legitimacy of charisma as one basis of authority in his now-classic threefold scheme (Max Weber, *The Theory of Social and Economic Organization*, ed. Talcott Parsons [New York: Oxford University Press, 1974], p. 328). Ann Ruth Wilner and Dorothy Wilner attribute some of the confusion to a "misreading" of Weber's definition of charisma ("The Rise and Role of Charismatic Leaders," *Annals of the American Academy of Political and Social Sciences* 358 [March 1965], p. 78). Reinhart Bendix refers to

the "unthinking frequency with which the term has come to be applied," and attempts to "restate" Weber's original formulation ("Reflections on Charismatic Leadership," <u>Asian Survey</u> 7:6 [June 1976], p. 342). Edward Shils sees Weber's use of the term as too narrow or restrictive and attempts to see the "charismatic phenomenon in a more comprehensive perspective" ("Charisma, Order, and Status," <u>America Sociological Review</u> 30 [April 1965], p. 200), and Friedrich concludes that much of the confusion has been occasioned by Weber's unfortunate coining of the term "charismatic leadership" in the first place (<u>Man and His Government</u>, p. 114).

85. Carmen Blacker, "Millenarian Aspects of the New Religion of Japan," in Donald H. Shivley, ed., <u>Tradition and Modernization in Japanese Culture</u> (Princeton: Princeton University Press), p. 564.

86. See Irwin J. Schulman, "Mao as Prophet," <u>Current Scene</u> (Hong Kong) 7:13 (June 7, 1970). Also see Myers 1972a, pp. 7-8.

87. <u>Renmin ribao</u> [People's daily] (Beijing), October 1, 1958.

88. <u>Renmin ribao</u> (Beijing), October 13, 1960.

89. Liu Lantao, "The Communist Party Is the Supreme Commander of the Chinese People in Building Socialism," <u>Renmin ribao</u> (Beijing), September 28, 1959. Cf. Myers 1972a, p. 8.

90. Robert A. Dahl, <u>Modern Political Analysis</u> (Englewood Cliffs, N.J.: Prentice-Hall, 1965), p. 19. Lasswell and Kaplan call "miranda" those symbols whose function is "setting forth and strengthening faiths and loyalties" (Harold D. Lasswell and Abraham Kaplan, <u>Power and Society: A Framework For Analysis</u> [New Haven: Yale University Press, 1952], p. 116).

91. Lucian W. Pye, <u>The Spirit of Chinese Politics: A Psychocultural Study of the Authority Crisis in Political Development</u> (Cambridge, Mass.: MIT Press, 1968), p. 9.

92. Ibid., p. 7.

93. Chalmers Johnson's view of values is very close to the one suggested in this chapter. He writes, "Values are both <u>explanations</u> of a situation . . . and <u>standards</u> of appropriate action designed to produce some desired ('envalued')

resolution or management of the situation" (<u>Revolutionary Change</u> [Boston: Little, Brown and Company, 1966], p. 21). In other words, values are directions for performance or, in Peckham's words, "normative verbal redundancies" (1979, p. 197). Peter Sederberg adds, "Power is a form of explanation and explanation is a form of power" (<u>Politics of Meaning</u>, p. ii). Peckham actually separates the concept of "values" from "value semiosis," a concept that is perhaps best left for a later essay (see Peckham 1979, pp. 191-206).

94. Snow, <u>Red Star Over China</u>, p. 75.
95. Ibid., p. 79.
96. Mao Zedong, "In Memory of Norman Bethune," <u>Selected Works</u>, vol. 2 (Beijing: Foreign Language Press, 1965), pp. 331-338. The story of Norman Bethune still appears in the elementary Chinese readers published today.
97. See pp. 302-305.
98. <u>China Youth</u>, February 1, 1959, p. 35.
99. Becker writes: "In the invisible world everything is more perfect, permanent, changeless. If you can get some of this eternal perfection to erupt into our visible dimension, it renews us: that is the basis of miracles--a breakthrough of power from the invisible world that enriches and transforms our own" (1971, pp. 121-122). Mao's most famous essay on the miraculous is probably "The Foolish Old Man Who Removed the Mountains," in <u>Selected Readings from the Works of Mao Tse-tung</u> (Beijing: Foreign Language Press, 1967), pp. 260-263.
100. Frederick Wakeman, Jr., "The Chinese Mirror," in Michel Oksenberg, ed., <u>China's Developmental Experience</u> (New York: Academy of Political Science, 1973), p. 217.
101. See Myers 1972a.
102. Andre Malraux, <u>Anti-Memoirs</u>, tr. Terrence Kilmartin (New York, Holt, Rinehart and Winston, 1968), p. 357.
103. Ibid., p. 354.
104. Ibid., p. 360.
105. This heading is also the title of a paper I published a number of years ago, which anticipated in a preliminary way the point made in this section (see James T. Myers, "The Fall of

Chairman Mao," *Current Scene* [Hong Kong] 7:10 [June 15, 1968]).

106. *Chinese Communist Affairs: Facts and Features* (Taipei) 1:5 (December 27, 1967). It was later reported that a farmer was sentenced to fifteen years for "allowing his wife to humiliate Chairman Mao by putting his picture under a hen roost" and that a similar sentence was given a man whose portrait of Chairman Mao was chewed up by cockroaches attracted by the rice paste he used to mount it to his wall (see "Defiling the Image," *Time*, January 26, 1970).

107. Peckham 1979, pp. 229f.

108. See Merle Goldman, *Literary Dissent in Communist China* (New York: Atheneum, 1971), pp. 158-202.

109. The "Mao-against-the-Party bureaucracy" view of the Cultural Revolution is essentially the view that Jürgen Domes and I argue in Jürgen Domes, James T. Myers, and Erik Von Groeling, *Cultural Revolution in China: Documents with Analysis* (Brussels: Centre d'Etude du Sud-Est Asiatique et de l'Extreme Orient), especially General Introduction, pp. 1-34.

110. Malraux, *Anti-Memoirs*, p. 373.

111. Ibid., p. 370.

112. Ibid., p. 366.

113. Ibid., p. 375 (emphasis added).

114. That is, "emphasizing the institution of customs and values which are thought to have been in the mazeway of previous generations but are now absent" (Wallace, "Revitalization Movements," p. 267).

115. That is, "characterized by strong emphasis on elimination of alien persons, customs, values and/or materiel from the mazeway" (ibid.).

116. Pye, *Spirit of Chinese Politics*, p. 10.

117. Hu Yaobang, "Create a New Situation in All Fields of Socialist Modernization," p. 26.

118. Ibid. (emphasis added).

119. Anthony F.C. Wallace, *Culture and Personality*, 2d ed. (New York: Random House, 1970), pp. 191-192. Wallace adds: "Once severe cultural distortion has occurred, the society can with difficulty return to the steady state without the institution of a revitalization process. Without revitalization, indeed, the society is likely to

disintegrate as a system" (ibid., p. 192).
120. Hu Yaobang, "Create a New Situation in All Fields of Socialist Modernization," p. 26.
121. Ibid., p. 22.
122. Morse Peckham, "Arts For the Cultivation of Radical Sensitivity," in Peckham, *Romanticism and Behavior*, p. 287.
123. *Nanfang ribao* (Guangzhou), February 21, 1981, p. 1.
124. *Wen hui pao* (Shanghai), November 21, 1981, p. 3.
125. *Sichuan ribao* (Chengdu), March 10, 1981, p. 1. The "five stresses" are decorum, manners, hygiene, discipline, and morals. The "four beauties" are beautification of the (1) mind, (2) language, (3) behavior, and (4) environment.
126. *China Daily* (Beijing), December 9, 1982.
127. E.g., "Being Rich in Both Pocket and Mind," Shandong, Jinan, *Dazhong ribao*, November 2, 1983; "Trade Unions Should Resist Spiritual Pollution," Beijing, *Renmin ribao*, November 10, 1983; "Experience in Teaching Patriotism at School," *Guangming ribao*, November 16, 1983; "Wang Dian on Spiritual Pollution," Yunnan, Kunming Radio, November 23, 1983; "Chongqing CPC Meeting Criticizes Pollution," Sichuan Radio, November 23, 1983; "Faith in Communism," *Guangming ribao*, November 28, 1983; "Guangdong Forum on Spiritual Pollution," *Nanfang ribao*, December 1, 1983; "Heilongjiang Holds Forum on Spiritual Pollution," Harbin Radio, December 1, 1983; "Henan Reports on Spiritual Pollution," Zhengzhou Radio, December 1, 1983; "Shanxi Education Officials Discuss Spiritual Pollution," Taiyuan Radio, December 12, 1983.
128. Hu Yaobang, "Create a New Situation in All Fields of Socialist Modernization," p. 21 (emphasis added).
129. Peckham 1979, p. 222.
130. *Renmin ribao* (Beijing), November 4, 1958.
131. *Renmin ribao* (Beijing), October 1, 1958.
132. *Xinhua* (Beijing), June 30, 1981 (in English).
133. See Chen Kuan-sheng, *Lei Feng, Chairman Mao's Good Fighter* (Beijing: Foreign Language Press, 1968).
134. Ibid., p. 100.
135. Ibid., p. 101.

136. The official biography contains a facsimile of Mao's handwritten inscription to "learn from Comrade Lei Feng" and another by Lin Biao to "follow the example set by Comrade Lei Feng and be Chairman Mao's good fighters."
137. Shen Hui-min, "The Screw," in *A Young Pathbreaker and Other Stories* (Beijing: Foreign Language Press, 1975), pp. 75-76.
138. Chen Kuan-sheng, *Lei Feng*, p. 28.
139. Ibid., p. 102.
140. Ibid., p. 30.
141. *Beijing ribao*, March 6, 1981, p. 3.
142. *Beijing ribao*, March 4, 1981, p. 3.
143. *Wen hui pao* (Shanghai), March 4, 1981.
144. Xinhua Domestic Service in Mandarin, March 4, 1982.
145. "Moral Lesson Can Be Art," *China Daily* (Beijing), January 24, 1984, p. 5. Zhu Boru, himself said to be worthy of emulation, was recently honored with the title "Glorious Pacesetter in Learning from Lei Feng" (see "Emulate Zhu Boru," *Beijing Review*, August 8, 1983, p. 6).
146. "Moral Lesson Can Be Art," p. 5.
147. "New Play Exposes Backdoor Relations," *China Daily* (Beijing), January 27, 1984, p. 5.
148. "Break Up 'Net' of Ill Practices in Party," *China Daily* (Beijing), January 27, 1984, p. 4 (reprinted from Hongqi).
149. Ibid.
150. Yue Ping, "Preventing Idological Pollution," *Beijing Review*, November 21, 1983, p. 22. Another article by Deng Liqun, member of the Secretariat of the CCP Central Committee, cited four main categories of cultural contamination: (1) "Spreading things which are obscene, barbarous or reactionary," (2) "Vulgar taste in artistic performances," (3) "Efforts to seek personal gain, indulgence in individualism, anarchism, liberalism, etc.," and (4) "Writing articles or delivering speeches that run counter to the country's social system" ("Clearing Cultural Contamination," *Beijing Review*, November 7, 1983, p. 13).
151. Ibid.
152. "Opposing Ideological Pollution," *Beijing Review*, October 31, 1983, pp. 6-7 (emphasis added).
153. Yue Ping, "Preventing Ideological Pollutio

154. *China Daily* (Beijing), January 24, 1984, p. 4.
155. Ibid.
156. *Notes from the National Committee* 14:1 (Winter 1984), p. 1.
157. *China Daily* (Beijing), November 10, 1982, p. 4.
158. Becker 1971, p. 191.
159. Robert N. Bellah, *Beyond Belief: Essays On Religion In a Post-Traditional World* (New York: Harper and Row, 1970), pp. 11-12.
160. Becker 1971, p. 191.
161. Peckham 1979, p. 223.
162. Ibid., p. 187.
163. Ibid., p. xviii.
164. Ibid.
165. Ibid., p. 230.
166. Pye, *Spirit of Chinese Politics*, p. 27.
167. Goldman, *Literary Dissent in Communist China*, p. 275.
168. *Beijing Review*, March 19, 1984, p. 16.
169. "The Democratic Parties in Action," *Beijing Review*, November 7, 1983, pp. 22-23; "Jiangxi CPPCC Standing Committee Holds Session," Jiangxi Radio, November 7, 1983; "CPPCC Meeting Ends," *Beijing Review*, December 20, 1982; "Democratic Parties Play Their Role," *Beijing Review*, July 20, 1981; "Fewer Communists in CPPCC," *Beijing Review*, May 9, 1983, are only a few examples of the enormous coverage these activities have received.
170. See "Watching the Death Notices," *Far Eastern Economic Review*, February 16, 1984. See also David Bonivia, "Repent Or Die," ibid. Bonivia reports "more than 6000" executions between July 1983 and February 1984.
171. See the *Far Eastern Economic Review*'s cover stories on intellectuals, February 9, 1984, pp. 32-43.
172. Ian Findlay, "Few Can Escape the Dead Hand of Party Control," ibid., pp. 41-42.
173. *Beijing Review*, December 12, 1983, p. 11.
174. James T. Myers, "The Catholic Church in China: An Eyewitness Report," *Commonweal* (New York), October 7, 1983.
175. Calvin Greenham, "A Church of Survivors Faces New Form of Attack in China," *Far Eastern*

Economic Review, March 8, 1984, pp. 70-72.
    176. Peckham 1979, p. 243.

Part 2

Economics in the PRC

11
Mainland China's Economic System: A New Model or Variations on an Old Theme?

Robert F. Dernberger

I

In the conclusion to my evaluation of China's post-Mao economic reform program, "Communist China's Industrial Policies: Goals and Results," presented to the Tenth Sino-American Conference in 1981, I argued that because of the problems created by the program of economic reforms, the Chinese leaders had been forced to reassert the centralized control of the traditional Soviet-type economic system. Nonetheless, while admitting this need to reassert "centralization and unification at the present time [1981] as necessary to achieve readjustment" of the economy, the leadership went on to insist that "once readjustment is achieved, the economic reform program will not only be feasible, it will be carried out."[1] Yet, in the absence of true systemic reform, I believed the attempt to introduce the economic reforms in a piecemeal fashion in the future, as in the past, would merely generate the same problems, and I did not foresee that the Chinese leader would behave any differently in response to these future problems than they had in 1981, i.e., they would fall back on their traditional economic system of highly centralized decision making and control by means of the bureaucratic administration of the economy.
In a second evaluation of China's post-Mao program of economic reforms, "The Chinese Search for the Path of Self-sustained Growth in the 1980s: An Assessment," written in 1982, I

remained convinced that the Chinese would retain their basic Soviet-type economic system, but with considerably less certainty. "At the present time [1982] there are ample reasons for believing that the Chinese will retain the basic features of the traditional Soviet economic model. . . . However, . . . it is far from certain that the campaign to reform China's Soviet-type economic system, initiated in the mid-1950s, renewed in the early 1960s, and vigorously pursued after the death of Mao, will not succeed."[2]

In yet a third review of China's post-Mao program of economic reforms written at the end of 1982, on the basis of many speeches by the Chinese leaders and articles in Chinese journals, I had become convinced that the Chinese leaders did intend to modify their traditional Soviet-type economic system but had no intention of abandoning that system.[3] For example, in his speech to a conference on industrial and transportation work (March 1982), Zhao Ziyang made what, to me, is the clearest statement on economic reforms. According to Zhao:

> We have domestically implemented the policy of activating our economy, delegating some powers to the local authorities and enlarging the enterprise's decision-making powers for the purposes of whipping up the enthusiasm of the local authorities, the various departments and enterprises and the masses, turning human talents and land and other material resources to good account and vigorously developing China's national economy. Efforts to expand decision-making powers and activate the economy are also apt to foster the trend toward departmentalism, decentralism, and liberalism, to weaken and depart from the state's unified plan, to interfere with and break up the unified market of socialism and to affect our efforts to take the whole country and the overall situation into consideration. . . . Ours is a unified socialist nation. We must have a unified plan and a unified

domestic market. . . . In order to strengthen centralization and unification in economic work, we must adhere to the overall plan on major issues while allowing freedom on minor issues. We must advocate centralism on major issues while allowing decentralism on minor issues. . . . The products to be transferred according to state plans, including farm and sideline products, must be transferred strictly according to such plans. The commodity price and revenue system must be centralized and unified. . . . No matter what reform is to be carried out, the general guideline is to combine the strengthening of centralization and unification with the activation of the economy and to bringing into full play the initiative of localities, departments, enterprises and people under the guidance of state planning and the principle of taking the whole country into account.[4]

Although I may be convinced that the guidelines or limits to the post-Mao program of economic reforms being pursued by the current leaders in China is a modification, not a replacement, of the traditional Soviet-type economy, this basic conclusion, which is expressed in most of my writings on this topic, has been contested by my critics. Among the many counterarguments I have encountered, I believe the following are the most creditable. Whatever the intentions of the Chinese leaders,

1. The economic results of the economic reforms introduced thus far are so impressive that the leadership, which has given economic objectives a very high priority, will be convinced of the economic benefits of continuing the program of economic reforms, even including systemic reform.

2. The economic reforms introduced thus far have already given increased material benefits and/or created rising expectations of those benefits in such a large segment of the population that the leadership will be unable to implement its intended limits to the program of

economic reform but will be forced by the masses to continue on, even to including true systemic reforms.

3. The leadership is dedicated to economic reform in a desire to make its economic system work better, and as the leaders learn that a piecemeal attempt to patch up the shortcomings of the traditional system won't work, they will be forced to seek a better alternative economic system for the sake of successful economic modernization.

4. Although unintended, the attempt at economic reforms has involved considerable decentralization of authority and decision making to the extent that the leadership at the top has lost control over the program of economic reform, which is now being introduced and carried out at the local level. The result will be a new and uniquely Chinese economic system, relying to a great extent on traditional Chinese institutions and patterns of behavior.

5. The leadership's attempt to experiment with economic reform has meant that the economists or experts have acquired a considerably greater role in formulating policy at the top of the political network. These experts are a leading focus of support for true systemic reform, and having learned from their mistakes (both economic and political) in the past, they will be much more successful in achieving their objective of systemic reform during the next phase of experimental reforms in the future.

Although I have never been reticent to engage in speculations about the future, that is not my purpose in this chapter. Rather than engage in one more round of a debate between those of us who are labeled as pessimists (China's economy will basically remain a Soviet-type economic system) and those who enjoy being called optimists (having opened Pandora's box with their experiments in economic reform, whether intended or not, the process of reform now under way will inevitably lead to the abandonment of the traditional Soviet-type economic system), my purpose here is more limited and is based on a desire to clarify some of the fundamental concepts involved in the debate.

What do I consider to be the basic features of a Soviet-type economic system? What reforms of their economy have the Chinese introduced thus far? Why do I argue that those reforms do not constitute a change in China's traditional Soviet-type economic system? What changes would be necessary before I would accept the argument that the Chinese traditional Soviet-type economy had been rejected in favor of a different economic system? If we can obtain agreement about these features of the existing developments in China's program of economic reforms, I believe that we can understand better the extent to which we agree or disagree about the future.

Before proceeding directly to those questions, however, I can be excused if I briefly list the reasons why I reject the counterarguments of the critics of my earlier published arguments on this topic. In other words, if those critics are correct, then the logic of the developments now taking place on the mainland mean that China's traditional Soviet-type economic system will inevitably, and in the near future, be replaced by a new and different economic system and the basic theme of my analysis in this chapter is erroneous. I will state my disagreement with each of the criticisms in the same order in which they were presented above:

    1. The success of the reforms will create the necessary force for their continuation and expansion until the Soviet-type economic system is completely dismantled in favor of a new and different economic system. There can be little argument that the Chinese economy did very well in the seven years after 1977. The statistics in Table 11.1 clearly indicate that a significant upsurge occurred in the economy after 1977, especially when the immediate post-Mao period (1977-1980) is compared with the immediately preceding three-year period (1975-1977). Yet, as Milton Friedman concluded after a visit to the mainland in the fall of 1980:

> There clearly has been a decided improvement in the economy over the past three years or so. The Chinese attribute this to the new "pragmatic" policies adopted

Table 11.1. Selected macroeconomic indicators, 1952–1982
(in billion yuan at comparable prices)

	1952	1957	1962	1965	1970	1975	1977	1980	1982
A. National income[1]									
Total Sources[2]	58.9	90.1	77.1	116.3	173.6	226.6	237.7	303.0	341.1
Agriculture	34.0	42.2	37.0	53.7	71.7	89.3	88.2	120.6	152.1
Industry	11.5	25.5	25.3	42.3	69.6	100.8	107.4	138.8	143.9
Construction	2.1	4.5	2.7	4.4	7.1	10.2	11.2	13.9	15.7
Transportation	2.5	3.9	3.2	4.9	6.6	8.6	9.5	9.7	10.6
Commerce	8.8	14.1	8.9	10.9	18.6	17.7	21.4	20.0	18.8
Uses[3]									
Consumption	46.3	67.7	69.1	84.8	116.5	149.8	160.9	207.3	242.2
Accumulation	12.6	22.4	8.0	31.5	57.1	76.8	76.8	95.7	98.9
B. Population statistics[4]									
Population	574.8	646.5	673.0	725.4	829.9	924.2	949.7	987.1	1,015.4
Labor Force	207.3	237.7	259.1	286.7	344.3	381.7	393.8	419.0	447.1
C. Per capita statistics									
Per capita national income	102.5	139.4	114.6	160.3	209.2	245.2	250.3	307.0	335.9
National income per worker	284.1	379.0	297.6	405.7	504.2	593.7	603.6	723.2	762.9
Per capita consumption	80.5	104.7	102.7	116.9	140.4	162.1	169.4	210.0	238.5

Table 11.1 (continued)

	1952–1957	1957–1962	1962–1965	1965–1970	1970–1975	1975–1977	1977–1980	1980–1982	1952–1977	1977–1982
D. Annual rates of growth										
National income	8.9	-3.1	14.7	8.3	5.5	2.4	8.4	6.1	5.7	7.5
Agriculture									3.9	11.5
Industry									9.4	6.0
Construction									6.9	7.0
Transportation									5.5	2.2
Commerce									3.6	-2.6
Consumption	7.9	0.4	7.1	6.6	5.2	3.6	8.8	8.1	5.1	8.5
Population									2.0	1.4
Per capita national income	6.3	-3.8	11.8	5.5	3.2	1.0	7.0	4.6	3.6	6.1
Per capita consumption	5.4	-0.4	4.4	3.7	2.9	2.2	7.4	6.6	3.0	7.1

[1] The Chinese definition of national income is the sum of net material product in five sectors: agriculture, industry, construction, transportation, and commerce. National income in this table is estimated on the basis of absolute value given on p. 22 and the index for all years, 1949–1982 (1952=100) on p. 23 of PRC, State Statistical Bureau, Statistical Yearbook of China, 1983 (Beijing: Statistical Publishers of China, 1983).

[2] Total national income multiplied by relevant percentages for structure of national income for all years, 1949–1982, on p. 24, Statistical Yearbook of China, 1983.

[3] Total national income multiplied by relevant percentage shares of consumption and accumulation in national income for all years, 1952–1982, on p. 25, Statistical Yearbook of China, 1983.

[4] Population, in millions of persons at the end of each year, from p. 103, and labor force (including peasants), in millions of persons at the end of each year, from p. 120 of Statistical Yearbook of China, 1983.

> under Vice-premier Deng, who is clearly
> the person in charge. My own impression
> is somewhat different. . . . The mere
> restoration of order on the death of Mao
> and the gaining of power by Deng was
> bound to permit a rapid recovery and a
> jump in economic level. I believe that
> this is a far more fundamental explana-
> tion than the Deng reforms, most of which
> are so far only on paper.[5]

Moreover, those reforms that were implemented during this period soon created very serious problems--budget deficits, unemployment, import surpluses, inflation, etc.--which led the leadership to reassert central control over the economy, to put many of the reform proposals on hold, and to single out readjustment of the economy as the major objective of economic policy. Furthermore, a second check of the data in Table 11.1 also reveals, with the significant exception of agriculture and per capita consumption, that the results for 1980-1982 were not noticeably greater than the trends and achievements in earlier periods. Finally, most observers agree that China's leading advocate of economic reform in a position of real authority, Chen Yun, began to give much greater emphasis to the planned economy versus the market sector in his speeches in 1981 and 1982.[6]

Thus, I do not believe that the favorable economic results of the seven years after 1977 are completely attributable to the economic reform program or that all of the results of that program have been favorable. More important, I believe there are major elements of the present leadership that would agree with this interpretation.

2. There can be little doubt that the program of economic reform has created sizable interest groups who have benefited from the reforms and would like to see them continued and even expanded so as to result in true reform of the economic system. Any policy change or change in development strategy creates winners and losers, in both economics and politics. Although the general upsurges in economic activity and

standard of living have obviously benefited a large majority of the Chinese people, the economic reform program has largely created opportunities for the more productive to get rich first--the coastal urban areas versus the interior, people associated with industrial and sideline activities versus those associated with fieldwork in the countryside, etc. Although the argument used to justify the economic reforms is that the nation and everyone will benefit in the long run, it is obviously a minority that will directly and significantly benefit in the immediate future.

Furthermore, I do not believe that the Chinese political system has become a matter of consensus politics. Rather, various factions and interest groups have an unequal influence on the top leadership, and the proreform factions and interest groups are <u>not</u> those factions and interest groups that have traditionally played a dominant role among the top leadership. I see no reason to believe that the military, the central planners, the bureaucrats, the political leaders from the interior, the industrial workers, etc., have lost their political clout, and I would need to be convinced that these groups have benefited from and become strong advocates of the continued expansion of systemic reform.

3. There can be no doubt that a modification of China's traditional economic model of the past quarter of a century--i.e., a rejection of the Maoist economic principles, a more balanced investment program (rejecting the Stalinist, big-push development strategy), and allowing a private-market sector to supplement a dominant centrally planned sector--would lead to significantly improved economic performance and growth. It can also be argued that there exists, in theory at least, an economic system that would perform even better. Even allowing for the existence of a superior alternative economic system, I am yet to be convinced that the "rational" implementation of a Soviet-type economic system, which allows a supplemental role for private-market activity, will either fail or perform so badly that the Chinese leadership, in the near future, will be forced to abandon the Soviet-type economic system

in favor of a superior alternative economic system. <u>All</u> economic systems in the world today rationally accept considerable inefficiencies for the sake of other objectives, and the maintenance of a socialist economy that has control over the allocation of resources is a very important objective for the current leadership in China.

4. There can be no doubt that the presence and force of China's tradition is a very important and active factor in present-day China, a force that is made more evident during periods of relaxed central control and liberalization. The people who believe in the theory of an ever-repeating dynastic cycle for China's future, as well as in the past, argue that we are about to see the dawn of a new era in Chinese history. The modern version of the Ch'in dynasty has been brought to a close, and the dawn of a new Han dynasty is just beginning. This new era, including its new and unique Chinese economic system, will be built upon elements from Chinese tradition, and it will not be built by the present leaders but by the Chinese masses. This situation is made possible because the current leadership has lost control as a result of the decentralization introduced by the economic and political reforms of the seven years after 1977.

I disagree with this argument on two grounds. The early reform policies, which introduced decentralization of decision making in the economy, did involve a loss of control, but the leaders quickly reasserted central control over the economy in the last half of 1981. Although they have encountered some problems, i.e., in the areas of investment decisions and the expenditures of local governments, they have been able to stem the tide, and the speeches of the leaders make it clear that they had regained their confidence in this regard by the end of 1982. Furthermore, their loss of control was greatest in the economy; I do not believe that their loss of control was anywhere near as great in the areas of politics, the military, literature, migration, or any other area of life in China today. Second, the central authorities never lost control over the "commanding heights" of the economy, and it would have been very difficult for the local authorities and population to introduce and implement an economic system that did not complement the existing elements of the centrally controlled economy.[7]

5. As a group, the economists who survived the Cultural Revolution have not only been rehabilitated but been given a more prominent position of respect and importance than they have enjoyed at any time since 1949. Not only have they been appointed to high-level advisory positions, but they are publishing a veritable flood of articles on economic problems and reform in China. Nonetheless, the most powerful men in China today, in terms of setting the broad outlines of policy, are Deng Xiaoping, Chen Yun, Cheng Zhen, Li Xiannian, and Ye Jianying. None are economists. Only two have had considerable experience in economic administration (Chen and Li), and they are strong supporters of the Soviet-type economic system.

Furthermore, the top leaders are Leninists and will not tolerate a departure from a socialist path of economic development achieved by means of centralist bureaucratic systems dominated by the Communist Party. It is unlikely that the economists, because of their skills and knowledge, will achieve positions of political leadership in such a system or dictate the policies that those who are the political leaders will adopt and implement. In any event, the argument that the achievement of true systemic reform of the economy is just around the corner in China because the political leadership will be forced to rely on the economists to achieve economic development is based upon a flawed assumption: that the economists as a group support a systemic reform of the economy. I know of no empirical evidence to support this assumption, and in fact, the Chinese themselves have told us that the advocates of systemic reform are in the minority.[8]

Thus, I reject the arguments of those people who claim that even though the artifacts of a Soviet-type economic system can still be found in China, its days are numbered and true systemic reform of the economy is the inevitable result of the current period of economic reform in China. In rejecting their counterarguments and criticisms, I do not reject or even comment on those general theories or hypotheses that claim that the Soviet-type economic system is impossible to maintain in the long run, i.e., it contains the seeds of its own destruction and will eventually collapse or be abandoned in favor of a superior alternative.[9] Whether or not these predictions of what is inevitable in the long run are valid does not interest us here; we are interested in the past, the present, and the foreseeable future, i.e., the rest of our lifetime. The classical economists may have been correct in saying that the problems of unemployment in a free-market system will cure themselves in the long run, but that is of little interest to us because, in the long run, all of us will be dead.

II

Just what institutional organization of the economy do I identify by means of the term "Soviet-type economic system"? This economic system is called "Soviet-type" because it was first developed and adopted in the Soviet Union. The basic texts of Marxism and Leninism held few clues for the economic system in a socialist country, and the brief attempt at war communism following the success of the Russian revolution ended in disaster. This economic disaster forced Lenin and his followers to adopt the new economic mechanism to rehabilitate the economy and restore incentives, essentially by relying on markets to determine outputs and their distribution. This mechanism set the stage for the industrialization debates of the late 1920s in the Soviet Union, and it has been common wisdom to depict Stalin as the deciding force, not only for resolving the debate in favor of the big-push development strategy, but also for developing the Soviet economic system to facilitate the implementation of the strategy. Furthermore, by means of an ex post facto rationalization of these developments, this strategy and economic system have been interpreted as the logically and ideologically dictated economic system for the developing socialist countries. Thus, by the post-World

War II period, this Soviet model (i.e., economic system) had been widely accepted as the only orthodox socialist system. As one Chinese central planner has argued, a believer even three years after the death of Mao, "the central planning of production and allocation of investment is socialism."[10]

More recent scholarship, however, has been less generous to Stalin in regard to the role he played in the adoption of this economic system and development policies and to the belief that its adoption was based on theoretical or ideological considerations. Rather, Stalin is now being interpreted as exhibiting great political skill rather than ideological or theoretical creativity. Stalin was really not a major figure in the industrialization debate, and both Nikolai Bukharin, the loser of the debate, and Eugene Preobrazhensky, the winner, were later purged. As for the system of central control and planning in the allocation of resources, it was Leon Trotsky who called the system of material balances "the rhapsody of socialism." Gosplan was originally created to collect statistics and serve as a forecasting service, with the planners suggesting policies to achieve changes on the margin to move the economy in a direction desired by the policymakers, the so-called generic approach to planning. The advocates of this approach suffered a loss of support because of the terrible errors in their forecasts, while the advocates of the teleological ("creating by design") approach, or the direct interference into the production and investment decisions by the central planners on the basis of their "material balance" accounts, had a natural appeal to the central political authorities.

Thus, the implementation of the First Five-Year Plan by direct, administrative decrees rather than by means of indirect instruments had a more practical and political rather than an ideological or a theoretical origin. As for the collectivization of agriculture, this concept was not part of the scheme when the First Five-Year Plan began in 1928, but the collectivization movement was already under way. Several studies argue that the collectivization movement was actually adopted and implemented in the field by the cadres who were sent out to collect the agricultural surplus from the peasants after the state's failure to obtain the necessary agricultural surplus as a result of the dismal agricultural year of 1928. Once in place, however, with its proven ability to achieve the fulfillment of the leadership's most basic economic objectives, this economic system became entrenched as part of that leadership's program of basic institutions and policies for socialist countries, i.e., a country in the transition stage between capitalism and communism.

The above may explain the origin of this economic system and provide justification for why we call it the Soviet-type economic system, but I still have not described it. On the basis of historical experience throughout the socialist world, the basic components of the Soviet-type economic system consist of the following:

1. The means of production in industry are nationalized as are enterprises in the commerce, transportation, and banking sectors.
2. These enterprises have state-managers appointed who are assigned output and input targets. The reward system is based on the managers' exceeding their output targets while minimizing their use of inputs.
3. The output and input targets are determined centrally by the planners on the basis of material balance accounts (a T-account of sources and needs) for all major products.
4. The government's budget acquires the profits of the state enterprises as revenue, along with indirect taxes levied on commodities and agricultural land. Government expenditures are allocated to cover the losses of state enterprises, normal government operating costs, defense, and all major investment expenditures.
5. These budget expenditures are also determined centrally by the planners who control, therefore, the rate and

allocation of investment as well as the product mix of current output in the economy. Investments are financed by unilateral budget grants to the enterprises.
6. The banking system holds cash deposits of the state enterprises, acts as a clearinghouse for transactions between state enterprises, finances approved budget expenditures, and makes loans for the state enterprises' working capital.
7. The economic plan (output and input mix, investment, transfers among enterprises and sectors, etc.) is in physical terms. Both the economic plan in physical terms and its counterpart, the financial plan in monetary terms, are to be balanced, but the planners try to correct imbalances by rationing or reallocating scarce inputs, outputs, or money as bottlenecks arise.
8. Prices for most commodities are set by the state, as are wages for the various grades of labor.
9. Trade and transport of most commodities are included in the plan and carried out by state enterprises, including the distribution of consumer goods through state retail stores. All foreign trade is nationalized and carried out according to plan by state trading companies.
10. Agricultural production and capital, including land, are collectivized, and peasants are members of a collective. They work on assigned tasks in exchange for work points, which represent a share of the collective's net income at the end of the production year. The collectives are assessed an agricultural tax and a fixed output quota that must be delivered to the state at a price that is below "a market price." Collectives can organize industrial and sideline activities, and the individual peasant household can have a private plot and can engage in private production

and trade in rural markets after fulfilling a minimum obligation for work to be done for the collective. State farms are operated as state enterprises, the peasant becoming wage earners.

This definition of the Soviet-type economic system is a descriptive one based on a summary of the key elements of that economic system as it has been adopted throughout the socialist world. The detailed implementation of this economic system has varied considerably throughout the socialist world, i.e., in addition to the above institutions, the Chinese added rationing of necessities and strict control over internal migration. Furthermore, the various programs of economic reform in Eastern Europe after the death of Stalin and in China after the death of Mao have significantly changed the characteristics of that economic system and have reduced greatly its uniformity in implementation among the various countries of the socialist world. Those reforms have significantly changed or modified China's Soviet-type economic system, so it is necessary for me to spell out the essential or basic elements of what I call a Soviet-type economic system; i.e., if and when these elements are eliminated as a result of economic reform, then the Chinese Communists will have rejected or replaced their traditional Soviet-type economic system in favor of a new and different economic system. The importance of their failure to engage in true systemic reform, despite the many and significant modifications of their economic system, will be discussed in the conclusion of this chapter.

Allowing for considerable variability in institutional detail, I believe that the essential elements that define a Soviet-type economic system <u>and</u> differentiate it from other systems are the following:

1. Because of the nationalization of resources and enterprises, most land and raw materials are owned by the state, and the state is the major employer of labor in the industrial, construction, communication, and commercial enterprises owned by the state. Households may

be the basic unit of production in the agricultural sector, and a large and active private sector may exist side by side with the state sector in the nonagricultural economy. Nonetheless, state ownership of the means of production and economic units throughout the economy predominates economic activity. This is a basic principle of socialism.

2. The allocation of resources and the operation of enterprises within the state sector are largely carried out according to centrally determined plans. These plans include the budget, credit plan, input allocations, output quotas, trade and transportation, foreign trade, and employment. The plans can be based on information or decisions made at lower levels of the economic bureaucracy, or even the level of the production units themselves. Yet, no matter how strongly influenced by the lower levels, the plan is the result of conscious decisions about the central planners' (political leaders') priorities concerning the allocation of resources, and once approved, the plan assigns targets for the lower-level units of production. Targets can also be assigned to units of production outside the state sector, i.e., as quotas to be met by households. On the other hand, once the targets have been met, a unit of production or enterprise in the state sector may produce for and sell in a private market. A private, unplanned sector will exist and can be significant. Nonetheless, in a Soviet-type economic system, the planned allocation-- i.e., the production and economic activities undertaken to meet the plan--of resources and commodities is determined by the preferences of the planners and the political leaders. This was the major reason the Soviet-type economic system was originally developed.

3. Obviously, given the above two principles, prices play a secondary role in the allocation of resources. That role may be important, but it is not a dominant one. In the Soviet-type economic system, the plan targets are determined in quantities and as nonsubstitutable entities, and prices and values have a largely accounting function in the planned sector of the economy. In other words, when a gap appears

between the supply and demand of an important commodity in the planned sector, the planner in a Soviet-type economic system will react by changing the plan targets, not by changing prices.[11]

I firmly believe that these three elements clearly define an economic system that differs from all others that have been either developed and implemented in reality or suggested in theory. The Soviet-type economic system fundamentally relies upon the nationalization (state ownership) of most resources and enterprises, the allocation of most resources and the direction of most economic activities according to a plan in nonconvertible physical units, and, as a corollary to the first two elements, an administered price system with prices playing a secondary role in the allocation of resources. Some people may object to these three defining elements of a Soviet-type economic system, arguing that a private, market, non-planned sector can be introduced (i.e., when market prices direct economic behavior and the allocation of resources) and grow to the extent that these two sectors exist side by side and that neither can be said to dominate the long-sought-after and dreamed of perfect mixed system. My answer to this argument is, not that such a system has never existed (and it hasn't), but that there are a host of theoretical and practical arguments as to why it cannot exist. I once pointed out to a Chinese who claimed that this ideal mixed system was the objective of China's economic reform program that nobody had solved the problem of being only "a little bit pregnant." There is no need to get involved in another debate over an "impossibility theorem" for, as will be made clear in my argument in the next section, the current economic reform program in China has a long way to go before anything like parity can be claimed between the private-market sector and the state-planned sector.

III

Having defended what I consider to be the essential elements of any Soviet-type economic system, it readily can be shown why I believe that the many major economic institutional, strategy, and policy changes that were introduced in the seven years after 1977 may have considerably modified that economic system but they have not rejected or replaced it. A discussion of why the retention or rejection of this economic system is a very important question in determining China's economic future is presented in the last section of this chapter.

A major change in the post-Mao economy is the restoration of a significant private-market sector as a supplement to the state-planned sector of the economy. In the cities, unemployed workers are urged to create cooperatives or to set up private businesses to provide goods and services demanded not only by consumers but by state enterprises as well and to sell those goods and services in "officially controlled," but relatively free, markets. The Chinese have reacted to the renewed opportunity to engage in "penny capitalism" with vigor, and the host of private or cooperative ventures has certainly captured the imagination of the Western observer. Many of these observers, on the basis of a brief visit down a side street in Beijing, have loudly hailed the return of capitalism to China. Yet, the existence of a cooperative and private sector and "free market" transactions in goods and services is nothing new in a Soviet-type economic system, in which a nonplanned sector is used to "fill in the cracks" left by the state-planned sector. Such a cooperative and private sector was also permitted in the Soviet-type economic system of the 1950s in China, and at that time, it was much larger than it is today.

For example, between 1979 and 1982, the number of private individual workers in the urban areas increased by over 50 per year to total 1.47 million in 1982; only 23 percent of the number of 1955 and 65 percent of the average level in 1962-1964.[12] Retail sales in the private sector did double between 1981 and 1982, but they still amounted to less than 3 percent of the total retail sales (compared to 20 percent in the mid-1950s).[13] In other words, the volume of trade handled by state trading agencies still accounts for over three-fourths of the total retail trade. When the collectives' participation in that trade is included, the state/collective share is well over 90 percent of the total.

These statistics, however, are downward-biased estimates for the role of the market sector in China's economy today as the state enterprises were allowed, as part of the program of economic reform, to utilize their resources to produce goods "for the market" after their plan targets for output were fulfilled. According to one estimate, these products by industrial producers accounted for approximately 20 percent of urban production, and when added to the collective, cooperative, and private-market sales, they would bring the market-allocated sales up to a level of one-fourth of all retail sales.[14] When account is taken of above-quota and negotiated-price sales of agricultural products to state procurement agencies,[15] the estimate that one-fourth of all economic activity in China is governed by market forces, not the plan, is probably a reasonable estimate. There is sufficient evidence to show that the state intends to control these market activities and that the state-planned sector remains the clearly dominant sector in the Chinese economy today.[16]

In an even more direct challenge to the planned sector, the economic reform program has called for the creation of collective, cooperative, and private production as well as commercial, transportation, and service activities that directly parallel and compete with the state-planned sector. The encouragement of cooperatives and private individuals to directly compete with the state sector is a rational response to the legacy of economic policy in China before the death of Mao. The extreme emphasis given to material products in the producers' goods industry and the attempts to achieve self-sufficiency, as well as the concomitant neglect of "nonproductive" activities, had left the Chinese economy seriously bereft of infrastructure and without well-developed service-sector facilities (transport, trade, banking, etc.).

A major objective of China's leaders at the present time is to develop a commodity economy based on specialization and the division of labor. However, their attempt to develop such an economy is seriously limited by the very poorly developed commercial network for trade and exchange. In an attempt to remedy bottlenecks, collectives and private individuals are urged to provide these desired commodities and services even if they compete with the state-planned sector in doing so. Nonetheless, if and when the activities of a unit that has been created and developed in the private-market sector grows to any significance, it will then become a leading candidate for transition and absorption into the state or collective sector. Furthermore, a major share of its activities probably will have been included in the state plan well before that ultimate transfer of ownership has become necessary to maintain the dominance of the planned sector in the economy.[17]

An important argument in the debate between planned or market allocation of goods and services involves the optimum degree of centralization-decentralization in decision making. Even the most ardent advocate of a Soviet-type economic system must admit the need to rely on some decentralization in decision making so as to ensure the utilization of knowledge available only at the local level and for incentive purposes.[18] Thus, the history of any Soviet-type economy reveals an ebb and flow between periods of centralization to reestablish coordination and control of the macrolevel and periods of decentralization to stimulate greater efficiency and enthusiasm at the microlevel. The economic reform program in China in the seven years after 1977 launched a major wave of decentralization in China's economy, so much so that by the end of 1980 and in early 1981, the Chinese leadership had begun to admit that it had lost control over the budget, the money supply, prices, employment, wages, the balance of payments, and investment decisions. If allowed to continue, this decentralization movement would have severely undercut the basic principles of a Soviet-type economic system, and during that period, it was somewhat misleading to refer to economic activities in China as resulting from a centrally determined economic plan.

This period obviously taught the Chinese economic reformers that experiments with reforms could have dangerous consequences for the economy, and the Chinese quickly reintroduced centralized control over the budget, prices, investment, and foreign trade. However, this effort has not been completely successful: The inflationary pressures have been dampened, but the budget has been balanced in an accounting sense only--investment expenditures outside the plan remain a serious problem, and efforts to correct the deficit in the balance of payments have resulted in overkill and an unnecessary accumulation of foreign exchange. Nonetheless, the Chinese leadership has regained its confidence along with its restoration of greater central control over the economy. More important, the people at the highest level of authority who were advocates of economic reform have been very careful ever since to admit that China's economy was and will continue to be a centrally planned economy, with the state sector dominating, and that national-level priorities will prevail over local and private interests.

As one astute student of the economic policies advocated by China's leaders concludes about Zhao Ziyang (the highest-level advocate of economic reform in China today), "what Zhao's speeches reveal during this time is a redefinition of 'reform'," "moving away from 'reform' meaning development of the market (sector) to 'reform' meaning the use of economic levers."[19] Still others see the recent establishment of economic regions to be planned and administered by the major municipality of a region as the resulting compromise of centralization-decentralization <u>within</u> the traditional Soviet-type economic system: decentralization, but to a level far above the individual enterprise, with no implication that the individual enterprise will become more heavily engaged in activities in the market sector.

One of the most crucial economic activities included in the planned allocation of resources, i.e., determined by the central authorities, is investment. To stimulate initiative in problem solving at the local level and to ensure a more responsible use of investment funds, the program of economic reform allowed enterprises and local authorities to retain a share of their profits or budget revenues and use these retained funds for investment purposes. In addition, investment projects in certain sectors and for certain purposes are to be financed by means of bank loans, which have to be repaid with interest.

Inasmuch as the retained earnings and revenue sharing by local units remains in effect, and some investment projects are to be financed by bank loans, the amount of "outside-the-plan" investment is considerably larger than had been the case in the preeconomic reform period. Furthermore, the central authorities have encountered considerable problems in asserting the degree of central control over investment that they desire.

Nonetheless, while attempting to reassert the state's central control over investment, the program of economic reform does intend to change the manner in which investment is financed. A considerable portion of planned investment will be financed by unilateral budget grants, as in the past. In addition, a significant portion of planned investment will be financed by bank loans and/or retained earnings and shared revenue.[20] Finally, the central authorities will establish priorities or guidelines for investment outside the state plan, and any project not within the state plan that is to be financed by means of retained earnings, shared revenue, or bank loans must receive the approval of higher-level authorities, the particular level depending on the size of the project.[21] Thus, I have no quarrel with the conclusions of a Japanese analysis of China's fiscal and financial reforms:

> To sum up, while basic investments in new plant construction have been shifted to Construction Bank loans and away from treasury funds, funds for enterprise innovation and improvements are henceforth to come from retained profits, loans for the tapping of potential, technical innovation and improvement of the Construction Bank and the medium and short-term loans for facilities by

the People's Bank of China. In addition, the increased ratio of depreciation funds retained by enterprises is expected to play a bigger role as a financial resource for innovation and improvement to push financial reform in this direction.[22]

There is no doubt that the program of economic reform does intend to shift the burden of <u>financing</u> investment onto the local units and to reduce the burden of unilateral budget grants on the resources of the central government. At the same time, however, the central authorities intend to keep central control over the determination of what those investment projects will be and who will undertake them, decisions to be based on national, not local, interests. It is the central authorities' making the decisions as to the rate of accumulation and the structure of investment that is the important principle of a Soviet-type economic system, and who pays and how are undoubtedly important determinants of how efficiently the system works.

A second major institutional reform created by the program of economic reforms in China also refers to the relations between state enterprises and the budget. Traditionally, the profits of state enterprises were submitted to the state budget as revenues, and losses were subsidized from the state budget. From time to time, profit or loss targets were included in the plan as major objectives assigned to the enterprises, but fulfilling the quantity of output or gross value of output was always the foremost target. Again, for the purpose of generating local initiative and efficiency in operations, the program of economic reform has created a new system: profit taxes, with the state enterprises responsible for their own losses and profits. In the short run, of course, with the structure of administered prices and assigned planned targets for outputs and allocated inputs, profit rates and losses vary widely, even within an industry.

With each industry now responsible for its own profits and/or losses, the profits tax initially must be tailored to fit the situation in each enterprise--high taxes for very profitable enterprises, negative taxes for those that traditionally suffer losses. Nonetheless, despite the many technical problems that will have to be faced, i.e., how to value capital costs or what are allowable deductions for costs, the desire is to create an incentive system for enterprises so that cutting losses and increasing profits are rewarded by more retained earnings. However, a second, more serious problem is, Are the increased profits or reduced losses due to factors external to the firm, i.e., windfall profits, or are they due to greater efficiencies in the operation of the firm? Finally, this change merely creates one more issue of debate between the local units and the center, the tax rate on a unit's profits and its profit or loss norm. The ideal, of course, is to eventually reach the point at which there is one profit tax rate for all, and firms suffering losses will go bankrupt and close.

If achieved, this change <u>could</u> succeed in transforming the Chinese economic system into a new and different system. As now intended, however, the planned targets for outputs and inputs in physical quantity are still the dominant objective of the enterprises; the application of a profit tax with the enterprises' retaining the after-tax profits is an incentive mechanism to achieve the realization of those planned targets more efficiently. If the desire is to achieve a single-rate profit tax to be applied to all enterprises, with those suffering losses being forced to close down, it would be necessary to rationalize the system of administered prices to that they reflected and were consistent with the planners' preferences as expressed in the planners' targets for inputs and outputs.[23]

Although this system of enterprises' being responsible for their own profits and losses would be unique to the socialist countries employing a Soviet-type economic system, it would not violate any of the principles of that system: The administered price system would be rationalized, but only to more accurately reflect the planners' preferences as those preferences are already revealed in their determination of the output and input targets. On the other hand, if the planners were to stop issuing physical-quantity planned output and input targets and to rely only on the economic levers of the rationalized, but still administered, prices that reflect their preferences (along with a profits tax and a capital use tax levied for budget revenue purposes) to regulate the enterprises' production, the economic system would no longer be a Soviet-type economic system. Rather, it would have become a Lange-Lerner model, a market socialist system with planners' preferences instead of consumers' preferences determining the administered prices.[24] Although the Chinese leaders have called for increased reliance upon economic levers for the purpose of achieving a more efficient operation of enterprises, they have not indicated that these levers will replace the mandatory plans that dominate the allocation of resources and commodities in the economy for a price-taking, profit-maximizing operation of the units of production throughout the economy.[25]

Perhaps the most radical (from the institutional aspect of a traditional Soviet-type economy) institutional changes in the economy have occurred in the agricultural sector: the adoption of a contract responsibility system and the permitting of some households (approximately 13 percent of all farm households) to specialize in sideline or completely commercial farming, with no limit on household income.[26] Time and space do not permit a detailed discussion of this institutional change, but such a discussion is not necessary here. Obviously, the Chinese leadership after the Third Plenum in 1978 encouraged, or at least allowed, the peasants in some areas to experiment with various forms of the contract responsibility system that had been introduced in the early 1960s. This change proved so popular with the peasants and the local authorities and was so successful in achieving an increase in production (especially the form that made the household the basic unit of production and accounting; really the restoration of tenant farming with the state becoming the landlord) that this "correct policy" has been adopted as the basic strategy, along with science and technology, for solving China's agricultural problems.

This restoration of tenant farming by individual households, with leases longer than fifteen years and the ability to trade and amalgamate land in the hands of the most skillful farmers, plus giving them permission to hire farm laborers, could well make both Stalin and Mao turn over in their graves. As for those households that are allowed to cease crop production altogether, specialize in a sideline or noncrop commercial agricultural activity, buy considerable amounts of capital goods for that purpose, and engage in long-distance transportation and trade, some have become downright wealthy capitalists. This new policy, despite all the ideological, social, and political problems it causes, has been defended by the leadership for a very simple reason--it works. At least it has worked very well in the past. Whether it will continue to do so in the future is another matter, but China's leaders have certainly pinned their hopes on its continued success.

Comparing the average annual rates of growth in the agricultural sector in 1977-1982 and 1952-1977, the Chinese accomplished as much in the five-year period after 1977 as they did over a period of fifteen years before 1977. More important, the average per capita income of the peasants increased at a remarkable rate during the same five-year period doubling between 1978 and 1982, while the per capita disposable income of the families of workers and staff members (nonagricultural workers) increased by 50 percent.[27] The per capita income of the peasants was still only 50 percent that of the nonagricultural family members, but if the rates of growth of the seven years after 1977 were to continue, the gap between these per capita incomes would be eradicated and the peasants' income would be 20 percent higher than that of a family member in the nonagricultural sector in only ten years. It obviously will be very difficult to maintain these rates of agricultural growth in the future; nonetheless, the economic conditions and prospects improved considerably in the Chinese countryside in the seven years after 1977, and China's leaders clearly believe the contract responsibility system is a major explanatory factor in that success, and they suggest that this same system should be adopted in other sectors of the economy.

The current leadership initially accepted and then strongly advocated the contract responsibility system in agriculture, not only because it was very popular with the peasants and was very successful in stimulating production, but also because it did not alter the three basic principles of the Soviet-type economic system. All discussions of this system have made it very clear, first, that there is to be no private ownership or market sales of land--the land remains public property and the state is the landlord. Second, the tenants' contracts with the state assign to the peasant tenant households the planned targets for output included in the state plan: their tax delivery obligations, their quotas for deliveries to the state-purchasing agencies at the administered prices set by the state, their contributions to the welfare fund, and their other obligations to the local collective or government. All of these obligations are to be negotiated, but the same was true of these same obligations when they were assigned to the collectives in the past.

The big difference with the past, of course, is that now the household is free to organize the resources at its disposal (including the land, capital goods, and inputs allocated to it by the local collective or township government) to produce the output required to meet the contract quota. Households are also allowed to keep and/or dispose of any surplus produced. On the other hand, the agricultural sector is still included in the plan drawn up by the central authorities as it was in the past insofar as the quantities of output, in major commodity categories, are required to be delivered to the state as quota deliveries at below market prices. The state may, if it chooses, purchase additional quantities at above-quota premium prices at negotiated prices, or any output beyond the amount required by their tax or assigned quota deliveries may be sold by the peasants on the market.

Despite the increased level of production

and available supplies of agricultural commodities, the Chinese are clearly aware that the state-planned sector could not obtain the products needed if they were to abandon their assignment of "planned" quotas in agriculture. The administered agricultural price system is such that if the peasants were not required to produce certain products in quantities beyond their own needs, they would shift to more profitable crops, to the neglect of the most important and basic crops in agriculture.[28] A partial rationalization of most major agricultural prices occurred in 1978, and many piecemeal agricultural price adjustments have occurred since then and will undoubtedly continue in the future. Yet, a price reform that would rationalize prices to the point at which planned quotas assigned to the contract households were no longer necessary has been ruled out (for obvious reasons), at least for the foreseeable future.

IV

It should be clear that the great many economic policy, strategy, and institutional changes that were introduced as part of the economic reform program in the seven years after 1977 and the economic changes associated with that program have significantly transformed the Chinese economy so that the economy of today is very different from the Chinese economy of 1975. None of my arguments are intended to deny that these important changes have occurred; my major purpose has been to point to the important changes that have not occurred and are unlikely to occur in the near future. By concentrating on the many changes that have taken place, as evidenced by the flood of articles published both within China and by specialists outside of China on China's economic reform program, the implicit or explicit argument is that reform of China's basic economic system has either already taken place, is in the process of taking place, or is an inevitable and a logical outcome of the changes that have already occurred. My argument in this chapter is that the three basic principles of a Soviet-type economic system have not been changed by the economic reform program that was adopted in the seven years after 1977 and, on the basis of both the intentions of China's leaders and the logic of the economic reform program itself, will not be abandoned in the foreseeable future.

What difference does this failure to reform the economic <u>system</u> make? Why not concentrate on the many significant changes in economic policy institutions and strategy that have been introduced in evaluating both what happened in the seven years after 1977 and in predicting what is likely to happen in the future? My answer to these questions is quite simple. Our predictions of what will happen in the future should depend, to a large extent, on whether or not the changes have been true systemic changes or not. In other words, inasmuch as the economic reforms have been changes <u>within</u> China's Soviet-type economic system, i.e., changes introduced to make that system work better, the current economic results are more likely to be one-time improvements, and it is likely that the long-term trend will still be constrained by the traditional problems of inefficiency associated with the Soviet-type economic system.

The only true systemic reforms that have been carried out in the countries that have adopted the Soviet-type economic system are those in Hungary and Yugoslavia. Both of those countries discarded the system of central planning based on physical output and input targets derived from material balances for commodities and adopted a reliance on economic levers (prices, taxes, interest rates, exchange rates, etc.) to guide production and allocation decisions. A necessary complement of these systemic reforms was a serious attempt to establish a rational set of prices. In all other socialist countries in Europe that have a Soviet-type economic system, the last two decades have seen an endless program of economic reforms. Yet, without true systemic reform of the second and third principles of the Soviet-type economic system (mandatory input and output targets determined by the central authorities or planners and an administered price system in which the administered prices do not represent rational prices on the basis of either the planners' or the consumers' preferences), the economic authorities have become experts in the process of annually reforming the reforms introduced in the previous year, without ever solving the fundamental economic problems associated with the Soviet-type economic system that the reforms are trying to cure. A key element is the need for price reform, without which decentralized decision making and the use of economic levers instead of mandatory plans will not work.

Thus, despite the many important changes in economic policy, strategy, and institutions the Chinese have adopted as part of their economic reform program in the seven years after 1977, on the basis of those changes adopted thus far, I expect the Chinese to repeat the experience of the Russians: continually reforming the reforms in an attempt to reduce the inefficiencies of their Soviet-type economic system without really coming to grips with the basic cause of those inefficiencies. Perhaps the best summary of the argument can be taken from a study of economic reforms in the Soviet Union:

> Over the past dozen years, the Soviet government has undertaken a series of measures unprecedented in scope and intensity, in an effort to improve efficiency in the economy's use of resources and the quality of its products. Since the problems stubbornly refused to go away, the period since 1970 has witnessed a continuous process of reforming these initial reforms. The reformed "reforms" and the "improved" plans also have not made matters much better. Yet another round of reforming the reforms is now on the drawing board. If, as in the past, these new reforms leave the essentials of the system unaltered, they, too, will not alleviate the <u>system-based</u> malaise."[29]

NOTES

1. Robert F. Dernberger, "Communist China's Industrial Policies: Goals and Results," in *Mainland China's Modernization: Its Prospects and Problems*, Institute of International Studies and Institute of East Asian Studies (Berkeley: University of California, 1981), p. 160.

2. Robert F. Dernberger, "The Chinese Search for the Path of Self-sustained Growth in the 1980s: An Assessment," in U.S. Congress, Joint Economic Committee, *China Under the Four Modernizations*, pt. 1 (Washington, D.C.: Government Printing Office, 1982), p. 76.

3. Robert F. Dernberger, "The Domestic Economy and the Four Modernizations Program," in Atlantic Council, *China Policy for the Next Decade* (Boston: Oelgeschlager, Gunn and Hain, 1984), pp. 139-179.

4. "Zhao Ziyang Speech at Industry Conference," Foreign Broadcast Information Service, April 1, 1982, pp. K6-8.

5. Milton Friedman, "Report to the Committee on Scholarly Communications with the People's Republic of China on Trip to China" (mimeograph).

6. See David Bachman, "Differing Visions of China's Post-Mao Economy: The Ideas of Chen Yun, Deng Xiaoping, and Zhao Ziyang" (Unpublished paper, March 1984), pp. 5-12. Bachman sums up his analysis of Chen's views by arguing, "Chen appears to emphasize readjustment and control more than he does reform" (p. 12).

7. There are additional considerations that argue against the creation of a new Chinese economic system at the local level in contradiction to the wishes of the leadership at the national level: the size of the economy, the level of development, and the very large number of surplus workers in the rural areas. Certain groups, sectors, and regions could do very well on their own, but as they developed and/or became rich on the basis of their own devices, a much greater number of people and areas would be condemned to severe poverty. This result may well come to pass, but it is better described as anarchy or the reappearance of the "cellular" economy, not a flourishing of a unique new

Chinese economic system in the upswing of the dynastic cycle.

8. See Jiang Yiwei, "The Theory of an Enterprise-based Economy," *Social Sciences in China*, no. 1 (1980), pp. 53-54. Additional evidence to be used in rejecting this criticism of my conclusion is a "rumor" cited by many Chinese I have talked to during their visits to the United States: A well-known advocate of systemic reform openly criticized the traditional Soviet-type economic system and called for true systemic reform in an article published in the *Renmin ribao*; although he obviously had the support of a high-level authority in publishing this article and a year or so later was appointed to a high-level advisory position, it was widely acknowledged that he had encountered considerable problems as a result of publishing the article.

9. I list and discuss these long-run theories or hypotheses, which predict the eventual demise of the Soviet-type economic system, in Robert F. Dernberger, "The State-planned, Centralized System: Comparative Analysis of the Socialist Economies of the People's Republic of China, the Democratic People's Republic of Korea, and the Democratic Republic of Vietnam," in *Asian Economic Development--Present and Future*, ed. Robert Scalapino, Seizaburo Sato, and Jusuf Wanand: (forthcoming), especially manuscript pp. 21-25. These hypotheses can be labeled the convergence hypothesis, the empirical law of uniformity, the technological-imperative hypothesis, the dead-weight-loss argument, the inevitable triumph of pragmatism over utopianism thesis, and the exhaustion of mass mobilization and failure of the permanent lie.

10. Stated by a member of the State Planning Commission in an interview with the author, Beijing, November 1979.

11. A good illustration of this point in the Chinese context was the recent discussions about the excess supply of tobacco produced because the reforms had allowed the peasants to have a larger role in determining what to produce and how to produce it, as well as allowing them to keep a larger share of the profits. Because the administered price system indicated that the

profit from producing tobacco was much greater than that for most other crops, the peasants did what comes naturally--produced more tobacco. In response to the resulting surplus, however, the leaders did not lower the price of raw tobacco, they reduced the allotted acreage for planting tobacco in the plan.

12. PRC, State Statistical Bureau, <u>Statistical Yearbook of China, 1983</u> (Beijing: Statistical Publishers of China, 1983), p. 120.

13. Ibid., p. 372.

14. Zhang Zhuoyuan and Xing Junfang, "Give Full Play to the Superiority of the Socialist Planned Economy," <u>Jingzi yangjiu</u>, no. 4 (1981).

15. The same article cited in note 13 claims that 34 percent of the total output of agricultural <u>sideline</u> products was purchased outside the plan.

16. For a detailed list of the many controls imposed on the private-market-sector activities, see "State Regulations on Rural Private Industry, Trade," Foreign Broadcast Information Services, March 13, 1984, pp. K10-13, and "State Council Rules on Transportation Marketing," ibid., pp. K13-15.

17. To the extent that the private-market sector relies on inputs, supplies, and orders from the state-planned sector, it can be said to already be a part of that sector. In fact, many articles in the Chinese press urge authorities at the local level to include the needs of cooperative and private/individual economic units in the planned allocation of scarce goods so they can operate their businesses effectively.

18. Obviously, any local-level knowledge can be had at the central level, but the sheer volume of such information would overwhelm any decision-making group at the central level and make rational decisions impossible. Thus, the microinformation is aggregated so as to make it manageable, but the mere process of aggregation destroys the original information that is time, place, and item specific.

19. See note 6.

20. In some cases, the retained earnings or shared revenue from one unit may be used to finance the investment of another. Surplus

retained earnings or shared revenue are expected to be used to buy central government bonds or may even be taxed away by means of a special assessment; either source is listed as budget revenue, which can be used on the expenditure side to finance investment in any unit in the economy. If these retained earnings or shared revenues are deposited in the bank, they become funds available to the bank for making loans to finance investment projects in any unit in the economy.

21. This stipulation would result even if not intended, because, as in the case of all similar reforms in Soviet-type economies, with the shift from unilateral budget grants to bank loans as a means for financing investment, the interest rates on the loans are set far too low to serve as a means for rationing the available investment funds among the alternative demands. Thus, with demand exceeding supply, the planners (or bankers acting on behalf of the planners) must allocate the available funds on the basis of some other criteria, usually the same set of allocative priorities they were pursing when investment funds were allocated by means of unilateral budget grants.

22. Akira Fujimoto, "China's Fiscal and Financial Reforms," Japan External Trade Organization (JETRO), China Newsletter, no. 44 (May-June 1983), p. 6.

23. This level of success in the program of economic reforms would mean that the Chinese had achieved the objectives of Evsey Lieberman's reform proposals in the Soviet Union. Never intending to challenge the basic principles of a Soviet-type economy, Lieberman argued that the single indicator of profits could be used to determine how efficiently the plan targets were being achieved by enterprises, and the enterprises should be awarded on the basis of the profits they earned. Following their experiment with the Lieberman proposals, Soviet economists acknowledge the Lieberman proposal will not work in the absence of rational prices, even if those prices were to be made rational on the basis of planners'--not the consumers'--preferences.

24. Oskar Lange actually described such a system in an article published in Poland near

the end of his life (i.e., the late 1950s).

25. A recent analysis of mandatory versus guidance planning in China clearly specified that mandatory plans would continue to dominate most economic activities. Yet the author did admit that the present situation in Shanghai Municipality, where more than 90 percent of all industrial output was produced for the plan, probably was a bit excessive.

26. I have not read the often-referred-to Document no. 1 that was adopted in January and spells out these new radical policies for the agricultural sector, but many articles in the Chinese press indicate that it does allow the concentration of land under a single household and the hiring of farm laborers.

27. PRC, <u>Statistical Yearbook of China, 1983</u>, p. 483.

28. A study of production costs for forty-six brigades in Henan from 1980 to 1982 showed that the production of foodgrams resulted in very low rates of profit (7.91 yuan per mou for the five basic grains, or about 20 percent) while commercial crops were very profitable (118.21 yuan per mou for tobacco, or about 75 percent). In 1981, the producers of the five basic grains suffered a loss (see <u>Rural Financial Accounting</u>, no. 7 [1983], pp. 12-13).

29. Gertrude E. Schroeder, "The Soviet Economy on a Treadmill of 'Reforms'," in U.S. Congress, Joint Economic Committee, <u>Soviet Economy in a Time of Change</u> (Washington, D.C.: Government Printing Office, 1979), pp. 312-313 (emphasis added).

12
Mainland China's Special Economic Zones

Jan S. Prybyla

HISTORY

In July 1979, as part of the general reorientation of economic policy toward the outside world, and especially toward the advanced capitalist component of that world, Communist China's State Council authorized the provinces of Guangdong (Kwangtung) and Fujian (Fukien) to establish special economic zones (SEZs) "where foreign trade and investment are granted broader facilities than elsewhere in the country."[1] Four SEZs were designated: Shenzhen (Shenchen), Zhuhai (Chuhai), and Shantou (Swatow) in Guangdong Province, and Xiamen (Amoy) in Fujian Province. Administrative adjustments were made to reduce bureaucratic red tape (e.g., in anticipation of the move, Baoan and Zhuhai Counties were made into municipalities and placed directly under provincial government control); laws and regulations were issued dealing with investment, enterprise operations, and other matters in the SEZs; and steps were taken to upgrade the areas' deficient infrastructural facilities (transportation, communications, ports, power supply, housing).

Although cautious, the initial response of outside investors, especially Hong Kong businessmen, to China's open-door policy cast in the SEZ format was positive. By the end of 1981, the total foreign direct investment commitment in the four SEZs came to $1.7 billion, or 60 percent of all direct foreign investment commitment on the mainland at that time. The bulk of the committed investment was in Shenzhen: $1.4 billion, most of which came from Hong Kong and took the form of flexible coproduction arrangements.[2]

The concept of special economic zones designed to encourage foreign investment, technology transfers, upgrading of managerial and labor skills, and the promotion of exports (i.e., acquisition of hard currencies) is not original to mainland China's newly pragmatic leaders. It has long been practiced by more than seventy market-economy countries in some 300 zones. Among the more successful have been the export processing zones established by the Republic of China on Taiwan in the mid-1960s.[3] In a sense, Hong Kong is a large very special zone, one of the most dynamic in the world. The special economic zone concept found its earliest application in China's treaty ports: a politically unacceptable arrangement for China, as is well known, but despite its bad reputation, an economically constructive one over the long term.

Today, the rest of mainland China is exhorted to "learn from Shanghai," not because of Shanghai's socialist construction of the 1950s or its flirtation in the late 1960s and early 1970s with leftist radicalism (which nearly destroyed it), but because of the advanced infrastructure, commercial and organizational sophistication, and technological aptitude acquired, by and large, in the bad old days of the treaty ports. In fact, in 1982 Shanghai was designated as the fulcrum of one of two regional economic cooperation zones (the other, suggestively, being Canton), which in the future are to carry the special economic zones idea beyond its present limits. With 0.5 percent of mainland China's land area, the--as yet loose--Yangtze River Delta Zone centered on Shanghai generates 20 percent of the mainland's gross value of industrial and agricultural output (GVIAO), 25 percent of the country's total revenue, and 20 percent of the foreign trade turnover, and it has a per capita GVIAO of more than $1,000 a year--a level the rest of the mainland is unlikely to achieve even in the year 2000.[4]

In the early 1970s, a concept of special export commodity production bases gained currency for awhile under the sponsorship of Zhou Enlai. The key idea was to cut through artificial administrative divisions and establish economically meaningful links between the government's various foreign trade organizations and industrial and agricultural enterprises for the purpose of encouraging the export of certain targeted commodities. Although there was no question at that time of inviting direct foreign participation in this export drive, the experience gained was probably useful in later efforts to establish the SEZs.

The backward historical linkages of the SEZ concept in China to the treaty ports and its forward linkages to large regional economic cooperation zones, with the present SEZs in between, and the many practical variants of the idea (export processing zones, free trade zones, industrial zones) in the outside world, suggest that the SEZs are experimental, fluid, and transitional phenomena intended primarily to accomplish certain specific objectives, among which hard currency export earnings and technology acquisition rank high in the minds of mainland China's policymakers. But history also suggests, as in the cases of Shanghai and Canton (and to a lesser extent, Amoy) that the concept has effects that go well beyond the narrow short- and medium-term purposes for which the SEZs are designed; that they spill over into the social and personal psychologies of the people caught up in their maelstrom and, indeed, that they have lasting repercussions on the system of economic organization. The Marxist purists on the mainland intuitively, and I think correctly, approach Hong Kong, Shanghai, Canton, and the new special economic zones with a wariness that is but a step removed from horror.

The SEZs, despite many caveats and restrictions, are capitalist conceptual constructs and capitalist engines of development. They feed on ideas such as profit maximization and minimization of administrative intervention, license to hire and fire, freedom to make and break, factor mobility, extensive privatization of property rights, and contractual legality. They are creatures of money and the competitive world market. To advance material prosperity, they necessarily cause dislocations in socialist structures and philosophical disturbance in the realm of Marxist-Leninist theory. Because of these threats, the

SEZs are treated as phenomena separate from the body politic and economic of central planning and socialized property. They are "special," and they are "zoned" to minimize the ethical side effects of capitalism. But these factors mean that the linkage effect between the SEZs and the rest of the mainland economy is impeded in terms of the transfer of managerial expertise, work attitudes, technical experience, and so on.

Linkage effect problems between the export processing zones and the rest of the domestic economy were also at one time experienced by Taiwan, but to a smaller extent and of a different socioeconomic order. In Taiwan (as elsewhere in the market economies), the break between the zones and the rest of the economy was primarily technical. In mainland China, it is both technical and systemic: The SEZs there operate on economic principles that are qualitatively different from those which govern the operation of the bulk of the domestic economy. The difference is one of contradictory economic cultures. If modern casts of mind imported into the zones from capitalist countries are to benefit the retarded mainland economy, the spillover effect from the zones must be encouraged and enhanced rather than the opposite.

PURPOSE

The establishment of the enclaves is intended to help mainland China promote the following objectives:[5]

   Attract foreign investment in the form of
      advanced plant and equipment
   Import up-to-date technology, which can
      then be subjected to reverse and
      enhancement engineering
   Stimulate the development of exports to
      hard currency areas
   Earn hard currencies through tourism in
      the zones
   Acquire managerial know-how and knowledge
      of modern business procedures
   Serve as controlled experiments with alien
      forms of socioeconomic organization

(markets, private property, incentive systems)
Provide employment and training for the labor force
Stimulate the development of domestic industry
Keep in touch with economic, scientific, and technological trends in the world market
Provide an apparently "autonomous" socio-economic model for the incorporation of Hong Kong, Macao, and Taiwan into the PRC[6]

These objectives are to be realized through controlled concessionary policies.

POLICIES

Controls

The government of mainland China reserves the right to exercise a far-reaching control over the activities of the SEZs. These controls include the following:

1. Enterprises and individuals in the SEZs must abide by the laws, decrees, and related regulations of the PRC, including specific provisions that apply to the zones only. As of early 1984, there were about forty major pieces of legislation applicable to foreign investment in China that had actually been published. However, as the National Council for U.S.-China Trade warns, these laws are by no means the only ones: "Because so many Chinese laws are kept secret and out of the hands of foreigners, it is very important that investor understand that their enterprises in China may come under laws they do not know about and are not allowed to see."[7] Such laws can be discovered if foreigners consult Communist internal documents (neibu), if they can get hold of them--an act, however, that in itself constitutes a breach of the law.

2. Customs offices of the SEZs are agencies of the central government, and administrative offices are under the provincial governments. The

latter are charged, among others, with the examination and approval of investment projects submitted by potential investors, the registration of enterprises, and land allotment. "Contentions and contradiction between the two offices can only be resolved by relevant ministries of the central government."[8] Investors have found that approval by the Ministry of Foreign Economic Relations and Trade (created in March 1982) is increasingly a must. There are also, of course, Communist Party offices in each zone, and a great deal of power ultimately resides in them. Separate agencies have been established to act as agents of the government in economic dealings with foreign investors in the SEZs (e.g., fund raising, trust investment, operating enterprises or joint ventures with foreign investors, and acting as agents for investors in matters related to sales and purchases with other parts of the mainland).[9] These agencies include, among others, the Guangdong Provincial SEZ Development Company and the China Merchants Steam Navigation Company registered in Hong Kong (in the Shekou industrial district of the Shenzhen SEZ).

3. Foreign exchange control within the SEZs is exercised by offices of the Bank of China.

4. The People's Insurance Company of China (PICC) is the sole admitted carrier in mainland China handling foreign and domestic risks. Foreign insurance firms are regarded as nonadmitted carriers: They cannot seek insurance in the PRC, although they can insure foreign investments in China other than joint equity ventures. One such nonadmitted carrier is the American Insurance Company, a fifty-fifty joint venture formed in 1983 by the New York registered American International Group and the PICC. The restrictions placed by the mainland Chinese on insurance have resulted in underinsurance or no insurance at all of foreign investments in the SEZs and elsewhere in the country.[10]

5. Land in the SEZs remains the property of the PRC. It is leased to investors by the Chinese authorities according to actual needs.

6. Workers to be employed in SEZ enterprises are recommended by state labor service companies in the zones. Wage rates and other

payments (e.g., labor insurance) are stipulated in contracts concluded between employers and employees in accordance with the guidelines laid down by an SEZ's administrative office. Wage rates in the SEZs are invariably higher than the industry average, and most of the difference is retained by the government. Enterprises are also required to pay for labor insurance, medical care, and a number of subsidies that are about 1.3 times the basic wage. Similar provisions apply to the salaries of Chinese managerial personnel in the SEZs. In this regard, the rule insisted on by the Chinese is comparability, i.e., equal compensation for Chinese and foreign managers of equal rank, even though domestic Chinese salaries for that rank are much smaller. Most of the difference between the domestic salary rate and the SEZ rate is retained by the government--in effect, it represents a subsidy paid by the foreign partner to the PRC. Although in principle workers can be dismissed by SEZ employers, such dismissals must be in line with the provisions of the labor contracts and guided by China's socialist practice, which means, in effect, that it is very difficult to dismiss workers. At the very least, a lengthy haggling process is involved.

Concessions

To attract foreign capital and expertise, the SEZs offer a number of inducements to potential foreign investors that are, in general, somewhat better than the concessions granted to foreign investors outside the zones:[11]
 1. The SEZ administrations undertake (with foreign participation whenever possible) to provide basic infrastructural facilities. These have been badly lacking to date, particularly in the Zhuhai, Shantou, and Xiamen zones in such areas as telecommunications, electricity supply (Zhuhai, Shantou--electricity for Shenzhen is supplied from Hong Kong), water supply (Xiamen), rail transportation (Zhuhai, Shantou), roads, and port facilities (Shenzhen, Zhuhai, Shantou).
 2. Land availability is guaranteed at rents that are competitive with, say, those in Hong Kong. In 1980, annual land rental in Shenzhen

came to HK $2-4 a square foot; in Xiamen it was HK $0.92--a figure that is rising at the rate of 10 percent a year.[12] Targeted industries can receive preferential treatment with regard to choice and use of land sites. In the case of joint equity ventures, the Chinese partner contributes the right to land use, the value of that contribution being determined by the contributor. Land leases are normally available for periods of up to twenty-five years.

3. Means of production and inputs (machinery, spare parts, raw materials, vehicles) for SEZ enterprises are exempt from the consolidated tax and customs duties. However, tax is levied if these goods are later resold in China. Consumer items that are deemed necessary to the conduct of SEZ enterprise business can be fully or partially exempted from import duties, and SEZ-produced exports are not subject to customs duties.

4. There is a flat enterprise income tax rate of 15 percent (compared with 20 percent elsewhere in mainland China) levied on SEZ enterprises with no local surtax. The rate applies to all enterprises in an SEZ: equity joint ventures, cooperative production arrangements, foreign companies with SEZ contracted projects, and (the few) enterprises that are wholly owned by foreign investors or overseas Chinese. Depending on the amount of the investment, the nature of the technology transferred, and the period of time for which the investment is made, tax holidays within the SEZs are generally superior to those granted to investors outside the zones. Normally for investments of $5 million or more, extended over a long period and involving high technology, a tax holiday of up to five years can be granted, or the tax rate can be reduced 20 to 50 percent. Foreign and overseas Chinese investors who reinvest SEZ enterprise profits in the SEZs for five years or longer may apply for a reduction of or an exemption from income tax on the sums reinvested.

5. The share of enterprise after-tax profits accruing to the foreign investor can be repatriated in hard currencies with a 10 percent withholding tax applying to such repatriated profits. Only 50 percent of the after-tax salaries paid to foreigners in China can be repatriated, a concession

that, in fact, represents a serious obstacle to attracting foreign personnel to mainland China.

6. Personal income tax rates in the SEZs are more favorable than outside the zones. In the Guangdong SEZs, the applicable tax rates range from 3 to 30 percent compared to 5-45 percent nationwide, and it is reported that in the Xiamen SEZ, individual income tax rates might be applied that would be only 50 percent of the national rate. Monthly income of less than 800 yuan is exempt from tax.[13]

7. Equity joint venture shares are normally 51 percent Chinese and 49 percent foreign, but majority foreign holdings are permitted.[14]

8. In equity joint ventures, the chairman of the joint venture is Chinese. The post of vice-chairman and other managerial positions can be filled by foreigners.

9. In principle, the law on joint ventures implies that joint venture employers have the right to dismiss workers, but, as already noted, this right has been seldom exercised. Also in principle, enterprise managers have the right to make their own hiring decisions, although here, too, practice falls short of principle. Managers are allowed to test workers before hiring and to stipulate probationary periods, but these rights apply explicitly to joint equity ventures. In other forms of enterprise organization (e.g., co-production or sole foreign ownership), these privileges have to be specifically negotiated.

10. Although the products of SEZ enterprises are intended primarily for export, it is possible to negotiate the sale of some products or some part of the total output on the domestic Chinese market. In such cases, the pricing of the goods is done by the Chinese authorities, not by the SEZ enterprises according to world market rules.

11. SEZ enterprises are encouraged to avail themselves of China-made means of production and inputs. These are offered at preferential prices compared with similar commodities exported by the PRC.

12. Entry and exit procedures for foreigners and overseas Chinese (including residents of Hong Kong and Macao) doing business in the zones are simplified.

13. To make life in the Shenzhen SEZ less arduous, three measures were taken early on: First, the practice of small private trading on the Hong Kong border was restored, and six trading points were opened. After fulfilling the state procurement plan, rural communes and brigades near the border were permitted to export small amounts of their farm and sideline products to the colony. Second, several border farming areas were allowed to send peasants across the border to help grow cash crops in the New Territories. The foreign exchange earned in this way could be used to purchase agricultural means of production. Commune members working across the border were permitted to bring back to China various articles of daily use from Hong Kong. Third, communes and brigades along the Hong Kong border were encouraged to develop fish farms by cooperating directly with Hong Kong firms or through compensation trade.

CATEGORIES

Zones

The four SEZs can be classified into two broad categories: (1) comprehensive economic system zones covering industry, agriculture, commerce, services, housing, and tourism (Shenzhen and Zhuhai) and (2) primarily export processing and tourism-oriented zones (Shantou and Xiamen).

Enterprises

Enterprises in the SEZs, and elsewhere, involving foreign as well as Chinese overseas and "compatriot" participation are of four principal kinds: (1) equity joint ventures, (2) coproduction arrangements (cooperative enterprises), (3) compensation trade, and (4) processing.

In the early years (1979-1982), the institutionally most structured equity joint ventures were the least popular, and by the end of 1982, there were ten times as many coproduction enterprises and fifteen times as many compensation trade arrangements as equity joint ventures. This unpopularity probably had much to do with the fluid situation of China's economic legislation at that time, since joint ventures involve a fairly complex organizational form of limited liability company with articles of association and numerous ancillary agreements, which are in general more complicated than those involved in looser forms of organization.

Coproduction arrangements are more adaptable. Each is subject to a separate contract between the Chinese and the foreigners, and the two sides cooperate in operations and management in line with the contract but without forming a united organ of authority. Normally, the Chinese only provide the land and buildings and supply labor, and the foreign investor provides all the funds and takes the risks, including the risk of the coproduction venture's not being included in the state plan-- and thus not being assured of the supply of needed domestic materials. The positive side of remaining outside the state plan is that such coproduction arrangements are somewhat less hamstrung by the ministerial bureaucracy.

Compensation trade requires that the foreign partner supply, free of charge, equipment that later is paid for with the goods produced by that equipment. This equipment becomes the property of the Chinese at any time stipulated by the contract. The foreign partner is responsible for marketing abroad the goods produced, and financing the deal with foreign exchange is also the foreigners' problem.

The last enterprise form involves the supply by the foreign partner of equipment and materials to be processed or assembled in China for which a fee is then paid by the foreigner. The equipment may either become China's property at the expiration of the contract or be returned to the foreign investor.[15]

IDEOLOGY

Joint equity ventures and other forms of foreign participation in mainland China's socialist economy do not constitute an ideological deviation. Even if they did, dialectical logic can be used to rationalize anything. The explanation proceeds along several paths:

1. "Using capitalist funds, technology, and experience of management and administration to build socialism"[16] is one explanation that had Lenin's blessing. In his less guarded moments, Lenin called such capitalist partners "useful idiots."

2. On the other hand, there is the danger of spiritual pollution, a by-product, if one is not vigilant, of united front tactics. To counteract bourgeois influences on raw young workers and wily old cadres in the zones, it is thought necessary "to strengthen their powers of resistance against decadent capitalist ideology and to enhance their cultural, technical, and professional standards so as to help them grow and dedicate themselves to the construction of the special economic zones."[17] One way of accomplishing these goals is to strengthen the Party school of the local district and conduct training courses for leading cadres from the SEZs at higher educational institutions at the provincial level.

3. Although spiritual contamination represents a real danger, the scale of capitalist penetration is too small to pose a serious threat to the system of central planning and public property. "Even if all the capital were advanced by the foreigners in setting up factories in certain special zones in China, it is too small a fraction in the national economy to undermine socialism."[18] In any event, the government has many controls over the capitalists, and capitalist property will eventually revert to the Communist state.

4. What about exploitation? "The exploitation of surplus value exists objectively in China's special economic zones, which is in contradiction with China's socialist system. However, in the long term, the exploitation of surplus value in the special zones is a 'buying-out' policy," a policy of redemption earlier practiced toward China's "national capitalists." In the early 1950s, the idea was to obtain the national capitalists' cooperation. Today, a similar policy is followed with respect to foreign capitalists, overseas Chinese businessmen, and compatriots from Hong Kong and Macao. In essence, joint equity ventures both inside and outside the SEZs have the

ideological characteristics of state capitalism. "They constitute a link and a form of cooperation between China's state administration and capitalism."[19] "To fulfill the four modernizations and develop socialist economy, we will allow investors their share of reasonable profits. Foreign investors are after profits, and we are after socialist modernization. Because of our different aims, there is the potential for economic cooperation."[20]

5. The existence of state capitalism (and even of small areas of pure capitalism in the form of ventures wholly owned by foreign investors) accords with Marx's stage theory of development (historical materialism). It is the skipping of objectively necessary historical stages--tried by the Gang of Four--that represents the real deviation.

PROBLEMS

As might be expected, after years of isolation, experimentation with open-door policies and neocapitalist forms of economic organization and procedures (e.g., market competition) was bound to raise problems for both the mainland government and the foreign investors. Even sympathetic Western observers of the evolving mainland economic scene caution potential investors in and outside the SEZs about the many difficulties and pitfalls of doing business in Communist China. The problems revolve around three main issues: laws, system, and ideology.

Laws

Whereas before 1979 mainland China was a lawless society in the literal meaning of that term (there were practically no laws), today there are many laws, decrees, and regulations. Since 1979, some 300 laws and regulations have been adopted, 250 of them dealing with economic matters. However, as already noted, many of these are confidential, known only to the lawmakers; most are very general, vague, hortatory, and murky; interpretation depends more on the moral "spirit" as it

moves Chinese judges than on the letter of the
law; and there are big gaps in the legal edifice
(e.g., mainland China has no corporation or tort
law).

Numerous examples of the perils inherent in
this situation could be cited, but only a few can
be given here to typify the general problem:

1. A regulation governing technology imports
into the Shenzhen SEZ requires that to benefit
from concessions, the technology must produce
"remarkable economic results."[21]

2. In contract negotiations with foreign
businessmen, the Chinese counter the foreigners'
insistence on specificity regarding issues likely
to give rise to contention by assurances that
"China honors contracts and keeps promises." If
anyone doubts, proof of that proposition is offered,
for example, by referring to Premier Zhao Ziyang's
public assurances to this effect.

3. A tricky problem has to do with mainland
China's regulations on foreign exchange rates,
which can significantly affect the flow of enterprise funds into and out of China. There is
apparently considerable uncertainty and confusion
on this subject.[22] The PRC has two exchange rates
for the yuan: an official rate of roughly two yuan
to the dollar and an internal rate of almost three
yuan to the dollar. The latter applies, with a
good deal of flexibility upward, to Chinese
domestic exporting enterprises and is designed
to encourage exports. The question--unresolved
in law--is which rate will apply to the dollars
earned by exports from SEZ (and other PRC/foreign)
exporting enterprises? Obviously, the use of one
or the other rate can make a lot of difference to
the financial position of a joint firm. Demands
that the rate be pinned down in the enterprise
contract are not satisfied by the Communist
authorities' assurances that "China honors
contracts and keeps promises."

4. Another question that causes anxiety
for foreign investors is the still ill-defined,
recently promulgated law on the protection of the
confidentiality of industrial property rights.
Although proprietary rights to the technology
brought in by the foreign partner may indeed be
safeguarded in the contract concluded between the

foreign investor and the Chinese partner, there is evidence that other Chinese enterprises are not bound by the provisions of the contract and that a discreet dissemination of trade secrets occurs, sometimes in response to instructions given by a superior authority to the Chinese partner in the venture. In formal (not dialectical) logic, this situation is known as cheating.[23]

5. Yet another collection of problems besetting joint business arrangements both within and outside the SEZs concerns dispute resolution. The 1979 law on joint ventures makes no mention of conflict resolution through litigation in the courts. It would appear that the Chinese partners prefer arbitration in mainland China by the Arbitration Commission of the China Council for the Promotion of International Trade, or abroad by a less partisan but understanding agency such as the Arbitration Institute of the Stockholm Chamber of Commerce. But the clear preference of the PRC is to resolve disputes informally through consensus.[24]

6. In line with the PRC's propensity to rely on the "spirit" rather than on the letter of legal contracts and to interpret that spirit in ways that may be at odds with the foreign partners' understanding of the agreement, there have been instances in which the Chinese have linked performance under one contract with conduct under other quite unrelated contracts. For example, the U.S. decision to limit China's access to the U.S. textile market in the absence of legally binding agreements on the subject has had repercussions on other areas of U.S.-PRC economic relations (e.g., grain and cotton trade, airline landing rights, and offshore oil exploration ventures). According to one mainland official, the PRC sees Sino-U.S. trade as one entity. "If you hurt us in one area, we'll respond in another," irrespective of the letter of the law.[25]

System

Many other problems and misunderstandings arise because of mainland China's system of economic organization, which is based on central planning, the quasi-absence of a market-generated price system, public property, and administrative labor allocation; the country's preoccupation with full, lifelong employment (at least in state sector firms); and the context of an economy of scarcity. The most important by far is the presence of a large, self-serving, enormously complex and unwieldy, highly politicized bureaucracy that is characterized by overlapping and ill-defined jurisdictions: the system's surrogate for the market mechanism. Foreign businessmen quickly learn that obtaining agreement with one administrative authority does not necessarily bind other authorities, higher up or parallel. By and large, it is easier to deal with province-level bodies, but their authority can be--and has been known to be--countermanded by the central offices, which themselves are poorly coordinated or at loggerheads. Which of the seemingly countless bureaucracies is the best partner in a joint undertaking is a question that most often cannot be answered at the time the contract is concluded. This situation means, in effect, that "the best that the foreign and Chinese partners can do is check with every Chinese agency that might have a say in some aspect of their agreement."[26] This task is easier said than done, because--like some laws--many power-wielding agencies operate in the twilight of secrecy. Finding out who's who may amount to breaking some clandestine law.

There can be trouble with the mainland managers who are everyday partners in the joint enterprises. They are not conditioned to exercising the authority that is required for operational and strategic business decisions, they tend to respond to often baroque administrative success indicators (i.e., the system judges them by criteria that are not exclusively economic), and their professional competence sometimes leaves much to be desired. Such problems can cause frustrations, delays, contradictions, and losses to the joint firm that cannot be fully captured by a purely accounting calculation of costs, even when such costs are carefully evaluated beforehand and spelled out in the contract.

Grief can also result from the fact that workers are hired and retained under a system that sets great store on employing as many people as possible (productivity-crippling overstaffing) for as long a period as possible (lifelong employment). There is a feeling in some foreign business quarters that labor insurance and other social charges the joint firms must pay are excessive and that the wage rates paid to often unskilled, first-generation ex-peasant industrial workers are not justified by even a liberal estimation of the workers' marginal productivity. In short, the incentive mechanism of joint enterprises is impaired by the economic system's reluctance (despite special provisions) to grant the needed decision-making powers to the people who are directly in charge of the basic economic units, especially the foreign partners, who are suspected--if not in so many words--of wanting to exploit the local labor force and profit from China's weakness.[27]

In an economy of scarcity in which there is no reliable instrument for measuring opportunity costs, the tendency is to use to the hilt any physical product that is actually produced, irrespective of the product's quality, comparative advantage, or other economic dimensions suggested by a market type of calculation. There have been instances in which goods produced by a joint enterprise that--for quality or other reasons--should not have been marketed show up in the Chinese domestic market under the joint firm's trademark or, worse still, pop up in the international market without being marked as a Chinese domestic export. The latest worry is that the Chinese mainland authorities may insist on production from marginally profitable oil wells in the South China Sea, if and when deposits are found there by the joint venture exploration teams. In the Chinese mainland system, the distinction between economically profitable production and uneconomical production has not been fully grasped.

The physical orientation of the system also manifests itself in a lack of understanding on the part of the Chinese of intangible business value (business goodwill). This issue will loom large when the time comes for the transfer of a joint enterprise's property to China. The difficulty is ultimately traceable to Marxist economic theory, which considers that only activities which result in tangible output are productive.

Ideology

The biggest problem is the Communist Party apparatus, a sprawling giant that imposes its a priori scientological view of the world on the conduct of economic affairs, including the everyday business transactions of SEZ-based joint enterprises. The proliferation of government bureaucracies is compounded by the presence of the Party bureaucracy which has its ideological watchdog offices in every SEZ. The problems each cause cannot but further inhibit each and every well-intentioned move in the direction of economic rationality.

The Marxist-Leninist dialectical understanding of "correctness" (i.e., the relativization of truth) casts a shadow over all Party-sponsored laws, decrees, and regulations--their spirit as well as the letter--and, hence, on the meaningfulness and permanence of contracts. Similar reservations apply to the Party's interpretation of the voluntariness, spontaneity, and competitiveness of economic transactions ("anarchy"); private property ("exploitation"); the role of the individual in the social process (derivative and subsidiary to the state); the function of the venture entrepreneur ("class oppressive"); and other market aspects that are to be tolerated in the SEZs.

The fragility (from the perspective of the foreign investor) of the philosophical foundations of the SEZs is increased by the track record of mainland China's paramount leaders since 1949. Unpredictability, violent swings, and factionalism have been the rule. The current regime of wizened old men, who are pragmatists by necessity, is not reassuring on historical and gerontological grounds alone. At best, the foreign investor, driven by the prospect of short-run gain, like the Chinese peasant with his or her subcontracted new economic policy-like plot, can make some hay while the sun shines on the Western horizon. Concretely, this fragility implies the risk of sudden expropriation or more gentle strangulation stretched over a period of years. In the present climate of open-door united-front euphoria, such a risk appears remote, but its probability is supported by the philosophical postulates of Marxism-Leninism and the historical record of socialist operational systems deriving from those postulates--mainland China's prominently included.

PROSPECTS

The SEZs, with their controlled hothouse capitalist sprouts, have, in my view, a short future under either of two opposite assumptions. Under the first assumption of a continuance for the foreseeable future of the current, relatively moderate and pragmatic, "no matter what the color of the cat" policies, the SEZs will be either (a) overtaken by concessionary developments outside the zones or (b) absorbed into larger, interregional cooperative entities such as the Yangtze River Delta and Pearl River Delta zones. Both probabilities are taking shape right now.

Foreign investments outside the SEZs, in various enterprise forms (but mainly equity joint ventures and coproduction arrangements), are outstripping investment in the zones both in volume and in number of projects, and concessions inside and outside the zones are becoming more comparable.[28] It is, therefore, possible that the time of the SEZs has passed before it began. From a Communist control perspective, the spreading out of foreign investments over the country and adjacent seas could be seen as a desirable development. Within the zones, market and private property forces are highly concentrated. Although it is overstating the case a bit, "the law of value governs [with reservations] economic activity in the special zones."[29] Outside the zones, Sino-foreign joint ventures are more thinned out and surrounded by socialism, hence, they are more easily supervised. There are cogent practical considerations affecting a decision on the part of foreigners to invest outside the zones. In many ways, the SEZs are not the potentially most lucrative places to invest in. There is nothing particularly appealing about Zhuhai, for instance (apart from its location next to run-down Macao), or about Shentou (next to nothing). Shenzhen's attractiveness hinges only on its proximity to Hong Kong,[30] and Xiamen is largely intended to be a "me too" showcase vis-à-vis booming Taiwan. By and large, prospects in the SEZs are small potatoes when compared to the coal, power, oil, and other large project developments elsewhere on the mainland.

Plans to implement the concept of trans-regional zones (the first two to be based on Shanghai and Canton) are proceeding. Hong Kong and Macao are scheduled to join the Canton-based zone when the time comes, and doubtless, so will Shenzhen, the mainland's biggest SEZ so far. The SEZs' distinct status will be much diluted by such mergers.

The second assumption is that mainland China will at some point, well before the leases run out in the SEZs, swing away from the comparative pragmatism of recent years and foreign holdings will be expropriated or slowly strangled. Precedents for this course of action may be found in Communist China's early history. State capitalism will become an outcast again, and the people involved in it will be punished for their revisionism and exploitation. Perhaps in anticipation of this particular scenario, Hong Kong's "national capitalist" compatriots, in ever larger numbers, try to curry favor with the Xhinhua agency representatives in the colony (Hong Kong's shadow government) and fall over themselves to earn insurance points with Peking by investing in the SEZs: a curious case of reverse redemption. The more powerful, mobile, and jaded Hong Kong capitalists are moving their operations to Bermuda and putting their money in Japan, Taiwan, Singapore, and the United States.

NOTES

1. "Xiamen Special Economic Zone," interview with Lu Zifen, vice-chairman of the preparatory office and administrative committee of the Xiamen (Amoy) Special Economic Zone, China Reconstructs, no. 6 (June 1981), pp. 68-69.

2. James B. Stepanek, "Direct Investment in China," China Business Review (hereafter CBR) (September-October 1982), p. 21.

3. George Fitting, "Export Processing Zones in Taiwan and the People's Republic of China," Asian Survey (August 1982), pp. 732-744. For a less sanguine evaluation of the benefits derived by the host countries from the export processing zones, see "Export Enclaves: How Much Benefit for Developing Countries?" UNCTAD Bulletin, no. 200 (March 1984), pp. 1-2, 8-9.

4. Teresa Ma, "The Canton Connection," Far Eastern Economic Review (hereafter FEER), July 28, 1983, pp. 48-49; "Facts Behind the Shanghai Economic Zone," Beijing Review (hereafter BR), April 16, 1984, pp. 16-23.

5. Sun Ru, "The Conception and Prospects of the Special Economic Zones in Guangdong," Chinese Economic Studies (Fall 1980), pp. 68-78.

6. Present indications are that Hong Kong and Macao would be merged into the Shenzhen and Zhuhai SEZs, respectively, which, in turn, would be incorporated at some future time into the Pearl River Delta regional economic cooperation zone centered on Canton. The proposed zone would cover seventeen major cities and counties with a combined population of 318 million people.

7. CBR (September-October 1982), p. 22.

8. David K.Y. Chu and Y. T. Ng, "The Chinese Special Economic Zones: A Geographical Appraisal," Asian Geographer 1:2 (1982), p. 14. This article contains an exhaustive bibliography on the many economic, social, legal, and other aspects of the SEZs. An excellent summary presentation of the SEZs may be found in Thierry Pairault, Politique industrielle et industrialisation en Chine, Notes et Etudes Documentaires, no. 4735-4736 (Paris: La Documentation Francaise, October 12, 1983), pp. 49-56.

9. "Regulations on Special Economic Zones

in Guangdong Province," China Trade Report (October 1980), p. 14. For other laws governing foreign investment in mainland China, see CBR (September-October 1982), pp. 22-23.

10. D.C. Chan Wai-Kown, M. E. Cohen, and J. F. Ladman, Jr., "Insuring the China Trade," CBR (January-February 1984), p. 20.

11. "China's Special Economic Zones," BR, January 23, 1984, pp. 25-26.

12. China Trade Report (March 1980), p. 5. According to China's Foreign Trade, no. 4 (1983), p. 9, the annual fee per square meter in the Xiamen SEZ is between one and twenty yuan. The lease period is twenty years with a maximum of fifty years.

13. T. A. Gelatt and E. Theroux, "Tax Treatment in China," CBR (January-February 1984), pp. 22-27.

14. China Trade and Economic Newsletter (January 1984), p. 3.

15. Stepanek, "Direct Investment in China," pp. 21-22.

16. Wen wei po (Hong Kong), interview with the leader of the PRC Import and Export Control Committee, June 29, 1981, p. 2, in Foreign Broadcast Information Service, July 6, 1981, p. W3. "When Lenin introduced the new economic policy in the early 1920s, he put forward a proposal calling for cooperation with foreign capital. Because of various political factors in the USSR and abroad, the proposal fell through" (Sun Ru, "Conception and Prospects," p. 75).

17. Nanfang ribao, November 16, 1981, p. 4.
18. Sun Ru, "Conception and Prospects," p. 75.
19. BR, January 23, 1984, pp. 29, 31.
20. Sun Ru, "Conceptions and Prospects," p. 77.
21. Amanda Bennett, "China's Legal System Irks Westerners," Wall Street Journal, April 5, 1984, p. 34.
22. Jerome Alan Cohen, "Equity Joint Ventures: 20 Potential Pitfalls That Every Company Should Know About," CBR (November-December 1982), pp. 23-30.
23. Ibid., pp. 27-28.
24. Ibid., pp. 28-29.
25. Wall Street Journal, April 5, 1984, p. 34.
26. CBR (September-October 1983), p. 29.
27. Ibid., p. 27.

28. "Flexible economic policies will be practised in 14 more Chinese coastal cities, according to a forum which closed in Beijing on April 6 [1984]. The flexible policies to be adopted will be similar to those now practised in the four special economic zones in south China" (BR, April 16, 1984, p. 6). The designated ports include Dalian (Talien), Qinhuangtao (Ch'inhuangtao), Tianjin (T'ientsin), Yantai (Yent'ai), Qingdao (Ch'ingtao), Lianyungang (Lienyunkang), Shanghai, Nigpo, Wenzhou (Wenchou), Fuzhou (Fouchou), Guangzhou (Kuangchou), Zhanjang (Chanchiang), and Beihai (Peihai).
29. BR, January 23, 1984, p. 31.
30. "A Conversation with Shenzhen's Mayor," Asian Wall Street Journal, April 27-28, 1984, p. 8.

APPENDIX 12A
Shenzhen SEZ, 1979–1983

Subject	1979	1980	1981	1982	1983	Total
Capital construction investment (in millions of renminbi)	49.88	124.87	270.39	632.65	885.93	1,963.72
Gross value of industrial product (in millions of renminbi)	60.61	84.44	242.82	362.12	720.41	1,470.40
Imports of foreign capital						
Contracts signed	170.00	303.00	578.00	583.00	878.00	2,512.00
Investment according to agreements [commitments] (in millions of HK $s)	234.98	2,135.57	6,800.00	1,419.49	2,633.94	13,223.98
Actual investment (in millions of HK $s)	0.12	0.25	0.59	0.88	1.13	2.97
Economic forms (number of)						
Joint ventures	7	4	13	11	92	127
Joint projects [coproduction]	30	24	39	47	149	289
Sales agencies		5	18	8	13	44
Construction area						
Area constructed (in sq. meters)	130,113	346,303	545,944	926,662	1,464,000	3,413,022
Dwelling house area (in sq. meters)	52,617	178,546	234,067	455,687	624,000	1,544,917

Appendix 12A (continued)

Subject	1979	1980	1981	1982	1983	Total
Type of project (number of)						
Industry	112	243	321	457	714	1,847
Commerce, food, service	5	10	5	25	87	132
Communication and transportation	3	4	5	1	15	28
Real estate	2	9	25	6	17	59
Tourism and recreation	2	5	3	2	4	16
Agriculture, animal husbandry, aquatic products industry and others	46	32	218	86	41	423

Source: Renmin ribao, March 29, 1984, p. 5.

APPENDIX 12B

Composition of Investment in Shenzhen SEZ, 1979-1983

	Type of Project					
	Industry	Real Estate	Tourism Food, Service	Communication, Transportation	Husbandry	Others
Actual Investment (in millions of HK $s)	1,299.01	789.35	150.80	224.65	37.04	44.79	435.17

Source: Renmin ribao, March 29, 1984, p. 5.

13
Review of Studies on the Mainland Economy

K. C. Yeh

Since the late 1970s, studies on the mainland economy have proliferated on an unprecedented scale mainly as a result of several recent developments. First, drastic changes in the leadership's development strategy, institutional reforms, and economic programs have generated new interest among scholars in the mainland economy as a case study of economic development. Second, the rapidly expanding economic relations between mainland China and other nations have created the need to understand better the recent changes on the mainland. Third, a large volume of statistical data has now become available. These developments pose many new problems and make possible the reassessment of old ones with new insights. The result is an upsurge in the literature on the mainland economy. For obvious reasons it will not be feasible to cover all the studies in this review. I shall limit the scope of this chapter to recent studies by scholars outside the mainland and only those directly relevant to the theme of the Thirteenth Sino-American Conference on Mainland China, i.e., economic reform and its impact on the PRC's economic future. I interpret economic reform broadly to include both policy reform and institutional reform. However, in the period since 1978, the primary concern of the leadership's economic policy was the former. With the exception of organizational changes in the agricultural sector, major institutional reforms are still in an experimental stage. Consequently, serious research in this area is just beginning, and the few articles available will not be reviewed here. The following sections focus on studies in four main areas: overall assessment of economic growth in the next two decades, measurement of economic growth, development problems in two key sectors, and models of the mainland economy.

OVERALL ASSESSMENT OF THE PRC's ECONOMIC FUTURE

How fast will mainland China's economy grow in the 1980s and beyond? What are the principal obstacles to economic growth and the prospects of overcoming these difficulties? These are the main issues many scholars address in their overall assessment of the PRC's economic future. Let me turn first to the question of future growth.

Table 13.1 summarizes four projections of annual rates of gross national product (GNP) growth in the 1980s by Dwight Perkins (1981, 1982), Nai-Ruenn Chen (1978), Robert Dernberger (1978), and Chu-yuan Cheng (1982). There are, of course, other major contributions in this area: Ishikawa (1984), Prybyla (1980), Lardy (1978), the World Bank (1981), and Barnett (1981). Interesting as these studies are, they are not reviewed here mainly because their focus is on the period prior to the economic adjustment and reform or when such reforms were still at the initial stage, or because they make no quantitative projections.

To provide a basis for comparison, selected estimates by the PRC's State Statistical Bureau (SSB) and economists on the mainland are also presented. Thus far, the only official projections published are the planned growth rate of 4 percent per annum for net material product (NMP) in the Sixth Five-Year Plan period, 1981-1985, and the quadrupling of the gross value of industrial and agricultural output (GVIAO) in 1980 by the year 2000.[1] Apparently, economists on the mainland have universally accepted the target of quadrupling GVIAO as feasible, but there is no consensus as to whether NMP can grow at the same pace as GVIAO. Some, like Ma Hung (1982, p. 226), believe that it can and project a growth rate of 7.2 percent for the period 1980-2000. Others like Chang Shu-kuang (1983, p. 31), are more cautious and foresee a slightly lower NMP growth rate of 6.5 percent over

Table 13.1. Projected GNP Growth Rates, 1975-2000

	Past Performance	Projected Growth Rates (% per year)			
		1975-85	1985-2000	1980-85	1985-90	1980-2000

	Past Performance	1975-85	1985-2000	1980-85	1985-90	1980-2000
PRC estimates*						
SS3 (comparable prices)	6.0 (1952-1982)			4.0		
Chang (comparable prices)	6.1 (1952-1982)					6.5
Wang (comparable prices)	5.9 (1952-1981)		7.0		6.3	
Ma (U.S. $)	–					7.2
Other estimates						
Perkins (1978 prices)	4.8 (1952-1979)					7.0
(1952 prices)	6.0 (1952-1979)					
Chen (1976 U.S. $)	6.0 (1952-1976)	6.5-8.5	6-7.8			
Dernberger (1976 U.S. $)	–	6.5				
Cheng (1979 U.S. $)	5.9 (1952-1979)	5.0	4.5			
	5.7 (1960-1976)					

Sources: People's Daily, December 13, 1982, p. 1; Chang 1983, p. 31; Wang 1983; Ma 1983; Perkins 1981, 1982; Chen 1978; Dernberger 1978; Cheng 1981.

*NMP instead of GNP

the same period. Still others argue that the NMP growth rate will be somewhat below that of GIVAO.[2]

Historical data show that the GVIAO growth rate always exceeds the NMP growth rate by 1 percentage point or more.[3] For the future, the feasibility of matching the two growth rates depends on the relative growth rates of agricultural production and industrial production, changes in the input-output relationships in these two sectors, and the growth rates of net output in other material sectors. It appears likely that industry will grow faster than the other sectors, including agriculture, and that the trends toward more modern inputs in agriculture and possibly also in industry will continue. If so, NMP will grow less rapidly than GVIAO, i.e., less than 7.2 percent. Hence, for the present purpose, the median estimate of 6.5 percent by Chang, though less authoritative than Ma's, will be used as the baseline estimate.

A comparison of the four estimates by economists outside the mainland suggests two interesting contrasts. First, although these estimates are sometimes not strictly comparable because they are not based on the same price weights and refer to different time periods, it is clear that the assessments of future growth differ. Perkins's estimate of the future GNP growth rate, 7 percent per year for 1980-2000, is the highest, those of Chen and Dernberger are slightly lower, and that of Cheng is lower still. Second, virtually all of the estimates of past performance are the same--around 6 percent (Perkins's estimate in 1978 prices being an exception)--but all except Cheng expect that the future growth rate will exceed that of the past.

What is significant, perhaps, is not so much the difference between the levels of these forecasts but the different rationales behind them. Let me review briefly the analyses underlying the high and low estimates by Perkins and Cheng.

According to Perkins, GNP growth depends on how successfully the PRC leadership can overcome the following major potential bottlenecks: political upheavals, economic constraints (slow agricultural growth, energy shortage, and limited foreign exchange), and rigidity of Chinese bureaucratic management and planning. Regarding political upheavals, Perkins believes that "perhaps periodic upheavals are inherent in governing a country of such great size in accordance with China's authoritarian traditions," that "it is not at all difficult to envision a turn away from some of the efforts that have characterized the late 1970s and early 1980s," and that "political in-fighting severe enough to disrupt the economy could still occur."[4] Despite such uncertainties, Perkins believes that any such upheavals would be less serious than those of the past, so that one can reasonably expect GNP growth to be higher than in the past.

As for economic constraints, Perkins projects a 3 percent growth of agriculture in the future. There will be problems in energy supply, expansion of manufacture exports, and bureaucratic rigidity for some time to come, but Perkins is confident that these bottlenecks can be and will be overcome: "A 7 percent GNP growth rate is not a pipe dream: it is a reasonable forecast." In his judgment, the negative effects of the drags on economic growth will be more than offset by the effects of several positive factors: greater use of foreign technology, a relatively high rate of capital formation, and the tens of thousands of skilled workers, foremen, and engineers.[5]

The problem with Perkins's argument is that these positive factors are not independent of the constraints and might well be weakened or undermined by the bottlenecks. For example, Perkins believes that the PRC can achieve an annual increase in exports and imports of 10 percent in real terms. By 1990, total trade would be about U.S. $80 billion and exports, over U.S. $35 billion.[6] If this projection turns out to be correct, the PRC will face a trade deficit of U.S. $10 billion in 1990, and given such a large trade deficit, one wonders if the PRC would be willing to import foreign technology on a scale large enough to generate the positive effects that Perkins expects or capable of doing so.

The second positive factor, an investment rate as high as 30 percent, is indeed important, but its impact is by no means certain. Historically, in fourteen of the twenty-three years after 1952, the investment rate exceeded 30 percent, and yet the GNP growth rate, according to Perkins's estimate, was only 4.8 percent, markedly lower than the 7 percent projected for the future. The main problem lies in the inefficiency of management, which, in my opinion, has been underestimated.

Compared to Perkins's, Cheng's projections of GNP growth are markedly different in several ways. Not only is his projected growth rate considerably lower than Perkins's, he expects the future growth rate to fall below the level in the past, whereas Perkins expects an acceleration. More interestingly, Cheng estimates that the GNP growth in the two periods 1976-1985 and 1985-2000 will decline, in sharp contrast to the PRC leadership's expectations.[7]

Cheng's projection is based on a regression of the GNP growth rate on the growth rates of agriculture and industry, using Central Intelligence Agency data for 1949-1979.[8] Assuming the latter to be 4 and 7 percent, respectively, in the 1976-1985 period, Cheng derives a GNP growth rate of 5 percent for this period. For 1986-2000, the growth rates for agriculture and industry are expected to decline to 2.5-3 percent and 5-6 percent, respectively, resulting in a GNP growth rate of 4-4.5 percent.

The regression approach would have been more interesting if the estimates of GNP on the one hand and agricultural and industrial production indexes on the other had been derived independently of each other. Unfortunately, this is not the case. The GNP series used is that developed by Ashbrook, which is actually a weighted average of the agricultural and the industrial production indexes, the weights being two and one, respectively.[9]

What is interesting, however, is the assessment of the growth rates for agricultural and industrial production in the future. After a careful analysis of the factors affecting agricultural growth, Cheng concludes that a high rate of investment in agriculture and a thorough reform of the management and incentive systems are required to accelerate agricultural growth, and since these requirements are not likely to be met, agricultural growth will probably average about 4 percent in the period 1977-1985 and continue at a lower pace of 2 and 3 percent thereafter. In the case of industry, the significant growth in the past was attributable to a high rate of investment in physical capital, but now, the leadership faces difficulty in maintaining a high rate of industrial investment. Consequently, the industrial growth rate is not likely to exceed 7 percent during the period 1978-1985 and probably will decline to 5-6 percent thereafter.[10]

Unlike Perkins, Cheng emphasizes more the importance of investment, incentives, and management efficiency. Other factors such as major ideological modifications, institutional reforms, large-scale foreign aid, and technological breakthroughs have been considered but assigned a relatively minor role. Partly to allow for some positive effects of the current adjustment and reform program, and partly because of greater difficulties in maintaining a high growth rate as the economic base becomes larger, Cheng predicts higher growth rates for agriculture and industry in the pre-1985 than in the post-1985 period.

The incisive analyses of both Perkins and Cheng are primarily based on their assessments of constraints that are significant during the current period of adjustment and reform. Understandably, many problems that emerge as a result of these reforms have not yet been fully taken into account, yet these problems may yet become serious constraints in the not too distant future. To illustrate, one distinctive feature of the new development strategy is the shift from regional and local self-sufficiency to greater degrees of specialization and interdependency, and an important corollary is the open-door policy that greatly expands the PRC's involvement in international trade. Consequently, the policy shift places an enormous burden on a transportation system that was designed for a much smaller volume of commodity flow. The bottleneck will intensify the demand for investment in a sector that is characterized by relatively long construction periods and high capital output ratios.

Another example is the rise in consumption

both in absolute terms and in relation to national income.[11] The upward trend may well continue as the urban population continues to increase faster than the total population, the demand for consumer durables continues to expand, and the large amount of government subsidies to consumers remains at a high level.[12] If, indeed, the share of consumption continues to rise, investment will be affected.[13] In addition, the share of investment in residential housing also has been increasing, further reducing the amount of resources available for renovating or expanding productive capacity.

MEASUREMENT OF ECONOMIC GROWTH

Economists projecting the PRC's GNP or GVIAO growth often base their projections on past records. In so doing, they all follow a basic rule of the game: A consistent series is used to calculate the growth rate for both the past and the future. The only major exception is the SSB. In calculating the rate of growth of GVIAO in 1952-1982, 8.1 percent, the SSB used an index based on <u>comparable prices</u>. This growth rate is compared with that for 1980-2000, 7.2 percent, which is based on an index in <u>1980</u> prices, and the conclusion is then drawn that the latter is attainable because a higher growth rate has been achieved in the past under much more difficult conditions.[14]

The index based on comparable prices is actually a linked index. For example, the index for 1957-1970 is calculated in constant 1957 prices and that for 1970-1980 in constant 1970 prices. An index for 1957-1980 in comparable prices is simply a linked index of the two series, the link being the ratio of GVIAO in 1970 weighted by 1957 prices to that weighted by 1957 prices. The linked index is not the same as that in constant 1957 prices or that in constant 1970 prices.

The question of comparability is important because the calculation of aggregate growth rates is rather sensitive to the weights used. In the present case, the linked index of GVIAO, i.e., the index in so-called comparable prices, rises faster than the index based on 1980 prices. This fact can be demonstrated as follows. First, because industrial prices relative to agricultural prices were higher in 1957 than in 1970 and in 1970 than in 1980 and industrial output grew much faster than agricultural output over the entire period 1957-1980, the growth rate for GVIAO in constant 1957 prices will be higher than that in constant 1970 or 1980 prices.[15] Let P_0, P_1, and P_2 represent prices in 1957, 1970, and 1980, and Q_0, Q_1, and Q_2, quantities in 1957, 1970, and 1980, respectively. The SSB index of GVIAO in comparable prices in 1980, with 1957 as the base, is

$$(\Sigma P_1Q_2 \cdot \Sigma P_0Q_1 / \Sigma P_1Q_1) / \Sigma P_0Q_0$$

$$= \frac{\Sigma P_0Q_1}{\Sigma P_0Q_0} \cdot \frac{\Sigma P_1Q_2}{\Sigma P_1Q_1}$$

Now, for the reasons noted,

$$\frac{\Sigma P_0Q_1}{\Sigma P_0Q_0} > \frac{\Sigma P_1Q_1}{\Sigma P_1Q_0}$$

This can be rewritten

$$\frac{\Sigma P_0Q_1}{\Sigma P_1Q_1} > \frac{\Sigma P_0Q_0}{\Sigma P_1Q_0}$$

Multiplying both sides by the positive ratio $\Sigma P_1Q_2 / \Sigma P_0Q_0$, the inequality becomes

$$\frac{\Sigma P_0Q_1}{\Sigma P_1Q_1} \cdot \frac{\Sigma P_1Q_2}{\Sigma P_0Q_0} > \frac{\Sigma P_0Q_0}{\Sigma P_1Q_0} \cdot \frac{\Sigma P_1Q_2}{\Sigma P_0Q_0}$$

or

$$\frac{\Sigma P_0Q_1}{\Sigma P_0Q_0} \cdot \frac{\Sigma P_1Q_2}{\Sigma P_1Q_1} > \frac{\Sigma P_1Q_2}{\Sigma P_1Q_0}$$

Because of the difference in relative weights noted earlier, the index of GVIAO weighted by 1970 prices will be higher than that weighted by 1980 prices, i.e.,

$$\frac{\Sigma P_1 Q_2}{\Sigma P_1 Q_0} > \frac{\Sigma P_2 Q_2}{\Sigma P_2 Q_0}$$

Hence,

$$\frac{\Sigma P_0 Q_1}{\Sigma P_0 Q_0} \cdot \frac{\Sigma P_1 Q_2}{\Sigma P_1 Q_1} > \frac{\Sigma P_2 Q_2}{\Sigma P_2 Q_0}$$

The term on the left-hand side is the SSB's index of GVIAO in comparable prices for 1980 with 1957 as base. The one on the right-hand side is the index in constant 1980 prices. The former is greater than the latter.

The implication of this exercise is that if the SSB calculates the growth rate for 1953-1981 in constant 1980 prices, as it should, the result would surely be lower than the one in comparable prices. Whether or not it will be higher than the projected growth rate of 7.2 percent for 1980-2000 is not known. In any event, the comparison of the two indexes based on different price weights is totally misleading.

The proper way to measure growth is to use a consistent set of prices weights, preferably prices of a more recent year. However, this is not feasible at present because of a lack of data. To approximate a series in 1980 prices, several attempts have been made to deflate the component series separately. The following estimates of NMP growth rates based on totals in 1980 prices for 1957-1981 by Perkins, Wharton Econometric Forecasting Associates, and Yeh are compared with those by SSB:[16]

	NMP Growth Rate (% per year)
SSB (1957-1981)	5.3
Wharton (1957-1981)	5.5
Perkins (1952-1979)	4.8
Yeh (1957-1981)	4.6

The Wharton estimate, based on 1980 prices, is very close to the SSB figure based on comparable prices. It is hard to judge whether this

similarity is coincidental, since the derivation
of deflators has not been explained in the Wharton
publication. Both the estimates by Perkins and
Yeh are lower than the SSB figure. Apart from
the difference in price weights, another reason
for the disparity is that the SSB uses a single
deflator for both gross and net value of output,
whereas different deflators for outputs and inputs
are used in Yeh.[17] Crude as these approximations
may be, they are sufficient to show that in
measuring economic growth, methodological refinements of the SSB estimates are necessary.

STUDIES OF CRITICAL SECTORS

Energy

In addition to studies of the mainland
economy in the aggregate, there are important
contributions to the study of some critical
sectors such as agriculture, energy, foreign trade,
technology, and population. Because of space
limitations, I shall review only those relating
to two sectors: energy and science and technology.[18]
Among the recent studies of the PRC's energy
problems, the following five are the more important ones: Kim Woodward (1980, 1982), Chu-yuan
Cheng (1983), Vaclav Smil (1981), the World Bank
(1981), and Robert M. Field and Judith A. Flynn
(1982). For convenience of exposition, let me
outline the key issues and explain how the various
studies deal with these issues.

At this stage, the PRC leadership is facing
a serious energy shortage. An estimated 20 percent of industrial capacity remains idle because
of inadequate power supply,[19] and about 45 percent
of the farm households do not have enough fuel
for their daily use.[20] The energy shortage not
only affects industrial production, it also
restricts growth of energy exports, which in
recent years contributed over 20 percent of total
export earnings. The current energy gap notwithstanding, a relatively high GNP growth rate
of 7.2 percent of energy production is planned
for the Sixth Five-Year Plan period and
1980-2000.[21]

	Planned Growth Rate (%)	
	1980-1985	1980-2000
GNP	4.0	7.2
Energy output	1.4	4.1
Coal	2.5	3.4
Oil	-1.1	4.1
Natural gas	-6.9	4.0
Hydroelectric power	3.8	

    The energy crunch was the combined result of declining growth of energy production since the late 1970s, the rapid increase of domestic consumption and exports, and enormous wastes in energy use. The leadership's policy is to rely on energy conservation and expanding oil production in the 1980s. Thereafter, oil exploration, hydroelectric power development, and nuclear power plants currently under construction and planning are expected to increase the energy supply. Will this program bring about an energy supply that will adequately meet future needs?

    All of the studies under review foresee a sizable gap in the future energy production-consumption balance. The consensus is that the projected GNP growth rate will generate such a large demand for energy that, in all likelihood, increases in domestic energy production and energy conservation will not be sufficient. Cheng concludes that a sizable energy gap will emerge after 1985 and will reach unmanageable proportions by 2000 unless the growth of industrial and agricultural output slows to about 5.2.[22] The World Bank also expects that the slow-growing energy supply will severely constrain economic growth in the 1980s and that by 1990, the PRC will probably be a net importer of oil.[23] Field and Flynn believe that energy constraints alone will slow the industrial growth rate to -3.5 percent through 1985 but that in the 1990s, the situation could improve with the introduction of coal conservation technologies and the development of hydroelectric and nuclear power.

    The interesting issue, again, is the rationale underlying these projections. On this point, Cheng's analysis is perhaps representative. He attributes the causes of the current shortage to errors in the PRC's energy development strategy,

the overemphasis on exploitation to the neglect
of oil exploration, the problem of transportation
caused by the predominance of coal in the output
mix, the backward technology, and the inefficient
bureaucratic system. Turning to the future,
Cheng succinctly analyzes such problems as the lack
of a national long-term development program, a
shortage of development funds, and the pressing
problem of insufficient energy supply in the
rural areas.

One reason why these studies come to
similar conclusions is that they are based on
essentially the same methodology. Consequently,
they also share the same methodological limitations. In the first place, the projection model
is too aggregative, thus completely suppressing
the effect of structural changes. For example,
Cheng relates energy consumption to growth of
GVIAO, and Woodward uses a linear regression of
energy consumption on GNP. Over such a long
period as two decades, the compositions of GVIAO
and GNP are bound to change significantly, and
these changes will have profound effects on the
aggregate elasticity measure.[24]

Second, projections of energy production and
consumption are made independently.[25] GVIAO or
GNP growth determines future needs, and resource
availability and past trends provide the basis
for output projections. The difference between
energy output and consumption represents the
export potential if the residual is positive and
an energy gap if it is negative. The problem
with this approach is that production and consumption may not be independent in a dynamic
context. Not only does GNP growth increase
energy consumption, it could also increase energy
production in a subsequent period if the leadership should decide to invest the current increase
in GNP in the energy sector. On the other hand,
if an increase in energy production is used to
increase energy exports, the foreign exchange
earnings could be used to finance technology
imports, which in turn could increase GNP after
a time lag. Because of the interdependence
between future needs and production, it seems unrealistic to ignore the possible effects of resource allocation among alternative uses over the

two decades.

R&D and Technological Change

One important determinant of economic growth is science and technology. Clearly the goal of a fourfold increase in GNP in the next two decades is unattainable without rapid technological advance.[26] This raises a crucial issue: Will the PRC's research and development (R&D) base be able to develop the technological capability to generate and sustain a high rate of economic growth? Up until now, the contribution of R&D to economic growth has been quite limited. According to one estimate, less than 10 percent of economic growth can be attributed to technical change, compared to 40-60 percent in the developed countries.[27] The issue thus resolves into one of barriers to innovation, policies to remove these barriers, and the prospects of their success. Several recent studies by Simon, Fischer, Conroy, Suttmeier, and others address various aspects of these problems incisively.[28]

The barriers to innovation identified by these studies can be conveniently grouped into two categories: constraints within the research unit,[29] and problems arising from the inefficiency of the R&D system as a whole. Within the research organization, three major problems have impeded R&D development. The first is the lack of a driving force for innovation on the part of both the management of the research unit and the management of the production enterprise. Until recently, managers of a research unit had little incentive to innovate because there was no patent system to protect the interests of the innovator. Nor are they under pressure to innovate because the amount of funds allocated to a unit is totally unrelated to the research performance of that unit. On the other hand, the production managers are primarily concerned with fulfilling their production quota and are loath to risk reaching this objective with new products or new processes. Second, the researchers are not motivated because the award system is not working well owing to the widespread practice of sharing the award among most, if not all, of the workers. A third impediment is the inadequate resources, including equipment, information, and qualified personnel.

At the macrolevel, the following problems have been noted. First, the R&D system is so compartmentalized that technical specialization has been sacrificed and a unit's concern with its self-interests has led to information blockades and a duplication of effort. Second, not only are the research personnel inadequate in relation to the country's needs, they are mostly middle-aged and their technical training falls behind the advanced levels in other countries. Furthermore, the distribution of these personnel among research units is very uneven so that their talents have not been fully utilized, and restrictions on their mobility among units perpetuate this situation. Finally, in the area of technology transfer, the leadership has failed to grasp the importance of a substantial indigenous R&D program.

To cope with these problems, a series of reforms have been instituted. There has been a reorientation of priorities toward research projects that are directly relevant to the development of new products or processes. A contracting system has been introduced to permit the research institutes to work directly for the users. The leadership also established a national science fund to encourage individual effort in research. To fully utilize the science and technology resources, the State Council promulgated regulations to encourage four transfers of technical personnel: from the cities to rural areas, from large to small cities, from developed to remote areas, and from research institutes with a surplus of trained workers to those critically short of such personnel. How effective these measures are remains to be seen.

In any event, it is worth noting that the major barriers to innovation have their roots in the defective R&D system. In this connection, two aspects of the problem have been somewhat neglected in studies on the topic. The first relates to bottlenecks in the transformation of R&D results into actual production. All too often, the R&D process is considered to be completed after the new product or process has been successfully evaluated. Consequently, only 10-30 percent of the R&D results have been utilized.[30] The reasons for this relatively low utilization include the lack of user participation in the R&D process (except, perhaps, in the military sector); a shortage of funds to support such necessary steps as pilot-plant design and construction, testing, and tooling; and the fact that the research unit frequently chooses projects that are unrelated to production problems. Whatever the bottleneck may be, the contribution of R&D to economic growth will remain limited unless and until a close link between the R&D unit and the production enterprise has been established.

Another aspect of the R&D problem that needs to be explored further is the workings of the R&D system rather than the system itself, and and implementation of the S&T policy rather than the statement of that policy. For example, given the acute shortage of technical workers, perhaps the scarcest resource in the PRC today, the need for a policy of greater mobility of such workers is clear. However, when one considers the problem of housing for the relocated researcher, the possibility of separation from his or her family, the uncertainty of good working relationships in a new environment, and the reluctance of the management of the existing unit to let a capable worker go, the difficulties of implementing such a policy are understandable. For these reasons, the effectiveness of the R&D system cannot be properly evaluated unless we understand better how the system actually works.

MODELING THE MAINLAND ECONOMY

Although some scholars focus on specific sectors, others attempt to bring together the different sectors in input-output models and econometric models. Studies of input-output relations in the mainland economy are by no means new. Niwa (1970) and Liu and Yeh (1971) have compiled input-output tables for 1956 and 1957. More recently, Wiens (1979) reconstructed Niwa's table for 1956, and Taylor (1983) used his work to compile a table for 1980.

Wiens's 28-sector table is based on the crucial assumption that the structure of inter-industry of the 1956 mainland economy was similar to that of Japan's in 1952. Wiens converted a 166-sector Japanese input-output matrix for 1952 from the Japanese yen to 1952 yuan and consolidated it into 28 sectors. In so doing, he faced three formidable problems. First, are the physical input-output coefficients reflecting the technologies of the two economies in two different time periods similar enough to justify direct borrowing? Second, the Japanese transaction table was in yen, which raises the question, What are the appropriate exchange rates at which the transactions in 1952 yen can be realistically converted into 1956 yuan? Third, quite independent of the conversion problem, the relative prices of outputs and inputs for each sector in the two economies might well differ. Hence, even if the technical input-output coefficients are the same, the coefficients in value terms may be different because of different relative prices. Is it realistic, for example, to assume that the relationship of the price of cotton cloth on the mainland (which was rationed) to the price of domestically produced cotton in 1956 would be the same as that in Japan in 1952 (where cotton was mainly imported)? Not surprisingly, the matrix in Wiens's study turned out to be unbalanced as the total value added derived from the production sectors fell short of the total final demand. But even if all these statistical problems are satisfactorily solved, at best, such a table can tell us only what the pattern of production would be like, given the gross output of each of the 28 sectors in 1956, if the mainland economy in 1956 had an industrial structure similar to that of Japan in 1952. It is the uncertainty about the similarity that leaves open the question of how useful such a table is.

Taylor began with Wiens's table, adjusted its classification to include twenty sectors, converted the 1956 table to 1980 prices, and updated the 1956 table to 1980. Hence, in addition to all the difficulties in Wiens's table, Taylor faced another formidable problem in updating

the coefficients over the rather long period of
twenty-four years. The crucial assumption is that
the technology in 1980 was similar enough to the
1956 technology that a simple updating of a 1956
table will produce a matrix that roughly depicts
1980 interindustry demands. The difficulties of
projecting input-output coefficients are well
known,[31] and the task is even more complex when,
over a period of twenty-four years, technology
in some industries has changed markedly (e.g.,
the introduction of oil-fired thermal power
plants), new industries have emerged (e.g., petrochemicals), and structural changes have occurred
(e.g., small industries). If it is hazardous to
assume a cross-country similarity in industrial
structure, it may even be more so when one
projects the industrial structure over two decades
or more.

The contribution of Wiens's and Taylor's
tables is that some approximation, however rough,
is better than none, provided that the users of
these tables are well aware of their limitations.
In any event, the heroic effort of these two men
must be recognized. Theirs is scholarly, pioneering work, and as such, their tables will be useful
as stepping-stones for further exploration when
more information becomes available. In particular,
it will be interesting to compare Taylor's results
with the SSB's own twenty-one sector table for
1980, which reportedly is being drawn up.

Turning now to the macroeconomic models of
the mainland economy, one finds quite a number of
recent contributions since Ishikawa presented his
projection model in 1965. They include Lau (1978,
1981); Niwa and Ichimura (1981); Chow (1981,
forthcoming); Kwack, Fromm, and Tu (1980); and
Data Resources (1980). The purposes of these
models vary. Lau and Niwa and Ichimura have
given us basically simulation models. Chow's
model is intended to provide a theoretical framework to deal with allocative problems, and the
models drawn up by Kwack, Fromm, and Tu and Data
Resources are designed for forecasting purposes.
The size of these models also differs, ranging
from Lau's 24-equation model to Kwack, Fromm,
and Tu's 86-equation model.

It is not feasible to attempt even a tabular

survey of the characteristics of these models, let alone an evaluation of them.[32] However, some general comments in light of recent developments may be useful. First, the SSB has released data that are sometimes different from those published before and from those used in these models. Population, industrial production, and trade figures are examples. These models are somewhat dated since they are tied to the unrevised data. Second, and perhaps more significant, major structural and institutional changes have taken place so that the specification of some of the equations in these models needs be modified. For example, with all the changes in both the output and input structure in the agricultural sector since the 1950s, the equation for value added as an almost constant ratio of gross value of agricultural output based on the sample period 1952-1957 in Lau's model is not likely to fit the data for the 1980s. Another example is the effect of decentralization of decision-making power on some of the assumptions. The relatively large proportion of fixed investment outside the state investment plan in the 1980s raises the question, How realistic is the assumption in Lau's model that asymptotically gross fixed investment in industry will be a constant proportion of gross fixed investment? In the early 1980s at least, investment in industry increased much more rapidly than investment in other sectors because of the uncontrolled expansion of industrial investment outside the state plan. The recent emphasis on residential housing construction is another element that further undermines the assumption. Again, these issues merely point to possible refinements of these models and should not detract from their contributions to our understanding of the mainland economy.

CONCLUSION

This chapter has reviewed only a small subset of a large body of literature on the mainland economy. Many studies have not been discussed here, and in particular, I have left out the important issue of economic reform.[33] Nonetheless, this brief review is sufficient to show that we are now entering a new stage in the study of the mainland economy. Not only have the recent publications multiplied in quantity, the quality of these studies has greatly improved. Not only are old problems being reexamined in light of new data, new ones are being explored. Not only are traditional methodologies being employed, new ones such as quantitative research are being used and further refined. To be sure, there are many weak spots in these studies, and many issues have yet to be researched. Like the mainland economy itself, these studies are in a state of flux, but unlike the mainland economy, such studies will almost certainly move ahead rapidly both in quantity and in quality in the years to come.

NOTES

1. For projected growth of NMP in 1981-1985, see People's Daily, December 13, 1982, p. 1. The target of quadrupling GVIAO was formally stated in the report on government work by Chao Tzu-yang (1981), p. 8. Earlier, Teng Hsiao-ping had reportedly set the target of per capita GNP at U.S. $1,000 for the year 2000, quadrupling the level in 1980 (see Teng 1980, p. 19). This target implies an annual growth of GNP higher than 7.2 percent, because the population growth rate, however small, will probably be positive. Note, however, that Ma Hung interpreted Teng's statement to mean a target of per capita GVIAO (instead of GNP) of U.S. $800-$1,000 by the year 2000 (see Ma 1982, p. 218).
2. See, for example, Chi Yan-chung 1984, p. 3; Cheng Chia-heng et al. 1984, pp. 32-36; and Shu Ta-chih 1984, pp. 15, 37-39.
3. State Statistical Bureau 1983, pp. 19, 23.
4. Perkins 1982, pp. 4-6.
5. Perkins 1981, p. 119, and Perkins 1982, pp. 10-11. It is interesting to note that Perkins has diametrically opposite views on the role of skilled workers in his two chapters. In his earlier chapter, the limited number of skilled workers is considered a major constraint to economic growth. Later, he lists the "tens of thousands of skilled workers" as an underlying

strength of the economy.
  6. Perkins 1981, p. 126.
  7. A statement by Sun Shan-ching is indicative of the official view: "Industrial and agricultural output growth will be 4-5 percent at the end of the Sixth Five Year Plan, and 5-6 percent at the end of the Seventh Five Year Plan at most. In the 1990s and thereafter, however, it will develop by leaps and bounds" (<u>Nihon keizai shimbun</u> [Tokyo], October 15, 1982, p. 6; see also <u>People's Daily</u>, November 19, 1982, p. 5).
  8. Cheng 1982, pp. 327-329.
  9. See Arthur G. Ashbrook, "China: Shift of Economic Gears in Mid-1970s," in JEC 1978, p. 231.
  10. Cheng 1982, pp. 329, 335-377. See also Chu-yuan Cheng, "The Modernization of Chinese Industry," in Baum 1980, pp. 21-48.
  11. State Statistical Bureau 1983, p. 25.
  12. Ibid., p. 103; <u>Ching-chi jih-pao</u>, December 13, 1983; <u>Nihon keizai shimbun</u> (Tokyo), April 24, 1984, p. 10; and Lardy 1983.
  13. Unless, of course, there is a large inflow of foreign capital or a drastic cut in government consumption.
  14. See, for example, JMJP, November 19, 1982, p. 5.
  15. For an algebraic proof, see Yeh forthcoming. The argument is essentially the same as that for the Gerschenkron effect (see Gerschenkron 1951).
  16. <u>Statistical Yearbook 1981</u>, p. 20; Wharton Econometric Forecasting Associates 1984; Perkins 1981, p. 119; and Yeh forthcoming. Perkins's estimates are in 1978 prices.
  17. The first studies using the double-deflation method are the World Bank 1982 and Field 1982.
  18. For those interested in the other three sectors, see Barnett 1982, Khan and Lee 1983, Lardy 1984, Surls and Tuan 1982; Davie and Carver 1982, Gullo 1982, Monk and Rich 1982; Emerson 1982, Orleans 1982, and Tuan 1982.
  19. Wang Qingui and Gu Jian 1983, p. 15.
  20. <u>Ching-chi jih-pao</u>, December 3, 1983.
  21. See Table 13.1; Ma Hung and Sun Shan-ching 1981, pp. 274-284; <u>China in Focus</u> 1983,

p. 20; and Sixth Five-Year Plan, pp. 18, 55-61. The planned GNP growth rate in 1980-1985 refers to that of NMP.

22. Cheng 1983, pp. 107-111.
23. World Bank 1981, Annex E, p. 14.
24. Woodard believes that his approach "avoids the difficulties of growth rate elasticities" (Woodard 1980, p. 582), but this is an illusion. The linear equation he uses implicitly assumes a changing elasticity of energy consumption with respect to GNP. For example, his equation for median growth has a negative constant and a coefficient of 1.15 (Woodard 1980, p. 581), which implies an elasticity greater than 1 and declining as GNP increases. His baseline equation has a positive constant and thus will always have an elasticity that is less than 1.
25. The study by Field and Flynn (1982) is an exception. Their model is of the iterative type, linking supply and demand.
26. The PRC leadership apparently is fully aware of this fact. See, for example, the JMJP editorial of December 7, 1983.
27. Lu Yeh-chai 1982.
28. Simon 1982, 1982a, 1983b; Fischer 1982, 1983; Conroy 1982, 1984; Suttmeier 1982; Orleans 1982; Baum 1980; and Sigurdson 1980.
29. The R&D system is composed of five major components: the Chinese Academy of Sciences, institutes under the Ministry of Education; institutes under other ministries; institutes under local governments; and institutes in the defense sector. By a research unit, I refer to an institute in any of the four civilian components. Little is known about the military R&D sector so no generalization is possible.
30. Lu Yeh-chai 1982, p. 3.
31. See, for example, the discussion in Lecomber 1975.
32. Mainly because documentation of the procedures and data employed in some of the models are unavailable.
33. Despite the fact that the reforms are still in progress, a number of interesting articles have been written on the subject. See, for example, Ishikawa, 1982; Lee 1983; Lardy 1983; Naughton 1983; Wiens 1983; Reynolds 1983; and

Byrd 1983.

REFERENCES

Barnett, A. Doak. *China's Economy in Global Perspective*. Washington, D.C.: Brookings Institution, 1981.
———. "China's Food Prospects and Import Needs." In Harrison Brown, ed., *China Among the Nations of the Pacific*, pp. 59-67. Boulder, Colo.: Westview Press, 1982.
Baum, Richard. *China's Four Modernizations: The New Technological Revolution*. Boulder, Colo.: Westview Press, 1980.
Byrd, William. "Enterprise-Level Reforms in Chinese State-Owned Industry." *American Economic Review* (May 1983), pp. 329-332.
Chang Shu-kuang. "Growth of National Income, Social Product, and Gross Value of Industrial and Agricultural Output at the Same Pace." *Ching-chi yen-chiu* [Economic research], no. 10 (1983), pp. 26-31.
Chao Tzu-yang. "The Current Economic Condition and Guidelines for Future Economic Constructions." *Wen hui pao* (Hong Kong), December 18, 1981.
Cheng, Chu-yuan. *China's Economic Development*. Boulder, Colo.: Westview Press, 1982.
———. *The Demand and Supply of Primary Energy in Mainland China*. Taipei: Chung-Hua Institution for Economic Research, 1983.
Cheng Chia-heng, Tu Tieh-chang, and Li Tieh-chun. "It Is Difficult for Our Country to Achieve the Synchronous Increases of National Income and the Gross Value of Industrial and Agricultural Output from a Long Term Point of View." *Ching-chi yen-chi*, no. 1 (1984), pp. 32-36.
Chen Nai-Ruenn. "Economic Modernization in Post-Mao China: Policies, Problems, and Prospects." In JEC 1978, pp. 165-203.
China in Focus: China's Modernization Programmes. Beijing: Beijing Review, 1983.
Chi Yan-chung. "Preliminary Analysis of National Income, Gross Value of Industrial and Agricultural Output, and Social Product

Growing at the Same Pace." *Kuang-ming jih-pao*, February 12, 1984.

Chow, Gregory C. *Outline of an Econometric Model for Chinese Economic Planning.* Princeton: Princeton University, 1981.

―――. *The Chinese Economy: Analyses of Selected Problems.* Forthcoming.

Chung-hua jin-min Kung-ho--uo Kuo-min ching-chi ho she-hui ja-chan ti-liu-ke wu-nien chi-hua 1981-1985. Beijing: People's Press, 1983.

Conroy, Richard. "Supply of and Demand for Technological Innovations in China's Present Phase of Industrial Modernization." Paper presented at a conference on China in transition, Oxford, England, 1982.

―――. "Technological Innovation in China's Recent Industrialization." *China Quarterly*, no. 97 (March 1984), pp. 1-23.

Data Resources Incorporated. "DRI Economitric Model of the PRC." 1980. Mimeograph.

Davie, John L., and Dean W. Carver. "China's International Trade and Finance." In JEC 1982, pt. 2, pp. 19-47.

Dernberger, Robert F. "The Chinese Search for the Path of Self-sustained Growth in the 1980s: An Assessment." In JEC 1982, pp. 19-76.

Emerson, John Philip. "The Labor Force in China, 1957-80." In JEC 1982, pp. 224-267.

Field, Robert M. "China's Net Material Product: 1957-1980." 1982. Mimeograph.

Field, Robert Michael, and Judith A. Flynn. "China: An Energy-Constrained Model of Industrial Performance Through 1985." In JEC 1982, pp. 334-364.

Fischer, William A. "China's Scientific and Technological Policy: An Assessment." In *China's Scientific and Technological Modernization: Domestic and International Implications*, pp. 1-15. Washington, D.C.: Wilson Center, 1982.

―――. "The Chief Engineer." *China Business Review* 10:6 (November-December 1983), pp. 30-34.

Gerschenkron, A. *A Dollar Index of Soviet Machinery Output, 1927-28 to 1937.* Santa Monica, Calif.: Rand Corporation, 1951.

Gullo, Duncan T. "China's Hard Currency Export Potential and Import Capacity Through 1985." In JEC 1982, pt. 2, pp. 83-108.

Ishikawa, Shigera. "Long Term Projections of Mainland China's Economy: 1957-1082." Economic Bulletin for Asia and the Far East 16:2 (September 1965), pp. 10-56.

___. China's Economic System Reform: Underlying Factors and Prospects. 1982. Mimeograph.

___. "China's Economic Growth Since 1949--An Assessment." China Quarterly (January-March 1984).

Joint Economic Committee (JEC). Chinese Economy Post-Mao. Vol. 1, Policy and Performance. Washington, D.C.: Government Printing Office, 1978.

___. China Under the Four Modernizations. Parts 1 and 2. Washington, D.C.: Government Printing Office, 1982.

Khan, Azizur Rahman, and Eddy Lee. Agrarian Policies and Institutions in China After Mao. Bangkok: International Labor Organization, Asian Employment Programme, 1983.

Kwack, Sung, Gary Fromm, and Samson W. Tu. A Model of the People's Republic of China. SRI International and Wharton Econometric Forecasting Associates World Economic Program Discussion Papers no. 8. 1980.

Lardy, Nicholas R. "Recent Chinese Economic Performance and Prospects for the Ten Year Plan." In JEC 1978, pp. 48-62.

___. "Subsidies." China Business Review (November-December 1983), pp. 21-24.

___. Agriculture in China's Modern Economic Development. Cambridge: Cambridge University Press, 1984.

Lau, Lawrence J., W. F. William, Chao, Lin Wuu-Long, and Shea Jia-Dong. An Econometric Model of China. 1978. Mimeograph.

___. Near-Term Outlook for the Chinese Economy. 1981. Mimeograph.

Lecombe, J.R.C. "A Critique of Methods of Adjusting, Updating, and Projecting Matrices." In R.I.G. Allen and W. F. Gossling, eds., Estimating and Projecting Input-Output Coefficients, pp. 1-25. London: Input-Output Publishing Company, 1975.

Lee, Edmund. "Economic Reform in Post-Mao China: An Insider's View." *Bulletin of Concerned Asian Scholars*, no. 5 (1983), pp. 16-25.

Liser, Florizella B. "China and the General Agreement on Tariffs and Trade (GATT)." In JEC 1982, pt. 2, pp. 137-149.

Liu Ta-chung and Yeh Kung-chia. "Input-Output Relationships and Economic Development of the Chinese Mainland, 1952-65." In *Collected Documents of the First Sino-American Conference on Mainland China*. Taipei: Institute of International Relations, 1971.

Lu Yeh-Chai. "Expedite the Transformation of Science and Technology into Productivity." *Kuang-ming jih pao*, November 12, 1982.

Ma Hung and Sun Shan-ching, eds. *Chung-kuo ching-chi chieh-kou wen-ti yen-chiu* [Studies in the problems of China's economic structure]. Beijing: People's Press, 1981.

———. *Chung-kuo ching-chi tiao-cheng kai-ke yu fa-chan* [Adjustment, reform, and development of the Chinese economy]. Taiyuan: Shansi People's Press, 1982.

———. *Prospects of China's Modernization: An Economic Perspective*. Hong Kong: Almanac of China's Economy, 1983.

Monk, Liliana B., and A. Jackson Rich. "Recent Developments in China's Trade Practices, 1978-81." In JEC 1982, pt. 2, pp. 210-234.

Naughton, Berry. "The Profit System." *China Business Review* (November-December 1983), pp. 14-18.

Niwa, Haruki. *A Summary of the Estimate of China's Input-Output Table in 1956*. Tokyo: Asian Economic Research Institute, 1970.

Niwa, Karuki, and Shinichi Ichimura. *An Econometric Model of the Chinese Economy*. 1981. Mimeograph.

Orleans, Lao A. "China's Urban Population: Concepts, Conglomerations, and Concerns." In JEC 1982, pp. 268-302.

———. "Science, Elitism, and Economic Adjustment." In JEC 1982, pp. 475-488.

Perkins, Dwight A. "The International Consequences of China's Economic Development." In Richard H. Solomon, *The China Factor*, pp. 114-136. Englewood Cliffs, N.J.: Prentice-Hall, 1981.

———. "The Chinese Economy in the 1980s." In Harrison Brown, ed., China Among the Nations of the Pacific, pp. 1-14. Boulder, Colo.: Westview Press, 1982.
People's Republic of China, State Statistical Bureau. See State Statistical Bureau.
Prybyla, Jan. "China in the 1980s." Challenge 23:2 (May-June 1980), pp. 4-20.
Reynolds, Bruce L. "Economic Reforms and External Balance in China, 1978-81." American Economic Review (May 1983), pp. 325-328.
Shirk, Susan L., and James B. Stepanek. "China's Five-Year Reform Program." China Business Review (November-December 1983), pp. 8-9.
Shu Ta-chih. "National Income and Gross Social Product Are Difficult to Increase Synchronously in the Near Future." Ching-chi yen-chiu, no. 1 (1984), pp. 15, 37-39.
Sigurdson, J. Technology and Science in the PRC. Oxford: Pergamon Press, 1980.
Simon, Denis F. "China's Capacity to Assimilate Foreign Technology: An Assessment." In JEC 1982, pp. 514-552.
———. Implementing the S&T Modernization Program: China's Experience After the Third Plenum. Boston: Sloan School of Management, Massachusetts Institute of Technology, 1983.
———. "Rethinking R&D," China Business Review (July-August, 1983), pp. 25-31.
Smil, Vaclav. "China's Energy Technology." In Richard Baum, ed., China's Four Modernizations, pp. 207-233. Boulder, Colo.: Westview Press, 1980.
State Statistical Bureau. Chung-Kuo t'ung-chi nien-chien 1983 [Statistical yearbook of China 1983]. Beijing: State Statistical Press, 1983.
Surls, Federic M., and Francis C. Tuan. "China's Agriculture in the Eighties." In JEC 1982, pp. 419-448.
Suttmeier, Richard P. "Research Innovation and the Chinese Political Economy." In JEC 1982, pp. 489-513.
Taylor, Jeffrey R. Methodology Used in Constructing an Input-Output Table for 1980 China. Washington, D.C.: Department of Commerce, 1983.

Teng Hsiao-ping. "Report on Current Situation and Tasks." *Cheng ming* (Hong Kong), no. 29 (1980), pp. 11-23.

Tuan, Chi-hsien. "China's Population in Perspective." In Harrison Brown, ed., *China Among the Nations of the Pacific*, pp. 69-83. Boulder, Colo.: Westview Press, 1982.

U.S. Congress, Joint Economic Committee. See Joint Economic Committee.

Walder, Andrew G. "Rice Bowl Reforms." *China Business Review* (November-December 1983), pp. 18-21.

Wang Qingui and Gu Jian. "How Will China Solve Energy Problem?" *Beijing Review*, no. 35 (August 29, 1983), pp. 13-18.

Wang Shaofei. "Strategic Objective of Public Finance." *Tsai-mou ching-chi* [Economics of trade and finance], no. 12 (1983), pp. 17-21.

Wang Tong-eng. *Economic Policies and Price Stability in China*. Berkeley: Institute of East Asian Studies, University of California, 1980.

Wharton Econometric Forecasting Associates. *Centrally Planned Economies Current Analysis* 4:4-5 (January 25, 1984).

Wiens, Thomas B. *Towards a Model of the Economy of the People's Republic of China: The 1956 Input-Output Table*. Bethesda, Md.: MATH TECH, 1979.

_____. "Price Adjustment, the Responsibility System, and Agricultural Productivity." *American Economic Review* (May 1983), pp. 319-324.

Woodard, Kim. *The International Energy Relations of China*. Stanford: Stanford University Press, 1980.

_____. "China's Role in the Energy Development of Asia and the Pacific: The Next Twenty Years." In Harrison Brown, ed., *China Among the Nations of the Pacific*, pp. 85-103. Boulder, Colo.: Westview Press, 1982.

World Bank. *China: Socialist Economic Development*. World Bank, 1981.

Yeh, K. C. *Gross Domestic Product of Mainland China, 1957-82*. Forthcoming.

14
How Well Did U.S. Economists Understand Communist China's Economy?

Ramon H. Myers

By the late fifties, U.S. economists were studying the Chinese economy; even after the Peking regime stopped publishing statistics in the early sixties, some still persevered in their research. How well did they do their job? If poorly, can similar mistakes be avoided in the future? In a recent assessment of economic studies of China, Dwight Perkins contended that most economists did a pretty good job of understanding Communist China's economic development.[1]

In 1980, however, Chinese Marxist economists were presenting a very different evolution of the Chinese economy than the one described by the economists Perkins praised. Those Marxist economists perceived China's economy as being in a state of crisis caused by the regime's policies of the past, and they argued that only major reforms could resolve that crisis. Paradoxically, a few U.S. economists also had argued that serious troubles had characterized the Chinese economy, but their findings had never influenced academic circles. Why was that the case?

THE ASSESSMENT BY DWIGHT PERKINS

Written at Harvard, Dwight Perkins's doctoral thesis examined how the Communist government had combined planning and the free market to obtain more grain while imposing collective controls upon rural society. He later supervised various Harvard doctoral candidates who contributed to Chinese economic studies, organized conferences on the Chinese economy, and served as a consultant to the prestigious Social Science Research Council, which heavily supports research on the Chinese economy. Because Perkins greatly influenced the research agenda in the field and participated in the important debates, his assessment of the state of Chinese economic studies should be taken seriously.

Perkins analyzed over 100 works written by experts studying the Chinese economy. Rather than evaluating them according to any criteria, he merely focused on issues such as the quantitative indicators of economic growth, macromodels, economic difficulties related to planning and management, sectoral developments and debates, and the economic heritage the new regime had inherited from the past. After comparing the findings of many economists, especially U.S. economists, he offered this general conclusion:

> The record of most specialists on the Chinese economy in describing what happened over the past two decades on the world has been quite good. Those who suggested that China had effectively implemented across-the-board revolutionary changes that could serve as an ideal for others to strive toward were wrong, but they were a tiny majority of the field. Those who argued that little had changed and that China's economy was only marginally above pre-revolutionary levels by the 1970s were also wrong. The latter position still enjoys some vogue in the 1980s, but it too will die as the implications of decade after decade of substantial per capita GNP growth make themselves felt.[2]

On the basis of quantitative estimates by U.S. economists of economic growth and sectoral development, Perkins argued that they had produced estimates that were very similar to the official Communist figures.[3] The major finding he drew attention to is that the economy grew at a compound growth rate of 5 percent a year between

1958 and 1980 and the per capita income, at 3 percent. U.S. economists also had agreed that the "growth in industry has been rapid and has accounted for most of the increase in GDP, while the pace of development in agriculture has lagged badly."[4]

Perkins did not fail to mention that some scholars had compared China's economic system to that of the Soviet Union and noted that China had accumulated excessive inventories, so that "in both countries the emphasis on production targets leads to a neglect of quality."[5] But he never related these inefficiencies to China's growth performance, nor did he cite with approval scholars who had discussed that relationship and its implications for China's development.

Perkins did note these general findings. Income distribution had become more equal in the early 1950s, but later it probably became more unequal, especially among regions. Agricultural development had barely kept pace with population growth, but many people disagreed whether the main source of agricultural growth derived from more inputs being used or from some combination of new technology with those inputs. Because the regime had released few statistics about industrial growth and employment, economists had neglected those topics, but foreign trade had been accurately tracked. Finally, some economists had correctly identified certain historical antecedents that had made possible the rapid, post-1949 industrial spurt. As for future economic research, Perkins urged economists to "describe what is happening in China with as much objectivity and accuracy as possible," analyze "the important macro and micro relations," and integrate as much of their findings into the work produced by the economic profession.

To sum up, Perkins concluded that most U.S. economists studying Communist China had done a good job, particularly in constructing reliable quantitative indicators. Those who had praised Maoist policies and their results were in error, and the handful of economists who persistently described the PRC's performance as very poor were wrong.

CHINESE MARXIST ECONOMIC RESEARCH IN 1979-1980

The analytical and empirical studies by Chinese Marxist economists that were produced shortly after Mao's death give a very different overview of mainland China's economic development. One study, in particular, examined all aspects of economic development between 1949 and 1978.[6]

We are told, for example, that China's first three decades of socialist economic management and growth resembled the Soviet economic development experience of the thirties. When Stalin came to power, he "over-emphasized the development of heavy industry by adopting the strategy of developing heavy industry first, thus making that sector dominate the economic structure."[7] This strategy demanded a tremendous mobilization of resources from agriculture, which naturally had to pay the price. Because farmers were unwilling to supply the raw materials needed by industry, the state created new organizations and initiated policies to squeeze an agricultural surplus from the farmers. This strategy meant "eliminating the free market and collectivizing the organizations required to mobilize labor, materials and financial resources" and then integrating them under centralized, collective control.[8] "The development of [the Chinese] national economy was exactly like the process of development in the Soviet Union."[9]

Chinese Marxist economists rarely have admitted that their economy shared the same characteristics as the Soviet Union's during its most inhumane phase of rapid industrialization. But even more interesting in these essays was the interpretation that a distorted economic structure in China had evolved as the rate of economic growth declined and low living standards persisted over the period. What developments produced those trends?

First, these economists point out there had been a systematic and continuous misallocation of scarce resources. By devoting so many resources to building industries that produced only machines and materials or intermediate products, the economy never produced enough consumer goods to raise the living standards of the people but only overproduced intermediate products that never were used. Meanwhile, consumer goods had been in short supply, and personal disposable income barely rose over the period. Between 1952 and 1978, the average percentage of household expenditures for food and drink only declined from 56 to 51 percent, which meant that the living standards were extremely low.[10] Just as in the case of food and drink, which absorbed one-half of household spending, the quality and quantity of housing also declined over the same period.[11]

Meanwhile, as this planned economy created more industrial plant and capacity than it could effectively use, the new capital produced was also inefficiently utilized. Stockpiles of industrial products rusted away, factories operated far below their capacity,[12] and railroad lines and manufacturing plants were built in the wrong areas. As industry steadily became inefficient and unproductive, the productivity of the capital stock also declined during much of the period. For example, the annual income generated by each annual increment of capital declined during the Second, Third and Fourth Five-Year Plans.[13] Productivity in the energy producing sector showed an overall decline as well as huge fluctuations.[14]

The following description of the energy sector gives an idea of how these economists viewed their national economic development:

> In 1970 the total output of coal came to 350 million tons, 18 million tons of steel, and 87,000 automobiles. The petroleum industry was just beginning to grow, so that our industrial foundations were still comparatively weak. Under these conditions the rapid development of that industry made it impossible to free enough resources for other activities, and that industry soon could not sustain its rapid growth. Moreover, because of the backwardness of transport and the chemical processing industries, we could not efficiently use the petroleum we produced in a rational manner.[15]

Finally, the economy had experienced output and income fluctuations of incredible magnitude in some years. These major economic dysfunctions characterized the structural evolution of this planned economy, whereby a high rate of capital accumulation occurred and a very high proportion of national income was devoted to capital accumulation. Associated with this economic structure was the absence of productivity in the economy.

By 1978, the Chinese economy had become a cancer-stricken patient in urgent need of therapy, but we certainly do not find this same view or assessment reported in the mainstream writings of U.S. economists. It is also paradoxical that the Marxist economists did not entirely blame Maoist policies for these dysfunctions and the distorted economic structure. They also criticized the economic policies that had created this unbalanced sectoral development and an excessively high rate of capital formation.

Most U.S. economists certainly were surprised by the economic reforms introduced in 1979 and 1982, and their research had never hinted that an economic crisis of such severity had occurred to necessitate that such reform policies might be forthcoming. Finally, they never argued that China's economic growth possessed the same features of early Soviet industrialization.

Of course, those Chinese Marxist economic studies might have exaggerated the long-term dysfunctions of Chinese economic development in order to justify the reforms they recommended, but I do not think that was the case. If anything, their writings probably downplayed the true economic conditions in the country as of the late seventies. Yet I think we can take these Marxist economists at their word. That being the case, why had so many U.S. economists described the Chinese economy in such favorable terms?

TRYING TO UNDERSTAND CHINESE
ECONOMIC DEVELOPMENT

The predicament that confronted the U.S. economists in the late fifties, and even today, was that Communist regimes like China have published very little statistical evidence about the country's economic activity. Therefore, an inordinate amount of work had to be done to search out evidence, judge its veracity, and fill gaps in order to construct the national income accounts and other quantitative indicators that describe economic development.

Most U.S. economists studying China's economy shared the general positivist philosophy of social scientists trained in the United States after World War II. Namely, they eschewed value judgments and tried to measure and explain behavior or performance. That meant constructing certain quantitative indicators to show what kind of development had taken place, because without any uniform, standard measurements, further analysis of the economic system could not follow. This research approach placed enormous importance upon measuring economic activity, but it also undervalued the measurement of the sources of economic growth, particularly productivity, economic waste, and inefficiency.

Most economists agree that countries can become wealthy only when their output of goods and services grows at a more rapid rate and their organizations of production and distribution become increasingly productive over time. In other words, organizations must use a new technology, produce more goods and services, and consume fewer resources.

Looked at in this way, we note the paradox of twentieth-century socialist regimes' expanding their output and services at higher growth rates but not becoming increasingly more productive. The Soviet Union is certainly a world superpower, yet much of its wealth is channeled into producing more military hardware and capital goods while economic organizations remain incredibly unproductive. Even though some firms use very advanced capital and technology, they are still very inefficient.

As little attention was given to productivity in Chinese economic studies, many economists instead examined those Maoist policies that were designed to make the distribution of income more equal. The issue of income inequality had become very important in the sixties and seventies, so that economists in general neglected analyzing how much more economic growth would have occurred had greater productivity originated in the economy.[16]

We now know that the Chinese people paid an enormous price for the growth that took place, and that countless scarce resources were wasted to create a small, modern industrial sector. Even though the Chinese have traditionally possessed unique organizational capabilities, the Communist regime never used those effectively, preferring instead to reorganize the economy drastically according to Communist principles.

Most U.S. economists also ignored or downplayed the many dysfunctions of the Chinese economy. While concentrating their research upon constructing measurements of output growth for the economy and its various sectors, they tended to ignore the high costs an economic system will experience when rapid policy changes are continuously introduced and property rights are radically restructured.

But some U.S. economists were also very correct in their interpretations of Chinese economic growth. I now turn to describe three groups of scholars who analyzed the Chinese economic development experience between 1949 and 1978 but interpreted that historical period very differently. I refer to these three groups as the apologists for Chinese socialism, the positivists, and the critics of China's socialism.

APOLOGISTS FOR CHINESE SOCIALISM

There were a small number of U.S. scholars of a certain political persuasion who shared similar views about China's economy and the policies that were needed to modernize that economy and improve the people's welfare. First, they generally agreed that the system of resource ownership in pre-1949 China and the very unequal distribution of income it had produced had been largely responsible for the country's long-term poverty and backwardness. Second, they believed that the Communist Party's redistributive policies of the early 1950s had liberated new productive forces and at the same time had improved the living standards of the people. Finally, they applauded the Maoist policies and organizations by arguing that these had positively influenced economic development because they encouraged a greater equality of income distribution, placed wealth under collective-state ownership, and brought workers and farmers into organizational decision making.

For example, Carl Riskin and Victor Lippit have argued that the pre-1949 rural property system produced a large surplus and that the rural and urban elite never invested enough of that surplus in productive activities to increase GNP.[17] Therefore, when the Communist Party initiated land reform, the new government allegedly siphoned off much of that surplus, which the traditional property owners had supposedly used for their own consumption. Lippit concluded a study of the Communist land reform by saying, "the change in property relations wrought by the land reform in the agricultural sector of the economy and by increasing socialization in the industrial sector redirected income flows which had sustained luxury consumption in the financing of both higher levels of investment and higher consumption for those most in need."[18]

According to Lippit, by 1952-1953, new capital stock had been created and consumption per capita had increased without any painful costs for society. Lippit also did not believe that restoring peace and order and expanding employment after a decade of war might have greatly contributed to the growth of output and consumption. Further, he ignored the enormous trade-off costs the economy might have suffered when the Communist Party rapidly socialized the country and greatly reduced private trade and the activities of service enterprises.

Even though many scholars condemned the Great Leap policies of the Communist regime as being disastrous, economists like Riskin pointed to some of the benefits that flowed from those policies, particularly for the urban areas. He argued that "suffice it to say for the present that there is no evidence that workers were not motivated to upgrade skills during the Great Leap."[19] Although this might have been the case for some workers, the fact that 20 million to 30 million people, both rural and urban, died unnecessarily strongly suggests that most workers and farmers were far more concerned with conserving their energy and finding enough food to eat. Other scholars like Stephen Andors also pointed to alleged positive developments during the Great Leap period, as did Phyllis Andors who contended that those policies changed the working roles of women and improved their status.[20]

Some of these same scholars also praised the Cultural Revolution and the new policies the Maoist faction tried to impose upon the country. Stephen Andors was very impressed by the way the authorities tried to eliminate piece wages and bonuses and develop a different web of work rules in factories.[21] Benedict Stavis argued that the regime also had supposedly developed areas of high, stable food yields, an achievement made possible only by the new collective farming system, which was based upon more egalitarian principles of income reward and distribution.[22] All of these socialist policies were glowingly praised by one economist in these terms:

> China has shown, especially during the 1960s, *how* to industrialize without generating social problems that threaten to blow a society sky-high. China has involved increasing numbers of people, especially in the rural areas, in industrial activities in order to break down the potentially antagonistic relations between city and country, between workers and peasants; to spread knowledge of industrial processes as widely as possible so as to promote talent, ingenuity, confidence, and the scientific attitude among masses of workers and peasants; and to transform rural areas into self-reliant agrarian-industrial-cultural local economies which are attractive places to live in, and can become at least partly independent of high political units, including the state.[23]

Since 1978, however, the admissions made by Peking's leaders and the revelations published by U.S. journalists have seriously undermined much of the validity of those research findings that were advanced by the apologists of Chinese socialism.[24]

THE POSITIVISTS

Although the apologists for Chinese socialism had completely misunderstood how badly the system had worked, how well have the interpretations of the mainstream U.S. economic researchers held up? Some of their research did describe economic dysfunctions. Moreover, they made a powerful case that unless reliable quantitative indicators of economic change were constructed and agreed upon, there was no way to analyze the performance and behavior of the economy. Aside from these considerations, however, what major assessments of the Chinese economy did many of their studies share?

First, most of these researchers agreed that the new regime in 1949 had inherited conditions of unfavorable economic factor endowment along with great poverty and low per capita income. Second, they agreed that the leadership possessed a remarkable capability of mobilizing resources, particularly labor, and producing a rapid growth rate of output, which no developing economy with an equivalent low per capita income has been able to do. Finally, they emphasized that the regime had fed and supported a huge population without the usual pathologies of unemployment and low nourishment levels that had afflicted so many developing countries. These shared perceptions of the regime's capabilities and performance, therefore, distinctly conveyed the impression that China's economic development performance had been rather successful even though the regime still struggled with severe difficulties.

Alexander Eckstein and Dwight Perkins strongly emphasized that China's historical heritage and factor endowment exercised a strong influence upon the leadership's policies and the kinds of organizations that had been created. Eckstein claimed the new leaders had "inherited an economy which by practically all available measures was near the bottom of the world development scale."[25] In 1949, China's economy was characterized by low labor productivity, a small modern industrial sector, a population of around half a billion people, and a limited amount of good farmland. Even the Soviet Union had inherited a much more advanced economy with a favorable resource endowment to launch its industrialization drive.[26] Eckstein also argued that this factor endowment tended to be related to commodity scarcities and shifts in leadership ideology, so that the interaction of all three factors greatly shaped the pattern of economic development in China in a very distinctive way.

> All these features, combined with China's approaches to agricultural development, rural industrialization, methods of industrial planning, and economic administration do add up to a distinctive development model. Basically this model reflects an interplay between scarcity, ideology and organization. The harsh realities of poverty and of scarce land, capital, and highly skilled manpower are imposed by China's factor endowments. The objectives of development, stressing a strong, powerful, self-reliant, egalitarian state and society, grow out of China's modern history and contemporary ideology. The systematic massing of labor and its substitution for land and capital is a manifestation of the scarcity of these resources. The methods of mobilizing and motivating labor and all of the human factors in the system is a function of ideology and organization.[27]

For Perkins, however, limited land proved to be one of the most critical obstacles for the economy to overcome, for the regime had failed to achieve a rapid rate of agricultural output even after it had devoted more resources to that sector in the late sixties and seventies. Writing in 1975, he argued that "the main reason why agriculture has not been faster appears to be simply that China is attempting to achieve large farm output increases under basically unfavorable conditions."[28] Perkins did not believe that the cumulative dysfunctions generated by the collective farming organizations and bad economic policies might have accounted for why total factor productivity failed to rise in agriculture when more modern inputs were being introduced.

The mainstream economists generally accepted the official statistics and only adjusted them slightly to construct their economic indicators. Not surprisingly, their results showed high rates of GNP, industrial output growth, and capital stock growth that compared favorably with the official statistical claims.[29] Therefore, China's economy appeared to perform well because of these unusually high, sustained economic growth rates.

Writing in the 1972 Joint Economic Committee report of Congress on economic conditions in China, Philip W. Vetterling and James J. Wagy stated that in the previous twenty years, there had been "no indications of general shortages of locomotives or freight cars on the Chinese rail system" and the country had made "great progress toward its goal of developing an efficient transportation system capable of supporting a modern industrialized economy."[30] In the same report, Arthur G. Ashbrook, claimed that the policies after the Great Leap had been timely and effective and that the Great Proletarian Cultural Revolution had "proved to have no palpable effect on agriculture and only short-lived effects on industry."[31] According to Ashbrook, GNP had expanded at slightly over 4 percent yearly between 1952 and 1971. Robert Michael Field also reported an impressive growth of industry,[32] but Alexander Eckstein argued that for the 1970s, the growth rate would be lower than the 6 percent annual growth rate estimated for the years 1952-1974.[33] Even though this prediction might be interpreted as a declining rate of economic growth, Eckstein never gave any explanation for this slowdown in economic growth.

In spite of economic setbacks in the late fifties and the uncertain direction of the economy during the Cultural Revolution, favorable reviews of the Chinese economy filtered out of the 1975 and 1978 Joint Economic Committee reports to

Congress. Then in 1980, another conference volume based upon papers presented several years earlier confidently asserted that "nothing released in the Chinese press to this date reduces the validity of the evaluations in this volume of the economic model in the quarter-century after 1949."[34]

According to that economic model, China had achieved an average rate of GNP growth of around 5 percent per year and an industrial output growth ranging between 8 and 9 percent per year. By mobilizing great quantities of labor, allocating a large scale of the resources to the producer sector, and minimizing dependency on trade and foreign assistance, the regime had developed a small but resilient modern industrial sector while still managing to feed the growing population.[35] More important, this performance apparently had been achieved without any serious costs to society or severe dysfunctions afflicting the economy. Thomas Rawski had concluded that modern industrial growth centers like Shanghai tried to maximize rapid output growth at the expense of costs, product quality, and consumer welfare but that those costs did not really matter in the long run because a large producer goods sector had been created along with some impressive industrial innovations.[36]

The studies just cited greatly shaped interpretations about China's economy both within and outside academic circles. They gave the impression that official statistics were reliable and could be used to measure and evaluate Chinese economic development. They pointed to China's impressive growth rates, which seemingly had been achieved without any real cost to the people and without any major difficulties developing in the economic system. In none of these studies do we find any hint that the economy would be overtaken by crisis in 1978, forcing the Communist leadership to adopt new, unprecedented policy measures to resolve it.

CRITICS OF CHINA'S ECONOMIC SYSTEM

The final group of scholars failed to

influence public and scholarly opinion, but in retrospect, their interpretations appear to have been on the mark and correct. What common views did they share? First, some believed that economic growth in the first fifteen years of development had been much slower than official claims and that much of the growth had derived from policies to increase investment in capital accumulation at the cost of greatly restricting consumption and living standards. T. C. Liu and K. C. Yeh, for example, repeatedly made this claim, and while some of their time series were used by mainstream economists, the lower estimates for economic welfare were readjusted upward by those same economists so that their results invariably matched the official claims.

Even so, writing in 1968, Liu and Yeh pointed out that the 1952 level of GNP certainly was slightly higher than in 1933 but per capita consumption was lower. They agreed the regime had made higher investment expenditures in 1952 than in 1933, but it had done so only at the expense of "a smaller proportion of consumption expenditures in total domestic expenditures."[37] By 1957, they continued, there indeed had been a substantial shift in the economic structure because of the growth of industry and the widening gap between the relative products per worker in agriculture and industry. But because there had not been any major shift of labor from agriculture to industry and because GNP in the early thirties was higher than the benchmark used by officials estimating China's GNP growth, GNP increased by only 6 percent in those years rather than the near 9 percent claimed by the regime and later endorsed by many mainstream economists.

Liu and Yeh described the period 1958 to 1965 as one of "further industrialization without growth," a fitting assessment for the years until 1978.[38] They expressed skepticism of whether sustained growth was likely in the future because of low productivity in agriculture. They also pointed out that the population was relentlessly increasing and that economic growth for the rest of the decade and the next was not likely to be orderly and rapid. As we now know, their analyses and predictions have been borne out by Chinese

Marxist economists, who stressed in 1979-1980 that the distorted economic structure reflected a poor productivity performance and a misallocation of scarce resources.

A second view that was shared by many of these scholars was that the economic system had become riddled with serious dysfunctions.[39] That is to say, economic organizations had progressively become more inefficient and wasteful after 1949 because (1) the people were not provided with economic incentives to work, save, and innovate as in the past; (2) the market system of planned economy no longer sent correct market signals to organizations to allow them to efficiently minimize costs and maximize output; and (3) the state bureaucracy, the planned economy, and Communist Party policies were producing conflicting developments that merely wasted scarce resources. As a result of these three factors, factories continued to produce goods that failed to find buyers, communes inefficiently used fertile land to plant grain, and the modern industries producing machine tools, iron, and steel operated very inefficiently. Also, the service sector greatly contracted, and exchange and specialization were discouraged.

The final view held by these scholars was that the economy had generated very little, if any, real productivity. Certainly, the most vigorous advocate of this assessment was Anthony Tang, who devoted a great deal of research to showing that total factor productivity had actually declined over the period and as early as 1952-1953.[40] In an essay rarely referred to and of considerable importance for his later research, Tang also argued that the agricultural sector had probably not really regained its prewar level until around 1955 and that most of the output growth until then had been due to putting idle land and labor back to work.[41]

CONCLUSION

It is ironic that just when the new revelations by Peking's leaders, Chinese Marxist economists, and Western journalists have forced many people to reinterpret previous political and social developments, the interpretation advanced by the mainstream U.S. economists that China has experienced impressive economic growth is still endorsed as being correct. Why is that the case?

To answer this question we have to understand how social sciences are organized in U.S. universities, how research is funded, and how research findings are published. I think there is something called the politics of social science research funding and publication, but I must quickly state that that is only part of the problem. In other words, I would certainly argue that the mainstream economists who I have labeled the positivists have enormously influenced the agenda of research in Chinese Communist economic studies, and therefore their stamp of interpretation is quite heavy on the field. But I still believe their monopoly-hold could have been broken and their influence challenged more effectively by the critics of Chinese socialism. But that never happened. Why? That group remained small, fragmented, and without any leadership to challenge the mainstream, positivist group.

But there is a more important reason for the failure of those critics to be considered more seriously than they were. The reason is that somehow, they too had failed, and their failure to mount a significant methodological challenge to the flawed, narrow approach of the positivists is still evident even today. In other words, they failed to advance a theory to relate productivity, costs, and the growth of output of goods and services and to conceptualize how different systems of pricing, property rights, and economic organization relate to the state and its institutions.

Until those new theoretical advances are made, the many scholars who are critical of the operation and performance of socialist economic systems will neither persuade other scholars nor influence public opinion and policy. Therefore, there is an urgent need to develop an interdisciplinary methodology that can compare, analyze, and interpret economic development in various societies that are governed by different political systems, by different market economies and systems of property ownership, and by very different ideologies.

NOTES

1. Dwight H. Perkins, "Research on the Economy of the People's Republic of China: A Survey of the Field," *Journal of Asian Studies* 62:2 (February 1983), pp. 345-372.
2. Ibid., p. 361.
3. Four out of the six economic estimates of GNP Perkins cites were by Americans, eight out of ten estimates of gross industrial output were by Americans, and four out of five estimates for gross agricultural output were by Americans (see ibid., pp. 349-351).
4. Ibid., p. 351.
5. Ibid., p. 354.
6. Ma Hung and Sun Shang-ch'ing, eds., *Chung-kuo ching-chi chieh-kuo wen-t'i yen-chiu* [Studies of the problems concerning China's economic structure], 2 vols. (Beijing: Jen-min ta-ch'ang-she ch'u-pan, 1981). Other conference volumes dealing with prices, etc., could also be referred to, but this work is without doubt the best all-around study of Chinese economic development between 1949 and 1978 by Chinese Marxist economists.
7. Ibid., 2:796.
8. Ibid., 2:797.
9. Ibid.
10. Ibid., 2:545.
11. Ibid., 2:579.
12. Although neither volume gives much pertinent information for supporting these assertions that I make, Chapters 2 and 3 strongly indicate that these dysfunctions existed. Moreover, these economic phenomena certainly were widespread and reflected the poor use made of capital allocated to the producer goods industries. For a source that also confirms the idleness of workers in factories and low worker productivity, see Liang Heng and Judith Shapiro, *Son of the Revolution* (New York: Vintage, 1984), chap. 19.
13. Ma Hung and Sun Shang-ch'ing, *Chung-kuo*, 1:78.

14. Ibid., 1:267-268.
15. Ibid., 1:273. For evidence of little or no productivity growth in energy sector, see 1:280.
16. See the interesting argument by Amartya Sen in his essay "Economic Development: Objectives and Obstacles," in Robert F. Dernberger, ed., China's Development Experience in Comparative Perspective (Cambridge, Mass., and London: Harvard University Press, 1980), pp. 19-37, which reviews the literature discussing barriers to development but nowhere speaks to the issue of the importance of generating productivity in the early stages of economic development. Few studies in the theory of economic development relate employment, productivity, and income distribution in early economic growth.
17. Carl Riskin's essay can be found in Dwight H. Perkins, ed., China's Modern Economy in Historical Perspective (Stanford: Stanford University Press, 1975). For Victor Lippit's study, see his Land Reform and Economic Development in China (White Plains, N.Y.: International Arts and Sciences Press, 1974).
18. Victor Lippit, "Economic Development and Welfare in China," Bulletin of Concerned Asian Scholars 4:2 (Summer 1972), p. 84.
19. Carl Riskin, "Maoism and Motivation: Work Incentives in China," Bulletin of Concerned Asian Scholars 5:1 (July 1973), p. 11.
20. Phyllis Andors, "Social Revolution and Woman's Emancipation in China During the Great Leap Forward," Bulletin of Concerned Asian Scholars 7:1 (January-March 1975), pp. 33-42.
21. Stephen Andors, China's Industrial Revolution: Politics, Planning, and Management, 1949 to the Present (New York: Pantheon Books, 1977), p. 221.
22. Benedict Stavis, "How China Is Solving Its Food Problem," Bulletin of Concerned Asian Scholars 7:3 (July-September 1975), pp. 22-38.
23. John G. Gurley, China's Economy and the Maoist Strategy (New York and London: Monthly Review Press, 1976), p. 259.
24. See, in particular, works by Richard Bernstein, From the Center of the Earth (Boston

and Toronto: Little, Brown and Company, 1982); Fox Butterfield, China: Alive in the Bitter Sea (Toronto, New York, Sydney: Bantam Books, 1983); and Steven W. Mosher, Broken Earth: The Rural Chinese (New York: Free Press, 1983). For revelations from Peking, see Marshal Yeh Chien-ying's comment that "the Cultural Revolution forced the country to endure an entire decade of oppression, tyranny, and bloodshed" (Jen-min jih-pao [People's daily], October 1, 1979, p. 1) and Hu Yao-pang's remark to the Greek Communist editor Vasilidis Konstantinides in mid-December 1980 that "the decade between 1966 and 1976, or the period referred to as the Great Proletarian Cultural Revolution, were years of catastrophe. There was nothing correct nor positive about these ten years" (Jen-min jih-pao, December 15, 1980, p. 1).

25. Alexander Eckstein, "The Economic Heritage," in Alexander Eckstein, Walter Galenson, and Ta-chung Liu, eds., Economic Trends in Communist China (Chicago: Aldine Publishing Company, 1968), p. 79.

26. Alexander Eckstein, China's Economic Development (Ann Arbor: University of Michigan Press, 1976), p. 213.

27. Alexander Eckstein, China's Economic Revolution (Cambridge: Cambridge University Press, 1977), p. 314.

28. Dwight H. Perkins, "Constraints Influencing China's Agricultural Performance," in U.S. Congress, Joint Economic Committee, China: A Reassessment of the Economy (Washington, D.C.: Government Printing Office, 1975), p. 365.

29. For a good example of how these data from Communist China have been adjusted to compare comparably with the economic indicators published by Peking, see Alexander Eckstein, Quantitative Measures of China's Economic Output (Ann Arbor: University of Michigan Press, 1980).

30. See Philip W. Vetterling and James J. Wagy, "China: The Transportation Sector, 1950-71," in U.S. Congress, Joint Economic Committee, People's Republic of China: An Economic Assessment (Washington, D.C.: Government Printing Office, 1972), p. 174.

31. A. G. Ashbrook, "China: Economic Policy

and Economic Results, 1949-71," in ibid., pp. 3-58.

32. Robert Michael Field, "Chinese Industrial Development, 1949-70," in Eckstein, *Quantitative Measures*, pp. 61-85.

33. U.S. Congress, Joint Economic Committee, *Chinese Economy Post-Mao* (Washington, D.C.: Government Printing Office, 1978), p. 97.

34. Dernberger, *China's Development Experience*, p. vi.

35. This model is spelled out by Dwight Perkins's chapter, "The Central Features of China's Economic Development," in Dernberger, *China's Development Experience*, pp. 120-150. Perkins' penchant for the importance of growth rates is reflected in the following statement he made in that chapter: "There is value in knowing that a nation's GNP grew at an average rate of 5 percent a year while that of another was rising at 3 percent. If the differences are due to real factors and not distorted price structure, it follows that the 5 percent country is leaving the ranks of the poor faster than the 3 percent country" (p. 120). This is clearly not the case if the 3 percent expanding GNP country develops rising factor productivity and the 5 percent expanding GNP country does not.

36. See Thomas Rawski, "Choice of Technology and Technological Innovation in China's Economic Development," in Dernberger, *China's Development Experience*, pp. 191-229.

37. Ta-chung Liu, "Quantitative Trends in the Economy," in Eckstein, Galenson, and Liu, *Economic Trends*, p. 143. I have added K. C. Yeh's name to Liu's because both cooperated to produce these estimates, although the specific reference in this chapter comes from the work by Liu.

38. Ibid., p. 168.

39. Although many sources could be cited here, I mention only Kang Chao, *Agricultural Production in Communist China, 1949-1965* (Madison: University of Wisconsin Press, 1970); Yuan-li Wu, *The Steel Industry in Communist China* (New York, Washington, London: Frederick A. Praeger, Publishers, 1965); Ramon H. Myers, "Wheat in China--Past, Present, and Future," *China Quarterly*, no. 74 (June 1978), pp. 297-333; and Jan S.

Prybyla, <u>The Political Economy of Communist China</u> (Scranton, Pa.: International Textbook Company, 1970).

40. Anthony M. Tang and Bruce Stone, <u>Food Production in the People's Republic of China</u> (Washington, D.C.: International Food Policy Research Institute, 1980).

41. Anthony M. Tang, "Policy and Performance in Agriculture," in Eckstein, Galenson, and Liu, <u>Economic Trends</u>, pp. 459-508.

15
Agricultural Reform in Mainland China: Problems and Prospects

Feng-hwa Mah

> *We fear no flood and fear no drought,*
> *All that we fear is*
> *frequent policy turnabout.*
>
> *Mainland Chinese peasant proverb,*
> *early 1980s*[1]

INTRODUCTION

Agricultural policy in mainland China since 1949 has followed a zigzag path of changes. All of the policy changes can be considered as tactical in nature, designed to achieve the basically unchanged goals of raising agricultural production without substantially increasing state investment in the rural sector and increasing government acquisition of farm output within the framework of continued Communist control of the agricultural sector. Dwight H. Perkins has characterized mainland China's agricultural policies up to the 1960s as alternatively centralization and decentralization.[2] Although centralization would certainly include the control of the free market for farm products, decentralization would not necessarily be accompanied by an expansion of the function of the market. Decentralization may even result in the concentration of the controlling power in the hands of lower-level Party cadres, as happened during the Great Leap Forward in 1958. Therefore, the centralization-decentralization interpretation may not adequately describe the post-Mao rural reforms. More recently, Nicholas R. Lardy suggested that agricultural policies in mainland China since 1949 have shifted between price and quantity controls (or price planning and quantity planning),[3] yet the reality has never been neat and clear-cut. For example, it was during Lardy's price planning period of 1949-1957 that the "three-fix" grain quota policy of quantity control was implemented, and throughout his quantity planning period of 1966-1977, price controls continued to be in force. Recent agricultural reforms may not easily fit into such a cyclical interpretation either.

In an attempt to portray and explain the frequent policy changes, the late Alexander Eckstein developed the concept of "policy cycle" in mainland China. The essence of Eckstein's policy cycle revolves around the "resource mobilization-production nexus" on the one hand and the "dichotomy between the model Communist Man and Economic Man" on the other. He argues that the kind of measures imposed to mobilize resources tend to (a) produce strong disincentive effects and (b) lead to losses in productive efficiency. Therefore, while the mobilization measures may produce "positive input expansion effects," the severe curtailment of consumption of such measures will give rise to the "negative incentive and efficiency effects" on the production process. Initially, the mobilization measures tend to lead to a high rate of growth until the negative effects begin to cancel out the positive effects. At that point, the rate of growth would slow down, and policy adjustments would follow, so as to reduce the mobilization pace and to restore the incentive effects. As policies allowing freer play of the incentive effects are pursued and the growth rate begins to rise again, a point may be reached beyond which another slowdown occurs because the savings rate may be reduced. Thus, the incentive gains are at least partially canceled out. This situation will lead to another input mobilization phase, so the cyclical pattern repeats itself.[4]

Such phenomena are of course not unnoticed in China. In the early 1960s, mainland Chinese economists used such expressions as "saddle-shaped development" or "wavelike movement" to describe cyclical fluctuations in the Chinese economy. In recent years, frequent policy shifts have been neatly summarized by mainland Chinese economists as "I-fang chiu-luan, i-luan chiu-shou; I-shou chiu-szu, i-szu tsai-fang" (relaxation of controls leads to dislocation, dislocation leads to the tightening of controls; tight controls result in stagnation, and stagnation results in another relaxation"). Therefore, while interpretations may be somewhat different, there seems to be a general recognition that fluctuations in agricultural policy have characterized the Communist system in the mainland of China from its inception. Such cyclical policy changes inevitably would generate uncertainties and risks in production and investment decision making on the part of the Chinese peasants, who are on the receiving end of these frequent and often unpredictable policy shifts.

I wish to submit that the post-Mao agricultural reforms should be observed within such a historical context, and it will be argued that it ought not to be assumed that the current reforms are a permanent change of the socialist agricultural system in mainland China. The next section will briefly review the situation of mainland Chinese agriculture on the eve of the post-Mao reforms. The third section summarizes concrete reform measures since 1977, and the fourth and fifth sections examine some of the problems and prospects of these reforms.

MAINLAND CHINESE AGRICULTURE ON THE EVE OF THE REFORMS

The agricultural sector contains about 80 percent of mainland China's nearly 1 billion population.[5] The entire sector has been collectivized since 1956, and all land is publicly owned. The Chinese peasants are organized into communes, production brigades, and production teams. In the mid-1970s, each commune consisted of approximately 3,000 farm households, and each team averaged about 30 farm families. Since 1962, with some exceptions during the Cultural Revolution period, production teams have been the basic units of agricultural operation and accounting. Private plots and rural free markets are periodically permitted or abolished at the discretion of the Party and state authorities.

As in other sectors of the economy, mainland

China's agricultural organizations are intertwined with political organizations. The economic activities of the communes and production teams are controlled and directed by Communist Party cadres who are not necessarily experienced managers or efficient farmers. Resources are allocated primarily through administrative channels, and prices of farm products are determined by the government rather than in the market. For example, food grains, edible vegetable oil, and its raw materials were placed under a scheme of "planned purchase and planned supply" in November 1953, with compulsory quotas for sale to the government at prices substantially below the free market prices. Tighter controls of food grains were instituted in 1955 by adopting the "three-fix" policy to set output quota, government purchase quota, and government supply quota before each planting season[6] and by instituting a nationwide food-rationing system in August of that year.[7] For these commodities, the free market mechanism has been essentially abolished. This was the system in operation in the mid- and late 1970s, and it is basically still in force today. Political indoctrination and various forms of coercion together mold the pattern of peasant behavior, which, supposedly, can be described as dedication and self-denial for the building of socialism in China and for a promised better future.

Distribution of collective income is carried out at the level of the production teams. First, there is the grain ration (k'ou-liang) distributed to each member. Then, after fulfilling the obligations of agricultural tax and compulsory sales quotas, and after deducting for production and management expenses, reserve funds, and welfare funds, the remaining part is distributed to the team members in proportion to their contribution to work (work points). Thus, the relationship between the quality and quantity of work and reward is less direct than under the private ownership of farmland. According to official statistics for the mid-1960s and early 1970s, the share of collective income distributed to the farmers was around 50 percent of the total income of the team.[8] In 1977, the average per capita total income for the rural population was 117 yuan per year (equivalent to US $73.13 at the then-official exchange rate of 1.6 yuan to US $1).[9] This amount included both the collective income and the income from private sideline production and production on the private plots. The private plots were limited to 5 percent of the cultivated land before the agricultural reform. In 1978, the average per capita total income for the rural population was reported to be 133.57 yuan (US $83.48), of which 66.28 percent came from the collectives.[10] It should be noted that in 1978, the officially defined "basic subsistence level" of income was set at 116 yuan per capita per year.[11] Thus, the average annual income per capita of the rural population in 1977 and 1978 was either barely at the subsistence level or not much above it.

Such a low level of rural income clearly reflects the low level of agricultural productivity, which, in turn, is the combined result of a very high ratio of labor to land, the lack of technological improvement, and the disincentive effect of collectivization and market controls. In 1977, cultivated land was about 0.1 hectare per capita.[12] Rural underemployment was a serious problem, as is evidenced by the large "surplus rural labor" suddenly revealed since the introduction of the household responsibility system in 1980. Yet because of the Communist Party's inability to provide nonagricultural employment opportunities in the cities, farmers are not allowed to leave their agricultural communes and teams.

Hu Ch'iao-mu, president of Peking's Academy of Social Sciences at the time, stated in a 1978 article that the per capita food grain production in 1977 was the same as the 1955 level, concluding that mainland China's grain production was increasing at about the same rate as the population.[13] However, Hu's statement obscured the fact that there were periods when food grain production lagged behind the increase of population. Thus, according to another Chinese source, the average per capita grain output decreased from 603 catties (301.5 kilograms) in 1957 to 598 catties (299 kilograms) in 1977. In 1978, it was 636 catties

(318 kilograms), only slightly higher than 1957 but not as high as the prewar level of 660 catties (330 kilograms) in 1936.[14]

Per capita grain consumption, however, is much smaller than per capita production. It is now known that in 1976, 1977, and 1978, the average per capita food grain ration for the rural population was even lower than that in 1956 and 1957.[15] It is reported that in 1978, a year of good harvest, over 20 percent of the counties (hsien) in North China had a per capita distribution of unpolished grain less than 300 catties (150 kilograms) a year. In South China, in over 20 percent of the counties, the per capita unpolished grain distributed was less than 450 catties (225 kilograms) a year. Because of such widespread food shortages in that year, large numbers of peasants fled from their communes to beg for food in other regions.[16] Teng Hsiao-p'ing admitted in a 1978 speech that "to feed several hundred million people, our food grain production has not really passed the turning point."[17] Li Hsien-nien, the then-vice-premier, also reported on the food deficiency in April 1979, saying that "China now has 10 percent of its population [about 100 million people] who do not have enough to eat."[18]

In fact, since 1961, mainland China has been importing 5-10 million tons of food grain a year depending on harvest conditions. Hsüeh Mu-ch'iao, Peking's leading government economist, has pointed out that in 1978, "at least one-fourth of the urban population's food rations [k'ao-liang] depended on imported grain."[19] This is likely to be an understatement. Other evidence indicates that in the late 1970s, imported food grain accounted for at least 30 percent of the total food grain consumption (including grain rations and above-ration consumption) of mainland China's urban population.[20] The imported food grain most likely had contributed to as much as 40 percent of the grain rations of the urban population in the late 1970s.[21]

The severe agricultural situation at that time obviously had convinced Peking's leaders that China's dependence on foreign food grain would continue for some time. Therefore, during his visit to Peking in November 1978, U.S.

Secretary of Agriculture Robert Bergland was told by Li Hsien-nien that for the near future, China would be importing "something over 10 million tons of foreign grain a year" and that "5 to 6 million tons would come from the United States."[22] Actually, agricultural sales since 1972 have dominated U.S. exports to the Chinese mainland. Early in 1981, it was officially reported that "as many as an estimated 12 million acres are now planted annually in the United States for the Chinese market."[23]

In early 1978, Hua Kuo-feng declared that because of the faults of the Gang of Four, the Chinese economy by 1976 had "almost reached the brink of collapse,"[24] but Hsüeh Mu-ch'iao was more forthright. In a 1981 report he wrote, "For over twenty years, the continuous 'leftist' mistakes made since 1958 . . . have dragged our economy to the brink of collapse." Hsüeh further made the point that "the Cultural Revolution [of 1966-1976] had already reduced people's support, and lowered the Party's prestige. If this is followed by a few more years of increasingly deteriorating living conditions, people's confidence [in the CCP] would be shaken even more, and it is highly possible that a politically unstable situation would occur."[25] I believe that in addition to the food shortage and the extremely low level of rural income, the realization of a possible situation of political instability must have also contributed to the decision in 1978 to introduce economic reforms in general and agricultural reforms in particular.

POST-MAO AGRICULTURAL REFORMS

After the death of Mao in 1976, the new leadership of the CCP faced an agricultural sector that clearly called for new approaches to save it from further deterioration and to improve production. The new policies adopted since 1978 can be divided into two distinctive phases. The first, from February 1978 to mid-1979, can be identified as the modernization policies. The second phase, starting from late 1979 and still in force, is what is generally referred to as the policies of agricultural reform.

A major part of the first-phase policies was agricultural modernization. On February 26, 1978, Hua Kuo-feng announced the Ten-Year Plan for the Development of the National Economy (1976-1985) at the First Session of the Fifth National People's Congress. In the agricultural aspect, the plan set out targets for the total value of farm output to increase 4-5 percent annually during 1978-1985. Grain output was planned to be 400 million tons in 1985, implying a rate of increase of 4 percent per year. Since grain output had been increasing at roughly the same rate as population growth, these targets were quite ambitious. To achieve such high goals, the new policy emphasized increased mechanization along with plans for farmland improvement. The plan called for the mechanization of at least 85 percent of the "major processes" of farm work by 1985, without defining the meaning of that phrase. As to land improvement, the plan specified that by 1985, farmland giving stable high yields would be one mu (one-fifteenth of a hectare) per person in the rural areas. With regard to the improvement of irrigation, it called for the harnessing of rivers on a large scale, including the diversion of water from the Yangtze to areas north of the Yellow River.[26]

Another major component of the first-phase policies was to stimulate agricultural production through a substantial increase in the state procurement prices.[27] A December 1978 directive of the Central Committee of the CCP ordered increases in the procurement price of quota grains by an average of 20 percent, the price of above-quota grain by 50 percent, and the procurement price for cotton by 30 percent. At the same time, the prices of food grains in the urban areas were kept stable in order to avoid significant inflationary wage increases. The December 1978 directive also specified the expansion of production and the lowering of the state sales prices of agricultural equipment, chemical fertilizer, and other modern inputs by 10-15 percent in 1979 and 1980.[28] It was assumed that the increased funds in the agricultural sector would be used to purchase farm machinery and other modern inputs for a rapid technological transformation of agriculture. The higher procurement prices of farm products, the lower state sales prices of agricultural inputs, and the more than a billion yuan subsidization of grain supplies in the cities all contributed to large deficits in the state budget in 1979 and 1980.

By mid-1979, the authorities in Peking realized that they had miscalculated in their mechanization efforts. Production of farm equipment could not be expanded rapidly, nor could the prices of the equipment be reduced significantly. It was expected that the prices of raw materials for the agricultural machinery industry (metals, fuel, etc.) would remain constant, but they went up. It was assumed that profit margins in farm machinery industries could be reduced, but the factory managers refused to do so because their performances were evaluated in part on the profit earned. Therefore, by the autumn of 1979, it was clear that the modernization policies were unrealistic and therefore simply not feasible. It was time for another policy shift.

For the leadership in Peking,[29] 1979 was a year of general rethinking and drastic readjustment of mainland China's development strategy, not just a search for a new agricultural policy. The "eight-character" policy adopted in that year was readjusting (t'iao-cheng), restructuring (kai-ke), consolidating (cheng-tun), and improving (t'i-kao). That is, readjusting the imbalance of the economy by shifting high priority from heavy industry to agriculture and light industry; restructuring the management system to give production units greater degree of freedom over their finances; consolidating the industries by closing down money-losing, low-productivity factories; and finally, the improvement of management and technology in production.[30]

In actually carrying out the new policies, the emphasis seemed to be on readjustment and restructuring, or reform (kai-ke). Although there were indications of high-level debates on the priority of readjustment versus reform,[31] it became increasingly clear that agricultural reform had quickly become the center of attention of the new program. This was the second phase of the post-Mao agricultural policy, which began in late 1979.

This is not the place for a lengthy treatment of the historical development of agricultural reforms in China, but it needs to be pointed out that the post-Mao rural reform actually is the reincarnation of the agricultural reform of the early 1960s, which became a victim of the Cultural Revolution. Both the pre-Cultural Revolution and the post-Mao agricultural reform programs are the grand designs of Teng Hsiao-p'ing, who in the early 1960s, was a close associate of the then-state chairman, Liu Shao-ch'i, and is now the powerful leader of Peking's new economic programs. The similarities of the two agricultural reform programs are evident.[32] The 1960s agricultural reform was adopted to revive agricultural production after the disruption and economic crisis brought about by the Great Leap Forward of 1958-1959. The post-Mao agricultural reform was introduced to revitalize the agricultural sector after the disruption and agricultural stagnation caused by the Cultural Revolution and to overcome the impasse created by Hua Kuo-feng's ambitious modernization program. One can also point out that the pre-Cultural Revolution reform took place within the context of widespread economic reforms in East European countries and the Soviet Union in the early and mid-1960s[33] and that Peking showed considerable interest in the "Yugoslavian-Romanian experiences" (Nan-lo ching-yen) in the late 1970s.[34] An international comparison may be useful, but it is beyond the scope and space of this chapter.

The post-Mao agricultural reform policies focus on the decentralization of management and diversification of farm production, with greater emphasis on material incentives and a greater use of the price mechanism to determine cropping patterns, instead of the use of production quotas.[35] The new policies also include the expansion of the rural free market (late 1980) and the increase in the size of private plots from 5 percent to 15 percent of cultivated land. But the whole program is crystallized in the "agricultural production responsibility system" (nung-yeh sheng-ch'an tse-jen-chih), which is designed to solve the problem of management inefficiency in the production team. It encourages a variety of new forms of labor organization and method of remuneration by assigning the responsibility of production on designated plots of land (still collectively owned) to work groups, households, or individuals. A preliminary decision on this arrangement was made in late 1979 and formalized in late 1980.

In its initial, experimental stage, the agricultural responsibility system encompassed many different forms, which can be classified into two types: (1) remuneration according to the fulfillment of work quotas and (2) remuneration on the basis of farm output. Both were different from the previous method of payment according to work points. However, the first type of responsibility system, which links reward to work quotas, still had some "egalitarian" elements because the quality and intensity of work cannot be reflected in remuneration. The second type, which links farmers' income to their output, was much more favored. Therefore, the responsibility system linking remuneration to output (lien-ch'an tse-jen-chih) has been emphasized since 1980. By November 1983, over 90 percent of all the rural households were organized under the household responsibility system with remuneration linked to output.[36] This type of responsibility system includes the following two forms:[37]

   1. Pao-ch'an tao-hu, or contracting output quotas to individual households, with the production team conducting unified accounting. In this form, the production team contracts the collectively owned farmland to individual households for separate cultivation. The quota output is surrendered to the production team for unified distribution among team members. The above-quota output is either shared between the team and the contractor or goes entirely to the contractor as a bonus.

   2. Pao-kan tao-hu (also called ta pao-kan), or contracting output quotas to individual households, without the production team's conducting unified accounting. This arrangement has a pronounced character of individual family operation. The production team divides the collectively owned

land and small farm tools among individual households. By contract, each household has to surrender to the team specified crops in specified amounts as payment of agricultural tax and as contributions to the team's public accumulation and welfare funds. Apart from this stipulation, the household may grow any crops and treat the above-quota output as its own possession. In effect, under this system, the relationship between the production team and the farm household is not too different from the landlord-tenant relationship in traditional China.

The pao-kan tao-hu system is quickly becoming the major form of organization of production and distribution in the countryside. In many regions, the farmers praise it as "the second land reform," referring to the brief period in the early 1950s when farmland was distributed to the farmers for private cultivation. During the last few years, the household responsibility system has resulted in increased yield, changes in cropping patterns, higher income for the peasants, and some complicated problems with important implications.

PROBLEMS

The agricultural reform since 1979 has been in existence for too short a period to allow one to draw firm conclusions about its success or failure or about its long-run influence on agricultural productivity. Some problems, however, are obvious, and each may have significant implications on the future of Chinese agriculture. In this section, I summarize some of these problems in lieu of an evaluation of the program.

Recovery Versus Sustained Growth

The first phase of post-Mao agricultural policy stressed technological transformation to solve mainland China's agricultural problems. The agricultural reform since 1979, on the other hand, emphasizes organizational changes as a means to stimulate peasant incentive. This change of strategy resembles the policy cycles as analyzed by Alexander Eckstein. Peking's past experiences show clearly that attempted technological transformation without a significant allocation of resources to the agricultural sector would not produce the desired results. The past experiences also show that using organizational changes to increase peasant incentive can often lead to quick recovery as expressed in a high rate of growth of farm output in the short run. But the incentive effects cannot be long lasting.

Organizational changes such as the household responsibility system and the very visible incentive effects it generates cannot solve China's basic agricultural problems because the rural labor-to-land ratio is either unchanged or gradually deteriorating. Since 1979, there has not been any significant increase of resource allocations to the agricultural sector, and there seem to be no major technological changes in sight. The extremely high rate of growth of agricultural production (5.6 percent average annual rate for 1980 and 1981) simply reflects the fact that resources were not used to their fullest capacity in the past. Once the increase of output reaches the production frontier defined by the level of resources available to the rural sector and the state of technology, further expansion would not be possible. Wan Li, vice-premier and chairman of the State Agriculture Commission, admitted in 1983 that the rapid growth in recent years was, to a considerable extent, recovery in nature,[38] and Thomas Wiens has demonstrated the limits of agricultural intensification in the Soochow district.[39] To a large extent, Wiens's analysis ought to be valid for other regions in China as well, because his findings are well within the framework of the law of diminishing returns.

Inefficiencies in Resource Allocation

The reform program calls for greater use of the market mechanism to increase production efficiency. Yet the planners do not seem to understand the fact that in order to take advantage of the market mechanism, prices must be allowed to perform the allocating function. That is, prices should be allowed to serve as signals to guide the allocation of resources.[40] For example, it has been reported that in many regions, government purchase prices of farm and sideline products are fixed by the government with no flexibility. Farmers respond to low government prices of some commodities by producing fewer of them or refusing to sell whatever amount is produced. These responses create shortages, yet the prices are not allowed to go up. For some other commodities for which the prices are set high, the farmers respond by producing and selling more of them. This situation simply leads to excessive government inventories, but the greater supplies do not result in lower prices.[41] If prices had been allowed to freely adjust to supply and demand conditions, such shortages and stockpiling could have been avoided, and therefore, resources could have been used more efficiently.

To use another example, in April 1981, there was an increase in the government purchase price of tobacco. As a result, there was a 50 percent increase (to 9 million mu) of land area planted in tobacco. This increase led to a 70 percent increase in leaf tobacco production to a record high of 1.25 million tons, turning a 1980 shortage into a 1981 surplus of 150,000 tons. Yet the tobacco price remained at the high level. As a result, an additional expansion of 50 percent of the land area planted in tobacco was expected in 1982.[42] In this case, profits must have been made, not because of efficiency in production, but simply because of the guaranteed high price. Again, this type of inefficiency can be avoided if prices are allowed to be determined by supply and demand. A market mechanism without a rational price system to reflect relative scarcity and supply and demand conditions will not help Peking use scarce resources such as farmland more efficiently.

Potential Income Gaps

Peking's policy of letting some farmers get rich first could create two entirely different problems with different situations.

One problem is the lack of a sense of

security on the part of the newly rich farmers (the <u>wan-yuan hu</u>, or the ten-thousand-yuan households). There have been numerous reports of discrimination against the <u>wan-yuan hu</u> in many provinces, with those who "became rich first" often being threatened by other team members. They are frequently reminded that "one of these days we will cut your [capitalist] tail" or that "your income is several times higher than a landlord in the past. You definitely will be in trouble in the near future."[43] As a result, some of the newly rich farmers are so scared they do not even dare to go to meetings called to honor them as model workers. Some of them genuinely feel they have made a mistake by working too hard and becoming rich.[44] Many of them decide to sell a major part of their harvest to the government, instead of selling in the free market, in order to avoid being criticized or threatened. According to information at the microlevel, many of the newly rich farmers sell 65-77 percent of their total output to the government in addition to fulfilling their regular obligations of agricultural tax, quota sales, and above-quota sales to the government.[45] In such cases, the relationship between creative and hard work and reward is less certain, and the incentive effect of the household responsibility system on production is at least partly eliminated.

The other potential problem in connection with income gaps could have even more serious implications. If the threats from the "leftist elements" in a team are silenced and the newly rich farmers are indeed allowed to keep and use their higher income without fear, then there will be real incentives for many more ingenious and hardworking farmers to become rich. Yet it is not possible for every farm household to become a <u>wan-yuan hu</u> because land fertility is not uniform, the number of workers in each household may be quite different, and different individuals naturally may have different skills, physical strengths, and work attitudes. Furthermore, many farmers under the age of thirty-five have never had the experience of working independently. Therefore, they cannot be expected to be able to work on and manage a small farm as efficiently as those who have had some such experience in the past. For all these reasons, income gaps between the rich and the poor farmers most likely will continue to widen.

Income inequality in the countryside may reach a point beyond which the authorities may find it unacceptable. If at that point measures are taken to restrict any further widening of the income gaps, many farmers would then feel that the days of reckoning had finally arrived, and the incentive effect of the household responsibility system would quickly disappear.

Conservation of Land Resources

Under the household responsibility system, land is still collectively owned, but since there are uncertainties as to how long the current policies will continue, there have been widespread practices of "predatory style" land use. Such practices include thoroughly removing all trees on the land and hills, destroying topsoil by building kilns to bake bricks on the farmland, nonmaintenance and nonimprovement of the land and the irrigation facilities on it, and building residential houses on farmland.

Available information indicates that farmers' production expenses are used mostly to purchase current inputs such as fertilizers, seeds, and occasionally small farm tools.[46] There is almost no report of investment by individual farm households to improve the farmland assigned for their use. The CCP Central Committee "Circular on Rural Work of 1984" (issued in January 1984) specifically requested that "peasants should be encouraged to invest more in the land to enrich the soil,"[47] implying that the peasants were not doing so. At the same time, public investment in agriculture also was reduced. The data in Table 15.1 clearly show that the amounts of both mechanical farming area and irrigation area have declined since 1979. These tendencies all point to a serious problem of the deterioration of land productivity in the long run.

Table 15.1. PRC: Mechanical farming area and irrigation area, 1979-1982 (unit: 10,000 hectares)

Year	Mechanical Farming Area	Irrigation Area	
		Total	Mechanical Irrigation Area
1979	4,221.9	4,500.3	2,532.1
1980	4,099.0	4,488.8	2,531.6
1981	3,647.7	4,457.4	2,523.1
1982	3,511.5	4,417.7	2,514.5

Source: Lu Liangshu, "Present Status and Prospects of Agriculture and Food Production in China" (Paper presented at a seminar on May 31, 1984, at the International Rice Institute, Los Baños, Philippines, Mimeographed), p. 14.

Population Problems in the Countryside

The assignment of land to each household according to the number of individuals in the family encourages a larger family size, and the prevailing method of production in mainland Chinese agriculture also favors families with more children since a larger labor force means more income.[48] The natural rate of increase of the population was 1.09 percent in 1980, the year the household responsibility system was generally adopted. Next year, in 1981, the rate went up to 1.46 percent.[49] As a result, in many localities, population control programs, including the enforcement of birth control quotas, abortion, and sterilization, have been pushed with vigor, harshness, and varying degrees of coercion.[50] But the problem obviously cannot be easily solved.

At the same time that agricultural production is successfully increasing, these agricultural and many other economic and social problems continue to cast gray shadows on Chinese agricultural development in the longer run.

PROSPECTS

Regardless of the economic performance of the

agricultural reform program, the future of the reform will most likely be determined by political factors. Many observers consider that mainland China's political situation is still not fully stable and that further changes are not impossible. Greater economic freedom and the rigid Communist system do not combine easily. There is the view that such Party elders as Li Hsien-nien, Ch'en Yun, and Yeh Chien-ying are more conservative in their economic thinking than Teng Hsiao-p'ing. If they can outlive Teng, they could steer mainland China away from economic reform to more orthodox Communist policies.[51]

Judging from the frequent statement of "two unchanges" from Peking, that is, the socialist collective system will not change and the agricultural production responsibility system will not change for a long time to come,[52] it would seem that as long as Teng and his associates are in control, the current reform program will continue. However, there are also indications that even if there is no opposition to the reform policies within the CCP, the household responsibility system in agricultural production may still not be a permanent institution and that further policy changes might indeed occur. The following quotation from Teng's Selected Works may provide some clue:

> Since the liberalization of rural policies, many localities have carried out the household responsibility system [pao-ch'an tao-hu]. The results are very good and the changes are very swift. . . . Some comrades are worrying as to whether such development would adversely affect the collective economy, I see no need for such worries. Our general direction is to develop the collective economy. In the places where the household responsibility system is practiced at the present time, the mainstay of the economy is still the production team. What will be the future of these places? It is certain that if only production is further developed, and if only the social division of labor and the commercial

economy are further developed in these rural areas, the currently low level of collectivization will be elevated to a higher level. The collective economy, although weak now, will be strengthened by then. The key is to develop productivity. We have to create the conditions for the advancement of collectivization by increasing productivity. Specifically, the following four conditions must be fulfilled: First, a higher level of mechanization is achieved. [This means mechanization in the broad sense, not just mechanization in planting and harvesting.] That is, the kind of mechanization that is appropriate for the local natural conditions and the local economic situation is realized to a certain extent. Second, the level of management is raised, experiences are gained, and a group of rural cadres who are capable of considerable managerial skills has emerged. Third, rural diversification is further developed, and as a consequence, a variety of specialized work groups or teams are established, thus significantly expanding the rural commercial economy. Fourth, collective income is increased, and its share in total income is expanded. Once these four conditions are realized, those areas in which the household responsibility system is practiced now would have changes in the form of organization [toward higher level of collectivization]. Such changes would not be imposed from the top, they would not be based on executive orders, but necessarily be demanded by the development of production itself.[53]

This passage goes a long way toward answering the question concerning the future of the current agricultural reform in the PRC. It may be recalled that in 1950, when Liu Shao-ch'i declared that the "rich peasant economy" would be preserved for a long period of time after the land reform, he also used the expression: "if only such a condition is fulfilled . . .that there is widespread mechanization in the rural area, ... only then will there be no need of the rich peasant economy, and only then can collective farms be organized, ... and that can only be achieved in the very remote future."[54] The First Five-Year Plan (1953-1957) called for the completion of agricultural collectivization in fifteen years, in addition to a three-year recovery period after the land reform.[55] In reality, mainland China's agricultural sector was completely collectivized by the end of the First Five-Year Plan in 1957, that is, ten years ahead of the promised fifteen-year period.

How long a period are the current land contracts to the households supposed to cover? Until the end of 1983, the contract period was generally between two and eight years. In January 1984, the CCP Central Committee extended the contract period to fifteen years in the hope of gaining greater peasant confidence in the reform program.[56] However, if the fifteen-year period for the "rich peasant economy" can be shortened to five years, there seems to be no assurance that the fifteen-year period for the household land contracts cannot be shortened and a higher level of rural collectivization re-initiated, if the conditions are ripe.

At this point, it may be appropriate to refer to the following comment on the Soviet economic reform of 1965 by Andrei Amalrik: "In order to remain in power, the regime must change and evolve, but in order to preserve itself, everything must remain unchanged. The contradiction can be noted particularly in the case of the economic reform, which is being carried out so slowly and yet is so vital to the regime."[57]

In addition to the "two unchanges" referred to above, Peking also has its Four Basic Principles, which Teng Hsiao-p'ing insists cannot be changed. These four are (1) socialism, (2) people's democratic dictatorship, (3) leadership of the CCP, and (4) Marxism-Leninism and the thought of Mao Tse-tung. When too many things are claimed to be unchangeable, and when some of these unchangeables are not consistent with one another, one can almost be certain that another turn of the policy cycle will occur sooner or later.

NOTES

I wish to thank Professors Gordon Bennett and Richard Y.C. Yin for their constructive comments when this chapter was given as a paper at the Thirteenth Sino-American Conference on Mainland China. I am particularly grateful to Professor Yin for suggesting reference materials useful for its revision. Following the practice of the Library of Congress, I have used the Wade-Giles system in romanizing Chinese names of persons, places, and titles of periodicals. For works by Chinese authors in English, the author's name is given as it appears in the original publication. Names of Chinese places originally appearing in Han-yu P'in-yin romanization are converted into Wade-Giles romanization to the extent that the Chinese characters can be identified.

1. "Pu p'a lao, pu p'a han, chiu p'a cheng-ts'e lai hui pien," <u>Nung-yeh ching-chi wen-t'i</u> [Problems of agricultural economics] (Peking), no. 4 (1982), p. 27.

2. Dwight H. Perkins, "Centralization and Decentralization in Mainland China's Agriculture, 1949-1962," <u>Quarterly Journal of Economics</u> 78 (May 1964), pp. 208-237. Shortly before this article, in 1963, Chu-yuan Cheng analyzed the cyclical fluctuations in the Chinese economy in terms of harvest cycle and confiscatory policy in his book, <u>Communist China's Economy 1949-1962: Structural Changes and Crisis</u> (South Orange, N.J.: Seton Hall University Press, 1963), pp. 160-165.

3. Nicholas R. Lardy, "Comparative Advantage, Internal Trade, and the Distribution of Income in Chinese Agriculture" (Paper presented for the Trade and Development Workshop, Yale University, January 25, 1982, Mimeographed).

4. Alexander Eckstein, "Economic Fluctuations in Communist China's Domestic Development," in Ping-ti Ho and Tang Tsou, eds., <u>China in Crisis</u>, vol. 1, bk. 2 (Chicago: University of

Chicago Press, 1968); reprinted as chap. 11 of Eckstein's book, China's Economic Development: The Interplay of Scarcity and Ideology (Ann Arbor: University of Michigan Press, 1975), see particularly pp. 311-313.

5. The 1982 census counted 79.4 percent of the total population as rural (Jen-min jih-pao [People's daily], October 28, 1982, p. 4.

6. Jen-min jih-pao, March 9, 1955.

7. For details, see Jen-min jih-pao, August 25, 1955.

8. Based on data for representative production teams given in Peking Review, March 25, 1966, p. 16, and China Reconstructs (September 1972), pp. 26-29.

9. Hsüeh Mu-ch'iao, The Adjustment and Reform of Our National Economy (in Chinese) (Peking [Beijing]: People's Publishing House, 1982), p. 39 (hereafter Hsüeh Mu-ch'iao 1982).

10. Lu Liangshu (president, Chinese Academy of Agricultural Sciences, Peking), "Present Status and Prospects of Agriculture and Food Production in China," (Paper presented at a seminar on May 31, 1984, at the International Rice Research Institute, Los Baños, Philippines, Mimeographed), p. 11. The income figure is based on a survey of 6,095 peasant households.

11. Beijing Review, March 7, 1983, p. 11. This figure refers to Shantung Province in 1978.

12. Per capita cultivated land was 1.55 mu (1 hectare equals 15 shih mu); see Ch'en Mu-hua article in Jen-min jih-pao, August 11, 1979, p. 2. The per capita figure for 1977 was also given in Jen-min jih-pao, editorial, June 1, 1982, p. 1. The amount of cultivated land per capita of the rural population was about 1.8 mu or 0.12 hectare (Fundamentals of China's Agricultural Economy [in Chinese], ed. Policy Research Office of the Ministry of Agriculture [Peking (Beijing): Agriculture Publishing House, 1982], p. 2).

13. Hu Ch'iao-mu article in Jen-min jih-pao, October 6, 1978, p. 3.

14. Chou Shu-lien article in Ma Hung and Sun Shang-ching, eds., Studies of the Structure of Chinese Economy (in Chinese) (Peking [Beijing]: People's Publishing House, 1981), vol. 1, pp. 28-29 (hereafter Ma and Sun 1981). These figures are

considerably higher than Western estimates. For example, Dwight H. Perkins estimated the 1957 per capita grain output in China was 572 catties (286 kilograms) (see Dwight H. Perkins, Agricultural Development in China 1368-1968 [Chicago: Aldine Publishing Company, 1969], p. 15). A U.S. government source estimated 295, 288, and 291 kilograms for the years 1957, 1977, and 1978, respectively (see National Foreign Assessment Center, China: Agriculture in 1978, ER 79-10206 [Washington, D.C., April 1973], p. 1).

15. Hsüeh Mu-ch'iao 1982, p. 27, and Hsüeh Mu-ch'iao, Some Problems in Our Current Economy (in Chinese) (Peking [Beijing]: People's Publishing House, 1980), pp. 37-38 (hereafter Hsüeh Mu-ch'iao 1980).

16. Chang Cho-yuan article in Ma and Sun 1981, vol. 1, p. 65. The Chinese source uses the expression "still had such phenomenon of large numbers of peasants . . . begging for food," indicating that such phenomena were not limited to 1978.

17. Teng Hsiao-p'ing, speech at the closing session of the National Science Conference, Jen-min jih-pao, March 22, 1978, pp. 1-2; the translation is mine.

18. United Press International, Hong Kong dispatch, June 14, 1979; here quoted from Shih-chieh jih-pao [World journal], June 16, 1979, p. 1. Li's speech was made in a work meeting of the Central Political Bureau held on April 5-29, 1979.

19. Hsüeh Mu-ch'iao 1980, p. 90. Hsüeh also wrote that "even raw cotton, edible oil and sugar, must also be imported" (ibid.).

20. Kenneth R. Walker estimated the 1978-1979 average annual grain consumption (including the ration and above-ration consumption) per capita of urban population to be 280 kilograms (see his Food Grain Procurement and Consumption in China [Cambridge: Cambridge University Press, 1984], p. 191). In 1978, mainland China's urban population was 119.94 million (PRC, State Statistical Bureau, PRC Statistical Yearbook 1981, Chinese ed. [Hong Kong: Ching-chi Tao-pao She, October 1982], p. 89). The amount of food grain imported in 1978 was 9.4 million tons (U.S.

Department of Agriculture, PRC Agricultural Situation: Review of 1978 and Outlook for 1979, Supplement 6 to WAS 18 [Washington, D.C., June 1979], p. 23). Thus, the imports amounted to 28 percent of mainland China's total urban grain consumption (280 kilograms multiplied by 119.94 million) in 1978. Walker's estimated consumption amount of 280 kilograms (or 560 catties) per head of urban population, however, is much too high, mainly because of his unrealistic assumption that Shanghai was representative of urban China in 1978-1979.

21. Hsüeh Mu-ch'iao reported that in 1978, "the average per capita grain consumption recovered to 393 catties (385 catties for the farmers)" (Hsüeh Mu-ch'iao 1980, p. 37). We may assume these were actually the ration figures and use a round figure of 200 kilograms (400 catties) as the 1978 average grain ration amount per capita of urban population. Hence the 9.4 million tons of grain imports would be 3.92 percent of the PRC's total grain ration amount for the urban population (200 kilograms times 119.94 million) in 1978.

22. National Foreign Assessment Center, China: Demand for Foreign Grain, ER 79-10073 (Washington, D.C., January 1979), p. 1.

23. Gist (Bureau of Public Affairs, U.S. Department of State) (April 1981), p. 1.

24. Hua Kuo-feng, "Report on Government Work at the First Session of the Fifth National People's Congress, February 26, 1978," Jen-min jih-pao, March 7, 1978, p. 2.

25. Hsüeh Mu-ch'iao 1982, pp. 40, 68.

26. See Peking Review, June 9, 1978, pp. 5-7. On June 26, 1978, at the closing session of the Third National Conference on Agricultural Mechanization, then-Vice-Premier Yu Chiu-li delivered a report calling for the basic realization of agricultural mechanization by 1980. "Basic realization" was defined as 70 percent of "main work" in agriculture, forestry, animal husbandry, sideline production, and fisheries to be mechanized. For details of this report, see Peking Review, February 17, 1978, pp. 9-10. According to mainland publications, at least 70 percent of agricultural productive activities were still done by

human labor in 1979.

27. Unless otherwise noted, this and the following paragraphs are largely based on Michel Oksenberg, "Economic Policy Making in China: Summer 1981," China Quarterly, no. 90 (June 1982), pp. 165-194. Oksenberg's excellent presentation and analysis are based on his interviews in Peking and several Western publications.

28. Communiqué of the Third Plenary Session of the Eleventh Central Committee of the CCP, China News Service (Peking), December 23, 1978.

29. Teng Hsiao-p'ing assumed leadership in August 1977, but his political power was firmly established only by the end of 1978.

30. As defined by Yuan Pao-hua, vice-chairman of the State Economic Commission (see Business Week, May 19, 1980, p. 46).

31. See John L. Davie and Dean W. Carver, "China's International Trade and Finance," in U.S. Congress, Joint Economic Committee, China Under the Four Modernizations, pt. 2 (December 30, 1982) (Washington, D.C.: Government Printing Office, 1982), p. 32.

32. For an excellent account of the reform of the 1960s, see Jan S. Prybyla, "Communist China's Strategy of Economic Development 1961-1966," Asian Survey 6:1 (October 1966), pp. 589-603, particularly pp. 589-595.

33. For a good discussion of East European economic reforms in the 1960s, see Gregory Grossman, "Economic Reforms: A Balance Sheet," Problems of Communism 15:6 (November-December 1966), pp. 43-55. For a survey of the 1965 Soviet agricultural reform program, see Solomon Schwarz, "Agriculture: The Curtain Is Lifted," Problems of Communism 15:2 (March-April 1966), pp. 12-20. It is interesting to note that even the parallelism between the Soviet 1965 reform and the PRC post-Mao agricultural reform since 1979 is remarkable.

34. See, for example, Hsu Kun-ming and Yang Cheng-ming, "A Preliminary Investigation of the Belgrade Agricultural Joint Enterprise [PKB]" (in Chinese), New China News Agency (Belgrade), December 28, 1978.

35. This paragraph is based on Zhang Yulin, "Readjustment and Reform in Agriculture," in Lin

Wei and Arnold Chao, eds., China's Economic Reforms (Philadelphia: University of Pennsylvania Press, 1982), pp. 123-146, and Oksenberg, "Economic Policy Making in China," p. 189.

36. Wan Li, "Speech at the National Rural Work Conference on November 29, 1983," Jen-min jih-pao, January 18, 1984, p. 1.

37. The description is based on Wei and Chao, China's Economic Reforms, pp. 273-274.

38. Wan Li, "Speech at the National Rural Work Conference," p. 1.

39. Thomas B. Wiens, "The Limits to Agricultural Intensification," in U.S. Congress, Joint Economic Committee, China Under the Four Modernizations, pt. 1 (August 13, 1982) (Washington, D.C.: Government Printing Office, 1982), pp. 462-474.

40. John L. Davie and Dean W. Carver also made this point in connection with their study of mainland China's international trade (see their joint article, "China's International Trade and Finance," p. 34).

41. "Urgent Problems in the Development of Rural Economy," Nan-fang jih-pao [Southern daily], January 18, 1982, p. 4.

42. Jen-min jih-pao, January 30, 1982.

43. Jen-min jih-pao, January 16, 1984, p. 2.

44. Nan-fang jih-pao, November 17, 1982, p. 1.

45. Calculated on the basis of data from Nan-fang jih-pao, January 14, 1982, p. 2, and Jen-min jih-pao, January 17, 1983, p. 1.

46. It was only after the issuance of Document no. 1 of 1983 that farmers were permitted to purchase farm machinery and transport equipment (see Wan Li, "Speech at the National Rural Work Conference," p. 1).

47. Beijing Review, February 20, 1984, p. 6. The full text of this document was published in Jen-min jih-pao, June 12, 1984, p. 1.

48. This problem is generally recognized in mainland China. See, for example, a discussion of it in Nan-fang jih-pao, October 11, 1982, p. 4.

49. Almanac of China's Economy (1983), Chinese ed. (Hong Kong: Almanac of China's Economy Company, 1983), pp. I-15.

50. See, for example, Christopher S. Wren's report in the New York Times, May 16, 1982,

p. Y-29; Nan-fang jih-pao, December 18, 1980,
p. 1; and Nan-fang jih-pao, January 20, 1982, p. 1.

51. For a discussion along this line, see "Peking Persona," Wall Street Journal, April 23, 1984, pp. 1, 16.

52. "Policies Must Be Consistently Stable," Jen-min jih-pao, April 3, 1982, p. 1.

53. "On the Problem of Rural Policy" (excerpts of a talk with responsible persons of the Party center on May 31, 1980), in Selected Works of Teng Hsiao-p'ing (in Chinese) (Peking [Beijing]: People's Publishing House, 1983), pp. 275-276; the translation is mine. It is significant that this talk was not made public until 1983.

54. Liu Shao-ch'i, "Report on the Land Reform Problem," speech at the Second Session of the First National Committee of the Chinese People's Political Consultative Conference, June 14, 1950, in 1951 People's Handbook, 2d ed. (Shanghai: Ta Kung Pao, February 20, 1981), p. Cheng-39; the translation is mine.

55. See First Five-Year Plan for the Development of the National Economy, 1953-1957 (Chinese edition) (Peking [Beijing]: People's Publishing House, 1955), pp. 167, 182.

56. Beijing Review, February 20, 1984, p. 6.

57. Andrei Amalrik, Will the Soviet Union Survive Until 1984? (New York: Harper and Row Publishers, 1970), p. 22 (also, New York: Harper Colophon Book ed., 1981, p. 28).

16
Agriculture in Mainland China: Reform and Problems

Ting-chung Ch'en

Misguided by Mao Tse-tung's leftist policy in the past several decades, mainland China's agricultural development has been greatly retarded,[1] and agriculture has actually become the weakest and most contradictory sector in the entire economy. Only after Mao's death in 1976 did the Chinese Communists begin to think about the real obstacles to mainland China's agricultural development.

They found that the first obstacle was the disproportionate development in agricultural production caused by the policy of "taking grain as the key link." In fact, excessive deforestation and efforts to fill up lakes to create more farmland have disturbed the ecological balance, and this change, in turn, has had an adverse effect on agricultural development. The Chinese Communists have admitted that the Yangtze River is now choked up with silt, creating a situation almost as serious as that of the Yellow River; as a result of progressive desert formation, Southwest China has become as desolate as North China; and an increase in the amount of floating sand has made the Heilungkiang area the second loess plateau in China.

The second obstacle was the loss of the peasants' enthusiasm for work under the collective production system and the rural policy that was then in force. The people's commune has proved to be an organization of no economic value, and the low growth rate in agriculture resulting from policy mistakes and low efficiency has made the peasants' life one of only bare subsistence.²

Following the economic readjustment in 1979, the Chinese Communists began to make efforts to boost agricultural production, and in July 1980, the slogan of "relying on policy and science" was advanced in rural work. Currently, mainland China's agricultural reform comprises three parts: (1) reform in management method, (2) reform in production structure, and (3) technical reform. Reform in management method includes the system of contracted responsibilities with payment linked to output, the separation of government administration from commune management, and the readjustment of the "system of planned management" and the "system of rural commodity circulation." Reform in production structure is to change the practice of growing only one kind of product, that is to say, efforts should be made to develop a diversified economy while taking grain as the key link. Technical reform is aimed at realizing agricultural modernization. Nevertheless, the task of effecting changes in agriculture is not an easy one as it involves many complicated questions.

With regard to reform in management method, the system of contracted responsibilities with payment linked to output and the policy of separating government administration from commune management have been enforced. The adjustment of the system of planned management and the system of rural commodity circulation lacks a concrete plan for fulfillment. The development of a diversified economy and reform in agrotechnology remain thorny problems. It can be said that the agricultural reform currently under way on the Chinese mainland is still at the stage of policy readjustment. Meanwhile, in the course of economic readjustment and reform, new probems have emerged. Whether the reform can succeed will have a great bearing, not only on mainland China's economic development, but also on Teng Hsiao-p'ing's political future. This chapter will analyze the agricultural reform in mainland China in terms of its present condition, its possible development, and the problems confronting it.

CONTRACTED PRODUCTION AND THE
NEW ECONOMIC SYSTEM OF THE COMMUNE

The distribution of land originally used for collective farming to peasants for individual farming began in September 1980. With contracted land, the peasants were first asked to do a fixed amount of work. Shortly thereafter, they were asked to fulfill a fixed target of output. Later, there were the system of "fixing output quotas for each production team with payment linked to output" and the system of "fixing output quotas for each household with planned distribution in accordance with the work point." Finally, there is the system of "assigning land to each household in exchange for fixed levies."

According to the Chinese Communists, the system of assigning land to each household in exchange for fixed levies means contracting land to commune households in accordance with the number of people or the size of work force in a given household. While implementing this system, the administrative framework of the production team and the ownership system of the basic means of production remain unchanged. After delivering a portion of the produce to the state and retaining a portion for the collective, the peasants can keep what is left.[3] Actually, the system of assigning land to each household in exchange for fixed levies is a return to the tenant system except that under the current system, the Chinese Communist cadres in the rural areas are the collectors of levies for the Chinese Communists. Up to the first half of 1983, about 93.5 percent of the production teams were implementing the system of contracted responsibilities, which mainly took the form of assigning land to each household in exchange for fixed levies.[4] Meanwhile, about 13.8 percent of the peasant households became key households or specialized households engaged in industrial or agricultural sideline occupations.[5]

As some of the peasants chose production activities other than farming, the Chinese Communists called all these individual operations by peasants an "output-related system of contracted responsibilities which is based mainly on operation by households." This system is now being eulogized as a "new development of Marx's theory on agricultural cooperativization in the course of practice."[6] Under the current tenant system and under the condition that some of the restrictions on individual economy have been removed, the peasants are now able to engage in the following economic activities:

1. To contract land from the production team according to the number of people and the size of labor force in each household. The duration of this kind of contract work, originally set at one to three years, is now extended to fifteen years. The duration of contract for work in the mountainous and lake areas is now extended from thirty to fifty years. Moreover, plants and forests thus contracted for can be passed down to descendants or transferred to others.[7]

2. To transfer the contract for the use of farmland to other people who are skilled in farming.

3. To engage in the processing of agricultural and industrial by-products, to raise livestock and to breed and catch fish so as to become specialized households or key households that can provide commodities.

4. To engage in individual economic activities in the rural areas, including industry, handicrafts, commerce, catering trade, service trades, repair service, transportation, and housing repair service. With approval, individual rural craftsmen and traders may have their own shops, choose names for their shops, and have two to five apprentices.[8]

5. To engage in passenger and cargo transportation individually or several households jointly by using motor vehicles and motorized vessels. With approval, passengers and cargoes can be transported outside counties or provinces.[9]

6. To transport and market agricultural and sideline products in both retail and wholesale operations after having fulfilled the state delivery and sales quotas. Motor vehicles and motorized vessels may be used to transport passengers and cargoes outside counties or provinces.[10]

7. With the approval of the local

administration of industry and commerce, peasants with special skills are allowed to set up stands in towns to engage in individual industry and commerce and service trade, provided they give up their grain rations and apply for temporary residence permits.[11]

8. To raise money to run cooperative economic organizations for the promotion of economic, educational, and cultural affairs and to draw dividends from their shares.

9. Herdsmen are allowed to transfer the contract for pastureland and livestock. Regulations on other matters concerning individual industry and commerce in the pastoral areas are the same as those in the agricultural areas.[12]

In addition, the more than 760,000 enterprises under the people's communes or production brigades and teams are now called "enterprises of villages and townships," and most of them have been contracted to cadres and common members for management. The state-owned supply and marketing cooperatives are to be changed into private enterprises after their stocks are cleared up. Even the state-owned farms are to be contracted to individual households, which will assume full responsibility for profits and losses.

After the implementation of the contract system, the 54,350 communes, 719,000 production brigades, and 5,977,000 production teams no longer will operate under the previous "three-level ownership system of the commune, production brigade, and production team with the production team as the basic accounting unit," nor is the system of "integrating government administration with commune management" to be continued. In October 1983, the CCP Central Committee and the State Council jointly issued a "Notice on Separating Government Administration from Commune Management and Establishing Township Governments,"[13] which stipulates that the basic administrative organizations are to be separated from the people's communes to become township people's governments and villagers' committees, thus turning the people's commune into a purely economic unit. The notice also stipulates that the name "people's commune" will be abandoned when township governments are established throughout mainland China by the end of 1984.

Based on the current reform of separating government administration from commune management, township people's governments and township Party committees will be set up, and the supply and marketing cooperatives, credit cooperatives, food grain administration offices, foodstuff management stations, stations for promoting agricultural technology, and enterprises originally run by the commune will be incorporated into a new economic organization. Each township people's government will have a chief and a deputy chief plus staff members to take charge of civil, judicial, financial, cultural and educational, sanitary, family planning, production construction, and secretarial work. Under the township people's government will be also the armed department and the public security substation. The township Party committee is the core of leadership of the town.[14] Although the above-mentioned Party, government, and enterprise units are said to be independent of one another, the township Party committee actually holds the reins of power as the township people's government is placed under the leadership of the township Party committee and the economic organizations are under the jurisdiction of the township people's government.

Under the new policy of separating government administration from commune management, the production brigade is renamed "the administrative village." In each administrative village, there will be a villagers' committee and an economic organization known as an "agricultural cooperative," and key positions in these two organizations can be filled by the same people.[15] Today, when all the farmland has been contracted to peasants, the production team actually has nothing to do.

According to the Chinese Communist news media, many of the questions concerning the reorganization of the commune are to be decided by the people after they have made experiments. These questions include the name for the commune and the newly incorporated economic organization and the establishment and size of administrative organizations. Different experiments have been made in different localities. In Honan Province, for example, the "township economic joint association" has been set up at the commune level, the "village economic joint association" at the production brigade level, and the "producer's cooperatives" at the production team level. In Shenyang, Liaoning Province, the production brigades have been replaced by "joint associations of agriculture, industry, and commerce" while the production teams have been replaced by "joint agricultural producer's cooperatives" or "agricultural producer's cooperatives." In Anhwei Province, the "joint economic association" has been set up at the commune level. In Szechwan Province, "integrated complexes of agriculture, industry, and commerce" and the "service companies on agricultural management and administration" have been set up at the commune level. In Kwangtung, Hopei, and Szechwan Provinces, the name "commune" no longer exists after the establishment of the township government.

When the CCP Central Committee issued a notice in October 1983 calling for the separation of government administration from commune management, township people's governments had already been established in many provinces on a trial basis. At that time, a total of 9,028 people's communes (or 16.6 percent of the total number) in 902 counties followed the policy of separating government administration from commune management, and a total of 12,786 township people's governments were established.[16] By the end of 1983, the work of establishing township government had been completed in 536 counties and Tientsin Municipality, and there were 2,897 township governments and over 171,000 villagers' committees.[17] At that point, the collective economic system of the people's commune--which had been known for its characteristics of "being large in size and collective in nature," "integrating government administration with commune management," and "three-level ownership of the commune, the production brigade, and the production team with the production team as the basic accounting unit"--ceased to exist.

ORIENTATION OF THE REFORM

The agricultural collective system began to meet with resistance from peasants as early as the 1950s. As a result of strong peasant demand, the system of "fixing output quotas for each household" had been applied several times in the past, but the official attitude toward that system had been inconsistent. Some leading members held that it violated the general orientation of socialism and that it restored capitalism because it encouraged peasants to farm on their own. People of this opinion included Mao Tse-tung, Chang Ch'un-ch'iao, and Hua Kuo-feng. Those supporting the system included Liu Shao-ch'i, Teng Hsiao-p'ing, and Chao Tzu-yang. The latter maintained that the system of fixing output quotas for each household is the most effective way to manage production and that it is only a measure of expediency. Because of the lack of consensus at the leadership level, the system has not been followed all the way through. According to the Chinese Communists, it had been adopted four times before: 1956-1957, 1959, 1961-1962, and 1964.[18] During the period from 1956 to 1957, the system was instituted in such provinces as Chekiang, Kwangtung, Kiangsu, Honan, and Shansi. It was later suspended under severe criticism. In 1959, the system was again adopted at Hsinhsiang and Loyang, Honan Province. At that time, the Maoists criticized the system as a "most backward, perverse and reactionary act."[19] In 1961 and 1964, the system was instituted again in Anhwei, Yunnan, Kweichow, andKansu Provinces.

During the Cultural Revolution, Liu Shao-ch'i's policy of san-tzu i-pao--i.e., more plots for private use, more free markets, more enterprises with sole responsibility for their own profits or losses, and fixing output quotas on a household basis--was criticized as an out-and-out counter-revolutionary revisionist line. After Mao's death, however, the system was again adopted in some places. For example, in some rural areas in Hopei Province in 1979, farmland was distributed to peasant households for individual farming, and collective property was also distributed among the peasants. The peasants would like to revive the system of fixing output quotas whenever such an opportunity should arise, and accepting the fait accompli in May 1980, the Chinese Communists began to speak affirmatively about the policy of san-tzu i-pao: The system of san-tzu was an effective policy, and i-pao was a measure of expediency practiced under specified conditions and within certain limitations for the purpose of trying to revive production.[20] Consequently, after September 1980, the system of fixing output quotas for each household was officially enforced.

Indeed, many of the agricultural reform measures were created by peasants on their own initiative. What the CCP Central Committee has done is only to accept the fait accompli. The Chinese Communist leadership has justified this fact as a "process of correcting mistakes by coming from the masses of people and going into the masses of people" and a "process of strengthening and perfecting the policy in the course of practice."[21] Following are some instances to show that many of the rural policies ratified by the CCP Central Committee are generally policies that had already been adopted in local areas as a result of a strong demand by the peasants.

In 1982, the CCP Kansu Party committee issued ten regulations relaxing control over the rural economy. Under these regulations, peasants were allowed a longer duration of contracts for cultivating mountainous and other areas; the right to engage in processing by-products; and the right to open clinics, schools, child-care centers, theaters, and bookstores.[22] At about the same time, peasants in Yunnan Province were allowed to hire helpers and have apprentices, borrow money from and lend it to each other and pay interest, and draw dividends from shares. Some of these regulations were later ratified by the CCP Central Committee in Document no. 1 issued in January 1983. In the spring of 1983, the duration of contracts for farm production in Chishan County, Shansi Province, was extended to seventeen years. In Taming County, Hopei Province, the duration was extended from fifteen to twenty years.[23] However, the CCP Central Committee did not ratify the extension of contract duration until it issued Document no. 1 of 1984.

That document stipulates that the duration can be extended to fifteen years.

Since the system of fixing output quotas for each household was reinstituted in 1979, the CCP Central Committee has issued some documents concerning changes in rural policy. They are:

1. Document no. 4 of 1979: Issued in February 1979, it comprises two parts: "Decision on Some Questions Concerning the Acceleration of Agricultural Development (Draft)" and "Regulations on the Work in Rural People's Communes (Draft for Trial Use)"
2. "Some Questions Concerning Further Strengthening and Perfecting of the Production Responsibility System in Agriculture," Document no. 75 of 1980 issued in September 1980
3. "Notice on Transmitting the Report Concerning Active Development of a Diversified Economy in the Rural Areas," Document no. 13 of 1981 issued in March 1981
4. "A Summary of the National Rural Work Conference," Document no. 1 of 1982 issued in January 1982
5. "Some Questions Concerning the Current Economic Policies in the Rural Areas," Document no. 1 of 1983 issued in January 1983
6. "Notice on Strengthening Ideological-Political Work in the Rural Areas," Document no. 2 of 1983 issued in January 1983
7. "Notice on Separating Government Administration from Commune Management and Establishing Township Governments," Document no. 35 of 1983 issued in October 1983
8. "Notice on the Work in the Rural Areas in 1984," Document no. 1 of 1984 issued in January 1984

From these documents, it is clear that the Chinese Communist authorities have not had a well-conceived plan for agricultural reform. The reform was first aimed merely at solving food problems. Although some of the individual economic activities spontaneously engaged in by peasants are not intervened by the government, many others have been banned. Also restrictions on production are sometimes removed for the purpose of fulfilling production targets. Following are some instances to show that the Chinese Communists have had to accept the fait accompli for the purpose of fulfilling production targets:

    1. In the two documents issued in 1979--"Decision on Some Questions Concerning the Acceleration of Agricultural Development (Draft)" and "Regulations on the Work in Rural People's Communes (Draft for Trial Use)"--the system of fixing output quotas on the basis of individual household was not permitted.[24] Nevertheless, in Document no. 75 of 1980, there was the stipulation that this system could be applied to 5 percent of the production teams that had material difficulties. Shortly thereafter, the scope was extended to cover from 15 percent to 20 percent of the production teams. Finally, the tide of contracted production became unchecked, and by the end of 1982, 78.7 percent of the production teams were applying the system of contracted production.[25] Consequently, in Document no. 1 of 1983, the ban on contracted production for individual households was completely lifted.

    2. After the system of fixing output quotas based on each household had been instituted in some rural areas, the CCP Central Committee issued Document no. 13 in March 1981 to the effect that in places where the system was not instituted, peasants could use no more than 15 percent of the arable land belonging to the production teams as private plots or grazing land. Meanwhile, they were allowed to utilize some semi-able-bodied and auxiliary workers in sideline occupations during the slack seasons.[26] It can be said that by the first half of 1981, the rural policy was carried out within the framework of collective farming, except that some of the semi-able-bodied and auxiliary workers were allowed to engage in some individual economic activities. Nevertheless, in view of the then-prevalent tendency for peasants to look for contracted production and,

moreover, to divide up collective property for private use, the CCP Central Committee issued Document no. 1 of 1982, which gave tacit consent to contracted production by saying that the economic operations by peasant households that have engaged in contracted production should be limited to what can be managed by themselves.

3. After the system of fixing output quotas for individual households was widely implemented in the rural areas, the Chinese Communists again put many restrictions on the peasants. For example, they were not allowed to sell, rent out, or transfer the land contracted to them, nor could they build houses, lay out tombs, operate mines, or make bricks by using the earth on their land. They were also prohibited from exploiting hired labor, practicing usury, or operating commercial activities. Later, they were allowed to transport goods for sale in the place they lived by carrying the goods themselves or by using bicycles (but not by using motorized vehicles or boats or tractors) and to transport goods outside their counties or provinces.

All the restrictions, however, were later removed upon the strong demand of the peasants. For example, Shansi Province issued a notice in early 1981 forbidding people to purchase motored vehicles and tractors. But another notice issued by the same province in August gave the peasants the right to purchase agricultural machines for commercial operations.[27] The same thing happened in many other places. Consequently, in 1983, the CCP Central Committee had to accept the fait accompli. In Document no. 1 of 1983, the peasants were said to be able to hire hands, have apprentices, purchase machine tools for the processing of agricultural by-products, and purchase motored vehicles and boats for production and transportation purposes. They were also said to be able to transport goods outside their counties and provinces, jointly operate industrial and commercial enterprises, and draw dividends from their shares. In Document no. 1 of 1984, the peasants were promised greater autonomy in production, and they were allowed to transfer contracted land to other skilled farmers, build houses on contracted land, operate transportation services, and undertake construction projects.

4. In 1983, the peasants were allowed to engage in commercial operations only in the townships where they lived. In 1984, however, they were allowed to make a living in cities provided they gave up their own grain rations. On February 16, 1984, the <u>People's Daily</u> emphatically popularized the experience of some peasants from Tsuli County, Hunan Province, who had settled in cities to open shops or run factories.

Despite the removal of many of the restrictions on rural affairs, mainland China's rural policy is still confined within the framework of "the socialist road." The system of public ownership and the system of production responsibility continue to be upheld, and the practice of "giving scope to the leading role of the planned economy and the supplementary role of regulation by market mechanism" is followed in agricultural production so as to satisfy the need of the state, the collectives, and individuals.[28] In addition, the system of contracted production by individual households has been put under the direction of joint economic organizations in order to realize the Chinese socialist cooperative economic system in the rural areas, which is characterized by collective ownership, contract for individual household, division of labor in accordance with one's specialization, and the two-level operation by the joint economic organizations and individual households. Nevertheless, this new policy orientation is contradictory in itself because planned economy under the socialist system of public ownership is incompatible with contracted production by individual households. Actually, many of the agricultural reform measures adopted in recent years have brought about more complicated problems.

THE NEW TENANCY RELATIONS

After the contracting of farmland to peasants for individual farming, the income of those who are more skilled in farming and can do heavy work has increased because, with material incentive, they become more enthusiastic in their work.

According to the Chinese Communists, the gross output value of agriculture in 1982 increased by 34 percent as compared to 7.5 percent in 1978 when the agricultural reform was first instituted. Meanwhile, the income of peasant families has increased by 102 percent, at an annual rate of 19 percent. Consequently, the food problem in most of the shortage areas has been solved.[29] There are also indications that the rural economy in mainland China has been revitalized to a certain extent. For example, there was no need to import cotton from abroad in 1983, the cloth coupon was not used in 1984, and people in some places are able to buy grain and nonstaple foods without having to use grain coupons or meat coupons.

The existence of individual economy and semi-free farming under the new tenancy relationship has given rise to greater liberalization. To make more money, peasants have sometimes even violated government regulations on economic activities. On the other hand, the reluctance of the rural cadres to carry out the system of contracted production has also given rise to problems. Generally speaking, there are four kinds of problems in the rural areas.

1. <u>Problems brought about by rural cadres</u>: There are more than 60 million grass-roots cadres in the rural areas. They used to have authority over everything in the rural areas, but with the collapse of the collective economy following the implementation of the system of contracted production, they no longer have authority either over the production work or over the distribution of produce. As a result, they strongly oppose the reform. Besides, dependents of workers, government staff members, and military personnel who live in the rural areas also oppose the reform because they no longer can enjoy the special privileges to which they were entitled under the system of collective economy. A commentary published by the New China Agency on June 1, 1982, under the title "Correctly Understand and Treat the Practice of Separating Government Administration from Commune Management," said: "At present a small number of cadres do not understand why it is necessary to separate government administration from commune management.

". . . Others have misgivings and are worrying about their own future. They asked: 'If townships are going to be set up in the countryside, who will serve as cadres?' As a result, they have relaxed their leadership over current work." Indeed, it has been said that some leadership cadres in the rural areas have even found ways to discourage peasants from undertaking contracted production.[30]

This situation did not change even after the CCP Central Committee issued the "Notice on Separating Government Administration from Commune Management and Establishing Township Governments" in October 1983, which assured commune cadres of the continuation of the treatment they used to receive. In his speech at the National Rural Work Conference on November 29, 1983, Vice-Premier Wan Li criticized this phenomenon by saying: "Some policies . . . have been established and promulgated, but there are cadres who do not agree with them. Such comrades are either overly worried and refuse to implement the policies or do not exercise leadership in this regard, or engage in endless haggling and shifting of responsibilities. As a result, many problems that can be resolved have not been resolved."[31] Wan Li also pointed out that a few grass-roots cadres had taken advantage of their power and position to seek personal gain: "Some cadres are seizing farmland to build houses, obtaining through special connections chemical fertilizers, diesel oil and other means of production which are in short supply, taking the lead in obstructing the use of land for key construction projects in order to get something from the state, and openly plundering state property. Some cadres secure 'contracts' and take 'shares' by illegal means."

According to a _People's Daily_ article, some cadres have demanded shares from contractors by setting a lower output quota for them, some have taken shares by purchasing raw materials for contractors or by promoting the sale of goods produced by them, and others have used their position to create job opportunities for peasants.[32] By taking advantage of their power and position, rural cadres have made a lot of money in business operations. It is said that about 43 percent of the rich households in the rural areas are those of cadres or commune members who were previously cadres, 42 percent are those of ex-servicemen or sent-down intellectuals, 9 percent are those of skilled workers, 5 percent are those of people who are apt at doing business, and only 1 percent are those of individuals who have committed "historical errors."[33]

2. <u>Problems resulting from the implementation of the system of contracting land to peasants</u>: How to divide the land and contract it to peasants for individual farming is a thorny problem because some of the lands are fertile while others are poor, some have a southern exposure while others are in the shade, some are arid while others are damp, some are flat while others are sloping, some are in large tracts while others are in small pieces, and some are alkaline while others are acid. Moreover, the number of people in each family is not the same,[34] and generally, the amount of land to be allocated to each household is decided by the number of family members. Besides, the fertile and impoverished lands and the nearby and distant lands are paired up in distribution.

The first problem is that the land distributed is too fragmentary. Take the land distribution in Kuanshan Commune of Chishui County, Kiangsi Province, for example. There are ten peasant households there that contracted a total of 190 mu of land (one mu is equivalent to one-sixth of an acre) in 285 pieces. Each household was contracted on an average of 19 mu of land in 29 pieces. The smallest piece of land distributed to them was only one li (equivalent to one one-hundredth of a mu or 7 square meters). One of the peasant households was even contracted a total of 31 mu of land in 70 pieces, and the distance between some of the pieces of land was as far as one kilometer.[35] In one production team, the arable land was divided into over 660 pieces, with the larger ones not up to one mu and the smaller ones only several li. In many of the pieces of land distributed, peasants can grow only forty to fifty corn plants or twenty to thirty cotton plants. These pieces of land are too small to be plowed even with draft animals.[36]

According to the Chinese Communists, the amount of land contracted by each household is 7.4 mu of flat ground in 11 pieces and 15 pieces of hill land.[37]

The second problem is that whenever the number of people in a family changes, the amount of land distributed needs to be readjusted. According to a survey conducted in Hsiao County, Hunan Province, the number of family members changed in 131 out of the 140 production teams there in one year's time. It can be imagined that the readjustment of the acreage of contracted land will inevitably give rise to many complicated problems.[38]

The third problem is that the practice of distributing land according to the number of people in each household has resulted in a situation that a big family with a weak labor force cannot cultivate all its land while a small family with a strong labor force does not have enough land to till.[39] Fourth, many peasants have used the land for purposes other than farming, or they have rented it out or even sold it even though they did not own the land. Some Party cadres have even served as the middlemen or contractors for this illegal sale of land. It is said that the rent for one mu of land ranges from several hundred to about ten thousand yuan, while the selling price of one mu of land ranges from several thousand to several tens of thousands yuan.[40]

The fifth problem is that because the duration of contracts for farm production is too short, peasants are reluctant to spend money to maintain soil fertility. As a result, the production yield has declined,[41] and currently, the duration of contracts for farm production has been extended to fifteen years, with the hope that peasants will pay attention to both the yield and soil fertility.

3. <u>The problem of heavy burden on the peasants:</u> In the past, financial expenditures in the rural areas were defrayed by the collective economy, but since the implementation of the system of contracted production, it is the individual peasant households that have to pay for rural financial expenditures. According to an editorial in the <u>China Peasant News</u> on November 17, 1983,

peasants have to apportion a multitude of financial expenditures, which amount to half the financial burden the peasants must share, to ensure collective reserves and to pay for the rise in the cost of production. In many places, each peasant has to pay an average of 30 to 40 yuan for the collective reserves alone; in other places, the sum is as much as 70 to 80 yuan, as compared with the annual per capita income of 140 yuan for each peasant in 1982.

In Anyueh County, Szechwan Province, for example, the production teams collect from peasant households five items of expenditures in accordance with the contract. These include the agricultural tax and contributions to the public accumulation fund, welfare fund, subsidies for cadres, and administrative outlays. In addition, the peasants there have to share the other seventy items of expenditures imposed on them by other units. As a result, each peasant has to pay an average of 42 yuan annually, and each household, an average of 178 yuan.[42]

In Taoyuan County, Hunan Province, each peasant has to contribute to more than twenty items of expenditure, for an annual total of 35 to 51 yuan. If calcualted on the basis of the land tilled by peasants, each peasant has to pay 20 to 23 yuan for every mu of land contracted to him.[43] In Mienyang County, Hupeh Province, each peasant household has to apportion about 300 yuan annually for the various kinds of expenditures. Besides, each labor force has to take part in fifty days of "voluntary" labor each year.[44]

In Heishan County, Liaoning Province, each peasant in a household that has contracted 14.9 mu of land has to pay 46.8 yuan in agricultural tax and contributions to the public accumulation fund, welfare fund, subsidies for cadres, administrative outlays, allowances for dependence of four kinds of people--i.e., martyrs, military personnel, workers, and cadres--and the fund to promote family planning. In some production teams in this county, each peasant has to pay 70 to 80 yuan.[45] In Ketung County, Heilungkiang Province, the production teams tax peasants 20 yuan for each mu of land they farm as public reserves. As a result, peasants have to pay on an average of 39.2 percent of their gross income to the production teams.[46]

In November 1983, the CCP Central Committee issued a notice to lessen the burden on the peasants. It stipulated that the amount of money paid into collective reserves should not exceed 8 percent of the income earned by peasants in contracted production, and that "voluntary" labor for each peasant every year should not exceed thirty days. Even so, the burden on the peasants is still heavy because peasants have to hand in 50 percent of their produce to the production teams as rent,[47] 4.1 percent as agricultural tax, and 8 percent as a contribution to the collective reserves. These three items alone amount to 62 percent of the peasants' total income. Besides, each peasant has to do "voluntary" labor for thirty days. The burden that the peasants in mainland China have to carry is heavy indeed; by contrast, farmers on Taiwan can keep 62.5 percent of their production for themselves.

Since the mainland peasants can retain only a limited amount of the produce they raise, some of them not skilled at farming or unable to do heavy work tend to choose other jobs instead. As a result, much of the farmland is left untilled. It is said that in 1983, over 40,000 mu of land in Mienyang County, Hupeh Province, was deserted.[48] Because of the heavy financial burden, some specialized and key households also choose other jobs.

4. <u>The social problem created by the poor households</u>: Although peasants in general have enjoyed an increase in their income, the number of poor households has also increased in the rural areas. In Anhwei Province alone, the number of such households increased by 100,000 in 1983.[49] In the Symposium on the Work of Social Relief in Nineteen Provinces, Municipalities, and Autonomous Regions held in Shenchiu County, Honan Province, in November 1983, it was said that the work of supporting the poor had been developed by over 31,000 people's communes in 1,814 counties in mainland China. The number of poor households receiving assistance had reached 3,270,000, and of them, 1,090,000 had been lifted out of poverty.[50] It was also said that there were 2,988,900 people in the households enjoying the

five guarantees (childless and infirm old persons, the deformed, and the orphans who are guaranteed food, clothing, medical care, housing, and burial expenses by the people's commune). Among them, there were 2,647,800 old people, 198,500 deformed, and 142,600 orphans.[51] In the past, the poor households and the households enjoying the five guarantees were supported by the people's communes. After the dismantling of the collective economy and the implementation of the system of contracted production, it is the peasant households that are given the responsibility of supporting the households enjoying the five guarantees. In signing a contract for production, it is a usual practice that several peasant households are asked to support one five-guarantee household, and sometimes, people from the five-guarantee households have to eat in peasant households by turn. As a result, they are like beggars and may not be welcomed by the peasant households, which is made evident by the following stipulations in the "Regulations on the Five-Guarantee Work in the Rural Areas (For Trial Implementation)," which was published in Yunnan Province in December 1982: "We should by no means make the five-guarantee households beg for food and money from other households or to eat by turn in other households. Not any more should we discriminate against or make things difficult for them."[52]

The poor households do not receive good care either. In the "Notice on Handling Well the Work of Helping Poor Households in the Rural Areas," jointly issued by over ten units including the Civil Affairs Ministry in December 1982, it is said that many local cadres are indifferent to the work of helping the poor. It is also said that since the implementation of the system of contracted production, a considerable number of the poor households in the rural areas are composed of martyrs and of the military personnel, workers, and cadres who are assigned to work in other places. As they are unable to help their families in production work, the production output of their households naturally cannot compare with that of other households. This situation makes these people rather depressed. In the symposium on the work of social relief in the rural areas, the

Chinese Communists admitted that about 40 percent of the people's communes throughout mainland China had made no effort to help the poor households and that because the ways adopted to help the poor are not effective, many poor households still cannot ward off poverty.[53]

CONCLUSION

Despite the Chinese Communists' claim that the production responsibility system is in line with the socialist principle of distribution according to work, the practice of individual farming under the current production responsibility system is actually not in accord with the socialist principle. This fact has incurred much criticism from those individuals who hold fast to Communist doctrines.

Although the practice of individual farming has brought some economic benefits, it has also resulted in ideological confusion not only among ordinary people but also among the cadres. Some cadres have criticized the new production system as being a return to the days before the Communist occupation of the Chinese mainland.[54] One cadre of the Peking Chemical Experimentation Plant openly expressed his doubt about the necessity of practicing individual economy,[55] and particularly strong opposition to the new production system comes from the army. How to secure the support of cadres and military personnel for the implementation of the production responsibility system is undoubtedly the most urgent task for Teng Hsiao-p'ing and his followers.

It should be noted that since the implementation of the system of contracted production, official investment in agriculture has declined as compared with the amount invested previously.[56] This decline in agricultural investment will in turn have an adverse effect on agricultural development.

Since the distribution of land originally owned by the people's communes to individual households, the past distribution relationship between the state, the collective, and individuals has been transformed into a new one of tenancy between the state and the peasants. This change in the production relationship notwithstanding, the sociopolitical, ideological, and economic structures have not been similarly changed. The Chinese Communists have continued to uphold the proletarian dictatorship, socialist road, Communist leadership, Marxism-Leninism, and Mao Tse-tung thought, and they have continued to propagate the Marxist-Leninist theory concerning economy. Without structural reform, one can hardly expect any real progress in agricultural development.

Another problem with the current system of contracted farming is the way land has been distributed. Redistribution of land is to be made whenever the number of family members is changed, which happens frequently, and repeated land redistribution gives rise to many complicated problems. Moreover, since the land is still owned by the state, peasants are reluctant to make investments in the land for fear that the current policy adopted at a time when economic development was stagnant may be discontinued when the situation gets better.[57]

For the purpose of agricultural development, mainland China in the past several decades has proceeded from cooperative transformation of agriculture to communization and then back to distribution of land for individual farming and separation of government administrative from commune management. The bankruptcy of the policy of agricultural collectivization is a clear indication that the degree of agricultural collectivization is inversely proportional to agricultural growth. It is really time for the Chinese Communists to learn from Taiwan in agricultural development.

NOTES

1. Tu Jun-sheng, "Strenuously Maintain and Develop the Excellent Situation in Agriculture," Liao wang [Look out] (Beijing), no. 3 (1984), p. 12.
2. "Agricultural Policy Should Be Relaxed and It Should Be Stabilized on the Basis of

Relaxation," *Kwangming Daily*, December 15, 1980, p. 3.

3. "Questions and Answers on the Current Rural Policy," *Nung-ts'un kung-tso t'ung-hsun* [Bulletin on rural work] (August 1982), p. 27.

4. "Persist in the Principle of Seeking Truth from Facts to Develop Our Country's Socialist Agriculture," *Ching-chi yen-chiu* [Economic research] (September 1983), p. 10.

5. "Sidelights on the National Rural Work Conference," *Economic Daily*, December 30, 1983, p. 2.

6. Wan Li, "Speech at the National Rural Work Conference," *People's Daily*, January 18, 1984, p. 1; "Document No. 1 of 1983," *People's Daily*, April 10, 1983, p. 1.

7. Speech by Ts'ao Wen-chü, governor of Hunan, at the Hunan Rural Work Conference, Radio Hunan, February 26, 1984; "Speech on Rural Work," *Economic Daily*, February 7, 1984, p. 2.

8. "Certain Regulations Governing Individual Industry and Commerce in Rural Areas," *China Peasant News*, March 12, 1984, p. 3.

9. "Certain Regulations Governing the Purchase of Motor Vehicles, Vessels, and Tractors by Individual Peasants or Peasant Households for Engaging in Transportation Business," *People's Daily*, March 11, 1984, p. 2.

10. "What Are the Policy Regulations for the Marketing and Transportation of Agricultural By-products by Peasants?" *Pan yueh t'an* [Semimonthly review], no. 18 (1983), p. 40; "Regulations on Some Questions Concerning Cooperative Commercial Organizations and the Marketing and Transportation of Agricultural By-products by Individuals," *China Peasant News*, March 13, 1984, p. 3.

11. "Speech on Rural Work," *Economic Daily*, February 7, 1984, p. 2; "Peasants Settle Down in Cities to Open Shops and Plants Provided They Manage Their Own Food Ration," *People's Daily*, February 16, 1984, p. 3.

12. "Report by Yin Fa-t'ang, first secretary of the CCP Tibet Autonomous Region Committee at the Rural Pastoral Work Conference for the Whole Area," New China News Agency dispatch from Lhasa, February 25, 1984.

13. *Communique of the State Council*, no. 23

(Beijing: Office or the State Council, December 25, 1983), p. 1045.

14. "Questions and Answers on the Separation of Government Administration from Commune Management and Establishment of Township Governments," Pan yueh t'an, no. 21 (1983), p. 12.

15. Ibid.

16. Ibid.

17. "Over 20,000 Townships and 170,000 Villagers' Committees Have Been Established Throughout the Country," Economic Daily, February 15, 1984, p. 1.

18. "Materials on Fixing Output Quotas for Individual Households," Nung-yeh ching-chi ts'ung-k'an [A Collection on agricultural economy], no. 3 (1981), pp. 16-50.

19. "An Exposure of the True Face of Fixing Output Quotas for Indivdual Households," People's Daily, November 2, 1959, p. 4.

20. "It Is Necessary to Make a Correct Analysis of san-tzu i-pao," People's Daily, May 12, 1980, p. 20.

21. Wan Li, "Further Develop the Already Created New Situation in Agriculture," People's Daily, December 23, 1982.

22. "Ten Regulations on Relaxing Restrictions on Rural Economy," CCP Kansu Committee, Radio Kansu, December 19, 1982.

23. "Contract Land for a Long Period of Time and Sign Contracts by Stages," Shansi Daily, October 11, 1983, p. 1; "Taming County Issued Certificates on the Long Period of Contract and Utilization of Land," People's Daily, August 25, 1983, p. 2.

24. "CCP Central Committee Document, 1979, no. 4," in Chung-kung nien-pao 1979 [Yearbook on Chinese communism 1979] (Taipei, Institute for the Study of Chinese Communist Problems, September 1979), pp. viii-76.

25. "New Changes in the Current Distribution Method in the Rural Areas," Kwangming Daily, February 27, 1983, p. 3.

26. "Notice on Transmitting the Report Concerning Active Development of a Diversified Economy in the Rural Areas," issued by the CCP Central Committee and the State Council, People's Daily, April 6, 1984, p. 1.

27. "An Investigation Carried Out by Yuncheng Area on Peasants' Using Tractors for Commercial Activities," Shansi Daily, September 28, 1983, p. 2.
28. CCP Central Committee "Notice on Strengthening Ideological-Political Work in the Rural Areas," Economic Daily, June 9, 1983, p. 4.
29. "Why Are There Bumper Harvests One After the Other in China?" Economic Reporter, November 7, 1983, p. 16.
30. "Sidelights on the National Conference for Agricultural Secretaries," People's Daily, January 4, 1983, p. 3.
31. Wan Li, "Speech at the National Rural Work Conference," p. 2.
32. "Don't Try to Make Money by Taking 'Illegal Shares,'" People's Daily, September 28, 1983, p. 2.
33. "Who Are the People That Become Rich First in the Rural Areas?" People's Daily, January 5, 1984, p. 1.
34. "Let the 800 Million Peasants Be the Master," People's Daily, December 27, 1982, p. 5.
35. "Fragmentation of Contracted Land Is Disadvantageous to Production," People's Daily, November 3, 1983, p. 5.
36. "Linchuan County Solved Problems Concerning the Fragmentation of Contracted Land," People's Daily, January 14, 1982, p. 2.
37. People's Daily, August 1, 1983, p. 2.
38. "It Is Necessary to Reach Unification in Three Aspects in the Readjustment of Responsibility Land," People's Daily, November 3, 1983, p. 5.
39. "My Personal Views on Some Questions Concerning Contracted Land," China Peasant News, October 9, 1983, p. 2.
40. "Wenhsi County Succeeded in Putting a Stop to Three Evil Tendencies," Hopei Daily, September 16, 1983, p. 3; "State Council's Notice on Halting the Sale and Rent of Land," Economic Daily, December 1, 1983, p. 1.
41. See note 38; see also "Soil Fertility Can Be Improved If the System Is Perfect," Shansi Daily, August 29, 1983, p. 1.
42. "Anyueh County Has Taken Measures to Lessen Peasants' Burden," People's Daily, October 16, 1983, p. 2.

43. "It Is Imperative to Lessen Peasants' Burden," *Bulletin on Rural Work*, no. 4 (1983), p. 19.

44. "Large Gap Between Income from Agricultural Production and Side-line Occupations and Excessive Burden on Peasants Damps Peasants' Enthusiasm for Work," *People Daily*, July 11, 1983, p. 1; "An Investigation into the Case That Some Peasants in Mienyang County Do Not Want to Contract Responsibility Land for Production," *People's Daily*, October 16, 1983, p. 2.

45. "Deeds Are More Precious," *China Peasant News*, October 11, 1983, p. 1.

46. "Recheck the Contracts for Production and Put a Stop to Illegal Apportionment," *People's Daily*, October 16, 1983, p. 2.

47. "People Should Be Told How the Collective Retained Portion Is Used," *People's Daily*, March 23, 1983, p. 2.

48. "A Warning Signal," *People's Daily*, July 11, 1983, p. 1.

49. Radio Anhwei, March 21, 1984.

50. New China News Agency dispatch from Chengchow on November 8, 1983, on the symposium.

51. "The Census of Five-Guarantee Households in Rural Areas Has Basically Been Completed," *People's Daily*, January 31, 1984, p. 2.

52. "Introduction to Documents," *Studies on Chinese Communism* 18:1 (April 1, 1984), p. 131.

53. See note 50.

54. "Where Does the Misunderstanding Come From?" *People's Daily*, December 22, 1981, p. 2.

55. "Is It Progress or Retrogression to Enforce Economic Reform?" *Economic Daily*, July 25, 1983, p. 2.

56. A comparison of agricultural investment for the period from 1978 to 1979, when the system of contract production was not yet in force, and the period from 1980 to 1982, when that system was in force, shows that agricultural investment declined by 30.9 percent.

57. "The Principle of Invigorating Rural Economy Will Not Be Changed," *China Peasant News*, November 15, 1983, p. 1.

Part 3
Foreign Policy of the PRC

17
The Evolution of Communist China's Foreign Policy

Ch'ing-yao Yin

I

A Chinese Communist dictionary defines foreign policy as "the policy of a nation in handling its relations with other countries. The foreign policy of a nation cannot be separated from its domestic policy which depends absolutely on the nature of its government; and the nature of a government thus decides the basic direction of its foreign policy."[1] As a government, Communist China has its national interests. F. S. Northedge asserts that in the field of foreign policy, the most important task of a nation's policymakers is to determine its precise interests in external relations and list them in accordance with their relative importance. The order of priority for most nations, Northedge suggests, is self-preservation, independence, and maintenance of influence, prestige, and position in the international arena.[2] Communist China has exactly this order of priority.

However, as a Communist government, Communist China also has international duties. Its analysis and handling of international affairs are bound to be influenced by its Marxist-Leninist ideology or its world outlook because the ultimate objective of its external activities is to transform the world in line with the designs of Marxism-Leninism. In this respect, Communist China is different from democracies.

The Chinese Communists regard foreign policy as an "extension of domestic policy"[3] and affirm that changes in domestic affairs may affect foreign policy. At present, in a world characterized by constant international contacts, Communist China cannot be freed from the influence of the international political environment. Of course, under a Communist totalitarian political system, personal factors in the decision-making process should never be neglected; however, they are of less importance in comparison with the ultimate objectives, strategies, and tactics of communism. Only from this perspective can we understand the continuity of Communist China's foreign policy.

Guided by the ultimate objective of achieving a world revolution, Communist China attaches great importance to its own political power and influence in the international arena. Negatively, it is unwilling to submit to the influence of other countries, and positively, it strives to influence other countries and gain control of the situation so as to create an international environment that is favorable for the execution of its plan. Communist China is not only part of a large international society, it is also a part of the Communist (or socialist) camp, and as such, it strives to ensure its independence; maintain and enhance its influence, prestige, and position; and even compete for leadership in the international Communist movement.

To place appropriate emphasis on ideology, national interest, and the power struggle in foreign policy, the Chinese Communists have to rely on their short-term (tactical) and long-term (strategic) plans. In foreign relations, the Chinese Communists distinguish state-to-state activities from state-to-people activities,[4] asserting that "after the formation of the socialist camp, each socialist country has to handle three kinds of relations in terms of its foreign affairs, i.e., relations with other socialist countries; relations with countries with different social systems; and relations with oppressed peoples and oppressed nations."[5] Thus, they are carrying out a state-to-state, people-to-people, and comrade-to-comrade (Party-to-Party) diplomacy.

On the basis of the above-mentioned concepts this chapter will examine the evolution of

Communist China's foreign policy and its basic foreign policy in the 1980s in particular.

II

The Soviet invasion of Czechoslovakia in August 1968 constituted the watershed of Communist China's foreign policy during the three decades from its establishment in 1949 to the end of the 1970s. Before the invasion, the Chinese Communists mainly pursued an anti-U.S. policy; after it, they gradually developed an anti-Soviet policy. However, each of these two periods may be further divided into several stages.

During the years from October 1949 to Stalin's death in March 1953, the Chinese Communists leaned one-sidedly toward the Soviets, a position that conformed with the ideology and practical interests of Communist China. Wu Hsiu-ch'üan, who accompanied Chou En-lai to the Soviet Union in 1950 to negotiate a treaty of friendship, alliance, and mutual assistance, spoke highly of the treaty in his memoirs. He asserted that the policy of leaning one-sidedly toward the Soviets not only dispelled Stalin's suspicion of the Chinese Communists but also disrupted U.S. policy toward Communist China.[6] At that time, under Stalin's authoritative influence, Communist China had no chance to act independently.

In 1953, the first year of Communist China's First Five-Year Plan, the Soviet Union provided the country with ample aid. By the conclusion of Khrushchev's visit to Peking in September and October 1954, several agreements had been reached: (1) All Soviet troops would be evacuated from Port Arthur (Lüshun) by May 31, 1955, and the installations of this naval base would be transferred to Communist China without compensation; (2) the Soviet Union would hand over to Communist China on January 1, 1955, all its shares in the joint companies, the value of which would be refunded in goods over a number of years; (3) the Soviet Union would grant Communist China a long-term credit of 520 million (old) rubles (about US $130 million); and (4) the Soviet Union would aid Communist China in building 15 new industrial undertakings and would increase deliveries of equipment to 141 enterprises, the total value of which amounted to 400 million (old) rubles. This was the honeymoon period in relations between Communist China and the Soviet Union.

Generally speaking, during the first half of the 1950s, Communist China aimed mainly at promoting its relations with other Communist countries, and its views concerning international affairs were identical with those of the Soviet Union. In November 1949, the Chinese Communists convened a meeting of representatives of Asian and Australian trade unions in Peking. In October 1952, they also hosted a peace meeting in Peking during which representatives from thirty-seven nations decided to set up a Peace Liaison Committee of the Asian and Pacific Regions in Peking. The Soviets attended both meetings. In April 1955, in an address to the Asian-African Conference in Bandung, Indonesia, Chou En-lai, as head of the Chinese Communist delegation, expanded the Five Principles of Peaceful Coexistence that he had advanced in April 1954 (when the Agreement on Trade and Communications Between Tibet and India was signed) into ten principles of peace. The Soviet observers present at this conference proposed no objections.

The dispute between the Chinese and Soviet Communists began with the Twentieth CPSU Congress in February 1956. Mao Tse-tung disagreed with Khrushchev on the de-Stalinization movement as well as on the concepts of peaceful coexistence, peaceful competition, and peaceful transition. The Chinese and Soviet Communists had different viewpoints about ideology and the tactics of revolution. Later, Khrushchev's repudiation of Stalin's policies led to open revolts against the Stalinist system in Eastern Europe, causing great disorder. In early 1957, at Khrushchev's request, Chou En-lai went to Eastern Europe to arrange for a settlement. As a result, Communist China acquired increased prestige while that of the Soviet Union declined. This change nourished Mao's ambition for power.

In November 1957, at the First World Conference of Communist and Workers' Parties in Moscow, Mao disagreed with the Soviet Communists on the question of war and peace, and there was also a debate about the principle of relations among fraternal parties. The Chinese Communists stressed the principles of solidarity and reaching unanimity through consultation on the basis of Marxism-Leninism and proletarian internationalism and maintained that there should be no "superior" or "subordinate" parties.[7] This stand constituted a challenge to the leadership position of the Soviet Communists in the international Communist movement.

Although the opening of the abortive forty-four-day Chinese Communist battle for Kinmen (Quemoy) and Matsu on August 23, 1958, was a sign of belligerency, Khrushchev's visit to the United States and his creation with President Eisenhower of the Camp David spirit in September 1959 constituted the climax of the Soviet peace offensive. In the latter half of the 1950s, the Chinese and Soviet Communists quarreled, and each went their own way. Their subsequent split in the 1960s affected not only Communist China's foreign policy but also the world situation.

III

The Chinese Communists asserted that the contents of the general line of foreign policy for socialist countries should consist of the following: to develop relations of friendship, mutual assistance, and cooperation among the countries of the socialist camp in accordance with the principle of proletarian internationalism; to strive for peaceful coexistence on the basis of the Five Principles with countries having different social systems and oppose imperialist policies of aggression and war; and to support and assist the revolutionary struggles of all the oppressed peoples and nations.[8]

The Chinese Communists contended that solidarity among socialist countries should be based on the principle of equality and that peaceful coexistence can be applied only to the relations between countries with different social systems and should never be extended to apply to the relations between oppressed and oppressor nations, between oppressed and oppressor countries, or between oppressed and oppressor classes.[9] They blamed the Soviet Union for making peaceful coexistence the general line of foreign policy. They constantly adhered to Lenin's tactics and attached great importance to the liberation of nations and the anti-imperialist struggle. They regarded the vast areas of Asia, Africa, and Latin America as the storm centers of world revolution dealing direct blows at imperialism. They contended that U.S. imperialism was the chief bulwark of world reaction, an international gendarme and the enemy of the people of the whole world.[10] These were the basic disagreements between the Chinese and Soviet Communists during the latter half of the 1950s and the 1960s.

On June 20, 1959, the Soviet Union halted assistance to the Chinese Communist effort to develop nuclear weapons by announcing unilaterally the cancellation of the Atomic Cooperation Agreement and the New National Defense Technology Agreement. On July 16, 1960, the Soviets informed the Chinese Communists that all 1,300 Soviet experts working on the Chinese mainland would be withdrawn within a month and that several hundred agreements and contracts would be canceled. The Agreement on Mutual Preferential Treatment Concerning the Distribution of Magazines was also annulled. The ideological difference between Peking and Moscow thus developed into a conflict of national interests.

On October 1, 1960, Communist China celebrated the eleventh anniversary of its establishment. No high-ranking personnel from the socialist camp except Abdyl Kellezi, vice-chairman of the Council of Ministers of Albania, attended the celebration. Most foreign guests came from Asia, Africa, and Latin America. On the Tienanmen rostrum, standing beside Mao, were Prime Minister U Nu of Burma and Abbas Ferhat, leader of the insurgent forces in Algeria. Of all the Chinese Communist regular troops, only the Guard of Honor joined the parade; the half a million people who took part in it consisted mainly of militiamen. This composition showed that the Chinese Communists were determined to oppose the Soviet foreign policy of peaceful coexistence and that they intended to initiate revolutions against imperialism and colonialism in Asia, Africa, and Latin America by launching so-called people's wars.

However, on June 30, 1961, in a speech at a meeting celebrating the fortieth anniversary of the founding of the CCP, Liu Shao-ch'i reiterated that the general line of Communist China's foreign policy was to develop relations of friendship, mutual assistance, and cooperation with the Soviet Union and other fraternal socialist countries; to strive for peaceful coexistence with countries of different social systems on the basis of the Five Principles; to oppose imperialist policies of aggression and war; and to support the revolutionary struggles of all oppressed peoples and nations against imperialism and colonialism. It is noteworthy that Liu always mentioned the Soviet Union first when referring to other fraternal socialist countries.

On July 5, 1963, Teng Hsiao-p'ing led a delegation to Moscow for negotiations to improve the relations between the CCP and the CPSU, but he returned to Peking on July 21 empty-handed. Only four days later, on July 25, a Partial Nuclear Test-Ban Treaty was initialed in Moscow by the Soviet Union, the United States, and Britain. It seemed that the Soviet Union was trying to ease tensions with Western nations in order to concentrate its forces to deal with Communist China. In response to an open letter of the CPSU Central Committee, the Chinese Communists published nine commentaries to carry out an ideological struggle against the Soviets on such questions as domestic construction, the tactics of revolution, and the general line of foreign policy. The commentaries were issued on September 6, 13, 26, 1963; October 22, 1963; November 19, 1963; December 12, 1963; February 4, 1964; March 31, 1964; and July 14, 1964, and they were collected in 1965 in a single volume (in Chinese) entitled <u>Polemics on the General Line of the International Communist Movement</u>. On January 21, 1964--in an article entitled "All the World's Forces Opposing U.S. Imperialism, Unite!"--the <u>People's Daily</u> advanced the theory of intermediate zones as the theoretical basis for organizing an international united front. From the end of 1963 to early 1964, Chou En-lai led a large delegation on visits to thirteen nations in Asia and Africa in preparation for the convocation of the Second Asian-African Conference "without white participants," which was an attempt to expel both U.S. and Soviet influence from Asia and Africa. On March 31, 1964, the Chinese Communists issued the eighth commentary on the open letter of the CPSU Central Committee entitled "The Proletarian Revolution and Khrushchev's Revisionism." In it, they openly accused the Soviet Communists of becoming revisionist for the first time. The conflict between the two Communist parties was thus further aggravated.

The spearhead of the theory of intermediate zones was directed mainly against U.S. imperialism. According to this theory, the first intermediate zone--consisting of Asia, Africa, and Latin America--would be the mainstay in the struggle against U.S. imperialism. The second intermediate zone--consisting of the whole of Western Europe, Oceania, and Canada (later Japan was also included)--could be united with to form an anti-U.S. international united front. The Soviet Union, whose leaders were hankering for U.S.-Soviet cooperation to dominate the world, was excluded from this united front.

Except for the establishment of formal diplomatic relations with France in January 1964, the Chinese Communists had no other achievements in the second intermediate zone. They stepped up their activities mainly in the first intermediate zone. In the early 1950s, Communist China's external activities focused mainly on the Asian and Pacific regions. Relations with Africa began with the establishment of diplomatic relations with Egypt in May 1956, but no high-ranking Chinese Communist leaders had ever set foot on African soil before Chou En-lai's visit to Cairo in December 1963. After that, Communist China made strenuous efforts to promote its relations with African nations and intended to further expand its influence to Latin America.

On November 4, 1964, twenty days after Khrushchev's downfall (October 15), Chou En-lai, as the head of a delegation from Peking, arrived in Moscow to take part in the celebration of the forty-seventh anniversary of the Russian October Revolution. He was refused when he approached the new Soviet leaders with a suggestion to improve relations between the two parties.[11] Beginning in 1965, Chinese Communist activities in Asia and Africa went downhill gradually, and on September 30, a coup supported by the Chinese Communists in Indonesia ended in failure. Later, the suspension of the Second Asian-African Conference was announced.

The failure of the Great Leap Forward in the 1950s led to Mao's withdrawal from the front-line position, and frustrations concerning foreign relations in the mid-1960s made Mao worry about the instability of his own leadership. He thus planned to organize a "small Central Committee" in Shanghai to launch counterattacks against the "big Central Committee" in Peking. At his instigation, Yao Wen-yuan published, on November 10, 1965, an article in the Wen hui pao (Shanghai) entitled "On the New Historical Drama: Hai Jui Dismissed From Office" to initiate the Cultural Revolution. The purpose of this revolution was to "implant Mao Tse-tung thought still more firmly among the people all over the country and completely dig out the roots of revisionism and of the restoration of capitalism."[12]

On November 11, the editorial departments of the People's Daily and Red Flag jointly published an article entitled "Refutation of the New Leaders of the CPSU on 'United Action,'" in which the Chinese Communists drew a clear demarcation between themselves and the Soviet Communists. They asserted that "on all the fundamental issues of the present epoch the relations [between the Chinese and Soviet Communists] are one of sharp opposition; there are things that divide us and nothing that unites us, things that are antagonistic and nothing in common," and added, "The characteristic of the present world situation is that with the daily deepening of the international class struggle, a process of great upheaval, great division and great reorganization is taking place." With the beginning of the Great Proletarian Cultural Revolution in 1966, Communist China's domestic and foreign policies both entered an era of violence.

The Cultural Revolution was aimed at opposing and preventing revisionism. Its main slogan was: Rebel and seize power. During this period, the Chinese Communists adopted a policy of so-called rebel diplomacy in their foreign relations and pursued a "splittist" line in the international Communist movement and within the socialist camp by supporting opposition factions or organizing new Marxist-Leninist parties. In non-Communist countries, they supported all forces (including individuals, groups, and political factions) that opposed the government to carry out "the people's line." In Asia, Africa, and Latin America and particularly in Southeast and South Asia and the Middle East, they armed Communist guerrillas and incited them to insurgency. They distributed Mao's quotations and photograph and even emblems with Mao's portrait everywhere and made great efforts to promote revolution.

Up to the mid-1960s, the Chinese Communists under Mao's leadership paid a great deal of attention to ideology, the tactics of revolution, and the power struggle in both domestic and foreign policies. However, they never admitted that they were trying to seize the leadership of the international Communist movement. In their seventh commentary on the open letter of the CPSU entitled "The Leaders of the CPSU Are the Greatest Splitters of Our Times," the Chinese Communists refuted the Soviet charge that they were attempting to seize the leadership.[13] They asserted: "Marx and Engels declared that the trade union movement in Britain and the political struggle of the French working class were successively in the van of the international proletarian movement. After the defeat of the Paris Commune, Engels said that 'the German workers have for the moment been placed in the vanguard of the proletarian struggle.'" They continued to quote Lenin's 1919 statement that "hegemony in the revolutionary proletarian international has passed for the time being--but not for long, it goes without saying-- to the Russians." They finally concluded: "When a Party which formerly held the position of vanguard takes the path of revisionism, it is bound to forfeit this position despite the fact that it has been the largest Party and has exerted the greatest influence." Obviously, they considered that the Soviet Union had already forfeited the vanguard position in the international Communist movement.

In the article "Refutation of the New Leaders of the CPSU on 'United Action,'" published on November 11, 1965, the Chinese Communists wrote:

> The founders of Communist theory, Marx and Engels, advanced the fighting slogan, "Workers of all countries, unite!" . . . The international unity of the proletariat advocated by Marx and Engels is one of struggle to fulfill its great historical mission on a worldwide scale.
>
> In the historical conditions of rising struggle by the oppressed nations against imperialism, Lenin put forward the fighting slogan, "Workers and oppressed nations of the world, unite!" This slogan stimulated united struggle by the working-class movement of the countries in the West and the national-liberation movement of the oppressed nations in the East. It represented a still broader unity of the international revolutionary forces.
>
> In the light of the new changes in international class relations and the balance of forces after World War II, Comrade Mao Tse-tung advanced the slogan of establishing an international united front against U.S. imperialism. This united front has the unity of the international proletariat as its core and the unity between the international proletariat and the oppressed nations as its foundation. . . . It is a strategic principle of vital importance formulated by Comrade Mao Tse-tung on the question of world revolution in the new historical conditions.[14]

In so saying, the Chinese Communists juxtaposed Mao with Marx and Lenin.

During the catastrophic decade-long Cultural Revolution, the Chinese Communists described Mao Tse-tung thought as the "acme of Marxism-Leninism at the present time."[15] They also asserted, "The world today has entered a new revolutionary era with Mao Tse-tung thought as its great banner."[16] Following this declaration, it was impossible for them to cover up their intention to seize the leadership of the international Communist movement.

The Chinese Communists did not send any delegates to attend the Twenty-third CPSU Congress held in March 1966, and they stopped inviting other Communist parties to take part in their own congresses. The relations between the CCP and the CPSU were broken off. In December of the same year, the Chinese Communists began calling their ambassadors and high-ranking diplomats in foreign countries back to the mainland to take part in the Cultural Revolution. Only Huang Hua continued to stay in Cairo, and Communist China became quite isolated in the international arena. In August 1967, all of its embassies in foreign countries were ordered to stop exporting the Cultural Revolution, but the greatest change in its foreign policy was caused by the invasion of Czechoslovakia by the Soviet Union and five nations of the Warsaw Pact on August 21, 1968. Realizing that military invasion could happen between Communist fraternal countries, the Chinese Communists were afraid that the same thing might occur on the Chinese mainland. Therefore, in foreign policy, they began to stress national security.

Although the Cultural Revolution stressed that to oppose imperialism, it is imperative to oppose modern revisionism, the communiqué issued by the Eleventh Plenary Session of the Eighth CCP Central Committee on August 12, 1966, emphasized only the need to establish the broadest possible international united front against U.S. imperialism. However, the Soviet Union was not included in this united front because the Soviet revisionist leaders were pursuing a policy of Soviet-U.S. collaboration for world domination.

After the Czechoslovakian invasion, the Chinese Communists had the following reactions. First, on August 23, 1968, in a commentary entitled "Total Bankruptcy of Soviet Modern Revisionism," the People's Daily blamed the Soviet leaders for degenerating into a gang of social imperialists. Second, on September 17, in a joint message to Enver Hoxha, first secretary of the Albanian Party of Labor, and Mehmet Shehu, chairman of the Council of Ministers of Albania, Mao Tse-tung, Lin Piao, and Chou En-lai expressed firm support of Albania's decision to withdraw from the Warsaw Treaty and announced that a new historic stage of opposing U.S. imperialism and Soviet revisionism had begun. This statement indicated that the Chinese Communists would revise their strategy and tactics in foreign relations. Third, on October 1, the Chinese Communist embassy in Czechoslovakia invited to a celebration Yugoslav officials whom they had previously denounced as the first to pursue modern revisionism.

Fourth, the Eighth CCP Central Committee held its Twelfth Plenary Session from October 13 through October 31. The communiqué issued on November 1 declared that "China's Khrushchev," Liu Shao-ch'i, was expelled from the Party once and for all. The communiqué also denounced the United States and the Soviet Union for allegedly colluding with and supporting each other and urged that all peoples oppressed by U.S. imperialism, Soviet revisionism, and their lackeys should form a broad united front, i.e., an anti-U.S. and anti-Soviet united front. Fifth, on November 26, the spokesman for the Information Department of Communist China's Ministry of Foreign Affairs announced that Communist China had suggested to the United States that the Warsaw talks between the two countries be resumed on February 20, 1969, and that Communist China had consistently urged the United States to sign an agreement on the Five Principles of Peaceful Coexistence.[17] Judging by all these reactions, because of the need to cope with the Soviet Union, the Chinese Communists chose to place their national interest above ideology.

Armed clashes took place on Damansky (Chenpao) Island between Communist China and the Soviet Union in March 1969, and on October 20, the two sides held negotiations in Peking on the boundary question at the level of vice-minister of foreign affairs. Before entering into negotiation, the Chinese Communists reiterated on October 8 their position since the border talks in February 1964. They asserted:

(1) The struggle of principle will continue for a long time but this will not obstruct the normalization of relations between the two countries on the basis of the Five Principles of peaceful coexistence. (2) On condition that the Soviet Union admits that all treaties signed between China and Czarist Russia are unequal ones, the Chinese side is willing to take them as a basis for determining the entire alignment of the boundary in a reasonable way. (3) The Chinese side will not lay claim to the 150,000 square kilometers of Chinese territory ceded to Czarist Russia according to these treaties, but the Chinese territory that the Soviets are occupying in violation of these treaties (referring to a disputed area of 33,500 square kilometers) must be returned in principle but may be subject to necessary readjustments. (4) Before a final solution is reached, the <u>status quo</u> of the border should be maintained. To avoid armed clashes, the armed forces of both sides should withdraw from or refrain from entering into all disputed areas.[18]

The Chinese Communists' intention to persevere in the struggle concerning ideology and the tactics of revolution and to apply the Five Principles of Peaceful Coexistence in their relations with the Soviet Union show that they no longer regarded the Soviet Union as a socialist country.

While negotiating with the Soviet Union on the boundary question, the Chinese Communists resumed the Warsaw talks with the United States in January 1970, and in April 1971, they introduced the so-called ping-pong diplomacy that finally led to Nixon's visit to the Chinese mainland in February 1972. The people-to-people contacts between Communist China and the United States were thus elevated to the state-to-state level. In this period, when the Chinese Communists were implementing the policy of carrying on both negotiation and struggle with the Soviet Union and United States, they declared that they themselves would never seek to become a superpower, and they advocated an international struggle against the superpowers.

V

At a meeting with the visiting Zambian President Kenneth D. Kaunda in February 1974, Mao Tse-tung said that the United States and the Soviet Union constituted the First World; the intermediate forces such as Japan, Europe, and Canada belonged to the Second World; and both Zambia and China belonged to the Third World (consisting of Asia, Africa, and Latin America). This statement was an expansion and a development of the theory of intermediate zones proposed during the 1960s.

On April 10, at the Sixth Special Session of the UN General Assembly on the problems of raw materials and development, Teng Hsiao-p'ing openly expounded Communist China's theory of three worlds, which was originally a strategic deployment planned for the establishment of an international antihegemony united front. According to this theory, the developing countries of the Third World are the mainstay in the struggle against hegemonism, the countries of the Second World are forces that can be united within the antihegemony united front; and the First World countries are to be isolated and overthrown. Teng asserted that the Soviet Union posed more danger to the world than the United States did, in other words, the greatest enemy of the world was the Soviet Union. He even claimed that the socialist camp no longer exists. As a result, the Soviet Union and other Communist parties, including even Albania's, criticized the theory of three worlds for abandoning the proletarian position.

The theory of three worlds evolved from Mao's statement that "the world today is divided into two families and three parts." Mao believed that "revolution is the main trend of the world today,"[19] so in this revolutionary world, there are only two families: the exploiting class and the proletariat.[20] But as far as the united front work is concerned, the world may be subdivided into three worlds to facilitate the implementation of the policy of uniting with the majority to deal blows at the minority. To establish an international united front, the governments of Third World countries may be won over to be the mainstay of the antihegemony struggle. However, the Chinese Communists will continue to support Communist parties of various countries in a revolution to overthrow their respective reactionary ruling classes. In other words, the Chinese Communists distinguish between state-to-state relations and Party-to-Party relations. Even after the establishment of formal diplomatic relations, they will not stop supporting the Communist parties or the leftist forces in other countries.

On Mao's death in September 1976, the Soviet Union tried to seize the opportunity to improve relations with Communist China, but the Chinese Communists refused to accept the condolences sent by the CPSU. On November 2, in an interview with a French journalist, Li Hsien-nien suggested that the Soviet Union should restore Stalinism. On November 6, T'an Chen-lin told a Philippine journalist that it would take at least a thousand or even ten thousand years to eliminate the ideological struggle between the CCP and the CPSU.[21] In the Constitution adopted on August 18, 1977, by the Eleventh Party Congress, the CCP also asserted that it would unite firmly with the genuine Marxist-Leninist parties and organizations the world over, unite with the proletariat and the oppressed people and nations of the whole world, and fight shoulder to shoulder with them to oppose the hegemonism of the two superpowers, the Soviet Union and the United States. It is noteworthy that the Soviet Union was named first.

Following the April 1978 coup in Afghanistan, the pro-Soviet Nur M. Taraki came to power. In June of the same year, Vietnam, whose relations with Communist China were deteriorating, became a member of the Council for Mutual Economic Assistance (COMECON) of the Soviet camp. For fear of being encircled, Communist China signed a treaty of peace and friendship with Japan on August 12, and in the same month, Hua Kuo-feng paid visits to Romania, Yugoslavia, and Iran. A few months later, on December 16, Communist China issued a joint communiqué with the United States saying that the two sides would establish diplomatic relations on January 1, 1979. Obviously, Communist China assumed a low posture to seek the friendship of the United States and Japan and other countries in order to internationalize the struggle against the Soviet Union. Robert O'Neill, head of the Strategic and Defence Studies Centre of London, asserted in 1983 that the Chinese Communist warning about the inevitability of war with the Soviet Union had actually disappeared since 1978 because the Chinese Communists thought that they were no longer directly menaced by the Soviet Union.[22] The disappearance of direct Soviet menace is, of course, closely related to Communist China's efforts in promoting its external relations.

At the Third Plenary Session of the Eleventh CCP Central Committee held from December 18 to 22, 1978, the "pragmatists" prevailed over the "whateverists" and firmly established the Teng Hsiao-p'ing line. The Chinese Communists decided to shift the focus of the work of their Party to socialist modernization. Naturally this decision affected Communist China's foreign policy.

In February 1979, Communist China sent troops to attack Vietnam and in April, informed the Soviet Union of its decision not to further extend the treaty of friendship, alliance, and mutual assistance. These actions caused tension between the two Communist governments, but in the same year, Communist China adopted a different approach toward the domestic and foreign affairs of the Soviet Union. It recognized the Soviet Union as a socialist country but continued to accuse the Soviets of pursuing hegemonism. In November, Fox Butterfield, a correspondent for the New York Times, reported that a Chinese Communist document for internal circulation had showed this trend.[23] In December, the Soviet troops invaded Afghanistan. Later, the Japanese obtained a classified Chinese Communist document written at the end of 1979 and circulated within the Party in early 1980; it asserted that Vietnam would become a burden to the Soviet Union by making Moscow share its difficulties and that the main forces of the Soviet Union were directed against the United States, not against Communist China.[24] In such an international situation, Communist China's foreign policy had a new orientation.

VI

The Soviet intervention in Afghanistan caused great tension in East-West relations. On January 4, 1980, the United States announced the adoption of sanctions against the Soviet Union and the relaxation of restrictions on the purchase by Communist China of certain technology for both commercial and military use as well as certain items for military use. From January 5 to 13, the U.S. defense secretary, Harold Brown, visited Peking. All of these events conformed to the interest of Communist China. On January 16, in a speech to a CCPCC cadre conference, Teng Hsiao-p'ing asserted that the three main tasks of the Party in the 1980s would be opposing hegemonism, reunification of the motherland, and socialist modernization. On January 19, Communist China unilaterally announced the postponement of the normalization negotiations with the Soviet Union at the vice-ministerial level (which had begun in September of the previous year) and that the talks would not be resumed before the withdrawal of Soviet troops from Afghanistan. On March 11, at a meeting with officials of the Japanese Defense Agency in Peking, Su Yü, Communist China's vice-minister of national defense, requested that Japan raise its defense expenditure to more than 0.9 percent of its gross national product.[25] On April 29, at a meeting with Yashuhiro Nakasone, secretary-general of the Japanese Liberal-Democratic Party, Wu Hsiu-ch'üan, Communist China's deputy chief of PLA general staff, stated that the withdrawal of U.S. troops from Japan was against the interest of Asia, that the Japan-U.S. mutual security treaty was conducive to peace and stability in East Asia, and that he supported a Japan-U.S. military alliance.[26] Later, he also requested that Japan raise its defense budget to 2 percent of its gross national product.²⁷

However, on February 23, 1980, the Chinese Communists placed wreaths before the monuments erected in various provinces in honor of Soviet officers and men killed in action, something that had not been done for a long time. On March 20, Mikhail Kapitsa, chief of the First Far East Section of the Soviet Foreign Ministry and deputy head of the Soviet delegation to the normalization talks, arrived in Communist China to solve some internal problems of the Soviet embassy in Peking. During his stay in that city, he held half-hour talks with Yü Hung-liang, chief of the Soviet and East European Affairs Department of the Chinese Communist Foreign Ministry. According to a dispatch from the Agence France Presse on April 9 (just one day before the lapse of the treaty of friendship, alliance, and mutual assistance between Communist China and the Soviet Union), the Peking municipal government had already renamed Anti-Revisionist Road, where the Soviet embassy was situated, Peichung Road of Tungchih Gate.²⁸

In early 1981, L. M. Gudoshnikov of the Institute of the Far East of the Soviet Academy of Sciences told a reporter from the Japanese Kyodo News Service that the term "Soviet revisionism" had already disappeared in Communist China and that it was no longer mentioned even on official occasions.²⁹ This was a big change signifying the removal of the ideological contradictions between the two countries.

According to an article about Peking-Moscow-Washington relations in the 1980s written by Wang Pao-ch'in and two others of the Institute of International Relations of the Chinese Communist Academy of Social Sciences--in <u>Shih-chieh ching-chi yü cheng-chih</u> [World economics and politics], a magazine for private circulation published by the Institute of World Economics and Politics--when the antagonism between the Soviet Union and the United States deepened after the Cancún Summit on October 22 and 23, 1981, Communist China seized the opportunity to readjust its foreign policy to ensure independence in external relations, to maintain a certain distance from the United States,

and to improve relations with the Soviet Union.
The Chinese Communists thought that they had
better adopt an independent and a flexible policy
between the Soviet Union and the United States.[30]

In the second half of 1978, Communist China
had shifted the focus of its diplomatic activities
to the United States, Japan, and Western Europe,
but its diplomatic thrust in the 1980s is directed
toward the Third World. At the election of the
UN secretary-general in December 1981, Communist
China supported Tanzania's Foreign Minister Salim
A. Salim and blackballed Kurt Waldheim's reelection by casting more than ten vetoes. Finally,
neither candidate was elected, and Communist
China's wish was not realized, but a senior African
diplomat indicated that Communist China's vetoes
were of great importance to the Third World. The
Chinese Communist behavior in the United Nations
proved that Communist China was trying to keep
its promise to the Third World and dared to
challenge the United States.[31]

At that time, Communist China's relations
with the United States were somewhat strained,
and the Chinese Communists often threatened to
downgrade them. On March 24, 1982, in a speech
in Tashkent, Brezhnev offered to improve relations
with Communist China, suggesting the following main
points. First, although the Soviet Union criticized
many aspects of Communist China's foreign policy as
being at variance with socialist principles and
standards, it had never denied the existence of a
socialist system in Communist China. Second, the
Soviet Union did not support the concept of "two
Chinas" and fully recognized Communist China's
sovereignty over Taiwan. Third, the Soviet Union
had no territorial claim on Communist China and
was ready to discuss the question of possible
measures to strengthen mutual trust in the border
areas. Fourth, the Soviet Union had never
considered that the state of hostility and
estrangement between the two sides was normal and
was prepared to come to terms, without any preliminary conditions, on measures acceptable to
both sides--but certainly not to the detriment
of third countries. Fifth, the Soviet Union
suggested that as preparation for the normalization of relations, concrete measures should be

adopted in the fields of economics, science, culture, and politics.³² The Chinese Communist response to this proposal was quite moderate.

At the Twelfth CCP National Congress in September 1982, the Chinese Communists formulated an independent foreign policy, and the major points of this policy were revealed in a report by Hu Yao-pang. First, Communist China's foreign policy is based on the scientific theories of Marxism-Leninism and Mao Tse-tung thought, and it proceeds from the fundamental interests of the people of Communist China and the rest of the world. It follows an overall long-term strategy and is definitely unswayed by expediency or by anybody's instigation or provocation. Second, Communist China never attaches itself to any big power or group of powers and never yields to pressure from any big power. Third, the Five Principles of Peaceful Coexistence are applicable to Communist China's relations with all countries, including socialist countries. Fourth, although some forces in Japan wish to revive Japanese militarism, Communist China will work to make the friendship between the two peoples flourish from generation to generation. Fifth, Communist China wishes to further improve relations with the United States but regards the existence of the Taiwan Relations Act as a barrier.

Sixth, the Soviet Union has pursued a hegemonist policy, and there are three obstacles to the improvement of relations between Communist China and the Soviet Union; namely, the stationing of a large number of Soviet troops along the Sino-Soviet and Sino-Mongolian borders, Soviet support of Vietnam during the latter's invasion of Cambodia, and the Soviet invasion of Afghanistan. If the Soviet Union takes practical steps to lift its threat to Communist China's security, normalization of relations between the two sides will be possible. Seventh, Communist China belongs to the Third World and regards the waging of a resolute struggle against imperialism, hegemonism, and colonialism together with the other Third World countries as its sacred international duty. Eighth, the CCP develops its relations with other Communist or working-class parties in strict conformity with Marxism and the principles of independence, complete equality, mutual respect, and noninterference in each other's internal affairs.[33]

In his opening speech to the Twelfth CCP National Congress, Teng Hsiao-p'ing modified the order of the three major tasks of the Chinese Communists in the 1980s into socialist modernization, reunification of the motherland, and combating hegemonism. This change indicated another strategic readjustment in Communist China's foreign policy.

VII

Ideology, national interest, and the power struggle (including the competition for influence, prestige, and position in the world and among Communist parties) are three essential factors that the Chinese Communists will never abandon in their foreign policy, but they may always shift the focus of emphasis from one factor to another to meet the needs of their domestic policy and to cope with the changes in the international situation.

The Chinese Communists continue to criticize the United States. However, in the latter half of May 1983, the United States relaxed the restrictions on the transfer of technology to Communist China by moving it from Country Group P to Country Group V among more than ten country groups identified by U.S. export regulations; on November 17, the U.S. State Department and Department of Commerce announced new guidelines for technology transfer to Communist China; and in March 1984, a Chinese Communist military delegation arrived in the United States to conduct negotiations on the purchase of weapons. All of these events are beneficial to Communist China. At present, instead of asking Japan to increase its defense expenditure, the Chinese Communists urge that country to limit its military strength to the level of defense needs.[34] They sometimes even criticize it for reviving militarism, but they will not stop wooing it for they need loans in yen, credits from the Japan Import-Export Bank, and investment by as well as the economic and technological cooperation of Japanese private companies. The economic and technological aid from the United States and Japan may increase Communist China's national strength and strengthen its position in implementing an independent foreign policy as well as in negotiating with the Soviet Union.

Without waiting for the withdrawal of Soviet troops from Afghanistan, the Chinese Communists have resumed vice-ministerial contacts with the Soviet Union, referring to them as "consultations" instead of "talks." At present, official contacts between the two sides have already been upgraded to the level of vice-premier. Exchanges in the field of tourism, sports, and culture, which had been interrupted for many years, have already been resumed, and bilateral trade is on the increase. Also, the Soviet Union may possibly help Communist China repair four old factories built in the 1950s.[35] All of this change is also to the advantage of Communist China.

Fearing that closer relations with the United States might hamper the improvement of relations with the Soviet Union, the Chinese Communists use "the Taiwan problem" to control the speed of the development of its relations with the United States. At the same time, they are afraid that improving relations with the Soviet Union might affect economic and technological aid from the United States and Japan; hence, they use "the three big obstacles" as a brake in developing relations with the Soviet Union. L. P. Deliusin, director of the Chinese Office of the Institute of the Far East of the Soviet Academy of Sciences, said, "The so-called 'three big obstacles' the Chinese Communists have publicized are only false prices given by businessmen"[36]--certainly a true statement.

Referring to Party-to-Party relations, Hu Yao-pang stressed only Marxism without mentioning Leninism in order to enhance the Chinese Communist attempt to improve relations with the anti-Leninist Euro-Communists. In fact, the Chinese Communists have improved their relations with many Communist parties, except the one in Vietnam, but they have not yet reestablished relations with the CPSU.[37] On this point,

Deliusin stated: "I think the state-to-state relations have already been normal. As we are both socialist countries, it is logical to say that the party-to-party contacts will be reestablished in the next phase."[38] He also emphasized, "Many ideological problems that caused serious controversies have actually disappeared." He was probably too optimistic, but it is undeniable that without ideological conflicts, it would be easier for the two parties to improve relations. If the CCP can really obtain the independence and complete equality that Hu Yao-pang mentioned in his report, relations between the two parties will be resumed.

Ideological conflicts have disappeared only between the CCP and the CPSU, not between Communist China and the free world. Just as Hu Yao-pang stressed in his report to the Twelfth CCP National Congress, Marxism-Leninism and Mao Tse-tung thought are the theoretical bases of Communist China's foreign policy as well as the bases of its strategy. Actually, the Chinese Communists still regard the burial of the free world as their ultimate aim; their current cooperation with the free world is only a tactical expedient.

In foreign policy, the Chinese Communists will continue to reduce the threat along their northern border by stabilizing their relations with the Soviet Union, and they will develop closer relations with Western nations to obtain economic and technological aid so as to strengthen their independent position, increase their influence in the world arena, and gradually achieve their ultimate aim of transforming the whole world. At the same time, they will try to improve their relations with all Communist parties to consolidate their position and increase their influence in the international Communist movement. They will also step up diplomatic offensives in the Third World since, in their plan for launching a world revolution, the national and democratic revolution of the Third World is considered an "important component part of the proletarian revolution at the present time."[39] Hu Yao-pang maintained that the common tasks of Third World countries are to safeguard national independence and sovereignty, take active measures to develop the national economy, and promote South-South cooperation. Wu Hsueh-ch'ien, Communist China's foreign minister, has blamed developed Western nations for making Third World countries the biggest victims of the economic crisis by transferring the crisis to them. He emphasized that the Third World countries strongly demand the establishment of a new international economic order, the promotion of the North-South dialogue, and improvement in North-South relations.[40] All of these diplomatic activities are in accord with the ultimate objective of Marxism-Leninism.

NOTES

1. <u>Hsin-ming-tz'u tz'u-tien</u> [A Dictionary of new terminology] (Shanghai: Ch'un-ming Publishing House, 1953), p. 77.
2. F. S. Northedge, "The Nature of Foreign Policy," in F. S. Northedge, ed., <u>The Foreign Policy of the Powers</u> (New York: Frederick A. Praeger, 1968), pp. 16-18.
3. <u>Hsin-ming-tz'u tz'u-tien</u>.
4. Writing Group of the CCP Hupeh Provincial Committee, "A Powerful Weapon for Uniting the People and Defeating Enemies--The Study of 'On policy,'" <u>Red Flag</u>, no. 9 (August 2, 1971), pp. 10-17.
5. "Two Diametrically Opposing Policies on Peaceful Coexistence--Sixth Comment on the Open Letter of the CPSU Central Committee," in <u>Kuan-yü kuo-chi kung-ch'an chu-i yun-tung tsung-lu-hsien te lun-chan</u> [Polemics on the general line of the international Communist movement], vol. 1 (Beijing: People's Publishing House, 1965), p. 303.
6. Wu Hsiu-ch'üan, "My Eight-Year-Long Experience in the Foreign Ministry," <u>Wen wei po</u> [Literary news] (Hong Kong), August 23 and 24, 1983, p. 3.
7. "A Proposal Concerning the General Line of the International Communist Movement--The Letter of the CCP Central Committee in Reply to the Letter of the CPSU Central Committee of March 30, 1963," in <u>Kuan-yü kuo-chi kung-ch'an</u>

chu-i yun-tung tsung-lu-hsien te lun-chan, pp. 44-45.

8. "Two Diametrically Opposing Policies on Peaceful Coexistence," in ibid., pp. 303-304.

9. "A Proposal Concerning the General Line of the International Communist Movement," in ibid., pp. 33-34.

10. Ibid., p. 13.

11. At that time, Brezhnev told Chou En-lai to his face that there was not a shade of difference between themselves (Brezhnev and other Soviet leaders) and Khrushchev on the question of the international Communist movement or of relations with Communist China (see editorial by the People's Daily and Red Flag, "Refutation of the New Leaders of the CPSU on 'United Action,'" in Red Flag, no. 12 [November 11, 1965], p. 4).

12. Editorial, "Long Live the Great Proletarian Cultural Revolution," Red Flag, no. 8 (June 8,1966), p. 11.

13. "The Leaders of the CPSU Are the Greatest Splitters of Our Times," in Kuan-yü kuo-chi kung-ch'an chu-i yun-tung tsung-lu-hsien te lun-chan, pp. 357-358.

14. "Refutation of the New Leaders of the CPSU," pp. 1-2.

15. Red Flag, no. 8 (June 8,1966), p. 11.

16. Commentary, "A Foul Performance in Budapest," People's Daily, March 18, 1968, p. 1.

17. People's Daily, November 27, 1968, p. 5.

18. Based on Red Flag, no. 11 (October 29, 1969), pp. 16-17.

19. Mao Tse-tung's statement issued on May 20, 1970, on the invasion of Cambodia by U.S. troops entitled "People of the World, Unite and Defeat the U.S. Aggressors and All Their Running Dogs!" People's Daily, May 21, 1970, p. 1.

20. "Ch'iao Kuan-hua's Address on the 'Current Situation of the World' and Peking's 'Foreign Policy' (May 20, 1975)," in Classified Chinese Communist Documents: A Selection (Taipei: Institute of International Relations, 1978), p. 546.

21. T'an seemed to repeat Mao's statement to Edgar Snow that ideological polemics would have to be carried on for ten thousand years if necessary (see Edgar Snow, The Long Revolution

[New York: Random House, 1972], p. 175).
22. Yomiuri shimbun, May 7, 1983, p. 2.
23. New York Times, November 10, 1979, p. 3.
24. Asahi shimbun, January 29, 1980, p. 7.
25. Sankei shimbun, March 14, 1980, p. 1.
26. Ta kung pao (Hong Kong), April 30, 1980, p. 1.
27. Asahi shimbun, May 16, 1980, p. 2.
28. Ta kung pao (Hong Kong), April 11, 1980.
29. Asahi shimbun, February 15, 1981, p. 7.
30. Yomiuri shimbun, December 17, 1983, p. 5.
31. Victoria Graham, "Peking Veto Helps Allay Third World Suspicions," South China Morning Post, December 10, 1981, p. 8.
32. Radio Moscow Mandarin Broadcast, March 25, 1982.
33. "Hu Yao-pang's Report to the 12th CCP National Congress--Create a New Situation in All Fields of Socialist Modernization," Beijing Review, no. 37 (September 13, 1982), pp. 29-33.
34. Reuters (Beijing) February 19, 1983; Lien-ho pao [United daily] (Taipei), February 21, 1983, p. 1.
35. The issue was discussed during the third round of consultations beginning on October 6, 1983.
36. Wen wei po (Hong Kong), October 18, 1983, p. 2.
37. Hu Yao-pang did not send condolences to the CPSU on the death of Yuri Andropov.
38. Wen wei po (Hong Kong), October 18, 1983, p. 2.
39. "A Proposal Concerning the General Line of the International Communist Movement," in Kuan-yü kuo-chi kung-ch'an chu-i yun-tung tsung-lu-hsien te lun-chan, p. 14.
40. Wen wei po (Hong Kong), December 8, 1983, p. 2.

18
Peking, Moscow, and the Indian Subcontinent: Cards, Triangles, and Possible Rapprochement

Richard J. Kozicki

In 1952, Franz Borkenau, an astute observer of the two Communist giants, the Soviet Union and China, said that a "profound conflict" between them was "in the long run as certain as anything predictable in politics," emphasizing that the Soviet totalitarian regime could not have a genuine ally and that this fact was incompatible with the Communist Chinese "quest for national independence." He went on to write that "India is obviously a natural object of both Russian and Chinese expansion. . . [and] that . . . India is bound in the long run to be an apple of discord between the two powers," although a "workable division of zones of influence" then existed between Peking and Moscow in Asia.[1] There are apples and there are apples, just as there are zones of influence and zones of contention, penetration, and armed conflict.

The purpose of this chapter is to discuss the varied relationships and competition of Peking and Moscow in the Indian subcontinent, particularly in regard to India and Pakistan, and how the Sino-Soviet conflict has apparently affected their respective perceptions, policies, and actions. Special reference is made to India, the predominant power in South Asia since 1971, and to recent Sino-Indian normalization efforts.

The setting for this brief study is clearly large. In terms of population, it involves the three most populous countries, China, India, and the Soviet Union, or about half of all humankind. The geographical dimensions are, of course, equally vast. In its central location, China shares a border of 4,500 miles with the Soviet Union. The contiguous Sino-Indian border is some 1,700 miles in length and separate from the intermediate Himalayan states of Nepal and Bhutan, both of which may be viewed as buffers or extensions of the Sino-Indian border. Borders commonly involve conflicts, and the lengthy frontiers between China and its two largest neighbors have been no exception.

Accordingly, geostrategic considerations and triangular relationships naturally come to mind quickly. One may note the beginnings of these relationships with the several events in the early 1960s, especially the Sino-Indian border clash in the fall of 1962, and perhaps more dramatically with the Indo-Pakistani war in late 1971 that led to the birth of Bangladesh. However, as one Indian analyst has written: "The triangular relationship between India, China and the Soviet Union has been developing ever since the power structure of Asia underwent a revolutionary change by the middle of the present century. . . . Since then three giants have emerged sprawling the continent of Asia and facing two oceans."[2] A short summary of the historical and political background of these developments must be made, focusing again on Sino-Indian relations.

PRE-1962 BACKGROUND AND THE 1954 SINO-INDIAN AGREEMENT ON TIBET

India gained its independence in August 1947, but that independence was accompanied by the painful partition of the Indian subcontinent, which resulted in the new and predominantly Islamic state of Pakistan, a curious bifurcation with two wings separated by 1,000 miles of Indian territory. The setting and political situation invited strife and possible foreign involvement. Independent India's prime minister for the first seventeen years was Jawaharlal Nehru, who also served as the country's foreign minister and mentor in foreign affairs until his death in 1964. His legacy has been that India should pursue a foreign policy of nonalignment (termed by many as "neutralism") and avoid the perils of the cold war, a stance that he had advocated even before independence, declaring in a radio address in September 1946 that his interim National government proposed, "as far as possible, to keep away from the power politics of groups, aligned against one another, which have led in the past to world wars and which may again lead to disasters on an even vaster scale."[3] Criticized by some people for being naive or simply opportunistic, Nehru also had as a futile dream of postwar international relations the idea of Asian unity, including particularly ties with India's great northern neighbor, China, then torn by civil war. It need hardly be added that the leadership of the new China in 1949 was not sympathetic to India's nonalignment. Mao Zedong bluntly said that his regime would "lean to one side," that of socialism (led by Moscow) and not that of imperialism (presumably led by Washington), and he rejected the notion of any "third path." Relations between New Delhi and Peking were tenuous, and following is a calendar of events that influenced Sino-Indian relations through 1962:

> December 1949--India decides to recognize the new People's Republic of China. (India would have been the first non-Communist country to do so but held back at the request of Burma, which became the first.)
>
> October 1950--Communist Chinese troops enter Tibet.
>
> April 1954--Conclusion of the Sino-Indian treaty on the "Tibet region" of China, which enunciated in the preamble the Five Principles of Peaceful Coexistence. (Indians generally refer to them as the Pancha Shila or Panchsheel, meaning "five principles," namely: (1) mutual respect for each other's territorial integrity and sovereignty, (2) mutual non-aggression, (3) mutual noninterference in each other's internal affairs,

(4) equality and mutual benefit, and (5) peaceful coexistence.)

June 1954--Peking denounces the presence of Indian troops in the disputed border area of Barahoti. (This is a small area lying between Nepal and Kashmir that India claims is part of India.)

October 1954--Jawaharlal Nehru makes a formal visit to China.

April 1955--Asian-African Conference held at Bandung, Indonesia. (At which, Nehru vied with China's Premier Zhou En-lai for the delegates attention but also took pains to introduce him to his fellow Asian delegations. This conference included those countries of Asia that had turned from the path of nonalignment, such as Pakistan, Thailand, and the Philippines.)

July 1956--Communist Chinese forces are revealed as having crossed disputed Sino-Burmese border areas and having removed border markers.

August-November 1958--Notes are exchanged between India and China on boundary differences. (These included the question of China's use of "old maps" prepared by the former Nationalist government, a sharpening of the differences in tone, and the revelation for the first time that during 1956-1957 the Communist Chinese had built a road across the eastern part of the Ladakh region of Kashmir. This road, some 100 miles in length, forms part of the Tibet-Sinkiang highway. The government of India did not let the Indian people in on the "secret" until 1959.)

March 1959--Abortive Tibetan revolt and the flight of the Dalai Lama with thousands of followers to India, where he is granted asylum. (This is commonly taken as the chief turning

point in the worsening Sino-Indian
relationship, exceeded only by the
major armed clashes on the border in
late 1962.)

October 1959--Chinese troops open fire on an
Indian patrol in southern Ladakh
(Kashmir), causing five Indian casualties.

April 1960--Communist Chinese Premier
Zhou En-lai visits India for a week
at New Delhi's invitation for talks
with Premier Nehru. No agreement is
reached, and representatives continue
the talks with no success. (It was
suggested in many quarters that China
offered to accept the McMahon Line,
India's eastern boundary, provided
India agreed to China's title to the
Aksai Chin road in Ladakh.)

October 20, 1962--Communist Chinese
forces attack India and humiliate
Indian troops in the border areas.

November 22, 1962--China declares a unilateral cease-fire.

In the initial period, down to 1953, Peking
regarded India with some suspicion and Nehru as
a "running dog of imperialism," partly because
of the evangelical zeal that is common to radical
movements and the ideological contempt for the
"bourgeois" leadership in India and its alleged
dependence on the West. Toward the mid-1950s,
it was apparent that there would be no early
Communist millenium in India or elsewhere in
Asia, as apparently envisioned by Mao, and Peking
reconsidered its views on the subject of India
and nonalignment. A new phase in Communist
Chinese foreign policy was unfolding as Peking
indicated its readiness to assume normal and
friendly diplomatic relations with its non-
Communist neighbors. In the case of India, an
important issue to be resolved was that of Tibet.

Since the early 1900s, Tibet had served as
the northern buffer of British India. Chinese
occupation of the area in October 1950 meant that
a major power was now on the Himalayan border of

India, a power that had shown an assertive posture and would be involved within a month in the fighting in Korea. But India, while concerned about the autonomy of the Tibetans and their classical Indian culture (Tibet also contains important pilgrimage sites for Hindus), did not seem publicly alarmed by the Communist Chinese establishment of authority in Tibet in the sense of a direct threat to the security of India. The Himalayas had always been viewed as virtually impregnable, and moreover, no major invasion of the Indian subcontinent had ever come from that direction. Historically, the land threat was from the northwest via the Khyber Pass. In addition, there was little or nothing that New Delhi could do to block China's plans to control Tibet. Nehru and his foreign policy associates evidently soon came to that conclusion, if they had not done so before the fall of 1950.

The influential K. M. Panikkar, then India's ambassador to Peking, later wrote with historical detachment:

> I knew like everyone else that with Communist China cordial and intimate relations were out of the question, but I was fairly optimistic about working out an area of cooperation by eliminating causes of misunderstanding, rivalry, etc. The only area where our interests overlapped was in Tibet, and knowing that every Chinese government, including the Kuomintang, had attached to exclusive Chinese authority over that area, I had, even before I started for Peking, come to the conclusion that the British policy (which we were supposed to have inherited) of looking upon Tibet as an area in which we had special political interests could not be maintained.[4]

Would Peking, however, reciprocate any special gestures from New Delhi and be content to remain north of the crest of the Himalayas?

It was in New Delhi's national interest to keep China's influence and, above all, physical presence north of the Himalayan crest, which would involve limiting the opportunities for Chinese influence in the Himalayan kingdoms of Nepal, Bhutan, and Sikkim. Their northern borders with Tibet along the Himalayan crest were viewed by New Delhi then--and continue to be--as India's northern strategic frontier. By 1950, India had concluded treaties with all three kingdoms containing security clauses and, in the cases of Bhutan and Sikkim, the statement that they would be "guided" by India in the conduct of their foreign relations.[5] Such guidance would understandably be aimed at maximizing India's presence prudently, but effectively, along the cis-Himalayan edge and, conversely, minimizing any Chinese penetration, political or other.

On the other hand, Indian professions of friendship toward the new China, early formal diplomatic recognition of Peking's international personality, acquiescence in the Communist Chinese incorporation of Tibet in 1950, a stated willingness to conclude a formal treaty that would recognize that incorporation, and India's repeated advocacy of the admission of the People's Republic of China to the United Nations might pay some political dividends in more harmonious relations between the two great Asian neighbors. The alternative for India to the steadfast pursuit of nonalignment was unacceptable (at least then): an Indian security relationship with the West that would result in a containment policy vis-à-vis China.

Patience may have its rewards in international relations, even if they prove to be only temporary. By 1953-1954, as noted earlier, Peking was adopting a new posture of friendly diplomatic relations with China's non-Communist neighbors, usually referred to as the period of peaceful coexistence. In late 1953, New Delhi decided to sound out Peking about negotiating an understanding on trade and cultural intercourse between India and the Tibet region of China, which Nehru hoped would lead to a rapprochement with Peking. China readily welcomed the proposed idea of a small Indian delegation's being sent to Peking. One of the participants on the Indian side later wrote that Nehru had refused to accept the thesis that China was the main threat to India's security and had argued that "if India and China could work out a modus vivendi of respecting each other's sovereignty and integrity and noninterference in internal affairs, it would be a step away from the cold war and prevent its penetration into Asia."[6]

In brief, the Indian mood seemed to be compromise if need be to get an agreement with China, but get an agreement. For example, the Indian side had suggested twenty-five years for the duration of the agreement, but the Chinese wanted only five years. Ultimately, it was agreed that it would last eight years. This compromise made the Indian negotiators "somewhat suspicious of the Chinese motives," and they reported their suspicion to New Delhi, but eight years was accepted anyway.[7] They did get the Chinese to agree that the Five Principles (Panchsheel) would form part of the agreement, if not a separate article (which India wanted), then in the Preamble. Through Zhou En-lai's reported intervention, the Five Principles were incorporated into the Preamble. This inclusion was welcomed by official India, which was to set great store by the Five Principles in India's foreign relations with China and the world in general, especially on the Asian scene. Indeed, they came to be closely associated, at least for India, with that country's general policy of nonalignment, and the term Panchsheel acquired a special symbolic content for India. The same cannot be said to hold for new China.

Nevertheless, the signing of the treaty did usher in a period of relative harmony between China and India, although it lasted only about three years. When Zhou En-lai visited India in June 1954, he was warmly received, and Indians everywhere chanted "Hindi Chini bhai bhai" (Indian and Chinese are brothers). Answering an Indian newspaperman, Zhou hailed the Sino-Indian agreement on Tibet as having "set a good example of co-operation among Asian States" and added that the "Chinese people respect the life-long devotion of Gandhi and his struggle for national independence. Such a life-long struggle has a profound influence on the Chinese people."[8] (He did not note, however, that Gandhi's political struggle was a nonviolent one.) When Nehru made a thirteen-day return visit to China in October 1954, he reportedly received an enthusiastic welcome. A few weeks later in his speech at India's National (Republic) Day reception, held in Peking on January 26, 1955, Zhou described the Five Principles of Peaceful Coexistence, "jointly advocated" by China and India, as an important factor in "enlarging the area of Peace" and observed, "China always attaches importance to the efforts made by India in safeguarding the peace of Asia and the world, and is ready to increase its co-operation with India in order to attain this common goal."[9] Time would tell for how long.

In retrospect, the terms of the 1954 Sino-Indian agreement, or treaty, on Tibet seem fairly straightforward, including the accompanying exchange of notes in which India gave up various installations and any "extraterritorial" rights it may have inherited from British India.[10] The highlights of the agreement can be summarized as follows:

1. The Preamble containing the Five Principles
2. The establishment of trade agencies (India's at Yatung, Gyantse, and Gartok; China's at New Delhi, Calcutta and Kalimpong)
3. The establishment of ten trade marts in Tibet for customary petty border trade by Indian traders (with none on the Indian side)
4. Ensuring entry and security of Indian and Tibetan religious pilgrims to each other's holy shrines (Kang Rimpoche [Kailas], Mavam Tso [Mansarowar], and Lhasa in Tibet; Banaras, Sarnath, Bodh Gaya, and Sanchi in India)
5. The recognition of six Sino-Indian border passes for travel by traders and pilgrims of both countries (Shipki La, Mana, Niti, Kungri Bingri, Darma, and Lipu Lekh)

One might also ask in retrospect what all the

excitement was about with regard to the conclusion of the agreement by India and China, particularly on the side of New Delhi. Goodwill could--and did--evaporate as the implementation of an eight-year accord became problematic and other border problems became paramount in Sino-Indian relations.

Nevertheless, for a time in the mid-1950s there did seem to be evidence of increased cooperation in Asian relations between China and India. One hallmark was the appearance of Nehru and Zhou in tandem at the Asian-African Conference at Bandung, Indonesia, in April 1955. There they tried with some success to reassure Communist China's southern neighbors of its commitment to peaceful coexistence (the <u>Panchsheel</u> were partly incorporated into the final conference communiqué); to answer the arguments of Pakistan, the Philippines, and other states that had entered into mutual security pacts (the right of collective self-defense was eventually recognized in the final communiqué also); and to promote the vague idea of Afro-Asian solidarity a la "Bandung spirit." It was admittedly an historic show, and contrary to the fears of various Western observers, no "Bamboo Curtain" emerged.[11] Bandung may have represented the high point in Sino-Indian cooperation in general Asian affairs and an apparent personal friendship between Zhou and Nehru.

This cooperation would be linked to the important factor of bilateral and multilateral alliances intruding into the "peace area," namely, South and Southeast Asia. In 1954, the Southeast Asia Treaty Organization (SEATO) emerged, the handiwork mainly of John Foster Dulles, the containment-minded U.S. secretary of state. For India, Pakistan's acceptance of U.S. arms aid and subsequent membership in SEATO and the Baghdad Pact (later CENTO) were especially disturbing. Pakistan's security fears with regard to India, against whom such arms might be and were directed, were the motivation here, not any concern with "containing" Chinese communism. India repeatedly berated its Islamic neighbor's alliances and upheld nonalignment for all to pursue if international peace were to be realized.¹² SEATO, born in 1954 and phased out in 1977, naturally became a favorite whipping boy for Peking. On some occasions Zhou En-lai would even quote and endorse critical remarks made about SEATO by his Indian counterpart, Premier Nehru.¹³

In passing, it must be noted that India never commented publicly as the foremost leader of the nonaligned movement on the Sino-Soviet treaty and alliance of 1950. Article 1 of that treaty (since abrogated) stated that in the event that one of the contracting parties (China or the Soviet Union) were attacked by Japan or "any state allied with her," the other contracting party "shall immediately render military and other assistance by all means at its disposal."¹⁴ (No such similar provision would appear in the Indo-Soviet treaty of 1971, which will be discussed later.)

Penetration of the Indian subcontinent by the Soviet Union soon followed the military ties concluded by the United States with Pakistan. This Soviet forward policy to the south, with strategic overtones of historic Russian ambitions in the direction of the Indian Ocean, moved slowly but steadily for a decade until the mid-1960s. It started with the famous "B and K" (Bulganin and Khrushchev) tour of India in late 1955 and intensified as Sino-Soviet relations in the early 1960s. However, one should be cautious about treating any Indo-Soviet, Sino-Soviet, Sino-Pakistani, or other relationships affecting the Indian subcontinent as simply a function or knee-jerk reaction of another adverse relationship. As William J. Barnds has written, it is important

> to keep in mind the inherent limitations of any attempt to evaluate the impact of the Sino-Soviet dispute on a particular region. A move by the Soviet Union or China is often only one of a number of influences in South Asia, which are usually a combination of domestic pressures, intraregional maneuvers, and the actions of external powers other than the USSR or China. The role of the

United States has often been as important as that of the Soviet Union or the PRC.[15]

By 1956 and the appearance of Communist Chinese forces across the friendly Burmese frontier,[16] the "Bandung spirit" had begun to evaporate. Nehru may have been almost as disturbed by this development as his neighbor and friend, Burma's Premier U Nu, but he spoke softly on the subject. His optimism about China's developing good relations with its southern neighbors was surely reflected in his failure to achieve any real Indian quid pro quo for New Delhi's acceptance of the fact of Chinese political control over Tibet. One such possibility might have been the working out a border agreement with Peking at the time, thereby reducing, if not avoiding, many of India's later problems with China.

Now, as Peking repeatedly took the position that the southern borders variously defined during British imperial rule in India, including the McMahon Line, were "illegal" products of imperialism, New Delhi began to face "cartographic aggression" in the form of Chinese maps claiming Indian-held territory plus the growing prospect of a political confrontation. These official Chinese maps showed that the Aksai Chin area of Ladakh (about 14,000 square miles), across which a strategic Chinese road had been completed in 1957, was Chinese. The same situation occurred in the case of the North East Frontier Agency (NEFA). Known today as the union (federal) territory of Arunachal Pradesh, NEFA involved some 38,000 square miles lying just below the McMahon Line and on the direct approach from the north to what was then India's only major oil-producing fields in Dibrugarh, Assam. This new assertive stance by Peking toward New Delhi was plainly serious, even though Nehru chose to play it down in the face of mounting Indian criticism, and it can be seen in part as a general stiffening of the Chinese Communist attitude toward the nonaligned states, which were allegedly "tilting" toward the United States.[17]

Any call by Indians on the ancient ties of

2,000 years of friendship between China and India or expression of "Hindi Chini bhai bhai" ended in early 1959 with the Tibetan revolt, its suppression by Peking, and the flight of the Dalai Lama to India with many of his followers. Asylum was given, and the Chinese ambassador in New Delhi was so informed soon afterward by the foreign secretary of India on April 3. The same Indian official soon confronted the Chinese ambassador again, protesting statements that had been made at the session of the National People's Congress in Peking to the effect that the Dalai Lama was "under duress" and that included references to "Indian reactionaries" who were supposed to be "working in the footsteps of the British imperialists and . . . harbouring expansionist ambitions towards Tibet."[18] The downward slide in Sino-Indian relations was clear.

On April 27, Nehru made a lengthy statement on the situation in Tibet before the lower house of the Indian Parliament. He declared that India's broad policy was governed by three factors: "(1) the preservation of the security and integrity of India; (2) our desire to maintain friendly relations with China; and (3) our deep sympathy for the people of Tibet. That policy we shall continue to follow, because we think that a correct policy not only for the present but even more so for the future." India's premier continued: "It would be a tragedy if the two great countries of Asia, India and China, which have been peaceful neighbours for ages past, should develop feelings of hostility against each other." He deplored the "unfounded charges" and the use of "cold war" language by Peking and rejected the Chinese charge that Kalimpong in India was a center of the Tibetan rebellion. He recalled separate talks he had had in India with Premier Zhou En-lai and the Dalai Lama regarding the problem of Tibetan autonomy and the challenge of Chinese Communist "reforms." He saw the circumstances as undoubtedly difficult, observing, "On the one side, there was a dynamic, rapidly moving society; on the other, a static, unchanging society fearful of what might be done to it in the name of reforms." He concluded that the revolt in Tibet was not simply the result of a number of so-called upper strata reactionaries (Peking's term) but that it was of "considerable magnitude" and that the basis of it must have been a "strong feeling of nationalism."[19]

A detailed Chinese commentary, "The Revolution in Tibet and Nehru's Philosophy," was published by the Editorial Department of People's Daily on May 6, 1959.[20] It treated Nehru and his alleged "contradictions" curiously, charging that he was "unvoluntarily pushed" into an alliance with "so-called sympathizers" of the Tibetan people. It was charged that this alliance was counterrevolutionary and included the U.S. State Department, British colonialists, Syngman Rhee, Ngo Dinh Diem, Chiang Kai-shek, and India's "reactionary parties." Nehru was described as a respected prime minister who was trying to safeguard world peace, but his denial that India never interfered in Tibet was rejected, and the Chinese editors placed special blame, in Marxist fashion, on India's "big bourgeoisie" and its "innumerable links with imperialism."

The Dalai Lama remained in India, where suspicions about the intentions of China toward India grew, peaceful coexistence seemed increasingly on trial, and the need for constructive diplomacy, perhaps at the summit level, had become apparent. But the week-long visit in April 1960 of Premier Zhou En-lai to New Delhi at India's invitation proved disappointing. Tensions along the Sino-Indian border had increased after the October 1959 incident, in which Chinese troops had opened fire on an Indian patrol in southern Ladakh facing the Aksai Chin area, resulting in several Indian casualties. The rapid deterioration of Sino-Indian relations might have been arrested if the reported "swap" proposal of the Chinese side in regard to territorial claims had been accepted by India. This proposal apparently would have involved Peking's accepting the McMahon Line as the legitimate boundary in the northeast, providing India would accept the fact of China's control over the Aksai Chin area in the northwest. Sino-Indian differences on the middle sector, running westward from Nepal to Kashmir (and Aksai Chin), would presumably have been resolved in future discussions. However, no Sino-Indian border agreement along these rather logical lines resulted, probably because New Delhi saw the problem from a legal as well as a historical perspective, since preindependence treaties on the subject had been signed. Peking believed these treaties were invalid "legacies" of imperialism regarding often vague boundary lines and conflicting maps. In any event, China did control the area surrounding the strategic access road across Aksai Chin, and, as if to demonstrate its willingness to negotiate boundaries along "traditional customary lines," Peking concluded border agreements in 1960 with both Burma and Nepal, thereby salvaging something of its image in the way of reasonableness.[21]

In the case of Nepal, developments between India and China, which was now clearly an influence south of the Himalayas, offered the opportunity to play Peking against New Delhi. But Katmandu wisely adopted a policy of "equidistance" in its relations with China and India as well as other major powers. Nepal did benefit as a recipient of aid programs from both sides, including the Katmandu-Tibet road built by the Chinese and east-west roads, among other projects, undertaken by the Indians. If the Nepalese held a Chinese or an Indian "card" from the early 1960s, they chose not to play it openly. In the meantime, Peking conducted a "flexible diplomacy" toward Katmandu, evidently as part of China's long-term design to achieve predominance in the Himalayan region.[22]

THE 1962 SINO-INDIAN BORDER CONFLICT AND AFTER

A series of incidents along the Sino-Indian border followed the failure of Zhou En-lai's 1960 mission to India, the last such Chinese diplomatic mission to India until the arrival, in June 1981, in New Delhi of the PRC's then foreign minister, Huang Hua. The anticipated major clash of arms came suddenly on October 20, 1962, when Chinese forces swept down on ill-prepared Indian troops in both the western and the eastern border sectors. Heavy damage was inflicted on the Indians, especially in the eastern sector, and all

India felt outraged and humiliated by the course of the conflict.[23] Why did China do it? Was Peking simply too irritated by the probes of Indian border patrols and the placing of pickets in territory it deemed to be Chinese? Was it a question of India, as a leader and an alternative model of development to China in the general Third World, having to be reduced considerably in stature? A number of views have focused on the latter theory and the matter of Sino-Indian competition in Third World affairs as an explanation.

T. N. Kaul, a former Indian ambassador who served in Peking, Moscow, Washington, and other major capitals, later wrote that the

> only valid, logical and reasonable surmise seems to be that China's radical leaders, isolated and beset with internal and international problems, wanted to divert the attention of their people by securing successes somewhere. They wanted China to become the leader of the communist world and the "Big Brother" in Asia, with a string of client states around it. . . . India seemed to be the main obstacle in extending China's hegemony over Asia and then [sic] assume the leadership of the Third World. . . . This was China's "forward policy" against India. She wanted to show the Third World that India was militarily weak, socially decadent and economically dependent on Western aid.[24]

The official explanation from Peking was stated in a lengthy letter from Zhou En-lai, dated November 15, 1962, to leaders of Asian and African countries.[25] In this letter, he paid tribute to the Five Principles of Peaceful Coexistence, emphasized the "friendly" manner of the Sino-Burmese and Sino-Nepalese border settlements, and accused the Indian government of having "covetous desires" on Tibet and of making a series of "encroachments" and "repeated inroads" into Chinese territory. Zhou emphatically charged, "All relevant facts show that the current grave Sino-Indian border conflict was wholly engineered by the Indian Government, deliberately and over a long period of time." He called for the disengagement of forces on both sides for a distance of twenty kilometers to the November 1959 line of actual control along the Sino-Indian boundary (a position that favored Peking and was rejected by New Delhi), and he welcomed the efforts of leaders of Asian and African countries to promote a peaceful Sino-Indian settlement. On November 22, 1962, China declared a unilateral cease-fire and effected a troop withdrawal along the lines of Peking's previously announced proposal. The diplomatic efforts of some third parties continued, notably those of a group of nonaligned countries headed by Ceylon (Sri Lanka today), but they were of no avail in achieving a solution to the Sino-Indian border conflict.

China evidently scored a major point as a result of that conflict: India reeled and anxiously solicited assistance from all quarters, East and West. The relative influence of the factors of Chinese history and Marxist ideology aside, Peking asserted its claims and forced New Delhi to call officially for help in the form of emergency military equipment from outside powers. A prompt response came from the United States, Britain, and other Western countries. The Soviet Union, already a supplier of military hardware to India and developing a closer relationship with New Delhi as Sino-Soviet relations worsened in the early 1960s, delayed responding to the initial Indian requests but eventually allowed spare MiG and other parts that were already in the pipeline to be delivered. But Moscow could not respond fully to India, as Khrushchev indicated to the Indian ambassador to Moscow in November 1962, reportedly stating: "You must remember that China is our brother but not a small brother. We cannot hit him as if he was a little brother."[26]

For the United States, an inherent dilemma existed in the conduct of its foreign policy in South Asia since 1953 and the supply of U.S. arms aid to Pakistan, a sort of "little brother" on the subcontinent. Anything Washington did for

Pakistan was resented strongly by India, and the reverse applied in the event of any U.S. military or economic assistance to India.[27] Pakistan was a member of SEATO and CENTO, was once described as the United States' "most allied ally," and objected to any U.S. help to India. This was the case in the instance of the Sino-Indian border conflict in 1962 but even more so three years later when the second Indo-Pakistani war took place and the United States and Britain placed an arms embargo on both India and Pakistan. By the time of this armed clash in September 1965, Pakistan had discovered Communist China as a potential ally against India and, to the consternation of Washington, had engaged in considerable diplomatic activity with Peking.[28] The simple principle here in realpolitik would seem to be, "the enemy of my enemy may be my new friend." It is nothing new in international relations.

China, however, was not necessarily a military "card" in Pakistan's rivalry with India, as events in 1965 and 1971 were to show. The change in Peking's policy toward Pakistan that began in the early 1960s was in part due to worsening relations between India and China, but it also reflected a growing Chinese geopolitical interest in light of what was seen by Peking as a growing Soviet attempt to isolate China and encircle it through a closer collaboration with India. Thus, ideological differences with Pakistan would not prevent China from supporting an Islamabad that had once been closely allied with the West.[29] The question was, How much support?

The projection of Chinese power across the Himalayas and into the Indian subcontinent did not rest with an armed Sino-Indian border clash or growing diplomatic activity with Pakistan. The Chinese nuclear explosion in the fall of 1964 was another factor, one that led New Delhi to decide not to foreclose on its nuclear option. (Ten years later, India's "peaceful" nuclear explosion was made.) Apart from some strong talk and rocket rattling in 1965, China did not go to Pakistan's aid in the second Indo-Pakistani war. In addition, neither China nor the United States was to provide the good offices and venue toward reaching an interim settlement between India and

Pakistan, the hostile neighbors. The honor fell to the Soviet Union, which hosted the meeting between India's Premier Lai Bahadur Shastri and Pakistan's president, Ayub Khan, at Tashkent in January 1966.

The stated agreement in the Tashkent Declaration was renunciation of force, noninterference in each other's internal affairs, a curbing of hostile propaganda, repatriation of war prisoners, and the restoration of normal diplomatic and trade relations. Both sides expressed their deep appreciation to the Soviet leadership for its "constructive, friendly and noble part" in bringing about the meeting in Soviet Uzbekistan.[30] Soviet prestige in the Indian subcontinent stood high, especially in the eyes of New Delhi and India's new prime minister, Indira Gandhi, who succeeded Shastri on his death in January 1966. As the daughter of Jawaharlal Nehru, she would emerge as a formidable politician, but she chose not to hold the portfolio of foreign affairs, although her influence on such decision making was critical, including developing closer ties with the Soviet Union and assisting the people of East Pakistan to break away in 1971 and form an independent Bangladesh.

Space does not permit any detailed discussion of the complex aspects related to the emergence of Bangladesh here, including the juxtaposition of the several powers--India, Pakistan, the Soviet Union, and China.[31] A summary must note that the peoples of the eastern "wing" (East Bengal) had been suffering from what their leaders termed "internal colonialism" and were inclined increasingly to separatism. Martial law and a vicious military crackdown in early 1971 denied them the fruits of a national electoral victory and, in due course, many lives. The die had been cast.

Refugees (mostly Hindus) poured into surrounding India, reaching an estimated total of 10 million by late August. India's sympathies were understandably with the Bangladesh freedom fighters (Mukhti Bahini), and New Delhi refused to accept the argument that this was really an internal Pakistani matter, as Washington and Peking, both allies of Pakistan, then did.

Moreover, the secessionist effort of the East Bengalis (the Bangladeshis) did point to a classic opportunity in realpolitik for India. If the effort succeeded, Pakistan would be reduced in size (55 percent of all the people of Pakistan lived in East Bengal), and the attempt by the United States to maintain an artificial balance of power in South Asia between India and Pakistan would be finally ended. It would also be a blow to Communist China's growing influence on the subcontinent.

What New Delhi needed was a sort of security treaty that would put Peking on notice that any intervention in the likely event of a third Indo-Pakistani war could be highly dangerous. It was provided by the Soviet Union in the Indo-Soviet Treaty of Peace, Friendship, and Cooperation concluded on August 9, 1971.[32] Article 4 contains the Soviet Union's avowed "respect" for India's policy of nonalignment, which is always cited by those defenders of the genuiness of India's continuing nonalignment. But Article 9 states, "In the event of either Party being subjected to an attack or a threat thereof, the High Contracting Parties shall immediately enter into mutual consultations in order to remove such threat and to take appropriate effective measures to ensure peace and the security of their countries." This provision has raised many eyebrows, probably including some in Peking. The duration of the treaty is for twenty years, but India needed only a few more months and the winter snows to block the Himalayan passes leading from China to India. Interestingly enough, Peking did not comment immediately on the new Indo-Soviet treaty, with its obvious implications, reserving its comments for the December meetings of the UN Security Council after the Indo-Pakistani fighting, the third war, had actually begun.

Both Peking and Washington in their unfolding relationship (President Nixon had already announced in July 1971 his pending visit to Peking in 1972) chose to stay with Islamabad in what was Pakistan's hopeless attempt to have its isolated forces in East Bengal survive the invading Indian army and the naval blockade. The Nixon-Kissinger "tilt" was toward Pakistan, was definitely related to the new Sino-American relationship, whatever it might hold, and demonstrated a singular inability to appreciate the new order that was clearly emerging in South Asia.[33] By December 17, the Pakistani forces had surrendered, the war ended, and Bangladesh became a political reality, although there was no further "dismemberment" of Pakistan by India as Islamabad's supporters had once claimed there would be.

The fact that China did not intervene militarily on Pakistan's behalf leads to several conclusions: (1) The recent Indo-Soviet treaty had served as a deterrent; (2) Peking had come to respect the capabilities of the Indian army, which had been greatly improved, largely with Soviet matériel and Indian ordnance, after 1962; (3) China was prepared to accept the preeminent status of India in South Asia, although China's relationship with Pakistan would remain close; and (4) China might be ready before long to normalize its relations with India--although this process did not get under way until 1976, when India and China once again exchanged ambassadors. This diplomatic exchange came less than two years after India's annexation of Sikkim as an "associate state" in 1974, an action Peking described as "intolerable bullying" by India and a "colonialist Policy."[34]

During the 1970s, the Soviet Union emerged as India's largest trading partner and continued as its major supplier of military hardware. This relationship included highly visible visits by Soviet Defense Minister Dmitri Ustinov to India in 1982 and 1984 and the acquisition of a sophisticated new weapons system from the Soviet Union.[35] In April 1984, an Indian air force officer was carried aloft with two Soviet cosmonauts to become India's first man in space, which was greeted with enthusiasm by the nation and Prime Minister Indira Gandhi. A few months earlier, in December, a Soviet Communist Party "fraternal" delegation had attended by invitation Gandhi's Congress Party plenary session, a gesture that demonstrated a stronger Soviet link with India's ruling party. It was also the first such attendance by the Soviets, who, since the early 1960s, had been attending only Communist Party of India (CPI) conferences.

Official relations between India and the Soviet Union undeniably remain close, with India apparently still getting the better share of the relationship. In its diplomacy, New Delhi has avoided direct criticism of the Soviet Union's invasion of Afghanistan in late 1979, which brought the presence of another great power to the borders of the subcontinent. At the risk of incurring the lasting displeasure of its Asian neighbors, the Islamic states, and many Third World nations, India has abstained on pertinent UN resolutions criticizing the Soviet occupation of Afghanistan. New Delhi also recognized both the Soviet-backed regime in Kabul in 1980 and the Vietnamese- (and Soviet-) supported Heng Samrin regime in Kampuchea (Cambodia).

But in the course of these developments, India has not become a Soviet satellite. Like neighboring China, India is too large and too independent for such a status. The Soviet Union's efforts to increase its influence with New Delhi will doubtless go on. Thus far, Moscow has acquired no naval base in India, and, although it would surely like one, it will not be able to convert Vishagapatnam or any other Indian installation into a Cam Ranh Bay.

China's competition with the Soviet Union remains an important factor in Peking's continued support of Islamabad, including emerging as the largest supplier of arms to Pakistan until the 1981 U.S. to Pakistan arms and economic assistance package of $3.2 billion. Peking has consistently and roundly condemned the Soviet occupation of Afghanistan and has made its termination as one of the three major issues that prevent a normalization of Sino-Soviet relations.

The process of normalization of Sino-Indian relations has continued since 1976, but slowly. A number of exchanges have taken place between India and China, including ping-pong teams. Trade between the two countries was never very significant, stopped in 1963, and now has been picking up. Most important, on the key question of the boundary between India and China, the two sides had held four rounds of talks through October 1983, when the Indian side reported no specific progress on the question but said that it would make "determined efforts to advance towards a solution of the boundary question."[36] An agreed border solution would certainly make a Sino-Indian rapprochement possible, but it is doubtful whether the two great Asian neighbors would ever be close as the lips and the teeth, let alone China and the Soviet Union.

NOTES

I would like to thank Hideki Maedomari for research assistance and the staff of the Center for Chinese Studies Library, University of California at Berkeley, for their kind help.

1. Text of paper as given in John E. Tashjean, "The Sino-Soviet Split: Borkenau's Predictive Analysis of 1952," China Quarterly, no. 94 (June 1983), pp. 342-361.
2. Maharaj K. Chopra, "The Sino-Soviet-Indian Triangle," U.S.I. Journal (United Service Institution of India, New Delhi) 110 (April-June 1980), p. 103.
3. See Jawaharlal Nehru, India's Foreign Policy: Selected Speeches, September 1945-April 1961 (Delhi: Publications Division, Ministry of Information and Broadcasting, Government of India, 1961), p. 2. See also B. R. Nanda, ed., Indian Foreign Policy: The Nehru Years (Honolulu: University Press of Hawaii, 1976), pp. 1-23, and Bimal Prasad, ed., India's Foreign Policy: Studies in Continuity and Change (New Delhi: Vikas, 1979), pp. 481-508.
4. K. M. Panikkar, In Two Chinas (London: George Allen and Unwin, 1955), p. 1. See also George N. Patterson, Peking Versus Delhi (New York: Praeger, 1963), pp. 102-107.
5. See Narendra Goyal, Prelude to India: A Study of India's Relations with Himalayan States (New Delhi: Cambridge Books, 1964), and Rama T.S. Rao, "The Himalayan Frontier Policy of India--A Historical Perspective," Indian Yearbook of International Affairs (Madras) 15-16 (1970), pp. 558-567.
6. T. N. Kaul, Diplomacy in Peace and War (New Delhi: Vikas, 1979), p. 98.

7. Ibid., p. 102.
8. *The Hindu* (Madras), June 23, 1954.
9. R. K. Jain, ed., *China-South Asian Relations, 1947-1980*, 2 vols. (New Delhi: Radiant Publishers, 1981), 1:83.
10. For the full text of the Sino-Indian agreement and related notes, see ibid., 1:61-67. The agreement was ratified by both governments on June 3, 1954.
11. The best account of the Bandung Conference, including the remarks made by Zhou and Nehru in the Political Committee, is still George Kahin, ed., *Asian-African Conference, Bandung, Indonesia, April, 1955* (Ithaca, N.Y.: Cornell University Press, 1956).
12. See Nehru, *India's Foreign Policy*, especially pp. 87f.
13. See Jain, *China-South Asian Relations*, pp. 80-81.
14. The full text, in English translation, is given in Theodore McNelly, ed., *Sources in Modern East Asian History and Politics* (New York: Appleton-Century-Crofts, 1967), pp. 297-300.
15. William J. Barnds, "The Impact of the Sino-Soviet Dispute on South Asia," in *The Sino-Soviet Conflict: A Global Perspective*, ed., Herbert J. Ellison (Seattle: University of Washington Press, 1982), p. 208. See also Alvin Z. Rubinstein, ed., *Soviet and Chinese Influence in the Third World* (New York: Praeger, 1975).
16. See Richard J. Kozicki, "The Sino-Burmese Frontier Problem," *Far Eastern Survey* 26 (March 1957), pp. 33-38.
17. See Vidya Prakash Dutt, *China and the World: An Analysis of Communist China's Foreign Policy* (New York: Praeger, 1964), pp. 155-166, 199-214. The author is a leading Indian specialist on China.
18. Jain, *China-South Asian Relations*, 1:121.
19. Extracts in ibid., pp. 122-124.
20. Ibid., pp. 125-131.
21. See Dutt, *China and the World*, pp. 165-185.
22. See Leo E. Rose, *Nepal: Strategy for Survival* (Berkeley: University of California

Press, 1971), especially the last five chapters, and Hemen Ray, "Communist China's Strategy in the Himalayas: Nepal, A Case Study," Orbis 11 (Fall 1967), pp. 826-845.

23. See Patterson, Peking Versus Delhi. Also for a pro-Chinese account, see Neville Maxwell, India's China War (New York: Pantheon Books, 1970), and for a critical Indian interpretation, see G. S. Bhargava, The Battle of NEFA: The Undeclared War (Bombay: Allied Publishers, 1964).

24. Kaul, Diplomacy in Peace and War, pp. 111-112.

25. Extracts in Jain, China-South Asian Relations, 1:230-235. For a dispassionate treatment by an Indian, see J. A. Naik, Soviet Policy Towards India from Stalin to Brezhnev (Delhi: Vikas, 1970).

26. Kaul, Diplomacy in Peace and War, p. 125. The Soviet Union had already supported India firmly in its position on another territorial dispute, that of Kashmir. See, for example, the strong statements by the Soviet UN delegate to the Security Council in May and June 1962 (texts given in R. K. Jain, ed., Soviet-South Asian Relations, 1947-1978, 2 vols. [Atlantic Highlands, N.J.: Humanities Press, 1979], 1:38-53).

27. See Norman D. Palmer, South Asia and United States Policy (Boston: Houghton Mifflin Company, 1966), especially pp. 177-183, 295-305; also William J. Barnds, "India and America at Odds," International Affairs 49 (July 1973), pp. 371-384.

28. See Mohammed Ayub Khan, "The Pakistan-American Alliance: Stresses and Strains," Foreign Affairs 42 (January 1964), pp. 195-209, and Frank N. Trager, "The United States and Pakistan: A Failure in Diplomacy," Orbis 9 (Fall 1965), pp. 615f.

29. Zubeida Mustafa, "Pakistan: The Focus of China's South Asian Policy," in Pakistan in a Changing World, ed. Masuma Hasan (Karachi: Institute of International Affairs, 1978), pp. 194-207. See also Anwar Syed, "The Politics of Sino-Pakistan Agreements," Orbis 11 (Fall 1967), pp. 798-825.

30. Full text in Jain, *Soviet-South Asian Relations*, 1:95-98. Indian Premier Shastri suffered a fatal heart attack in Tashkent within a few hours after the signing of the declaration, and his body was flown back to India for Hindu cremation rites.

31. See Mohammed Ayoob, *India, Pakistan, and Bangladesh--Search for a New Relationship* (New Delhi: Indian Council of World Affairs, 1975), especially pp. 69f; also Bhabani Sen Gupta, "Moscow and Bangladesh," *Problems of Communism* 24 (March 1975), pp. 56-68.

32. Full text in Jain, *Soviet-South Asian Relations*, 1:113-116.

33. Norman D. Palmer, "The New Order in South Asia," *Orbis* 15 (Winter 1972), pp. 1109-1121, and Christopher Van Hollen, "The Tilt Policy Revisited: Nixon-Kissinger Geopolitics and South Asia," *Asian Survey* 20 (April 1980), pp. 339-361.

34. See Jain, *China-South Asian Relations*, 1:446-450.

35. *Times of India* (Bombay), March 16-18, 1982; *The Hindu* (International edition), May 5, 1984; and *San Francisco Chronicle*, March 10, 1984.

36. *India News* (Embassy of India, Washington, D.C.), October 31, 1983, p. 1. See also S. P. Seth, "Sino-Indian Relations: Problems and Prospects," *Asia Pacific Community* 26 (Fall 1984), pp. 66-85.

19
Paris and London: Between Washington and Beijing

Douglas T. Stuart

This chapter will focus upon the strategies that have been employed by two West European nations to adjust their foreign policies to pressures from the United States and mainland China since World War II. I have chosen to study two specific West European states rather than West Europe as a whole in order to avoid the familiar errors associated with the homogenization of the very different and often competing foreign policies of the Western European governments. France and Britain were selected because they are the West European nations that had the greatest stake in Asia after World War II and because they provide some interesting contrasts in their responses to the often contradictory demands presented by the United States and mainland China.

The first parts of the British and French sections will present historical summaries of the recognition issue as it was managed by London (from 1949 to 1972) and Paris (from 1949 to 1964). I will then focus upon the development of British and French relations with mainland China since the establishment of diplomatic relations, emphasizing British and French responses to three successive strategies that have been pursued by Beijing over the last fifteen years. These correspond to the doctrines of "the strategic differentiation of the three worlds," "the global anti-hegemony front," and a substantially revised version of the three worlds approach, which is still being developed and has not yet been officially baptized.

Throughout the chapter I will stress British and French security policies and concerns. I will avoid questions of trade and economic relations, except in those cases in which such issues are closely related to security policy, as in the strategic embargo debate of the 1950s and the ongoing issues of arms sales and defense-related technology transfers to Beijing.

GREAT BRITAIN: 1949-1972

On the day that he was in Washington to sign the North Atlantic Treaty (April 4, 1949), British Foreign Secretary Ernest Bevin gave a top-secret briefing to members of the U.S. Policy Planning Staff headed by Secretary of State Dean Acheson. The briefing was meant as a <u>tour d'horizon</u> of recent developments with <u>potential implications</u> for the common security interests of the United States and Great Britain. Bevin made special reference to the situation in China at the time, advising his hosts that in his opinion, the Allies had to begin to face the fact that China seemed to be "lost to us." He reassured the group, however, that Britain would "stand firm" in Hong Kong to challenge the Communist forces on the mainland, noting that Hong Kong could be viewed by the United States as a kind of "Berlin of the East." In fact, however, the British Foreign Office was already attempting during this period to develop a policy of working with the Communist forces rather than a policy of "standing firm." Throughout the summer and fall of 1949, Britain pursued a strategy that Acheson described as "trying to keep a foot in the door [to] see what happens."[1] This effort was followed in December by a British decision to extend de jure recognition to the People's Republic of China, in spite of U.S. pressure for postponement of any Western decision on the issue of recognition.

Bevin attempted to explain the unique concerns of the British government that compelled him to support early recognition of Beijing in a letter to Acheson in December 1949:

There are some factors which affect us

> specially, not only our interests in
> China, but the position of Hong Kong,
> and also in Malaya and Singapore where
> there are vast Chinese communities.
> We are advised that continued non-
> recognition is liable to cause trouble
> there which we cannot afford to risk,
> and we have had to bear this in mind.[2]

This version of the role of Britain's residual colonial possessions in U.K. foreign policy was somewhat different from the Berlin of the East argument. British colonial possessions were presented here (and in several other discussions between London and Washington during the 1950s) as encumbrances and sources of British--and by extension, U.S.--vulnerability, an interpretation of the role of Britain's postwar imperial system that was shared by the majority of U.S. policy-makers at the time. Hong Kong, Malaya, and Singapore were not strong points from which the West could hope to control, contain, and eventually weaken the Beijing regime according to most U.S. security planners. Rather, they were strategic liabilities, which the British government was stuck with because of its continued unrealistic pretensions to empire and which the United States risked becoming saddled with because of its "special relationship" with England.

London's sense of vulnerability in the face of the threat from mainland China was attributable not only to the geostrategic placement of Hong Kong and (to a lesser extent) Malaya and Singapore but to the British economic assets that were vulnerable to the will of the Beijing leadership after 1949. According to estimates by Robert Boardman, capital and outstanding loans from the British government and the London market amounted to slightly over £200m by 1947. Boardman observes that "on none of these questions [investments or outstanding loans] was British official opinion optimistic about the outcome of any further negotiations with the Communist regime: but their existence added weight to the argument that an official relationship with it would serve British interests."[3]

Britain's sensitivity to mainland Chinese

threats to its colonial outposts in Asia, and the above-mentioned British concern for preserving their economic investments in China, ran counter to U.S. warnings that Britain should not move too far away from a coordinated Western position on the issue of recognition. But British leaders appear to have been laboring under a number of misapprehensions in this regard. According to many influential British policymakers of this period, the difference between the U.S. and the British positions was a matter of timing rather than a substantive disagreement on policy. British policymakers assumed that the United States was moving in the direction of recognizing the PRC at the time and that British recognition of Beijing would probably precede U.S. recognition by only a matter of months.[4] A U.S.-U.K. confrontation over the recognition issue was avoided as a result of developments during late 1949 and 1950, which froze negotiations between London and Beijing. Beijing accepted British recognition on January 9, 1950, but bilateral relations were to remain at the chargé d'affaires level until 1972.

Britain's decision to enter the Korean War was treated in Beijing as a confirmation of London's status as a lackey of the United States. An article in <u>Jen min jih pao</u> attributed the British decision to the inducements of "Marshall Plan aid."[5] Over time, however, Britain's perspectives regarding the appropriate policies for the pursuit of the Korean War came to differ in important respects from the policies actually pursued by Washington, in particular on the question of how to keep mainland China out of the war. London pressed for a policy of conciliating and reassuring Beijing while Washington leaned in favor of deterrence. Great Britain argued for giving Beijing the benefit of the doubt in regard to its support for the North Korean offensive and the more general issue of Sino-Soviet cooperation. Bevin developed the British position in a letter to Acheson dated June 15, 1950:

> You know our policy towards China, and I think it is the right policy. On the question of recognition you and

> we have differed, but I did think that,
> as a result of the official talks in
> London in May we were agreed that we
> did not want to see China irrevocably
> alienated from the West. What I am
> afraid of is that the present situation
> will, if we are not careful, push China
> further and further in the direction of
> the Soviet Union. On our information
> China, though reacting violently to
> your declaration on Formosa, has
> committed herself no more than Russia
> has over Korea, and I should doubt if
> she wishes to become involved in that
> conflict. . . . I think we must be
> careful not to accuse China of what
> she has not yet done, or to give her
> the impression that she is already
> so much beyond the pale, that she has
> no hope of re-establishing her position
> with the West.[6]

From Washington's perspective, the immediate need to discourage mainland China from intervening actively in the Korean conflict took precedence over the longer-term and somewhat ephemeral goal of weaning the regime in Beijing away from the Soviet Union, and the demands of deterrence could best be served by a show of strength.

History appears to have vindicated at least one aspect of Bevin's analysis. Mao Zedong was reticent to become embroiled in the Korean War at a time when the PRC leadership was very unsure of its power base and still developing its domestic and foreign policy identity. But Mao mismanaged his campaign to keep the UN forces below the thirty-eighth parallel. He attempted to conjoin the themes of deterrence (involving clear signals and warnings for the purpose of war avoidance) and tactical deception (involving the theme of surprise for the purpose of war winning). The result was a seriously diluted deterrent threat, which failed to discourage Douglas MacArthur from moving north, and a disadvantaged strategy of deception which succeeded only because of the self-delusion of the UN military intelligence gatherers.[7]

After China entered the war, Britain continued to press Washington to provide Beijing with opportunities to extricate itself from the conflict. London retained its diplomatic mission in Beijing after the Chinese intervention in Korea in order to be able to serve a mediating function if this was required. London also supported initiatives aimed at delimiting the area of conflict in Korea, opposed specific U.S. plans to attack North Korean targets that would be especially threatening or damaging to mainland China, and supported Soviet peace proposals during the course of the war.[8]

The dispute between Washington and London regarding how best to influence foreign and defense policy decisions in Beijing persisted throughout the cold war era. Differences over the relative merits of coercion and inducement became particularly intense over the issue of trade with mainland China. In early 1949, the United States began to press Britain to accept a "China differential" in its trade policy with the Communist bloc--a coordinated Western embargo of goods to mainland China that would be more stringent than the embargo imposed on the Soviet Union and other Eastern bloc states. London initially resisted such pressure from Washington on the grounds that any precipitate moves might "provoke retaliatory action against Hong Kong,"[9] but by the end of 1950, the general British position had been brought into line with Washington's approach.

Following the Korean War, the retention of a China differential again surfaced as a matter for U.S.-U.K. dispute. Britain challenged the U.S. argument on two points of principle and one point of pragmatism. The two issues of principle involved British claims that trade embargoes encouraged China to be less, rather than more, reasonable in its international behavior and a general British suspicion of the utility of economic instruments for achieving political ends. The pragmatic concern was that British and Hong Kong traders were being kept out of the mainland China market.[10] This latter concern became more intense and more important as a domestic political issue in Britain when other nations began to develop trade ties with Beijing during the mid-1950s.[11] These considerations led in 1957 to the British decision to break with Washington over the China differential. London was joined by most U.S. allies in a rejection of the U.S.-sponsored embargo policy, and by the end of 1958, the annual trade between mainland China and the four major West European governments had increased by an average of 200 percent over the previous two years.[12]

British policy also diverged from U.S. policy on questions relating to the security and status of Taiwan, with London once again taking a position that was more conciliatory toward Beijing than the U.S. position. At the time of the outbreak of the Korean War, Prime Minister Clement Attlee placed British naval forces at the disposal of the United States. But an analysis of this action by the Royal Institute of International Affairs at the time noted that "the fact that these forces were not also instructed to operate in Formosan waters emphasized the distinction drawn by the British between Korean and Formosan problems and betokened a British intention to steer clear of Formosan entanglements."[13] During 1954 and 1955, Britain sought to encourage the Eisenhower administration to press Chiang Kai-shek to withdraw from Quemoy and Matsu, and there is some indication that London influenced Eisenhower's decision to tone down his public security commitments to the security of the offshore islands in early 1955.[14] In general, however, Britain's efforts to encourage a more accommodating policy toward Beijing on the issue of Quemoy and Matsu were drowned out by cold war rhetoric in the U.S. Congress and in the executive branch during the 1950s.

Britain's cold war disputes with the United States over mainland China--the recognition issue, the management of the Korean War and the Taiwan Straits crises, and the question of the strategic embargo--reflected a fundamental suspicion of Washington's strategy of containing and isolating the PRC and a concern about the repercussions on Hong Kong of any toughening of the Western position. The British preference for bringing mainland China into the community of nations was reflected in particular in Anthony Eden's various proposals designed to bring Washington and Beijing together--in the United Nations and other international forums and/or in direct bilateral negotiations.[15] British sensitivity regarding the security of Hong Kong contributed to the difficulties London experienced in its efforts to articulate and maintain a coherent policy on the issue of sovereignty, particularly during the mid-1950s.

In its attempt to play a mediating role between Washington and Beijing, London usually found itself being criticized by both sides--on grounds of appeasement by U.S. policymakers and on grounds of aggression or deceit by mainland China. In its efforts to find de jure solutions that would satisfy all parties with the least amount of change in the de facto situation, London opened itself to criticisms of betrayal and bad faith from both sides of the Taiwan Strait. Finally, Britain's paramount concern to preserve its economic and political interests in Asia reinforced a suspicion, which had been held by many U.S. leaders following the end of World War II, that the "special relationship" involved special burdens for the United States rather than an additional source of strength for the West in its campaign to contain communism.

The contradictions inherent in Britain's policies toward Beijing are perhaps best illustrated by the fact that London maintained diplomatic ties with the People's Republic of China at the chargé d'affaires level from 1950 to 1967, without a formal exchange of ambassadors. Whatever interest London had in moving beyond this anomalous relationship was constrained by the need for Washington's imprimatur and Beijing's active cooperation. The contradictions were temporarily resolved for Britain in 1967 when the excesses of the Cultural Revolution forced London to downgrade its relations with the PRC, but this situation was finally reversed on March 13, 1972--just fifteen days after the Shanghai communiqué--when London and Beijing established full diplomatic relations.

LONDON AND BEIJING SINCE THE
SHANGHAI COMMUNIQUE

Robert Boardman has recounted in great detail the initiatives by British and PRC leaders between 1969 and 1972 that led to bilateral recognition.[16] The context for the discussions was provided by the Nixon administration, which had been telegraphing its own plans for the eventual recognition of the Beijing regime since coming to office. British politicians and, in particular, businessmen were anxious to avoid being caught unprepared by a U.S. opening to mainland China--especially if it led to a rapid preemption of what were considered to be the most lucrative sectors of the China market.

A special concern among British industrialists was the securing of a substantial portion of any market in weapons and defense-related technologies that might develop between the West and mainland China, and shortly after the formalization of diplomatic ties, the government of Edward Heath announced its support for negotiations for the sale of fifty Rolls Royce Spey engines to mainland China.[17] The negotiations outlived the Heath government and were concluded in 1975 by the Labour government of Harold Wilson. The successful completion of these talks encouraged the subsequent British governments of James Callaghan and Margaret Thatcher to press for further arms-related trade with Beijing. Special priority has been accorded to the sale of Harrier vertical takeoff and landing ground attack aircraft, the Chieftain tank, and the Lynx helicopter.[18]

Between 1972 and 1979, the British governments attempted to delimit the political implications of their pursuit of the China arms market by three strategies:

1. Placing their bilateral defense-related trade in the broader context of London-Beijing commercial transactions
2. Coordinating the sale of weapons and defense-related technologies with Organization for Economic Cooperation

and Development (OECD) allies and requiring Coordinating Committee for Export to Communist Areas (COCOM) approval as a precondition for sale
3. Resisting mainland China's efforts to place the issue of defense-related trade in an explicitly anti-Soviet context[19]

During the latter half of the 1970s, it became increasingly more difficult for London to maintain the third strategy of insulating its arms trade with Beijing from the politics of anti-Sovietism as the leadership in mainland China became more and more strident in its campaign to recruit West European governments into a global antihegemony front against Moscow. The Callaghan government in particular found it difficult to manage the conflicting demands from Moscow and Beijing during this period.

Beijing made no attempt to conceal its dissatisfaction with the ambivalent policies of the Callaghan government in the late 1970s or its preference for the politics of Callaghan's chief political opponent, Margaret Thatcher. With Thatcher's election in May 1979, Beijing acquired its most sympathetic and ardent West European supporter of the logic of the global antihegemony front. Unlike her predecessors, Thatcher was not at all reticent to criticize the Soviet Union or to express approval for quasi-alliance initiatives between mainland China and the OECD states for the explicit purpose of containing an increasingly dangerous USSR.

In public pronouncements between 1979 and 1982, Beijing rewarded Thatcher for her willingness to confront Moscow, comparing her at one point to Winston Churchill in her ability to recognize aggression and resist the pressures for appeasement. But Thatcher was consistently disappointed in her efforts to translate this rhetorical support into commercial advantage in negotiations with mainland China. Although the Thatcher government communicated to Beijing that it was willing to be more flexible than its predecessor had been in bilateral arms-related negotiations, and that it was content to accept the political implications of such defense deals in its relations with Moscow, Great Britain was still unable to close the important Harrier deal or the other previously mentioned arms contracts.

By 1982, Beijing was moderating its public support for Thatcher in accordance with its shift away from the more extreme elements of the global antihegemony front strategy. Arms-related trade talks have continued since that time, but the results have been no more or less impressive. A 1982 contract with Marconi Limited for the purchase of £14 million worth of avionics and radar equipment to modernize mainland China's Type-7 fighter aircraft represents one of the few significant deals since 1972.[20]

If Thatcher has been disappointed by the economic results of her policies toward mainland China, she cannot be any more satisfied with the political results, especially regarding the situation in Hong Kong. Sensitivity to the vulnerability of Hong Kong has been a major determinant of British foreign policy toward China since 1949, and Thatcher cannot claim to have reduced this vulnerability since coming to office. After a brief period of unrealistic assertiveness on the Hong Kong issue, the Thatcher administration negotiated the future of Hong Kong as a rearguard action, in effect, settling for what Beijing was prepared to give in terms of assurances regarding the political and economic status of Hong Kong after it reverts to mainland control.[21]

The reaction to this British approach on the part of the Hong Kong public and, in particular, the business community is not yet a stampede, but the sense of insecurity and the fear of abandonment have been growing steadily since Thatcher's visit to Beijing in the fall of 1982.[22] Mainland China's commitment to Hong Kong's retaining essential aspects of its present system for fifty years after the reversion in 1997 has been greeted with suspicion by many Hong Kong residents. Cynics within the Hong Kong establishment could point to Mao's observation to Henry Kissinger in 1972 that "we can do without Taiwan for the time being, and let it come after 100 years," and to the subsequent change in mainland China's position on this question by the start of the 1980s.[23] A quick back-of-envelope calculation using the Taiwan issue as a formula would encourage the more cautious elements in the Hong Kong community to expect a four-year grace period after Hong Kong's reversion to mainland Chinese control.

It would be gratuitous and unfair to argue that Thatcher should accept all or even most of the blame for the direction of events in Hong Kong since 1982. London-Beijing negotiations over Hong Kong were inevitable in view of the lease status of 90 percent of Hong Kong's territory, and no British government in the 1980s could have approached such negotiations from the position that Hong Kong was militarily defensible or economically viable in the long run in the face of a concerted mainland Chinese opposition. Nevertheless, a good case can be made for the argument that mainland China's assertive stance on the Hong Kong issue, beginning in the middle of 1982, was at least partly attributable to the policies pursued by the Thatcher government in its relations with Beijing during the period of the global antihegemony campaign. Just as U.S. support for a Beijing-sponsored global antihegemony front may have convinced mainland China by the end of the 1970s that Washington was becoming increasingly vulnerable to pressure from Beijing on the issue of reunification, so London may have also communicated a growing stake in mainland Chinese goodwill by its statements and policies between 1979 and 1982.

Hong Kong will continue to dominate London's relations with Beijing for the next few years at least. An appropriate position for Britain to take would be anchored in the propositions that mainland China has an interest in preserving an economically vital Hong Kong and that Beijing recognizes the damage that would be done to its international image if it does not demonstrate good faith in its dealings with the people of Hong Kong after reversion has been accomplished. From this point of view, it becomes clear that London is not without leverage during the transition period. Britain can, and indeed must, use this leverage to contribute to the orderly denouement of the issue, which has been at the core of its policy toward mainland China since 1949.

FRANCE: 1949-1964

Ambivalence and internal contradiction were likewise the hallmarks of French foreign policy in Asia during the 1950s and for many of the same reasons. France, like Britain, attempted in the early cold war years to maintain "the confetti of empire" in Asia without running afoul of either Washington or Beijing. De Gaulle set the direction of French postwar colonial policy in Asia during his brief tenure as head of the Provisional Government (1944-1946) by his announcement, on March 24, 1945, that France would retain its political control over Indochina and by his subsequent decision to send a French expeditionary force to the region to enforce this policy. But successive governments during the Fourth Republic were in general agreement on the principle that long-term peace and stability in Asia--and the preservation of an independent French presence in the region--could be achieved only with the support or at least the assent of China. General Philippe Leclerc articulated this principle shortly after his arrival in Saigon as commander-in-chief of the French expeditionary forces: "Indochina is, first of all, a Chinese problem."[24] This logic encouraged Paris to support policies that led to the signing of the Chungking treaty on February 28, 1946, and many French foreign policymakers subsequently tended implicitly or explicitly to transfer this logic to the Beijing regime after 1949 and to favor a long-term foreign policy goal of "adjustment to reality."

French Prime Minister Georges Bidault commented in May of 1950 that France's recognition of Beijing was largely contingent upon mainland China's self-restraint in Southeast Asia.[25] Beijing nonetheless apparently considered that the potential benefits from involvement in Southeast Asia in support of Ho Chi Minh would outweigh any possible gains that might accrue from official diplomatic ties with France. Mainland

China formally recognized the government of Ho Chi Minh in January 1950 and began to provide extensive arms and matériel support to the Vietminh forces. According to Pierre Rocalle, Beijing provided its own stocks and transhipped Soviet supplies to the Vietminh forces in steadily increasing quantities during the French Indochina conflict: "In the first quarter of 1952 [deliveries] were barely 250 tons per month; at the end of the year they were 450 tons per month; increasing to 900 tons [per month] in the first quarter of 1953 and raised to 2,000 tons by the month of June 1953."[26] By March 1954, the mainland Chinese were contributing to a $500-million Soviet-sponsored common fund in support of the Vietminh war effort and providing extensive military training for Ho Chi Minh's cadres at military schools, mostly located in Yunan.[27]

Under these circumstances, Paris found little opportunity to pursue accommodation with Beijing between 1950 and 1954. After an initial period of indecision, the French government came to accept the U.S. view that under present circumstances, Beijing was "beyond the pale" and could not be reasoned with.[28] The French therefore supported the U.S.-sponsored strategic embargo strategy against mainland China and encouraged a strong UN response to the invasion of South Korea to preserve "Western prestige" and forestall "grave repercussions in Indochina."[29]

French support for U.S. policy toward mainland China and Korea was at least partly a quid pro quo for U.S. aid in Indochina. Between 1950 and 1954, this financial support amounted to $2.6 billion, or 80 percent of the total cost of the French war effort.[30] Paris was also anxious to demonstrate its reliability as a U.S. ally in Asia in order to increase its influence over U.S. foreign policy in the region, but the vulnerability of this strategy for assuring the perservation of French vital interests was driven home in 1954 when Washington refused to assist Paris in its efforts to raise the siege of Dien Bien Phu.

The fundamental flaws in the strategy of seeking assurances from Washington were that it placed Paris in a permanent position of dependency upon U.S. goodwill in Asia and it encouraged

Washington to treat France accordingly. Many U.S. policymakers did, in fact, harbor considerable disdain for Paris during this period, as is reflected in a memo from the director of the U.S. Office of European Affairs to the secretary of state in 1949: "The French have basically only European and North African responsibilities, and inadequate strength to play any role in other theaters and therefore are not entitled to participate in consideration of global strategy."[31] The unavoidable reality for Fourth Republic French foreign policymakers was that U.S. decisions to provide or withhold support for French policies in Asia were determined in Washington. This reality, in turn, encouraged the aforementioned belief on the part of several Fourth Republic policymakers that France's only hope of establishing a foreign policy in Asia that was truly independent of Washington depended upon the support, or at least the approval, of mainland China.

Premier Pierre Mendès-France made an attempt at reconciliation with mainland China during the Geneva talks of 1954, but his efforts foundered on the reality that France was still very firmly entrenched in the Western camp and had very limited room for independent maneuver. Zhou Enlai was pleased to accept the status that was accorded to the Beijing regime by both Mendès-France and Eden during the Geneva negotiations, but he appears to have had no delusions about the limits to which French and British attentions could be translated into real leverage against the United States, the Soviet Union, or both, in the mid-1950s.

The limits of Beijing's interest in France during this period are illustrated by the special attention that mainland China accorded to the Algerian war. Mao Zedong accorded pride of place to this issue in his campaign to displace Khrushchev as the principle spokesman for Third World anticolonialism. Beijing was the first Communist regime to recognize the People's Revolutionary Government of Algeria in 1958 and focused much of its propaganda offensive against Paris during the era of the Algerian war. Mao intensified his public attacks on Paris following

Khrushchev's decision to support de Gaulle's proposals for a cease-fire in Algeria as one portion of the Soviet premier's campaign for peaceful coexistence. This decision provided Mao with ample ammunition for criticizing Khrushchev on grounds of inconsistency and even duplicity in his commitment to anticolonialism. Beijing publicly derided all proposals aimed at a negotiated cease-fire short of victory in Algeria and encouraged the National Liberation Front to uphold its struggle until it had won true independence. By the end of 1960, French policymakers were distinguishing between pro-Chinese and pro-Soviet factions in the National Libration Front--with the former being viewed as the more ferocious and unyielding forces of opposition.[32] Under these circumstances, any hopes that successive French governments harbored regarding rapprochement with Beijing had to await the resolution of the Algerian question.

BEIJING'S PLACE IN THE FIFTH REPUBLIC'S FOREIGN POLICY

In 1944, de Gaulle had warned Churchill that "our two old nations [will] find themselves simultaneously weakened" in the postwar era by "the rise of America and Russia, not to mention China!"[33] Churchill made it clear to de Gaulle at the time that Britain's response to the situation of the relative decline of West European power was to be a strategy of playing Greece to Washington's Rome. "The Americans have immense resources. They do not always use them to the best advantage. I am trying to enlighten them, without forgetting, of course, to benefit my country."[34] For de Gaulle, such a strategy was fundamentally flawed by the inevitability of competition between national interests. De Gaulle preferred instead to manipulate the natural tensions in great power competition as a means of enhancing French power. In the case of China (and in de Gaulle's vision, this meant any mainland Chinese government) the general was guided by an enduring faith in the prospects for special tension between Moscow and Beijing as a result of permanent factors of geography and race. Ultimately, the Soviet Union would have to accept the implications of its status as a "White European nation . . . confronting the yellow multitude."[35] Soviet détente initiatives toward Western Europe would be the logical concomitant, and West European governments would not have to do very much in order to benefit from this situation in the long term. De Gaulle saw himself as the appropriate West European leader to negotiate this new modus vivendi with Moscow, and he sought to position himself to be ready to accept and encourage Soviet solicitations when the time was right.

U.S. cold war dominance and the morass of Algeria were the overriding sources of foreign policy frustration for de Gaulle during the first four years of the Fifth Republic. He came to office convinced that France could not acquire the foreign policy independence that its status required under the existing system of U.S. hegemony. He utilized the directorate proposal of 1958 to confirm this belief publicly and then proceeded to lay the groundwork for his break with Washington. An essential precondition for the establishment of de Gaulle's politics of grandeur was the resolution of the Algerian dispute, which sapped French strength and assured French dependence upon the United States. A second precondition was a channel between Paris and Moscow to permit France to play a larger role in East-West relations. A third precondition for the acquisition of new foreign policy influence, particularly in the Asian region, was the achievement of some form of reconcilation with the PRC.

It should be mentioned at this point that there was nothing inherent in de Gaulle's view of a Sino-Soviet conflict that compelled the general to seek diplomatic ties with Beijing. He believed that a Sino-Soviet conflict would develop with or without the intervention of France and that benefits would inevitably accrue to Western Europe. De Gaulle's decision to recognize the Beijing regime as soon as practicable after Algeria had more to do with his plan for increasing French influence over Washington than over Moscow. The general's writings and actions indicate that he accepted the Leclerc thesis that a successful Asian policy for any Western nation required some accommodation to the reality of mainland Chinese power. He also believed that Washington would share the French fate in its efforts to extricate itself from Vietnam. As long as the United States was trapped in Vietnam, opportunities would arise for France to establish itself as an important and perhaps indispensable mediator between Washington and the regimes in Moscow, Beijing, and Hanoi. Furthermore, Washington's involvement in Vietnam seriously constrained U.S. foreign policy options among other states in Northeast and Southeast Asia--providing potentially rich opportunities for diplomatic maneuvers by de Gaulle. These opportunities could be pursued by France once formal diplomatic ties were established between Beijing and Paris.

De Gaulle stressed the theme of "adjustment to reality" in his press conference to announce the formalization of bilateral relations on January 31, 1964: "The weight of evidence and of reason increases day by day. The French Republic estimated, for its part, that the time had come to place its relations with the People's Republic of China on a normal, in other words a diplomatic, basis."[36] Jacques Vernant reflected the general French response to de Gaulle's initiative in an article published in March 1964:

> The merit of the decision can hardly be challenged, and in fact has been challenged by very few. . . .
> France . . . continues to have important material and moral interests in Southeast Asia. And one cannot feel confident of safeguarding these interests unless there is a regional solution, which presupposes a minimal political accord with China.[37]

As Jean-Luc Domenach observes:

> In the eyes of Washington officials

> and commentators, who were increasingly obsessed with the Vietnam War, General de Gaulle's spectacular gesture did not appear to be that "recognition of realities" which received the almost unanimous approval of French public opinion . . . but rather, pure and simple "treason."[38]

In the eyes of the Beijing leadership, which had sought geostrategic advantage at French expense in Indochina and propaganda advantage at French expense in Algeria, French willingness to extend recognition to the People's Republic of China in 1964 must have appeared as a gift and as further confirmation of the inevitability of recognition by all Western governments, on Beijing's terms.

During 1964 and 1965, neither the PRC nor France appears to have gained any useful leverage or special benefits in the international system as a result of their exchange of ambassadors. De Gaulle in particular appears to have been frustrated in his hopes of transforming the Paris-Beijing relationship into an instrument for advancing French global interests. Several French editorials during 1964 and 1965 focused on de Gaulle's disappointment, attributing it variously to the general's self-delusion, Mao's conscious deception, or both.[39] Self-delusion on de Gaulle's part is probably the most accurate explanation. The international system was still overwhelmingly bipolar in the mid-1960s, in spite of de Gaulle's numerous initiatives and Beijing's controversial challenges to Soviet authority. By 1966, any hopes that de Gaulle still entertained regarding the potential utility of ties with Beijing foundered on the hysteria of the Cultural Revolution, which began to occupy all of the attention and energy of mainland China.

With the waning of the Cultural Revolution, Paris and Beijing began to interact once more, providing Washington with a convenient channel for its early inquiries into the preconditions for a Washington-Beijing bilateral recognition. Nixon solicited de Gaulle's assistance in this regard during the U.S. president's visit to Paris in March 1969, and de Gaulle used that occasion to articulate his theory of the inevitability of further Sino-Soviet conflict and the direct and indirect benefits of such a situation for the Western powers.[40] It is to some extent a confirmation of the essential logic of de Gaulle's strategy that at the very end of his career, his assistance was solicited by a U.S. president because France commanded an independent diplomatic position between Washington and Beijing. It is nonetheless also a comment on the limitations of French power and influence that de Gaulle was being asked to serve as an intermediary, but not as the only intermediary and certainly not as an active participant, in the preliminary negotiations between Washington and Beijing.

During the period of Georges Pompidou's presidency (1969-1974), Paris and Beijing found common ground in their opposition to the post-World War II hegemonic order and in their suspicion of any U.S.-Soviet initiatives that contributed to the possibility of a great power condominium. Mainland China and France diverged, however, in their strategies for playing Washington against Moscow.

The threat posed by Moscow substantially reduced mainland China's foreign policy flexibility during the Pompidou era, and Beijing found itself at least temporarily in the <u>demandeur</u> position in negotiations with the United States. Chinese doctrine during the period, which stressed the three worlds theme of opposition to both superpowers, was thus a double fiction in that it camouflaged a foreign policy that was based upon a clear distinction between Washington and Moscow and it accorded priority to Second and Third World politics at a time when Beijing's overriding interest and attention was focused upon the nations of the First World.

Although détente with Moscow was impossible for Beijing during the Pompidou era, it was an important policy option for France. Following a Gaullist tradition dating back to the Franco-Soviet pact of December 1944, Pompidou attempted to establish himself as the principle spokesman for Europe in détente relations with the USSR. This placed an absolute limit on the prospects for foreign policy coordination with China. The French president made his nation's position clear during his visit to mainland China in September 1973 by borrowing Willy Brandt's formula ("détente plus defense equals security").[41] He expanded upon this theme in a press conference in Beijing:

> The situation in Europe is a situation which is at present moving toward détente and toward development and cooperation. Asia is a different matter, because there are still centers of conflict, there is the factor of China's immensity and the immensity of its frontier with the USSR, there is Japan, with its formidable development on China's border. There is the United States, which remains there even if it retreats from certain regions. All of this makes it obvious that the point of view of China and the point of view of France cannot coincide.[42]

French détente politics become an increasingly disruptive issue in Paris-Beijing relations in the second half of the 1970s as mainland China pursued a more confrontational strategy against Moscow under the banner of the global anti-hegemony front. This Chinese campaign presented Valéry Giscard d'Estaing with two political problems. It publicly encouraged greater French policy coordination with NATO at a time when Giscard was in fact attempting to adjust aspects of French defense planning to the requirements of coordinated Western defense without drawing public attention to these initiatives, and it contributed to the arguments of Giscard's political opponents who defined the president's détente policies in terms of Finlandization. It is not surprising, therefore, that Giscard was especially concerned about the possibility that Hua Quofeng would use the occasion of his visit to France during the fall of 1979 as an opportunity to either commend him for his progress toward greater NATO cooperation or scold him on his cooperation with the USSR.

In spite of policy differences, France and

mainland China did begin to develop a bilateral arms trade during the Giscard presidency. The most significant deals for France during the late 1970s were the sale of thirty Alouette and Super Frelon helicopters in 1977 and fifty Dauphin-II heliocopters in 1980.[43] Although such contracts were small by comparison with French arms deals with other Third World nations, they remain among the most important instances of successfully completed contracts between West European aerospace firms and mainland China, along with the previously cited British deals. They also represent the outer limits of Paris-Beijing security cooperation in a period when mainland China was sponsoring a new security framework based on extreme anti-Sovietism and France was attempting to make what profit it could out of the existing situation of declining superpower détente.

There is a nice irony in the fact that the arguments developed by Beijing in the late 1970s to enlist West European governments in the global antihegemony front bear a striking resemblance to the <u>guerre revolutionnaire</u> theory developed by French policy elites in the 1950s to convince Washington that France was doing more than its share to defend NATO interests by its military campaigns in Indochina and Algeria.[44] According to the <u>guerre revolutionnaire</u> thesis, Western governments were insufficiently attentive to the global nature of the Communist threat and to the geostrategic significance of the Third World for the survival of the industrialized democracies. Mainland China and Russia were generally depicted as being in close collaboration in these arguments, although Beijing was generally identified as the more immediate and direct threat to Western security. Communist strategy was described as a pincers movement against the West, by direct and indirect domination of strategic regions in the Third World. The ultimate goals for Moscow and Beijing were the encirclement of Western Europe and the strangulation of Western resource and trade lines, the separation of Western Europe from the United States.[45] Two decades later, the Giscard administration was treated to virtually the same arguments in the form of the global antihegemony front, with two important differences:

Beijing was now the hero of the piece, rather than the principal villain as it had been in the 1950s, and Soviet social imperialism was substituted for revolutionary communism as the ultimate source of global tensions.

To the extent that he was able, Giscard sought to discourage Beijing from pressing its case for a global anti-Soviet alliance in the 1970s, at least on French soil, but this attempt assisted Francois Mitterrand in his efforts to criticize Giscard on the grounds of subservience to Moscow during the presidential campaign of spring 1981. Mitterrand argued for a more assertive policy toward the Soviet Union in light of the growth of Soviet global military power, the SS-20 threat, and the Soviet invasion of Afghanistan. He did not discount the importance of détente, but he stressed the need for identifying the conditions under which détente could be expected to persist. Mitterrand also succeeded in casting doubt upon Giscard's ability to maintain independence from Washington in his foreign and defense policies.

All three of Mitterrand's campaign themes--sensitivity to the Soviet threat, conditional détente, and a policy of independence from Washington--found an attentive audience among a Beijing leadership that had begun, by this time, to move away from the more extreme elements of the global antihegemony campaign in favor of a more multifaceted foreign policy strategy. This interest led some analysts to predict an especially close relationship between Paris and Beijing in the early 1980s, but the results have been somewhat disappointing. In the realm of defense-related trade, there have been no major deals struck between France and mainland China although the Mitterrand government has been as active in its support of French arms exports as any of its predecessors.

French disappointment in its attempts to sell arms to mainland China is primarily due to the combination of reticence and poverty that has made Beijing a particularly frustrating trading partner for all West European arms merchants. But it is also symptomatic of more general diplomatic problems that have developed between

Paris and Beijing since 1981. Mitterrand has run afoul of Beijing on three issues in particular:

1. The priority that Mitterrand has accorded to relations with India and, in particular, his willingness to actively contribute to the modernization of the Indian armed forces by the sale of weapons and defense-related technology to New Delhi. The Indian purchase of coproduction rights for the Mirage-2000 was a special concern for Beijing in 1982.[46]
2. French attempts to "keep a foot in the door" in Southeast Asia by maintaining ties with the government of Vietnam. Paris was subjected to particularly strong criticism by mainland China in 1982 and 1983 when France extended financial aid to Hanoi--an action that was interpreted by Beijing as an indirect subvention of Vietnamese aggression in Cambodia.[47]
3. Periodic French criticisms of the Khmer Rouge faction within the Beijing-sponsored coalition of Cambodian opposition forces and, in particular, statements of "revulsion" regarding Pol Pot.[48]

To date, both sides have kept these specific disputes in context and under control, and during 1984, there were some policy adjustments by Beijing and Paris that may have reduced the prospects for a major confrontation over any of these issues. In the case of India, there have been noticeable improvements in the relations between New Delhi and Beijing, which may encourage mainland China to take a less alarmist view of Indian defense modernization in general and the Franco-Indian arms trade in particular. In the case of Southeast Asia, the French government continues to openly vilify Pol Pot, but President Mitterrand has accepted at least the principle of

Khmer Rouge participation in a coalition government in Cambodia, and France has increased its criticisms of Vietnam for its occupation of Cambodia.[49]

Foreign policy engagements over specific issues are likely to continue to surface between Paris and Beijing in the future, because both France and mainland China are now actively involved in world politics in general and in the Third World in particular. Such engagements will be characterized by conflict or cooperation, according to the issues involved, but in either case they should contribute to making the next few years an especially interesting period for Paris-Beijing relations.

Both Paris and Beijing are now in a better position to assert real foreign policy independence than at any time since the beginning of the cold war. This new power is primarily attributable to structural changes in the international system, but both France and mainland China have been positioning themselves to take advantage of such structural changes since 1944 in the case of Paris and at least since the mid-1950s in the case of Beijing. Given these parallel developments, it is not surprising that France and mainland China hold similar points of view on many questions of arms control, strategic doctrine, and East-West relations. Such similarities in world view should help Beijing and Paris manage foreign policy disputes when they arise, and they could also provide a context for increased cooperation between France and mainland China on issues relating to the aforementioned general topics.

ANALYSIS

At the end of World War II, France and Britain shared the problems associated with being relatively weak nations committed in principle to preserving as much of their former Asian empires as practicable. Great Britain attempted to solve the problems by relying upon its special relationship with the United States, hoping to "enlighten" Washington in such a way as to advance British security interests in Asia. France, on the other hand, initially sought to pursue a strategy of independent action, but it could not avoid the necessity of soliciting U.S. sponsorship. Both the British and the French approaches were frustrated by the realities of the power structure in the postwar international system. Both West European states were relatively dispensable in Washington's global security planning, in spite of their efforts to convince the United States to the contrary.

Under these circumstances, neither could be sure that it would receive the amount of U.S. backing that might be required to preserve their respective colonial holdings in Asia, particularly in view of the fact that anticolonialism remained an influential, if secondary, theme in U.S. foreign policy throughout the cold war years. For Britain, this situation gave rise, not to a solution, but to a series of accommodations in its policies toward Beijing and Washington, accommodations that continue to haunt British policymakers today. For France, a solution of sorts was imposed upon Paris at Dien Bien Phu. But having been "liberated" from the most severe constraints on and contradictions in its foreign policy toward Asia, France nonetheless found it difficult to acquire, and then to effectively play, its "China card" from a position of relative weakness in the still predominantly bipolar international system of the late 1960s.

Most other West European governments were spared the kinds of decisions faced by France and Britain in Asia. Since they had limited interests in the region as a whole, they could treat the choice between accommodation and containment of mainland China with relative indifference or academic objectivity. Since they tended as a group to understand the implications of their positions as junior partners in the Western system, they generally adopted positions that were in line with U.S. policy at very low cost to themselves. In a period of just two years (1971-1972), the majority of these West European governments established diplomatic relations with Beijing. In effect, this rush to Beijing was a foregone conclusion in light of the Nixon/Kissinger initiatives that preceded it, but it is important to note that West European governments were not being pulled in the direction of mainland China by the United States. Rather, the Nixon/Kissinger opening to Beijing was viewed in most West European capitals as a long overdue adjustment to reality and as an opportunity to pursue the mythical "China market" in earnest, without the encumbrances of cold war diplomacy.

From the point of view of Beijing, the opening of one West European embassy after another in the early 1970s must have been a source of considerable reassurance during a period of serious geostrategic vulnerability and after the diplomatic isolation and domestic chaos of the Cultural Revolution. In terms of economic development, the West European governments were recognized as potentially rich alternative sources of technology, expertise, and hard currency, which could be used to enhance Beijing's negotiating leverage in trade and arms transfer negotiations with the United States and Japan. In the realm of security and global diplomacy, the Beijing leadership also recognized that Western Europe provided new opportunities for "making foreign things serve China." The principle policy question for mainland China was how best to capitalize upon the opportunities provided by Western Europe in the 1970s.

Beijing's initial response was a strategy that emphasized the contradictions it saw in the U.S.-European relationship. In terms of its relations with Britain, this strategy underestimated the extent to which London continued to recognize the desirability of preserving its special relationship with Washington. As a basis for relations with France in the early 1970s, the three worlds thesis did correspond to the enduring Gaullist predisposition toward anti-Americanism, but it foundered upon the fact that Pompidou was unable to develop an independent position vis-à-vis Washington without entangling France in détente relations with Moscow.

Over time, Beijing's doctrine of indiscriminate opposition to both superpowers became impossible to maintain in the face of growing Washington-Beijing cooperation. This situation encouraged Beijing to shift its doctrinal and political emphasis to the global antihegemony campaign by the mid-1970s and to press the West European states to play a more active role in NATO. The global antihegemony campaign corresponded fairly well with Britain's continued commitment to the Anglo-American special relationship, particularly after the election of Margaret Thatcher in 1979, but Beijing's campaign presented special problems for Giscard d'Estaing, in both domestic and international politics, and helped to highlight the inconsistencies in Giscard's politics that made him vulnerable to attack by Mitterrand in 1981.

Since 1981, Beijing has moved away from the global antihegemony strategy and has pursued a foreign policy based upon mixed adversary relations with both superpowers. This more balanced policy toward the superpowers has been mirrored in Beijing's approach to Britain and France. Anti-Sovietism is no longer the overriding issue in London-Beijing or Paris-Beijing relations, and it is not likely to resurface as the central issue in these bilateral relationships in the foreseeable future. Instead, mainland China's discussions with Britain and France now center upon specific areas of converging and competing interests.

Mainland China's shift to a mixed adversary strategy is an encouraging sign since it reflects a trend toward moderation and pragmatism on the part of the Beijing leadership. It is also a more flexible and potentially a more beneficial strategy for mainland China in the long run. To the extent that this strategy represents a step away from the politics of diatribe that has characterized so much of mainland China's international relations since 1949, it should be welcomed by all actors on the international scene.

NOTES

1. Acheson's response to Bevin's reference to the Berlin of the East is informative: "The thought of another Berlin, if this involved another airlift, filled me with considerable

distaste" (cited in Foreign Relations of the United States (FRUS), vol. 6, Near East, South Asia, and Africa (1949), p. 315.

2. Bevin's letter to Acheson, December 16, 1949, in FRUS, vol. 9, Far East: China (1949), pp. 225-226.

3. Robert Boardman, Britain and the People's Republic of China, 1949-74 (New York: Barnes and Noble, 1976), pp. 12-13.

4. Ibid, passim.

5. Jen min jih pao [People's daily], August 13, 1950, quoted in Allen Whiting, China Crosses the Yalu (Stanford: Stanford University Press, 1968), p. 71.

6. FRUS, vol. 8, Korea (1950), p. 398. See also Mineo Nakajima, "The Sino-Soviet Confrontation: Its Roots in the International Background of the Korean War," Australian Journal of Chinese Affairs 1 (January 1979), pp. 19-46.

7. Discussed in D. Stuart and W. Tow, "The Theory and Practice of Chinese Military Deception," in Strategic Military Deception, ed. D. Daniel and K. Herbig (New York: Pergamon, 1982), pp. 298-301.

8. See, for example, British attempts to reassure mainland China that "there would be no crossing of the Yalu and no interference with essential installations along its course" (Survey of International Affairs, 1949-1950 [London: Royal Institute of International Affairs, 1953], pp. 497-498).

9. FRUS, vol. 6, East Asia and Pacific (1950), p. 643.

10. Robert Boardman quotes a British MP in 1953 describing the mood in the Hong Kong business community regarding the embargo policy, "much as a man would feel if you were to give him a knife and tell him that it was in his interests to go and cut his own throat" (Boardman, Britain and the People's Republic, p. 101). The China differential debate is discussed by D. Stuart and W. Tow in "Chinese Military Modernization: The Western Arms Connection," China Quarterly (June 1982), pp. 253-270.

11. Robert Boardman mentions British concern between 1953 and 1957 that other U.S. allies, in particular Japan, were taking advantage of

Britain's adherence to the embargo policy to acquire lucrative contracts with mainland China. He also notes the growing suspicion during this period that the United States was edging toward a reversal of its own embargo policy to get the jump on British businessmen (Boardman, *Britain and the People's Republic*, pp. 100-101).

12. From 1956 to 1958, trade with mainland China increased in West Germany (338 percent), France (95 percent), Italy (214 percent), and the U.K. (153 percent) (see D. Stuart and W. Tow, "Chinese Military Modernization," p. 253).

13. *Survey of International Affairs, 1949-1950*, pp. 481-482.

14. Boardman, *Britain and the People's Republic*, pp. 112-129.

15. See, for example, Richard Harris, "Britain and China: Coexistence at Low Pressure," in A. M. Halpern, ed., *Policies Toward China* (New York: McGraw-Hill, 1965).

16. Boardman, *Britain and the People's Republic*, pp. 143-154.

17. In testimony before the Joint Economic Committee of the U.S. Congress in 1979, Lt. General Eugene Tighe (director, Defense Intelligence Agency) observed that "new generation offensive systems [in the mainland Chinese air force] will be centered in the British Spey jet engine for which China has procured production rights . . . in addition, the Spey could also be used for a new generation of tactical transport aircraft and possibly a new light Bomber" (U.S. Congress, Joint Economic Committee, *Allocation of Resources in the Soviet Union and China, 1979*, Hearings before the Subcommittee on Priorities on Economy in Government, 96th Cong., 1st sess. 1979, pp. 123-124). For an updated analysis of the difficulties China has confronted in its aircraft development, see the chapter by Bill Sweetman on "Chinese Air Power" in G. Segal and W. Tow, eds., *Chinese Defense Policy* (London: MacMillan, forthcoming), and the more general study of *La modernisation de la defense chinoise et ses principales limites, 1977-1983*, Georges Tan Eng Bok, Fondation pour les Etudes de Defense Nationale, Convention du recherche no. 81-82.05 (Paris, December 1983).

18. Discussed in D. Stuart, "Prospects for Sino-European Security Cooperation," *Orbis* 26 (Fall 1982), pp. 721-747.

19. For further information, see D. Stuart and W. Tow, "China's Military Turns to the West," *International Affairs* (London) 26:3 (Spring 1981), pp. 289-290.

20. For details see Stuart, "Prospects," p. 732.

21. The text of the joint declaration between London and Beijing is published in the *Times* (London), September 27, 1984, p. 5.

22. For background, see Gordon Lawrie, "Hong Kong and the PRC: Past and Future," *International Affairs* (London) 56:2 (Spring 1980), pp. 280-295. An update, with analysis, is provided by Robert Sutter in "The United States and Hong Kong's Future: Important Interests, Limited Options," Congressional Research Service, Report no. 83-149-F (July, 1983). See also Chalmers Johnson's chapter on "The Mousetrapping of Hong Kong," chapter 5 of this book.

23. Henry Kissinger, *Years of Upheaval* (Boston: Little, Brown, 1982), p. 692.

24. Cited in Guy de Carmoy, *The Foreign Policies of France: 1944-1968* (Chicago: University of Chicago, 1970), p. 134.

25. Boardman, *Britain and the People's Republic*, p. 53.

26. Pierre Rocalle, ed., *Pourquoi Dien Bien Phu?* (Paris: Flammarian, 1968), p. 68, cited in Georgette Elgey, *La Republique des contradictions: 1951-54* (Paris: Fayard, 1968), p. 439 (translated by the author).

27. Ibid.

28. France initially hoped to be able to follow Britain's strategy of "keeping a foot in the door," as is evidenced by the fact that the first counselor of the French embassy remained in Canton until the summer of 1950 and a second French diplomat remained in Beijing until the middle of 1951. But as the conflicts in Korea and Indochina intensified, this conditional strategy became increasingly untenable (see, in particular, *FRUS*, vol. 6, *East Asia and the Pacific*, pp. 851-855, on the period of French indecision).

29. Ibid., pp. 175-176. See also the account in Alfred Grosser, La IVe Republique et sa politique etrangere (Paris: COLIN, 1961), pp. 280-281.

30. U.S. Senate, Congressional Record, February 21, 1966, p. 3410.

31. Quoted in Michael Harrison, The Reluctant Ally (Baltimore: Johns Hopkins University Press, 1981), p. 13.

32. On the role of Algeria in Sino-Soviet competition, see Roderick MacFarquhar, The Origins of the Cultural Revolution (London: Royal Institute of International Affairs, 1983), pp. 260-261, and Donald Zagoria, The Sino-Soviet Conflict: 1956-1961 (Princeton: Princeton University Press, 1962), pp. 270-272.

33. The War Memoirs of Charles de Gaulle: Salvation, 1944-46 (New York: Simon and Schuster, 1960), p. 58.

34. Ibid., p. 59.

35. See my analysis of de Gaulle's theory in "Sino-Soviet Competition: The View from Western Europe," in D. Stuart and W. Tow, eds., China, the Soviet Union, and the West (Boulder, Colo.: Westview Press, 1982), pp. 216-218.

36. Le Monde, February 2-3, 1964; quoted in Francois Fejto, "France and China: The Interaction of Two Grand Designs," in Halpern, Policies Toward China, p. 61.

37. Jacques Vernant, "La Reconnaissance de la Republique Populaire de Chine," Revue de defense nationale 20 (March 1964), pp. 514-515 (translated by the author).

38. Jean-Luc Domenach, "Sino-French Relations: A French View," in Chun-tu Hsueh, ed., China's Foreign Relations: New Perspectives (New York: Praeger, 1982), p. 89.

39. See, for example, Rene Debernat, "L'Elysee decu par Mao," Combat, October 14, 1964, and "M. Mabraux a Pekin," Le Monde, July 22, 1965.

40. Henry Kissinger, The White House Years (Boston: Little, Brown, 1979), pp. 107-110.

41. Le Monde, September 16-17, 1973, p. 6.

42. "La visite officielle du president de la Republique in Republique Populaire de Chine, 10-17 Septembre, 1973," Ministere des Affaires Etrangeres, Information et Presse, October 1973,

p. 17 (translated by the author).
43. Stuart and Tow, "China's Military," pp. 292-293.
44. The colonialist geostrategic perspective was reflected in a number of French journals in the 1950s, of which Revue de defense national is the most well known. For a survey of these writings, see Raoul Girardet, L'idee coloniale in France: 1871-1962 (Paris: Table Ronde, 1972), passim.
45. See, in particular, L. M. Chassim, "Vers un encirclement de l'occident," Revue du defense national 12 (May 1956), pp. 531-552.
46. On the French-Indian Mirage deal, see Far Eastern Economic Review, January 15, 1982, p. 20.
47. Mainland China's response to the French offer of aid to Hanoi is reported in Summary of World Broadcast (SWB), Far East, April 27, 1982 (FE/7012/A1-2).
48. See French Foreign Minister Claude Cheyson's comments during his 1982 tour of Southeast Asia, quoted in the Times (London), August 3, 1982.
49. See Mitterrand's comments while in Beijing, reported in Le Monde, May 5, 1983. On Beijing's efforts to improve its relations with New Delhi, see Yaakov Vertzberger, "China's Strategic Thinking, Defense Policy, and Diplomacy toward South Asia," in Segal and Tow, Chinese Defense Policy.

20
Sino-Soviet Relations and the Asian Quadrangle, 1984

William E. Griffith

Because it is now more than five years since the PRC[1] first reciprocated the 1964 Soviet proposal to improve mutual relations at the state level, the time has come to draw up a new balance sheet concerning its results. I shall consider two aspects, methodological and analytical. To begin with, we must formulate new methodological categories in four respects. First, we must replace the "break-reconciliation" dichotomy with one centering on the varying levels and extent of détente. Second, we must treat Sino-Soviet relations, as the USSR and the PRC now do, primarily on the realpolitik rather than on the ideological level. Third, we must analyze those relations as a part of global politics, especially those of the Asian quadrangle, which also includes Japan and the United States. Fourth, we must pay more attention to the role of peripheral middle powers in the relationship, notably Vietnam and Mongolia. Analytically, we must analyze the causes of the recent limited Sino-Soviet détente as well as its extent, direction, limits, and likely duration.

What has happened recently in Sino-Soviet relations may be briefly summarized, for it has been analyzed in detail elsewhere.[2] Since 1979, with an interruption caused by the Soviet invasion of Afghanistan, negotiations at the deputy foreign minister level have been going on intermittently between Moscow and Peking. They have resulted in some improvement in economic, cultural, and sport relations, but no progress has been made on the main substantive issues in dispute. Peking has demanded that the Soviet Union cut back the number of its troops on the Chinese frontier, withdraw all of its troops from Mongolia, withdraw from Afghanistan, settle the Sino-Soviet border disputes, abandon its support of Vietnam's invasion of Cambodia, withdraw from Danang and Cam Ranh Bay, and, recently, cut back sharply on its SS-20 deployment targeted on East Asia. Moscow has steadily rejected these demands and, instead, has proposed a nonaggression pact between the two countries.

In early and mid-1984, Sino-Soviet relations worsened again. The postponement of the visit to Peking of Soviet Deputy Premier Arkhipov, one day before it was scheduled, probably reflected Soviet resentment at the Reagan and Nakasone visits to Peking, the subsequent Sino-Japanese and Sino-U.S. defense discussions, and the escalation of Sino-Vietnamese border clashes. Behind this action probably lay Chernenko's domestic and foreign policy hardening and Deng Xiaoping's greater emphasis on domestic reforms and his renewed moves toward Washington and Tokyo, which, just like the contrast between Krhushchev's thaw and Mao's Great Leap Forward in the late 1950s, worsened Sino-Soviet relations. The Soviets also resented China's more active policy toward Eastern Europe, the more so because of their problems with East Germany's and Hungary's resistance to the Soviet Union's attempt to limit their ties with West Germany. Moscow and Peking exchanged sharpened polemics on these issues. The former emphasized the necessity of following the "general laws of socialist construction" (i.e., Soviet guidance), and the latter declared that "the real problem lies in the fact that while the Soviets attempt to control us, we are opposed to being controlled." The Chinese also criticized the Soviets, including Chernenko, for attacking China and supporting Vietnam.

However, Gromyko met Chinese Foreign Minister Wu at the United Nations in New York in September 1984 and reportedly said that the Arkhipov visit to Peking was still on the agenda. Thereafter Sino-Soviet polemics declined, and Moscow and Peking again tried to improve their relations.

Arkhipov finally went to Peking in late December 1984, in an atmosphere of Chinese cordiality unprecedented since 1958. His Chinese hosts referred to him as "comrade" and as an "old friend of China." (He had been in charge of Soviet aid to China after Mao came to power.) His visit produced a significant increase in Sino-Soviet trade and a trade agreement for the 1986-1990 period, to be coordinated with both countries' five-year plans. In November 1984, a Soviet parliamentary delegation, headed by Politburo member Kunayev and including Ponomarev's principal deputy Zagladin, visited Japan. They said that they wanted better Soviet-Japanese relations, but they gave no indication of any Soviet compromise on the Kuriles. Finally, Peking did not seriously retaliate militarily against Hanoi, despite the renewed Vietnamese attacks on the Cambodian rebels. Yet Sino-Soviet polemics intensified again in the last three months of Chernenko's rule.

Gorbachev's coming to power intensified this Soviet attempt to improve Sino-Soviet relations. His conciliatory phraseology was more striking than Brezhnev's attempts immediately after the death of Mao. This time, however, the Chinese reciprocated, going even further than Gorbachev did. Gorbachev called for "major improvements" in Sino-Soviet relations in his speech to a Soviet Central Committee plenum immediately after he was chosen. The Chinese representative at Chernenko's funeral, Vice-Premier Li Peng, referred to the Soviet Union and China as "two socialist countries" and Chinese Secretary-General Hu Yaobang congratulated Gorbachev on his election as Soviet secretary-general, thus hinting that Peking was prepared to discuss the reestablishment of Communist Party relations with Moscow. Later, Hu was quoted as having said to Hong Kong journalists visiting Peking, when they asked him about the Chinese "three obstacles," "What three obstacles?" However, he had shortly before said to a journalist from the Italian Communist daily L'Unità that he expected "no swift improvement" in Sino-Soviet relations.

This view seemed confirmed by the apparent lack of substantive progress during the April 9-22, 1984, sixth meeting of Soviet and Chinese deputy foreign ministers in Moscow. Not only did the final communiqué give no such indication, but was followed (in <u>Pravda</u>) by an item about a Vietnamese visit to Moscow³ and preceded, during the meeting, by a <u>Pravda</u> attack on Chinese policy in Afghanistan.⁴ Even so, Sino-Soviet relations had improved, at least in tone, but in May 1985, no rapid or decisive progress in them seemed likely.

In summary, the Soviets have tried to improve the peripheral, atmospheric aspects of Sino-Soviet relations and have hoped, albeit so far essentially in vain, that their adamant refusal to make any substantive concessions to Peking might gradually move the latter toward unilateral Chinese concessions. (Peking no longer demands that Moscow fulfill all of China's conditions. Apparently one would be enough, but Moscow has so far refused to do even that.)⁵

So much for what has happened; why has it? I shall analyze the causes in four respects: the Chinese response to the 1964 Soviet offer, the unforthcoming Soviet counterresponse, the most recent phase, and the increasing external involvement.

THE CAUSES OF THE CHINESE RESPONSE

The post-1979 Chinese response to the often-repeated Soviet offers for negotiation may best be seen as the second act in the Chinese response to the Soviet challenge to China after the Sino-Soviet break. The first was Mao's decision in 1969 to draw the logical consequence from the rising Soviet military buildup and hostility: to improve relations with the United States. (That the Vietnam War was still going on was, it is now clear, an incentive for Washington and not a disincentive for Peking to improve relations, for Chinese-Vietnamese relations were already worsening by that time.) Sino-U.S. relations improved further after Mao's death, for Deng Xiaoping, along with Zhou Enlai, the initiator of the process, and Zbigniew Brzezinski, the U.S. national security adviser during the Carter administration, both pushed it because of parallel concerns about the rising Soviet power.⁶ Mao's and Suslov's deaths made ideological factors no longer serious obstacles to Sino-Soviet détente.

The main analytical problem, therefore, is why Peking in 1979 and again since late 1984 has also favored improvement, however limited, of Sino-Soviet relations? Several reasons may be advanced. The PRC wanted to further improve its security by making less likely a Soviet attack on the PRC or, indeed, excessively high Soviet-U.S. tension, which would result in the disruption of Deng's overriding policy goal, modernization of the PRC. Second, the PRC believed that this goal would be safe as well as desirable because the United States, under Reagan, was stronger, more anti-Soviet, and therefore less likely to compromise with Moscow at Peking's expense while the Soviet Union was weaker and beset by Polish and Afghan troubles and a low growth rate. (Yet by 1984, Reagan was moving toward some improvement, however slight, in Soviet-U.S. relations, and Deng, perhaps in part for that reason, began to improve relations with him and, later, with Moscow.)

Third, even a partial Sino-Soviet détente might make the United States more fearful of a Sino-Soviet reconciliation and therefore be more forthcoming to Peking, especially on the Taiwan issue. Fourth, the PRC could finally afford to abandon any dependence on any foreign power and return to the traditional imperial policy of independence, i.e., of being opposed to all foreign hegemonic powers while championing the Third World and attempting to exercise influence in the (now much looser) international Communist movement. Such a policy, the PRC may well have believed, would give it greater flexibility vis-à-vis both superpowers and make the USSR and the United States more inclined to make concessions in regard to the PRC's demands.

These four conditions were essentially a PRC response to the continuing Soviet military buildup, which increased after the Sino-Soviet negotiations began in 1979. It included major conventional ground, air, and naval deployments around the PRC's frontiers, rising Soviet military presence in and military support of Vietnam, and continuation of the war in

Afghanistan. Although under Khrushchev there were at most only twenty Soviet divisions stationed east of the Urals, there are now fifty-two (180,000 versus 500,000 men), and Soviet tactical and strategic nuclear deployments in Asia continue to increase. Badgers are now stationed at Danang, and the Soviet Far Eastern Fleet uses Cam Ranh Bay regularly.[7]

As had been the case since the first Soviet offer in 1964, Soviet military policy and diplomacy, notably vis-à-vis Vietnam, were thus going in the opposite direction from the Soviet Union's declared policy toward the PRC. The more the Soviet military buildup increased, the more anxious the PRC was to stop or reverse it or, failing that, to engage in negotiations with Moscow, however inconclusive, which would restrain the USSR from using its military power for active aggression against the PRC. Thus, the Soviets were <u>demandeurs</u> tactically (that Peking respond to the Soviet offer), but the Chinese were <u>demandeurs</u> strategically (that the Soviets cut back their military buildup). This situation, however, is not new and certainly not unique in history: Wilhelm II believed that he could simultaneously build up the Imperial German High Seas Fleet and improve relations with London, and the Japanese Empire was not prepared in the 1930s to give up its conquests in China in order to improve relations with the United States.

It is not difficult, therefore, to understand why the PRC has demanded what it has from the Soviets, or why it continues negotiations and allows some peripheral improvement in Sino-Soviet relations despite the Soviet Union's refusal to meet or to compromise on its demands. What is more difficult is the analysis of Soviet policy toward the PRC.

CAUSES OF SOVIET POLICY TOWARD THE PRC

Soviet policy toward the PRC today still seems compounded out of two only apparently contradictory frames of mind: arrogant strength and fear caused by perceived weakness. Soviet military superiority over the PRC is great and getting greater still, but Moscow sees Siberia as empty, far away, and conquered and Soviet lines of communication to it vital but inadequate and potentially threatened. The Soviets fear and despise Japan and all other Asians, and their racism, plus their increasing problems with the Muslims of Soviet Central Asia, make them fear both more. The renewed closeness of the United States and Japan, of the United States and China, and most recently of Japan and China have accentuated Soviet concerns.

Professor Rozman has conclusively demonstrated that at least until very recently, the dominant view among Soviet experts and policymakers, notably Rakhmanin, Kovalenko, and even Kapitsa, remains one of great suspicion of the PRC ("Maoism without Mao") and of Japan, and that the Soviets favor military intimidation as the means to prevent these two countries from becoming dangerous to Soviet security.[8] (A smaller group of experts, which must have some high protectors in order to publish at all, has so far fruitlessly advocated compromise with both and by mid-1985, may have gained more influence.) This dominant view probably argues that the Soviet military buildup in the Far East has at least prevented any major Chinese-originated border incidents and has been the primary reason why the Chinese have agreed to negotiate at all with the Soviets. (As my previous analysis has indicated, this is in fact a very partial and oversimplified analysis of the Chinese motives, but, given Russian history and the Soviet experience, why should it not be?) The question may, then, more accurately be posed as follows: Why has this dominant view remained dominant, given the recently more forthcoming Chinese position?

First, Soviet bureaucratic interia has been intensified by the prolonged Soviet succession crisis. Second, the longer the Soviet military buildup proceeds, the more the Soviet military urges, for bureaucratic as well as for military reasons, its continuation. Third, the USSR, like the PRC and most other authoritarian governments, is not under public pressure for rapid success, so each is predisposed to wait the other out. Fourth, the Soviet buildup can be more effectively justified as anti-U.S.-Chinese, and -Japanese relations become closer in the anti-Soviet Asian strategic triangle (the United States, Japan, and China). (The fact that the Soviet military buildup is one of the major reasons for the consolidation of the triangle is perceived to be the case by its members but not by the Soviet ruling elite.) Fifth, two Soviet allies, Mongolia and Vietnam, have their own strong reasons for opposing a Sino-Soviet détente, and Moscow has so far not been prepared to overrule them in favor of a major Sino-Soviet compromise on any decisive substantive issue.

All this having been said, why did Gorbachev so strongly renew the frequent Soviet initiatives for détente with China, why did China respond so favorably, and what may result? Gorbachev's new initiative was only the latest in a series of similar Soviet moves, first after Khrushchev's removal and then after Mao's death. As earlier, Gorbachev did not indicate that he would compromise on the major Chinese demands. Peking wanted to improve Sino-Soviet relations, but only at the price of some Soviet compromises, and the Chinese were testing Gorbachev's readiness to do so by its cost-free rhetorical gestures within the context of the recent Chinese stress on an independent foreign policy. Peking would probably most of all like some Soviet troop draw-down along the Sino-Soviet and Sino-Mongolian frontiers and also some Soviet pressure on Vietnam toward a compromise in Cambodia.

The favorable Chinese reactions to Soviet gestures before and after Gorbachev came to power occurred at the same time Soviet-U.S. relations began to improve. Since Mao died, Peking has never wanted to be on worse terms with Moscow than Washington is. On the contrary, China's preferred position, like Moscow's and Washington's in this triangular relationship, is to be on better terms with the other two powers than they are with each other. Therefore, any improvement in Soviet-American relations would in theory make Peking improve its relations with Moscow and maintain good relations with Washington as well. This is exactly what Peking seemed to be doing in mid-1985.

However, the other imperatives on Chinese policy continued--their need for Western and Japanese technology, their opposition to Soviet control of the international Communist movement, and their resentment of Vietnam and Mongolia. Nor was it likely that Gorbachev will be able to compromise decisively with Peking, even if he were willing to do so, which is doubtful. Thus slow, peripheral, and limited improvement of Sino-Soviet relations still seemed the most likely near-term prospect.

THE ROLE OF MONGOLIA

Mongolia was a part of the empire of the Manchu (Ch'ing) dynasty. In 1954, he later declared, Mao unsuccessfully asked Khrushchev and Bulganin, during their visit to Peking, to return Mongolia to China. It has been a Russian satellite, except for several years after the 1917 revolution, since the Chinese Empire collapsed in 1911. Given the record of ethnic Chinese expansion into Inner Mongolia, Sinjiang, and Tibet, Mongolia understandably fears China more than Russia and thus is vitally interested in not being reabsorbed into it. Only Russia can guarantee it against this fate. Mongolia therefore can only guard what little independence remains to it if it can prevent Moscow from agreeing in this respect with Peking, over its head and against its interests. (Its predicament in this respect is similar to West Germany's vis-à-vis the United States and the USSR.)

In light of this predicament, an incident in April 1983 becomes more understandable. Mongolia, although it had given intermittent lip service to an improvement of Sino-Soviet and Sino-Mongolian relations, denounced the PRC for demanding that Moscow remove Soviet troops from Mongolia and expelled from its capital into rural areas some thousands of Han Chinese.[9] The PRC protested this Mongolian move, and the Mongolian press replied with fierce polemics against Peking, at least one of which was reprinted at length in <u>Pravda</u>. Thereupon, we may assume, the Chinese brought pressure on Moscow, perhaps even threatening to break off the Sino-Soviet negotiations, and Mongolia, presumably under Soviet pressure, capitulated. The USSR was in any case unlikely to make any concessions to the PRC in this respect because the Soviet tank divisions in Mongolia directly threaten Peking and any Soviet policy of intimidation of the PRC requires that they remain there. Nevertheless, Mongolia must have resented being told by the USSR, on whom Mongolia is extremely dependent for economic aid, to cease deporting the ethnic Chinese to the countryside.

THE ROLE OF VIETNAM

Sino-Vietnamese relations are worse than Sino-Mongolian ones, as has been demonstrated by the brief Chinese attack on Vietnam in 1979; by renewed Sino-Soviet border clashes in the spring and summer of 1984, most notably during President Reagan's visit to China; and by Chinese support in the form of arms shipments and money of the Khmer Rouge in Kampuchea against the Vietnam-controlled Heng Samrin government there. The historic Vietnamese heritage of nearly a millennium of Chinese rule and the traditional Chinese determination to divide and rule over Indochina make a Sino-Vietnamese comity anything but likely.

Conversely, when Hanoi saw the United States as its principal enemy, it tried to keep on good terms with both Moscow and Peking, but it needed the former more than the latter for modern weaponry. Once the United States left Saigon in 1975, and to some extent even before, Hanoi, like Ulan Bator, not surprisingly chose the farther away and stronger ally against close, historic Chinese imperialism. Vietnam needed the Soviet Union even more when, as it had long intended, it moved into Kampuchea. (Indeed, one of the functions of the massive Soviet military deployment on the Chinese frontier was to deter China from conquering Vietnam, thus making it possible for Vietnam to conquer Kampuchea.) Moscow's military and economic aid to Hanoi remains massive, including supplying almost all of Vietnam's petroleum. In return, Moscow has extracted from Hanoi, despite the latter's fierce nationalism, the use of the U.S.-built bases at Danang and Cam Ranh Bay, thereby fulfilling a double Soviet objective: to encircle the PRC militarily from the south and to lie astride the U.S. naval and air communications lines from U.S. bases in the Philippines to Diego Garcia and the Gulf. In April 1984, Soviet and Vietnamese forces held joint maneuvers off the Vietnamese coast.

It is true that the Russians and Vietnamese dislike each other, but that fact has so far not overridden Soviet and Vietnamese realpolitik.[10] Thus, the PRC demands that the Soviet Union abandon Vietnam, the Soviet Union refuses to do so, and the PRC is therefore pushed toward the United States and Japan.

NON-COMMUNIST ACTORS

The United States

The U.S. move toward the PRC was a consequence of the growth of Soviet military power and of the Sino-Soviet split.[11] It was delayed by ideological barriers on both sides: Mao's violent anti-Americanism until 1968 and hostility to the PRC in the United States as a result of the Korean War, the U.S. involvement with the ROC, and U.S. anticommunism. As ideology gave way to realpolitik in Washington and Peking, the Sino-U.S. rapprochement began. (It was begun by Peking and rapidly reciprocated by Washington.) Not surprisingly, it was pushed in Washington by the people who refused to give absolute priority to arms control agreements with Moscow and saw Moscow's realpolitik aim to be to persuade the United States that the price for arms control agreements was Washington's acceptance of Moscow's definition of "equal security": that Washington so limit the military power of its allies, and by implication of such a potential one as the PRC because it is a Soviet enemy, that the USSR would not be inferior to all of its opponents. Soviet exploitation of the opportunities it saw in Third World crises pushed Washington further toward Peking, for proponents of a Sino-U.S. rapprochement used these crises to move in that direction. (For example, Brzezinski used the 1978 Soviet involvement in Ethiopia to scuttle the Soviet-U.S. Indian Ocean negotiations and go to Peking, and he used the Soviet invasion of Afghanistan to put Washington on an even more anti-Soviet course.)

Initially, as Peking saw the situation, the Reagan administration took an anti-Moscow and less pro-Peking (because more pro-ROC) course. But by 1982, the administration's anti-Soviet priority ultimately enabled those in Washington who favored closer Sino-U.S. relations to move U.S. policy in that direction. Thus, the realpolitik adage that "the enemy of my enemy is my friend" reasserted itself. Peking was thus better able to improve its relations with both Moscow and Washington by declaring its "independence" of both hegemonic superpowers while in fact retaining closer relations with Washington.
The April 1984 Reagan visit to Peking made this fact even clearer. It is easy to see that this development served Chinese interests; it served U.S. interests as well.

The visit, preceded by one by U.S. Secretary of Defense Weinberger in September 1983, led to Washington's making China the only other socialist country besides Yugoslavia eligible for military sales and credits. The United States agreed to sell China advanced avionics for its jet fighters and to provide training for Chinese pilots at U.S. bases, and China sold the United States half a squadron of its F-7 copies of the Soviet MiG-2 jet fighter plane. Washington also agreed in principle to sell China antitank and antiaircraft weapons. These agreements were viewed with extreme disfavor by Moscow.[12]

Japan

The major recent development in Sino-Soviet relations, one that is very unfavorable to Soviet interests, has been the Sino-Japanese rapprochement, which culminated in the state visit of Prime Minister Nakasone to Peking in March 1984. Japan granted the PRC $2 billion in credits, and both countries declared that their economic and technological relations would be intensified throughout the twenty-first century and beyond. Japan and the PRC declared that both would work to have the Soviet Union withdraw its SS-20s from Asia, and Japan fully endorsed the PRC position on Vietnam and Kampuchea.

Why did Japan turn toward the PRC? First, because Soviet-Japanese relations have deteriorated sharply. Soviet policy toward post-1945 Japan has been steadily hostile. As Japan's economic power and self-confidence increased, and as Japan drew up to the United States in high technology and far ahead of the USSR and even of Western Europe, the adamant Soviet refusal to make any concessions to Japan on what has become the first national issue in postwar Japanese politics, the return by the Soviet Union to Japan of the four southern Kurile Islands, has become a key issue of conflict between Moscow and Tokyo.

As it does with China, Moscow incorrectly regards military intimidation as the most effective way to exercise influence over Tokyo. So far, as with Peking, the Soviet calculation has backfired--even more so after the KAL incident, probably a Soviet military blunder, which profoundly shocked Japanese public opinion. Because of the Soviet Union's lack of hard currency and concentration on selling natural gas to Western Europe, even Soviet-Japanese trade began to decline in 1983. Moreover, Moscow has steadily increased its military, naval, and nuclear deployments, which Japan sees as directed against itself. Because it is an island archipelago, allied with the United States, and the dominant naval and air power in the western Pacific, Japan is invulnerable to Soviet military pressure short of general war. Japanese nationalism was bound to revive anyway, but it has been speeded up by Soviet intransigence.

Prime Minister Nakasone is the most overt nationalist in post-1945 Japanese history. He publicly advocates autonomous and independent diplomacy and defense, he denies the need for Japan to make any concessions to the USSR, and he wants to cement relations with the United States on the basis of a community bound together by a common destiny. At the Williamsburg summit, he publicly associated Japan with the Western security consensus, and in March 1984, he cemented Sino-Japanese relations and identified Japan with the PRC vis-à-vis the Soviet Union and Vietnam.[13] Thus, the Soviet Union has contributed mightily to what it fears the most in Asia: the creation of a strategic triangle of the United States, Japan, and the PRC directed against it.

The 1984 Sino-Japanese quasi-alliance marked a new defeat for Moscow and a new step toward its encirclement because Japan and the PRC share two important common perceptions vis-à-vis the Soviet Union. Both are irredentist toward Moscow, China with respect at least to the "disputed" territories and Japan with respect to the four southern Kurile Islands. Both feel threatened by Soviet SS-20 deployment in Asia, but unlike Western Europe, where public opinion makes response to it difficult--although as intermediate nuclear force (INF) deployment demonstrated, not impossible--China, which does not permit pacifism, and Japan, which is invulnerable to a Soviet land attack, want to do something against it, a policy they share with Washington.

CONCLUSION

The main new factor in Sino-Soviet relations, and indeed in global politics in general, is the increasing role of Japan: its identification with Washington and Peking, its stronger anti-Soviet position, its rising self-assertive nationalism, and its gradually increasing defense budget. Japan, like the United States, is already a high technology superpower; will it become a high technology military superpower? Not likely, and at least not soon. Indeed, doing so would probably move China more toward the Soviet Union. It seems likely, rather, that Japan, like West Germany, will remain nonnuclear but will contribute greatly, even more than the United States, to the modernization of the PRC (more than West Germany will to the modernization of the Soviet Union, if only because only Japan and the United States will be high technology superpowers, not

West Germany).
   The PRC, on the other hand, has many reasons to prefer Japan as an industrial and a technological partner rather than the Soviet Union or (except in the military field) the United States. Japan can provide state-of-the-art high technology but is not a military threat. It is not involved in the Taiwan issue, it is menaced by the USSR and weaker than the PRC, and it is dependent on exports. The PRC enjoys a unique cultural prestige in Japan, and finally, Japan, unlike the United States, is not, except technologically, a hegemonic power. Conversely, given the partial Chinese détente with the USSR, the United States cannot as easily play the "Chinese card" against the USSR. Washington's current anti-Sovietism makes it want to improve its relations with Peking and not give top priority to arms control agreements with the USSR. Finally, the continued succession struggle in Moscow makes it unlikely that this situation will soon change.
   The stagnation in Soviet policy makes a move by Moscow toward compromise with Washington, Peking, or Tokyo unlikely in the near future. The same is probably true for Peking, at least as long as Deng Xiaoping is in power. Japanese policy moves slowly and consenually, so no rapid change is to be expected from that country. U.S. policy often moves rapidly--at least uncalculably, at most uncalculatedly--but U.S. policy toward China and Japan has become consensual and is likely to remain so.
   Sino-Soviet relations, like those between the U.S. and the USSR, seem to be, and are likely to remain, ones of limited conflict, in the former case because Moscow (reluctantly and Peking (confidently) each thinks that it is in its own self-interest. In the latter case the nuclear threat has made such a relationship necessary. A quadripolar world, therefore, has returned in Asia, one in which realpolitik plays an ever-greater role and ideology an ever-lesser one. Perhaps the Chinese will be the most lasting Gaullists.

NOTES

1. People's Republic of China. I shall use ROC (Republic of China) for the government in Taipei.
2. William E. Griffith, "Sino-Soviet Rapprochement?" Problems of Communism 32:2 (March-April 1983), pp. 20-29; Donald S. Zagoria, "The Moscow-Beijing Detente," Foreign Affairs 61:4 (Spring 1983), pp. 853-873; Jacques Levesque, "L'evolution des relations sino-sovietiques: 'Les trois obstacles' dans un monde changeant," Le monde diplomatique 31:361 (April 1984), pp. 1, 6; Harry Harding, "Change and Continuity in Chinese Foreign Policy," Problems of Communism 32:2 (March-April 1983), pp. 1-19; Joachim Glaubitz, "Akzentverschiebungen in der Aussenpolitik Chinas," Stiftung Wissenschaft und Politik, SWP-AP 2357 (April 1983); Allen S. Whiting, "Assertive Nationalism in Chinese Foreign Policy," Asian Survey 23:8 (August 1983), pp. 913-933; Jonathan D. Pollack, "The Sino-Soviet Rivalry and Chinese Security Debate," Rand report no. R-2907-AF (Santa Monica, Calif., October 1982); Herbert S. Yee,"The Three World Theory and Post-Mao China's Global Strategy," International Affairs 59:2 (Spring 1983), pp. 239-249; Alain Jacob, "La lente reinsertion, de la Chine dans le monde communiste," Politique etrangere 48:1 (Spring 1983), pp. 63-74; Robert L. Worden, "China's Balancing Act: Cancun, the Third World, Latin America," Asian Survey 23:5 (May 1983), pp. 619-636; Harry Gelman, "Soviet Policy Toward China," Survey 27:118/119 (Autumn-Winter 1983), pp. 165-174, "Soviet Expansionism in Asia and the Sino-Soviet-U.S. Triangle," (Paper presented at Security Conference on Asia and the Pacific, Marina del Rey, California, March 1983), "The Soviet Far East Buildup and Soviet Risk-Taking Against China," Rand report no. R-2943-AF (Santa Monica, Calif., August 1982), and a recent unpublished paper on Sino-Soviet relations; Donald S. Zagoria, "The Kremlin Looks Bad in East Asia," Journal of East Asian Affairs 3:1 (Spring-Summer 1983), pp. 113-152; and the papers and testimonies of Seweryn Bialer, Harry Gelman, and Kenneth Lieberthal

before the Subcommittee on Asian and Pacific Affairs of the U.S. House of Representatives Committee on Foreign Affairs, August 2, 1983 (Washington, D.C.: Government Printing Office, Committee Print, 1983). I differ with Segal's more optimistic view of Sino-Soviet relations in Gerald Segal, "Sino-Soviet Relations: The Road To Detente," World Today 40:5 (May 1984), pp. 205-212. I have profited from discussions with Gelman and from recent conversations in Moscow, Peking, and Tokyo.

3. Pravda, April 23, 1985, p. 4.
4. Ibid., April 18, 1985, p. 5.
5. For the Soviet view, see O. B. Borisov (pseud. for O. B. Rakhmanin, first deputy chief, CPSU CC Department for Liaison with Communist States and Ruling Parties), "Soyuz novogo tipa," Voprosi istorii KPSS, no. 4 (April 1984), especially pp. 45-56, and O. Drugov, "Proletarsky internatsionalizm: traditski i sovremennost'," Partiinaya zhizn', no. 12 (June 1984), pp. 13-22; analysis: see Sallie Wise, "What's Behind the Recent Sino-Soviet Chill?" Radio Liberty Research, no. 298/84 (August 6, 1984). The Rakhmanin article polemicized with an earlier article by Mátyás Szurös, "The Reciprocal Effect of the National and International Interests in the Development of Socialism in Hungary," Társadalmi Szemle 39:1 (January 1984), pp. 13-21. (FBIS/EE/30 Jan. 84/F1-9.) For an analysis of Soviet-East European tension, see Fred Oldenburg, "Werden Moskaus Schatten langer?" Deutschland Archiv, no. 8 (August 1984). For Rakhmanin's hard line on Sino-Soviet relations, see Gilbert Rozman, "Moscow's China-Watchers in the Post-Mao Era: The Response to a Changing China," China Quarterly, no. 94 (June 1983), pp. 215-241. For the Chinese view, see Wang Jinqing, "Why the Sino-Soviet Strains?" Beijing Review 27:28 (July 9, 1984), pp. 31-32, from which the quotation is taken; Wang Ziying, "Toughness in Diplomatic Postures," Beijing Review 27:30 (July 23, 1984), pp. 12-13; and Yu Sui, "Diplomacy Tends Toward Rigidity," Beijing Review 27:37 (September 10, 1984), pp. 11-12. A longer version of the last article is in Renmin ribao, August 28, 1984 (FBIS/CHI/28 Aug. 84/C1). For the

conversation between Gromyko and Wu Xueqian, see Tokyo KYODO in English, October 11, 1984, 0052 GMT (FBIS/SOV/11 Oct. 84/B1). For Chinese activity in Eastern Europe, see the New York Times, May 5 and August 5, 1984, pp. 4 and E4, respectively. For analysis of recent Sino-Soviet developments, see Dieter Heinzig, "Abkühlung zwischen Moskau und Peking," Europa-Archiv 39:22 (November 25, 1984), pp. 675-684, and Bohdan Nahaylo, "A New Stage in Sino-Soviet Relations?" Radio Liberty Research (April 3, 1985).

    6. Zbigniew Brzezinski, Power and Principle (New York: Farrar, Straus and Giroux, 1983).

    7. See an unpublished paper by Harry Gelman of Rand.

    8. Rozman, "Moscow's China-Watchers in the Post-Mao Era."

    9. See the authoritative analysis by William R. Heaton, "Mongolia in 1983: Mixed Signals," Asian Survey 24:1 (January 1984), pp. 127-133.

    10. Harry H. Kendall, "Vietnamese Perceptions of the Soviet Presence," Asian Survey 23:9 (September 1983), pp. 1052-1061; Douglas Pike, "Southeast Asia, the USSR, and Vietnam" (Paper prepared for a conference on Soviet policy toward the Third World at the Kennan Institute, Washington, D.C., March 2, 1984); Pao-min Chang, "Beijing Versus Hanoi: The Diplomacy over Kampuchea," Asian Survey 23:5 (May 1983), pp. 598-618; Dennis Duncanson, "Vietnam: A New Turning-point?" World Today 40:5 (May 1984), pp. 198-204.

    11. Kim Hak-joon, "North Korea's Foreign Relations Amidst Sino-Soviet Conflict, II," Vantage Point (Seoul) 7:5 (May 1984).

    12. The best analysis of recent U.S. policy toward China that I have seen is Robert A. Manning, "China: Reagan's Chance Hit," Foreign Policy, no. 54 (Spring 1984), pp. 83-101. For the arms sales aspect, see Nayan Chanda, "TOWing the Peking Line," Far Eastern Economic Review 124:26 (June 28, 1984), pp. 12-14.

    13. For this information, I have primarily drawn on the latest paper on Soviet-Japanese relations by Hiroshi Kimura of Hokkaido University, "USSR-Japanese Relations" (Paper prepared for a

conference on Soviet policy toward the Third World at the Kennan Institute, Washington, D.C., March, 1984). I am grateful to Kimura for many discussions on this subject.

21
Co-opting China: The Realization of an American Dream?

Peter Van Ness

> *They experienced similar excitement and danger, entertained similar hopes, learnt to bear with similar frustrations, and operated with a combination of integrity and deviousness. They bared their own souls and mirrored their own societies in their actions, yet in doing so they highlighted fundamental Chinese values. And they speak to us still, with a shared intensity, about the ambiguities of superiority, and about that indefinable realm where altruism and exploitation meet.*
>
> Jonathan Spence, describing Western advisers to China from the 1620s to the 1950s, in <u>To Change China</u>

The signs are everywhere. News magazines announce the ascendancy of Capitalism in China and Socialism's demise. Orville Schell despairs in the <u>New Yorker</u> that China may be losing its Maoist "national essence." And Prime Minister Zhao Ziyang, according to the <u>Washington Post</u>, a Chinese leader "cut from a different cloth," lectures leading U.S. business executives at a gala luncheon in Washington during his visit to the United States about the "objective necessity" of China's opening to the West, promising that the door will never again be closed.

Are Zhao Ziyang and CCP General-Secretary Hu Yaobang the "new generation" of Chinese pragmatists that the Modernization theorists for twenty years have promised would emerge in China and provide an opportunity for a true accommodation between China and the United States? Is the U.S. dream of a China willing to play by our rules finally becoming a reality?

This is not a new dream. From the first contacts with China in the early 1800s to Premier Zhao's visit in 1984, so many U.S. China-hands, old and new, have dreamed of bringing China into their particular fold: Christian missionaries, Cold Warriors, liberal academicians, ambitious capitalists, Machiavellian practitioners of realpolitik, and just plain good-hearted, ethnocentric Americans eager to bring progress to the world.

Since 1949, how to change China has been the number-one priority for American strategic thinkers with responsibility for U.S. Asian policy. A Communist China had either to be defeated militarily, subverted from within, or somehow enticed into voluntary transformation. Since the mid-1960s, the policy debate among China experts has increasingly revolved around alternative designs for co-optation. As things turned out, Richard Nixon was more audacious than the experts, negotiating in 1971 and 1972 an accommodation with Mao Zedong and Zhou Enlai that, as he immodestly but accurately put it, "changed the world."

This chapter will examine the principal features of that initial accommodation and then go on to explore the implications of the Sino-American relationship that has subsequently evolved through two different phases: the first, from 1971 until Mao's death, and the second, from the implementation of the Four Modernizations in 1978 to the present. In the final section, I will assess the probability for the success of a U.S. strategy that is based on attempting to co-opt China.

PHASE I: THE VIETNAM IMPERATIVE AND THE SOVIET THREAT

Seymour Hersh tells us that it was really Nixon, not Kissinger, who first conceived of taking the initiative toward China. In his book, <u>The Price of Power</u>, it is clear that Hersh was determined to find as much fault and to give as little credit as possible to Henry Kissinger, but with regard to this question at least, he is correct.[1]

The famous Nixon <u>Foreign Affairs</u> article, published a year before the tumultuous presidential election year of 1968 (when Henry Kissinger was still backing Nelson Rockefeller for president), described a particular strategic perception of China.[2] Like many U.S. analysts writing at the time, Nixon was trying to conceive of an Asia <u>beyond Vietnam</u>. The Vietnam War was clearly destroying the postwar Pax Americana global design, and no matter how Vietnam might be resolved, U.S. policy in Asia would have to change.

Nixon described Asian countries in the mid-1960s as sharing a common danger, the threat from Communist China. At the same time, he saw the hope for Asia in Capitalism. Pointing to the economic success of countries like Japan, Hong Kong, Taiwan, South Korea, and Singapore, Nixon came close to invoking Manifest Destiny when he wrote, "it could be said that a new chapter is being written in the winning of the West: in this case, a winning of the promise of Western technology and Western organization by the nations of the East."[3]

Acknowledging that "one of the legacies of Viet Nam almost certainly will be a deep reluctance on the part of the United States to become involved once again in a similar intervention on a similar basis," and that "the role of the United States as world policeman is like to be limited in the future," Nixon argued that "any American policy toward Asia must come urgently to grips with the reality of China." Nixon did not propose to appease a threatening China. Rather, "recognizing the present and potential danger from Communist China, and taking measures designed to meet that danger," Nixon urged, "we simply cannot afford to leave China forever outside the family of nations."

Nixon's answer to the China threat was outright co-optation. "The world cannot be safe until China changes," he asserted.

> Thus our aim, to the extent that we can influence events, should be to induce change. The way to do this is to persuade China that it _must_ change: that it cannot satisfy its imperial ambitions, and that its own national interest requires turning away from foreign adventuring and a turning inward toward the solution of its own domestic problems.

"If our long-range aim is to pull China back into the family of nations," Nixon argued, "we need a positive policy of pressure and persuasion, of dynamic detoxification, a marshaling of Asian forces both to keep the peace and to help draw off the poison from the Thoughts of Mao." The Nixon formula would combine carrot and stick: "Aggression has to be restrained while education proceeds." While the PRC was being wooed and won over, a U.S.-led "community embracing a concert of Asian strengths as a counterforce to the designs of China" would defend the status quo.[4]

As events transpired, it was not U.S. strength but Washington's decision to get out of Vietnam, not the attraction of U.S. enticements but Beijing's fear of the Soviet Union, that made the 1971 accommodation possible. Contrary to the insistence of many analysts that the United States would have to wait for a new post-Mao generation of Chinese leaders with whom to make an accommodation,[5] it was Mao and Zhou Enlai who initiated détente with the United States. Somewhat like Nixon's role in taking the initiative in the United States in regard to China, Mao was perhaps the only one of China's leaders with the audacity and insight to attempt a policy initiative that was so radical, and at the same time, Mao had the ideological credentials and authority to win the domestic political battle to implement and to defend such a marked departure from long-established policy.[6] Thus, Richard Nixon the anti-Communist and Mao Zedong the Marxist revolutionary made peace, each for his own particular reasons.

For the United States, three strategic considerations were most important: resolving the Vietnam conflict; finding a way to play China

and the Soviet Union off against each other; and
emasculating the revolutionizing influence of
the thought of Mao Zedong, especia-ly in the Third
World. A by-no-means inconsequential additional
consideration for Nixon was how an opening to
China might enhance the chances of his being
reelected.

Vietnam was inevitably in the forefront of
the minds of the Nixon administration, initially
elected to power in 1968, the most traumatic
political year since the Great Depression.
Political differences over the Vietnam War had
pushed the country to polar extremes--ending the
war was at the top of everyone's political
agenda--while throughout the Third World, the U.S.
intervention in Indochina had become the paramount
symbol of imperialism--undermining the ethical
claims of the postwar Pax Americana.[7] Somehow a
way had to be found to extract the United States
from Vietnam without the appearance of defeat, as
Nixon put it, the United States had to achieve
"peace with honor." Chinese pressure on Hanoi
was the key to success. The Soviets had been
willing to give some assistance to the United
States in its effort to achieve a negotiated
conclusion to the U.S. intervention, but without
China's cooperation, it seemed the war might go
on forever. The price of China's help would have
to include concessions regarding Taiwan, and, as
Hersh describes it: "In return for the concession on Taiwan, Nixon and Kissinger would seek
Chinese support for a negotiated settlement in
the Vietnam War. . . . Each side was asking the
other to betray an ally."[8]

Regarding the second consideration, seeking
to play China and Russia off against each other,
the tensions between China and Russia, obvious
to the world for a decade, had by 1970 still not
produced a U.S. global strategy that was designed
to benefit from this conflict. An opening to
China would permit the United States to exploit
Sino-Soviet differences for the first time in a
triangular strategic fashion.

The final objective of U.S. policy, but the
one least discussed in the subsequent analytical
literature, was the preoccupation at the heart of
Nixon's 1967 <u>Foreign Affairs</u> article: "detoxifying"

Maoist global influence. It is difficult to reconstruct today the U.S. view of Maoist China during the 1960s, especially given the current aura of Sino-American cooperation and détente, but twenty years ago, U.S. policymakers felt profoundly threatened by the political influence and ideological militance of China, a country that then had a GNP estimated to be about one-tenth that of the United States (with almost four times the number of mouths to feed) and military capabilities insufficient even to cross the Taiwan Strait much less to threaten North America. Nonetheless, for example, Robert McNamara, secretary of defense from 1961 to 1968, proposed that the United States install an antiballistic missile system for the sole purpose of defending against projected future Chinese military capabilities, despite the fact that China had tested its first nuclear device only in 1964 and, even today, Chinese nuclear weapons and missile delivery systems are but a tiny fraction of U.S. capabilities.[9]

There was something about the Chinese militance of the time that was deeply threatening to American defenders of the global status quo. One analyst argued that "when we speak of Communist aggressiveness we must . . . think not only in terms of traditional state relations and traditional military attacks, but also--and primarily--in terms of Communist revolutionary strategy, backed by military power." He continued, "Chinese communism has been both the test case and the proclaimed model for the strategy of creating 'national liberation movements' and promoting 'wars of national liberation.'" Assessing the different dimensions of Chinese support for this assault on the established world order, he concluded that "perhaps the most crucial supportive service provided by Peking lies in the area of psychological warfare."[10] Mao had made U.S. leaders begin to wonder whether or not the United States was indeed a "paper tiger" after all!

For the Chinese, there were also several important strategic benefits to be gained by an accommodation with the United States, among which, deterring the Soviet Union was probably the most important. Richard Wich, in his study of what he characterizes as a "geologic shift in the international political environment," begins his story with the August 1968 Soviet invasion of Czechoslovakia and the Brezhnev doctrine of limited sovereignty and spells out a resulting series of changes in PRC foreign relations, including identifying the Soviet Union as China's primary global adversary; the accommodation with the United States; reconciliation with Japan; and transformed Chinese relations with Vietnam, Yugoslavia, Romania, and Albania. Wich's analysis thoughtfully weaves together explanations at several levels of analysis (the global system, factional power struggles within the CCP leadership, and Sino-Soviet bilateral relations),[11] but there were additional implications of the Chinese decision for détente with the United States that reached even further afield.

We sometimes fail to recall that during the decade of 1960-1970, Beijing had adopted a strategic posture of confronting <u>both</u> superpowers. As Wich and other analysts have pointed out, during the late 1960s, probably initiated by the Soviet military intervention to destroy the Czech "Prague Spring" reforms, the Soviet Union superseded the United States in China's perception of threat to its national security. Nonetheless, as late as 1970, both superpowers were still perceived as very serious dangers to China. The accommodation concluded between Mao and Zhou on the one side and Nixon and Kissinger on the other amounted to an arrangement that, for the Chinese, was a way of dealing with the threat from <u>both</u> superpowers, not just with the Soviet threat alone. The accommodation with the United States would deter the Soviet Union, but it would also demolish, almost with the stroke of a pen, the U.S.-led anti-China alliance of Asian states that had been in place since the Korean War.

Moreover, détente with the United States meant that Washington would no longer attempt to deny the legitimacy of the People's Republic and stand in the way of China's taking its rightful place in international institutions and establishing formal diplomatic relations with countries around the world. The United Nations General Assembly's decision to accept Beijing and to expel the representatives of Taiwan's Republic of

China government on October 25, 1971, less than four months after the July announcement of President Nixon's planned trip to China, symbolized these changes. The accommodation with the United States had opened the door for the People's Republic to participate in established international institutions. China had gained access to a powerful and legitimate role in the United Nations and other international organizations that would prevent the United States at any subsequent time from being able to deny China legitimacy and label it "outlaw" and that would make it immensely difficult for the United States to rebuild the kind of hostile constellation of states to threaten the security of China as the United States had done during the previous twenty years.

Perhaps most profound of all, it was clear to the entire world (except perhaps to some people in the United States) that the U.S. withdrawal from Vietnam, which was a component part of the new arrangement with China, meant the end of Pax Americana. The world policeman was gradually retiring from service; the United States was a declining hegemonic power.

IMPLICATIONS OF THE 1971-1972 SINO-AMERICAN ACCOMMODATION

By and large, the United States and China both got what they had intended from the accommodation. China achieved a sense of security with respect to both superpowers;[12] it won recognition and legitimacy throughout the world while, at the same time, Taiwan was increasingly being isolated diplomatically;[13] and it observed a realignment of global power as the Soviet Union gained nuclear parity with the United States and, pursuant to the vague outlines of Nixon's Guam doctrine, Washington began to play a less interventionist role in global affairs. In fact, Beijing seems to have been concerned that U.S. power vis-à-vis that of the Soviet Union was declining too rapidly, until Ronald Reagan was elected in 1980 and began to commit additional funds to the U.S. military budget.

For its part, Washington won a "decent

interval" between a negotiated U.S. withdrawal from Vietnam (concluded in Paris in January 1973) and the inevitable Communist victory in Indochina in 1975, as well as new strategic opportunities to play the Chinese and the Russians against each other in a triangular diplomacy that Kissinger seemed especially to delight in. In 1972, Nixon won reelection, but within two years, he would have to resign under the pressure of the spreading Watergate scandal.

With respect to Nixon's early intention of "detoxifying" the thought of Mao Zedong, U.S. policy was also successful--at least as far as the international influence of Chinese ideology and the Maoist revolutionary model were concerned. Maoists around the world were shocked by the July 15, 1971, announcement. Making peace with the United States, the foremost imperialist power in their view, was a betrayal of principle and a betrayal of the common mission fostered by Chinese policy during the 1960s to build a joint effort ("the broadest possible united front") to oppose U.S. imperialism. One of the more articulate in his outrage was Enver Hoxha, first secretary of the Central Committee of the Albanian Workers' Party, whose government, for its own anti-Soviet and anti-Yugoslav reasons, had been one of the few in the world to support China through the most violent times of the Great Proletarian Cultural Revolution. Hoxha denounced China's withholding of support for its North Vietnamese ally, and commenting that the Chinese had played "America the Beautiful" during Nixon's visit in February 1972, he wrote in his diary:

> The orchestra at the banquet played the song "America the Beautiful!" The beautiful America of millionaires and multimillionaires! America, the center of fascism and barbarous imperialism! America, the murderer of Vietnamese and Arabs, the suppressors of peoples' freedom. . . . And they sing to this America in Peking so ardently that Nixon, in his reply to Chou En-lai at the banquet, said: "I have never heard American music played better than this

in a foreign country."[14]

During the 1960s (actually from 1958 through 1970), Chinese policy toward the Third World had been built around two main thrusts: the first, support for revolutionary national-liberation struggles, and, the second, the establishment of government-to-government relations with those non-Communist regimes that were willing to grant Beijing formal diplomatic recognition and to support a minimum of China's foreign policy objectives. The PRC economic aid program to non-Communist Third World countries, begun in 1956, was designed to sustain and develop relations with those regimes. This two-pronged PRC strategy continued through the 1960s, even though it was sometimes interrupted by spillover from the domestic chaos of the Cultural Revolution.

However, the foreign policy pattern of the 1960s was broken in 1971. In research with Satish Raichur, I have found that following the accommodation with the United States, Chinese support for Third World revolutions dropped off significantly while Beijing's more conventional government-to-government relations skyrocketed and the number of economic aid recipients increased in response to the willingness of other governments to establish formal diplomatic relations (see Figure 21.1). Yet, despite the fact that many new countries became recipients of Chinese economic aid after 1970, the total amount of Chinese aid began to drop at the same time, especially following Mao's death in 1976 as China began to conserve its available capital for investment in its own economic development (see Figure 21.2).

PHASE II: THE FOUR MODERNIZATIONS

For reasons having largely to do with U.S. and Chinese domestic leadership succession problems, the Sino-American relationship did not really advance much further until after Jimmy Carter became president of the United States and the new post-Mao leadership had consolidated its power in China following Mao's death and the

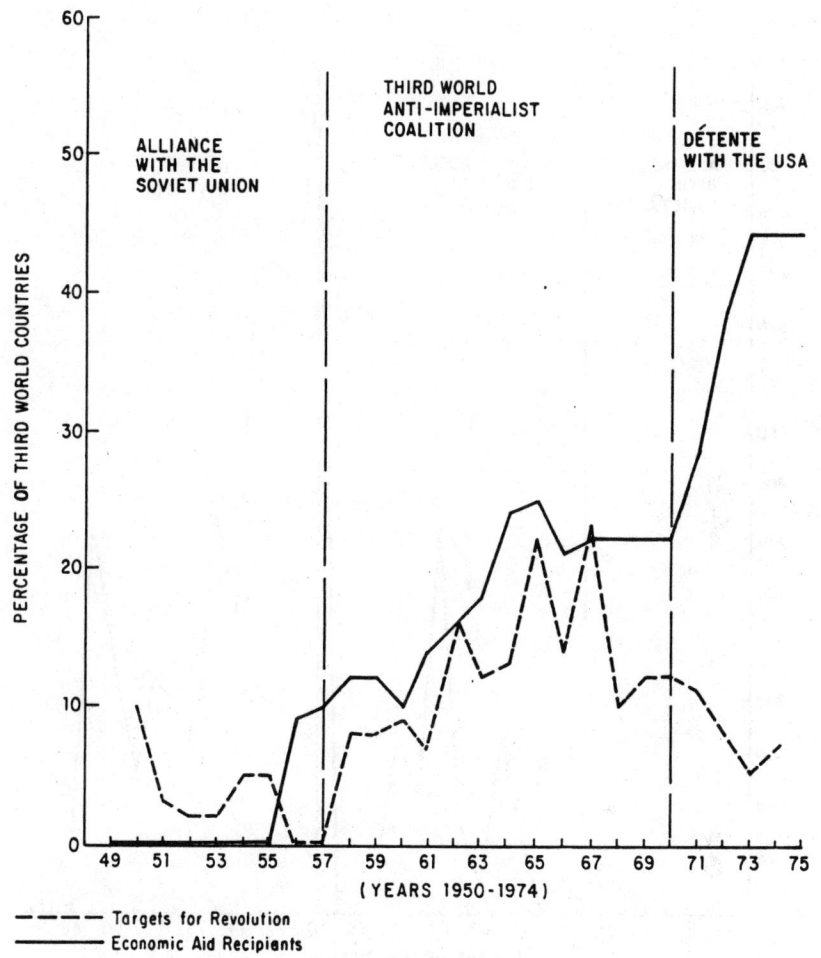

Figure 21.1. China's Relations with the Third World: Support for revolution, and economic assistance (percentage of total independent, non-Communist Third World countries identified as targets for revolution and percentage of total Third World countries that were active recipients of economic aid from the PRC by year). (Figure by Tom Van Ness and William McAninch)

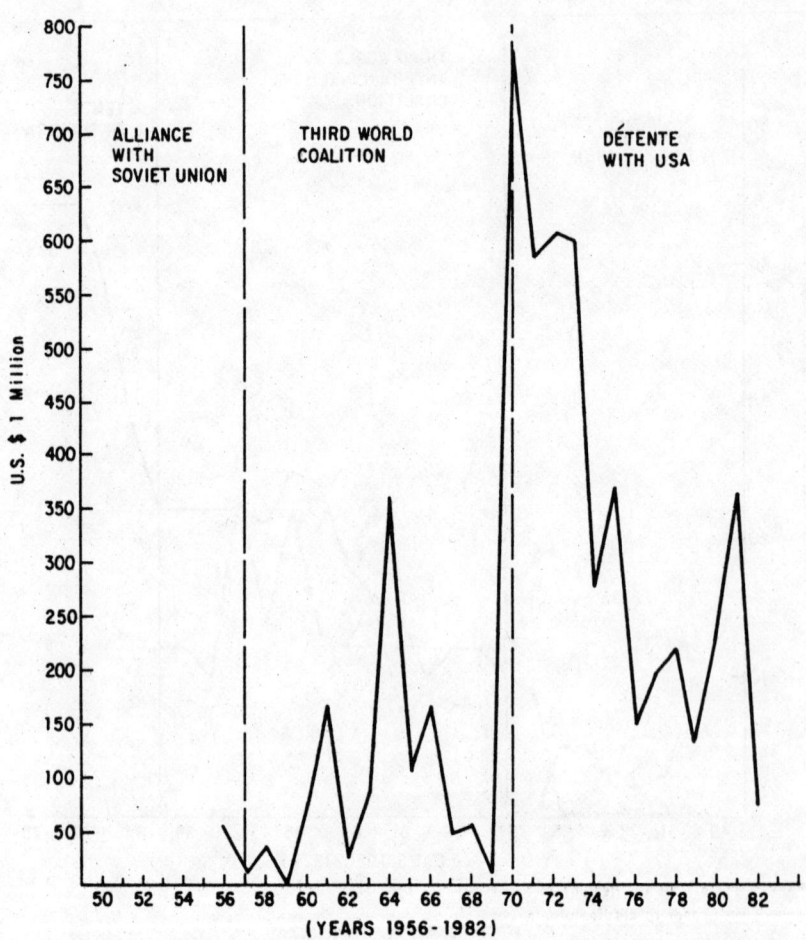

Figure 21.2. China's economic aid (total commitments by year to non-Communist less developed countries). (Figure by Tom Van Ness and William McAninch)

defeat of the Gang of Four in 1976. By 1978, however, events began to move at a rapid pace when the Carter administration decided to finally establish formal diplomatic relations with Beijing, and the Deng Xiaoping-led CCP leadership adopted and began to implement a market-socialist type of strategy for domestic development under the rubric of the Four Modernizations, which also included provisions for opening China to foreign direct investment.[15] Also in 1978, Beijing decided to send hundreds (later thousands) of Chinese students and scholars abroad to capitalist countries for training, and each year since 1978, there has been a deepening involvement of the People's Republic of China in the global capitalist system.

Although the Four Modernizations leadership has continued to speak of self-reliance and an independent foreign policy,[16] since 1978 China has systematically implemented policies that were anathema to Mao Zedong and obviously contrary to his sense of what self-reliance meant. In addition to sending large numbers of PRC citizens to capitalist countries for academic training, these policies include establishing joint ventures in China with multinational corporations; joining the International Monetary Fund and the World Bank, the two key multilateral institutions linking the capitalist industrialized countries with the Third World; seeking out long-term foreign loans; building a foreign tourist industry in China; importing foreign consumer goods for sale to PRC citizens; and organizing companies in China to sell the labor of Chinese workers and technicians to multinational corporations and foreign governments for projects abroad. Each of these policies, in Mao Zedong's view, had the potential either for making China dependent on foreign countries or for compromising the country's socialist relations of production.

These new policies have already begun to achieve results. For example, Premier Zhao Ziyang, during his visit to the United States in January 1984, announced that in the past five years, "we have absorbed foreign funds to the tune of 12 billion US dollars, and have carried out or set up about 2,000 projects and enterprises with direct foreign investment,"[17] and the authoritative China Business Review also reports that some $2,650 million in World Bank loans have either been made to China thus far or are currently under negotiation.[18] In 1980, China (like Taiwan in the mid-1960s) set up special economic zones (SEZs) designed to attract foreign investment. According to Beijing Review, by the end of 1983, Shenzhen, the largest of the four new SEZs, "had concluded 2,506 agreements with foreign and overseas Chinese businesses for a total of HK $13,220 million, of which 2,740 million dollars have already been put to use."[19] Beijing Review also reports that China's forty-two corporations, established to contract for engineering projects and labor services abroad, signed agreements with more than forty countries in 1983 to send Chinese workers and engineers overseas to work for foreign governments and multinational corporations.[20] Literally month by month since 1978, the web of ties between China and the capitalist world has grown: trade, loans, investment; licensing arrangements, offshore oil exploration, and communications technology deals; "dual use" arrangements with military applications and intelligence-sharing agreements.

In 1982, on the tenth anniversary of his historic trip to China, Nixon gave his blessing to the current phase of U.S. relations with the People's Republic of China, noting significantly that "China today seems to be making some progress in becoming more Chinese and less Marxist, embracing capitalist-style incentives rather than continuing to wear an ideological straight-jacket. If they continue on this course, they could become the major economic power in the world in the 21st century."[21] The "detoxification" effort was now focused on the domestic Chinese social system, and Deng Xiaoping and his men seemed to be doing an acceptable job.

Mainstream U.S. economists essentially have welcomed the Four Modernizations policies (China's new domestic and international programs both) as a long-overdue dose of economic common sense. If you are a less developed country and you want to modernize your economy, in their view, there is really only one way to do it: by using capitalist practices and in cooperation with the "developed" capitalist countries of the world. For them, China is finally beginning to see the light.[22]

Cultural and educational exchanges between the United States and China are now well advanced, permeating everything from urban planning to experimental physics to educational television. But there is a strange lack of symmetry in these relations. For example, under the educational exchange agreements, thousands of Chinese students and scholars come to the United States to study in return for only a few hundred U.S. academics going to work in China. Kenneth Prewitt, president of the Social Science Research Council, and Michel Oksenberg, member of Jimmy Carter's National Security Council staff during the critical years when the exchanges were begun, have written a report in which they argue that reciprocity in these exchanges is not important. Why? Because "it should be recognized that the United States is opening its science and technology to the Chinese mainly for reasons other than access for humanistic and social science scholars. Also involved are strategic national interests, the opportunity to train the next generation of technologists in China, and the recognition that many problems transcend national boundaries and require an international community of scientists for their solution."[23] Why are we so eager to train the next generation of scientists in the People's Republic? In order to change China.

CO-OPTING CHINA: WHY IT ISN'T GOING TO WORK

The co-optation policy, which began under Nixon, passed through an initial phase focused on destroying the international revolutionizing potential of the Chinese Communist experience and Maoist ideology--a radical force that seemed to threaten the very foundations of U.S. power throughout the non-Western world during the 1960s. That phase was successful. Third World revolutionaries saw Mao Zedong's accommodation with Nixon as a betrayal of both ethical principle and common political purpose.

A second phase began in 1978, when the ambitions of some Americans escalated even higher as China's domestic policies began to change and the CCP, under Deng Xiaoping, decided to cooperate with the capitalist West in order to more rapidly develop China's economy. Presently, we are several years into this phase, and in 1984, as Premier Zhao and President Reagan exchanged visits, hopes were high in the United States that there will be a fundamental transformation of the Chinese social system in a capitalist direction and the integration of China into the world capitalist economy in ways that seem likely to make China a friendly and cooperative partner for the foreseeable future. Beijing's rhetoric about an "independent foreign policy" to the contrary, China seems to be beginning to play the game by U.S. rules. So, why isn't co-optation going to work?

There are three main reasons: history, culture, and capabilities--any of which is probably sufficient by itself. Let's begin with history. Those Americans who dream today of co-opting China, of bringing civilization to the People's Republic, should take time out to read Jonathan Spence's book, To Change China.[24] There they will find the story of their predecessors--all of whom have not fared very well. Spence recounts the experiences of people who presumed to advise China, from the Jesuits Schall and Verbiest in the seventeenth century to the Russian technicians sent by Moscow to the People's Republic in the 1950s. The Chinese have a way of using what China needs or wants and rejecting the rest, especially designs by foreigners to control or manipulate them. Successors to one of the longest and most glorious historical traditions in recorded human history, the Chinese--no matter whether they are Communists, fascists, republicans, or whatever--have a strong sense of who they are, what China has been, and what China should be in the future. Especially after their experience at the hands of the imperialist powers during the latter half of the nineteenth century and the first half of this one, the Chinese are most unlikely to permit foreigners to make their important choices for them.

The second reason is culture. For those of you who are familiar with Chinese society, set yourself a test. Settle in one evening for a typical two or three hours of U.S. prime-time television. Almost any evening will do, but for good measure, be sure to include "Hill Street Blues," the police show on NBC. Then role play. Attempt to view the evening's programs through the eyes of a typical PRC citizen, not some leftover Maoist cadre or dogmatic official propagandist, just an everyday, urban man-on-the-street--a Xiao Zhang or a Lao Chen. Clearly, what you are looking at, to Chinese eyes, is <u>luan</u> ("chaos"). Things are out of control. Richard Solomon once wrote a whole book about the Chinese fear of <u>luan</u>--and one need not go that far--but order is a very important part of a Chinese sense of how things should be.[25] If there is one thing that the United States, especially since the 1960s, does <u>not</u> represent to the Chinese, it is order. From their point of view, U.S. crime rates are astronomically high, the American family is in total disarray, sexual relations are absolute chaos, and education is a disgrace. In short, the U.S. culture, for good or ill, is not something the Chinese want to emulate. They want aspects of it--the science, the productive capacity, even the vitality--but they don't want the cultural foundation, the social system.

The third reason co-optation isn't going to work concerns capabilities. In Nixon's 1967 <u>Foreign Affairs</u> article, he suggested an analogy that is true, I think, but not in the way he thought when he was writing the article. That was a time of U.S.-Soviet détente. Nixon argued that the United States and the West had created conditions following the end of World War II that had gradually forced an obstreperous Soviet Union into an accommodating posture: "Moscow finally changed when it, too, found that change was necessary."[26] Nixon suggested that China could be forced to follow the Soviet example. Today, when the Soviet Union has achieved nuclear parity with the United States, Moscow behaves quite differently, but Nixon, unknowingly, provided us with an instructive analogy. As Djilas warned in <u>The New Class</u>,[27] a leadership in that kind of system may behave defensively and even accommodatingly in foreign relations when it is weak, but when it has developed the resources and capabilities to support a more interventionist posture in the world, as we know now from the Soviet case, it is likely to behave in a rather less accommodating fashion.

To take seriously the illusion of civilizing China as the foundation of U.S. policy is to mislead the U.S. people and to invite new cultural despair in the United States' historic love-hate relationship with the Chinese. The policy won't work, and when it fails, isn't the United States likely to search for scapegoats--to carry out witch-hunts once again for those who "lost China"?

NOTES

1. Seymour M. Hersh, The Price of Power: Kissinger in the Nixon White House (New York: Summit Books, 1983), pp. 350-351.
2. Richard Nixon, "Asia After Vietnam," Foreign Affairs 46 (October 1967), p. 118.
3. Ibid.
4. Ibid., pp. 113-114, 121-124.
5. For example, Lucian W. Pye, "China in Context," Foreign Affairs 45 (January 1967), pp. 229-245.
6. Whether one assumes that there was a serious objective threat from the Soviet Union (i.e., that Moscow had considered the possibility of some kind of military attack on China) or that a significant part of the "Soviet threat" had been either provoked or fabricated by Lin Biao in his anti-Mao machinations, the perception by Mao and Zhou Enlai of a Soviet threat seems to have been real. See, for example, Hersh, Price of Power, chap. 26; Yao Ming-le, The Conspiracy and Death of Lin Biao (New York: Knopf, 1983); and Richard Wich, Sino-Soviet Crisis Politics: A Study of Political Change and Communication (Cambridge, Mass.: Harvard University Press, 1980).
7. See Ronald Steel, Pax Americana: The Cold War Empire and the Politics of Counter-

Revolution (New York: Viking, 1970).
   8. Hersh, Price of Power, p. 367.
   9. Robert S. McNamara, The Essence of Security: Reflections in Office (New York: Harper and Row, 1968), appendix 1.
   10. Franz Michael, "A Design for Aggression," Problems of Communism 20 (January-April 1971), pp. 63, 67.
   11. Wich, Sino-Soviet Crisis Politics, e.g., p. 93.
   12. Some immensely interesting evidence with respect to the Chinese sense of security appears in CIA estimates of PRC defense expenditures. According to these estimates, Chinese defense spending, after rising rapidly from 1965 to 1971, dropped off sharply after the Sino-American accommodation in 1971 and did not regain the 1971 level of expenditures again until 1979, when the Chinese military were obviously allocated additional resources in connection with the Sino-Vietnamese war of that year. Since 1979, Chinese defense expenditures have once again fallen (see, especially, Ronald G. Mitchell, "Chinese Defense Spending in Transition," in U.S. Congress, Joint Economic Committee, China Under the Four Modernizations, pt. 1 [Washington, D.C.: Government Printing Office, 1982], pp. 605-610).
   13. For details of the Chinese role in the United Nations and related organizations in the first years after the Sino-American accommodation, see Samuel Kim's comprehensive, China, the United Nations, and World Order (Princeton: Princeton University Press, 1979).
   14. Quoted in Hersh, Price of Power, pp. 495-496; see also, pp. 376-377.
   15. See, for example, Peter Van Ness and Satish Raichur, "Dilemmas of Socialist Development: An Analysis of Strategic Lines in China, 1949-1981," Bulletin of Concerned Asian Scholars 15 (January-February 1983), pp. 2-15.
   16. See, for example, Mu Youlin, "More on China's Independent Diplomacy," and Premier Zhao Ziyang's speech to the Canadian Parliament in January 1984, in Beijing Review, January 30, 1984.
   17. China Business Review 11:1 (January-February 1984), p. 29.

18. Ibid., p. 38.
19. *Beijing Review*, January 23, 1984, p. 28.
20. *Beijing Review*, January 30, 1984, p. 11.
21. *New York Times*, February 28, 1982, p. E19.
22. See, for example, Robert F. Dernberger, "The Chinese Search for the Path of Self-Sustained Growth in the 1980's: An Assessment," in U.S. Congress, *China Under the Four Modernizations*, pp. 19-76. See, also, Dwight H. Perkins, "The International Consequences of China's Economic Development," in Richard H. Solomon, ed., *The China Factor: Sino-American Relations and the Global Scene* (Englewood Cliffs, N.J.: Prentice-Hall, 1981).
23. Kenneth Prewitt, ed., *Research Opportunities in China for American Humanists and Social Scientists* (New York: Social Science Research Council, 1982), p. 46.
24. Jonathan Spence, *To Change China* (Boston: Little, Brown and Company, 1969).
25. Richard H. Solomon, *Mao's Revolution and the Chinese Political Culture* (Berkeley: University of California Press, 1971).
26. Nixon, "Asia After Vietnam," p. 122.
27. Milovan Djilas, *The New Class* (New York: Praeger, 1957), e.g., pp. 178-179.

22
The Washington-Moscow-Peking Triangle: An Analysis

Bih-jaw Lin

Although the growing volume of transnational activities has raised hope for an advance toward international order, modern states still live in an anarchic society that lacks effective central political institutions for preserving peace and regulating the behavior of its members. In such a society, states are bound to feel insecure and driven to lessen their sense of insecurity by cooperating with their friends against perceived enemies. They are convinced that a nuclear war cannot be waged because, in their view, it would lead to the extinction of the human race and the end of civilization. They are therefore compelled to seek allies, impose constraints on their adversaries, and do whatever else is possible to preserve peace. It is the resulting mutual fear as well as mutual benefit that produce the great-power tripolar relationship.

Today, in the U.S. strategic design to contain the Soviet Union, Communist China constitutes an important element. For its part, Moscow is extremely sensitive to the development of Washington-Peking relations because of the Soviet Union's fear that these relations might lead to an encirclement of the USSR. Peking tries to gain as much benefit as it can from the two superpowers. Does this triangular relationship promise a stable international system, or does it stimulate the propensity of international relations toward tension and crisis? What is the origin of the triangular relationship? What are the future prospects? In this chapter, I will cover both the theoretical and the empirical aspects of the situation.

I

It might be useful to begin with a discussion of three approaches to the origin of the triangular relationship. The most widely discussed analysis is found in the works of Henry Kissinger, Thomas Robinson, Allen Whiting, Doak Barnett, Robert Scalapino, Harold Hinton, and Michael Yahuda.[1] The point of departure is the view that the origin of the tripolar relationship lies in the nature of changing Moscow-Peking relations. It is unnecessary to trace the origin of the Sino-Soviet dispute in detail; for the purpose of this discussion, a summary of the relations between the two Communist giants will suffice. In the late 1950s, Peking opposed Soviet peaceful coexistence with the West and insisted that in order to defeat the imperialist camp, led by the United States, firm opposition and armed struggle were needed. Despite Peking's criticism of the Soviet policy, the theme of unity of the Soviet bloc under the leadership of the Soviet Union still dominated the thinking of the Chinese Communist leaders. This situation was to change after the signing of the Partial Nuclear Test-Ban Treaty in 1963. The treaty was regarded by Peking as a Soviet sellout of the interests of international communism and, furthermore, as showing Soviet collaboration with the United States against Communist China. From then on, the Soviet Union was to be regarded along with the United States as a target against which the people of the world should unite.

The removal of Khrushchev in 1964 brought a brief lull in Sino-Soviet polemics, but since the new Soviet leadership continued to adopt Khrushchev's foreign policy, Communist China soon resumed its intense polemic attack. Brezhnev and Kosygin were accused of pursuing the same objective of Soviet-U.S. collaboration for the domination of the world. Peking rejected the Soviet call for united action in support of North Vietnam and continued to charge the Soviet Union with revisionism and collaboration with the United States to sabotage the worldwide anti-imperialist movements. Then came the Soviet invasion of Czechoslovakia in August 1968. As Communist China saw the invasion, it was not only a violation of proletarian internationalism but also proof that the Soviets intended to establish a new colonial empire by threatening other countries with war. The Soviet Union had therefore become an imperialist power in the international community. The enunciation of the Brezhnev doctrine and the Sino-Soviet border clashes convinced the Peking leadership of the seriousness of the Soviet threat. The result was Peking's reconciliation with the United States, which was also supposed to resolve Washington-Peking differences. In short, the initial impetus toward a Washington-Peking détente came from Peking under the perceived threat of Moscow.

Richard Nixon's and Henry Kissinger's memoirs provide further information on the origin of the triangular relationship and the subtle maneuvers involved. According to Kissinger, the opening to Communist China was a policy instrument designed to attract Peking, impose constraint on Moscow, and increase the United States' freedom of maneuver in Vietnam. In his own words, "China needed us precisely because it did not have the strength to balance the Soviet Union by itself," and the United States should play the power game to "give each communist power a stake in better relations with us."[2] These comments are typical of Kissinger's Machiavellian type of diplomacy. The objectives of foreign policy were defined in terms of the national interest and should be supported by adequate power and skillful diplomacy.

II

The first alternative to the power politics approach is found in the works of Lowell Dittmer, Gerald Segal, and Michael Ng-Quinn.[3] According to Dittmer, the structure of the state system makes it necessary for states to develop patterned relationships with one another. They have to make deals, compromise, and impose sanctions, and these activities can be understood in terms of transaction and exchange. Because states differ in size, population, and economic capability, Dittmer says that exchanges may be positive, negative, symmetrical, or asymmetrical. The key variables that affect the type of exchange are (1) the behavior of the two players in a bilateral relationship vis-à-vis one another, (2) the power ratio between the two players, and (3) each player's relationship with a third player. Dittmer then advances three patterns of relationships: a stable marriage, a stable affair, and a romantic triangle. In Dittmer's study, the period 1949-1960 witnessed the existence of a stable marriage between Moscow and Peking. Subsequently, because of the U.S.-USSR détente and the Sino-Soviet dispute, the stable marriage was transformed into a kind of stable affair, or competitive-collusive relationship, in the years 1960-1970. The romantic tripolar relationship came into being when Peking decided to establish a rapprochement with Washington in 1970 as a counterweight to the Soviet Union relationship.

Segal begins from a perspective that is more historical than Dittmer's. He examines four cases--the Laotian crisis of 1961-1962; the Sino-Indian border dispute of 1962; the Vietnam War (1963-1968), and the nuclear weapons and arms control negotiations of 1963-1968--to demonstrate that the tripolar relationship began to take shape in the 1960s. For Segal, the triad does not refer to substantial, tangible, or measurable phenomena. Instead, it is merely an analytical tool for the observer to understand the interaction among the three powers. Having said that, Segal proceeds to define the concept of a pivot power as "a state that has the most cooperative and least conflictive relations with the other two members of the triad and desires to retain if not enhance its cooperative relationships." In a tripolar system, each power fears diplomatic isolation, and, therefore, each is likely to enhance its security by colluding with one of the other powers against the chief adversary or by preventing collusion between the two other powers. In the process, the guiding principle is not ideology but the national interest.

In Segal's analysis, the tripolar relationship contains a mechanism that is capable of adjusting or regulating the relations among the three powers. A pivot country's ability to play one power against the other depends upon three conditions: (1) a commonality of interests between the two powers, (2) the two powers are wooing the third power at the same time, (3) any two powers in the triangle are concerned about the consequence of the pivot aligning itself with one power against the other. The Laotian crisis, in Segal's view, is an ideal case for observation of the interaction among the three powers. His study of the other three cases also serves this purpose.

Segal's book is useful to students interested in international politics in general and the Washington-Moscow-Peking triangle relationship in particular, but his approach does not offer an adequate explanation. It is undoubtedly a long way from observing that Moscow has been concerned about the development of Peking-Washington relations to assuming the existence of a tripolar relationship. We can observe the foreign policy of the Soviet Union during the Vietnam War and say that Moscow acted in the context of a tripolar relationship, but we could never say that on the basis of studying just one country, because international politics and the foreign policies of Peking and Washington were much more complex and dissimilar than those of Moscow. Suppose we can observe a steady trend in Soviet or Communist Chinese policy, that trend, by itself, cannot be accepted as evidence of the existence of a tripolar relationship. Because the evidence in his book is often flimsy, Segal runs the danger of imposing his theory on the evidence rather than testing his theory against it.

In "Effects of Bipolarity on Chinese Foreign Policy," Michael Ng-Quinn has not sought to focus on the triangle relationship. His study of Peking's foreign policy is not an exercise in international relations theory or methodology but an attempt to examine Peking's perception of bipolarity. He contends that Peking's foreign policy and its dealings with the United States and the Soviet Union can best be explained in terms of strategic bipolarity. Since the end of World War II, the Communist Chinese leadership has constantly pursued its foreign policy objectives in accordance with its understanding of bipolarity.

In the 1950s, the United States was regarded by Peking as the principal enemy and as attempting to gain control over most of the world in order to attack the Soviet Union, Communist China, and the socialist system. Before this attack could be launched, the United States would have to be subjugated by a vast zone, including many capitalist, colonial, and semicolonial countries in Europe, Asia, and Africa. The concept of an intermediate zone and Mao's call to lean to one side, in Ng-Quinn's analysis, do not necessarily negate the concept of bipolarity because the zone could not be intermediate without two poles. As Peking's perception of Moscow began to change in the late 1950s, its foreign policy also shifted. According to Ng-Quinn, the Communist Chinese leadership suppressed its lean-to-one-side theory and used the intermediate-zone theory to defy strategic bipolarity from 1962 until 1969.

We all know that Peking proceeded swiftly in the early 1970s to establish diplomatic relations with foreign countries, and two factors were relevant to this change of policy. On the one hand, Peking was confronted with an expansionist Soviet Russia, and on the other, it was confronted with a United States that was deeply involved in the Indochina war. The United States could no longer, in Peking's view, pursue an aggressive imperialist policy but would linger on in Asia, Africa, and Latin America because of its economic and political interests. The two superpowers would then act either in collusion or in contention with each other to divide the world. Communist China appealed for unity among the developing nations against the superpowers' aggression and manipulation. The guiding principle of Peking's foreign policy was the concept of three worlds.

On this point, Ng-Quinn offers a very

interesting interpretation. He contends that there was no such thing as a three-world differentiation in operational perspective, because what Peking actually advocated was to unite the Third World against the First World. So, the leadership still viewed the international situation in terms of bipolarity: the Soviet pole versus the non-Soviet pole. Ng-Quinn also criticizes Dittmer and Segal for failing to provide a clear definition of a pole. Without that, the observer is unable to measure the asymmetrical capabilities and differentiate the poles from the nonpoles. Since Communist China does not possess the same capabilities as the Soviet Union and the United States, Ng-Quinn claims that tripolarity does not exist.

III

The second alternative, emphasizing "Pekingology" ("Beijinology"), focuses on the links between the domestic politics and the foreign policy of Communist China. Drawing its inspiration from Graham Allison, the approach tries to view Peking's foreign policy as resulting from the pulling and hauling of various factions. Thomas Gottlieb's <u>Chinese Foreign Policy Factionalism and the Origins of the Strategic Triangle</u> is the pathfinding study.[4] His central argument is that there were three factions contending over foreign policy during 1968 and 1969. The criteria used by Gottlieb to define factions are their different evaluations of Moscow and Washington's threat to Communist China, the nature of Sino-Soviet relations, and the strategic suggestions of those relations for the regime. The Gang of Four formed the radical group; Lin Piao led the military faction, and Chou En-lai gathered a group of bureaucrats and the PLA regional commanders around him known as the moderates. According to Gottlieb, Chou En-lai, with the blessing of Mao, first sought a rapprochement with the United States in 1968, but his initiative was opposed by Lin Piao and his associates. Because the army's cooperation was essential to the building of the country after the tumultuous decade-long Cultural Revolution, Chou and Mao decided to delay their initiative after the Sino-Soviet border clashes in 1969.

Following Gottlieb's work, John Garver, Harry Harding, and Kenneth Lieberthal use the same approach to examine the links between Communist China's domestic politics and its foreign relations.[5] The approach, however, is still subject to uncertainty and criticism. For instance, we know that there have been different opinions among the top leaders in Peking on the Vietnam War, Washington-Peking relations, and Moscow-Peking relations, but the information that is publicly available provides only a fragmentary account. Also, the essential factors that help us perceive the process of foreign policy-making are still lacking. The approach can be utilized to some extent, but it may not be empirically feasible to examine the relationship between factional strife and foreign policy on every issue that Communist China faces.

In summary, the three approaches are mutually complementary, and more books and articles on the subject will doubtless be written. It is true to say that the study of the strategic triangle can accommodate various approaches and that it will thrive on controversy. Having said that, it is important to bear in mind that the triangle includes the world's two superpowers and a much weaker power--weaker but the most densely populated state in the world. Any policy mistake will have grave consequences for Asia and the world. For this reason, it is necessary to address the question in the context of policy science. After all, political scientists are usually not content with hypotheses, models, and explanations but like to prescribe policy guidelines and evaluate policy options.

IV

As noted earlier, the Washington-Peking rapprochement was a result of a mutual fear of Moscow. The United States intended to use Communist China to balance the Soviet Union, and Communist China hoped to gain U.S. backing as leverage against "the mighty bear." The question that we in the Western world should ask ourselves is, How effective is the U.S. policy? When we look at the record of the Soviet Union's international behavior, we see a clear sequence of events linking a Soviet fear of a Washington-Peking rapprochement and Soviet foreign policy. The Soviet Union did sign the SALT I agreement with the United States in 1972 and the Vladivostok agreement in 1974--as Kissinger observed, after his and Nixon's visits to mainland China, the Soviets were "suddenly anxious to create the impression that more serious business could be accomplished in Moscow than in Peking."[6] However, a close examination of events in the 1970s and early 1980s shows that the Washington-Peking rapprochement also resulted in an acceleration of the arms race, and thus it has undermined the stability of the Pacific region.

It is no longer a secret that the Soviet Union has spent far more than the United States and Communist China on military development,[7] including building a first-class, combat-ready navy. The Soviet Pacific Fleet, for instance, accounts for 1.6 million tons, a third of the total Soviet naval tonnage. (The U.S. Seventh Fleet has decreased to 650,000 tons, and its vessels are not as up-to-date as they were before.) On the Asian continent, the Soviets have deployed more than fifty divisions along the Sino-Soviet border, and about a quarter of Moscow's ground and air forces are assigned for action in Asia. According to a report by Secretary of Defense Caspar Weinberger on Soviet military power, "the Soviet Navy has continued to focus developmental efforts on incorporating increasing levels of advanced technology and sophistication into all their ships." In the immediate future, the Soviet Union will "continue to build even larger ships with equally heightened levels of lethality in their weapons systems and greater endurance to facilitate deployments to all seas and oceans."[8]

It is very clear that the Soviet Union has transformed itself from a continental military power into one of the two most powerful countries in the world, and its military history reveals that Moscow's military buildup has proceeded in line with its foreign policy. For example, the Soviets began to deploy troops along the Sino-Soviet border in the early 1960s, and as a result of the March 1969 clashes on the Ussuri River, there was a conspicuous acceleration of the Soviet military buildup along the border and in Mongolia. After the signing of the treaty of peace and friendship between Peking and Tokyo in 1978, Moscow increased its military deployment in the disputed territories north of Japan. According to intelligence estimates, the Soviets have built a submarine base at Simushir Island and stationed twenty to thirty MiG-23s on Etorofu (Iturup) Island both north of Hokkaido. They have seventy Backfire bombers in the Far East, some on Sakhalin Island within easy striking distance of Tokyo. In addition, thirty-five SS-20s capable of striking Japan and mainland China are poised at Siberian bases, and for the first time, Moscow has established a nonwartime operational military command in Siberia. All of these factors indicate that the Soviet Union regards security in the Far East as a matter of grave concern. The Soviet leaders are not likely to remain at ease in the Kremlin when U.S., Communist Chinese, and Japanese leaders are singing in tune.

Perhaps the clearest analysis of Soviet reaction toward the Washington-Peking rapprochement is given by Chi Su.[9] He demonstrates that since 1969, Soviet policy has gone through five distinct stages in accordance with the development of Washington-Peking relations: (1) moderate confidence, (2) excessive fear, (3) vigilant complacency, (4) embittered trepidation, and (5) renewed hope. The Soviet rationale for these changes in policy is based upon a thorough assessment of the world situation and U.S. policy toward mainland China and a carefully formulated concept of Soviet national interests. It is undeniable that the Soviets have been suspicious of the Chinese for centuries. Even Brezhnev was reported to have told Nixon in 1973 that in ten years, Communist China would be a major military power with a capability equal to that of the Soviet Union. According to

Nixon's account, Brezhnev did not think that Peking's foreign policy would change after Mao's death: "He was certain that the entire Chinese leadership was instinctively aggressive."[10] From his conversations with political prisoners, Andrei Sinyavsky learned that Soviet dissidents would fight with Russia against China despite their aversion to the Moscow regime.[11] It is therefore inconceivable that the Soviet leaders will allow Communist China or Japan to become a serious threat to the survival of the USSR. If the leadership in Moscow were to believe that Japan or Communist China had crossed the security threshold, it would certainly take appropriate action to deal with the situation. Aaron Friedberg is emphatic on this point: "The U.S. has sought to strengthen China through political support, economic aid, and, at times hesitantly, military assistance. American decision-makers may someday find themselves faced with the questions of whether or how to help defend the PRC if she is attacked by her powerful northern neighbour."[12]

V

We can now easily understand why Peking is sensitive to the danger of pushing the Soviet bear into a corner. The Peking leadership, in fact, has treated its country's relations with Moscow with great care. After the establishment of diplomatic relations between Peking and Washington in 1979, Communist China began to take steps to improve relations with the Soviet Union. On April 3, 1979, the Communist Chinese authorities informed the Soviets of their decision not to extend the Sino-Soviet treaty of friendship and alliance. The announcement was not unexpected; what deserves attention is the implied meaning that Peking intended to hold talks with Moscow without prior conditions.

Observers in the West generally agree that Peking's gesture was part of an ameliorative policy after the unsuccessful 1979 Sino-Vietnamese border war;[13] for obvious security reasons, Peking could not afford to face the danger of another war on two fronts. The talks between the two Communist giants took place in Moscow from September 27 through November 30, 1979.[14] The Communist Chinese were reported to have made the following proposals: (1) a reduction of the Soviet armed forces along the Sino-Soviet border area, (2) withdrawal of the Soviet armed forces from Mongolia, (3) discontinuance of Soviet aid to Vietnam, and (4) a settlement of the long-standing Sino-Soviet border dispute. In return, the Soviets furnished the Communist Chinese delegation with counterproposals. The two sides agreed to continue negotiations at the vice-ministerial level in Peking in early 1980, but the Peking leadership declined to engage in further talks after the Soviet invasion of Afghanistan in December 1979.

Various research reports indicate that the Chinese Communists have had no consensus on the Afghanistan issue.[15] Some quarters regard the Soviet invasion as part of a global Soviet design; others view it as a sign of weakness. The People's Daily has expressed doubts about Moscow's prospects in Afghanistan. In terms of policy, however, Peking has chosen not to provoke the Soviets[16] and has kept channels of communication with Moscow open. Following are a few examples of diplomatic feelers:

1. Mikhail Kapitsa, director of the Asian Department of the Soviet Ministry of Foreign Affairs, visited Peking in early 1981.
2. Athletes from Communist China were allowed to travel to Moscow in March 1981 and compete with their Soviet counterparts.
3. Moscow proposed resumption of the border negotiations in September 1981.
4. Moscow proposed scientific exchanges with Peking in December 1981.
5. Brezhnev proposed an improvement of Sino-Soviet relations at Tashkent on March 24, 1982.
6. Mikhail Kapitsa visited Peking again in May 1982.

7. Athletes and scientists from mainland China visited Moscow in May 1982.
8. *Pravda* carried an article on May 20, 1982, urging a Sino-Soviet rapprochement.
9. In his report to the CCP's Twelfth National Congress on September 1, 1982, Hu Yao-pang said: "We note that Soviet leaders have expressed more than once the desire to improve relations with China. But deeds, rather than words, are important."[17]
10. Brezhnev again proposed an improvement of Sino-Soviet relations at Baku on September 26, 1982.

The first round of talks after the Soviet invasion of Afghanistan was resumed in Peking in October 1982, and Peking later used the occasion of Brezhnev's funeral to express its desire for a rapprochement with Moscow. Andropov reportedly singled out Huang Hua, Peking's representative, for a long talk at the funeral, and Huang also met Gromyko at that time. On his return to Peking, Huang disclosed that he was very optimistic about the prospects of improved Sino-Soviet relations. The subsequent announcement of Huang's retirement was probably coincidental and not a repudiation of his dealings with the Soviet leaders, and Wu Hsueh-ch'ien's promotion to the position of foreign minister reflected no change in Communist China's policy toward the Soviet Union. Up to the time of writing, four rounds of talks had been conducted by Peking and Moscow, and their contacts had been upgraded to the vice-premier level.

Thus, the most interesting developments from 1979 to 1984 are Peking's changes in attitude toward the Soviet Union and the United States. These changes can be further illustrated by comparing some of the recent statements by top leaders with previous statements. In February 1979, for instance, Teng Hsiao-p'ing told Carter that

Our two countries have different social

> systems and ideologies, but both governments are aware that the interests of our peoples and of world peace require that we view our bilateral relations in the context of the overall international situation and with a long-term strategic perspective. This was the reason why the two sides easily reached agreement on normalization. Moreover, in the joint communiqué on the establishment of diplomatic relations, our two sides solemnly committed themselves that neither should seek hegemony and each was opposed to efforts by any other country or group of countries to establish such hegemony.[18]

Chao Tzu-yang issued this statement to the U.S. press when he visited Washington in January 1984: "We determine our position on international issues, each according to its own merit. As I have said, China is critical of some U.S. policies towards Third World countries. This being the case, it is not possible to establish a strategic partnership between China and the United States."[19] He went on to assert that "China pursues an independent foreign policy and is ready to establish, develop and improve relations with all countries, including the Soviet Union, on the basis of the Five Principles of Peaceful Coexistence."[20]

In October 1978, Teng Hsiao-p'ing visited Tokyo and stressed that

> the Treaty [China-Japan treaty of peace and friendship] explicitly stipulates that neither China nor Japan should seek hegemony and that each is opposed to efforts by any other country or group of countries to establish such hegemony. This is the first time that such a stipulation is included in an international treaty. . . . it is a heavy blow to hegemonism which is today the main threat to international security and world peace.[21]

When Hu Yao-pang visited Japan in November 1983, he announced that "it is our intention to seek friendly coexistence and contact with other countries around the world on the basis of the Five Principles of Peaceful Coexistence."[22]

It is therefore quite safe to predict that the talks between Moscow and Peking will continue, but the process is bound to be slow and frustrating. Both sides may be willing to make some reductions of troops along the Sino-Soviet border for economic reasons, but it remains to be seen whether Moscow and Peking can work out some kind of arrangement to do so.

VI

What, then, is the role of the United States? Washington clearly occupies a pivotal position in the triangular relationship, and over the years, the aims of U.S. foreign policy have remained unchanged: to contain Soviet power, preserve peace and order, and promote regional stability. The United States continues to stress its ties with Communist China, but its assessment of Peking has become sober, realistic, and balanced.

When President Reagan took office in 1981, Washington-Peking relations were under a dark cloud. Gallons of ink have been spilled over the cause,[23] and I do not intend to add much to them, but the core of the problem was the issue of arms sales to Taiwan. It should be remembered that during the negotiations between Washington and Peking for normalization of their relations, the United States had made no attempt to seek an agreement with Communist China on this issue. It was deemed impossible to reach an agreement, so the issue was put aside temporarily.[24] In view of Peking's eagerness for Washington's friendship, Carter and Brzezinski believed that they could handle the issue of arms sales to Taiwan with Peking's cooperation in the future. However, later events proved that what Carter and Brzezinski regarded as their major breakthrough turned out to be a liability for the Reagan administration.[25]

The administration began to consider how to solve the arms sales issue in October 1981, and the ultimate objective was to reach a mutual understanding with Peking on this issue in the hope that future development of relations would be on the right track. In addition, the administration was greatly concerned about the development of Moscow-Peking relations as there were clear indications that Moscow was trying to improve relations with Peking at Washington's expense. In retrospect, the arrival of John Holdridge in Peking in January 1982 was the harbinger of the long negotiations that were to culminate in a August 17, 1982, joint communiqué.

The communiqué, albeit carefully drafted, did not solve the differences that divided Washington and Peking. First, there were still basic differences on many issues. As Paul Wolfowitz has indicated, "some of the bilateral difficulties now plaguing U.S.-China relations may be said to stem from an insufficient understanding of our differing legal systems and societies."[26] The second factor concerns interpretation of the communiqué. According to the Reagan administration, the communiqué "is not a treaty or an agreement but a statement of future U.S. policy."[27] Future arms sales to Taiwan would be tied to Peking's commitment to solve the dispute between Taiwan and the mainland peacefully. Reagan even emphasized that there had been no retreat and no change in the U.S.-Taiwan arms sales policy. The United States would continue to supply Taiwan with arms in accordance with the Taiwan Relations Act. Peking, however, maintained that the communique should supersede the Taiwan Relations Act and that there was no link between the arms sales and a continuation of Communist China's peaceful policy toward Taiwan. Thus, the strained Washington-Peking relations continued throughout the second half of 1982.

It appears that by the end of 1982, the Reagan administration had concluded that its China policy should concentrate on economic, cultural, and technological exchanges. Although negotiations between Moscow and Peking were in progress, their differences could not be easily overcome. Peking would need substantial assistance for its modernization programs that Moscow could not supply, and close economic relations with the United States, other Western industrial nations, and Japan would remain in Peking's best interest. The Reagan administration was confident that enduring conflicts of interest would limit any new Peking-Moscow friendship. The three major obstacles were, and still are, the presence of a large number of Soviet troops along the Sino-Soviet border, the presence of Vietnamese troops in Kampuchea, and the presence of Soviet troops in Afghanistan.

During his visit to Peking in February 1983, U.S. Secretary of State George Shultz told the Chinese Communist leaders that the United States was prepared to help their modernization programs. Paul Wolfowitz later reconfirmed that "developing a strong, stable and enduring U.S.-China relationship is an important element of President Reagan's foreign policy"[28] and that the United States would provide Communist China with a broad range of U.S. technology. In a speech to the World Affairs Council of San Francisco on March 5, 1983, Shultz urged Peking and Washington to "reduce impediments to expanding trade in technology, as well as other economic relations, consistent with our long-term security needs."[29]

Subsequently, Secretary of Commerce Malcolm Baldrige and President Reagan's science adviser, George Keyworth, made separate trips to Peking in accordance with this general policy guideline.[30] At the conclusion of his trip, Baldrige announced that the United States would begin talks with Communist China on an industrial agreement to facilitate the use of U.S. technology to develop mainland China's energy resources, communications network, and manufacturing industries. Keyworth signed agreements with Communist China for joint research in the fields of transportation, aeronautics, nuclear physics, and biomedical science. The visit of Defense Secretary Caspar Weinberger in September 1983 gave further substance to U.S. policy toward Communist China. We know from his statement that the United States had approved the sale of

forty-three items of high technology to
Communist China; in addition, the two sides agreed
to exchange military officers in 1984 to study
each other's training, logistics, battle tactics,
and other fighting skills. U.S. Navy ships might
also visit mainland China.[31]

From reports of the visit of Chao Tzu-yang
to Washington in January 1984, one can get a sense
of the realism shown by the Reagan administration.[32]
Throughout his visit, Chao appeared as a man of
goodwill, emphasizing that he came as a friendly
envoy of the Chinese people for the purpose of
seeking increased mutual understanding. Reagan's
remarks were also warm and friendly. He spoke of
the growing trust and cooperation between the two
countries and stated that the United States stood
ready to nurture, develop, and build upon the
many areas of accord to strengthen the ties
between them. The two leaders did not mention
the Soviet Union or hegemonism and chose to stress
the economic aspects of their own relations. At
the end of his visit, Chao signed an agreement
on industrial and technical cooperation with
Reagan.

VII

Although the future of U.S.-Red China
relations appears bright, powerful elements of
uncertainty still hover over Peking and Washington.
Will Peking's present foreign policy line continue
after the passing of Teng Hsiao-p'ing? What
political fortunes are in store for Hu Yao-pang
and Chao Tzu-yang? Some observers believe that
the process of succession will be smooth and
that with the support of Teng, Hu and Chao will
gradually bolster their power bases by building
up their own networks of contacts within the
Party and the bureaucracy. Others see a source
of conflict between the two. At present, Hu is
responsible for Party affairs, and Chao handles
the economy. The division of labor between Hu
and Chao and, indeed, the balance of power
between them do not guarantee the future
stability of Communist China. Who is actually
Teng's choice as his true successor? To what

extent will the change in leadership affect foreign policy?

The Reagan administration will continue to support Peking's drive for modernization in the hope of building up a strong Communist China as a counterweight to the Soviet Union. For economic reasons, Peking will continue to be friendly with Japan and the United States in order to secure financial and technological assistance, a policy that has been shaped by expediency and material benefits. Thus, the question arises, Will Communist China remain a friend of the United States when Peking becomes economically strong and militarily powerful?

Another question is, What will be the impact on the development of Washington-Peking relations? In the immediate future, there will be increases in exchange, trade, and diplomatic contacts between them. Communist China will continue its independent foreign policy, and, at the same time, U.S. policy toward Peking will become more independent of the vicissitudes of Washington-Moscow relations. If this is the case, will the concept of the strategic triangle still be valid and meaningful? Answers to these questions will enable scholars to evaluate the future Washington-Moscow-Peking relationship.

NOTES

1. Henry A. Kissinger, *White House Years* (Boston: Little, Brown and Company, 1979), pp. 161-194; Thomas Robinson, "Soviet Policy in East Asia," *Problems of Communism* 22:6 (November-December 1973), pp. 32-51; Allen Whiting, "The Sino-American Détente: Genesis and Prospects," in Ian Wilson, ed., *China and the World Community* (London: Angus and Robertson, 1973), pp. 70-72; A. Doak Barnett, *China and the Major Powers in East Asia* (Washington, D.C.: Brookings Institution, 1977), pp. 193-201; Robert A. Scalapino, *Asia and the Road Ahead: Issues for the Major Powers* (Berkeley: University of California Press, 1975), pp. 75-76; Harold Hinton, "Peking-Washington: Chinese Foreign Policy and the United States," *Washington Papers*, no. 34 (Washington,

D.C.: Center for Strategic and International Studies, Georgetown University, 1976), pp. 30-40; Michael B. Yahuda, China's Role in World Affairs (London: Croom Helm, 1978), pp. 206-209.
   2. Kissinger, White House Years, p. 192.
   3. Lowell Dittmer, "The Strategic Triangle: An Elementary Game-Theoretical Analysis," World Politics 33:4 (July 1981), pp. 485-515; Gerald Segal, The Great Power Traingle (New York: St. Martin's Press, 1982); Michael Ng-Quinn, "Effects of Bipolarity on Chinese Foreign Policy," Survey 26:2 (1982), pp. 102-130; idem, "The Analytic Study of Chinese Foreign Policy," International Studies Quarterly, no. 27 (1983), pp. 203-224.
   4. Thomas M. Gottlieb, Chinese Foreign Policy Factionalism and the Origins of the Strategic Triangle (Santa Monica, Calif.: Rand Corporation, 1977).
   5. John Garver, "Chinese Foreign Policy in 1970: The Tilt Toward the Soviet Union," China Quarterly, no. 82 (June 1980), pp. 214-249; Harry Harding, "The Domestic Politics of China's Global Posture," in Thomas Finger, ed., China's Quest for Independence: Policy Evolution in the 1970s (Boulder, Colo.: Westview Press, 1980), pp. 96-98; Kenneth Lieberthal, "The Background in Chinese Politics," in Herbert J. Ellison, ed., The Sino-Soviet Conflict: A Global Perspective (Seattle: University of Washington Press, 1982), pp. 3-28.
   6. Henry Kissinger, The White House Years (Boston: Little Brown, and Company, 1979), p. 766.
   7. The following discussion is based upon Noel Gayler, "Security Implications of the Soviet Military Presence in Asia," in Richard H. Solomon, ed., Asian Security in the 1980s: Problems and Policies for a Time of Transition (Santa Monica, Calif.: Rand Corporation, 1979), pp. 54-65; Far Eastern Economic Review, December 15, 1983, pp. 28-34; Peter Duignan, "The World-Wide Threat of Soviet Communism," Journal of East Asian Affairs 2:2 (Fall 1982), pp. 235-259; and Coit D. Blacker, "Military Power and Prospects," Washington Quarterly 6:2 (1983), pp. 55-69.
   8. See Caspar W. Weinberger, Soviet

Military Power, 1984 (Washington, D.C.: Government Printing Office, 1983), p. 67.

9. Chi Su, "U.S.-China Relations: Soviet Views and Policies," Asian Survey 23:5 (May 1983), pp. 555-579.

10. Quoted in William G. Hyland, "The Sino-Soviet Conflict: A Search for New Security Strategies" in Solomon, Asian Security in the 1980s, p. 42.

11. Donald S. Zagoria, "The Moscow-Beijing Detente," Foreign Affairs 61:4 (Spring 1983), p. 861.

12. Aaron L. Friedberg, "The Collapsing Triangle: U.S. and Soviet Policies Toward China 1969-1980," Comparative Strategy 4:2 (1983), pp. 113-114.

13. See, for instance, William G. Hyland, "The Sino-Soviet Conflict: Dilemmas of the Strategic Triangle," in Richard H. Solomon, ed., The China Factor: Sino-American Relations and the Global Scene (Englewood Cliffs, N.J.: Prentice-Hall, 1981), pp. 141-143; Donald Hugh McMillen, "China in Asia's International Relations," International Journal 38:2 (Spring 1983), pp. 214-221; Herbert S. Yee, "China: De-Maoization and Foreign Policy," World Today 37:3 (March 1981), pp. 93-101; and Douglas T. Stuart, "China Between the Superpowers," World Today 39:3 (March 1983), pp. 90-97.

14. For background and development, see William E. Griffith, "Sino-Soviet Rapprochement?" Problems of Communism 32:2 (March-April 1983), pp. 20-30, and Zagoria, "Moscow-Beijing Detente."

15. Gerald Segal, "China and Afghanistan," Asian Survey 21:11 (November 1981), pp. 1158-1174; Jonathan D. Pollack, "Chinese Global Strategy and Soviet Power," Problems of Communism 30:1 (January-February 1981), pp. 54-69; and Yaacov Vertzberger, "Afghanistan in China's Foreign Policy," Problems of Communism 31:3 (May-June 1982), pp. 1-23.

16. See Cyrus Vance's memoirs, Hard Choices: Critical Years in America's Foreign Policy (New York: Simon and Schuster, 1983), pp. 390-391.

17. Beijing Review 25:37 (September 13, 1982), p. 31.

18. Ibid., 22:6 (February 9, 1979), p. 9.
19. *Beijing Review* 27:4 (January 23, 1984), p. 20.
20. Ibid., p. 21.
21. *Peking Review* 21:43 (October 1978), p. 4.
22. *Beijing Review* 26:49 (December 5, 1983), p. 8.
23. For example, John Garver, "Arms Sales, the Taiwan Question, and Sino-U.S. Relations," *Orbis* 26:4 (Winter 1983), pp. 999-1041; John Copper, "Sino-American Relations: On Track or Off Track?" *Asia Pacific Community*, no. 19 (Winter 1983), pp. 13-24; Robert A. Scalapino, "Uncertainties in Future Sino-U.S. Relations," *Orbis* 26:3 (Fall 1983), pp. 681-686; Allen Whiting, "Sino-American Relations: The Decade Ahead" *Orbis* 26:3 (Fall 1983), pp. 697-720; and Michel Oksenberg, "A Decade of Sino-American Relations," *Foreign Affairs* 61:1 (Fall 1982), pp. 175-195.
24. Zbigniew Brzezinski, *Power and Principle* (New York: Farrar, Straus and Giroux, 1983), pp. 225-232.
25. For two brief but excellent discussions of the issue, see Charles T. Cross, "Taipei's Identity Crisis," *Foreign Policy*, no. 51 (Summer 1983), pp. 48-55, and Robert A. Manning, "China: Reagan's Chance Hit," *Foreign Policy*, no. 54 (Spring 1984), pp. 87-94.
26. *Department of State Bulletin* 83:2073 (April 1983), p. 65.
27. See John Holdridge's statement in U.S. Congress, Senate, *Hearing Before the Committee on Foreign Relations*, 97th Cong., 2d Sess., August 17, 1982, p. 10.
28. *Department of State Bulletin* 83:2073 (April 1983), p. 63.
29. Ibid., p. 33.
30. See *Business America* 6:12 (June 13, 1983), pp. 7-8, and *International Herald Tribune*, May 12, 1983.
31. *International Herald Tribune*, September 27, 1983.
32. "Sweet-and-Sour Politics," *Time*, January 23, 1984, pp. 6-10; Robert Manning, "White House Red Carpet," *Far Eastern Economic Review*, June 12, 1984, pp. 15-15; and "Zhao and Reagan Sup with Shortened Spoons," *Economist*, January 14, 1984, p. 19.

23
Interpretations of Mainland China's Recent Foreign Policy

Harold C. Hinton

After agreeing, with what I should have known as undue lightheartedness, to write a paper on mainland China's recent foreign policy for the Thirteenth Sino-American Conference on Mainland China, I asked an obliging colleague, Dr. Stuart Goldman of the Congressional Research Service, to have a computer search made for writings on this subject published since 1975. The yield from this request was a list of approximately 1,000 titles in various languages, most of them being articles--rather than books--in English and by U.S. writers. With only a fraction of them was I already familiar.

In view of this situation and the decidedly limited time available, the list obviously had to be shortened drastically. But on what principle? I decided to begin by laying out my own framework of analysis, a relatively congenial objective inasmuch as I always prefer to write about my own views rather than about those of others.

A FRAMEWORK OF ANALYSIS

Although according to Henry Kissinger, Mao Tse-tung was actually a supreme realist,[1] he insisted on injecting a high ideological ("revolutionary") content into both his domestic and his foreign policies. The most significant recent overall trend in mainland Chinese foreign policy, with little doubt, has been the shift away from a Maoist approach to a more pragmatic and predictable one. The widespread impression

that this shift occurred after Mao's death in
September 1976, implicitly for the reason that he
was in full command until then and delayed the
policy transition while he lived, is incorrect.
The origins of the shift date from March 1969,
when the previously powerful ultra-Maoist Lin Piao
inaugurated his own political decline and fall by
idiotically arranging for the ambush of a Soviet
patrol by one of his own. This blunder led to
the rapid rise of his archrival Chou En-lai; in
December 1970 Mao told Edgar Snow that Chou was
making all decisions and bringing only some of
them to him for confirmation.[2] This trend was,
of course, finalized by Lin's death in September
1971, whatever its exact circumstances may have
been.

    Chou En-lai, first assisted and then virtually replaced after 1973 by a rehabilitated
Teng Hsiao-p'ing, attached the highest importance
to the stabilization of the political system after
the turmoil of the Cultural Revolution, to the
modernization of the economy as the ultimate
source of national power, and to the cultivation
of a viable relationship with the United States
as a necessary constraint on the Soviet Union and
a means of acquiring technology. Teng was
intended by Chou to succeed him as premier, with
a figurehead (Wang Hung-wen) succeeding Mao as
Party chairman. The plan was sound and was only
briefly derailed by the one serious mistake
Chou made: He died before Mao. After Teng's
return to the political leadership in 1977, and
still more after the Third Plenum of the Eleventh
CCP Central Committee at the end of 1978, Chou's
priorities were clearly reinstated, with significant although not crucial variations over
time, and this approach has continued in operation
down to the present.

    On the domestic front, a reasonably innovative economic policy--especially in agriculture,
high technology, and foreign trade--has been
accompanied by a contrasting political approach
marked by bureaucratic centralization and
tighter police controls. This mixture was
probably inevitable--it existed under Lenin
during the new economic policy period--but it has
been intensified by a general desire on the part

of the Chinese leadership to avoid anything like
a repetition of the Polish experience and by a
determination on the part of conservative Maoists,
formerly regarded as radicals, to spare the
country spiritual pollution, even at the cost of
restricting contacts with the outside world.

In foreign policy, as Teng reemerged at the
top of the political system, he loudly advocated
a more or less worldwide united front, including
the United States, against Soviet "hegemonism."[3]
This policy was rapidly dropped after he discovered that the Carter administration, even
though it sought and achieved normalization,
was distinctly unreceptive to it. By mid-1980,
Teng was recommending to a visiting U.S. delegation simply that mainland China and the United
States pursue parallel strategies in such a way
that the Soviet Union could never feel certain
of being able to fight either one without also
being able to fight the other.

Irritation with the Reagan administration,
mainly but by no means exclusively on account of
its attitude toward Taiwan, led to an un-
publicized decision by the CCP leadership in
June 1981 to take up a more overtly uncooperative
stance with respect to the United States, at least
until U.S. policy on the two key issues—Taiwan
and sensitive technology—became more acceptable.
It would have been unwise, however, to promote
worse relations with the United States without
seeking better relations with the Soviet Union.
Fortunately for Teng, his archenemy Mikhail
Suslov died in January 1982, and a few weeks
later Leonid Brezhnev, seeing an opportunity,
began to propose talks on the entire range of
issues between the Soviet Union and mainland
China. These talks began later that year,
but the Chinese have used them mainly to hold
the Soviets in play while continuing to demand
a drastic reduction of the Soviet military
threat to mainland China and to maintain a tense
confrontation with Moscow's partner, Vietnam.

In August 1982, mainland China reached a
limited but reasonably satisfactory accommodation
with the United States on the touchy issue of
arms for Taiwan. In mid-1983, the United States,
although it had meanwhile shifted to a Far Eastern

policy that stressed Japan rather than mainland China, agreed to make a much wider range of "dual use" technology available to mainland China. A year later, Peking, which had consistently given the impression of wanting access of that kind before buying U.S. arms, was showing signs of finally taking that ultimate step. This Sino-U.S. relationship appeared to be moving into the realm of reality and at least partly out of that of rhetoric, friendly or hostile.

THE PROCESS OF SELECTION

Against this analytical background, I considered the problem of shortening my long list of titles to a brief list of manageable proportions. Among the items listed on my computer printout, I regretfully decided to exclude all of the articles from nonscholarly periodicals such as the Far Eastern Economic Review and from newspapers, valuable though such sources often are (the best newspaper coverage in the United States of events in mainland China is to be found in the Washington Post and the Los Angeles Times), because of the generally transitory character of their usefulness. Turning to the printout, I also decided to exclude all books, as distinct from pamphlets. My reason was that whereas in the nineteenth century it was possible to publish a book in the United States in twenty-four hours, in this era of high technology, it takes about a year, so that a book on a contemporary subject is generally out of date when it is published--or even by the time the manuscript is finished.

That left pamphlets and articles in more or less scholarly journals and periodicals, most of them published in the United States. The list still amounted to about 600 titles. I immediately excluded the rather large number that, although published since 1975, dealt mainly or entirely with developments antedating the deaths of Chou En-lai and Mao Tse-tung. I further ruled out articles that treated mainland China's policy toward or relations with a single country, other than one of the superpowers. That left articles

covering the recent aspects of general mainland
Chinese foreign policy, its policy toward one or
both of the superpowers, or its policy toward
some region that is important to it or vice
versa. Shifting to subjective criteria, I then
began to evaluate the remaining articles on the
basis of the importance of the topic, the quality
of the analysis, and the conspicuousness of the
author or the periodical. Some of the survivors
of this ruthless winnowing I could not find, at
least on short notice. The survivors I could find
numbered eight, and it is with these articles
that I am concerned hereinafter.

GENERAL ANALYSES OF MAINLAND CHINA
FOREIGN POLICY AND STRATEGY

On the basis of the framework of analysis I
have already suggested and the subjective criteria
I have just mentioned, I had to admit that none
of the articles lying under my scrutiny did justice
to the subject of Chinese foreign policy. In
part, this situation was because of an advantage
of mine of which I grew more and more conscious
as I worked: that of writing later than someone
else, and therefore presumably with keener hind-
sight. In any event, my objective and my subjective
criteria combined left me with six general
articles--three of them actually pamphlets--
that struck me as important for one reason or
another. I summarize and comment on them here
in strict chronological order of publication,
although my remarks will no doubt betray a
preference for one or another.

William R. Heaton, Jr., a U.S. Air Force
officer with a record as a very perceptive East
Asian analyst, published a few years ago a
pamphlet stressing the concept of a united front
against Soviet (not U.S.) hegemonism as the key-
note of Teng Hsiao-p'ing's foreign policy.[4] He
sees mainland China's foreign policy in general
as being underlain by the motivating forces of
ideology (especially the three worlds theory),
bureaucratic politics (based on personalities,
differing outlooks, career patterns, and issues),
and perceptions of the international environment

(especially factors thought to affect mainland China's modernization, the integrity of its existing political system in the face of possible spiritual pollution, and its sovereignty and territory). According to Heaton, the mainland Chinese leadership perceives the United States as a constraint on the Soviet Union and as a source of modern technology, the Soviet Union as an ideological monstrosity and a military threat, and Asia as the area where mainland China is destined to attain regional prominence. He concludes that mainland China will continue to seek a united front against Soviet hegemonism as long as the Soviet threat persists.

I see, or I think I see, flaws in this analysis, which is generally excellent. One is that Teng dropped the united front concept about a year before the publication of Heaton's pamphlet, in my opinion because of the Carter administration's wanting no part of it. The other is that Heaton, like many other scholars, sees a mere propaganda rationalization in mainland China's theory of the three worlds, which lumps the two superpowers together in the First World; for one thing, it would make little sense to seek a united front with the United States if it was really as bad as the Soviet Union, as the three worlds theory taken at face value seems to imply.

Michael Pillsbury, another keen U.S. analyst of Chinese foreign policy and strategy, has written an extraordinarily stimulating article entitled "Strategic Acupuncture."[5] Too much space would be required for even a summary of his remarkably sophisticated argument, but the essence of it is that "the recognition that it may be emotion more than reason that deters a national leadership from war is the most striking difference between Chinese and Western strategic doctrines." "The Chinese seek to strengthen their deterrence posture by manipulating the perceptions of their adversaries." They also "stress the value of coalitions and cooperation in war and deterrence."[6] They have been trying to persuade the United States to take a similar approach to the Soviet problem--even though they (the mainland Chinese) fully realize the importance of actual military power and still consider that the

United States is slightly superior to the Soviet Union in strategic weapons--and want the United States to make appropriately vigorous, although nonprovocative, responses to Soviet actions. Pillsbury believes that through a cooperative strategic relationship with mainland China, the United States can learn to understand and cope better with the Soviet Union and political trends in the Third World.

Parris H. Chang, an eminent and a prolific analyst of mainland China's politics and foreign policy, has written a perceptive article about that country's strategy toward the Soviet Union.[7] He points out that during the preliminaries to normalization, the mainland Chinese did not like either Secretary of State Vance's alleged "softness" toward the Soviet Union or the school in Washington that favored "evenhandedness" between Moscow and Peking. Instead, they preferred Brzezinski's clearly anti-Soviet stance, even if--as he denies--he believed that he was "playing the China card." Writing before the beginning of the recent apparent improvement in Sino-Soviet relations, Chang correctly considers the "likelihood of a sweeping Sino-Soviet rapprochement" to be "rather remote." He concludes that "the Sino-Soviet conflict, albeit controlled, will continue for years to come, and Southeast Asia will become the most important arena for the rivalry."[8] Nothing that has happened since then has invalidated that analysis.

Among the many writings of the distinguished U.S. East Asian specialist Robert A. Scalapino is one that presents his overall interpretation of mainland China's foreign policy, both historical and recent.[9] He believes that recent Sino-American relations have been riled by a coinciding of mainland China's irritation at Reagan's comparatively pro-Taiwan line and Teng Hsiao-p'ing's growing sense of urgency (on account of the passage of time) about the Taiwan issue. In spite of the opportunity seemingly created by this situation, Sino-Soviet relations are not making any real progress, largely because Peking still feels threatened. Mainland China dislikes the Solidarity movement and does not support the West on the Polish question. As elsewhere in his writings, Scalapino overstates Peking's commitment to North Korea; a number of developments that have occurred since the publication of his pamphlet (originally a lecture), such as the remarkable proliferation of "unofficial" contacts between Peking and Seoul, cast serious doubt on his analysis of this important point. Although rather vaguely stated, Scalapino's conclusion seems to be that mainland China will eventually have to modify its current somewhat ambiguous stance and work harder to establish a viable relationship with one superpower or the other.

Very unusual among the articles on mainland China published in the West is one by "Edmund Lee," described by his editor as a "scholar from the People's Republic of China specializing in Far Eastern politics."[10] This author believes the basic domestic trends that have molded recent mainland Chinese foreign policy are the strong conservative bureaucratic trend, a desire to import and make use of Western technology without becoming dependent on the West, and the felt need for a relaxation of tension with the Soviet Union in order to promote the international stability that Peking considers essential to China's modernization. "China's new generation of leaders is determined to rebuild a Soviet-type system." He makes the sweeping and questionable statement that "Chinese and Soviet interests are more compatible than Soviet and American interests," and he correctly points out that Peking has stopped talking about an anti-Soviet united front.[11] Hu Yao-pang has a particular interest in restoring "normal" relations with other Communist Parties, apparently including even the Soviet Party. Peking does not want to attack Taiwan, but its sense of urgency about this issue tends to increase with the passage of time. "Lee" takes a rather bearish view of the Sino-U.S. relationship; trade between the two countries has probably peaked, and "Sino-American military cooperation seems increasingly unlikely, at least under the Reagan administration." Recent developments call both of these views into serious question. On the other hand, it would be hard to quarrel with "Lee's" conclusion that mainland "China has not joined the

Soviet camp. Peking will continue to look out for its own interests first."[12]

A policy paper published by the Atlantic Council's Committee on China Policy presumes quite reasonably that mainland China "may move further toward an independent position between Moscow and Washington, tactically continuing to shift its balance between them, in order to increase its leverage with each of the superpowers."[13] Perhaps the main interest of this analysis and this document lies in the facts that the committee included some of the United States' best-known China watchers and that its conclusions were discussed in advance with officials and specialists in a number of foreign capitals, including Taipei and Peking.

SOME REGIONAL ANALYSES

If mainland China does come to exercise the regional prominence anticipated by Heaton, it is likely to be in Southeast Asia, an area on whose relations with Peking he has written recently and well.[14] His conclusion is that, although for various reasons of domestic and foreign policy Peking will not disavow its historic relationship with the Communist Parties of Southeast Asia, in fact it has considerably reduced its contacts with them in the hope of encouraging the governments of the states belonging to the Association of Southeast Asian Nations (ASEAN) to support its stand on the Cambodian issue and oppose Hanoi's. Although this conclusion is true, there still remain deep suspicions about mainland China's intentions in Southeast Asia--on the part of Indonesia and Malaysia in particular.

Another region of great importance to Peking, especially at the present time, is the Middle East and Southwest Asia. A recent article by a perceptive and prolific U.S. writer on China's policy toward this region[15] holds, entirely persuasively, that Peking perceives a serious threat both to mainland China and to Southwest Asia from the Soviet military intervention in Afghanistan. As the best countermeasure, Peking wants stability, unity (although not with Israel), and moderation on the part of the states of the region. It cultivates friendly states, especially Egypt and Pakistan, and it supports both the Camp David agreement and the Palestine Liberation Organization--a neat trick.

SOME FINAL IMPRESSIONS AND CONCLUSIONS

Looking back once more over the full list of titles from which the articles I have discussed were drawn, I am struck, as one would be in the case of any other important and complex area or subject, with the immense variety of the authors' origins (Asia, North America, and Europe), points of view, and conclusions. What I do not detect, at least from the evidence presently available to me, is a perception of the real policy problem that, in my judgment, mainland China is likely to pose over the coming decades for Asia and, through that area, for the rest of the world.

Mainland China has long been very secretive about its technological progress and its military modernizations, mainly, it would appear, in order to avoid possibly alarming the superpowers and its Asian neighbors before it was ready to deal with them from a position of strength. The advisability of this low posture was almost certainly borne in on Peking, very forcefully, by the period of great tension with the Soviet Union in 1964, which arose to a large extent out of Moscow's concern about Peking's rapid progress toward having a nuclear weapons capability. At that time, Mao Tse-tung gave the order, with reference to Peking's military research and development facilities, to "disperse them to mountain caves" (san shan tung). This move was made, with missiles among other things, and by now major complexes of such facilities exist in South Central China, Southwest China, and Tibet. From a technical point of view, mainland China's military modernization program is making considerable progress,[16] and now that mainland China has reserves of over $20 billion in gold and foreign exchange and, apparently, at least some access to U.S. arms, it may become, say in the early part of the next century, a considerably more formidable military power than it is now. If this situation occurs, it could render real the fears of mainland China that are felt in Southeast Asia, which, until now, have been largely imaginary. The problem could become especially serious if a significant level of military modernization and capability for force projection on mainland China's part should happen to coincide with a period of intense preoccupation on the part of the superpowers with developments elsewhere, in Southwest Asia for example.

In any event, it would be highly desirable for the United States and other industrial countries to monitor very closely the pace and direction of mainland China's industrial and military development, rather than unconsciously supporting a process whose results they and others may have cause to regret. It is desirable that mainland China have a reasonable defensive capability against the Soviet Union but not a major offensive capability against the rest of Asia. Unfortunately, it is not likely that Peking will attain the first of these capabilities without also eventually attaining the second.

NOTES

1. "Kissinger on Mao: Brilliance and Cold Blood," *Time*, September 20, 1976, p. 49.
2. This passage was omitted, probably at Chou En-lai's request, from all of Snow's writings about the interview.
3. For example, in his interview in *Time*, February 5, 1979, p. 34.
4. William R. Heaton, Jr., *A United Front Against Hegemonism: Chinese Foreign Policy into the 1980's* (Washington, D.C.: National Defense University Press, March 1980).
5. Michael Pillsbury, "Strategic Acupuncture," *Foreign Policy*, no. 41 (Winter 1980-1981), pp. 44-61.
6. Ibid., pp. 49, 53, 59.
7. Parris H. Chang, "Peking's Strategy Against Moscow," *Asian Affairs* 8:3 (January-

February 1981), pp. 131-147.

8. Ibid., pp. 145, 146.

9. Robert A. Scalapino, In Quest of National Interest--The Foreign Policy of the People's Republic of China (Berkeley: University of California Press, 1983).

10. Edmund Lee (pseud.), "Beijing's Balancing Act," Foreign Policy, no. 51 (Summer 1983), pp. 27-46.

11. Ibid., pp. 31, 33, 35.

12. Ibid., pp. 28, 46.

13. China Policy for the Next Decade (Washington, D.C.: Atlantic Council, October 1983), p. 30.

14. William R. Heaton, Jr., "China and Southeast Asian Communist Movements: The Decline of Dual Track Diplomacy," Asian Survey 22:8 (August 1982), pp. 779-800.

15. Lillian Craig Harris, "China's Response to Perceived Soviet Gains in the Middle East," Asian Survey 20:4 (April 1980), pp. 362-372.

16. See, for example, Bradley Hahn, "China in the SLBM Club," Pacific Defence Reporter 10:8 (February 1984), pp. 17-20.

About the Contributors

C. Montgomery Broaded is an assistant resident dean of Earl Warren College, University of California at San Diego.

Hsien-yun Chao is a research fellow at the Institute of International Relations, Taipei.

Ting-chung Ch'en is an associate professor at the National Taiwan University, Taipei.

Cal Clark is a professor of political science and director of International Studies at the University of Wyoming. He is the coauthor of The Communist Balkans in International Politics (1976) and co-editor of North-South Relations: Studies in Dependency Reversal (1983).

Robert F. Dernberger is a professor of economics and director of the Center for Chinese Studies, University of Michigan. He is the coauthor of China Trade and U.S. Policy (1971).

Lowell Dittmer is an associate professor of political science and chairman of the Center for Chinese Studies at the University of California, Berkeley. He has also taught at the University of Michigan and the State University of New York, Buffalo.

William E. Griffith has been Ford Professor of Political Science at the Massachusetts Institute of Technology since 1972. He is the author of Albania and the Sino-Soviet Rift (1963),

The Sino-Soviet Rift (1964), Sino-Soviet Relations, 1964-65 (1967), The Ostpolitik of the Federal Republic of Germany (1978), and The Superpowers and Regional Tensions (1981).

Harold C. Hinton is a professor of political science and international affairs, Institute for Sino-Soviet Studies, George Washington University, Washington, D.C. His principal publications include The Bear at the Gate: Chinese Policymaking Under Soviet Pressure (1972), An Introduction to Chinese Politics (1973), Peking-Washington: Chinese Foreign Policy and the United States (1976), The People's Republic of China, 1949-1979: A Documentary Survey (1980), and The China Sea: The American Stake in Its Future (1980). He is also the editor of The People's Republic of China: A Handbook (Westview, 1979).

Chalmers Johnson is Walter Haas Professor of Asian Studies at the University of California, Berkeley. Among his recent books are: METE and the Japanese Miracle (1982) and The Industrial Policy Debate (1984).

Richard J. Kozicki is chairman and professor of government at the University of San Francisco and is the author of International Relations of South Asia, 1947-80 (1981).

Tai-chun Kuo is an assistant researcher at the Institute of International Relations, Taipei, and the coauthor of Communist China-Watching in the United States and the Republic of China (forthcoming).

Wen Lang Li is a professor of sociology at Ohio State University.

Bih-jaw Lin is an associate professor and acting dean of the Graduate School of International Law and Diplomacy, National Chengchi University, Taipei.

Alan P.L. Liu is a professor of political science at the University of California, Santa Barbara.

Feng-hwa Mah is a professor of economics at the University of Washington, Seattle. He is the author of Communist China's Foreign Trade: Price Structure and Behavior, 1955-1959 (1963) and The Foreign Trade of Mainland China (1971).

James T. Myers is an associate professor in the department of government and international studies at the University of South Carolina. He is the coauthor of Cultural Revolution in China: Documents with Analysis (1974), Conversations in American Government: A Guide for Students (1974; 2nd ed. 1976), The American Way: An Introduction to U.S. Government and Politics (1977), American Government: Telecourse Workbook for Students (1983), and An Introduction to the U.S. Constitution (in Chinese) (1984).

Ramon H. Myers is curator-scholar of the East Asian Collection and senior fellow at the Hoover Institution. His publications include Two Chinese States (1978) and The Chinese Economy: Past and Present (1980).

Jan S. Prybyla is a professor of economics at Pennsylvania State University. He is the author of The Political Economy of Communist China (1970), Issues in Socialist Economic Modernization (1980), and The Chinese Economy: Problems and Policies (1981).

Douglas T. Stuart is an associate professor of international relations, The Johns Hopkins University, Bologna Center, Italy. He is the coeditor of China, The Soviet Union, and the West: Strategic and Political Dimensions in the 1980s (1982), and coauthor of The Limits of Alliance: Out-of-Area Challenges to NATO (1984) and International Communism (1984).

Peter Van Ness is an associate professor and director of the Institute for the Study of Development, Graduate School of International Studies, University of Denver, Colorado, and is the author of Revolution and Chinese Foreign Policy: Peking's Support for Wars of National Liberation (1970).

Lynn T. White III is an associate professor in the Woodrow Wilson School, politics department, and East Asian Studies Program, Princeton University.

K.C. Yeh is an economic adviser at the Rand Corporation, Santa Monica, California. He is the author of many studies and coeditor of The Economy of the Chinese Mainland, National and Economic Development, 1939-59 (1965).

Ch'ing-yao Yin is a specialist on Soviet and Chinese Communist affairs at the Institute of International Relations, Taipei. His publications include History Has Given the Answer (1968), From Marx and Lenin to Mao Tse-tung: The Origin of Mao's Thought (1973), and Foreign Policy and External Relations of Communist China (1973), all in Chinese.